INDEX
TO SELECTED
BIBLIOGRAPHICAL
JOURNALS
1933-1970

LONDON

THE BIBLIOGRAPHICAL SOCIETY

1982

Oxford University Press, Walton Street, Oxford OX2 6DP
London Glasgow New York Toronto
Delhi Bombay Calcutta Madras Karachi
Kuala Lumpur Singapore Hong Kong Tokyo
Nairobi Dar es Salaam Cape Town
Melbourne Auckland
and associate companies in
Beirut Berlin Ibadan Mexico City
Published in the United States by
Oxford University Press, New York

BIBLIOGRAPHICAL SOCIETY PUBLICATION
FOR THE YEARS 1969 AND 1970
PUBLISHED 1982

British Library Cataloguing in Publication Data

Index to selected bibliographical journals. —
(Bibliographical Society publication for the
years . . . ; 1969 and 1970)
1. Bibliography—Periodicals—Bibliography
I. Series
016'.002   Z1001

ISBN 0-19-721777-X

Printed in Great Britain
by John S. Speight Ltd.,
Parkside Works, Guiseley, Nr. Leeds.
A Division of Hawthornes of Nottingham

INTRODUCTION

In 1963, during the Presidency of Mr. Simon Nowell-Smith, the Society adopted a suggestion from him that the card-index to bibliographical articles kept in the Upper Reading Room of the Bodleian Library might be published by the Society as a continuation of George Watson Cole's *Index to Bibliographical Papers published by the Bibliographical Society and the Library Association, London 1877 - 1932* (Chicago, 1933).

Nearly twenty years later, after many delays, and much editorial work, the *Index* is in print

Its intention is to provide an author and subject index to articles published not only in *The Library* but in other bibliographical journals which are listed below. The opening date is the publication date of Cole's *Index*; the closing date is (approximately) 1970.

The Society has become aware of what it should perhaps have known at the outset that a reference tool compiled on cards by a number of people for use in one particular library is very difficult to translate into a piece of continuous and coherent print. The work was began before such refinements as standard abbreviations for periodical titles, standard citations for articles and, indeed codes of cataloguing were generally accepted. Those familiar with the catalogues of the Bodleian Library will at once recognise some of the eccentricities of the Library's cataloguing rules; notably use of lower case letters for honorifics.

It cannot be denied that the present index contains inconsistencies and even inaccuracies which have escaped the eyes of several editors and of two members of the Society who read the proofs. The Society's Council nevertheless believes that the utility of having a consolidated index to the bibliographical papers published in this period, in British and American journals, but having a truly international scope, will outweigh the defects.

The period 1933 - 1970 will probably be seen in retrospect as that in which historical bibliography matured; in which it freed itself from the some-times dangerous influences of a rather vague bibliophily and offered itself as a serious discipline both independently and as an auxiliary to literary and historical studies. Some of the Society's most eminent gold medallists are extensively cited in these pages, and the bibliography they represent is that of the textual study of the great monuments of English literature, the application of scientific tests to the authenticity of literary documents, the history of the book-trade, and the substitution, in the study of book-binding, of detailed study of tools, rolls and blocks, combined with archival evidence, for mere impressionism. We may also see in these pages the enormously vigorous growth of bibliographical studies in America based in large part on the great rare book collections built up by collectors in the twenties and by universities in the following forty years.

The object has been to record the contents of English-language journals which were primarily concerned with historical bibliography. Journals which recorded the acquisitions of particular libraries — the British Museum Quarterly, the Bodleian Library Record and the publications of the major American research libraries come to mind — have been omitted.

The arrangement of the entries is alphabetical, by letter rather than by word; so that for example NEW ENGLAND follows NEWCOME. Within an author or subject heading it is alphabetical by periodical and chronological thereafter.

The Council of the Society wishes to record its gratitude to those whose work appears in this volume, and chiefly to Mr. Giles Barber, Mr. Michael Turner and Miss Georgina Warrilow.

ABBREVIATIONS

BC   Book Collector

BH   Book Handbook

BTHK   Bibliotheck

EBST   Edinburgh Bibliographical Society Transactions

GBSR   Records of the Glasgow Bibliographical Society

JPHS   Journal of the Printing Historical Society

LIB   The Library. Transactions of the Bibliographical Society. Fourth series volume 14 — Fifth series volume 25

OBSP   Oxford Bibliographical Society Proceedings and Papers

PBSA   Papers of the Bibliographical Society of America

SB   Studies in Bibliography

TCBS   Transactions of the Cambridge Bibliographical Society

A

A., R. F.
Sterne: *Sentimental Journey*. First edition. (Query, 9) BC, i (52), 57.

ABBEY, John Roland
British signed bindings in my library. Illus. TCBS, i (49/53), 270-9.

John Roland Abbey. (Contemporary collectors, 26). Illus. BC, x (61), 40-8.
A. R. A. Hobson and A. N. L. Munby.

ABBEY OF THE HOLY GHOST
The first edition of *The Abbey of the Holy Ghost*. SB, vi (54), 101-6.
C. F. Bühler.

Notes on two incunables: *The Abbey of the Holy Ghost* and *A ryght profytable treatyse*. LIB, x (55) 120-1.
H. S. Bennett.

ABECEDARIA
The Elizabethan ABC with the Catechism. Illus. LIB, xvi (35/6), 32-48.
H. Anders.

'An English ABC imitating handwriting'. (Note, 56) BC, iv (55), 329-30.
C. Clair.

Abecedaria and their purpose. Illus. TCBS, iii (59/63), 181-6.
B. L. Ullman.

ABERCROMBIE, Lascelles
Abercrombie and Housman: a coincidence in parodies. PBSA, xlviii (54), 98-9.
W. White.

ABERDEEN *univ. libr.*
Some early law books in Aberdeen University Library. Illus EBSP, xv (32/5), 1-16.
W. Menzies.

Aberdeen University Library special collections, printed books. BTHK, iii (60/2), 35-40.
H. J. H. Drummond.

German bindings in Aberdeen University Library: iconographic index, and indices of initials, binders, and dates. LIB, xvii (62), 46-55.
W. S. Mitchell.

William Oughtred's *Arithmeticae in numeris* or *Clavis mathematicae*, 1647; an unrecorded (unique?) edition in Aberdeen University Library. BTHK, (67/70), 147-8.
P. J. Wallis.

ABERDEEN INTELLIGENCER
The *Aberdeen Journal* and the *Aberdeen Intelligencer* 1752-7: a further note on a Raban device. BTHK, v (67/70), 204-6.
W. R. McDonald.

ABERDEEN JOURNAL
The *Aberdeen Journal* and the *Aberdeen Intelligencer* 1752-7: a further note on a Raban device. BTHK, v (67/70), 204-6.
W. R. McDonald.

ABERDEEN MAGAZINE
Robert Burns and the *Aberdeen Magazine*. BTHK, v (67/70), 102-5.
G. R. Roy.

ABERDEEN PHILOSOPHICAL SOCIETY
David Skene and the Aberdeen Philosophical Society. BTHK, v (67/70), 81-99.
B. Fabian.

ABERDEENSHIRE
Court song in Scotland after 1603: Aberdeenshire. Illus. EBST, iii (48/55), 159-68.
P. M. Giles and H. M. Shire.

ABGARIAN, G.
The Matenadaran at Erevan. (Unfamiliar libraries, 6). Illus. BC, ix (60), 146-50.

ABINGER CHRONICLE
The *Abinger Chronicle*, 1939-44. (Note, 229). BC, xiii (64), 352.
S. Nowell-Smith.

ACCOUNT OF A VOYAGE
An Account of a Voyage for the discovery of a North-West Passage. London, 1748-9. [?By Charles Swain]. PBSA, xxxvii (43), 308.
B. Solis-Cohen.

ACCURSIUS, Franciscus
Accursius, Franciscus (1225-1293). *Casus in terminis super Codice*. [Strassburg, about 1485]. PBSA, xxxiv (40), 267.
R. B. Anderson.

ACOLASTUS
See GNAPHEUS, Gulielmus

ACQUISITION POLICY
The Acquisition of manuscripts by institutional libraries. PBSA, liv (60), 1-15.
A. N. L. Munby.

Bibliography and the collecting of historical material. PBSA, lviii (64), 141-5.
H. H. Peckham.

AD IMPRIMENDUM SOLUM
Ad imprimendum solum. LIB, ix (54), 242-7.
Sir W. W. Greg.

ADAGIA
'A thing called *Adagia*'. LIB, iv (49/50), 71-3.
J. Crow.

ADAM *OF Rottweil*
Adam Alamanus. Illus. LIB, i (46/7), 237-42.
J. V. Scholderer.

ADAM, Robert
An Adam binding, 1764 [for R. Adam's *Ruins of the palace of the emperor Diocletian at Spalatro*]. (English bookbindings, 57). Illus. BC, xv (66) 184.
H. M. Nixon.

ADAMS, Charles M.
Mr. Ciardi, Mr. Adams, and Mr. White. PBSA, lv (61), 393.
C. E. Feinberg.

ADAMS, Dickinson W.
The New Testament 1611 (Dublin: George Grierson 1799) (Query, 242). BC, xviii (69), 520-1.

ADAMS, Donald K.
"A certain 4to *Elegy*". [Re T. J. Wise, Sir Edmund Gosse and editions of Gray's *Elegy*]. PBSA, lv (61), 229-31.

ADAMS, Frederick Baldwin
Mr. Roosevelt continues, as President and author. PBSA, xxxvii (43), 223-32.

ADAMS, Henry Hitch
A prompt copy of Dryden's *Tyrannic Love*. SB, iv (51/2), 170-4.

ADAMS, Herbert Mayow
A catalogue of sixteenth-century foreign printed books in Cambridge. LIB, x (55), 79-85.

Tables for the identification of octavo Books of Common Prayer, 1553-1640. LIB, xiii (58), after 284.

Tables for identifying the edition of imperfect copies of the Book of Common Prayer, 1600-1640. TCBS, i (49/53), 61-3.

A catalogue of sixteenth-century foreign books in Cambridge [A report]. TCBS, i (49/53), 90-1.

ADAMS, James
James Adams: the first printer of Delaware. PBSA, xxviii (34), 28-63.
D. L. Hawkins.

ADAMS, Joseph Quincy
The *Massacre at Paris* leaf. Illus. LIB, xiv (33/4), 447-69.

Hill's list of early plays in manuscript. LIB, xx (39/40), 71-99.

Another fragment from Henslowe's Diary. Illus. LIB, xx (39/40), 154-8.

The author-plot of an early seventeenth century play.[*Philander King of Thrace*]. Illus. LIB, xxvi (45/6), 447-69.

ADAMS, Katherine
A binding by Katherine Adams. (English bookbindings, 66). Illus. BC, xvii (68), 331.
H. M. Nixon.

ADAMS, Randolph Greenfield
Title variants of Hubley's *American Revolution*. Illus. PBSA, xxx (36), 85-90.

William Hubbard's *Narrative*, 1677. A bibliographical study, PBSA, xxxiii (39), 25-39.

Remarks [on bibliography]. PBSA, xxxvi (42), 59-60.

ADAMS, Raymond
The bibliographical history of Thoreau's *A Week on the Concord and Merrimack Rivers*. PBSA, xliii (49), 39-47.

ADAMS, Robert Martin
Light on Joyce's *Exiles*? A new MS, a curious analogue, and some speculations. SB, xvii (64), 83-105.

ADAMS, Thomas Randolph
The authorship and printing of *Plain Truth* by Candidus. PBSA, xlix (55), 230-48.

A rediscovered Dante *Credo*. PBSA, l (56), 181-2.

Bibliotheca Americana: a merry maze of changing concepts. PBSA, lxiii (69), 247-60.

ADDISON, Joseph
See also SPECTATOR; TATLER

The early editions of Addison's *Campaign*. SB, iii (50/1), 256-61.
R. D. Horn.

Richard Steele, 1672-1729; Joseph Addison, 1672-1719. (English literary autographs, 25). Illus. BC, vii (58), 63.
T. J. Brown.

Two scenes by Addison in Steele's *Tender Husband*. SB, xix (66), 217-26.
S. S. Kenny.

ADDRESS TO A DEIST
See VAIL, Joseph

ADDRESS TO THE INHABITANTS
An address to the inhabitants of the new settlements in the Northern and Western parts of the United States. New Haven [1793 and 1795]. PBSA, xxxiv (40), 187.
A. C. Bates.

ADELIO *pseud.*
A Journey to Philadelphia. By Adelio. Hartford. 1804. PBSA, xxxv (41), 205.
C. S. Brigham.

ADELMAN, Seymour
The first American edition of the Brontës' *Poems* (Query, 121). BC, ix (60), 201.

ADEN, John M.
Swift, Pope, and "the sin of wit". PBSA, lxii (68), 80-5.

ADERMAN, Ralph M.
Contributors to the *American Quarterly Review*, 1827-1833. SB, xiv (61), 163-76.

James Kirke Paulding's contributions to American magazines. SB, xvii (64), 141-51.

Publication dates of three early works by James Kirke Paulding. SB, lix (65), 49-50.

ADKINS, Nelson Frederick
The early projected works of Nathaniel Hawthorne. PBSA, xxxix (45), 119-55.

Chapter on American Cribbage: Poe and plagiarism. PBSA, xlii (48), 169-210.

Notes on the Hawthorne canon. PBSA, lx (66), 364-7.

ADMONITION
An admonition to borrowers [in the sale catalogue of the library of Ralph Willet, 1813]. (Note, 220). BC, xiii (64), 211.
A. Ehrman.

ADVANCE COPIES
Crane's *Red Badge of Courage* and other advance copies. SB, xxii (69), 273-7.
F. T. Bowers.

ADVERTISEMENTS
An early blurb. (Query, 12). BC, i (52), 130.
E. M. Dring.

Advertisements in Cruikshank's *The Bee and the Wasp*. (Query, 150). BC, xi (62), 352.
J. M. Shaw.

A 17th-century bookseller's circular. (Query, 153). BC, xi (62), 484-5.
B. Weinreb.

Was Mr. Spooner advertising? (Note, 195). BC, xii (63), 204.
D. Parikian.

'Minerva Press' publicity — a publisher's advertisement. LIB, xxi (40/1), 207-15.
M. Sadleir.

On the use of advertisements in bibliographical studies. LIB, viii (53), 174-87.
W. B. Todd.

[A letter]. LIB, ix (54), 134-5.
J. R. Moore.

Two unrecorded early book advertisements. LIB, xi (56), 114-15.
J. V. Scholderer.

John Newbery, projector of the *Universal Chronicle*: a study of the advertisements. SB, xi (58), 249-51.
G. J. Kolb.

The laureate as huckster: Nahum Tate and an early eighteenth century example of publisher's advertising. SB, xxi (68), 261-6.
S. Astor.

ADVOCATES' LIBRARY
See NATIONAL LIBRARY OF SCOTLAND

AELFRIC *abbot of Eynsham*
The first book printed in Anglo-Saxon types. [Aelfric, *A testimonie of antiquitie*]. Illus. TCBS, iii (59/63), 265-91.
J. Bromwich.

AESOP
The undated *Aesop* attributed to Jakob Wolff de Pforzheim (Hain-Copinger, 327). LIB, xii (57), 119-21.
C. C. Rattey.

A post-incunable edition of Aesop. LIB, xiv (59), 281-2.
D. E. Rhodes.

Aesopus Moralisatus. Brescia, Jacobus Britannicus, 1485. PBSA, xxxiv (40), 84.
F. R. Goff.

AGREEMENTS
A publishing agreement of the late seventeenth century. [Re *Henrici Mori Cantabrigiensis Opera Theologica,* 1675]. LIB, xiii (32/3), 184-7.
R. B. McKerrow.

Three eighteenth-century American book contracts. PBSA, xlvii (53), 381-7.
R. G. Silver.

AILLEVARD, Jean *pseud.*
Crabbe's *Inebriety,* 1775. (Query, 53). BC, iii (54), 309-10.

AILLY, Pierre d' *card., bp. of Cambrai*
See ALLIACO, Petrus de *card., bp. of Cambrai*

AITKEN, Robert
A note on Robert Aitken, printer of the 'Bible of the Revolution', BTHK, v (67/70), 36-7.
R. L. Crawford.

AITKEN, William Russell
William Soutar, bibliographical notes and a checklist. BTHK, i/2 (56/8), 3-14.

Further notes on the bibliography of James Leslie Mitchell/Lewis Grassic Gibbon. BTHK, i/2 (56/8), 34-5.

C. M. Grieve/Hugh MacDiarmid. BTHK, i/4 (56/8), 3-23.

Neil Miller Gunn. BTHK, iii (60/2), 89-95.

Eric Linklater. BTHK, v (67/70), 190-3.

AITKEN BINDERY
The Aitken shop. Identification of an eighteenth-century bindery and its tools. Illus. PBSA, lvii (63), 422-37.
W. *and* C. Spawn.

AKENSIDE, Mark
Akenside's *The Pleasures of Imagination.* (Note, 62). BC, v (56), 77-8.
D. F. Foxon.

ALAMNUS, Adam
See ADAM *of Rottweil*

ALBERT *prince consort*
An illuminated vellum binding for the Prince Consort, 1843. (English bookbindings, 26). Illus. BC, vii (58), 284.
H. M. Nixon.

ALBION PRESS
The Albion press. Illus. JPHS, ii (66), 58-73.
R. Stone.

— Addenda and corrigenda. JPHS, iii (67), 97-100.
R. Stone.

ALBIONS TRIUMPH
Albions Triumph: a further corrected state of the text. LIB, xvi (61), 294-9.
E. Veevers.

The art of selling books: notes on three Aldus catalogues, 1586-1592. SB, i (48/9), 83-101.
R. Hirsch.

The errata lists in the first Aldine editions of Caro's *Rime* and of the *Due orationi* of St. Gregorius Nazianzenus. SB, xv (62), 219-22.
C. F. Bühler.

ALDIS, Owen Franklin
Aldis, Foley, and the collection of American literature at Yale. PBSA, xliii (48), 41-9.
D. C. Gallup.

ALDRICH, Thomas Bailey
T. B. Aldrich and *Household Words*. PBSA, xlii (48), 70-2.
G. J. L. Gomme.

ALDUS *family*
See ALDINE PRESS

ALEXANDER VI *pope*
Two unrecorded incunabula [Alexander VI, *Regulae cancellariae*, Strassburg, Johann Prüss, 1495. and *Almanach auf das Jahr 1492*, [[Leipzig, Gregor Boettiger]]. Illus. BC, vi (57), 259-62.
G. Borsa.

Two issues of an indulgence of Alexander VI. LIB, xv (60), 206-7.
D. E. Rhodes.

ALEXANDER *the great*
A ghost edition of the *Historia Alexandri Magni*. (Note, 125). BC, ix (60), 67-8.
D. J. A. Ross.

The printed editions of the French Alexander Romance. LIB, vii (52), 54-7.
D. J. A. Ross.

The French prose Alexander romance. LIB, xx (65), 243-4.
L. W. Riley.

ALEXANDER *grammaticus*
The early London editions of the *Doctrinale* of Alexander Grammaticus: with a note on Duff 224. LIB, xxiv (69), 232-4.
D. E. Rhodes.

ALEXANDER, Elizabeth H.
A further bibliography of the writings of John Ferguson, M.A., LL.D., F.S.A., Regius Professor of Chemistry in the University of Glasgow, 1874-1915. Illus. GBSR, xii (36), 82-127.

ALEXANDER, Peter
Two notes on the text of Shakespeare. [*A Midsummer-Night's Dream*, II, i, 77; *The Merry Wives of Windsor*, II, ii]. EBST, ii (38/45), 409-13.

ALEXANDER, sir William
Sir William Alexander's *Supplement* to Book III of Sidney's *Arcadia*. Illus. LIB, xxiv (69), 234-41.
A. Mitchell *and* K. Foster.

The date of publication and composition of Sir William Alexander's supplement to Sidney's *Arcadia*. PBSA, l (56), 387-92.
A. G. D. Wiles.

ALEXANDROVNA, princess Marie
See MARIE *duchess of Edinburgh*

ALEYN, Charles
Aleyn's *The Historie of that Wise Prince, Henrie the Seventh*. (Query, 80). BC, vi (57), 181.
G. B. Lowe.

ALGAR, F.
Engravings by Isaac Taylor. (Note, 3). BC, i (52), 126-7.

ALL THE YEAR ROUND
The American edition of *All the Year Round*. PBSA, xlvii (53), 301-4.
G. G. Grubb.

ALLEN, C. G.
The sources of 'Lily's Latin Grammar': a review of the facts and some further suggestions. LIB, ix (54), 85-100.

Certayne Briefe Rules and 'Lily's Latin Grammar'. LIB, xiv (59), 49-53.

ALLEN, Don Cameron
Some contemporary accounts of Renaissance printing methods. LIB, xvii (36/7), 167-71.

ALLEN, Gay Wilson
Walt Whitman's reception in Scandinavia. PBSA, xl (46), 259-75.

ALLEN, Robert R.
Variant readings in Johnson's *London*. PBSA, lx (66), 214-15.

ALLENTUCK, Marcia
Where are Fuseli's letters? (Query, 199). BC, xv (66), 69.

ALLESTREE, Richard
Richard Allestree and *The Whole Duty of Man*. LIB, vi (51/2), 19-27.
P. Elmen.

ALLIACO, Petrus de *card., bp. of Cambrai*
Ailly, Pierre d', *cardinal* (1350-1420?). *Destructiones modorum significandi*. [Lyons] Jason Carcain, [about 1492] PBSA, xxxv (41), 293.
H. R. Mead.

Imago Mundi. [Sir Walter Raleigh's copy of the work by Pierre d'Ailly]. (Collector's piece, 1). Illus. BC, xv (66), 12-18.
W. Oakeshott.

ALLISON, Antony Francis
Early English books at the London Oratory, a supplement to *STC*. LIB, ii (47/8), 95-107.

A note on the authorship of three works against Thomas Bell. LIB, ii (47/8), 286-9.

Robert Howard, Franciscan. LIB, iii (48/9), 288-91.

— *and others*. List of books acquired by the British Museum from Chatsworth. Part II. English books 1501-1640. Part III. Bindings. BC, viii (59), 52-9.

ALLOTT, Mary
Philip Chetwind and the Allott copyrights.
LIB, xv (34/5), 129-60.
H. Farr.

ALLOTT, T. J. D.
Jean Bertaut and the French anthologies about
1600. LIB, xxii (67), 136-42.

ALMANACKS
Woodcuts for an almanac. (Query, 64). Illus.
BC, iv (55), 254-5.
M. Frost.

—. BC, v (56), 174-5.
B. A. Gross.

Notes on further addenda to English printed
almanacks and prognostications to 1600. LIB,
xviii (37/8), 39-66.
E. F. Bosanquet.

Some English mock-prognostications. LIB, xix
(38/9), 6-43.
F. P. Wilson.

An almanac for the year 1478. LIB, xix (38/9),
99-102.
J. V. Scholderer.

The distribution of almanacks in the second
half of the seventeenth century. SB, xi (58),
107-16.
C. Blagden.

Thomas Carnan and the almanack monopoly.
SB, xiv (61), 23-43.
C. Blagden.

Franklin's *Poor Richard Almanacs:* their
printing and publication. SB, xiv (61), 97-115.
C. W. Miller.

ALSPACH, Russell King
Some textual problems in Yeats. SB, ix (57),
51-67.

ALSTON, Robin Carfrae
Bibliography and historical linguistics. LIB,
xxi (66), 181-91.

ALTHOLZ, Josef Lewis
Bibliographical note on the *Rambler* [1848-62].
PBSA, lvi (62), 113-4.

ALTICK, Richard Daniel
Cope's Tobacco Plant: an episode in Victorian
Journalism. Illus. PBSA, xlv (51), 333-50.

English publishing and the mass audience in
1852. SB, vi (54), 3-24.

From Aldine to Everyman: cheap reprint series
of the English classics, 1830-1906. SB, xi (58),
3-24.

Nineteenth-century English best-sellers: a
further list. SB, xxii (69), 197-206.

AMBROSE, Issac
Isaac Ambrose (1604-1663) & William Bates
(1625-1699). *Christ in the Clouds coming to
Judgement.* [Various American eds., 1752-1811].
PBSA, xxxiv (40), 187.
C. S. Brigham.

AMERICAN AUTHORS
The descriptive bibliography of American
authors. SB, xxi (68), 1-24.
G. T. Tanselle.

AMERICAN FICTION
Propaganda in early American fiction. PBSA,
xxxiii (39), 98-106.
L. M. Wright.

AMERICAN POETRY
American poetry of the first world war and the
book trade. PBSA, lxi (67), 209-24.
J. A. Hart.

AMERICAN-PRINTED HISTORICAL WORKS
Evidence indicating the needs for some bibliographical analysis of American-printed historical works. PBSA, lxiii (69), 261-77.
E. Wolf *2nd.*

AMERICAN QUARTERLY REVIEW
Contributors to the *American Quarterly Review,*
1827-1833. SB, xiv (61), 163-76.
R. M. Aderman.

AMERICAN REVOLUTION
A nineteenth-century view of the historiography of the American Revolution: a footnote
on plagiarism. PBSA, lviii (64), 164-9.
R. K. Newmyer.

AMERICAN STATE UNIVERSITY LIBRARIES
Rare books in American State university libra-
ries. BC, vi (57), 232-43.
R. B. Downs.

AMERICAN TRACT SOCIETY
The printing and publishing activities of the
American Tract Society from 1825 to 1850.
Illus. PBSA, xxxv (41), 81-114.
L. S. Thompson.

AMERICANA
Americanum nauticum. PBSA, xli (47), 343-4.
H. M. Lydenberg.

A 1642 Americana item. PBSA, xlii (48), 321.
E. E. Willoughby.

Some bibliographical adventures in Americana.
PBSA, xliv (50), 17-28.
C. W. Barrett.

The first trans-Mississippi imprint. PBSA, lii
(58), 306-9.
D. Kaser.

Tracing western territorial imprints through
the National Archives. PBSA, lix (65), 1-11.
W. A. Katz.

Bibliotheca Americana. PBSA, lxii (68), 351-9.
C. K. Shipley.

Bibliotheca Americana: a merry maze of changing concepts. PBSA, lxiii (69), 247-60.
T. R. Adams.

AMORY, Hugh
A preliminary census of Henry Fielding's legal
manuscripts. PBSA, lxii (68), 587-601.

AMSTERDAM
Amsterdam — cradle of English newspapers.
Illus. LIB, iv (49/50), 166-78.
F. Dahl.

The exiled English Church at Amsterdam and
its press. Illus. LIB, v (50/1), 219-42.
A. F. Johnson.

J. F. Stam, Amsterdam, and English Bibles.
Illus. LIB, ix (54), 185-93.
A. F. Johnson.

ANBUREY, Thomas
Thomas Anburey's *Travels through America*:
a note on eighteenth-century plagiarism.
PBSA, xxxvii (43), 23-36.
W. J. Bell.

ANDERS, H.
The Elizabethan ABC with the Catechism.
Illus., LIB, xvi (35/6), 32-48.

ANDERSEN, Hans Christian
Hans Anderson. (Query, 52). BC, iii (54),
308-9.
P. H. Muir.

ANDERSON, A.
Gray's *Elegy* in *Miscellaneous pieces,* 1752.
LIB, xx (65),144-8.

ANDERSON, Alexander
Joel Munsell prints Lossing's *Memorial of
Alexander Anderson.* PBSA, xlv (51), 351-5.
D. S. Edelstein.

ANDERSON, Andrew H.
The books and interests of Henry, lord Stafford, 1501-1563. Illus. LIB, xxi (66), 87-114.

ANDERSON, G. L.
The authorship of *Cato Examin'd,* 1713.
PBSA, li (57), 84-90.

ANDERSON, Hans Christian
See ANDERSEN, Hans Christian

ANDERSON, Howard
The manuscript of M. G. Lewis's *The Monk*:
some preliminary notes. PBSA, lxii (68),
427-34.

ANDERSON, Maxwell
Maxwell Anderson (1876-). *Saturday's
Children.* New York, 1927. PBSA, xxxiv (40),
89.
M. K. Howes.

Additions to the bibliography of Maxwell
Anderson. PBSA, lvii (63), 90-1.
G. T. Tanselle.

Addenda to the Maxwell Anderson bibliography; *The Measure.* PBSA, lxiii (69), 31-6.
L. G. Avery.

ANDERSON, Robert Bolvie
Franciscus Accursius (1225-1293). *Casus in
terminis super Codice.* [Strassburg, about 1485].
PBSA, xxxiv (40), 267.

ANDERSON, Sam Follet
A variant specimen of Anton Sorg's *Bücheranzeige* of 1483-1484. Illus. PBSA, lii (58),
48-52.

ANDERSON, Sherwood
Additional reviews of Sherwood Anderson's
work. PBSA, lvi (62), 358-65.
G. T. Tanselle.

The first printing of Sherwood Anderson's
Winesburg, Ohio. SB, iv (51/2), 211-13.
W. L. Phillips.

ANDERSON, Wallace Ludwig
Letters of Edwin Arlington Robinson. (Query,
224). BC, xvii (68), 219.

ANDREWS, John
John Andrews' *History of the War with America*:
a further note on eighteenth-century plagiarism.
PBSA, lv (61), 385-92.
R. K. Newmyer.

ANGLE, Paul McClelland
Four Lincoln firsts. PBSA, xxxvi (42), 1-17.

ANGLING BOOKS
A new line for the *Angler,* 1577. LIB, x (55),
123-5.
D. E. Rhodes.

ANGLO-LATIN POETRY
Musae Anglicanae: a supplemental list. LIB,
xxii (67), 93-103.
L. Bradner.

ANGLO-SAXON STUDIES
The dispersal of the monastic libraries and the
beginnings of Anglo-Saxon studies; Matthew
Parker and his circle: a preliminary study. Illus.
TCBS, i (49/53), 208-37.
C. E. Wright.

The first book printed in Anglo-Saxon types.
[Aelfric *A testimonie of antiquitie*]. Illus.
TCBS, iii (59/63), 265-91.
J. Bromwich.

The non-runic scripts of Anglo-Saxon inscriptions. Illus. TCBS, iv (64/8), 321-38.
E. Okasha.

ANGOULÊME, Margaret of
See MARGARET, *consort of Henry II king of
Navarre.*

ANGUS, Norman S.
A manuscript of James White's translation of
The Clouds. LIB, xxvi (45/6), 304-7.

ANGUS, William
An eighteenth-century social and economic
survey of the Highlands. EBST, ii (38/45),
426-9.

ANNAN, Gertrude L.
Regimen sanitatis. [14]99. PBSA, xxxiv (40),
185.

*An Abstract of the Patent Granted by His
Majesty King George to Benj. Okell.* London,
1731. PBSA, xxxiv (40), 186.

ANNOTATION
Preliminary short-title list of bibliographies containing manuscript notes. PBSA, xliii (49), 209-26.
T. Besterman.

Principles of annotation: some suggestions for editors of Shakespeare. SB, ix (57), 95-105.
A. Walker.

ANNUAL ANTHOLOGY
The contributors to *The Annual Anthology.* PBSA, xlii (48), 50-65.
K. Curry.

ANNUAL REGISTER
A bibliographical account of the *Annual Register,* 1758-1825. LIB, xvi (61), 104-20.
W. B. Todd.

Edmund Burke's friends and *The Annual Register.* LIB, xviii (63), 29-39.
T. W. Copeland.

Burke's authorship of the historical articles in Dodsley's *Annual Register.* PBSA, li (52), 244-9.
J. C. Weston.

Editorial mannerisms in the early *Annual Register.* PBSA, lii (58), 131-7.
B. D. Sarason.

Predecessors to Burke's and Dodsley's *Annual Register.* SB, xvii (64), 215-20.
J. C. Weston.

ANT AND THE NIGHTINGALE
The early editions of *The ant and the nightingale.* PBSA, xliii (49), 179-90.
G. R. Price.

ANTHOLOGIES
Jean Bertaut and the French anthologies about 1600. LIB, xxi (67), 136-42.
T. J. D. Allott.

ANTIGUA
A checklist of early printing on the island of Antigua, 1748-1880. PBSA, l (56), 285-92.
B. F. Swan.

ANTI-JACOBIN
The authorship of poems in *The Anti-Jacobin.* (Query, 180). BC, xiii (64), 214.
H. Shine.

ANTONIA *de Salamanca*
See MARTINEZ, Antonia

ANTONINUS *st., abp. of Florence*
A Lyonese book, 1506. [Antoninus, *Summa theologica*]. PBSA, xl (46), 229-30.
C. F. Bühler.

APOSTROPHES
Some early apostrophes to printing. PBSA, liv (66),113-15.
R. H. Bowers.

APPIANUS *of Alexandria*
A manuscript of the Latin version of Appian's *Civil Wars.* Illus. LIB, xxvi (45/6), 149-57.
A. M. Woodward.

APPLEGATH, Augustus
Augustus Applegath, some notes and references. JPHS, ii (66), 49-57.
W. T. Berry.

APPRENTICES
Apprenticeship in the Stationers' Company, 1555-1640. LIB, xiii (58), 292-9.
D. F. McKenzie.

A list of printers' apprentices, 1605-1640. SB, xiii (60), 119-41.
D. F. McKenzie.

AQUINAS, Thomas, *st.*
An incunabulum of Esslingen. [Aquinas's *Catena aurea*]. LIB, xii (57), 270-1.
J. V. Scholderer.

ARBROATH
An Arbroath book inventory of 1473. BTHK, iii (60/2), 144-6.
J. Durkan.

ARCHANGEL GOSPELS
The binding of the Archangel Gospels. Illus. BC, xiii (64), 481-5.
B. van Regemorter.

ARCHER, Horace Richard
The writings of William Faulkner: a challenge to the bibliographer. PBSA, l (56), 229-42.

ARCHPRIEST CONTROVERSY
The Archpriest Controversy and the printers, 1601-1603. LIB, ii (47/8), 180-6.
G. Jenkins.

ARDAGH, Philip
St. Andrews University Library and the Copyright Acts. EBST, iii (48/55), 179-211.

ARDEN OF FEVERSHAM
The Southeast text of *Arden of Feversham.* LIB, v (50/1), 113-29.
J. M. Nosworthy.

ARENTS, George
Where there's smoke there's — literature. PBSA, xxxv (41), 145-50.

ARGENTINA
Incunabula and fine printing in Argentina. PBSA, xxxvi (42), 315-18.
M. B. Stillwell.

ARGENTINE, John
Provost Argentine of King's and his books. Illus. TCBS, ii (54/8), 205-12.
D. E. Rhodes.

— Addendum. TCBS, iii (59/63, 263).
J. M. Fletcher.

ARISTOPHANES
A manuscript of James White's translation of *The Clouds.* LIB, xxvi (45/6), 304-7.
N. S. Angus.

ARISTOTLE
Variants in the 1479 Oxford edition of Aristotle's *Ethics.* SB, viii (56), 209-12.
D. E. Rhodes.

ARLAUD-DUCHANGE PORTRAIT OF
SHAKESPEARE
The Arlaud-Duchange portrait of Shakespeare.
Illus. LIB, xvi (35/6), 290-4.
G. E. Dawson.

A note on the Arlaud-Duchange portrait of
Shakespeare. LIB, xviii (37/8), 342-4.
G. E. Dawson.

ARMITAGE, C. M.
Identification of New York Public Library
manuscript 'Suckling Collection' and of Huntington manuscript 198. SB, xix (66), 215-16.

ARMSTRONG, Charles E.
The *Voyage to Cadiz* in the second edition of
Hakluyt's Voyages. PBSA, xlix (55), 254-62.

ARMSTRONG, James C. *and* CARPENTER,
Kenneth E.
James Russell Lowell *On Democracy.* PBSA,
lix (65), 385-99.

ARMSTRONG, John
A seventeenth-century Cambridge book and its
cost. [John Armstrong's *Secret and family
prayers* and *The souls worth and danger*].
TCBS, ii (54/8), 376-81.
F. Barnes *and* J. C. Dickinson.

ARMSTRONG, Samuel T.
Belcher & Armstrong set up shop: 1805.
SB, iv (51/2), 201-4.
R. G. Silver.

ARMY PRINTING
Army field printing in the New World. Illus.
PBSA, l (56), 169-80.
E. H. Carpenter.

ARNOLD, John Henry *and* EELES, Francis Carolus
Some leaves of a thirteenth-century missal
probably from Jedburgh Abbey. [*With*] Notes
on the music. EBST, iii (48/55), 1-15.

ARNOLD, Matthew
Matthew Arnold in private collections. (Query,
lll). BC, viii (59), 73.
R. L. Brooks.

Matthew Arnold, 1822-88. (English literary
autographs, 46). Illus. BC, xii (63), 195.
T. J. Brown.

The autograph of Arnold's *Sohrab and Rustum.*
(Note, 209). BC, xii (63), 494.
T. J. Brown.

Matthew Arnold's *Stanzas from Carnan* and
A Southern Night. (Note, 259). BC, xiv (65),
543.
R. L. Brooks.

An unrecorded American edition of the *Selected Poems of Matthew Arnold.* LIB, xvi (61),
213-14.
R. L. Brooks.

The *Strayed Reveller* myth. LIB, xviii (63),
57-60.
R. L. Brooks.

A census of Matthew Arnold's *Poems* 1853.
PBSA, liv (60), 184-6.
R. L. Brooks.

A neglected edition of Matthew Arnold's
poetry and a bibliographical correction.
PBSA, lv (61), 140-1.
R. L. Brooks.

A Danish *Balder Dead.* PBSA, lvi (62), 253-4.
R. L. Brooks.

The Story manuscript of Matthew Arnold's
New Rome. PBSA, lviii (64), 295-7.
R. L. Brooks.

Matthew Arnold and Percy William Bunting:
some new letters, 1884-1887. SB, vii (55),
199-207.
R. L. Lowe.

Some unaccomplished projects of Matthew
Arnold. SB, xvi (63), 213-16.
R. L. Brooks.

ARSDEL, Rosemary van
John Chapman and *The Westminster Review.*
BC, v (56), 171-2.

ARUNDEL *castle*
The Harington manuscript at Arundel castle
and related documents. Illus. LIB, xv (34/5),
388-444.
R. Hughey.

ARUNDEL *12th earl of*
See FITZALAN, Henry *12th earl of Arundel*

ASHE, Dora Jean
The text of Peele's *Edward I.* SB, vii (55),
153-70.

ASSHETON, Ralph
The library of Ralph Assheton: the book
background of a colonial Philadelphia lawyer.
PBSA, lviii (64), 345-79.

ASSOCIATION COPIES
Association copies. Illus. BC, ii (53), 241-6.
Sir S. C. Roberts.

A much-travelled association copy of Calvin's
Institutes. (Collector's piece, 3). Illus. BC,
xvii (68), 458-62.
C. S. Bliss.

Association copies. EBST, ii (38/45) 447-8.
J. A. Petrie.

ASTELL, Mary
Mary Astell, 1666-1731. (Some uncollected
authors, 27). BC, x (61), 58-65.
J. E. Norton.

Two facts about Mary Astell. (Note, 163).
BC, x (61), 334.
R. Halsband.

Mary Astell's *Serious Proposals to the Ladies,*
1694. (Note, 164). BC, x (61), 334-5.
W. B. Todd *and* BC, x (61), 448. J. E. Norton.

ASTOR, Stuart L.
   The laureate as huckster: Nahum Tate and an
   early eighteenth century example of publisher's
   advertising. SB, xxi (68), 261-6.

ASTROLABES
   A note on the astrolabe of Regiomontanus.
   LIB, xv (60), 209.
   J. V. Scholderer.

ATHENIAN ORACLE
   The Athenian Oracle. 2nd ed. London, 1704.
   PBSA, xxxvi (42), 320.
   F. R. Goff.

ATHENS, *Gennadius libr.*
   Two anonymous translations of pseudo-
   Xenophon [in the Gennadius Library]. (Query,
   219). BC, xvi (67), 512-13.
   F. R. Walton.

ATKINS, Samuel B. *and* KELLEY, Maurice
   Milton and the Harvard Pindar. SB, xvii (64),
   77-82.

ATTO, Clayton
   The Society for the Encouragement of Learning.
   LIB, xix (38/9), 263-88.

ATTRIBUTIONS
   Evidence of authorship. (Query, 175). BC, xiii
   (64), 71.
   J. B. Shipley.

   Authorship attributions in early play-lists,
   1656-1671. EBST, ii (38/45), 303-29.
   Sir W. W. Greg.

ATWATER, V. G. B. *and* FUSSELL, George
   Edwin
   Travel and topography in seventeenth-century
   England. A bibliography of sources for social
   and economic history. LIB, xiii (32/3), 292-311.

AUBIGNY, Bernault d'
   A work assigned to Bernault d'Aubigny. EBST,
   iii (48/55), 81.
   G. Dickinson.

AUDEN, Wystan Hugh
   W. H. Auden's first book. LIB, xvii (62),
   152-4.
   B. C. Bloomfield.

   The printing of Auden's *Poems*, 1928, and
   Spender's *Nine experiments*. LIB, xxii (67),
   149-50.
   A. T. Tolley.

AUERBACK, P.
   An unknown edition of the Ilias. [Paris, Jean
   Vatel, 1520]. LIB, xvii (36/7), 448-53.

AUGSBURG
   Notes on early Augsburg printing. Illus.
   LIB, vi (51/2), 1-6.
   J. V. Scholderer.

   An unidentified 'incunable' printed at Augsburg
   not before 1502. LIB, xiii (58), 54-6.
   D. E. Rhodes.

AUGUSTINE *st.*
   A palimpsest in the National Library of
   Scotland: early fragments of Augustine *De
   Trinitate,* the *Passio S. Laurentii* and other
   texts. Illus. EBST, iii (48/55), 169-79.
   N. R. Ker.

   The first pirate. [The priority of Fust or
   Mentelin's editions of St. Augustine's *De Arte
   Praedicandi*]. LIB, xxiv (43/4), 30-46.
   F. W. Householder.

   The first collected edition of Saint Augustine.
   LIB, xiv (59), 46-9.
   J. V. Scholderer.

AUNGERVYLE, Richard *bp. of Durham*
   Richard de Bury and the Philobiblon. BH, i
   (47/51), 282-92.
   W. M. Dickie.

AUSONIUS Decimus Magnus
   Decimus Magnus Ausonius: *Opera.* Venice
   [Epon. Press] 1472. LIB, v (50/1), 270-1.
   C. C. Rattey.

   The first edition of Ausonius. PBSA, xli (47),
   60.
   C. F. Bühler.

AUSTEN, Jane
   Who was Sophie Sentiment? Was she Jane
   Austen? BC, xv (66), 143-51.
   Sir Z. V. Cope.

   The first American editions of Jane Austen.
   (Query, 218). BC, xvi (67), 512.
   D. J. Gilson.

   The early American editions of Jane Austen.
   Illus. BC, xviii (69), 340-52.
   D. J. Gilson.

   The manuscript of Jane Austen's Volume the
   First. LIB, xvii (62), 231-7.
   B. C. Southam.

   Austen, Jane (1775-1817). *Emma: a novel.*
   Philadelphia, 1816. PBSA, xxxiv (40), 89-90.
   C. B. Hogan.

AUSTEN-LEIGH, Richard Arthur
   See LEIGH, Richard Arthur Austen—

AUSTIN, C. S.
   Girault de Sainville. (Note, 48). BC, iv (55), 171.

AUSTIN, Gabriel
   The earliest catalogue of incunabula. (Query,
   196). BC, xv (66), 213.

AUSTRALIA
   Lost incunabula of S. Australia. (Query, 66).
   BC, v (56), 78-9.
   K. T. Borrow.

AUTHOR PAYMENTS
   Longfellow's income from his writings, 1840-
   1852. PBSA, xxxviii (44), 9-21.
   W. Charvat.

   Fees paid to authors by certain American
   periodicals, 1840-1850. SB, ii (49), 95-104.
   J. A. Robbins.

Hawthorne's income from *The Token*. SB, viii (56), 236-8.
S. L. Gross.

AUTHOR'S CERTIFICATE
Author's certificate to the printer. (Note, 37). BC, iii (54), 226.
J. Wellesley.

AVERY, Laurence G.
Addenda to the Maxwell Anderson bibliography: *The Measure*. PBSA, lxiii (69), 31-6.

AXTELL, James L.
Concerning James Tyrrell, 1642-1718. (Query, 159). BC, xii (63), 72.

AYERS, Robert W.
A suppressed edition of Milton's *Defensio Secunda* 1654. PBSA, lv (61), 75-87.

The John Phillips — John Milton *Angli Responsio*: editions and relations. PBSA, lvi (62), 66-72.

AYSCOUGH, William
Ayscough's *Weekly Courant*. [A letter]. LIB, xxv (44/5), 80-1.
W. A. Potter.

AYTOUN, sir Robert
Ralegh and Ayton: the disputed authorship of *Wrong Not Sweete Empress of my Heart*. SB, xiii (60), 191-8.
C. B. Gullans.

The Rogers editions of Sir Robert Aytoun. PBSA, lviii (64), 32-4.
W. Roberts.

B

B., A. C. *pseud.*
Extant copies of Tennyson's *Timbuctoo,* 1829. (Query, 101). BC, vii (58), 296.

BABB, James Tinkham
Thomas Jefferson Hogg. (Query, 7). BC, i (52), 56-7.

—. BC, i (52), 130.

In memoriam: James Tinkham Babb, 1899-1968. PBSA, lxiii (69), 1-3.
M. G. Wynne.

BABCOCK, Robert Witbeck
A supplement to the bibliography of *Shakespeare Idolatry* [by R. W. Babcock]. SB, iv (51/2), 164-6.
M. L. Wiley.

BACKUS, Azel
Azel Backus, (1765-1817): *Absalom's conspiracy a sermon.* Suffield, 1798. PBSA, xxxiv (40), 271.
A. C. Bates.

BACON, Francis *visct. St. Albans*
A Baconian and Cervantes. (Note, 146). BC, ix (60), 454.
D. H. Woodward.

Fine paper copies of Bacon's *Essays,* 1625. (Note, 263). BC, xiv (65), 545.
R. S. Pirie.

Francis Bacon, 1561-1626. (English scientific autographs, 8). Illus. BC, xv (66), 185.
T. J. Brown.

Bacon's copy of a Douai-Reims Bible. LIB, iii (48/9), 54-6.
E. E. Willoughby.

The 1613 editions of Bacon's *Essays.* LIB, iii (48/9), 122-4.
P. S. Dunkin.

BACON, sir Nicholas
The origin of Sir Nicholas Bacon's book-plate. TCBS, ii (54/8), 373-6.
E. R. Sandeen.

BADER, Arno Lehman
Captain Marryat and the American pirates. LIB, xvi (35/6), 327-36.

BADINSSE Louis de
A "lost" poet of Louisiana [Louis de Badinsse]. Illus. PBSA, xlvi (52), 387-91.
J. F. McDermott.

BAENDER, Paul
The meaning of copy-text. SB, xxii (69), 311-18.

BAGE, Robert
The life of Robert Bage, papermaker and novelist. Illus. BH, i (47/51), 18-30.
C. Hutton.

A preliminary survey for a bibliography of the novels of Robert Bage. BH, i (47/51), 30-6.
E. A. Osborne.

BAIL, Hamilton Vaughan
James Russell Lowell's *Ode Recited at the Commemoration of the Living and Dead Soldiers of Harvard University,* July 21, 1865. PBSA, xxxvii (43), 169-202.

BAILDON, John
De Beau Chesne, John and Baildon, John. *A booke containing divers sortes of hands.* London, Thomas Vautrouillier, 1581. PBSA, xxxv (41), 293.
F. R. Goff.

BAILEY, David
Addenda to Irish [*The modern American muse*]: Theodora Taylor, Rixford J. Lincoln, David Bailey, Lester S. Parker. PBSA, lxiii (69), 198-200.
R. C. Johnson.

BAILEY, Nathan
Notes on serialization and competitive publishing: Johnson's and Bailey's *Dictionaries,* 1755. OBSP, v (40), 305-22.
P. B. Gove.

Bailey's folio *Dictionary:* a supplementary note. OBSP, i (40/48), 45-6.
P.B. Gove.

Bibliographical information concerning N. Bailey and John Kersey. (Query, 216). BC, xvi (67), 225.
G. Freeman.

BAILEY, Philip James
English editions of Philip James Bailey's *Festus.* PBSA, xliv (50), 55-8.
M. Peckham.

BAIN, D. C.
Some notes on the printing of the *Summa de Exemplis,* 1499. LIB, xxi (40/1), 192-8.

BAIN, Iain S.
Thomas Ross & Son: copper and steel-plate printers since 1833. Illus. JPHS, ii (66), 3-22.

James Moyes's Temple printing office of 1825. Illus. JPHS, iv (68), 1-10.

BAINE, John
A note on John Baine. EBST, iii (48/55), 22.
R. P. Doig.

BAINE, Rodney M.
The publication of Steele's *Conscious Lovers.* SB, ii (49/50), 169-73.

The first anthologies of English literary criticism, Warton to Haslewood. SB, iii (50/1), 262-5.

BAIRD, John D.
MSS by or relating to William Cowper. (Query, 214). BC, xvii (68), 217.

BAKER, Charles Henry Collins
Some illustrators of Milton's *Paradise Lost,* 1688-1850. Illus. 2 pts. LIB, iii (48/9), 1-21; 101-19.

BALD, Robert Cecil
The Shakespeare folios. Illus. BH, i (47/51), 100-5.

The *Locrine* and *George-A-Greene* title page inscription. Illus. LIB, xv (34/5), 295-305.

Sir William Berkeley's *The Lost Lady*. Illus. LIB, xvii (36/7), 395-426.

Arthur Wilson's *The Inconstant Lady*. Illus. LIB, xviii (37/8), 287-313.

A. E. Housman — an annotated check-list. Additions and corrections. LIB, xxiii (42/3), 43-4.

The foul papers of a revision. Illus. LIB, xxvi (45/6), 37-50.

Landor's *Sponsalia Polyxenae*. LIB, iv (49/50), 211-12.

Early copyright litigation and its bibliographical interest. PBSA, xxxvi (42), 81-96.

Editorial problems — a preliminary survey. SB, iii (50/1), 3-17.

Dr. Donne and the booksellers. SB, xviii (65), 69-80.

BALDWIN, Anne
Richard and Anne Baldwin, Whig patriot publishers. PBSA, xlvii (53), 1-42.
L. Rostenberg.

BALDWIN, Joseph Glover
Baldwin's *Flush Times of Alabama and Mississippi*—a bibliographical note. PBSA, xlv (51), 251-6.
J. F. McDermott.

BALDWIN, Richard
Richard and Anne Baldwin, Whig patriot publishers. PBSA, xlvii (53), 1-42.
L. Rostenberg.

BALE, John *bp. of Ossory*
Books and manuscripts formerly in the possession of John Bale. LIB, xvi (35/6), 144-65.
H. McCusker.

The resurreccion of the Masse, by Hugh Hilarie —or John Bale (?). LIB, xxi (40/1), 143-59.
C. Garrett.

A bibliography of John Bale. Illus. OBSP, v (40), 201-79.
W. T. Davies.

— Additions and corrections. OBSP, i (49), 44-5.
J. G. McManaway.

BALFOUR-MELVILLE, Evan Whyte M.
See MELVILLE, Evan Whyte M. Balfour-

BALLADS
Scottish ballads and music in the Robert White collection in the University Library, Newcastle-upon-Tyne. BTHK, v (67/70), 138-41.
C. Hunt.

Notes on the ballad market in the second half of the seventeenth century. SB, vi (54), 161-80.
C. C. Blagden.

British authorship of ballads in the Isaiah Thomas collection. SB, ix (57), 225-8.
T. L. Philbrick.

BALLEY, Richard.
A London binding by Richard Balley, 1700. (English bookbindings, 13). Illus. BC, iv (55), 144-5.
H. M. Nixon.

BALSTON, Thomas
Whatman paper in a book dated 1757. (Query, 108). BC, viii (59), 306-8.

John Martin, 1789-1854, illustrator and pamphleteer. LIB, xiv (33/4), 383-432.

Some illustrators of Milton's *Paradise Lost*. [A letter]. LIB, iv (49/50), 146-7.

BALTIMORE
An unoticed first issue relating to the Baltimore Riot of 1812. PBSA, lvii (63), 222-4.
E. G. Howard.

An unrecorded Baltimore imprint from Philadelphia [*The romance of real life* by Mrs. Charlotte Turner Smith]. PBSA, lxi (67), 121-3.
E. G. Howard.

BALTIMORE *Walters art gallery*
The Baltimore binding exhibition. BC, vii (58), 419-26.
H. M. Nixon.

BALTIMORE LIBRARIES
Rare books and other bibliographical resources in Baltimore libraries. PBSA, lv (61), 1-16.
M. N. Barton.

BAMBURGH CASTLE
The Bamburgh Library. (Unfamiliar libraries, 4). Illus. BC, viii (59), 14-24.
A. I. Doyle.

BANBURY
Early Banbury chap-books and broadsides. Illus. LIB, xvii (36/7), 98-108.
C. R. Cheney.

BANCROFT *libr.*
See CALIFORNIA *univ., Bancroft libr.*

BANCROFT, George
Promoting a book: Prescott to Bancroft, December 20, 1837. PBSA, li (57), 335-9.
C. H. Gardiner.

BANCROFT, Hubert Howe
See also CALIFORNIA *univ., Bancroft libr.*

Leland Stanford and H. H. Bancroft's *History*. A bibliographical curiosity. PBSA, xxvii (33), 12-33.
G. T. Clark.

BANDELLO, Matteo *bp. of Agen*
Sidney and Bandello. Illus. LIB, xxi (66), 326-8.
J. Robertson.

BANKS, John
The variant sheets in John Banks's *Cyrus the Great,* 1696. SB, iv (51/2), 174-82.
F. T. Bowers.

BANNATYNE, George
Bishop Percy's annotated copy of Lord Hailes's *Ancient Scottish poems* [by G. Bannatyne]. EBST, ii (38/45), 432-7.
A. F. Falconer.

BANVARD, John
Banvard's Mississippi panorama pamphlets. Illus. PBSA, xliii (49), 48-62.
-J. F. McDermott.

— [A letter]. PBSA, xliii (49), 245.
B. L. Heilbron.

BARBADOS HILL
See PENNSYLVANIA *Devon Barbados Hill.*

BARBARINI, Manfred
The St. Andrews University copy of Glareanus and Barbarini. BTHK, iv (63/6), 72-5.
C. Hill.

BARBER, Giles Gaudard
In search of an archetype. (Query, 125). BC, ix (60), 80.

Catchwords and press figures at home and abroad. BC, ix (60), 301-7.

French illustrations in English books of the Romantic period. (Note, 159). BC, x (61), 200-1.

Les Liaisons Dangereuses in Dublin. (Note, 165). BC, x (61), 335-6.

Henry Saint John, Viscount Bolingbroke, 1678-1751. (Some uncollected authors, 41). BC, xiv (65), 528-37.

Parisian binding prices in 1649. (Note, 268). BC, xv (66), 210.

Les reliures vernis sans odeur. [An addition to A. Ehrman's list]. BC, xv (66), 351-2.

J. J. Tourneisen of Basle and the publication of English books on the continent *c.* 1800. LIB, xv (60), 193-200.

Galignani's and the publication of English books in France from 1800 to 1852. LIB, xvi (61), 267-86.

Notes on some English centre- and corner-piece bindings *c.* 1600. Illus. LIB, xvii (62), 93-5.

An example of eighteenth-century Swiss printer's copy. Euler on the calculus of variations [*Methodus inveniendi lineas curvas*]. LIB, xxii (67), 147-9.

Treuttel and Würtz: some aspects of the importation of books from France, *c.* 1825. Illus. LIB, xxiii (68), 118-44.

De Thou and Theophilus's Institutes [in the library of Trinity College, Cambridge]. TCBS, iii (59/63), 160-3.

— , WARRILOW, Alice Georgina *and* GASKELL, Philip. An annotated list of printers' manuals to 1850. Illus. JPHS, iv (68), 11-32.

BARBER, M. J.
The books and partonage of learning of a 15th-century prince [John, Duke of Bedford, 1389-1435]. BC, xii (63), 308-15.

BARCLAY, Andrew
The amazing career of Andrew Barclay, Scottish bookbinder, of Boston. SB, xiv (61), 145-62.
H. D. French.

BARI
The first book printed at Bari [N. A. Carmignano's *Operette*]. Illus. [and] Additional notes. SB, vii (55), 208-11. xi (58), 227-8.
D. E. Rhodes.

BARKER, J. R.
Cadell and Davies and the Liverpool booksellers. LIB, xiv (59), 274-80.

John McCreery: a radical printer, 1768-1832. Illus. LIB, xvi (61), 81-103.

BARKER, Nicolas John
The aesthetic investor's guide to current literary values. An essay in bibliometry. BC, ix (60), 414-22.

So Gosse was in it after all? (Note, 235). BC, xiii (64), 501-3.

The works of William Dole, a judicial inquiry. Illus. BC, xv (66), 296-302.

The Biblioteca nazionale at Florence. Illus. BC, xviii (69), 11-22.

Richard Taylor, a preliminary note. Illus. JPHS, ii (66), 45-8.

A note on the bibliography of Gibbon, 1776-1802. LIB, xviii (63), 40-50.

Some notes on the bibliography of William Hayley. Illus. 3 pts. TCBS, iii (59/63), 103-12, 167-76, 339-60.

BARKER, William
William Barker, Tudor translator. PBSA, li (57), 126-40.
G.B. Parks.

BARLEY, William
William Barley: Elizabethan printer and bookseller. SB, viii (56), 218-25.
J. L. Lievsay.

William Barley, draper and stationer. SB, xxii (69), 214-23.
J. A. Lavin.

BARLOW, sir Thomas Dalmahoy
Books illustrated by Albert Dürer. [A summary]. LIB, xv (34/5), 385-7.

BARNARD, John
Dryden, Tonson, and subscriptions for the 1697 Virgil. PBSA, lvii (63), 129-51.

BARNBOUGLE CASTLE
Barnbougle castle. (Unfamiliar libraries, 7). Illus. BC, xi (62), 35-44.
Eva Primrose, *countess of Rosebery.*

Books from Beckford's library now at Barnbougle. Illus. BC, xiv (65), 324-34.
Eva Primrose, *countess of Rosebery.*

BARNES, Daniel R.
Washington Irving: an unrecorded periodical publication. SB, xx (67), 260-1.

BARNES, F. *and* DICKINSON, J. C.
A seventeenth-century Cambridge book and its cost. [John Armstrong's *Secret and family prayers* and *The souls worth and danger*]. TCBS, ii (54/8), 376-81.

BARNES, Jack C.
A bibliography of Wordsworth in American periodicals through 1825. PBSA, lii (58), 205-19.

BARNES, Robert
The sixteenth-century editions of *A Supplication unto King Henry the Eighth* by Robert Barnes, D.D.: a footnote to the history of the royal supremacy. TCBS, iii (59/63), 133-42.
W. D. J. C. Thompson.

BARR, C. B. L.
An unrecorded pamphlet by Archdeacon Wrangham. (Note, 203). BC, xiii (64), 64-5.

—. BC, xiii (64), 206.

More books from Ben Jonson's library. (Note, 223). BC, xiii (64), 346-8.

A misprinted title in a *Prudentius* of 1499? (Note, 256). BC, xv (66), 207.

Bindings with the device of a pelican in its piety. (Note, 291). BC, xvii (68), 351.

Proposals for printing Jackson's *Works* 1672. (Query, 230). BC, xviii (69), 224-5.

Early Scottish editions of *The seven sages of Rome*. Illus. BTHK, v (67/70), 62-72.

— *and* POLLARD, M. The *Historia Plantarum* of John Ray. TCBS, iii (58/63), 335-8.

BARRETT, Clifton Waller
The Barrett collection. (Contemporary collectors, 10). Illus. BC, v (56), 218-30.

Some bibliographical adventures in Americana. PBSA, xliv (50), 17-28.

BARROS, Alonso de
A Cervantes item from Emmanuel College library: Barros's *Filosofía cortesana* 1587. Illus. TCBS, iv (64/8), 363-71.
E. M. Wilson.

BARTGIS, Matthias
[Additions to the bibliography of M. Bartgis. A letter]. PBSA, lv (61), 393-4.
K. G. Wust.

BARTHOLD, Allen J.
Gazette Française, Newport, R.I., 1780-81. PBSA, xxviii (34), 64-79.

BARTHOLOMAEUS *Anglicus*
Wynkyn de Worde's use of the Plimpton manuscript of *De Proprietatibus Rerum*. Illus. LIB, vi (51), 7-18.
R. W. Mitchner.

BARTLET, John
Joseph Pote of Eton and Bartlet's *Farriery*. LIB, xvii (36/7), 131-54.
R. Austen-Leigh.

BARTLETT, Henrietta Collins
First editions of Shakespeare's quartos. LIB, xvi (35/6), 166-72.

BARTLETT, Phyllis
A copy of Tennyson's *The princess*, 1848. (Query, 207). BC, xv (66), 356-7.

A copy of Meredith's *Poems*, 1851. (Query, 208). BC, xv (66), 357.

BARTLETT, Roger
An Oxford binding by Roger Bartlett, c. 1670. (English bookbindings, 67). Illus. BC, xvii (68), 463.
H. M. Nixon.

Roger Bartlett, bookbinder. Illus. LIB, x (55), 233-43.
I. G. Philip.

Roger Bartlett's bookbindings. Illus. LIB, xvii (62), 56-65.
H. M. Nixon.

BARTON, Mary N.
Rare books and other bibliographical resources in Baltimore libraries. PBSA, lv (61), 1-16.

BARTON, Thomas Pennant
America's first [Thomas Pennant Barton's] Shakespeare collection. PBSA, lviii (64), 169-73.
J. E. Alden.

BARZIZIUS, Gasparinus
A grammarian's fraud. [A MS. copy of *De Orthographia* by Gasparino de Barziza]. (Note, 132). BC, ix (60), 188-92.
A. M. Woodward.

BASEL
The beginnings of printing at Basel. Illus. LIB, iii (48/9), 50-4.
J. V. Scholderer.

BASHAN
Bound for Bashan. [Rev. R. B. Stratton's *Captivity of the Oatman Girls, being an interesting narrative of Life among the Apache and Mohave Indians*]. PBSA, lvii (63), 449-53.
R. H. Dillon.

BASKERVILLE, Charles Read
Sir Richard Morison as the author of two anonymous tracts on sedition. [*A Lamentation in whiche is shewed what Ruyne and destruction cometh of seditious rebellyon;* and *A Remedy for Sedition*]. LIB, xvii (36/7), 83-7.

BASKERVILLE, John
John Baskerville's books. BC, viii (59), 185-9.
J. Dreyfus.

The Baskerville punches 1750-1950. Illus. LIB, v (50/1), 26-48.
J. Dreyfus.

John Baskerville: a bibliography. LIB, xv (60), 201-6.
L. W. Hanson.

Baskerville and James Whatman. SB, v (52/3), 187-9.
A. T. Hazen.

John Baskerville, proposals for a revised edition of Straus and Dent's bibliography and memoir. TCBS, i (49/53), 191-2.
J. Dreyfus *and* R. J. L. Kingsford.

Baskerville's ornaments. Illus. TCBS, i (49/53), 273-7.
J. Dreyfus.

Prolegomena to the revised edition of Straus and Dent's *John Baskerville*. TCBS, i (49/53), 288-95.
J. P. W. Gaskell.

BASSAN, Maurice
A bibliographical study of Stephen Crane's poem *In the Night*. PBSA, lviii (64), 173-9.

BASSETT, J. G. Tilney-
Edmund Tilney's *The Flower of Friendshippe*. Illus. LIB, xxvi (45/6), 175-81.

BASTARD, Thomas
Thomas Bastard's disclaimer of an Oxford libel. LIB, xvii (62), 145-9.
J. L. Sanderson.

BATDORF, Franklin P.
An unrecorded edition of Crabbe. PBSA, xliii (49), 349-50.

Notes on three editions of George Crabbe's *Tales*. PBSA, xliv (50), 276-9.

An unrecorded early anthology of Crabbe. SB, iii (50/1), 266-7.

The Murray reprints of George Crabbe: a publisher's record. SB, iv (51/2), 192-9.

BATE, George
A bibliography of George Bate's *Elenchus Motuum Nuperorum in Anglia*.
LIB, vi (51), 189-99.
F. F. Madan.

BATES, Albert Carlos
Some notes on early Connecticut printing. PBSA, xxvii (33), 1-11.

An address to the Inhabitants of the New Settlements in the Northern and Western Parts of the United States . . . New Haven, [1793, 95]. PBSA, xxxiv (40), 187.

The New-England Primer Improved. Litchfield 1792; — Norwich 1795; and, — Litchfield 1798. PBSA, xxxiv (40), 189.

Backus, Azel (1765-1817). *Absolam's conspiracy: a Sermon, Preached at the General Election, at Hartford . . . May 10th, 1798 . . .* Suffield, 1798. PBSA, xxxiv (40), 271.

Great Britain. Parliament. *Anno Regni Georgii II . . . At the Parliament begun and holden at Westminster, the Tenth Day of November, Anno Dom. 1747.* London: 1751. Re-printed by Timothy Green, Connecticut, 1752. [An Act for Regulating the commencement of the Year . . .]. PBSA, xxxiv (40), 271-2.

The Renowned History of Giles Gingerbread. Boston, 1768. PBSA, xxxvi (42), 320.

Early Connecticut laws. PBSA, xl (46), 151-8.

BATES, William
Ambrose, Issac (1604-1663) & Bates, William (1625-1699). *Christ in the clouds coming to judgment*. A sermon. V.p., v.d. PBSA, xxxiv (40), 187.
C. S. Brigham.

BATEY, Charles Edward
The Oxford partners, some notes on the administration of the University Press, 1780-1881. JPHS, iii (67), 51-65.

BATHO, Edith Clara
Notes on the bibliography of James Hogg, the Ettrick Shepherd. Illus. LIB, xvi (35/6), 309-26.

BATHO, Gordon Richard
The library of the "Wizard" Earl: Henry Percy, Ninth Earl of Northumberland, 1564-1632. Illus. LIB, xv (60), 246-61.

BATTESTIN, Martin Carey
Fielding's revisions of *Joseph Andrews*. SB, xvi (63), 81-117.

BATTLE, Guy A.
The case of the altered "C" — a bibliographical problem in the Beaumont and Fletcher first folio. PBSA, xlii (48), 66-70.

The box rule pattern in the first edition of *Paradise Lost*. PBSA, xlii (48), 315-21.

A bibliographical note from the Beaumont and Fletcher first folio. SB, i (48/9), 187-8.

BAUER, Konrad Friedrich
Metal cuts at the Gutenberg workshop [Tr. by E. L. Hauswedell]. Illus. PBSA, lxii (68), 581-6.

BAUGHMAN, Roland
Washington's manuscript diaries of 1795 and 1798. PBSA, xlv (51), 117-24.

BAUMGARTNER, Paul R.
The date of *Cocke Lorelles bote* [pr. by Wynkyn de Worde]. SB, xix (66), 175-81.

BAXTER, James Houston *and* FORDYCE, Christian James
Books published abroad by Scotsmen before 1700. GBSR, xi (33), 1-55.

BAY, Jens Christian
Bibliographical reminiscences and prophesies. PBSA, xlix (55), 289-99.

BAYLEY, Daniel
Daniel Bayley's *The American Harmony:* a bibliographical study. PBSA, xlix (55), 304-54.
A. P. Britton *and* I. Lownes.

BEARD, Charles A.
Charles A. Beard in the *Freeman*. PBSA, lvii (63), 226-9.
G. T. Tanselle.

BEARE, Robert L.
Kinder- und Hausmärchen of the brothers Grimm. (Note, 258). BC, xiv (65), 542-3.

Notes on the text of T. S. Eliot: variants from Russell Square. SB, ix (57), 21-49.

BEATTIE, James
The manuscript background of James Beattie's *Elements of moral science*. BTHK, v (67/70), 181-9.
B. Fabian *and* K. Kloth.

BEATTIE, William
A hand-list of works from the press of John Wreittoun at Edinburgh, 1624-*c.* 1639. EBST, ii (38/45), 89-104.

Supplement to the Handlist of incunabula in the National library of Scotland. Illus. [*And*] Second supplement. EBST, ii (38/45), 151-251: 331-51.

An early printed fragment of the *Buke of the Howlat*. Illus. EBST, ii (38/45), 393-7.

Fragments of *The Palyce of Honour* of Gawin Douglas, printed by Thomas Davidson at Edinburgh *c.* 1540. Illus. EBST, iii (48/55), 31-46.

Two notes on fifteenth-century printing. I. Jacobus Ledelh. II. Jacques Le Forestier and Noel de Harsy, Printers at Rouen, 1490. EBST, iii (48/55), 75-7.

Walter Chepman's signature. EBST, iii (48/55), 81-2.

'Ulric in personas'. EBST, iii (48/55), 82-3.

— *and* DOBIE, Marryat R. The first twenty years of the National Library of Scotland, 1925-1945. EBST, ii (38/45), 285-302.

BEATTY, sir Alfred Chester
The Chester Beatty Library. (Contemporary collectors, 18). Illus. BC, vii (58), 253-64.
R. J. Hayes.

Some early bindings from Egypt in the Chester Beatty Library. Additional notes. Illus. LIB, xviii (63), 218-23.
R. Powell.

BEAUCHAMP, Charles Louis
Chorégraphie. The dance notation of the eighteenth century: Beauchamp or Feuillet? Illus. BC, xvi (67), 450-76.
F. Derra de Moroda.

BEAUCHESNE, Jean de
De Beau Chesne, John, and Baildon, John. *A booke containing divers sortes of hands.* London, Thomas Vautrouillier, 1581. PBSA, xxxv (41), 293.
F. R. Goff.

BEAULIEU *abbey*
Beaulieu Abbey account book, xiii. (Note, 50). BC, iv (55), 252.
A. Ehrman.

BEAUMONT, Francis
The printing of the Beaumont and Fletcher folio. Illus. LIB, iii (48/9), 233-64.
J. Gerritsen.

Beaumont, Francis (1584-1616) and Fletcher, John (1579-1625). *A king and no king.* London, for Thomas Walkley, 1619. PBSA, xxxiv (40), 270.
E. M. Sowerby.

The case of the altered "C" — a bibliographical problem in the Beaumont and Fletcher first folio. PBSA, xlii (48), 66-70.
G. A. Battle.

The text of *The maid's tragedy*. PBSA, lxi (67), 173-200.
H. B. Norland.

A bibliographical note from the Beaumont and Fletcher first folio. SB, i (48/9), 187-8.
G. A. Battle.

The second quarto of *A King and No King*, 1625. SB, iv (51/2), 166-70.
B. Sturman.

The shares of Fletcher and his collaborators in the Beaumont and Fletcher canon. 7 pts. SB, viii (56), 129-46.
C. Hoy.

—. Pt. 2. SB, ix (57), 144-62.
C. Hoy.

—: Pt. 3. SB, xi (58), 85-106.
C. Hoy.

—. Pt. 4. SB, xii (59), 91-116.
C. Hoy.

—. Pt. 5. SB, xiii (60), 77-108.
C. Hoy.

—. Pt. 6. SB, xiv (61), 45-67.
C. Hoy.

—. Pt. 7. SB, xv (62), 71-90.
C. Hoy.

The printing of Beaumont and Fletcher's *The Maid's Tragedy*, Q1, 1619. SB, xiii (60), 199-20.
R. K. Turner.

Notes on the text of *Thierry and Theodoret*, Q1. SB, xiv (61), 218-31.
R. K. Turner.

The printers and the Beaumont and Fletcher folio of 1647, section 2. SB, xx (67), 35-59.
R. K. Turner, *jr.*

The printers and the Beaumont and Fletcher folio of 1647, sections 4 and 8 D-F. SB, xxii (69), 165-78.
S. Henning.

BEAURLINE, L. A.
An editorial experiment: Suckling's *A Sessions of the Poets*. SB, xvi (63), 43-60.

BEAUTIES OF MAGAZINES
The Beauties of Magazines and an engraving of William Cullen. BTHK, i/4 (58), 40-2.
R. H. Carnie.

BECKFORD, William
Beckford's *Vathek*, 'Londres 1791'. (Note, 99). BC, vii (58), 297-9.
A. Parreaux.

BC, xi (62), 211.
H. Marlow. *pseud.*

Beckfordiana. (Query, 120). BC, viii (59), 432.
A. R. A. Hobson.

Books from Beckford's library now at Barnbougle. Illus. BC, xiv (65), 324-34.
Eva Primrose, *countess of Rosebery.*

The Lausanne edition of Beckford's *Vathek*. LIB, xvii (36/7), 369-94.
J. Carter.

An annotated checklist of the works of William Beckford. PBSA, lxi (67), 243-58.
R. J. Gemmett.

BEDE *the venerable*
The *editio princeps* of Bede's life of St. Cuthbert, and its printer's XIIth century 'copy'. Illus. LIB, xix (38/9), 289-303.
B. Colgrave *and* I. Masson.

BEDFORD, Francis
A London binding by Francis Bedford, 1866. (English bookbindings, 33). Illus. BC, ix (60), 178.
H. M. Nixon.

BEE BOOKS
Old bee books. BH, ii (51/2), 206-10.

More bee books. (Note, 10). BC, i (52), 193-4.
M. Frost.

BEEBE, Charles William
Beebe, William (1877-1962). *Edge of the Jungle.* New York, 1921. PBSA, xxxv (41), 207.
H. S. Mott.

BEEBE, William
See BEEBE, Charles William

BEECHAM, H. A.
John Gauden and the authorship of the *Eikon Basilike*. LIB, xx (65), 142-4.

BEERBOHM, sir Henry Maximilian
A note on *Carmen Becceriense*. Illus. BC, i (52), 215-8.
C. Evans.

BEETHOVEN, Ludwig van
Thomson's collections of national song with special reference to the contributions of Haydn and Beethoven. Illus. EBST, ii (38/45), 1-64.
C. Hopkinson *and* C. B. Oldman.

— Addenda et corrigenda. EBST, iii (48/55), 121-4.

BEHN, Aphra
Aphra Behn's first biography [*Life and memoirs . . . by one of the fair sex*]. SB, xxii (69), 227-40.
R. H. Day.

BEKENHUB, Johann
The Strasbourg *Speculum Iudiciale,* 1473: with a note on the career of Johann Bekenhub. LIB, xi (56), 273-7.
J. V. Scholderer.

BELCHER, Joshua
Belcher & Armstrong set up shop: 1805. SB, iv (51/2), 201-4.
R. G. Silver.

BELKNAP, George Nicholas
Authentic Account of the Murder of Dr. Whitman: the history of a pamphlet. PBSA, lv (61), 319-46.

An Oregon miscellany. PBSA, lvii (63), 191-200.

Oregon printing before the *Spectator*. PBSA, lix (65), 50-5.

Addendum to Belknap, Oregon imprints, no. 7: Nesmith's *To the world!!* PBSA, lxiii (69), 128-9.

BELL, H. E.
The price of books in medieval England. LIB, xvii (36/7), 312-32.

BELL, John
John Bell's *A Discourse on Witchcraft* — a query. BTHK, ii (59/60), 72.
E. G. Jack.

BELL, Thomas *fl. 1573-1610*
A note on the authorship of three works against Thomas Bell. LIB, ii (47/8), 286-9.
A. F. Allison.

BELL, Thomas *1792-1880*
Part-issues of Bell's *History of the British Crustacea*, 1844-53. (Query, 112). BC, viii (59), 73-4.
H. O. Bull.

BELL, Whitfield Jenks
Thomas Anburey's *Travels through America*: a note on eighteenth-century plagiarism. PBSA xxxvii (43), 23-36.

BELLAMY, John
John Bellamy: 'Pilgrim' publisher of London. PBSA, l (56), 342-69.
L. Rostenberg.

BELLANTIUS, Lucius
The date of the Florentine incunable of the *De astrologica veritate* by Lucius Bellantius. PBSA, lx (66), 99-100.
C. F. Bühler.

BEMBO, Pietro *card., bp. of Bergamo*
Manuscript corrections in the Aldine edition of Bembo's *De Aetna*. PBSA, xlv (51), 136-42.
C. F. Bühler.

BENEDETTI, Alessandro
See BENEDICTUS, Alexander

BENEDICTUS, Alexander
Stop-press and manuscript corrections in the Aldine edition of Benedetti's *Diaria de bello Carolino*. PBSA, xliii (49), 365-73.
C. F. Bühler.

BENGER, F. B.
John Wolfe and a Spanish book. [Bartolome Felippe's *Tractado del consejo y de los consegeros*]. LIB, iii (48/9), 214-16.

BENKOVITZ, Miriam Jeanette
Ronald Firbank in periodicals. PBSA, liv (60), 295-7.

BENNET, Thomas *1664/5-1706*
The notebook of Thomas Bennet and Henry Clements, 1686-1719, with some aspects of book trade practice. OBSP, vi (56).
N. Hodgson *and* C. C. Blagden.

BENNET, Thomas *1673-1728*
Thomas Bennet, a forgotten bibliographer. LIB, vi (51), 43-7.
S. Gibson.

BENNETT, Henry Stanley
Medieval English manuscripts and contemporary taste. EBST, ii (38/45), 382-3.

The production and dissemination of vernacular manuscripts in the fifteenth century. LIB, i (46/7), 167-78.

Printers, authors, and readers, 1475-1557. LIB, iv (49/50), 155-65.

Notes on English retail book-prices, 1480-1560. LIB, v (50/1), 172-8.

A check-list of Robert Whittinton's grammars. LIB, vii (52), 1-14.

Notes on two incunables: *The Abbey of the Holy Ghost* and *A Ryght Profytable Treatyse*. LIB, x (55), 120-1.

An unrecorded Sarum Book of Hours of 1526. Illus. TCBS, i (49/53), 178-9.

The Syndics' library at the University Press. TCBS, iv (64/8), 253-6.

BENNETT, Josephine Waters
The woodcut illustrations in the English editions of *Mandeville's Travels*. PBSA, xlvii (53), 59-69.

Benson's alleged piracy of *Shake-speares sonnets* and of some of Jonson's works. SB, xxi (68), 235-48.

BENNETT, Josiah Q.
Portman Square to New Bond Street, or, How to make money though rich. [Henry Yates Thompson]. BC, xvi (67), 323-39.

BENNETT, Scott
A concealed printing in W. D. Howells [i.e. in his *A travler from Altruria*]. PBSA, lxi (67), 56-60.

BENSLEY, Thomas
A printed text of a portion of Macpherson's *Ossian*. [*Speciment of the intended edition of Ossian's poems*, pr. by T. Bensley, 1830]. BTHK, v (67/70), 111-13.
I. Henderson.

BENSON, Carolyn
The advertisement in the *Sentimental Journey*. (Query, 9). BC, ii (53), 157.

BENSON, John
Benson's alleged piracy of *Shake-speares sonnets* and some of Jonson's works. SB, xxi (68), 235-48.
J. W. Bennett.

BENTHAM, Jeremy
A Jeremy Bentham collection. Illus. LIB, i (46/7), 6-27.
A. Muirhead.

Bentham's publication on evidence. LIB, ix (54), 205-7.
T. H. Bowyer.

BENTLEY, Gerald Eades *jr.*
Blake's Hesiod. LIB, xx (65), 315-20.

A new Blake document: the 'Riddle' manuscript. Illus. LIB, xxiv (69), 337-43.

Blake's engravings and his friendship with Flaxman. Illus. SB, xii (59), 161-88.

Thomas Taylor's biography. SB, xiv (61), 234-6.

The date of Blake's Pickering manuscript: or, the way of a poet with paper. SB, xix (66), 232-43.

BENTLEY, Richard
The Bentley papers. LIB, vii (52), 178-200.
G. N. Ray.

Colburn-Bentley and the march of the intellect. SB, ix (57), 197-213.
R. A. Gettman.

Melville's *Mardi*; Bentley's binder? PBSA, lxii (68), 361-71.
J. F. Guido.

BERG, Albert Ashton
See also NEW YORK *city, publ. libr., Berg collection.*

BERGERON, David M.
Two compositors in Heywood's *Londons Ius honorarium*, 1631. SB, xxii (69), 223-6.

BERKELEY, George *bp. of Cloyne*
George Berkeley, 1685-1753; David Hume, 1711-1776. (English literary autographs, 26). Illus. BC, vii (58), 181.
T. J. Brown.

Establishing Berkeley's authorship of *Guardian* papers. PBSA, liv (60), 181-3.
P. Kaufman.

BERKELEY, Norborne *baron Botetourt*
The reconstruction of the Library of N.B., Baron de Botetourt, Governor of Virginia, 1768-1770. PBSA, xxxvi (42), 97-123.
G. Yost.

BERKELEY, sir William
Sir William Berkeley's *The Lost Lady*. Illus.
LIB, xvii (36/7), 395-426.
R. C. Bald.

BERKENMEYER, Wilhelm Christoph
The colonial parish library of Wilhelm Christoph
Berkenmeyer. PBSA, liii (51), 114-49.
J. W. Montgomery.

BERNARDIN, Charles W.
John Dos Passos' textual revisions. PBSA,
xlviii (54), 95-7.

BERNE
The collections of Hollis bindings at Berne. Illus.
BC, vii (58), 165-70.
C. Ramsden.

The Berne legal manuscript. EBST, ii (38/45),
379-81.
T. M. Cooper.

BERNERS, Juliana
Sources of the *Boke of St. Albans*. (Query, 220).
BC, xvii (68), 83.
R. Hands.

Notes on the Wynkyn de Worde editions of the
Boke of St. Albans and its separates. SB, v
(52/3), 43-52.
E. Pafort.

BEROL, Alfred C.
Gosse and Henry Patmore's *Poems*. (Note, 155).
BC, x (61), 71-2.

Lanrick — a game for two players, by Lewis
Carroll. PBSA, liii (59), 74.

The Daniel Press. PBSA, lv (61), 40.

BERRY, Lloyd Eason
Thomas Charde, printer and bookseller. LIB,
xv (60), 57-8.

Giles Fletcher the elder's *Licia*. LIB, xv (60),
133-4.

Another booklist of Thomas Charde. PBSA, lv
(61), 381-2.

— Addendum. PBSA, lvi (62), 115.

Richard Hakluyt and Turberville's poems on
Russia. PBSA, lxi (67), 350-1.

Giles Fletcher, the elder: a bibliography. TCBS,
iii (59/63), 200-15.

BERRY, William Turner
Augustus Applegath, some notes and references.
JPHS, ii (66), 49-57.

— *and* FERN, Alan M.
Typographical specimen books. A checklist of
the Broxbourne collection with an introduction.
Illus. BC, v (56), 256-72.

BERTAUT, Jean
Jean Bertaut and the French anthologies about
1600. LIB, xxii (67), 136-42.
T. J. D. Allott.

BERTHELET, Thomas
The protocollum of Thomas Berthelet. Illus.
LIB, i (46/7), 47-9.
S. Gibson.

BESSEMER, Anthony
Anthony Bessemer, London, 1830. (19th-century
type-specimen books, no. 1). JPHS, v (69), 99.

BESTERMAN, Theodore
Preliminary short-title list of bibliographies
containing manuscript notes. PBSA, xliii (49),
209-26.

A modern instance [of an error in pagination in
T. Besterman, *World bibliography of bibliographies*, vol. 1, 2nd ed.] Illus. PBSA, l (56),
302-4.
J. D. Thomas.

BETHESDA Maryland *nat. libr. of med.*
See UNITED STATES *nat. libr. of med.*

BETJEMAN, sir John
Betjemaniana. (Note, 140). BC, ix (60), 199.
J. Carter.

— BC, ix (60), 452.

BETSON, Thomas
Thomas Betson of Syon Abbey. LIB, xi (56),
115-18.
A. I. Doyle.

BETTERTON, Thomas
See also FLETCHER, John *and* BETTERTON,
Thomas

A bibliographical history of the Fletcher-
Betterton play, *The prophetess,* 1690. LIB, xvi
(61), 169-75.
F. T. Bowers.

BEVERIDGE, John
See ST. ANDREWS *univ. libr.*

BEWICK, Thomas
Bewick, *Quadrupeds*, 1st edition, 1790. (Query,
14). BC, i (52), 130-1.
S. Roscoe.

— BC, i (52), 195.
W. A. Jackson.

Bibliography of Thomas Bewick. (Note, 40).
BC, iv (55), 73.
S. Roscoe.

A Bewick prospectus. (Query, 133). BC, ix (60),
457.
P. C. G. Isaac.

— BC, x (61), 72.
G. Chandler.

Bewick, Catnach, and William Davidson.
(Query, 161). BC, xii (63), 72.
P. C. G. Issac.

An unrecorded children's book illustrated by
Thomas Bewick. LIB, v (50/1), 272-3.
T. C. D. Eaves.

— LIB, vii (52), 59-60.
S. Roscoe.

BEWLEY, William
William Bewley and *The Monthly Review:* a problem of attribution. PBSA, lv (61), 309-18.
R. Lonsdale.

BIBLE
Gutenberg Bible census. (Note, 1). BC, i (52), 53
P. H. Muir.

The binding of the Coronation Bible. Illus. BC, ii (53), 139.
L. Lamb.

A note on Robert Aitken printer of the 'Bible of the Revolution'. BTHK, v (67/70), 36-7.
R. L. Crawford.

The printers of the Coverdale Bible, 1535. Illus. LIB, xvi (35/6), 280-9.
L. A. Sheppard.

Bacon's copy of a Douai-Rheims Bible. LIB, iii (48/9), 54-6.
E. E. Willoughby.

J. F. Stam, Amsterdam, and English bibles. Illus. LIB, ix (54), 185-93.
A. F. Johnson.

The Ferrara Bible at press. Illus. LIB, x (55), 244-69.
S. Rypins.

— LIB, xi (56), 124.
S. Rypins.

— LIB, xii (57), 44-53.
W. B. Todd.

The Ferrara Bible: an addition to the census. LIB, xiii (58), 128.
S. Rypins.

The evolution of a book form: the octavo Bible from manuscripts to the Geneva version. Illus. LIB, xvi (61), 15-28.
M. H. Black.

The folio Bible to 1560. Illus. LIB, xviii (63), 191-253.
M. H. Black.

Bible. English. *The Holy Bible* . . . London: R. Barker, 1618. PBSA, xxxiv (40), 185.
E. W. Willoughby.

The Continental Congress considers the publication of a Bible, 1711. SB, iii (50/1), 274-81.
W. H. Gaines.

The problem of the pre-1776 American Bible. PBSA, xlviii (54), 183-94.
H. M. Lydenberg.

BIBLIOGRAPHICAL DESCRIPTION
Thomas J. Wise's descriptive formula. (Query, 181). BC, xiii (64), 214-15.
J. Carter.

— BC, xiii (64), 355-6.
M. Trevanion.

A formulary of collation. LIB, xiv (33/4), 365-82.
Sir W. W. Greg.

Purposes of descriptive bibliography, with some remarks on methods. LIB, viii (53), 1-22.
F. T. Bowers.

The specification of binding cloth. LIB, xxi (66), 246-7.
G. T. Tanselle.

Tolerances in bibliographical description. LIB, xxiii (68), 1-12.
G. T. Tanselle.

Problems in the bibliographical description of nineteenth-century American books.. PBSA, xxxvi (42), 124-36.
J. Blanck.

Certain basic problems in descriptive bibliography. PBSA, xlii (48), 211-28.
F. T. Bowers.

Principles and standards of bibliographical dsescription. PBSA, xliv (50), 216-23.
W. Parker.

The identification of type faces in bibliographical description. PBSA, lx (66), 185-202.
G. T. Tanselle.

The first edition of Ficino's *De Christiana Religione*: a problem in bibliographical description. SB, xviii (65), 248-52.
C. F. Bühler.

A system of color identification for bibliographical description. SB, xx (67), 203-34.
G. T. Tanselle.

The descriptive bibliography of American authors. SB, xxi (68), 1-24.
G. T. Tanselle.

BIBLIOGRAPHICAL PRESSES
The bibliographical press movement. JPHS, i (65), 1-13.
J. P. W. Gaskell.

BIBLIOGRAPHICAL SOCIETY
A gift to the [Bibliographical] Society's library. [A letter. The gift by Mr. A. R. A. Hobson of line-blocks for G. D. Hobson's *Les Reliures à la fanfare. Le Problème de l'S fermé*, 1935. and three sets of slides intended to illustrate lectures on bindings.] LIB, xiii (58), 63.
C. C. Blagden.

BIBLIOGRAPHICAL SOCIETY OF AMERICA
The Bibliographical Society of America — its leaders and activities, 1904-1939. PBSA, xxxv (41), 177-202.
H. B. Van Hoesen.

BIBLIOGRAPHICAL STUDIES
Bibliography — an apologia. LIB, xiii (32/3), 113-43.
Sir W. W. Greg.

The aims of bibliography. LIB, xiii (32/3), 225-58.
Sir S. Gaselee.

Recent bibliographical work. LIB, xxiii (42/3), 108-26.
Sir F. C. Francis.

Bibliographical work in Germany, 1939-1945. LIB, xxvi (45/6), 193-4.
E. von Rath.

Bibliographical miscellanea. LIB, i (46/7), 131-34.
F. T. Bowers.
Religio Bibliographici. LIB, viii (53), 63-76.
Sir G. L. Keynes.

Spelling and the bibliographer. LIB, xviii (63), 1-28.
T. H. Hill.

Physical and reference bibliography. LIB, xx (65), 124-34.
L. Hibberd.

Bibliography revisited. LIB, xxiv (69), 89-128.
F. T. Bowers.
Bibliographical reflections of a biologist. Illus. OBSP, v (39), 167-86.
F. J. Cole.

Microphotography and bibliography. PBSA, xxxii (38), 65-70.
K. D. Metcalf.

Problems in nineteenth-century American bibliography. PBSA, xxxv (41), 35-47.
R. G. Silver.

Remarks [on bibliography]. PBSA, xxxvi (42), 59-60.
R. G. Adams.
Early copyright litigation and its bibliographical interest. PBSA, xxxv (42), 81-96.
R. C. Bald.

Bibliography the world over: some recent developments. PBSA, xlv (51), 257-64.
J. B. Childs.

Bibliography, pure bibliography, and literary studies. PBSA, xlvi (52), 186-208.
F. T. Bowers.

Bibliography and the rare book trade. PBSA, xlviii (54), 212-29.
J. Carter.

A calendar of bibliographical difficulties. PBSA, xlix (55), 1-18.
J. Blanck.

Bibliographical files for research in the Yale University libraries. PBSA, xlix (55), 199-211.
M. G. Wynne.

Bibliographical reminiscences and prophesies. PBSA, xlix (55), 289-99.
J. C. Bay.
The well-tempered bibliographer. PBSA, l (56), 28-39.
N. Harlow.

Some bibliographical errors concerning the romantic age. PBSA, li (57), 159-62.
K. S. Guthke.

Literary research and bibliographical training. PBSA, li (57), 303-11.
C. F. Bühler.

A journey of bibliographical exploration. PBSA, lvii (63), 33-41.
R. W. Hale, *jr.*

Thoughts on books and libraries. PBSA, lvii (63), 438-44.
E. Wolf, *2nd.*

Historical research and bibliography. PBSA, lviii (64), 133-40.
J. J. Heslin.

Pursuits, problems and pitfalls in sixteenth- and seventeenth-century bibliography. PBSA, lix (65), 355-66.
R. W. Gibson.

Bibliographical blessings. PBSA, lxi (67), 307-14.
D. C. Weber.

A proposal for recording additions to bibliographies. PBSA, lxii (68), 227-36.
G. T. Tanselle.

Bibliotheca Americana: a merry maze of changing concepts. PBSA, lxiii (69), 247-60.
T. R. Adams.

Evidence indicating the need for some bibliographical analysis of American-printed historical works. PBSA, lxiii (69), 261-77.
E. Wolf, *2nd.*
Some relations of bibliography to editorial problems. SB, iii (50/1), 37-62.
F. T. Bowers.

Bibliography and the editorial problem in the eighteenth century. SB, iv (51/2), 41-55.
W. B. Todd.

Bibliography and the novelistic fallacy. SB, xii (59), 59-73.
B. Harkness.

Reappearing types as bibliographical evidence. Illus. SB, xix (66), 198-209.
R. K. Turner, *jr.*

Printers of the mind; some notes on bibliographical theories and printing-house practices. SB, xxii (69), 1-75.
D. F. McKenzie.

Copyright records and the bibliographer. SB, xxii (69), 77-124.
G. T. Tanselle.

BIBLIOGRAPHY OF AMERICAN LITERATURE
See BLANCK, Jacob Nathaniel.

'BIBLIOMETRY'
'An essay in bibliometry' [A letter inspired by N. Barker's 'An essay in bibliometry']. BC, x (61), 48.
O. L. Shaw.

BIBLIOTECA NAZIONALE
See FLORENCE *bibl. naz. centrale*

BIBLIOTECA OVETENSE
See OVIEDO Y VALDÉS, Gonzalo Fernández de

BIBLIOTHECA BODMERIANA
See BODMER, Martin

BIBLIOTHECA PARISINA
Bibliotheca Parisina. Illus. BC, xviii (69), 307-17.
A. Rau.

BIBLIOTHECA THORDARSONIANA
See THORDARSON, Chester H.

BIBLIOTHECOHIMATIOURGOMACHIA
Bibliothecohimatiourgomachia. PBSA, xlviii (54), 23-8.
R. H. Taylor.

BICHI, Celio
See BICHIUS, Coelius

BICHIUS, Coelius
The second edition of Celio Bichi's *Decisiones.* PBSA, liii (59), 196-7.
D. E. Rhodes.

BICKHAM, *family*
The Bickhams and their *Universal Penman.* Illus. LIB, xxv (44/5), 162-84.
P. H. Muir.

— LIB, xxvi (45/6), 196.
P. H. Muir.

— [A letter]. LIB, i (46/7), 247-8.
P. H. Muir.

BIERCE, Ambrose Gwinnett
BAL addendum: Ambrose Bierce — entry No. 1112*. PBSA, lxii (68), 451.
G. T. Tanselle.

BILL, Edward Geoffrey W.
Lambeth palace library. LIB, xxi (66), 192-206.

BILL, John
A binding supplied by John Bill to James I, *c.* 1621. (English bookbindings, 40). Illus. BC, xi (62), 62.
H. M. Nixon.

BILSON, Thomas *bp. of Winchester*
The two editions of Thomas Bilson's *True difference between Christian subjection and unchristian rebellion.* TCBS, ii (54/8), 199-203.
W. D. J. Cargill.

BINGHAM, Caleb
Caleb Bingham's '*American preceptor*', Lexington, 1805. PBSA, lix (65), 177-82.
R. J. Wolfe.

BIOLOGICAL STUDIES
Bibliographical reflections of a biologist. Illus. OBSP, v (39), 167-86.
F. J. Cole.

BIOREN, John
John Bioren: printer to Philadelphia publishers. PBSA, xliii (49), 321-34.
M. S. Carson *and* M. W. S. Swan.

BIRCH, Brian
Henry James: some bibliographical and textual matters. Illus. LIB, xx (65), 108-23.

BIRCH, J. G.
A letter of Petrus Savorgnanus to Bilibald Pirckheimer. Illus. LIB, ii (47/8), 153-8.

BIRCHENOUGH, Edwyn
The Prymer in English. LIB, xviii (37/8), 177-94.

BIRKBECK, J. A.
The history of Little goody two-shoes. (Query, 179). BC, xiii (64), 503.

BIRLEY, sir Robert
The Storer collection in Eton College Library. Illus. BC, v (56), 115-26.

Press-marks of the de Thou library. (Note, 69). BC, v (56), 173-4.

The history of Eton College library. Illus. LIB, xi (56), 231-61.

Roger and Thomas Payne: with some account of their earlier bindings. LIB, xv (60), 33-41.

The library of Louis-Henri de Loménie, Comte de Brienne, and the bindings of the Abbé Du Seuil. Illus. LIB, xvii (62), 105-31.

Additions from Eton College library to the record of copies in Sir. W. W. Greg's *A Bibliography of the English Printed Drama to the Restoration.* LIB, xviii (63), 228-9.

Some unrecorded Cambridge books in the library of Eton College. TCBS, i (49/53), 441-3.

BIRMINGHAM LIBRARY
Some pamphlets connected with the early history of the Birmingham library. (Note, 294). BC, xvii (68), 78-80.
J. L. Marks.

BISHOP, John
John Bishop, 1665-1737. (Query, 15). BC, i (52), 195.
M. Frost.

BISHOP, Terence Alan M.
Notes on Cambridge manuscripts. Illus. TCBS, i (49/53), 432-41.

—. TCBS, ii (54/8), 185-99.

—. TCBS, ii (54/8), 323-6.

—. TCBS, iii (59/63), 93-5.

—. TCBS, iii (59/63), 412-23.

—. TCBS, iv (64/8), 70-6.

An early example of the square minuscule. [Trinity College MS. 368]. Illus. TCBS, iv (64/8), 246-52.

The Corpus Martianus Capella. [Corpus Christi coll. 153]. Illus. TCBS, iv (64/8), 257-75.

An early example of insular-Caroline [University Lib. Ee.2.4]. Illus. TCBS, iv (64/8), 396-400.

'BISHOPS' WARS'
A bibliography of the Bishops' Wars, 1639-40. GBSR, xii (36), 21-40.
J. D. Ogilvie.

BISSELL, E.
Peter Rabbit. (Query, 18). BC, ii (53), 77.

Grahamiana. (Query, 30). BC, ii (53), 79.

Swinburne problems. (Query, 51). BC, iii (54), 227-8.

Gosse, Wise and Swinburne. (Note, 115).
BC, viii (59), 297-9.

BISWANGER, Raymond A.
Thomas D'Urfey's *Richmond Heiress*, 1693:
a bibliographical study. SB, v (52/3), 169-78.

BJÖRKBOM, Carl
Undescribed copy-books in the Ekström collection, Svenska Skolmuseet, Stockholm. LIB, xiv
(33/4), 107-13.

BLACK, Hester Mary
An Irish Parliamentary binding in Glasgow
University Library. Illus. BTHK, iii (60/2),
101-2.

Archbishop Law's books in Glasgow University
Library. Illus. BTHK, iii (60/2), 107-21.

— BTHK, v (67/70), 100-1.

— *and* GASKELL, John Philip W.
Special collections in Glasgow University Library.
Illus. BC, xvi (67), 161-8.

BLACK, Michael Hugh
The evolution of a book-form: The octavo
Bible from manuscripts to the Geneva version.
Illus. LIB, xvi (61), 15-28.

The evolution of a book-form: II The folio
Bible to 1560. Illus. LIB, xviii (63), 191-203.

BLACK HILLS
Printing in the Black Hills. PBSA, xxxvii (43),
37-60.
D. C. McMurtie.

BLACKMORE, Richard Doddridge
Blackmore, *Fringilla* 1895. (Query, 239). BC,
xviii (69), 226.
W. B. Todd.

BLACKSTONE, sir William
Sales of and profits on some early editions of
Sir William Blackstone's *Commentaries*. PBSA,
lviii (64), 156-63.
R. D. Harlan.

BLACKWATER CHRONICLE
The Blackwater Chronicle, New York, 1853.
PBSA, xxxvi (42), 67-8.
H. S. Mott.

BLACKWOOD'S MAGAZINE
*See also TALES FROM BLACKWOOD
NOCTES AMBROSIANAE*

BLACKWOOD'S MAGAZINE
Michael Scott and *Blackwood's Magazine*:
some unpublished letters. LIB, viii (53), 188-96.
E. A. Nolte.

Writers on German literature in *Blackwood's
Magazine*, with a footnote on Thomas Carlyle.
LIB, ix (54), 35-44.
A. L. Strout.

The authorship of articles in *Blackwood's
Magazine*, numbers xvii-xxiv, August 1818-
March 1819. LIB, xi (56), 187-201.
A. L. Strout.

BLADES, William
Three notes on Caxton. [Concerning the recovery by W. Blades of fragments from the
Boethius in the King Edward VI grammar
school at St. Albans]. LIB, xvii (36/7), 155-66.
C. F. Bühler.

William Blades. LIB, xvi (61), 251-66.
J. Moran.

BLAGDEN, Cyprian Claud
Charter trouble. Written on the occasion of the
quater-centenary of the grant of a charter to
the Stationers' Company. BC, vi (57), 369-77.

The first edition of Switzer's *Brocoli*. [A letter].
LIB, vii (52), 211-12.

The genesis of the *Term Catalogues*. LIB, viii
(53), 30-5.

The English stock of the Stationers' Company.
LIB, x (55), 163-85.

The English stock of the Stationers' Company
in the time of the Stuarts. LIB, xii (57), 167-86.

The Stationers' Company in the Civil War
period. LIB, xiii (58), 1-17.

The missing *Term Catalogue*. [Michaelmas
1695]. SB, vii (55), 185-90.

The accounts of the Wardens of the Stationers'
Company. SB, ix (57), 69-93.

The distribution of almanacks in the second
half of the seventeenth century. SB, xi (58),
107-16.

The 'Company' of printers. SB, xiii (60), 3-17.

Thomas Carnan and the almanack monopoly.
SB, xiv (61), 23-43.

Early Cambridge printers and the Stationers'
Company. TCBS, ii (54/8), 275-89.

BLAIZOT, Georges
The International League of Antiquarian
Booksellers. BC, ii (53), 147-9.

BLAKE, Norman Francis
Some observations on William Caxton and the
Mercers' Company. Illus. BC, xv (66), 283-95.

BLAKE, William
William Blake, 1752-1827. (English literary
autographs, II). Illus. BC, iii (54), 218-19.
T. J. Brown.

Blake exhibitions in America on the occasion
of the bicentenary of the birth of William Blake.
BC, vi (57), 378-85.
E. Wolf *2nd*.

Blake's *Holy Thursday* in Anne and Jane
Taylor's *City Scenes*. (Note, 128). BC, ix (60),
75-6.
Sir G. L. Keynes.

A Blake engraving in Bonnycastle's *Mensuration*,
1782. Illus. BC, xii (63), 205-6.
Sir G. L. Keynes.

Blake's *Little Tom the sailor*. Illus. BC, xvii
(68), 421-7.
Sir G. L. Keynes.

A census of copies of William Blake's *Poetical Sketches*, 1783. LIB, xvii (36/7), 354-60.
M. R. Lowery.

Blake, Tulk, and Garth Wilkinson. LIB, xxvi (45/6), 190-2.
Sir. G. L. Keynes.

Blake's *Hesiod*. LIB, xx (65), 315-20.
G. E. Bentley, *jr*.

A new Blake document: the 'Riddle' manuscript. Illus. LIB, xxiv (69), 337-43.
G. E. Bentley, *jr*.

The Blake-Linnell accounts in the library of Yale University. PBSA, xxxvii (43), 1-22.
E. Wolf *2nd*.

Blake's engravings and his friendship with Flaxman. SB, xii (59), 161-88.
G. E. Bentley, *jr*.

The supressed and altered passages in Blake's *Jerusalem*. Illus. SB, xvii (64), 1-54.
D. V. Erdman.

Blake's *Jerusalem*: Plate 3 fully restored. SB, xviii (65), 281-2.
D. V. Erdman.

The date of Blake's Pickering manuscript or The way of a poet with paper. SB, xix (66), 232-43.
G. E. Bentley, *jr*.

BLAKISTON, Jack M. G.
Winchester College. (Unfamiliar libraries, 11). Illus. BC, xvi (67), 297-304.

A Dublin reprint of Thomas Warton's *History of English Poetry*. LIB, i (46/7), 69-70.

Winchester College library in the eighteenth and early nineteenth centuries. Illus. LIB, xvii (62), 23-45.

BLANCHARD, Jean Pierre
Blanchard, Jean Pierre (1753-1809). *Journal de ma quarante-cinquième ascension, la première faite en Amérique le 9. janvier, 1793*. Philadelphie, 1793. PBSA, xxxiv (40), 358.
E. M. Sowerby.

Blanchard, Jean Pierre (1735-1809). *Journal de ma quarante-cinquième ascension, la première faite en Amérique le 9. janvier, 1793*. Philadelphie, 1793. PBSA, xxxv (41), 70.
F. Bowe.

BLANCHARDIN AND EGLANTINE
Caxton's *Blanchardin and Eglantine*: notes on the leaf preserved in the British Museum. PBSA, xxxix (45), 156-61.
C. F. Bühler.

BLANCK, Jacob Nathaniel
Edwards, Harry Stillwell (1854-1938). *Eneas Africanus*. [Macon, Georgia, 1919]. PBSA, xxxiv (40), 273.

Problems in the bibliographical description of nineteenth-century American books. PBSA, xxxvi (42), 124-36.

Salmagundi and its publisher. PBSA, xli (47), 1-32.

A calendar of bibliographical difficulties. PBSA, xlix (55), 1-18.

[BAL. List of authors in Vol. 1]. PBSA, lii (58), 159.
W. White.

Washington Irving's *Life of Capt. James Lawrence*. PBSA, liii (59), 338-40.

Artemus Ward his book, 1862. PBSA, liv (60), 121-5.

BAL [Bibliography of American Literature] Addenda. PBSA, lv (61), 46-7.

— PBSA, lv (61), 152-3.

The star spangled banner. [A bibliography]. PBSA, lx (66), 176-84.

BAL Addenda. Ralph Waldo Emerson — entry no. 5272. PBSA, lxi (67), 124-6.

BAL addenda. M.E.W. Freeman — entry no. 6380. PBSA, lxi (67), 127.
R. B. O'Connor.

BAL Addendum. Joel Chandler Harris — entry no. 7115. PBSA, lxi (67), 266.

BAL addendum: Ambrose Bierce — entry no. 1112*. PBSA, lxii (68), 451.
G. T. Tanselle.

BAL addendum 3479: Twain's *A dog's tale*. PBSA, lxii (68), 617.

BAL addendum: Harold Frederic's *Gloria mundi*? —entry 6293. The first four printings of Harold Frederic's *Gloria mundi*. PBSA, lxiii (69), 197-8.
J. Katz.

BLAND, David Farrant
Fine books of 1954. Illus. BC, iv (55), 229-35.

BLAYNEY, Glenn H.
An error in microfilms. LIB, viii (53), 126-7.

Variants in the first quarto of *The Miseries of Inforst Mariage*. LIB, ix (54), 176-84.

Variants in Q1 of *A Yorkshire Tragedy*. LIB, xi (56), 262-7.

BLEDSOE, Albert Taylor
Bledsoe's *Is Davis a Traitor*? A note on an imprint changed without cancellation. PBSA, lii (58), 220.
J. C. Wyllie.

BLISH, Mary
A. C. Bradley: a summary account. PBSA, lxii (68), 607-12.

BLISS, Carey S.
Cancel slips. (Note, 33). BC, iii (54), 307.

Stubbe and Wotton. (Note, 63). BC, v (56), 276.

Bulmer and the Roxburghe Club Catalogue. (Query, 82). BC, vi (57, 291.

Bloomfield's *Rural Tales*, 1802. (Query, 119). BC, ix (60), 199.

An unexplained 17th-century cancel. (Query, 129). BC, x (61), 72.

Montagu Butler's translations of Tennyson. (Query, 162). BC, xii (63), 356.

Poe and Sarah Helen Whitman. (Note, 206). BC, xii (63), 490.

A much-travelled association copy of Calvin's *Institutes*. (Collector's piece, 3). Illus. BC, xvii (68), 458-62.

Cobden-Sanderson pattern books. (Note, 308). BC, xviii (69), 93.

Dating of Walter Crane toy books. (Query, 228). BC, xviii (69), 223.

BLISS, Philip
Philip Bliss 1787-1857, editor and bibliographer. [*And*] Additions and corrections. OBSP, iii (33), 173-260, 367-8.
S. Gibson *and* C. J. Hindle.

— Additions and corrections. OBSP, i (47), 40-2.
I. G. Philip.

BLOCK-BOOKS
Two block-books in the Hunterian Library, Glasgow University. BTHK, iii (60/2), 103-4.
R. Donaldson.

BLOOMFIELD, Barry Cambray
An unrecorded article by T. S. Eliot. (Note, 186). BC, xi (62), 350.

Bloomfield's *Rural Tales*, 1802. (Note, 188). BC, xi (62), 482.

An unrecorded pamphlet by Archdeacon Wrangham. (Note, 203). BC, xii (63), 355.

T. B. Mosher and the Guild of women binders. (Note, 285). BC, xvi (67), 82.

W. H. Auden's first book. LIB, xvii (62), 152-4.

BLOOMFIELD, Robert
Robert Bloomfield, 1766-1823. (Some uncollected authors, 20). BC, viii (59), 170-9.
John Gathorne-Hardy *earl of Cranbrook and* J. Hadfield.

Robert Bloomfield (Summer 1959, pp. 173-79). Addenda. (Note, 116). BC, viii (59), 299.
J. Sparrow.

Bloomfield's *Rural Tales*, 1802. (Query, 119). BC, viii (59), 431-2.
A. Bridge.

— BC, ix (60), 199.
C. S. Bliss.

Early editions of Bloomfield's poems. (Note, 179). BC, xi (62), 216-7.
J. Clements.

Bloomfield's *Rural Tales*, 1802. (Note, 188). BC, xi (62), 482.
B. C. Bloomfield.

BLOOMINGDALE, Judith
Haiku: An annotated checklist. PBSA, lvi (62), 488-94.

— Correction. PBSA, lvii (63), 196.

Three decades in periodical criticism of Hart Crane's *The Bridge*. PBSA, lvii (63), 360-71.

BLOSSOM, Henry A.
Stone & Kimball addendum: Blossom's *Checkers*. PBSA, lxii (68), 451-2.
G. T. Tanselle.

BLOUNT, Charles
Charles Blount, 1654-1693. (Some uncollected authors, 17). BC, vii (58), 182-7.
J. S. L. Gilmour.

BLUDDER, Sir Thomas
A Cavalier library — 1643, [i.e. that of Sir Thomas Bludder]. SB, vi (54), 141-60.
J. L. Lievsay *and* R. B. Davis.

BLURB
See ADVERTISEMENTS

BLYENBURG, Damas van
See BLYENBURGIUS, Damasus.

BLYENBURGIUS, Damasus
Blyenburg corrects his book. PBSA, lv (61), 382-3.
R. H. Bowers.

BOBER, Harry
A Book of Hours for the use of Autun printed for Simon Vostre (*c.* 1507). A correction to the Stillwell census. PBSA, xli (47), 341-2.

BOCCACCIO, Giovanni
A Boccaccio manuscript in Australia. PBSA, lvi (62), 56-65.
K. V. Sinclair.

BOCQUET, Edward
Edward Bocquet's illustrated edition of the *Letters of Junius*. PBSA, xlvi (52), 66-7.
F. Cordasco.

BODLEIAN LIBRARY
See OXFORD *univ., Bodleian libr.*

BODLEY HEAD PRESS
The Bodley Head Press: some bibliographical extrapolations. PBSA, lxi (67), 39-50.
R. D. Brown.

BODMER, Martin
The Rosenbach-Bodmer Shakespeare collection. BC, i (52), 112-16.
J. Hayward.

Bibliotheca Bodmeriana. (Contemporary collectors, 19). Part 1. Manuscripts; Part II. Printed books. Illus. BC, vii (58), 386-95; viii (59), 31-45.
A. Rau.

Date of a MS in Bibliotheca Bodmeriana. (Note, 105). BC, viii (59), 69.
A. I. Doyle.

BODONI, Giovanni Battista
Two untraced Bodoni items. (Query, 100). BC, vii (58), 295-6.
R. F. Lane.

— BC, viii (59), 300.
R. F. Lane.

Count MacCarthy-Reagh and Bodoni. (Note, 104). BC, vii (58), 418.
R. F. Lane.

— (Note, 127). BC, ix (60), 72-5.
R. F. Lane.

Two states of a Bodoni type specimen. (Note, 218). BC, xiii (64), 207-10).
M. J. Faigel.

Bodoni's *Manuale Tipografico* and the recent facsimile. LIB, xvii (62), 132-8.
R. F. Lane.

Bodoni's first hundred printing commissions. PBSA, liii (59), 21-36.
R. F. Lane.

BOECE, Hector
See BOETHIUS, Hector

BOERHAAVE, Hermann
Boerhaave's *Elementa Chemiae*, 1732. (Note, 121). BC, viii (59), 428-9.
R. G. Neville.

— BC, ix (60), 64.
F. N. L. Poynter.

BOETHIUS, Anicius Manlius T. S.
Three notes on Caxton. [Concerning the recovery by W. Blades of fragments from the *Boethius* in the King Edward VI Grammar School at St. Albans]. LIB, xvii (36/7) 155-66.
C. F. Bühler.

BOETHIUS, Hector
A manuscript of Hector Boece. EBST, ii (38/45), 392-3.
G. Watson.

BOHANNON, Mary Elizabeth
A London bookseller's bill: 1635-1639. LIB, xviii (37/8), 417-46.

BOHEM, Hilda
A collection of poems by several hands, 1693. [Identity of the authors]. (Query, 227). BC, xvii (68), 352-3.

A special copy of Galluci's *Theatrum mundi*. (Note, 307). BC, xviii (69), 92-3.

The device on plate E5v of Vegetius's *De re militari*. (Query, 240). BC, xviii (69), 226-7.

BOHN, Henry George
Do you know your Lowndes? A bibliographical essay on William Thomas Lowndes and incidentally on Robert Watt and Henry G. Bohn. PBSA, xxxiii (39), 1-22.
G. W. Cole.

BOLDONI, Sigismondo
A manuscript from Queen Christina's library: the *Amores* of Sigismondo Boldoni. Illus. LIB, xvii (62), 281-315.
J. H. A. Sparrow.

BONAPARTE, prince Louis-Lucien
The private press and publishing activities of Prince Louis-Lucien Bonaparte. BC, ix (60), 31-7.
A. Ehrman.

Prince Louis-Lucien Bonaparte's publications. (Note, 137). BC, ix (60), 198.
S. G. Gillam.

Prince L. L. Napoleon's first catalogue. (Note, 154). BC, x (61), 70-1.
A. Ehrman.

Prince Louis-Lucien Bonaparte's publications. (Note, 224). BC, xiii (64), 348-50.
D. J. Gilson.

BONAVENTURE *st.*
Three English books of the sixteenth century. (*Opuscules or smale werkes of saynt bonaventure; The Pomander of Prayer; The doctrynall of symple people*). Illus. LIB, xvii (36/7), 184-9.
Sir F. C. Francis.

Bonaventura, S. *Meditationes vitae Christi*. [Paris], ? Jean Petit [n.d.]. PBSA, xxxiv (40), 84.
F. R. Goff.

BOND, Donald Frederick
The text of the *Spectator*. SB, v (52/3), 109-28.

BOND, Richmond Pugh
Early lending libraries. LIB, xiii (58), 204-5.

John Partridge and the Company of Stationers. SB, xvi (63), 61-80.

BOND, William Henry
Arthur Amory Houghton *jr.* (Contemporary collectors, 12). Illus. BC, vi (57), 28-40.

Alice in Wonderland: proof illustrations. (Query, 79). BC, vi (57), 181.

The Houghton Library's vernis binding. [A revised description]. BC, xv (66), 352.

W. A. Jackson's *Dibdin*: a revised entry. (Note, 275). BC, xv (66), 352-3.

Imposition by half-sheets. Illus. LIB, xxii (41/2), 163-7.

Two ghosts: Herbert's *Baripenthes* and the Vaughan-Holland portrait of Sidney. LIB, xxiv (43/4), 175-81.

Henry Hallam, *The Times* newspaper, and the Halliwell case. LIB, xviii (63), 133-40.

Casting off copy by Elizabethan printers: a theory. PBSA, xlii (48), 281-91.

A printer's manuscript of 1508. [J. J. Pontanus's *De Prudentia* — B. M. Add. MS. 12,027]. Illus. SB, viii (56), 147-56.

BONE, Gavin
Jeremy Taylor and Elizabeth Grymeston. [A letter]. LIB, xv (34/5), 247-8.

BONNELL, Alice H.
Binding for Pope Paul IV. PBSA, liii (59), 68-9.

BONNYCASTLE, John
A Blake engraving in Bonnycastle's *Mensuration,* 1782. Illus. BC, xii (63), 205-6.
Sir G. L. Keynes.

BOOK CLUBS
Book club in Huntingdon. (Query, 68). BC, v (56), 79.
A. Ehrman.

A bookseller's record of eighteenth-century book clubs. Illus. LIB, xv (60), 278-87.
P. Kaufman.

BOOK COLLECTING
An early ownership rhyme. (Query, 27). BC, ii (53), 222.
B. Harris.

Trends in modern first edition collecting since 1939. BC, iv (55), 58-62.
A. T. Miller.

Sidelights on American bibliophily. BC, v (56), 357-67.
J. Carter.

Country collecting. BC, vi (57), 54-9.
A. Walbank.

The aesthetic investor's guide to current literary values. An essay in bibliometry. BC, ix (60), 414-22.
N. Barker.

Three opportunities [for buying Irish MSS. in the 19th century]. BC, xv (66), 437-45.
A. N. L. Munby.

Adventures in book-collecting. BH, ii (51/2), 105-10.
L. J. Lloyd.

Armorial book stamps and their owners. LIB, xx (39/40), 121-35.
H. J. B. Clements.

Prices, collectors and librarians. PBSA, xxxvi (42), 46-55.
F. M. Sweet.

An imp with Uncle Sam. PBSA, xl (46), 247-58.
W. S. Merwin.

Spanish books in England: 1800-1850. TCBS, iii (59/63), 70-92.
N. Glendinning.

BOOK COLLECTOR
[*The Book Collector*] After ten years. BC, x (61), 402-7.
J. Carter.

BOOK COLLECTORS
Some unconventional women before 1800. Printers, booksellers and collectors. PBSA, xlix (55), 300-14.
F. Hamill.

BOOK DESIGN
Fine books of 1954. BC, iv (55), 229-35.
D. Bland.

BOOK ILLUSTRATION
See ILLUSTRATION

BOOK IMPORTS
Treuttel and Würtz: some aspects of the importation of books from France, *c.* 1825. Illus. LIB, xxiii (68), 118-44.
G. G. Barber.

BOOK LABELS
Early book labels. (Query, 48). BC, iii (54), 227.
A. N. L. Munby.

—. BC, iv (55), 172.
G. B. Lowe.

An admonition to borrowers. (Note, 220). BC, xiii (64), 211.
A. Ehrman.

BOOK OF COMMON PRAYER
See PRAYER, Book of Common

BOOK OF HAWKING, HUNTING AND HER-ALDRY
See BERNERS, Juliana

BOOK OF ST. ALBANS
See BERNERS, Juliana

BOOK PLATES
The earliest dated woodcut book plate. (Note, 119). Illus. BC, viii (59), 426-7.
A. Ehrman.

(Note, 119). Illus. BC, ix (60), 326.
A. Ehrman.

The earliest extant French armorial ex-libris. (Note, 161). Illus. BC, x (61), 331-2.
A. Rau.

The earliest extant French armorial ex-libris. (Note, 161). BC, xi (62), 212.
W. L. Hanaway, *jr.*

—. BC, xi (62), 212.
R. Mortimer.

—. BC, xi (62), 212-3.
W. H. McCarthy, *jr.*

John Ruskin's bookplates. (Note, 303). BC, xxiii (69), 88-9.
J. S. Dearden.

Australian book plates. Some makers and owners. Illus. BH, i (47/51), 381-401.
R. H. Croll.

The origin and evolution of the book-plate. Illus. LIB, i (46/7), 39-44.
G. H. Viner.

The origin of Sir Nicholas Bacon's book-plate. TCBS, ii (54/8), 373-6.
E. R. Sandeen.

BOOK PRICES
An 18th-century list of books with prices. (Note, 212). BC, xiii (64), 65-6.
D. H. Woodward.

Book prices past [referred to in *A critical and historical account of all the celebrated libraries in foreign countries* ascribed to W. Oldys]. (Note, 278). BC, xv (66), 356.
W. Rees-Mogg.

Is this a record? BC, xviii (69), 353-9.
J. Carter.

The price of books in medieval England. LIB, xvii (36/7), 312-32.
H. E. Bell.

A London bookseller's bill: 1635-1639. LIB, xviii (37/8), 417-46.
M. E. Bohannon.

Notes on English retail book-prices, 1550-1640. LIB, v (50/1), 83-112.
F. R. Johnson.

[Notes on English retail book-prices, 1550-1640. [A letter]]. LIB, v (50/1), 275-6.
G. B. Evans.

Prices, collectors and librarians. PBSA, xxxvi (42), 46-55.
F. H. Sweet.

Prices of some second-hand law books in 1620. PBSA, lvii (63), 212-17.
A. G. Watson.

BOOK REPAIRS
See BOOKBINDING TECHNIQUES

BOOK STAMPS
The book-stamps of the Tollemache family of Helmingham and Ham. Illus. BC, xvi (67), 178-85.
E. Wilson.

Armorial book-stamps and their owners. LIB, xx (39/40), 121-35.
H. J. B. Clements.

Sir Christopher Hatton's book stamps. Illus. LIB, xii (57), 119-21.
R. J. Roberts.

BOOKBINDERS
See also under names of individual bookbinders.

French bookbinders, 1789-1848. (Note, 78). BC, v (56), 383-4.
C. Ramsden.

Grolier's binders. Notes on the Paris exhibition. 2 pts. BC, ix (60), 45-51, 165-70.
H. M. Nixon.

—. (Note, 171). BC, xi (62), 79.
H. M. Nixon.

—. BC, xi (62), 213-14.
H. M. Nixon.

London bookbinders: masters and men, 1780-1840. LIB, i (46/7), 28-38.
E. Howe.

Bookbinders to George III and his immediate descendants and collaterals. LIB, xiii (58), 186-93.
C. Ramsden.

Early American bookbinders. PBSA, xxxv (41), 210-11.
A. Ehrman.

Cambridge books of congratulatory verses, 1603-1640, and their binders. Illus. TCBS, i (49/53), 395-421.
J. C. T. Oates.

BOOKBINDERS CASE UNFOLDED
The Bookbinders Case Unfolded. Illus. LIB, xvii (62), 66-76.
B. C. Middleton.

BOOKBINDERS' CLOTH
The nomenclature of nineteenth-century cloth grains. Illus. BC, ii (53), 54-8.
J. Carter *and* M. Sadleir.

Colour variations in 19th-century publishers' bindings. (Note, 302). BC, xvii (68), 490.
J. Carter.

Canvas and bookcloth, an essay on beginnings. Illus. LIB, iii (48/9), 39-49.
D. Leighton.

The specification of binding cloth. LIB, xxi (66), 246-7.
G. T. Tanselle.

BOOKBINDERS' TICKETS
The earliest Newcastle binder's ticket. (Note, 296). BC, xvii (68), 81-2.
W. S. Mitchell.

BOOKBINDING COSTS
Binding costs, 1735. LIB, iii (48/9), 222-3.
J. H. P. Pafford.

BOOKBINDING FRAGMENTS
Fragments of accounts relating to the Royal Works from Oxford bindings. LIB, xxv (44/5), 66-7.
A. Deeley *and* S. Gibson.

Fragments from a binding. LIB, xxvi (45/6), 172-5.
L. A. Sheppard.

Here the frailest leaves. PBSA, xlvii (53), 201-17.
D. M. Schullian.

BOOKBINDING TECHNIQUES
To bind or not to bind. (Note, 166). BC, x (61), 336.
A. Ehrman.

The development of bookbinding methods — Coptic influence. Illus. LIB, xiii (32/3), 1-19.
D. Cockerell.

The ethics of book repairs. LIB, ix (54), 194-8.
A. Gardner.

Changes in the style of bookbinding, 1550-1830. Illus. LIB, xi (56), 71-94.
H. G. Pollard.

The construction of English twelfth-century bindings. Illus. LIB, xvii (62), 1-22.
H. G. Pollard.

The Lichfield St. Chad's Gospels: repair and rebinding, 1961-1962. Illus. LIB, xx (65), 259-76.
R. Powell.

BOOKBINDING TOOLS
A late use of a crested roll. (Note, 12). BC, i (52), 264.
A. N. L. Munby.

—. BC, ii (53), 154-5.
A. I. Doyle.

An early English panel-stamped binding. (English bookbindings, 6). Illus. BC, ii (53), 140-1.
H. M. Nixon.

Bindings with the device of a pelican in its piety. (Note, 291). BC, xvii (68), 351.
C. B. L. Barr.

Some early bindings and binders' tools. Illus. LIB, xix (38/9), 202-47.
G. D. Hobson.

Notes on Nuremberg panel stamps before the Reformation. Illus. PBSA, xliv (50), 59-62.
E. Kyriss.

The Aitken shop. Identification of an eighteenth-century bindery and its tools. Illus. PBSA, lvii (63), 422-37.
C. *and* W. Spawn.

Early binding stamps of religious significance in certain American libraries: a supplementary report. Illus. SB, ii (49/50), 63-77.
E. Wead.

— Addendum. SB, v (52/3), 210.
E. Kyriss.

Parisian panel stamps between 1480 and 1530. Illus. SB, vii (55), 113-24.
E. Kyriss.

An unrecorded Cambridge panel. Illus. TCBS, i (49/53), 179-80.
J. B. Oldham.

Katherine of Aragon's pomegranate. TCBS, ii (54/8), 88-92.
K. P. Harrison.

BOOKBINDINGS
Early trade bindings. (Query, 2). BC, i (52), 54.
J. Carter.

—. BC, i (52), 128-9.
A. N. L. Munby.

—. BC, i (52), 194.
A. N. L. Munby.

—. BC, i (52), 266.
J. P. Harthan.

—. Illus. BC, ii (53), 221-2.
A. R. A. Hobson.

A waterproof binding. (Query, 42). BC, ii (53), 283.
C. Ramsden.

A trade binding. (Note, 70). BC, v (56), 276.
A. Rogers.

—. BC, v (56), 383.
A. W. G. Lowther.

Gilt tooling on macabre bindings. (Query, 98). BC, vii (58), 295.
A. Rau.

The Baltimore binding exhibition. BC, vii (58), 419-26.
H. M. Nixon.

List of books acquired by the British Museum from Chatsworth. Part II. English books 1501-1640. Part III. Bindings. BC, viii (59), 52-9.
A. F. Allison.

An international binding design. (Note, 198). BC, xii (63), 206-7.
T. W. Hanson.

A binder's mosprint. (Note, 244). BC, xiv (65), 214.
W. B. Todd.

Rebound in the 16th-century? (Query, 202). BC, xv (66), 214.
A. Ehrman.

—. [An answer to Query 202]. BC, xv (66), 487.
H. P. Kraus.

Bindings with the device of a pelican in its piety. (Note, 291). BC, xvii (68), 351.
C. B. L. Barr.

Two unusual cancel bindings. Illus. BTHK, ii (60/1), 71-2.
I. R. Grant.

Some cuir-ciselé bookbindings in English libraries. Illus. LIB, xiii (32/3), 337-65.
E. P. Goldschmidt.

Some early bindings and binders' tools. Illus. LIB, xix (38/9), 202-47.
G. D. Hobson.

Individual binding. LIB, xxiii (42/3), 197-8.
R. W. Chapman.

Bindings in the M. Wodhull library. [A letter]. LIB, viii (53), 279.
C. Ramsden.

Early binding stamps of religious significance in certain American libraries: a supplementary report. Illus. SB, ii (49/50), 63-77.
E. Wead.

—. Addendum. SB, v (52/3), 210.
E. Kyriss.

Bookbindings in the libraries of Prague. Illus. SB, iii (50/1), 105-30.
E. Kyriss.

British signed bindings in my library. TCBS, i (49/53), 270-9.
J. R. Abbey.

BOOKBINDINGS: American
Scottish-American bookbindings. Six examples from colonial North America. Illus. BC, vi (57), 150-9.
H. D. French.

The Aitken shop. Identification of an eighteenth-century bindery and its tools. Illus. PBSA, lvii (63), 422-37.
W. *and* C. Spawn.

The amazing career of Andrew Barclay, Scottish bookbinder, of Boston. SB, xiv (61), 145-62.
H. D. French.

'Bound in Boston by Henry B. Legg'. Illus. SB, xvii (64), 135-9.
H. D. French.

BOOKBINDINGS: Belgian
Comments on a Belgian "Sammelband" of the early sixteenth century in the Pierpont Morgan Library. PBSA, lviii (64), 154-6.
C. F. Bühler.

BOOKBINDINGS: Byzantine
A Byzantine silver binding. Illus. LIB, xvii (36/7), 295-7.
E. H. Minns.

BOOKBINDINGS: Coptic
The development of bookbinding methods — Coptic influence. Illus. LIB, xiii (32/3), 1-19.
D. Cockerell.

Early book-bindings from a Coptic monastery. Illus. LIB, xx (39/40), 214-33.
C. T. Lamacraft.

BOOKBINDINGS: Egyptian
Some early bindings from Egypt in the Chester Beatty Library: additional notes. LIB, xviii (63), 218-23.
R. Powell.

BOOKBINDINGS: English
Collecting English signed bindings. Illus. BC, ii (53), 177-93.
A. N. L. Munby.

Notes on bindings from English collections at Stuttgart. BC, v (56), 158-61.
E. Kyriss.

An unidentifiable English binder. (Query, 144). BC, x (61), 202.
H. D. Lyon.

—. BC, xi (62), 86.
P. E. Hall.

A London panel-stamped binding, c. 1530, rebacked for James West, c. 1755. (English bookbindings, 59). Illus. BC, xv (66), 460.
H. M. Nixon.

Note on some new tools by the 'Unicorn binder'. Illus. LIB, ii (47/8), 283-4.
J. B. Oldham.

BOOKBINDINGS: English: 12th c.
The construction of English twelfth-century bindings. Illus. LIB, xvii (62), 1-22.
H. G. Pollard.

BOOKBINDINGS: English: 15th c.
A binding from the Caxton bindery, c. 1490. (English bookbindings, 48). Illus. BC, xiii (64), 52.
H. M. Nixon.

The binding of books printed by William Caxton. PBSA, xxxviii (44), 1-8.
C. F. Bühler.

BOOKBINDINGS: English: 16th c.
Gilt binding by John Reynes, c. 1521-4. (English bookbindings, 2). Illus. BC, i (52), 94-5.
H. M. Nixon.

London binding for King Edward VI, c. 1550. (English bookbindings, 4). Illus. BC, i (52), 244-5.
H. M. Nixon.

An early English panel-stamped binding. (English bookbindings, 6). Illus. BC, ii (53), 140-1.
H. M. Nixon.

A binding presented to Edward VI, c. 1552. (English bookbindings, 7). Illus. BC, ii (53), 272-3.
H. M. Nixon.

A binding for King Henry VIII, c. 1540. (English bookbindings, 14). Illus. BC, iv (55), 236.
H. M. Nixon.

A binding by the Morocco binder, c. 1563. (English bookbindings, 22). Illus. BC, vi (57), 278.
H. M. Nixon.

A binding for Archbishop Parker, c. 1574 (English bookbindings, 23). Illus. BC, vi (57), 386.
H. M. Nixon.

A binding by the Dudley binder, c. 1558. (English bookbindings, 30). Illus. BC, viii (59), 282.
H. M. Nixon.

A binding for Elizabeth I by the Initial binder, 1563. (English bookbindings, 35) Illus. BC, ix (60), 444.
H. M. Nixon.

A binding for William Bullein by the Initial binder, c. 1562. (English bookbindings, 37). Illus. BC, x (61), 184.
H. M. Nixon.

A London binding by the Medallion binder, c. 1545. (English bookbindings, 44). Illus. BC, xii (63), 60.
H. M. Nixon.

A binding attributed to John de Planche, c. 1572. (English bookbindings, 50). Illus. BC, xiii (64), 340.
H. M. Nixon.

A binding by the Flamboyant binder, c. 1540-45. (English bookbindings, 53). Illus. BC, xiv (65), 200.
H. M. Nixon.

A binding for the Earl of Arundel, c. 1555. (English bookbindings, 60). Illus. BC, xvi (67), 54.
H. M. Nixon.

A binding by the Macdurnan Gospels binder, c. 1570. (English bookbindings, 69). Illus. BC, xviii (69), 200.
H. M. Nixon.

Binding in Oxford in A.D. 1520. (Note, 311). BC, xviii (69), 220.
A. Ehrman.

Cambridge binding by Garrett Godfrey, c. 1522. (English bookbindings, 71). Illus. BC, xviii (69), 490.
H. M. Nixon.

The gilt binding of the Whittington *Epigrams*, MS. Bodley 523. LIB, vii (52), 120-1.
H. M. Nixon.

The Virgin and Child binder, LVL, and William Horman. Illus. LIB, xvii (62), 77-85.
N. R. Ker.

Notes on some English centre- and corner-piece bindings *c.* 1600. Illus. LIB, xvii (62), 93-5.
G. G. Barber.

Note on the binding of Ushaw College XVIII c. 9b. TCBS, i (49/53), 46-7.
A. N. L. Munby [from information supplied by J. B. Oldham].

BOOKBINDINGS: English: 17th c.
Restoration binding *c.* 1680. (English bookbindings, 1). Illus. BC, i (52), 2-3.
H. M. Nixon.

A Cambridge binding perhaps by David Boyse, *c.* 1627. (English bookbindings, 9). Illus. BC, iii (54), 50-1.
H. M. Nixon.

A binding by the Naval binder, *c.* 1675. (English bookbindings, 12). Illus. BC, iv (55), 45-7.
H. M. Nixon.

A London binding by Fletcher, 1660. (English bookbindings, 16). Illus. BC, v (56), 53-4.
H. M. Nixon.

A London binding by Fletcher, *c.* 1662. (English bookbindings, 17). Illus. BC, v (56), 150.
H. M. Nixon.

A Cambridge binding by Titus Tillet, 1677. (English bookbindings, 27). Illus. BC, vii (58), 396.
H. M. Nixon.

A London binding by Queen's binder B, *c.* 1675. (English bookbindings, 28). Illus. BC, viii (59), 50.
H. M. Nixon.

A binding by Lewis for Oliver Cromwell, 1656. (English bookbindings, 29). Illus. BC, viii (59), 168.
H. M. Nixon.

A binding by Daniel Search. (Query, 117). BC, viii (59), 184.
H. M. Nixon.

Another binding for Oliver Cromwell. (Note, 117). BC, viii (59), 299-300.
H. M. Nixon.

A binding from the Mearne shop, *c.* 1680. (English bookbindings, 22). Illus. BC, ix (60), 52.
H. M. Nixon.

A London binding by Henry Evans, *c.* 1655. (English bookbindings, 34). Illus. BC, ix (60), 316.
H. M. Nixon.

A binding by the Small Carnation binder, *c.* 1680. (English bookbindings, 26). Illus. BC, x (61), 56.
H. M. Nixon.

A binding from Charles Mearne's shop, 1685. (English bookbindings, 38). Illus. BC, x (61), 320.
H. M. Nixon.

A binding from the Samuel Mearne bindery, *c.* 1669. (English bookbindings, 29). BC, x (61), 440.
H. M. Nixon.

A binding supplied by John Bull to James I, *c.* 1621. (English bookbindings, 40). Illus. BC, xi (62), 62.
H. M. Nixon.

A little Gidding binding, *c.* 1635-40. (English bookbindings, 42). Illus. BC, xi (62), 330.
H. M. Nixon.

A Pyramus and Thisbe binding, *c.* 1616. (English bookbindings, 46). Illus. BC, xii (63), 338.
H. M. Nixon.

A London binding by Queen's binder A, *c.* 1670 (English bookbindings, 47). Illus. BC, xii (63), 488.
H. M. Nixon.

A binding by Lord Herbert's binder, *c.* 1633. (English bookbindings, 52). Illus. BC, xiv (65), 60.
H. M. Nixon.

A binding by Alexander Cleeve, *c.* 1690. (English bookbindings, 54). Illus. BC, xiv (65), 348.
H. M. Nixon.

A binding by the Centre-rectangle binder. (English bookbindings, 62). Illus. BC, xvi (67), 345.
H. M. Nixon.

A binding by the Royal heads binder, *c.* 1665. (English bookbindings, 64). Illus. BC, xvii (68), 44.
H. M. Nixon.

An Oxford binding by Richard Sedgley, 1699. (English bookbindings, 68). Illus. BC, xviii (69), 62.
H. M. Nixon.

Roger Bartlett's bookbindings. Illus. LIB, xvii (62), 56-65.
H. M. Nixon.

BOOKBINDINGS: English: 18th c.
Binding by Richard Montagu for Thomas Hollis, 1758. (English bookbindings, 3). Illus. BC, i (52), 182-4.
H. M. Nixon.

An eighteenth-century London binding, *c.* 1764. (English bookbindings, 5). Illus. BC, ii (53), 66-7.
H. M. Nixon.

A London binding by Richard Balley, 1700. (English bookbindings, 13). Illus. BC, iv (55), 144-5.
H. M. Nixon.

A binding for John Carteret, 2nd earl Granville, 1741. (English bookbindings, 19). Illus. BC, v (56), 368.
H. M. Nixon.

A mosaic binding for Lord Kingsale, 1720. English bookbindings, 20). BC, vi (57), 60.
H. M. Nixon.

A binding by the Settle Bindery, 1704. (English bookbindings, 25). Illus. BC, vii (58), 180.
H. M. Nixon.

A binding by John Brindley, 1743. (English bookbindings, 43). Illus. BC, xi (62), 466.
H. M. Nixon.

An Eton binding by Roger Payne, 1764. (English bookbindings, 45). Illus. BC, xii (63), 194.
H. M. Nixon.

A Harleian binding by Thomas Elliot, 1721. (English bookbindings, 49). Illus. BC, xiii (64), 194.
H. M. Nixon.

A binding designed by James Stuart, 1762. (English bookbindings, 55). Illus. BC, xiv (65), 538.
H. M. Nixon.

A London panel-stamped binding, c. 1530, rebacked for James West, c. 1755. (English bookbindings, 59). Illus. BC, xv (66), 460.
H. M. Nixon.

An Adam binding, 1764 [for R. Adam's *Ruins of the palace of the emperor Diocletian at Spalatro*]. (English bookbindings, 57). Illus. BC, xv (66), 184.
H. M. Nixon.

Harleian bindings by Chapman, 1721. (English bookbindings, 58). Illus. BC, xv (66), 321-2.
H. M. Nixon.

A London binding for Jonas Hanway, 1783. (English bookbindings, 61). Illus. BC, xvi (67), 194.
H. M. Nixon.

A Cambridge binding by Ed. Moore, c. 1748. (English bookbindings, 63). Illus. BC, xvi (67), 481.
H. M. Nixon.

An emblematic rococo binding, 1781. (English bookbindings, 70). Illus. BC, xviii (69), 360.
H. M. Nixon.

Chirm's banded bindings. Illus. TCBS, i (49/53), 181-6.
A. N. L. Munby.

Windham and Gauffecourt. TCBS, i (49/53), 186-90.
A. N. L. Munby.

BOOKBINDINGS: English: 19th c.
Binding by T. J. Cobden-Sanderson, 1888. (English bookbindings, 7). Illus. BC, ii (53), 212-13.
H. M. Nixon.

Binding variants in the Brontës' *Poems*. (Note, 25). BC, ii (53), 219-21.
D. F. Foxon.

A waterproof binding. (Query, 42). BC, ii (53), 283.
C. Ramsden.

A London binding by Charles Lewis, 1812. (English bookbindings, 10). Illus. BC, iii (54), 134-5.
H. M. Nixon.

A binding from Southey's 'Cottonian' library. (English bookbindings, 11). Illus. BC, iii (54), 298-9.
H. M. Nixon.

A George III binding, c. 1810-20. (English bookbindings, 15). Illus. BC, iv (55), 308-9.
H. M. Nixon.

An angling binding by Thomas Gosden, c. 1825. (English bookbindings, 21). Illus. BC, vi (57), 170.
H. M. Nixon.

A binding by James Hayday, c. 1845. (English bookbindings, 24). Illus. BC, vii (58), 62.
H. M. Nixon.

An illuminated binding for the Prince Consort, 1843. (English bookbindings, 26). Illus. BC, vii (58), 284.
H. M. Nixon.

A Newcastle binding by Lubbock, c. 1820. (English bookbindings, 31). Illus. BC, viii (59), 416.
H. M. Nixon.

A London binding by Francis Bedford, 1866. (English bookbindings, 33). Illus. BC, ix (60), 178.
H. M. Nixon.

A gift from the maidens of the United Kingdom, 1874. (English bookbindings, 41). Illus. BC, xi (62), 204.
H. M. Nixon.

Variant bindings on Moxon authors. (Query, 183). BC, xiii (64), 356-7.
N. Colbeck.

A London binding by John MacKinlay, c. 1810. (English bookbindings, 51). Illus. BC, xiii (64), 486.
H. M. Nixon.

The 'green' Tennysons. (Note, 246). BC, xiv (65), 215.
P. F. Hinton.

Variant binding of Clough's *Poems*. (Note, 257). BC, xiv (65), 542.
D. A. Randall.

Four designers of English publishers' bindings, 1850-1880, and their signatures. Illus. PBSA, lv (61), 88-99.
S. Pantazzi.

Nineteenth-century cloth bindings. PBSA, lxi (67), 114-19.
M. Hartzog.

BOOKBINDINGS: English: 20th c.
A binding variant. [H.O. Sturgis: *Belchamber*. Constable, 1904]. (Query, 13). BC, i (52), 130.
J. Carter.

The binding of the Coronation Bible. Illus. BC, ii (53), 139.
L. Lamb.

A mosaic binding by A. de Sauty, c. 1904. (English bookbindings, 18). Illus. BC, v (56), 248.
H. M. Nixon.

A Guild of Women-Binders binding *c.* 1903. (English bookbindings, 56). Illus. BC, xv (66), 46.
H. M. Nixon.

A binding by Katherine Adams. (English bookbindings, 66). Illus. BC, xvii (68), 331.
H. M. Nixon.

BOOKBINDINGS: Ethiopian
Ethiopian bookbindings. LIB, xvii (66), 85-8.
B. van Regemorter.

BOOKBINDINGS: French
L'Encyclopédie in contemporary morocco. (Note, 76). BC, v (56), 383.
A. Rau.

French bookbinders, 1789-1848. (Note, 78). BC, v (56), 383-4.
C. Ramsden.

Grolier's *Chrysostom.* Illus. BC, xi (62), 64-70.
H. M. Nixon.

A faked Henri II/Diane de Poitiers binding. (Note, 236). BC, xiv (65), 72.
F. R. Walton.

Les reliures vernis sans odeur, autrement dit 'Vernis Martin'. Illus. BC, xiv (65), 523-7.
A. Ehrman.

Parisian binding prices in 1649. (Note, 268). BC, xv (66), 210.
G. G. Barber.

Les reliures vernis sans odeur. [An addition to A. Ehrman's list, BC, Winter 1965]. (Note, 273). BC, xv (66), 351-2.
G. G. Barber.

The Houghton Library's vernis binding. [A revised description]. (Note, 274). BC, xv (66), 352.
W. H. Bond.

Les reliures vernis sans odeur. [A further addition]. (Note, 273). BC, xv (66), 484.
A. Rau.

A 'vernis sans odeur' binding. (Foreign bookbindings, 3). Illus. BC, xviii (69), 361.
G. Colin.

—. (Note, 325). BC, xviii (69), 520.
A. Rau.

French bookbinding 1789-1848. LIB, v (50/1), 258-60.
C. Ramsden.

Parisian panel stamps between 1480 and 1530. Illus. SB, vii (55), 113-24.
E. Kyriss.

BOOKBINDINGS: German
German Renaissance patrons of bookbindings. Illus. 2 pts. BC, iii (54), 171-89, 251-71.
G. D. Hobson.

Bindings by Jacob Krause and his school in English collections. Illus. BC, viii (59), 25-30.
I. Schunke.

An Erfurt binding of the 15th century. (Foreign bookbindings, 1). BC, xviii (69), 63.
E. Kyriss.

A Bavarian monastic binding, *c.* 1480. (Foreign bookbindings, 4). Illus. BC, xviii (69), 491.
E. Kyriss.

German bindings in Aberdeen University Library; iconographic index, and indices of initials, binders and dates. LIB, xvii (62), 46-55.
W. S. Mitchell.

A portrait of John-George of Brandenburg on presentation bindings: a footnote to Haebler. Illus. LIB, xvii (62), 88-92.
D. M. Rogers.

Notes on Nuremberg panel stamps before the Reformation. Illus. PBSA, xliv (50), 59-62.
E. Kyriss.

BOOKBINDINGS: Hungarian
Two Renaissance bindings. BC, vii (58), 265-8.
A. R. A. Hobson.

BOOKBINDINGS: Irish
The Irish Parliamentary bindings. Illus. BC, ii (53), 24-37.
M. Craig.

An Irish bookbinding probably bound for Lord Carteret, *c.* 1725-30. Illus. BC, iii (54), 216-17.
H. M. Nixon.

A binder's misprint. (Note, 244). BC, xiv (65), 214.
W. B. Todd.

An Irish Parliamentary binding in Glasgow University Library. Illus. BTHK, iii (60/2), 101-2.
H. M. Black.

The origin of the publisher's binding in Dublin. TCBS, ii (54/8), 92-4.
J. W. Phillips.

BOOKBINDINGS: Italian
Two Renaissance bindings. BC, vii (58), 265-8.
A. R. A. Hobson.

Italian Renaissance bookbindings: Bologna 1519. (Foreign bookbindings, 2). BC, xviii (69), 201.
I. Schunke.

Binding for Pope Paul IV. PBSA, liii (59), 68-9.
A. H. Bonnell.

An Italian panel-stamped binding of the fifteenth century. TCBS, i (49/53), 37-40.
E. F. Goldschmidt.

BOOKBINDINGS: Romanesque
Further notes on Romanesque bindings. Illus. LIB, xv (34/5), 161-211.
G. D. Hobson.

BOOKBINDINGS: Russian
Russian bookbinding from the 11th to the middle of the 17th century. Illus. BC, x (61), 408-22.
S. A. Klepikov.

Russian bookbinding from the middle of the 17th to the end of the 19th century. Illus. BC, xi (62), 437-47.
S. A. Klepikov.

The binding of the Archangel Gospels. Illus. BC, xiii (64), 431-5.
B. van Regemorter.

BOOKBINDINGS: Scottish
Scottish-American bookbindings. Six examples from colonial North America. BC, vi (57), 150-9.
H. D. French.

An early seventeenth-century Scottish binding. Illus. EBST, ii (38/45), 416-18.
G. D. Hobson.

BOOKBINDINGS: Ukrainian
Historical notes on Ukrainian bookbinding. Illus. BC, xv (66), 135-42.
S. A. Klepikov.

BOOKS
Books in pictures. Illus. BC, xi (62), 175-83.
D. Gordon.

BOOKS PUBLISHED ABROAD
Books published abroad by Scotsmen before 1700. GBSR, xi (33), 1-55.
J. H. Baxter and C. J. Fordyce.

BOOKSELLERS
A bookseller's donation-label. (Note, 134). Illus. BC, ix (60), 192-5.
J. C. T. Oates.

BOOKSELLERS' GUARANTEES
Booksellers' guarantees. LIB, vi (51), 212-13.
J. C. T. Oates.

—. LIB, x (55), 125-6.
J. C. T. Oates.

BOOKSELLER'S RUNNER
Adventures of a bookseller's runner. BH, ii (51/2), 172-5.
B. J. Farmer.

BOOKSELLER'S STAMP
A bookseller's stamp. (Query, 37). BC, ii (53), 222-3.
J. C. T. Oates.

—. BC, ii (53), 223.
L. W. Hanson.

—. BC, iii (54), 149.
T. R. Francis.

—. BC, iii (55), 254.
H. A. Hammelmann.

BOOKSELLING
Sales talk in 1823. (Query, 24). BC, i (52), 269.
A. N. L. Munby.

Fragment of a bookseller's day-book of 1622. BC, iii (54), 302-6.
A. N. L. Munby.

A 17th-century bookseller's circular. (Query, 153). BC, xi (62), 484-5.
B. Weinreb.

Hawkshaw rides again. BC, xii (63), 178-83.
J. Carter.

Terms of the trade. (Note, 194). BC, xii (63), 203-4.
J. H. P. Pafford.

A London bookseller's bill: 1635-1639. LIB, xviii (37/8), 417-46.
M. E. Bohannon.

A bookseller's subscription in 1669. LIB, vii (52), 281-2.
P. Morgan.

Booksellers' trade sales. LIB, xxiv (69), 241-3.
S. Parks.

Bibliography and the rare book trade. PBSA, xlviii (54), 219-29.
J. Carter.

Some unconventional women before 1800: printers, booksellers, and collectors. PBSA, xlix (55), 300-14.
F. Hamill.

A Russian bookstore catalogue of the eighteenth century. PBSA, lvi (62), 106-7.
N. Reingold.

The art of selling books: notes on three Aldus catalogues, 1586-1592. SB, i (48/9), 83-101.
R. Hirsch.

Notes on the ballad market in the second half of the seventeenth century. SB, vi (54), 161-80.
C. C. Blagden.

The booksellers' "Ring" at Strawberry Hill in 1842. SB, vii (55), 194-8.
A. T. Hazen.

Scottish printers and booksellers 1668-1775: a supplement. SB, xii (59), 131-59.
R. H. Carnie and R. P. Doig.

Scottish printers and booksellers 1668-1775: a second supplement (I).-(II). SB, xiv (61), 81-96, xv (62), 105-20.
R. H. Carnie.

Fragment of a bookseller's list, probably Antwerp, about 1533-35. Illus. TCBS, ii (54/8), 14-37.
M. E. Kronenberg.

BOOKTRADE
See also BOOKSELLING, PUBLISHING.

Caxton and the trade in printed books. BC, iv (55), 190-9.
M. J. M. Kerling.

'Drawback' in the booktrade. (Query, 68). BC, xii (63), 356.
A. Wesson.

The production and dissemination of vernacular manuscripts in the fifteenth century. LIB, i (46/7), 167-78.
H. S. Bennett.

Booksellers' trade sales 1718-1768. LIB, v (50/1), 243-57.
C. C. Blagden.

Christopher Plantin's trade-connexions with England and Scotland. LIB, xiv (59), 28-45.
C. Clair.

Book-trade publicity before 1800. PBSA, xxxii (38), 47-56.
C. T. Hallenbeck.

—. Correction. PBSA, xxxiv (40), 60.
C. T. Hallenbeck.

The book trade and the protective tariff: 1800-1804. PBSA, xlvi (52), 33-44.
R. G. Silver.

Bibliography and the rare booktrade. PBSA, xlviii (54), 219-29.
J. Carter.

The origin of the booktrade sales. PBSA, l (56), 296-302.
D. Kaser.

The changing world of rare books. PBSA, lix (65), 103-41.
G. N. Ray.

Some additional figures of distribution of eighteenth-century English books. PBSA, lix (65), 160-70.
R. D. Harlan.

American poetry of the First World War and the booktrade. PBSA, lxi (67), 209-24.
J. A. Hart.

BOOKTRADE: America
Book distribution in mid-nineteenth century America illustrated by the publishing records of Ticknor and Fields, Boston. PBSA, xli (47), 210-30.
W. S. Tryon.

BOOKTRADE: England
See also TERM CATALOGUES

The history of the book trade in the north, a review of a research project. Illus. JPHS, iv (68), 87-98.
P. C. G. Isaac *and* W. M. Watson.

Parliament and the press 1643-7. 2 pts. LIB, xiii (32/3), 399-424; xiv, 39-58.
W. M. Clyde.

Counterfeit printing in Jacobean times. Illus. LIB, xv (34/5), 364-76.
W. A. Jackson.

Some Exchequer cases involving members of the book-trade, 1534-1558. LIB, xvi (35/6), 402-17.
H. J. Byrom.

The price of books in medieval England. LIB, xvii (36/7), 312-332.
H. E. Bell.

Entrance, licence, and publication. LIB, xxv (44/5), 1-22.
Sir W. W. Greg.

Papers and documents recently found at Stationers' Hall. LIB, xxv (44/5), 23-36.
S. Hodgson.

Printers' 'copybooks' and the black market in the Elizabethan book trade. LIB, i (46/7), 97-105.
F. R. Johnson.

Printers, authors, and readers, 1475-1557. LIB, iv (49/50), 155-65.
H. S. Bennett.

Booksellers' trade sales 1718-1768. LIB, v (50/1), 243-57.
C. C. Blagden.

Notes on English retail book prices, 1550-1640. LIB, v (50/1), 275-6.
G. B. Evans.

Pills and publishing: some notes on the English book trade, 1660-1715. LIB, vii (52), 21-37.
J. E. Alden.

Publications of 1623. LIB, xxi (66), 207-22.
J. Simmons.

The history of the book trade in the north: a preliminary report on a group research project. LIB, xxiii (68), 248-52.
P. C. G. Isaac.

Notes on serialization and competitive publishing: Johnson's and Bailey's *Dictionaries*, 1755. OBSP, v (36/9 or 40), 305-22; NS, i (47 or 49), 45-6. Bailey's folio *Dictionary*: a supplementary note.
P. B. Gove.

Literary piracy in the Elizabethan age. OBSP, i (49), 1-23.
P. Simpson.

The notebook of Thomas Bennet and Henry Clements, 1686-1719, with some aspects of book trade practice. OBSP, vi (56).
N. Hodgson *and* C. C. Blagden.

Licensers for the press, &c. to 1640. A biographical index based mainly or Arber's *Transcript of the Registers of the Company of Stationers*. OBSP, x (62).
Sir W. W. Greg.

Publishers and sinners: the Augustan view. SB, xii (59), 3-20.
I. Watt.

Printers and stationers in the parish of St. Giles Cripplegate, 1561-1640. SB, xix (66), 15-38.
W. E. Miller.

Stationers made free of the City in 1551-2 and 1552. TCBS, i (49/53), 194-5.
B. Dickins.

Two licences granted to Cambridge stationers. TCBS, i (49/53), 443-4.
C. P. Hall.

A seventeenth-century Cambridge book and its cost. [John Armstrong's *Secret and family prayers* and *The souls worth and danger*]. TCBS, ii (54/8), 376-81.
F. Barnes *and* J. C. Dickinson.

The press under the early Tudors, a study in censorship and sedition. TCBS, iv (64/8), 29-50.
D. M. Loades.

Restrictive practices in the Elizabethan book-trade: the Stationers' company *v.* Thomas Thomas. TCBS, iv (64/8), 276-90.
J. Morris.

Some aspects of the Norfolk book-trade, 1800-24. TCBS, iv (64/8), 383-95.
T. Fawcett.

BOOKTRADE: Germany
A survey of books printed in Germany between 1501 and 1530. The book production in the German speaking cultural area. PBSA, xxxiv (40), 117-36.
R. Hirsch.

BOOKTRADE: Ireland
Deception in Dublin: problems in seventeenth-century Irish printing. SB, vi (54), 232-7.
J. E. Alden.

Deception compounded: further problems in seventeenth-century Irish printing. SB, xi (58), 246-9.
J. E. Alden.

BOOKTRADE: Netherlands
Forged addresses in Low Country books in the period of the Reformation. LIB, ii (47/8), 81-94.
M. E. Kronenberg.

BOOKTRADE: Wales
Developments in the booktrade in eighteenth-century Wales. LIB, xxiv (69), 33-43.
E. Rees.

BORDE, Andrew
Andrew Borde's *Dyetary of Health* and its attribution to Thomas Linacre. LIB, ii (47/8), 172-3.
J. L. Thornton.

Some remarks on a nineteenth-century reprint. [Andrew Borde's *The fyrst boke of the Introduction of Knowledge*]. PBSA, xli (47), 53-9.
C. F. Bühler.

BORLAND, Catherine Robina
Notes on C. R. Borland's *A Descriptive Catalogue of Western Medieval Manuscripts in Edinburgh University Library*. 1916. BTHK, iii (60/2), 44-52.
C. P. Finlayson.

BORRENSTEIN, David A.
David A. Borrenstein: a printer and publisher at Princeton, N.J., 1824-28. Illus. PBSA, xxx (36), 1-56.
G. J. Miller.

BORROW, George Henry
Borrow: *The Death of Balder*. London, Jarrold, 1889. (Query, 6). BC, i (52), 56. [An enquirer].

Borrow: *The Death of Balder*. (Query, 6). BC, i (52), 129.
E. Schlengemann.

Borrow, *The Death of Balder*, 1889. (Query, 6). BC, i (52), 266-7.
J. P. W. Gaskell.

—. BC, iv (55), 78-81.
J. Rubinstein.

George Borrow's *The Zincali*. (Note, 58). BC, v (56), 75.
K. T. Borrow.

Tales of the wild and wonderful, 1825. (Query, 104). BC, vii (58), 417.
J. Park.

T. J. Wise and *Tales of the Wild and Wonderful*. (Query, 104). BC, viii (59), 300-3.
J. E. Alden.

—. BC, viii (59), 303-6.
J. Rubinstein.

Borrow's *Lavengro* and *Faustus*. (Note, 153). BC, x (61), 70.
W. B. Todd.

BORROW, Keith Travers
George Borrow's *The Zincali*. (Note, 58). BC, v (56), 75.

Lost incunabula of S. Australia. (Query, 66). BC, v (56), 78-9.

Bulmer Lytton and George Stevenson. (Query, 84). BC, vi (57), 291-2.

BORSA, Gedeon
Two unrecorded incunabula. [Alexander VI., Papa: *Regulae cancellariae*, 8. August 1495. [Strassburg: Johann Prüss, nicht vor 8. August 1495]; and *Almanach auf das Jahr 1492*, lat. [Leipzig: Gregor Boettiger]. Illus. BC, vi (57), 259-62.

Early printed books in Hungary. BC, vii (58), 15-27.

BOSANQUET, Eustace Fulcrand
The personal prayer-book of John of Lancaster, Duke of Bedford, K.G. Illus. LIB, xiii (32/3), 148-54.

Three little Tudor books. 1. Xenophon's *Treatise of Household*. Tr. G. Hervet. T. Berthelet, 1532. 2. Philip Moore's *The Hope of Health*. J. Kingston, 1564. 3. *The Viniard of Devotion*. Newly corrected for Edw. White, 1599. Illus. LIB, xiv (33/4), 178-206.

The Lyf of our Lady. Fragments of the so-called second edition. [A letter]. LIB, xvii (36/7), 362-3.

Notes on further addenda to English printed almanacks and prognostications to 1600. Illus. LIB, xviii (37/8), 39-66.

The Flye, 1569. Illus. LIB, xviii (37/8), 195-200.

BOSTON
Abstracts from the wills and estates of Boston printers, 1800-1825. SB, vii (55), 212-8.
R. G. Silver.

BOSTON. *Lincs, St. Botolph's*
Some documents printed by Pynson for St. Botolph's, Boston, Lincs. LIB, xv (60), 53-7.
D. E. Rhodes.

BOSTON *Mass., publ. libr.*
Benjamin Levy imprints in Boston Public
Library. PBSA, lv (61), 48-50.
J. E. Alden.

BOSTON POST
The "famous *Boston Post* list": mid-nineteenth
century American best-sellers. PBSA, lii (58),
93-110.
H. T. Meserole.

BOSWELL, Alexander
Alexander Boswell's copies of *The Anatomy of
Melancholy*, 1621 and 1624. (Note, 88). BC, vi
(57), 406-7.
R. A. Hunter *and* I. Macalpine.

BOSWELL, James
Boswell's crest. (Query, 23). BC, i (52), 268.
J. W. Turner.

The anonymous designations in Boswell's
Journal of a tour to the Hebrides and their
identification. EBST, ii (38/45), 353-71.
L. F. Powell.

Dr. Burney and the integrity of Boswell's
quotations. PBSA, liii (59), 327-31.
R. Lonsdale.

BOSWORTH, Newton
Bosworth, Newton (d.1848). *The Accidents of
Human Life.* New York, 1814. PBSA, xxxv
(41), 207.
R. S. Wormser.

BOTANY
America — a hunting ground for eighteenth-
century naturalists with special reference to
their publications about trees. PBSA, xxxii
(38), 1-16.
J. R. Butler.

BOTETOURT, *baron*
See BERKELEY, Narborne, *baron Botetourt.*

BOUCHER, François
A cancel in the Boucher Molière, 1734. (Query,
190). BC, xiv (68), 367.
H. A. Hammelmann.

BOUCK, Constance W.
On the identity of Papyrius Geminus Eleates.
[The author of *Hermathena*, i.e. Sir Thomas
Elyot]. TCBS, ii (54/8), 352-8.

BOURGUIGNON D'ANVILLE, Hubert-François
English eighteenth-century book illustrators.
[Including a list of "English books illustrated
by Gravelot".] Illus. BH, ii (51/2), 127-35.

Gravelot in England. Illus. BH, ii (51/2),
176-90.
H. A. Hammelmann.

BOURNE, Nicholas
Nathaniel Butter and Nicholas Bourne, first
'Masters of the Staple'. LIB, xii (57), 23-33.
L. Rostenberg.

BOWE, Forrest B.
[Lullin de Châteauvieux, Frédéric] (1772-1841)
*Napoleon's own memoirs printed from a manu-
script.* Pittsburgh, 1817. PBSA, xxxiv (40),
188-9.

[Lavoisier, Antoine Laurent] (1743-1794). *The
art of manufacturing alkaline salts and pot-
ashes.* Tr. by Charles Williamos[!] [Phila-
delphia, 1820?]. PBSA, xxxiv (40), 359.

—. PBSA, xxxv (41), 72.

Racine, Jean Baptiste (1639-1699). *The suitors.
A comedy.* Tr. by a member of the Detroit bar.
Detroit, 1862. PBSA, xxxiv (40), 361.

Blanchard, Jean Pierre (1735-1809). *Journal de
ma quarante-cinquième ascension, la première
faite en Amérique le 9. janvier, 1793.* Philadelphia, 1793. PBSA, xxxv (41), 70.

[Gérard de Rayneval, Joseph Mathias] (1746-
1812). *Observations on the Justificative
memorial of the court of London.* Philadelphia, 1781. PBSA, xxxv (41), 159.

[Martainville, Alphonse Louis Dieudonné]
(1776-1830). *The life of Lamoignon Malesherbes.* New York, 1806. PBSA, xxxv (41),
159-60.

Racine, Jean (1639-1699). *The distrest mother;
a tragedy.* New York, 1761. Translated by A.
Philips. PBSA, xxxv (41), 160.

[Rapin-Thoyras, Paul de] (1661-1725). *A dissertation on the rise, progress, views, strength,
interests and characters, of the two parties of
the Whigs and Tories.* Boston, 1773. PBSA,
xxxv (41), 161.

[Le Sage, Alain René] (1668-1747). *The comical
adventures of Gil Blas of Santillane.* Philadelphia, 1790. PBSA, xxxv (41), 205-6.

[Caraccioli, Louis Antoine de] (1721-1803).
Advice from a lady of quality to her children,
tr. by S. Glasse. Newbury-Port, [1789]. PBSA,
xxxvi (42), 64-5.

*The uncertainty of a death-bed repentance,
illustrated under the character of Penitens.*
[Germantown, 1756?]. PBSA, xxxvi (42),
231-2.

BOWER, Patrick
Patrick Bower. LIB, xxiii (42/3), 23-30.
G. H. Bushnell.

BOWER, Walter
The debt of Bower to Fordun and Wyntoun.
EBST, ii (38/45), 386-9.
E. W. M. Balfour-Melville.

BOWERS, Fredson Thayer
Bibliographical problems in Dekker's *Magnificent Entertainment.* LIB, xvii (36/7), 333-9.

Thomas Dekker: two textual notes. [*The roaring
girle*, 1611; and *The honest whore*, 1605].
LIB, xviii (37/8), 338-41.

Notes on running-titles as bibliographical evidence. LIB, xix (38/9), 315-38.

A possible Randolph holograph. LIB, xx
(39/40), 159-62.

Marriot's two editions of Randolph's *Aristippus*. Illus. LIB, xx (39/40), 163-6.

Bibliographical miscellanea. LIB, i (46/7), 131-4.

An examination of the method of proof correction in *Lear*. LIB, ii (47/8), 20-44.

The first series of plays published by Francis Kirkman in 1661. LIB, ii (47/8), 289-91.

Bibliographical evidence from a resetting in Caryll's *Sir Salomon*, 1691. LIB, iii (48/9), 134-7.

The first edition of Dryden's *Wild Gallant*, 1669. LIB, v (50/1), 51-4.

The supposed cancel in Southerne's *The Disappointment* reconsidered. LIB, v (50/1), 140-9.

The problem of the variant forme in a facsimile edition. LIB, vii (52), 262-72.

Purposes of descriptive bibliography, with some remarks on methods. LIB, viii (53), 1-22.

Underprinting in Mary Pix, *The Spanish Wives,* 1696. LIB, ix (54), 248-54.

A bibliographical history of the Fletcher-Betterton play, *The Prophetess*, 1690. LIB, xvi (61), 169-75.

Bibliography revisited. LIB, xxiv (69), 89-128.

Notes on standing type in Elizabethan printing. PBSA, xl (46), 205-24.

Criteria for classifying hand-printed books as issues and variant states. PBSA, xli (47), 271-92.

—. [A letter]. PBSA, xlii (48), 341-3.

Two notes on running-titles as bibliographical evidence. [George Sandys: Ovid's *Metamorphosis*, 1632; and George Sandys: *Christ's Passion*, 1640]. PBSA, xlii (48), 143-8.

Certain basic problems in descriptive bibliography. PBSA, xlii (48), 211-28.

The cancel leaf in Congreve's *Double Dealer*, 1694. PBSA, xliii (49), 78-82.

Thomas D'Urfey's *Comical History of Don Quixote*, 1694. PBSA, xliii (49), 191-5.

Printing evidence in Wynkyn de Worde's edition of *The Life of Johan Picus* by St. Thomas More. PBSA, xliii (49), 398-9.

Nathaniel Lee: three probable seventeenth-century piracies. PBSA, xliv (50), 62-6.

The prologue to Nathaniel Lee's *Mithridates*, 1678. PBSA, xliv (50), 173-5.

The first editions of Sir Robert Stapylton's *The Slighted Maid*, 1663, and *The Step-Mother*, 1664. PBSA, xlv (51), 143-8.

Bibliography, pure bibliography, and literary studies. PBSA, xlvi (52), 186-208.

Ogilby's coronation *Entertainment*, 1661-1689: editions and issues. PBSA, xlvii (53), 339-55.

Motteux's *Love's a Jest*, 1696: a running-title and presswork problem. PBSA, xlviii (54), 268-73.

Another early edition of Thomas Jevon's *Devil of a Wife*. PBSA, xlix (55), 253-4.

The manuscripts of Whitman's *Song of the Redwood-Tree*. PBSA, l (56), 53-85.

Running-title evidence for determining half-sheet imposition. SB, i (48/9), 199-202.

Bibliographical evidence from the printer's measure. SB, ii (49/50), 153-67.

Some relations of bibliography to editorial problems. SB, iii (50/1), 37-62.

The variant sheets in John Banks's *Cyrus the Great*, 1696. SB, iv (51/2), 174-82.

The pirated quarto of Dryden's *State of Innocence*. SB, v (52/3), 166-9.

Shakespeare's text and the bibliographical method. SB, vi (54), 71-91.

Whitman's manuscripts for the original *Calamus* poems. SB, vi (54), 257-65.

The printing of *Hamlet* Q2. SB, vii (55), 41-50.

—. Addendum. SB, viii (56), 267-9.

The textual relation of Q2 to Q1 *Hamlet* (1). SB, viii (56), 39-66.

Some principles for scholarly editions of nineteenth-century American authors. SB, xvii (64), 223-8.

Today's Shakespeare texts, and tomorrow's. SB, xix (66), 39-65.

Crane's *Red badge of courage* and other advance copies. SB, xxii (69), 273-7.

—, GERRITSEN, Johan *and* LASLETT, Peter Further observations on Locke's *Two Treatises of Government*. TCBS, ii (54/8), 63-87.

BOWERS, Robert Hood
Sir Simonds [D'Ewes] buys a manuscript. PBSA, l (56), 379-81.

Some Folger academic drama manuscripts. SB, xii (59), 117-30.

Some early apostrophes to printing. PBSA, liv (60), 113-15.

Blyenburg corrects his book. PBSA, lv (61), 382-3.

BOWLES, William Lisle
William Lisle Bowles, 1762-1850. (Some uncollected authors, 18). 2 pts. BC, vii (58), 226-94, 407-16.
C. Woolf.

BOWMAN, Mary Virginia
The Hallam-Tennyson *Poems*, 1830. SB, i (48/9), 193-9.

BOWTELL, John
Two medieval calendars and other leaves removed by John Bowtell from University Library MSS. TCBS, i (49/53), 29-36).
A. I. Doyle.

BOWYER, Tony Harold
Bentham's publications on evidence. LIB, ix (54), 205-7.

The published forms of Sir Josiah Child's *A New Discourse of Trade*. LIB, xi (56), 95-102.

BOWYER, William
Bowyer's paper stock ledger. Illus. LIB, vi (51), 73-87.
H. Davis.

BOX RULES
Center rules in folio printing; a new kind of bibliographical evidence. SB, i (48/9), 188-91.
J. S. Steck.

BOYCE, George K.
A letter of Mercator concerning his *Ptolemy*. PBSA, xlii (48), 129-39.

The costs of publishing Gibbon's *Vindication*. PBSA, xliii (49), 335-9

BOYD, James
Boyd, James (1888-1944). *Drums*. New York. London, 1925. PBSA, xxxv (41), 207-8.
F. Stone.

BOYD, Julian Parks
Higgins, Jesse. *Sampson against the Philistines*. Philadelphia, 1805. PBSA, xxxiv (40), 87.

BOYLE, hon. Robert
Cancellandum R2 in Boyle's *Sceptical Chymist* 1661. (Note, 176). BC, xi (62), 215.
E. A. Osborne.

Robert Boyle, 1627-1691. (English scientific autographs, 2). Illus. BC, xiii (64), 487.
T. J. Brown.

A bibliography of the honourable Robert Boyle. Fellow of the Royal Society. [And] Addenda. Illus. OBSP, iii (32) 33, 1-172, 339-65; (49), Second Addenda.
J. F. Fulton.

BOYLE, Roger *1st earl of Orrery*
A bibliographical study of *Parthenissa* by Roger Boyle, earl of Orrery. SB, ii (49/50), 115-37.
C. W. Miller.

BOYSE, David
A Cambridge binding, perhaps by Daniel Boyse, *c*. 1627. (English bookbindings, 9). Illus. BC, iii (54), 50-1.
H. M. Nixon.

BOZ *pseud.*
See DICKENS, Charles

BRACHER, Peter
The Lea & Blanchard editions of Dickens's *American notes*, 1842. PBSA, lxiii (69), 296-300.

BRACK, O. M.
Smollett's *Roderick Random* 1754. (Query, 215). BC, xvi (67), 225.

Account books of Benjamin Collins of Salisbury. (Query, 232). BC, xvii (68), 492.

Goldsmith's *A survey of experimental philosophy* 1776. (Note, 324). BC, xviii (69), 519-20.

Thomas James Mathias' *The Pursuits of Literature*. PBSA, lxii (68), 123-7.

BRADBURY, Henry
Henry Bradbury's nature-printed books. Illus. LIB, xxi (66), 63-7.
G. Wakeman.

BRADFORD, John
The *Kentucky Gazette* and John Bradford its founder. PBSA, xxxi (37), 102-32.
S. M. Wilson.

BRADFORD, William
William Bradford and the *Book of Common Prayer*. PBSA, xliii (49), 101-10.
B. McAnear.

Elias Burling, *A Call to back-sliding Israel*, New York, 1694: an unrecorded tract printed by William Bradford. Illus. SB, xiv (61), 251-3.
A. N. L. Munby.

BRADFORTH, John
The copye of a letter sent by John Bradforth to the Right Honorable Lordes The Erles of Arundel, Darbie, Shrewsbury and Pembroke, STC 3480.
See CAPSTOCKE, John

BRADLEY, Andrew Cecil
A. C. Bradley: a summary account. PBSA, lxii (68), 607-12.
M. Blish.

BRADNER, Leicester
Musae Anglicanae: a supplemental list. LIB, xxii (67), 93-103.

BRAMAH, Ernest *pseud.*
See SMITH, Ernest Bramah

BRANDENBURG, Hilprand
Hilprand Brandenburg and his books. Illus. LIB, iv (49/50), 196-201.
J. V. Scholderer.

BRANDER LIBRARY
See HUNTLY *Brander libr., George Macdonald collection.*

BRANT, Sebastian
Brant's *Narrensachiff*, 1494. (Query, 117). BC, viii (59), 431.
H. Eisemann.

BRASH, James
Brash and Reid, booksellers in Glasgow and their collection of *Poetry original and selected*. Illus. GBSR, xii (36), 1-20.
J. C. Ewing.

BRAUD, Denis
Denis Braud, some imprints in the Bancroft library. PBSA, lxii (68), 252-4.
D. Roaten.

BRAUN, Frank X. *and* BROWN, Robert Beneway
The tunebook of Conrad Doll. PBSA, xlii (48), 229-38.

BRENNAN, Joseph X.
The *Grammaticœ Artis Institutio* of Joannes Susenbrotus: a bibliographical note. SB, xiv (61), 197-200.

BRENTIUS, Andreas
The bibliography of a small incunable [i.e. Andreas Brentius's *C.Iul. Cesaris oratio Vesontione belgice ad milites habita*]. Illus. LIB, xvii (36/7), 36-61.
Sir I. Masson.

BRESLAUER, Bernard H.
The origin of offprints. (Query, 85). BC, vi (57), 403.

Jean Furstenberg. (Contemporary collectors, 25). Illus. BC, ix (60), 423-34.

BRETON, Nicholas
Nicholas Breton's *I would and would not*, 1619. LIB, xii (57), 273-4.
F. P. Wilson.

Nicholas Breton (?1545-?1626). *A Poste with a Packet of Madde Letters.* PBSA, xxxvii (43), 233.
F. Sullivan.

BRETT, Oliver *3rd viscount Esher*
Once upon a time: an autobiographical fragment. BC, vii (58), 398-400.

BRETT, Philip
Edward Paston, 1550-1630: a Norfolk gentleman and his musical collection. TCBS, iv (64/8), 51-69.

BRETTLE, Robert Edward
Marston bibliography; a correction. LIB, xv (34/5), 241-2.

BREVIARIES
A note on GW 5231. [Second edition of the Premonstratensian Breviary, printed by Johann Grüninger at Strassburg, 1490]. PBSA, li (57), 236-7.
C. F. Bühler.

BREVIARIUM COLONIENSE
Breviarium Coloniense (Cologne: Petrus in Altis, de Olpe, 1478; G W 5305). (Note, 287). BC, xvi (67), 508.
J. S. G. Simmons.

BREVISSIMA INTRODUCTIO AD LITTERAS GRAECAS
Notes on two incunabula printed by Aldus Manutius. [*Brevissima Introductio ad Litteras Graecas* and *Horae ad Usum Romanum*]. Illus. PBSA, xxxvi (42), 18-26.
C. F. Bühler.

BRÉZÉ (Diane de) *duchesse de Valentinois*
A faked Henri II/Diane de Poitiers binding. (Note, 236). BC, xiv (65), 72.
F. R. Walton.

BRIDGE, Alexander
Byron's *The Corsair*, 1814. (Note, 98). BC, vii (58), 191.

Bloomfield's *Rural Tales*, 1802. (Query, 119). BC, viii (59), 431-2.

Edward Fitzgerald's *Six dramas of Calderon* 1854 edition? (Query, 229). BC, xvii (68), 491.

BRIDGEMAN, sir Orlando
1st bart. Whereabouts of books owned by Traherne, Hopton, Bridgeman. (Query, 236). BC, xviii (69), 225-6.
L. Sauls.

BRIDGES, Robert Seymour
Robert Bridges, 1844-1930. (English literary autographs, 20). Illus. BC, v (56), 369.
T. J. Brown.

Mosher and Bridges. (Note, 189). BC, xi (62), 482-3.
S. Nowell-Smith.

Bridges, Robert (1844-1930). *A Case of Thickening of the Cranial Bones in an Infant, due to Congenital Syphilis.* In *Transactions of the Clinical Society of London.* London, 1897. PBSA, xxxv (41), 161.
T. P. Fleming.

BRIEFS
Seventeenth-century briefs at Cambridge. (Note, 11). BC, i (52), 264.
J. C. T. Oates.

BRIGGS, W. G.
The early editions of Magnall's *Questions.* LIB, ix (54), 53-5.

BRIGHAM, Clarence Saunders
Ambrose, Isaac (1604-1663) & Bates, William (1625-1699). *Christ in the Clouds coming to Judgment.* A Sermon. v.p., v.d. PBSA, xxxiv (40), 187.

Keach, Benjamin (1640-1704). *Instructions for Children.* New-York, 1695. PBSA, xxxv (41), 72.

A Journey to Philadelphia: . . . , by Adelio, . . . Hartford, 1804. PBSA, xxxv (41), 205.

An Address to a Deist, a poem. New London, 1796. PBSA, xxxvi (42), 64.

The Mother-in-Law; or Memoirs of Madam De Morville. By Maria-Ann Burlingham. Boston, 1817. PBSA, xxxvi (42), 66-7.

Goodrich, S. G. Juvenile histories, 1831-1852. PBSA, xl (46), 161-2.

The *Spirit of the Times.* [A letter]. Illus. PBSA, xlviii (54), 300-1.

BRIGHT, Timothy
Manuscript notes in the Bodleian copy of Bright's *Characterie.* Illus. LIB, xvi (35/6), 418-24.
M. Doran.

BRIMMELL, R. A.
Holmesiana. (Note, 84). BC, vi (57), 183.

BRINDLEY, John
A binding by John Brindley, 1743. (English bookbindings, 43). Illus. BC, xi (62), 466.
H. M. Nixon.

BRINKLEY, Roberta Florence
Poems, by S. T. Coleridge, Esq. PBSA, xxxix (45), 163-7.

BRINLEY, George
George Brinley, Americanist. PBSA, lx (66), 465-72.
D. B. Engley.

BRISTOL LIBRARY SOCIETY
The Bristol Library borrowings of Southey and Coleridge, 1793-8. LIB, iv (49/50), 114-32.
G. Whalley.

BRITISH CRITIC
The British Critic and the Oxford Movement. SB, xvi (63), 119-37.
E. R. Houghton.

BRITISH LIBRARY OF POLITICAL AND ECONOMIC SCIENCE
The Bray collection in the British Library of Political and Economic Science. EBST, ii (38/45), 440-3.
W. C. Dickinson *and* M. Plant.

BRITISH MUSEUM
A list of the printed books recently acquired by the British Museum from the Earl of Leicester, Holkham Hall. 3 pts. BC, i (52), 120-6, 185-9, 259-63.
L. A. Sheppard *and others*.

A royal manuscript by Arrighi Vicentino in the British Museum. (Note, 91). Illus. BC, vii (58), 78-9.
B. Wolpe.

The Royal Music Library. Some account of its provenance and associations. Illus. BC, vii (58), 241-52.
A. H. King.

List of books acquired by the British Museum from Chatsworth. Pt. I: Incunabula. BC, vii (58), 401-6.
G. D. Painter.

—. Pt. II: English books 1501-1640. [*And*] Pt. III: Bindings. BC, viii (59), 52-9.
A. F. Allison *and* H. M. Nixon.

Chatsworth incunabula in the British Museum. Addenda & corrigenda. (Note, 108). BC, viii (59), 180-1.
G. D. Painter.

—. (Note, 108). BC, viii (59), 294.
G. D. Painter.

The Henry Davis collection I. The British Museum gift. (Contemporary collectors, 44). Illus. BC, xviii (69), 23-44.
M. M. Romme.

King Henry VI's claim to France in picture and poem. Illus. LIB, xiii (32/3), 77-88.
B. J. H. Rowe.

A bibliographical paradox (*re Gawain and the Green Knight*, MS. Cotton Nero A.x). LIB, xiii (32/3), 188-91.
Sir W. W. Greg.

The scribal errors of the MS. Cotton Nero A.x. LIB, xiv (33/4), 353-58.
J. P. Oakden.

An unrecognized document in the history of French Renaissance staging. [British Museum MS. Harl. 4325]. LIB, xvi (35/6), 232-5.
S. L. England.

The liturgical music incunabula in the British Museum. Germany, Italy, and Switzerland. LIB, xx (39/40), 272-94.
K. Meyer.

The early ownership of the British Museum copy of Caxton's *Recuyell of the Histories of Troy*. LIB, iii (48/9), 216-18.
L. A. Sheppard.

British Museum Additional MS. 31432. William Lawes' writing for the theatre and the court. LIB, vii (52), 225-34.
J. P. Cutts.

Notes on the texts of William Lawes's songs in B.M. MS. Add. 31432. LIB, ix (54), 122-7.
M. C. Crum.

Two unrecorded items of 1603. [*The seuen soueraigne medicines* and *A godly exhortation*, found in MS. Harley 514]. Illus. LIB, xvi (61), 299-302.
A. G. Watson.

Caxton's *Blanchardin and Eglantine*: notes on the leaf preserved in the British Museum. PBSA, xxxix (45), 156-61.
C. F. Bühler.

The history of the Sneyd-Gimbel and Piggott-British Museum copies of Dr. Johnson's *Dictionary*. PBSA, liv (60), 286-9.
G. J. Kolb *and* J. H. Sledd.

Traherne's Ficino notebook. [MS. Burney 126]. PBSA, lxiii (69), 73-81.
C. M. Sicherman.

BRITTAIN, Frederick
Four "Q" rarities. Illus. BH, ii (51/2), 26-35.

BRITTAIN, Robert Edward
Christopher Smart in the magazines. LIB, xxi (40/1), 320-36.

Christopher Smart's *Hymns for the Amusement of Children*. PBSA, xxxv (41), 61-5.

BRITTON, Allen P. *and* LOWENS, Irving
Daniel Bayley's *The American Harmony*: a bibliographical study. PBSA, xlix (55), 340-54.

BROADSIDES
Broadsides concerning early printing. (Query, 147). BC, x (61), 337.
A. Ehrman.

Italian broadside catalogues. [A letter]. LIB, iv (49/50), 281.
A. Ehrman.

Textual problems in Restoration broadsheet prologues and epilogues. LIB, xii (57), 197-203.
R. Morton.

Unrecorded verse broadsides of seventeenth-century New England. Illus. PBSA, xxxix (45), 1-19.
H. S. Jantz.

BROCKWAY, Duncan
Some new editions from the reign of James II. PBSA, lv (61), 118-30.

The printing history of Uberto Foglietta's *De sacro foedere in Selimum*. Illus. PBSA, lxii (68), 77-80.

BROCKWELL, Maurice Walter
W. H. James Weale, the pioneer. LIB, vi (51), 200-11.

BROME, Richard
The early quartos of Brome's *Northern Lasse*. PBSA, liv (60), 179-81.
H. Fried.

BROMWICH, John
The first book printed in Anglo-Saxon types. [Aelfric's *A testimonie of antiquitie*]. Illus. TCBS, iii (59/63), 265-91.

BRONTË *family*
Binding variants in the Brontës' *Poems*. (Note, 25). BC, ii (53), 219-21.
D. F. Foxon.

The Brontës. (English literary autographs, 17). Illus. BC, v (56), 55.
T. J. Brown.

The first American edition of the Brontë's *Poems*. (Query, 121). BC, viii (59), 432.
J. Haywood.

—. BC, ix (60), 199-201.
D. A. Randall.

—. BC, ix (60), 201.
S. Adelman.

BRONTË, Charlotte
An early state of Charlotte Brontë's *Shirley*, 1849. (Note, 204). BC, xii (63), 355-6.
W. B. Todd.

Unrecorded newspaper reviews of Charlotte Brontë's *Shirley* and *Villette*. PBSA, liii (59), 270-1.
R. L. Brooks.

BROOKE, Rupert Chawner
The first American edition of *1914 and other poems*. (Query, 185). BC, xiii (64), 359.
D. A. Randall.

—. BC, xiii (64), 503.
Sir G. L. Keynes.

Brooke, Rupert (1887-1915). *The Collected Poems*. New York, 1915. PBSA, xxxvi (42), 68.
D. A. Randall.

BROOKS, Cleanth
The country parson as research scholar: Thomas Percy, 1760-1770. PBSA, liii (59), 219-39.

BROOKS, Eric St. John
The *Piers Plowman* manuscripts in Trinity College, Dublin. LIB, vi (51), 141-53.

BROOKS, Harold Fletcher
A bibliography of John Oldham, the Restoration satirist. OBSP, v (36/9), 1-38.

Rump songs: an index with notes. OBSP, v (36/9), 28-304.

BROOKS, Roger L.
Matthew Arnold's *Stanzas from Carnac* and *A southern night*. (Note, 259). BC, xiv (65), 543.

Matthew Arnold in private collections. (Query, 111). BC, viii (59), 73.

An unrecorded American edition of the *Selected Poems of Matthew Arnold*. LIB, xvi (61), 213-14.

The *Strayed Reveller* myth. LIB, xviii (63), 57-60.

Unrecorded newspaper reviews of Charlotte Brontë's *Shirley* and *Villette*. PBSA, liii (59), 270-1.

A census of Matthew Arnold's *Poems*, 1853. PBSA, liv (60), 184-6.

A neglected edition of Matthew Arnold's poetry and a bibliographical correction. PBSA, lv (61), 140-1.

A Danish *Balder Dead*. PBSA, lvi (62), 253-4.

The Story manuscript of Matthew Arnold's *New Rome*. PBSA, lviii (64), 295-7.

Some unaccomplished projects of Matthew Arnold. SB, xvi (63), 213-16.

BROPHY, Robert J.
A textual note on Robinson Jeffers' *The beginning and the end*. PBSA, lx (66), 344-8.

BROUGHTON, Thomas Duer
Melville's copy of Broughton's *Popular poetry of the Hindoos*. PBSA, lxi (67), 266-7.
H. Cohen.

BROWN, Andreas
Tennessee Williams by another name. PBSA, lvii (63), 377-8.

BROWN, Arthur
A proof-sheet in Thomas Heywood's *The Iron Age*. Illus. LIB, x (55), 275-8.

Editorial problems in Shakespeare: semi-popular editions. SB, viii (56), 15-26.

The rationale of old-spelling editions of the plays of Shakespeare and his contemporaries: a rejoinder [to an article by J. R. Brown]. SB, xiii (60), 69-76.

BROWN, Beth
Chorégraphie. F. Le Roussaü. (Note, 298). BC, xvii (68), 216-17.

BROWN, Carleton F. *and* ROBBINS, Rossell Hope
A bibliography and first-line index of English verse printed through 1500. A supplement to Brown and Robbins' *Index of Middle English Verse*. PBSA, xlix (55), 153-80.
W. F. Ringler.

BROWN, Charles Brockden
Charles Brockden Brown, America's first important novelist: a check list of biography and criticism. PBSA, lx (66), 349-62.
R. E. Hemenway *and* D. H. Keller.

BROWN, David D.
The text of John Tillotson's sermons. LIB, xiii (58), 18-36.

The Dean's dilemma: a further note on a Tillotson passage. Illus. LIB, xiv (59), 282-7.

BROWN, Everett Somerville
Bryce, James Bryce, viscount (1838-1922). *The American commonwealth*. London, 1888. PBSA, xxxvi (42), 65-6.

BROWN, Frances Swan
Addenda to Irish [*The modern American muse*]: Brown, North, and Wild. PBSA, lxii (68), 452.
G. T. Tanselle.

BROWN, Harry Glenn
Philadelphia contributions to the book arts and book trade, 1796-1810. PBSA, xxxvii (43), 275-92.

BROWN, Isabel
A short account of the Town's Hospital in Glasgow. BTHK, i/3 (58), 37-41.

BROWN, John
'Estimate' Brown, 1715-1776. (Some uncollected authors, 24). BC, ix (60), 180-7.
Sir S. C. Roberts.

Bibliography of 'Estimate' Brown. (Note, 157). BC, x (61), 198.
Sir S. C. Roberts.

BROWN, John Buchanan-
The first publication of Abraham Woodhead's translation of St. Teresa [The *Works* of St. Teresa of Avila]. LIB, xxi (66), 234-40.

BROWN, John Russell
The printing of John Webster's plays, I. SB, vi (54), 117-40.

—, II. SB, viii (56), 113-27.

—. III. *The Duchess of Malfi*. SB, xv (62), 57-69.

The compositors of *Hamlet* Q2 and *The Merchant of Venice*. SB, vii (55), 17-40.

A proof-sheet from Nicholas Okes' printing-shop. Illus. SB, xi (58), 228-31.

The rationale of old-spelling editions of the plays of Shakespeare and his contemporaries. SB, xiii (60), 49-67.

BROWN, R. D.
The Bodley Head press: some bibliographical extrapolations. PBSA, lxi (67), 39-50.

BROWN, Robert Benaway
The Lenox-Eames classification scheme at the William L. Clements Library. PBSA, xliv (50), 87-100.

Texans in leopard-skin pants. [Capt. Sam J. Richardson and W. W. Heartsill's *Fourteen Hundred and 91 Days in the Confederate Army*]. PBSA, xliv (50), 373-8.

— *and* BRAUN, Frank X.
The tunebook of Conrad Doll. PBSA, xlii (48), 229-38.

BROWN, Thomas Julian
Percy Bysshe Shelley, 1792-1822. (English literary autographs, 1). Illus. BC, i (52), 4-5.

William Makepeace Thackeray, 1811-63. (English literary autographs, 2). Illus. BC, i (52), 96-7.

John Dryden, 1631-1700. (English literary autographs, 3). Illus. BC, i (52), 180-1.

Alexander Pope, 1688-1744. (English literary autographs, 4). Illus. BC, i (52), 240-3.

The detection of faked literary MSS. Illus. BC, ii (53), 6-23.

Jonathan Swift, 1667-1745. (English literary autographs, 5). Illus. BC, ii (53), 68-9.

Samuel Johnson, 1709-1784. (English literary autographs, 6). Illus. BC, ii (53), 142-3.

Thomas Gray, 1716-1771. (English literary autographs, 7). Illus. BC, ii (53), 214-15.

Horace Walpole, 1717-1797. (English literary autographs, 8). Illus. BC, ii (53), 274-5.

Edward Gibbon, 1737-1794. (English literary autographs, 9). Illus. BC, iii (54), 52-3.

Thomas Chatterton, 1752-1770. (English literary autographs, 10). Illus. BC, iii (54), 136-7.

William Blake, 1757-1827. (English literary autographs, 11). Illus. BC, iii (54), 218-19.

Samuel Taylor Coleridge, 1772-1834. (English literary autographs, 12). Illus. BC, iii (54), 300-1.

Wordsworth and his amanuenses. (English literary autographs, 13). Illus. BC, iv (55), 48-50.

John Clare, 1793-1864. (English literary autographs, 14). Illus. BC, iv (55), 146-7.

Charles Dickens, 1812-1870. (English literary autographs, 15). Illus. BC, iv (55), 237.

Dante Gabriel Rossetti, 1828-1882. Christina Georgina Rossetti, 1830-1894. (English literary autographs, 16). Illus. BC, iv (55), 309.

The Brontës. (English literary autographs, 17). Illus. BC, v (56), 55-6.

William Morris, 1834-1896. (English literary autographs, 18). Illus. BC, v (56), 151.

Thomas Hardy, 1840-1928. (English literary autographs, 19). Illus. BC, v (56), 249.

Robert Bridges, 1844-1930. (English literary autographs, 20). Illus. BC, v (56), 369.

William Congreve, 1670-1729. (English literary autographs, 21). Illus. BC, vi (57), 61.

John Locke, 1632-1704. (English literary autographs, 22). Illus. BC, vi (57), 171.

Matthew Prior, 1664-1721. (English literary autographs, 23). Illus. BC, vi (57), 279.

Daniel Defoe, 1661?-1731. (English literary autographs, 24). Illus. BC, vi (57), 387.

Richard Steele, 1672-1729. Joseph Addison, 1672-1719. (English literary autographs, 25). Illus. BC, vii (58), 63.

George Berkeley, 1685-1753. David Hume, 1711-1776. (English literary autographs, 26). Illus. BC, vii (58), 181.

Laurence Sterne, 1713-1768. (English literary autographs, 27). Illus. BC, vii (58), 285.

Lord Chesterfield, 1694-1773. (English literary autographs, 28). Illus. BC, vii (58), 397.

Gilbert White, 1720-1793. (English literary autographs, 29). Illus. BC, viii (59), 51.

Robert Burns, 1759-1796. (English literary autographs, 30). Illus. BC, viii (59). 169.

English literary autograph number one [i.e. of the Venerable Bede]. (Note, 107). BC, viii (59), 180.

Alfred Edward Housman, 1859-1936. (English literary autographs, 31). Illus. BC, viii (59), 283.

Oliver Goldsmith, 1730?-1774. (English literary autographs, 32). Illus. BC, viii (59), 417.

John Bunyan, 1628-1688. (English literary autographs, 33). Illus. BC, ix (60), 53-5.

Thomas de Quincey, 1785-1859. (English literary autographs, 34). Illus. BC, ix (60), 179.

Elizabeth Barrett Browning, 1806-1861, and Robert Browning, 1812-1889. (English literary autographs, 35). Illus. BC, ix (60), 317.

John Keats, 1795-1821. (English literary autographs, 36). Illus. BC, ix (60), 445.

Algernon Charles Swinburne, 1837-1909. (English literary autographs, 37). Illus. BC, x (61), 57).

John Ruskin, 1819-1900. (English literary autographs, 38). Illus. BC, x (61), 185.

Gerard Manley Hopkins, 1844-1889. (English literary autographs, 39). Illus. BC, x (61), 321.

James Joyce, 1882-1941. (English literary autographs, 40). Illus. BC, x (61), 441.

William Wycherley, 1640?-1716. Sir John Vanbrugh, 1664-1726. (English literary autographs, 41). Illus. BC, xi (62), 63.

Lord Byron, 1788-1824. (English literary autographs, 42). Illus. BC, xi (62), 205.

William Cowper, 1731-1800. (English literary autographs, 43). Illus. BC, xi (62), 331.

Edmund Burke, 1729-1797. (English literary autographs, 44). Illus. BC, xi (62), 467.

Lord Tennyson, 1809-1892. (English literary autographs, 45). Illus. BC, xii (63), 61.

Matthew Arnold, 1822-1888. (English literary autographs, 46). Illus. BC, xii (63), 195.

Thomas Carlyle, 1795-1881. (English literary autographs, 47). Illus. BC, xii (63), 339.

Wilfred Owen, 1893-1918. (English literary autographs, 48). Illus. BC, xii (63), 489.

The autograph of Arnold's *Sohrab and Rustum*. (Note, 209). BC, xii (63), 494.

William Butler Yeats, 1865-1939. (English literary autographs, 49). Illus. BC, xiii (64), 53.

George Bernard Shaw, 1856-1950. (English literary autographs, 50). Illus. BC, xiii (64), 195.

Thomas Linacre, 1460?-1524. (English scientific autographs, 1). Illus. BC, xiii (64), 341.

Robert Boyle, 1627-1691. (English scientific autographs, 2). Illus. BC, xiii (64), 487.

William Harvey, 1578-1657. (English scientific autographs, 3). Illus. BC, xiv (65), 61.

Sir Hans Sloane, 1660-1753. (English scientific autographs, 4). Illus. BC, xiv (65), 201.

Henry Cavendish, 1731-1810. (English scientific autographs, 5). Illus. BC, xiv (65), 349.

Joseph Priestley, 1733-1804. (English scientific autographs, 6). Illus. BC, xiv (65), 539.

James Watt, 1736-1819. (English scientific autographs, 7). Illus. BC, xv (66), 47.

Francis Bacon, 1561-1626. (English scientific autographs, 8). Illus. BC, xv (66), 185.

Latin palaeography since Traube. TCBS, iii (59/63), 361-81.

BROWN, Thomas Edward
Thomas Edward Brown, 1830-1897. (Some uncollected authors, 33). BC, xi (62), 338-44.
S. Nowell-Smith.

BROWNE, Annie Leigh
The Leigh Browne collection at the Keats Museum. LIB, xvii (62), 246-50.
P. Kaufman.

BROWNE, Charles Farrar
Artemus Ward his book, 1862.
PBSA, liv (60), 121-5.
J. N. Blanck.

—. PBSA, lv (61), 392.
N. Kane.

BROWNE, Samuel
Samuel Browne, printer to the University of Heidelberg, 1655-1662. LIB, v (50/1), 14-25.
E. Weil.

BROWNE, sir Thomas
The iniquity of oblivion foil'd. [Sir Thomas Browne's *Hydriotaphia*: an author-corrected copy]. (Collector's piece, 2). Illus. BC, xv (68), 279-82.
J. Carter.

The correspondence between Sir Thomas Browne and John Evelyn. LIB, xix (38/9), 103-6.
F. S. de Beer.

A newly discovered *Urn Burial*. Illus. LIB, xix (38/9), 347-53.
J. S. Finch.

Sir Thomas Browne's autograph collections. [A letter]. LIB, xix (38/9), 492-3.
J. Carter.

Browne's *Urn Burial*. LIB, ii (47/8), 191-2.
J. Carter.

Sir Thomas Browne: early biographical notices, and the disposition of his library and manuscripts. SB, ii (49/50), 196-201.
J. S. Finch.

BROWNING, Elizabeth Barrett
Elizabeth Barrett Browning, 1806-1861, and Robert Browning, 1812-1889. (English literary autographs, 35). Illus. BC, ix (60), 317.
T. J. Brown.

A unique copy of *The Runaway Slave*, 1849. (Note, 191). BC, xii (63), 202-3.
J. Carter.

Mrs. Browning's contribution to periodicals: Addenda. PBSA, xliv (50), 275-6.
G. B. Taplin.

Edmund Gosse and the *Sonnets from the Portuguese*. PBSA, xlvi (52), 67-70.
R. Hagedorn.

Elizabeth Barrett and R. Shelton MacKenzie. SB, xiv (61), 245-50.
D. B. Green.

BROWNING, Robert
Elizabeth Barrett Browning, 1806-1861, and Robert Browning, 1812-1889. (English literary autographs, 35). Illus. BC, ix (60), 317.
T. J. Brown.

BROXBOURNE LIBRARY
The Broxbourne Library. (Contemporary collectors, 2). Illus. BC, iii (54), 190-7.
A. Ehrman.

Typographical specimen books. A checklist of the Broxbourne collection with an introduction. BC, v (56), 256-72.
W. A. Berry *and* A. M. Fern.

Three rare Paduan catalogues [in the Broxbourne Library]. (Note, 249). BC, xiv (65), 361-2.
D. E. Rhodes.

BRUCCOLI, Matthew Joseph
A mirror for bibliographers: duplicate plates in modern printing. PBSA, liv (60), 83-8.

Concealed printings in Hawthorne. PBSA, lvii (63), 42-9.

Notes on Ring Lardner's *What of It?* PBSA, lvii (63), 88-90.

A further note on Lardner's *What of It?* PBSA, lvii (63), 377.

States of *Fanshawe*. PBSA, lviii (64), 32.

Ring Lardner's first book. PBSA, lviii (64), 34-5.

Negative evidence about *The Celestial Rail-Road*. PBSA, lviii (64), 290-2.

Five notes on Ring Lardner. PBSA, lviii (64), 297-8.

F. Scott Fitzgerald's first book appearance. PBSA, lix (65), 58.

Cora's mouse. [Stephen Crane's gift of Kipling's *The seven seas* to Cora Taylor]. PBSA, lix (65), 188-9.

A sophisticated copy of *The house of the seven gables* [by N. Hawthorne]. PBSA, lix (65), 438-9.

A collation of F. Scott Fitzgerald's *This Side of Paradise*. SB, ix (57), 263-5.

Textual variants in Sinclair Lewis's *Babbitt*. SB, xi (58), 263-8.

Bibliographical notes on F. Scott Fitzgerald's *The Beautiful and Damned*. SB, xiii (60), 258-61.

Hidden printings in Edith Wharton's *The Children*. SB, xv (62), 269-73.

A further note on the printing of *The Great Gatsby*. SB, xvi (63), 244.

Material for a centenary edition of *Tender is the Night*. SB, xvii (64), 177-93.

Notes on the destruction of *The Scarlet Letter* manuscript. SB, xx (67), 257-9.

Scholarship and mere artifacts: the British and Empire publications of Stephen Crane. SB, xxii (69), 277-87.

—. *and* RHEAULT, Charles A.
Imposition figures and plate gangs in *The Rescue*. Illus. SB, xiv (61), 258-62.

— *and* KATZ, J.
Towards a descriptive bibliography of Stephen Crane: *Spanish-American war songs* [by S. A. Witherbee]. PBSA, lxi (67), 267-9.

BRUNHOUSE, Robert L.
David Ramsay's publication problems, 1784-1808. PBSA, xxxix (45), 51-67.

BRUNI, Leonardo
The *Epistolae Familiares* of Leonardo Bruni, Venice, 1495. PBSA, xxxvii (43), 157-8.
E. H. Wilkins.

BRUNO, Giordano
The location of copies of the first editions of Giordano Bruno. Illus. BC, v (56), 152-7.
J. Hayward.

First editions of Giordano Bruno. BC, v (56), 381-2.
J. Hayward.

Early editions of Giordano Bruno in Leningrad. (Note, 145). BC, ix (60), 453.
J. S. G. Simmons.

Early editions of Giordano Bruno in Poland. BC, xiii (64), 342-5.
A. Nowicki.

Early editions of Giordano Bruno at the University of Southern California. (Note, 238). BC, xiv (65), 74-5.
W. Nethery.

BRYANT, Jacob
Jacob Bryant and the Sunderland Library. Illus. LIB, ii (47/8), 192-9.
A. N. L. Munby.

Jacob Bryant's Caxtons: some additions to De Ricci's *Census*. LIB, iii (48/9), 218-22.
A. N. L. Munby.

BRYANT, Jerry H.
John Reynolds of Exeter and his canon. LIB, xv (60), 105-17.

BRYANT, William Cullen
Manuscript resources for the study of William Cullen Bryant. PBSA, xliv (50), 254-68.
H. E. Spivey.

Bryant's *The Prairies*: notes on date and text PBSA, lvi (62), 356-7.
C. D. Eby, *jr*.

BRYCE, James *visct.*
Bryce, James Bryce, viscount (1838-1922). *The American commonwealth*. London, 1888. PBSA, xxxvi (42), 65-6.
E. S. Brown.

BRYER, Jackson Robert
Thornton Wilder and the reviewers. PBSA, lviii (64), 35-49.

F. Scott Fitzgerald as book reviewer. PBSA, lx (66), 369-70.

BRYN MAWR *coll.*
The medieval library at Bryn Mawr. PBSA, xlvi (52), 87-98.
P. W. G. Gordan.

BUCHANAN, George
George Buchanan: some French connections. BTHK, iv (63/6), 66-72.
J. Durkan.

An unpublished commentary by George Buchanan on Virgil. EBST, iii (48/55), 209-88.
C. P. Finlayson.

George Buchanan's Latin poems from script to print: a preliminary survey. Illus. LIB, xxiv (69), 277-332.
I. D. Mcfarlane.

BUCHANAN-BROWN, John
See BROWN, John Buchanan-

BUCKLER, Edward
Edward Buckler, 1610-1706, poet and preacher. LIB, xvii (36/7), 349-53.
W. H. Buckler.

Three issues of *A Buckler against the Fear of Death*. LIB, xxi (40/1), 199-206.
H. R. Mead.

BUCKLER, William Earl
Household Words in America. PBSA, xlv (51), 160-6.

BUCKLER, William Hepburn
Edward Buckler, 1610-1706, poet and preacher. LIB, xvii (36/7), 349-53.

BÜHLER, Curt Ferdinand
Who printed the *Missale Speciale Constantiense*? BC, vi (57), 253-8.

The Dictes and Sayings of the Philosophers. LIB, xv (34/5), 295-329.

Caxton variants. Illus. LIB, xvii (36/7), 62-9.

Three notes on Caxton. [Concerning the recovery by W. Blades of fragments from the *Boethius* in the King Edward VI Grammar School at St. Albans]. LIB, xvii (36/7), 155-66.

George Maynyal: a Parisian printer of the fifteenth century? LIB, xviii (37/8), 84-8.

Notes on a Pynson volume. [*Old Tenures; Natura Brevium*; and Littleton, *Tenures Novelli*]. LIB, xviii (37/8), 261-7.

Three *Horae ad usum Sarum* printed by Philippe Pigouchet. Illus. LIB, xix (38/9), 304-10.

Two Caxton problems. [*Morte Darthur*; and *Lyf of our Lady*]. LIB, xx (39/40), 266-71.

The Churl and the Bird and *The Dictes and Sayings of the Philosophers* — two notes. LIB, xxi (40/1), 279-90.

Some documents concerning the Torresani and the Aldine press. LIB, xxv (44/5), 111-21.

An undescribed *Ars Poetica* printed at Paris about 1500. Illus. LIB, i (46/7), 127-31.

Two unrecorded Jacobean proclamations. LIB, iii (48/9), 121.

Some observations on *The Dictes and Sayings of the Philosophers*. LIB, viii (53), 77-88.

Another view on the dating of the *Missale Speciale Constantiense*. LIB, xiv (59), 1-10.

A letter written by Andrew Alciato to Christian Wechel. LIB, xvi (61), 201-5.

Aldus's *Paraenesis* to his pupil, Leonello Pio. LIB, xvii (62), 240-2.

Caxton's *History of Jason*. PBSA, xxxiv (40), 254-61.

A bibliographical curiosity. [Caxton's *Doctrinal of Sapience* and Duff's *Fifteenth Century English Books*]. PBSA, xxxv (41), 58-60.

Notes on two incunabula printed by Aldus Manutius. [*Brevissima Introductio ad Litteras Graecas* and *Horae ad Usum Romanum*]. Illus. PBSA, xxxvi (42), 18-26.

A note on Zedler's Coster theory. PBSA, xxxvii (43), 61-8.

Burley, Walter. *De vita et moribus philosophorum*. Augsburg, 1490. PBSA, xxxvii (43), 75.

A hitherto undescribed incunabulum. Missa. *De utilitate missae*. [Rome: Johann Besicken, after 1500?]. PBSA, xxxvii (43), 158.

The binding of books printed by William Caxton. PBSA, xxxviii (44), 1-8.

Caxton's *Blanchardin and Eglantine*: notes on the leaf preserved in the British Museum. PBSA, xxxix (45), 156-61.

Two undescribed incunabula. Justiniano, Leonardo. *Sonetti d'amore. El desperato*. [Rome: Johann Besicken, *c.* 1500]: [and] *Strambotti D'Ogni Sorte e Sonetti alla Bergamasca*. [Rome, Eucharius Silber, *c.* 1500]. PBSA, xxxix (45), 162-3.

The margins in mediaeval books. Illus. PBSA, xl (46), 32-42.

An undescribed indulgence. [Innocentius VIII. *Indulgence*. [Antwerp: Thierry Martens, 1497]] PBSA, xl (46), 229.

A Lyonese book, 1506. Antoninus. *Summa theologica*. [Lyons]: Johann Klein, [no date]. PBSA, xl (46), 229-30.

Some remarks on a nineteenth-century reprint. [Andrew Borde's *The fyrst boke of the Introduction of knowledge*]. PBSA, xli (47), 53-9.

The first edition of Ausonius. PBSA, xli (47), 60.

A Paris incunable. Seneca, Lucius Annaeus. *Proverbia. De moribus*. [Paris: Ulrich Gering, *c.* 1483]. PBSA, xli (47), 342-3.

Chaucer's *House of Fame*; another Caxton variant. PBSA, xlii (48), 140-3.

The first Aldine. [*Musarum Panagyris*]. PBSA, xlii (48), 269-80.

Seven variants in *The Chastising of God's Children*. PBSA, xliii (49), 75-8.

A Spanish incunable? Comas, Guillermus Petrus. *Quaestio de sudore sanguinis Christi*. [Barcelona: Johann Luschner, ca. 1498]. PBSA, xliii (49), 191.

Stop-press and manuscript corrections in the Aldine edition of Benedetti's *Diaria de bello Carolino*. PBSA, xliii (49), 365-73.

The British Museum's fragment of Lydgate's *Horse, Sheep, and Goose* printed by William Caxton. PBSA, xliii (49), 397-8.

Aldus Manutius: the first five hundred years. PBSA, xliv (50), 205-15.

A previously undescribed Horace. [*Sermones*. Paris, G. Marcand, 1492]. Illus. PBSA, xlv (51), 70-2.

Manuscript corrections in the Aldine edition of Bembo's *De Aetna*. PBSA, xlv (51), 136-42.

An edition of the *Sonetti* by Matteo Franco and Luigi Pulci. PBSA, xlv (51), 356-7.

A Prêtre Jean from Poitiers. PBSA, xlvi (52), 151-4.

Paulus Manutius and his first Roman printings. PBSA, xlvi (52), 209-14.

Wynkyn de Worde's printing of Lydgate's *Horse, Sheep and Goose*. PBSA, xlvi (52), 392-3.

Corrections in Caxton's *Cordiale*. PBSA, xlviii (54), 194-6.

Erhard Ratdolt's vanity. PBSA, xlix (55), 186-8.

Studies in the early editions of the *Fiore di virtù*. Illus. PBSA, xlix (55), 315-39.

The Constance Missal and two documents from the Constance diocese. PBSA, l (56), 370-5.

A note on GW 5231. [Second edition of the Premonstratensian Breviary, printed by Johann Grüninger at Strassburg, 1490]. PBSA, li (57), 236-7.

Literary research and bibliographical training. PBSA, li (57), 303-11.

A misprint in the Venetian *Filocolo* of 1472. PBSA, li (57), 319-22.

Corrected misprinting in the *Vida de Cristo*, Lisbon, 1495. PBSA, liv (60), 290-1.

An undescribed incunable: *Le lit de justice*, [Paris, circa 1488]. PBSA, lvi (62), 481-2.

Johannes Consobrinus and his English connections. PBSA, lvii (63), 211-12.

Comments on a Belgian 'Sammelband' of the early sixteenth century in the Pierpont Morgan Library. PBSA, lviii (64), 154-6.

A Caxton ghost — made and laid. PBSA, lix (65), 316.

The date of the Florentine incunable of the *De astrologica veritate* by Lucius Bellantius. PBSA, lx (66), 99-100.

The date of Michele Ricci's *Oratio ad Julium II*. PBSA, lxi (67), 349.

The headlines of William de Machlinia's *Year Book, 37 Henry VI*. SB, i (48/9), 123-32.

Observations on two Caxton variants. [In Lydgate's *The Pilgrimage of the Soul*, 1483; and Christine de Pisan's *The Book of the Fayttes of Armes and of Chyvalrye*, 1489]. Illus. SB, iii (50/1), 97-104.

The laying of a ghost? Observations on the 1483 Ratdolt edition of the *Fasciculus Temporum*. SB, iv (51/2), 155-9.

The Morgan copy of Machlinia's *Speculum Christiani*. SB, v (52/3), 159-60.

The first edition of *The Abbey of the Holy Ghost*. SB, vi (54), 101-6.

The printing of a *Valerius Maximus* dated 1671. SB, vii (55), 177-81.

A volume from the library of Sebald Pirckheimer. [Ovid's *Metamorphoses*, Parma, 1480]. SB, viii (56), 212-15.

Watermarks and the dates of fifteenth-century books. SB, ix (57), 217-24.

The second edition of the *Compagnia del Mantellaccio*. SB, xi (58), 225-7.

The errata lists in the first Aldine editions of Caro's *Rime* and of the *Due Orationi* of St. Gregorius Nazianzenus. SB, xv (62), 219-22.

The *Terence* of Turin, 1483. Illus. SB, xvii (64), 195-6.

The first edition of Ficino's *De Christiana Religione*: a problem in bibliographical description. SB, xviii (65), 248-52.

Dates in incunabular colophons. SB, xxii (69), 210-14.

—. *and* SCHULLIAN, Dorothy M.
A misprinted sheet in the 1479 *Mammotrectus super Bibliam* [of Johannes Marchesinus], Goff M-239. PBSA, lxi (67), 51-2.

BUFFALO
See NEW YORK *state, univ., Buffalo Lockwood Memorial libr.*

BUKE OF THE HOWLAT
An early printed fragment of the *Buke of the Howlat*. Illus. EBST, ii (38/45), 393-7.
W. Beattie.

BULGARINI, Belisario
Two autographs of a 'Sienese gentleman' in the Library of Congress. PBSA, liv (60), 291-3.
J. M. Edelstein.

Another Bulgarini book. PBSA, lvi (62), 482.
J. M. Edelstein.

Another Bulgarini volume. PBSA, lviii (64), 24.
J. M. Edelstein.

BULL, H. O.
Part-issues of Bell's *History of the British Crustacea*, 1844-53. (Query, 112). BC, viii (59), 73-4.

BULLEIN, William
A binding for William Bullein by the Initial binder, 1562. (English bookbindings, 37). Illus. BC, x (61), 184.
H. M. Nixon.

BULMER, William
Bulmer and the Roxburghe Catalogue. (Query, 82). BC, vi (57), 182.
P. C. G. Isaac.

—. BC, vi (57), 290-1.
B. Juel-Jensen.

—. BC, vi (57), 291.
C. S. Bliss.

Bulmer's *Poems of Goldsmith and Parnell*. (Query, 109). BC, viii (59), 72.
S. Roscoe.

Bulmer printed? (Query, 110). BC, viii (59), 73.
P. C. G. Isaac.

William Bulmer, 1757-1830: an introductory essay. Illus. LIB, xiii (58), 37-50.
P. C. G. Isaac.

BUNTING, sir Percy William
Matthew Arnold and Percy William Bunting: some new letters, 1884-1887. SB, vii (55), 199-207.
R. L. Lowe.

BUNYAN, John
Bunyan signatures in a copy of the Bible. (Note, 120). BC, viii (59), 427-8.
P. Kaufman.

John Bunyan, 1628-1688. (English literary autographs, 33). Illus. BC, ix (60), 53.
T. J. Brown.

Nathaniel Ponder; the publisher of *The Pilgrim's Progress*. LIB, xv (34/5), 257-94.
F. M. Harrison.

Some illustrators of *The Pilgrim's Progress*, part one: John Bunyan. Illus. LIB, xvii (36/7), 241-63.
F. M. Harrison.

Editions of *The Pilgrim's Progress*. LIB, xxii (41/2), 73-81.
F. M. Harrison.

John Bellamy: 'Pilgrim' publisher of London. PBSA, l (56), 342-69.
L. Rostenberg.

BURBY, Cuthbert
The English School-master: Dexter *v.* Burby, 1602. LIB, xxiii (42/3), 90-3.
Sir W. W. Greg.

BURDETT, Charles
Addenda to Wright [*American fiction 1774-1850*]: Burdett, Curtis, Judson, Weeks. PBSA, lxii (68), 452-3.
W. S. Kable.

BUREAU ACADÉMIQUE D'ÉCRITURE
The Bureau Académique d'Écriture: a footnote to the history of French calligraphy. Illus. PBSA, li (59), 203-13.
J. M. Wells.

BURKE, Edmund
Burke's *Reflections on the Revolution in France*. (Query, 58). BC, iv (55), 81.
W. B. Todd.

Edmund Burke, 1729-1797. (English literary autographs, 44). Illus. BC, xi (62), 467.
T. J. Brown.

Burke's *Vindication of Natural Society*. LIB, xviii (37/8), 461-2.
T. W. Copeland.

The bibliographical history of Burke's *Reflections on the Revolution in France*. LIB, vi (51), 100-8.
W. B. Todd.

Edmund Burke's friends and *The Annual Register*. LIB, xviii (63), 29-39.
T. W. Copeland.

Edmund Burke's library. PBSA, xliv (50), 153-72.
C. B. Cone.

Burke's authorship of the historical articles in Dodsley's *Annual Register*. PBSA, li (57), 244-9.
J. C. Weston, *jr*.

Predecessors to Burke's and Dodsley's *Annual Register*. SB, xvii (64), 215-20.
J. C. Weston, *jr*.

BURLEUS, Gualterus
Burley, Walter. *De vita et moribus philoso-phorum*, in German. Augsburg: Anton Sorg, 1490. PBSA, xxxvii (43), 75.
C. F. Bühler.

BURLEY, Simon
Two medieval book lists. [The libraries of Simon Burley and William de Walcote]. LIB, xxiii (68), 236-9.
V. J. Scattergood.

BURLEY, Walter
See BURLEUS, Gaulterus

BURLING, Elias
Elias Burling, *A Call to back-sliding Israel*, New York, 1694: an unrecorded tract printed by William Bradford. Illus. SB, xiv (61), 251-3.
A. N. L. Munby.

BURLINGHAM, Maria-Ann
The Mother-in-Law; or Memoirs of Madam de Marville, by Maria-Ann Burlingham. Boston, 1817. PBSA, xxxvi (42), 66-7.
C. S. Brigham.

BURNABY, Eustace
Eustace Burnaby's manufacture of white paper in England. Illus. PBSA, xlviii (54), 314-33.
A. T. Hazen.

BURNET, Gilbert *bp. of Salisbury*
Some reflections on the bibliography of Gilbert Burnet., Illus. LIB, iv (49/50), 100-13.
W. Rees-Mogg.

The bibliography of Gilbert Burnet. LIB, v (50/1), 61-3.
R. J. Dobell.

—. [A letter]. LIB, v (50/1), 151.
D. I. Masson.

—. LIB, vi (51), 126.
J. H. P. Pafford.

BURNETT, Frances Hodgson
A further printing of *That Lass o'Lowries*. PBSA, lvii (63), 222.
N. Kane.

BURNEY, Charles
Dr. Burney and the integrity of Boswell's quotations. PBSA, liii (59), 327-31.
R. Lonsdale.

Charles Burney's theft of books at Cambridge. Illus. [With an additional note by J. C. T. Oates]. TCBS, iii (59/63), 313-26.
R. S. Walker.

BURNEY, Frances
The publication of *Camilla*. (Note, 23). BC, ii (53), 219.
A. N. L. Munby.

BURNS, Robert
Robert Burns, 1759-1796. (English literary autographs, 30). Illus. BC, viii (59), 169.
T. J. Brown.

A slashed copy of *Reliques of Robert Burns*, 1808. (Note, 265). BC, xv (66), 67.
H. D. French.

Cromek's *Reliques of Robert Burns*, a footnote to Egerer 112. [*A bibliography of Robert Burns*]. BTHK, v (67/70), 33-5.
H. D. French.

Robert Burns and the *Aberdeen Magazine*. BTHK, v (67/70), 102-5.
G. R. Roy.

Scott's criticism of *The jolly beggars*. BTHK, v (67/70), 207-9.
D. A. Low.

Thomas Stewart, Robert Burns, and the law. PBSA, lvi (62), 46-55.
J. Egerer.

Robert Burns and William Creech — a reply [to an article by S. Parks]. PBSA, lxi (67), 357-9.
G. R. Roy.

The text of Burns' *The Jolly Beggars*. SB, xiii (60), 239-47.
J. C. Weston.

BURROW, Edward
Unpublished second volume of Edward Burrow's *A new and complete book of rates* 1774. (Note, 290). BC, xvi (67), 375-7.
D. H. Knott.

BURSCH, Frederick Conrad
An American typographic tragedy — the imprints of Frederick Conrad Bursch. Part I. Through the literary collector periods. PBSA, xliii (49), 1-38.
T. A. Larremore.

—. Part II Hillacre Bookhouse. Illus. PBSA, xliii (49), 111-72.

—. [Additions and corrections. A letter]. PBSA, xliii (49), 425-6.
T. A. Larremore.

BURTON, Robert
Alexander Boswell's copies of *The Anatomy of Melancholy*, 1621 and 1624. (Note, 88). BC, vi (57), 406-7.
R. A. Hunter *and* I. MacAlpine.

Two corrected forme readings in the 1632 *The Anatomy of Melancholy*. (Note, 276). BC, xv (66), 353-4.
D. G. Donovan.

A note on the text of *The Anatomy of Melancholy*. PBSA, lx (66), 85-6.
D. G. Donovan.

Robert Burton's *Anatomy of Melancholy* in early America. PBSA, lxiii (69), 157-75.
C. Heventhal.

BURY, Ricardus de
See AUNGERVYLE, Richard *bp. of Durham.*

BUSBY, John
The two John Busby's. LIB, xxiv (43/4), 81-6.
Sir W. W. Greg.

—. A correction. LIB, xxiv (43/4), 186.

—. A correction. LIB, xii (57), 203.

BUSHNELL, George Herbert
St. Andrews University Library. (Unfamiliar libraries, 3). BC, vii (58), 128-38.

William Schevez, Archbishop of St Andrews, d. 1497. (Portrait of a bibliophile, 4). BC, ix (60), 19-29.

Mr. John Govane, bibliothecary. EBST, ii (38/45), 419-20.

Patrick Bower. LIB, xxiii (42/3), 23-30.

BUSTI, Ubertino da
Ubertino da Busti. *Compendio devotissimo* [and other tracts]. Milan, Jacobus de Sancto Nazario and Philippus de Mantegatiis, 1496. PBSA. xxxvi (42), 318-9.
H. R. Mead.

BUTLER, Henry Montagu
How rare are Montagu Butler's translations of Tennyson? (Query, 162). BC, xii (63), 72-3.
R. L. Collins.

Montagu Butler's translations of Tennyson. (Query, 162). BC, xii (63), 356.
C. S. Bliss.

BUTLER, June Rainsford
America — a hunting ground for eighteenth-century naturalists with special reference to their publications about trees. PBSA, xxxii (38), 1-16.

BUTLER, Samuel *1612-1680*
The publication of *Hudibras*. Illus. PBSA, lx (66), 418-38.
J. L. Thorson.

BUTLER, Samuel *1835-1902*
Samuel Butler's revisions of *Erewhon*. PBSA, xxxviii (44), 22-38.
L. E. Holt.

BUTTER, Nathaniel
Nathaniel Butter and Nicholas Bourne, first 'Masters of the Staple'. LIB, xii (57), 23-33.
L. Rostenberg.

BUTTERFIELD, Lyman Henry
The American interests of the firm of E. and C. Dilly, with their letters to Benjamin Rush, 1770-1795. PBSA, xlv (51), 283-332.

BUTTERWORTH, Charles C.
Robert Redman's *Prayers of the Byble*. LIB, iii (48/9), 279-86.

—. [A letter]. LIB, v (50/1), 60.

Savonarola's expositions on the fifty-first and thirty-first Psalms. LIB, vi (51), 162-70.

Early primers for the use of children. PBSA, xliii (49), 374-82.

'BUZAGLOW' STOVES
Hot air from Cambridge. LIB, xviii (63), 140-2.
J. C. T. Oates.

BYLES, Alfred Thomas P.
William Caxton as a man of letters. LIB, xv (34/5), 1-25.

BYNNEMAN, Henry
Bynneman's books. LIB, xii (57), 81-92.
M. Eccles.

BYRD, Cecil Kash
Manuscript copies and printed editions of the Indiana Constitution, 1816. PBSA, xlviii (54), 390-402.

BYRNE, Muriel St. Clare
Bibliographical clues in collaborate plays. LIB, xiii (32/3), 21-48.

BYROM, H. J.
Edmund Spenser's first printer, Hugh Single-ton. LIB, xiv (33/4), 121-56.

Some exchequer cases involving members of the book-trade, 1534-1558. LIB, xvi (35/6), 402-17.

BYRON, Major G.
Major Byron. (Note, 31). BC, iii (54), 69-71.
T. G. Ehrsam.

BYRON, George Gordon N.
Byron's *The Corsair*, 1814. (Note, 98). BC, xii (58), 191.
A. Bridge.

Lord Byron, 1788-1824. (English literary autographs, 42). Illus. BC, xi (62), 205.
T. J. Brown.

Lord Byron and Mr. Coolidge of Boston. BC, xiii (64), 211-3.
E. M. Oldham.

Byron's dramas: three untraced MSS. (Query, 191). BC, xiv (65), 367.
T. G. Steffan.

A note on lord Byron's *Select Works*, 1823. LIB, i (46/7), 70-2.
T. C. D. Eaves.

Some notable errors in Parrott's edition of Chapman's Byron's plays. PBSA, lviii (64), 465-8.
J. B. Gabel.

The copyright of Byron's *Cain*. PBSA, lxiii (69). 5-13.
R. Mortenson.

C

C., J.
The Melancholy Cavalier [in relation to S. Rowlands' *The Melancholy Knight*]: a study in seventeenth-century plagiarism. SB, v (52/3), 161-3.
S. Dickson.

C., W.
See CRASHAW, William

C.A.L.M.
See CALENDARS OF AMERICAN LITER-ARY MANUSCRIPTS.

CABELL, Joseph Carrington
The reading of Joseph Carrington Cabell: 'A list of books on various subjects recommended to a young man . . .' SB, xiii (60), 179-88.
H. T. Colbourn.

CABINET DU ROI
Louis XIV, sa bibliothèque et le *Cabinet du Roi*. LIB, xx (65), 1-12.
A. Jammes.

CADELL AND DAVIES
Percy's relations with Cadell and Davies. LIB, xv (34/5), 224-36.
T. Shearer *and* A. Tillotson.

Cadell and Davies and the Liverpool book-sellers. LIB, xiv (59), 274-80.
J. R. Barker.

CADY, Edwin Harrison
Howells bibliography: a 'find' and a clarification. SB, xii (59), 230-3.

CAEDMON
Census of extant copies of Junius's *Caedmon*, 1655. (Query, 147). BC, xi (62), 218.
M. D. Clubb.

Junius's edition of *Caedmon*. [A letter]. LIB, xvii (62), 157.
M. D. Clubb.

A request for assistance. [Junius's *Caedmon*]. PBSA,. lvi (62), 116.
M. D. Clubb.

CAGLE, William R.
A 'lost' edition (1745) of Defoe's *Roxana*. (Query, 99). BC, xi (62), 483-4.

The publication of Joseph Conrad's *Chance*. Illus. BC, xvi (67), 305-22.

CAHOON, Herbert
A Scott facsimile. (Query, 78). BC, vi (57), 74.

CAIRNCROSS, Andrew Scott
Coincidental variants in *Richard III*. LIB, xii (57), 187-90.

Quarto copy for folio *Henry V*. Illus. SB, viii (56), 67-93.

CAITHNESS
Books and printing in Caithness. GBSR, vi (20), 84-94.
J. Mowat.

CAIUS, John
The Vesalian compendium of Geminus and Nicholas Udall's translation: their relation to Vesalius, Caius, Vicary and De Mandeville. Illus. LIB, xiii (32/3), 367-94.
S. V. Larkey.

CALDERÓN DE LA BARCA, Pedro
Edward Fitzgerald's *Six dramas of Calderón* 1854 edition? (Query, 229). BC, xvii (68), 491.
A. Bridge.

The two editions of Calderón's *Primera Parte* of 1640. Illus. LIB, xiv (59), 175-91.
E. M. Wilson.

On the *Tercera Parte* of Calderon - 1664. SB, xv (62), 223-30.
E. M. Wilson.

CALENDARS
Two medieval calendars and other leaves removed by John Bowtell from [Cambridge] University library MSS. TCBS, i (49/53), 29-36.
A. I. Doyle.

CALENDARS OF AMERICAN LITERARY MANUSCRIPTS
CALM addendum no. 1: Hart Crane. PBSA, lxiii (69), 130.
J. Katz.

CALHOUN, Philo Clarke
In memorium: Philo Clarke Calhoun, 1889-1964. PBSA, lxii (68), 421-5.
H. J. Heaney.

— *and* HEANEY, Howell J.
Dickens' *Christmas Carol* after a hundred years: a study in bibliographical evidence. PBSA, xxxix (45), 271-317.

Dickensiana in the rough. PBSA, xli (47), 293-320.

CALIFORNIA
Bibliographical notes on certain Eastern mining companies of the California Gold Rush, 1849-1850. Illus. PBSA, xliii (49), 247-8.
R. W. G. Vail.

Small renaissance: Southern California style. PBSA, l (56), 17-27.
J. Zeitlin.

Fifty-two early California imprints in the Bancroft Library, a supplementary list to Greenwood's *California Imprints, 1833-1862*. PBSA, lviii (64), 181-9.
J. R. K. Kantor.

The California *Constitution* of 1849. PBSA, lxiii (69), 25-9.
R. C. Johnson *and* M.P. Lowman II.

CALIFORNIA *univ., Bancroft libr.*
Fifty-two early California imprints in the Bancroft Library, a supplementary list to Greenwood's *California Imprints, 1833-1862*. PBSA, lviii (64), 181-9.
J. R. K. Kantor.

Denis Braud: some imprints in the Bancroft Library. PBSA, lxii (68), 252-4.
D. Roaten.

CALIFORNIA Southern, *univ.*
Early editions of Giordano Bruno at the University of Southern California. (Note, 238). BC, xiv (65), 74-5.
W. Nethery.

CALLIGRAPHY
An English *ABC* imitating handwriting. (Note, 56). BC, iv (55), 329-30.
C. Clair.

Handwritten books. (Query, 70). BC, v (56), 281.
H. E. James.

Writing masters and copybooks. (Note, 138). BC, ix (60), 198.
H. D. Lyon.

—. BC, ix (60), 326-7.
H. G. Pollard.

The adoption of the Latin uncial: a suggestion. EBST, ii (38/45), 375-9.
S. Morison.

Medieval writing-masters. Illus. LIB, xxii (41/2), 1-24.
S. H. Steinberg.

A French version of Duranti's prescriptions on the presentation of Papal Bulls. LIB, xxiii (42/3), 84-9.
S. H. Steinberg.

A hand-list of specimens of medieval writing-masters. LIB, xxiii (42/3), 191-4.
S. H. Steinberg.

—. [A letter]. LIB, ii (47/8), 203.
S. H. Steinberg.

An alphabet by Pieter Coecke van Aelst. LIB, xxiii (42/3), 195-7.
A. F. Johnson.

Early humanistic script and the first roman type. LIB, xxiv (43/4), 1-29.
S. Morison.

An American colonial calligraphic sheet of King Charles's *Twelve Good Rules* at Dartmouth College Library. Illus. LIB, vii (52), 111-16.
R. Nash.

An early example of the square minuscule. [Trinity College, Cambridge MS. 368]. Illus. TCBS, iv (64/8), 246-52.
T. A. M. Bishop.

The non-runic scripts of Anglo-Saxon inscriptions. Illus. TCBS, iv (64/8), 321-38.
E. Okasha.

An early example of insular-Caroline. [Cambridge university MS. Ee.2.4.]. Illus. TCBS, iv (64/8), 396-400.
T. A. M. Bishop.

CALVIN, Jean
A much-travelled association copy of Calvin's *Institutes*. (Collector's piece, 3). Illus. BC, xvii (68), 458-62.
C. S. Bliss.

CAMBRIDGE
Untraced MSS etc. relating to Cambridge institutions. (Query, 124). BC, ix (60), 79.
J. S. L. Gilmour *and* D. F. McKenzie.

A catalogue of sixteenth-century foreign printed books in Cambridge. LIB, x (55), 79-85.
H. M. Adams.

A catalogue of sixteenth-century foreign books in Cambridge. [A report]. TCBS, i (49/53), 90-1.
H. M. Adams.

Cambridge books of congratulatory verses, 1603-1640, and their binders. Illus. TCBS, i (49/53), 395-421.
J. C. T. Oates.

Notes on Cambridge manuscripts. Illus. TCBS, i (49/53), 432-41.
T. A. M. Bishop.

Two licences granted to Cambridge stationers. TCBS, i (49/53), 443-4.
C. P. Hall.

Slavonic books before 1700 in Cambridge libraries. Illus. TCBS, iii (59/63), 382-400.
J. S. G. Simmons *and* E. P. Tyrrell.

Greek manuscripts in Cambridge: recent acquisitions by college libraries, the Fitzwilliam museum and private collectors. TCBS, iv (64/8), 179-91.
P. E. Easterling.

Slavonic books of the eighteenth century in Cambridge libraries. TCBS, iv (64/8), 225-45.
J. S. G. Simmons *and* E. P. Tyrrell.

—. TCBS, ii (54/8), 185-99.
T. A. M. Bishop.

—. TCBS, ii (54/8), 323-36.
T. A. M. Bishop.

—. TCBS, iii (59/63), 93-5.
T. A. M. Bishop.

—. TCBS, iii (59/63), 412-23.
T. A. M. Bishop.

—. TCBS, iv (64/8), 70-6.
T. A. M. Bishop.

CAMBRIDGE *univ., Clare coll., libr.*
Medieval inventories of Clare College library. TCBS, i (49/53), 105-15.
R. W. Hunt.

CAMBRIDGE *univ., Corpus Christi coll., libr.*
A handlist of manuscripts in the library of Corpus Christi College, Cambridge, not described by M. R. James. TCBS, iii (59/63), 113-23.
J. Fines *and* R. Vaughan.

A sixteenth-century inventory of the library of Corpus Christi College, Cambridge. TCBS, iii (59/63), 187-99.
J. M. Fletcher *and* J. K. McConica.

The tracts of the Norman Anonymous: C.C.C.C. MS. 415. Illus. TCBS, iv (64/8), 155-65.
K. Pellens.

The Corpus Martianus Capella [C.C.C.C. MS. 153]. Illus. TCBS, iv (64/8), 257-75.
T. A. M. Bishop.

CAMBRIDGE *univ., Emmanuel coll., libr.*
Note on a copy of the *Book of Common Prayer* in the library of Emmanuel College, Cambridge. TCBS, iv (64/8), 79-83.
E. C. Ratcliffe.

A Cervantes item from Emmanuel College library: Barros's *Filosofía cortesana*, 1587. Illus. TCBS, iv (64/8), 363-71.
E. M. Wilson.

CAMBRIDGE *univ., Fitzwilliam musc., libr.*
A handlist of the additional manuscripts in the Fitzwilliam museum, received since the publication of the catalogue by Dr. M. R. James in 1895, excluding the McClean bequest. TCBS, i (49/53), 197-207.
P. M. Giles *and* F. Wormald.

—. TCBS, i (49/53), 297-309.
P. M. Giles *and* F. Wormald.

—. TCBS, i (49/53), 365-75.
P. M. Giles *and* F. Wormald.

—. TCBS, ii (54/8), 1-13.
P. M. Giles *and* F. Wormald.

—. Accessions 1953-60. TCBS, iv (64/8), 173-8.
P. M. Giles.

Description of Fitzwilliam Museum MS. 3-1954. Illus. TCBS, iv (64/8), 1-28.
P. M. Giles *and* F. Wormald.

Greek manuscripts in Cambridge: recent acquisitions by college libraries, the Fitzwilliam museum and private collectors. TCBS, iv (64/8), 179-91.
P. E. Easterling.

CAMBRIDGE *univ., King's coll., libr.*
The gifts of Elizabethan printers to the library of King's College, Cambridge. Illus. LIB, ii (47/8), 224-32.
A. N. L. Munby.

Notes on King's College library in the fifteenth century. TCBS, i (49/53), 280-6.
A. N. L. Munby.

Notes on King's College library, 1500-1570, in particular for the period of the Reformation. [*With*] Appendix, The inventory of 1556-7. TCBS, ii (54/8), 38-54.
W. D. J. C. Thompson.

Provost Argentine of King's and his books. Illus. TCBS, ii (54/8), 205-12.
D. E. Rhodes.

—. Addendum. TCBS, iii (59/63), 263.
J. M. Fletcher.

CAMBRIDGE *univ., libr.*
Incunabula in Cambridge university library. BC, iv (55), 51-7.
G. D. Painter.

Speght's Chaucer and MS. Gg.4.27 [a Canterbury Tales MS. in Cambridge university library]. SB, xxi (68), 225-35.
G. B. Pace.

Two medieval calendars and other leaves removed by John Bowtell from [Cambridge] University library MSS, TCBS, i (49/53), 29-36.
A. I. Doyle.

The sixteenth-century catalogues of the University library. Illus. TCBS, i (49/53), 310-40.
J. C. T. Oates *and* H. L. Pink.

The deposit of books at Cambridge under the Licensing Acts, 1662-79, 1685-95. TCBS, ii (54/8), 290-304.
J. C. T. Oates.

Fore-edge title in Cambridge university library. Illus. TCBS, iii (59/63), 163-5.
J. C. T. Oates.

Two Greek MSS. of Spanish provenance in bishop Moore's collection. TCBS, iii (59/63), 257-62.
P. E. Easterling.

Charles Burney's theft of books at Cambridge. Illus. TCBS, iii (59/63), 313-26.
R. S. Walker.

The University library catalogue of 1556; an addendum. TCBS, iv (64/8), 77-9.
J. C. T. Oates.

William Rysley's catalogue of Cambridge university muniments, compiled in 1420. TCBS, iv (64/8), 85-99.
C. P. Hall.

An early example of Insular-Caroline [University library MS. Ee.2.4.]. Illus. TCBS, iv (64/8), 396-400.
T. A. M. Bishop.

CAMBRIDGE, *univ., Magdalen coll., libr.*
A discovery in the Pepys Library. BC, ii (53), 278-9.
R. W. Ladborough.

The Pepys ballads. Illus. LIB, xxi (66), 282-92.
L. M. Goldstein.

A lost Pepys Library book recovered. Illus. TCBS, iii (59/63), 292-4.
R. W. Ladborough.

CAMBRIDGE *univ., Pembroke coll.*
The earliest printed statutes of Pembroke College. Illus. TCBS, i (49/53), 130-8.
A. I. Doyle.

CAMBRIDGE *univ., Trinity coll., libr.*
Halliwell Phillipps and Trinity College Library. LIB, ii (47/8), 250-77.
D. A. Winstanley.

—. Additional note. LIB, ii (47/8), 277-82.
R. W. Hunt.

Notes on the manuscript of *Generydes*. [Trinity College MS. 0.5.2]. LIB, xvi (61), 205-10.
D. A. Pearsall.

De Thou and Theophilus's *Institutes* [in Trinity College Library, Cambridge]. TCBS, iii, (59/63), 160-3.
G. G. Barber.

Trinity College Cambridge MS.B.14.52, and William Patten. Illus. TCBS, iv (64/8), 192-200.
B. Hill.

An early example of the square minuscule. [Trinity College MS. 368]. Illus. TCBS, iv (64/8), 246-52.
T. A. M. Bishop.

CAMBRIDGE PHILOSOPHICAL SOCIETY *libr.*
The function of a nineteenth-century catalogue belonging to the Cambridge Philosophical Library. TCBS, iv (64/8), 293-301.
N. C. Neudoerffer.

CAMBRIDGE PRINTING
Some unrecorded Cambridge books in the library of Eton College. TCBS, i (49/53), 441-3.
R. Birley.

Early Cambridge printers and the Stationers' company. TCBS, ii (54/8), 275-89.
C. Blagden.

Notes on printing at Cambridge *c.* 1590. TCBS, iii (59/63), 96-103.
D. F. McKenzie.

CAMBRIDGE UNIVERSITY PRESS *Syndics libr.*
The Syndics' library at the University Press. TCBS, iv (64/8), 253-6.
H. S. Bennett.

CAMBRIDGE [MASS.] PRESS
A document concerning the first Anglo-American press. Illus. LIB, xx (39/40), 51-70.
G. P. Winship.

The Cambridge Press, 1638-1692. PBSA, lviii (64), 24-5.
J. E. Alden.

The printing by the Cambridge press of *A platform of Church discipline*, 1649. SB, ii (49), 79-93.
L. G. Starkey.

Benefactors of the Cambridge press: a reconsideration. SB, iii (50), 267-70.
L. G. Starkey.

CAMELS
Camels in America. PBSA, xlvi (52), 327-72.
A. K. Greenly.

CAMERON, John *and* POTTLE, Frederick A.
Whereabouts of correspondence of J. G. Lockhart? (Query, 238). BC, xviii (69), 226.

CAMOENS, Luis Vaz de
An unknown impression by the printer of the first edition of the *Lusíadas.* Illus. LIB, xxi (40-1), 309-19.
H. Thomas.

CAMP, Charles L.
Wagner-Camp. [H. R. Wagner. *The Plains and the Rockies.* 3rd. ed., revised by C. L. Camp]. PBSA, lv (61), 45-6.
L. S. Thompson.

CAMPBELL, Ian
Carlyle's borrowings from the Theological library of Edinburgh University. BTHK, v (67/70), 165-8.

CAMPBELL, Isaac
An unknown Maryland imprint of the eighteenth-century. [I. Campbell's *A rational enquiry into the origin . . . of civil government,* 1785?] PBSA, lxiii (69), 200-3.
E. G. Howard.

CAMPBELL, James
Issues of Dylan Thomas's *The Map of Love.* (Note, 82). BC, vi (57), 73-4.

CANADA
Early Canadiana. BC, x (61), 28-9.
F. W. Watt.

CANCELS
Cancels. (Note, 19). BC, ii (53), 73.
R. J. Dobell.

Cancel slips. (Note, 33). BC, iii (54), 145.
J. C. T. Oates.

—. BC, iii (54), 307.
C. S. Bliss.

An unexplained 17th-century cancel [in Stubbe's *Legends, no histories*]. (Query, 129). BC, ix (60), 203-4.
H. W. Jones.

—. (Query, 129). BC, x (61), 72.
C. S. Bliss.

—. (Query, 129). BC, xi (62), 351-2.
R. J. F. Carnon.

A curious form of cancellation. (Query, 140). BC, x (61), 75.
Sir S. C. Roberts.

—. BC, x (61), 454-5.
W. B. Todd.

A cancel in the Boucher Molière, 1734. (Query, 190). BC, xiv (65), 367.
H. A. Hammelmann.

Deliberate preservation of cancellands. (Query, 241). BC, xviii (69), 387.
H. G. Pollard.

Cancels in Sir Walter Scott's *Life of Napoleon.* EBST, iii (48/55), 137-51.
W. Ruff.

A cancel in Southerne's *The Disappointment,* 1684. LIB, xiii (32/3), 395-8.
C. Leech.

A cancel in an early Milton tract. [*Animadversions upon the Remonstrant's Defence against Smectymnuus,* 1641.] LIB, xv (34/5), 243-6.
W. R. Parker.

—. [A letter.] LIB, xvi (35/6), 118.
H. C. H. Candy.

Lyrical Ballads, 1800: a paste-in. LIB, xix (38/9), 486-91.
J. E. Wells.

A political cancel in *The Coblers Prophesie.* LIB, xxiii (42/3), 94-100.
I. Mann.

Cancels in Malone's *Dryden.* LIB, xxiii (42/3), 131.
R. W. Chapman.

Cancels in Scott's *Minstrelsy*. LIB, xxiii (42/3), 198.
R. W. Chapman.

An uncancelled copy of the first collected edition of Swift's poems. [Vol. II of *The Works of J. S(wift)* Dublin, 1735]. LIB, xxii (67), 44-56.
M. J. P. Weedon.

The forms of twentieth-century cancels. PBSA, xlvii (53), 95-112.
J. C. Wyllie.

The cancels in Dr. Johnson's *Works* (Oxford, 1825). PBSA, xlvii (53), 376-8.
A. Sherbo.

A 19th-century American two-city cancel. PBSA, lii (58), 140.
J. C. Wyllie.

An unsuspected cancel in Tonson's 1691 *Rochester*. PBSA, lv (61), 130-3.
D. M. Vieth.

The cancels in Lockman's *Travels of the Jesuits*, 1743. SB, ii (49), 205-7.
J. R. Lucke.

CANDIDUS *pseud.*
The authorship and printing of *Plain Truth* by 'Candidus'. PBSA, xlix (55), 230-48.
T. R. Adams.

CANDY, Hugh Charles H.
Milton autographs established. Illus. LIB, xiii (32/3), 192-200.

Milton, N.LL. and Sir Tho. Urquhart. Illus. LIB, xiv (33/4), 470-6.

—. [A letter]. LIB, xv (34/5), 377-8.

Milton's *Prolusio* script. Illus. LIB, xv (34/5), 330-9.

A cancel in an early Milton tract. [*Animadversions upon the Remonstrant's Defence against Smectymnuus*. A letter]. LIB, xvi (35/6), 118.

CANNON, I. C.
The roots of organization among journeymen printers. Illus. JPHS, iv (68), 99-107.

CANON MISSAE
Canon missae [1457/8]. LIB, xii (57), 43-4.
Sir J. I. O. Masson.

CANT, Ronald Gordon
The St. Andrews University theses, 1579-1747: a bibliographical introduction. Illus. EBST, ii (38/45), 105-50.

The St. Andrews University theses, 1579-1747: supplement. EBST, ii (38/45), 263-72.

CANTERBURY *city, St. Augustine's monastery, libr.*
The 'Psalterium Hebraycum' from St. Augustine's Canterbury rediscovered in the Scaliger bequest at Leyden. Illus. TCBS, ii (54/8), 97-104.
G. I. Lieftinck.

CANTRELL, Paul L. *and* WILLIAMS, George Walton
Roberts' compositors in *Titus Andronicus* Q2. SB, viii (56), 27-38.

The printing of the second quarto of *Romeo and Juliet*, 1599. SB, ix (57), 107-28.

CANZLER, David G.
Quarto editions of *Play of the wether*. PBSA, lxii (68), 313-19.

CAPE TOWN *S. African publ. libr., Grey collection* The manuscripts of the Grey collection in Cape Town. Illus. BC, x (61), 147-55.
L. F. Casson.

CAPITALIZATION
Eighteenth-century capitalization. LIB, ix (54), 268-70.
G. Tillotson.

CAPSTOCKE, John
The authorship and publication of *The copye of a letter sent by John Bradforth to the right honorable lordes the erles of Arundel, Darbie, Shrewsbury and Pembroke,* S.T.C. 3480. TCBS, iii (59/63), 155-60.
D. M. Loades.

CARACCIOLI, Louis Antoine de.
[Caraccioli, Louis Antoine de] (1721-1803). *Advice from a lady of quality to her children.* Newbury-Port, by John Mycall for William Green of Boston [1789]. PBSA, xxxvi (42), 64-5.
F. B. Bowe.

CARACCIOLO, Peter
Some unrecorded variants in the first edition of Dryden's *All for Love*, 1678. (Note, 232). BC, xiii (64), 498-500.

CAREY, Mathew
The chronology of Carey imprints. PBSA, l (56), 190-3.
D. Kaser.

The printing [by M. Carey and P. Hall] of Jefferson's *Notes*, 1793-94. SB, v (52), 201.
P. J. Conkwright *and* C. Verner.

Mathew Carey's proof-readers. SB, xvii (64), 123-33.
R. G. Silver.

The costs of Mathew Carey's printing equipment. SB, xix (66), 85-122.
R. G. Silver.

CARLSON, Norman E.
Wither and the Stationers. SB, xix (66), 210-15.

CARLTON, W. J.
Samuel Pepys; his shorthand books. LIB, xiv (33/4), 73-84.

CARLYLE, Thomas
Thomas Carlyle, 1795-1881. (English literary autographs, 47). Illus. BC, xii (63), 339.
T. J. Brown.

A missing MS section of Carlyle's *Reminiscences*. (Query, 173). BC, xii (63), 496.
E. Sharples.

Thomas Carlyle's borrowings from Edinburgh University Library, 1819-1820. Illus. BTHK, iii (60/2), 138-43.
C. P. Finlayson.

Carlyle's borrowings from the Theological library of Edinburgh University. BTHK, v (67/70), 165-8.
I. Campbell.

Writers on German literature in *Blackwood's Magazine* with a footnote on Thomas Carlyle. LIB, ix (54), 35-44.
A. L. Strout.

CARMIGNANO, Niccolò Antonio
The first book printed at Bari [i.e. N. A. Carmignano's *Operette*]. Illus. SB, vii (58), 208-11.
D. E. Rhodes.

—. Additional note. SB, xi (58), 227-8.
D. E. Rhodes.

CARNAN, Thomas
Thomas Carnan and the Almanack monopoly. SB, xiv (61), 23-43.
C. Blagden.

CARNIE, Robert Hay
Perth booksellers and bookbinders in the records of the Wright calling, 1538-1864. BTHK, i/4 (56/8), 24-39.

The Beauties of Magazines and an engraving of William Cullen. BTHK, i/4 (56/8), 40-2.

Stationers and bookbinders in the records of the hammermen of St. Andrews. BTHK, iii (60/2), 53-60.

The Glasgow magazine 1770. BTHK, v (67/70), 142-3.

Lord Hailes's contributions to contemporary magazines. SB, ix (57), 233-44.

—. *and* DOIG, Ronald Paterson
Scottish printers and booksellers 1668-1775. A supplement. SB, xii (59), 131-59.

—. A second supplement (1). SB, xiv (61), 81-96.

—. A second supplement (2). SB, xv (62), 105-20.

CARNON, Ronald James F.
An unexplained 17th-century cancel [in Stubbe's *Legends, no histories*]. (Query, 129). BC, xi (62), 351-2.

The Infant Minstrel, 1816. (Query, 177). BC, xiii (64), 354-5.

Two anonymous translations of Pseudo-Xenophon [*Xenophon's Defence of the Athenian democracy*, tr. by H. J. Pye]. (Query, 219). BC, xvii (68), 218.

CARO, Annibale
The errata lists in the first Aldine editions of Caro's *Rime* and of the *Due Orationi* of St. Gregorius Nazianzenus. SB, xv (62), 219-22.
C. F. Bühler.

CARPENDER, William
The author of *Jura cleri* [ascribed to William Carpender]. PBSA, lxii (68), 241-5.
J. R. Jenson.

CARPENTER, Edwin Hagger
Government publication in late eighteenth-century Mexico. PBSA, xlvi (52), 121-38.

Checklist of the official imprints of the administration of Revilla Gigedo the younger, 1789-1794. PBSA, xlvi (52), 215-63.

Army field printing in the New World. Illus. PBSA, l (56), 169-80.

CARPENTER, Kenneth E.
An unrecorded Mark Twain. Illus. PBSA, lv (61), 236-9.

Copyright renewal deposit copies. PBSA, lx (66), 473-4.

—. *and* ARMSTRONG, James C.
James Russell Lowell *On democracy*. PBSA, lix (65), 385-99.

CARRIÈRE, Joseph M.
The manuscript of Jefferson's unpublished errata list for Abbé Morellet's translation of the *Notes on Virginia*. SB, i (48/9), 3-24.

CARROLL, Lewis, *pseud.*
See DODGSON, Charles Lutwidge

CARSON, Marian S. *and* SWAN, Marshall W. S.
John Bioren: printer to Philadelphia publishers. PBSA, xliii (49), 321-34.

CARSWELL, John
Bolingbroke's *Letters on history* 1738: a special copy. (Note, 300). BC, xvii (68), 351.

CARTER, Harry Graham
Caslon punches: an interim note. JPHS, i (65), 68-70.

The types of Christopher Plantin. Illus. LIB, xi (56), 170-9.

The longevity of a typeface. Illus. LIB, xvii (62), 242-6.

—. *and* WOLPE, Berthold
Pepys's copy of Moxon's *Mechanick Exercises*. LIB, xiv (59), 124-6.

—. *and others*
A list of type specimens. LIB, xxii (41/2), 185-204.

CARTER, John Waynflete
Early trade bindings. (Query, 2). BC, i (52), 54.

A binding variant. [H. O. Sturgis: *Belchamber*. Constable, 1904]. (Query, 13). BC, i (52), 130.

Beatrix Potter: *Peter Rabbit*, 1900-1902. (Query, 18). BC, i (52), 196.

Knox's *Absolute and Abitofhell*. (Query, 21). BC, i (52), 268.

Thomas J. Wise's *Verses*, 1882 &1883. (Query, 36). BC, ii (53), 158-9.

The A. E. Housman manuscripts in the Library of Congress. BC, iv (55), 110-14.

J. H. Newman. *The Dream of Gerontius*, 1866. (Note, 64). BC, v (56), 171.

Sidelights on American bibliophily. BC, v (56), 357-67.

George Eliot's *Agatha* 1869 — and after. BC, vi (57), 244-52.

A. E. Housman's contributions to an Oxford Magazine [*Ye Rounde Table*]. (Query, 90). BC, vi (57), 404.

Michael Sadleir: a valediction. BC, vii (58), 58-61.

William Ged and the invention of stereotype. (Query, 102). BC, vii (58), 296-7.

—. [A letter]. LIB, xiii (58), 141.

—. Illus. LIB, xv (60), 161-92.

—. A postscript. Illus. LIB, xvi (61), 143-5.

Thomas J. Wise and 'Richard Gullible'. (Note, 110). BC, viii (59), 182-3.

Betjemaniana. (Note, 140). BC, ix (60), 199.

—. (Note, 140). BC, ix (60), 452.

Housman manuscripts. (Query, 130). BC, ix (60), 204-5.

Trollope's *La Vendée*, London, Colburn, 1850. (Note, 152). BC, x (61), 69-70.

[An appraisal of *The Book collector*]. After ten years. BC, x (61), 402-7.

Housmaniana. (Note, 174). BC, xi (62), 84.

—. (Note, 247). BC, xiv (65), 215-7.

—. (Note 247,). BC, xvii (68), 215.

T. J. Wise and the technique of promotion. (Note, 184). BC, xi (62), 480-2.

—. (Note, 184). BC, xii (63), 202.

Who was Mr. Y. Z.? (Query, 152). BC, xi (62), 484.

Hawkshaw rides again. BC, xii (63), 178-83.

A unique copy of *The Runaway Slave*, 1849. (Note, 191). BC, xii (63), 202-3.

Thomas J. Wise's descriptive formula. (Query, 181). BC, xiii (64), 214-15.

Morisonianum. (Note, 253). BC, xiv (65), 365.

The iniquity of oblivion foil'd [Sir Thomas Browne's *Hydriotaphia*: an author-corrected copy.] (Collector's piece, 2). Illus. BC, xv (66), 279-82.

Wise forgeries in Doves bindings. (Query, 226). BC, xvii (68), 352-3.

Colour variations in 19th-century publishers' bindings. (Note, 302). BC, xvii (68), 490.

Ghosts. (Query,233). BC, xvii (68), 492-3.

An unsolicited review [of *New paths in Book Collecting*, 1934]. BC, xvii (69), 57-60.

Is this a record? BC, xviii (69), 353-9.

The Lausanne edition of Beckford's *Vathek*. LIB, xvii (36/7), 369-94.

Sir Thomas Browne's autograph collections. [A letter]. LIB, xix (38/9), 492-3.

Browne's *Urn Burial*. LIB, ii (47/8), 191-2.

Tennyson's *Carmen Saeculare*, 1887. LIB, ii (47/8), 200-2.

Thomas J. Wise's *Verses* 1882-1883. LIB, xxiv (69), 246-9.

Bibliography and the rare book trade. PBSA, xlviii (54), 219-29.

A hand-list of the printed works of William Johnson, afterwards Cory, fellow of King's College, Cambridge and assistant master at Eton. TCBS, i (49/53), 69-87.

—. Addenda and corrigenda. TCBS, iv (64/8), 318-20.

—. *and* SADLEIR, Michael
The nomenclature of nineteenth-century cloth grains. Illus. BC, ii (53), 54-8.

— *and* SPARROW, John
A. E. Housman, an annotated check-list. LIB, xxi (40-1), 160-91.

—. Additions and corrections. LIB, xxiii (42/3), 42-3.

— *and others*
John Hayward, 1904-1965: some memories. Illus. BC, xiv (65), 443-86.

CARTER, Paul J.
Mark Twain material in the *New York Weekly Review*. PBSA, lii (58), 56-62.

CARTERET, John *2nd earl Granville*
An Irish bookbinding probably bound for Lord Carteret, *c*. 1725-30. Illus. BC, iii (54), 216-17.
H. M. Nixon.

A binding for John Carteret, 2nd earl Granville, 1741. (English bookbinding, 19). Illus. BC, v (56), 368.
H. M. Nixon.

CARTOGRAPHY *See* MAPS

CARTWRIGHT, Thomas
Books printed at Heidelberg for Thomas Cartwright. LIB, ii (47/8), 284-6.
A. F. Johnson.

CARTWRIGHT, William
Comedies, Tragi-Comedies, with other poems, by mr. William Cartwright, 1651. LIB, xxiii (42/3), 12-22.
G. B. Evans.

CARVER, P. L.
John Palsgrave's translation of *Acolastus*.
LIB, xiv (33/4), 433-46.

CARY, Arthur Joyce L.
An authoritative text of *The horse's mouth*.
PBSA, lxi (67), 100-9.
A. Wright.

CARY, Henry Francis
Cary: *Dante*. (Query, 1). BC, i (52), 54.
H. Marlow *pseud*.

—. (Query, 1). BC, i (52), 127-8.
S. Roscoe.

CARY, Joyce
See CARY, Alfred Joyce L.

CARYE, Christopher, John & William.
Christopher and William Carye, collectors of monastic manuscripts, and 'John Carye'. LIB, xx (65), 135-42.
A. G. Watson.

CARYLL, John
Bibliographical evidence from a resetting in Caryll's *Sir Salomon*, 1691. LIB, iii (48/9), 134-7.
F. T. Bowers.

CASANOVA DE SEINGALT, Giacomo Girolamo
A clue to the mystery of Casanova's *Memoirs*.
PBSA, xlvi (52), 287-326.
J. R. Childs.

Further clues bearing on the mystery of Casanova's *Memoirs*. PBSA, xlviii (54), 248-62.
J. R. Childs.

An unknown work of Casanova identified.
PBSA, i (56), 264-78.
J. R. Childs.

CASE
The lay of the case. Illus. SB, xxii (69), 125-42.
J. P. W. Gaskell.

CASE, Arthur Ellicott
More about the Aldine Pliny of 1508. LIB, xvi (35/6), 173-87.

CASE, John
The Praise of Musicke, by John Case. PBSA, liv (60), 119-21.
W. Ringler.

John Case, *The Praise of Musicke*. PBSA, liv (60), 293.
D. G. Neill.

CASE, Leland D.
Origins of Methodist publishing in America.
Illus. PBSA, lix (65), 12-27.

CASE OF THE PLANTERS.
The Case of the Planters of Tobacco in Virginia, 1733: an extraordinary use of standing type.
SB, v (52), 184-6.
O. L. Steele.

CASHEI, *cathedral libr.*
Cashel cathedral. (Unfamiliar libraries, 14).
Illus. BC, xvii (68), 322-30.
F. Alderson.

CASHMORE, Herbert Maurice
Dodsley's *Collection of poems by several hands*. Additions. OBSP, i (47), 46.

CASLON, William
Caslon punches: an interim note. JPHS, i (65), 68-70.
H. G. Carter.

The early career of William Caslon. Illus.
JPHS, ii (67), 66-81.
J. Mosley.

Two Caslon specimens. LIB, ii (47/8), 199-200.
L. W. Hanson.

CASSON, L. F.
The manuscripts of the Grey collection in Cape Town. Illus. BC, x (61), 147-55.

CASTANO PRIMO
Castano psalter, 1486. (Note, 43). BC, iv (55), 78.
D. E. Rhodes.

—. BC, iv (55), 168.
A. Ehrman.

An unrecorded early printing centre [i.e. Castano Primo]. Illus. LIB, xviii (53), 128-9.
J. V. Scholderer.

CASTELMAN, Richard
The authenticity of the voyage of Richard Castleman, 1726. PBSA, xxxvii (43), 261-74.
E. D. Seeber.

CASTILLO SOLÓRZANO, Alonso de
Castillo Solórzano's *Garduña de Sevilla* in English translation. PBSA, xlvi (52), 154-8.
J. E. Tucker.

CATALOGUES
An untraced 18th-century catalogue. (Query, 142). BC, x (61), 201-2.
E. Wolf, *2nd*.

Threee rare Paduan catalogues [in the Broxbourne library]. (Note, 249). BC, xiv (65), 361-2.
D. E. Rhodes.

The earliest booksellers' catalogues of incunabula. (Query, 188). BC, xiv (65), 366.
A. Ehrman.

The earliest catalogues of incunabula. (Query, 196). BC, xiv (65), 546.
A. Ehrman.

Authors' catalogues of the 16th-century. (Note, 301). BC, xvii (68), 352.
A. Ehrman.

Italian broadside catalogues. [A letter]. LIB, iv (49/50), 281.
A. Ehrman.

Monthly catalogues of books published. LIB, xviii (63), 223-8.
D. F. Foxon.

The sixteenth-century catalogues of the University library [Cambridge]. Illus. TCBS, i (49/53), 310-40.
J. C. T. Oates *and* H. L. Pink.

CATCHWORDS
Catchwords and press figures at home and abroad. BC, ix (60), 301-7.
G. G. Barber.

CATECHISMS
The Elizabethan ABC with the Catechism. Illus. LIB, xvi (35/6), 32-48.
H. Anders.

CATESBY, Mark
Mark Catesby: the discovery of a naturalist. PBSA, liv (60), 163-75.
G. F. Frick.

CATHEDRAL LIBRARIES CATALOGUE
The Cathedral Libraries catalogue. [With] An appendix: Printed catalogues of books and manuscripts in cathedral libraries — England and Wales. LIB, ii (47/8), 1-13.
M. S. G. Hands *and* M. S. Smith.

CATHER, Willa Sibert
Cather, Willa Sibert (1876 -   ). *O. Pioneers!* Boston, 1913. PBSA, xxxv (41), 161.
B. D. Hitz.

CATHERINE *of Aragon, consort of Henry viii, King of England*
Katherine of Aragon's pomegranate. TCBS, ii (54/8), 88-92.
K. P. Harrison.

CATHOLICISM
Researches in early catholic America. PBSA, xxxiii (39), 55-68.
W. Parsons.

CATNACH, James
Bewick, Catnach and William Davison. BC, xii (63), 72.
P. C. G. Isaac.

CATO EXAMIN'D
The authorship of *Cato examin'd*, 1713. [By C. Gildon?] PBSA, li (57), 84-90.
G. L. Anderson.

CAUTHEN, Irby B.
Swinburne's letter concerning Poe. PBSA, xliv (50), 185-90.

The twelfth day of December: *Twelfth Night*, II, iii, 91. SB, ii (49/50), 182-5.

Poe's *Alone*: its background, source and manuscript. SB, iii (50/1), 284-91.

Compositor determination in the first folio *King Lear*. SB, v (52/3), 73-80.

John Esten Cooke on publishing, 1865. SB, viii (56), 239-41.

Gorboduc, Ferrex and Porrex [by T. Norton and T. Sackville] the first two quartos. SB, xv (62), 231-3.

CAVANAUGH, Jean Carmel
The library of Lady Southwell and Captain Sibthorpe. SB, xx (67), 243-54.

CAVENDISH, hon. Frederick
Did Mr. Cavendish burn his Caxtons? Illus. BC, xii (63), 449-66.
A. N. L. Munby *and* M. Pollard.

CAVENDISH, George
Cavendish's *Life of Wolsey*. (Query, 54). BC, iii (54), 310.
R. S. Sylvester.

CAVENDISH, hon. Henry
Henry Cavendish, 1731-1810. (English scientific autographs, 5). Illus. BC, xiv (65), 349.
T. J. Browne.

CAVENDISH, Margaret *duchess of Newcastle*
Duck and the Duchess of Newcastle. (Note, 14). BC, i (52), 265.
D. Grant.

CAXTON, William
Caxton and the trade in printed books. BC, iv (55), 190-9.
N. J. M. Kerling.

Did Mr. Cavendish burn his Caxtons? Illus. BC, xii (63), 449-66.
A. N. L. Munby *and* M. Pollard.

A binding from the Caxton bindery, *c.* 1490. (English bookbindings, 48). Illus. BC, xiii (64), 52.
H. M. Nixon.

Some observations on William Caxton and the Mercers' company. Illus. BC, xv (68), 283-95.
N. F. Blake.

William Caxton as a man of letters. LIB, xv (34/5), 1-25.
A. T. P. Byles.

The Dictes and Sayings of the Philosophers. LIB, xv (34/5), 295-329.
C. F. Bühler.

Caxton variants. Illus. LIB, xvii (36/7), 62-9.
C. F. Bühler.

Three notes on Caxton. LIB, xvii (36/7), 155-66.
C. F. Bühler.

The Caxton Indulgence of 1476. LIB, xix, 38/9), 462-4.
K. Povey.

Two Caxton problems. [*Morte Darthur* and Lydgate's *Lyf of our Lady*]. LIB, xx (39/40), 266-71.
C. F. Bühler.

A word on Caxton's *Dictes*. Illus. LIB, iii (48/9), 155-85.
G. Legman.

Jacob Bryant's Caxtons. Some additions to De Ricci's *Census*. LIB, iii (48/9), 218-22.
A. N. L. Munby.

An unrecorded Caxton at Ripon Cathedral. LIB, viii (53), 37-42.
J. E. Mortimer.

William Caxton's houses at Westminster. Illus. LIB, xii (57), 153-66.
L. E. Tanner.

The Caxton *Legenda* at St. Mary's, Warwick. Illus. LIB, xii (57), 225-39.
P. Morgan *and* G. D. Painter.

Caxton's *History of Jason*. PBSA, xxxiv (40), 245-61.
C. F. Bühler.

A bibliographical curiosity. [Caxton's *Doctrinal of Sapience* and Duff's *Fifteenth Century English Books*.] PBSA, xxxv (41), 58-60.
C. F. Bühler.

The bindings of books printed by William Caxton. PBSA, xxxviii (44), 1-8.
C. F. Bühler.

Caxton's *Blanchardin and Eglantine*: notes on the leaf preserved in the British Museum. PBSA, xxxix (45), 156-61.
C. F. Bühler.

Chaucer's *House of Fame*: another Caxton variant. PBSA, xlii (48), 140-3.
C. F. Bühler.

The British Museum's fragments of Lydgate's *Horse, Sheep, and Goose* printed by William Caxton. PBSA, xliii (49), 397-8.
C. F. Bühler.

Corrections in Caxton's *Cordiale*. PBSA, xlviii (54), 194-6.
C. F. Bühler.

Caxton as a literary critic. PBSA, li (57), 312-18.
D. B. Sands.

The variants in Caxton's *Esope*. PBSA, lv (61), 34-6.
R. T. Lenaghan.

A Caxton ghost made and laid. PBSA, lix (65), 316.
C. F. Bühler.

Observations on two Caxton variants [in Lydgate's *The Pilgrimage of the Soul*, 1483; Christian de Pisan's *The Book of the Fayettes of Armes and of Chyvalrye*, 1489]. SB, iii (50/1), 97-104.
C. F. Bühler.

CENSORSHIP
Libertine literature in England, 1600-1745. 3 pts. Illus. BC, xii (63), 21-36, 159-77, 294-307.
D. F. Foxon.

John Cleland and the publication of the *Memoirs of a Woman of Pleasure*. Illus. BC, xii (63), 476-87.
D. F. Foxon.

Ulysses and the Attorney-General 1936. LIB, xxiv (69), 343-5.
D. Thomas.

Robert Stephens, messenger of the press: an episode in 17th-century censorship. PBSA, xlix (55), 131-52.
L. Rostenberg.

'My squeamish public': some problems of Victorian magazine publishers and editors. SB, xii (59), 21-40.
C. Maurer.

The press under the early Tudors: a study in censorship and sedition. TCBS, iv (64/8), 29.50.
D. M. Loades.

CENTLIVRE, Susanna
Susanna Centlivre. (Some uncollected authors, 14). 2 pts. BC, vi (57), 172-8; 280-5.
J. E. Norton.

Mrs. Centlivre's *The Wonder*: a variant imprint. (Note, 93). BC, vii (58), 79-80.
A. D. McKillop.

A poem by Mrs. Centlivre. (Note, 95). BC, vii (58), 189-90.
D. G. Neill.

Two poems by Susanna Centlivre. (Note, 151). BC, x (61), 68-9.
J. Faure.

CENTRE-RECTANGLE BINDER
A binding by the centre-rectangle binder. (English bookbindings, 62). Illus. BC, xvi (67), 345.
H. M. Nixon.

CENTRE-RULES
See BOX RULES

CERTAMBERT, Louis Richard
Louis Richard Certambert and the first French newspapers in St. Louis, 1809-1854. PBSA, xxxiv (40), 221-53.
J. F. McDermott.

CERTAYNE BRIEFE RULES
Certayne briefe rules and 'Lily's Latin grammar'. LIB, xiv (59), 49-53.
C. G. Allen.

CERVANTES SAAVEDRA, Miguel de
A Baconian and Cervantes. (Note, 146). BC, ix (60), 454.
D. M. Woodward.

Some textual peculiarities of the first English *Don Quixote*. Illus. PBSA, xxxvii (43), 203-14.
E. B. Knowles *jr.*

Don Quixote abridged. Illus. PBSA, xlix (55), 19-36.
E. B. Knowles.

A Cervantes item from Emmanuel College library: Barros's *Filosofía cortesana*, 1587. Illus. TCBS, iv (64/8), 363-71.
E. M. Wilson.

CERVINI, Marcello *card.*
See MARCELLUS II *pope*

CHADWICK, Hubert
Stonyhurst College. (Unfamiliar libraries, 2).
BC, vi (57), 343-9.

CHADWICK, William Owen
The case of Philip Nichols, 1731. TCBS, i
(49/53), 422-31.

CHAIN LINES
See also WATERMARKS

Turned chain-lines. Illus. LIB, v (50/1), 184-
200.
I. J. C. Foster *and* K. Povey.

Chain-indentations in paper as evidence.
SB, vi (54), 181-95.
A. H. Stevenson.

CHAMBERS, David
An improved printing press by Philippe-Denis
Pierres. Illus. JPHS, iii (67), 82-92.

CHAMBERS, Robert
Serial publications of *Traditions of Edinburgh*
[by R. Chambers]. LIB, xiv (33/4), 207-11.
C. Parsons.

CHAMPION
The Champion. (Query, 61). BC, iv (55), 172.
S. B. Shipley.

CHANDLER, G.
A Bewick prospectus. (Query, 133). BC, x (61),
72.

CHANDLER, Raymond
Raymond Chandler. (Some uncollected
authors, 1). BC, ii (53), 209-11.

Raymond Chandler. (Note, 30). BC, iii (54), 69.
A. Lovell.

—. BC, iii (54), 69.
B. Johnston.

—. (Query, 45). BC, iii (54), 73.
B. Johnston.

The publications of Raymond Chandler's *The
long goodbye*. BC, xviii (69), 279-90.
R. H. Miller.

CHAN-TOON, Mabel Mary A.
Who wrote *For Love of the King*? Oscar Wilde
or Mrs. Chan-toon. BC, vii (58), 269-77.
G. Sims.

CHAPBOOKS
The Chapbook editions of the Lambs' *Tales
from Shakespear*. BC, vi (57), 41-53.
D. F. Foxon.

Scott's boyhood collection of chapbooks.
BTHK, iii (60/2), 202-18.
J. C. Corson.

Chapbooks with Scottish imprints in the Robert
White collection, the University Library,
Newcastle upon Tyne. BTHK, iv (63/6), 88-174.
F. W. Ratcliffe.

Early Banbury chapbooks and broadsides.
Illus. LIB, xvii (36/7), 98-108.
C. R. Cheney.

The Diceys and the chapbook trade. Illus.
LIB, xxiv (69), 219-31.
V. E. Neuburg.

Quevedo's *Buscón* as a chapbook. PBSA,
xliv (50), 66-9.
E. H. Hespelt.

Samuel Pepys's Spanish chapbooks. 3 pts.
Illus. TCBS, ii (54/8), 127-54, 229-68, 305-22.
E. M. Wilson.

Some Spanish verse chapbooks of the seventeenth century. Illus. TCBS, iii (59/63), 327-34.
E. M. Wilson.

CHAPIN LIBRARY
See WILLIAMSTOWN *Mass., Williams coll.,
Chapin libr.*

CHAPMAN, Christopher
Harleian bindings by Chapman, 1721. (English
bookbindings, 58). Illus. BC, xv (66), 321-2.
H. M. Nixon.

CHAPMAN, George
Some additional poems by George Chapman.
Illus. LIB, xxii (41/2), 168-76.
J. Robertson.

Chapman's text corrections in his *Iliads*. LIB,
xii (52), 275-81.
H. C. Fay.

Critical marks in a copy of Chapman's *Twelve
Books of Homer's Iliads*. LIB, viii (53), 117-21.
H. C. Fay.

A proof-sheet in *An humorous day's mirth*,
1599, printed by Valentine Simmes. Illus.
LIB, xxi (66), 155-7.
A. Yamada.

The whole works of Homer . . . by G. Chapman.
Lond., for Nathaniell Butter [1616?]. PBSA,
xl (46), 230-1.
P. S. Dunkin.

Some notable errors in Parrott's edition of
Chapman's Byron plays. PBSA, lviii (64),
465-8.
J. B. Gabel.

CHAPMAN, John
John Chapman and *The Westminster Review*.
(Note, 66). BC, v (56), 171-2.
R. von Arsdel.

CHAPMAN, Robert William
'Printed For'. [A letter]. LIB, xvi (35/6), 455.

Cancels in Malone's *Dryden*. LIB, xxiii (42/3),
131.

Individual binding. LIB, xxiii (42/3), 197-8.

Cancels in Scott's *Minstrelsy*. LIB, xxiii (42/3),
198.

End-papers. LIB, xxv (44/5), 79.

Gilt. LIB, iii (48/9), 223.

Dodsley's *Collection of Poems by several hands*. OBSP, iii (31/3), 269-316.

—. OBSP, i (47), 43-4.

— *and* HAZEN, Allen T.
Johnsonian bibliography, a supplement to Courtney. OBSP, v (36/9), 117-66.

CHARDE, Thomas
An additional letter and booklist of Thomas Charde, Stationer of London. LIB, xxi (40/1), 26-43.
D. Paige.

Thomas Charde, printer and bookseller. LIB, xv (60), 57-8.
L. E. Berry.

Another booklist of Thomas Charde. Addendum. PBSA, lv (61), 381-2; lvi (62), 115.
L. E. Berry.

CHARLECOTE HOUSE
The Charlecote House library. (Contemporary collectors, 20). BC, viii (59), 147-50.
D. Gordon.

CHARLES I *king of Gt. Britain*
For Eikon Basilike see GAUDEN, John *bp. of Worcester*

An unusual seal of King Charles I. Illus. BTHK, ii (59/60), 33.
D. J. W. Reid.

An American colonial calligraphic sheet of King Charles's Twelve Good Rules at Dartmouth College Library. Illus. LIB, vii (52), 111-16.
R. Nash.

CHARLESTON S. C.
French and Spanish works printed in Charleston, South Carolina. Illus. PBSA, xxxiv (40), 137-70.
J. F. Shearer.

CHARLESTON S. C. *Library soc.*
A classical debate of the Charleston, South Carolina, Library Society. PBSA, lxi (67), 83-99.
E. C. Reinke.

CHARVAT, William
Longfellow's income from his writings, 1840-1852. PBSA, xxxviii (44), 9-21.

Melville and the common reader. SB, xii (59), 41-57.

CHASTISING OF GOD'S CHILDREN
Seven variants in *The Chastising of God's Children*. PBSA, xliii (49), 75-8.
C. F. Bühler.

CHATSWORTH
List of books acquired by the British Museum from Chatsworth. BC, vii (58), 401-6.
G. D. Painter.

List of books acquired by the British Museum from Chatsworth. Pt. II, English books 1501-1640. BC, viii (59), 52-9.
A. F. Allison *and others*

Chatsworth incunabula in the British Museum. Addenda and corrigenda. (Note, 108). BC, viii (59), 180-1.
G. D. Painter.

—. BC, viii (59), 294.

CHATTERTON, Thomas
Thomas Chatterton, 1752-1770. (English literary autographs, 10). Illus. BC, iii (54), 136-7.
T. J. Brown.

The Rowley myth in eighteenth century Germany. PBSA, li (57), 238-41.
K. S. Guthke.

The authenticity of Chatterton's *Miscellanies in Prose and Verse*. PBSA, lv (61), 289-96.
D. S. Taylor.

Chatterton's brother-poet, William Roberts. PBSA, lvii (63), 184-90.
P. Kaufman.

CHAUCER, Geoffrey *Envoy to Allison*.
See ENVOY TO ALISON

Chaucer's *House of Fame*; another Caxton variant. PBSA, xlii (48), 140-3.
C. F. Bühler.

The text of Chaucer's *Purse*. SB, i (48/9), 103-21.
G. B. Pace.

Printer's copy for Tyrwhitt's *Chaucer*. SB, iii (50/1), 265-6.
A. L. Hench.

Chaucer's *Lak of Stedfastnesse*. SB, iv (51/2), 105-22.
G. B. Pace.

The Chaucerian *Proverbs*. SB, xviii (65), 41-8.
G. B. Pace.

Speght's Chaucer and MS. Gg.4.27 [a *Canterbury Tales* MS. in Cambridge university library]. SB, xxi (68), 225-35.
G. B. Pace.

CHAUNCY, Charles
Charles Chauncy and the Great Awakening: a survey and bibliography. PBSA, xlv (51), 125-35.
E. S. Gaustad.

CHEAP REPOSITORY TRACTS
Cheap Repository Tracts: Hazard and Marshall edition. LIB, xx (39/40), 295-340.
G. H. Spinney.

CHEMISTRY
The Duveen alchemical and chemical collection. (Contemporary collectors, 11). Illus. BC, v (56), 331-42.
D. I. Duveen.

The techno-chemical receipt book. (Among my books, 1.) BH, i (47/51), 58-60.
W. S. Field.

CHENEY, Christopher Robert
Early Banbury chapbooks and broadsides. Illus. LIB, xvii (36/7), 98-108.

CHEPMAN, Walter
Walter Chepman's signature. EBST, iii (48/9), 81-2.
W. Beattie.

CHERBURY LORD Herbert of
See HERBERT, Edward *1st baron.*

CHERRY, T. A. F.
The library of Henry Sinclair, Bishop of Ross, 1560-1565. BTHK, iv (63/6), 13-24.

CHERRY PICKERS
Chronicles of the 'Cherry Pickers'. BH, ii (51/2), 119-26.
J. Paine.

CHESTERFIELD *4th earl of*
See STANHOPE, Philip Dormer *4th earl of Chesterfield*

CHETTLE, Henry
Henry Chettle, *Englandes Mourning Garment*, 1603. [A letter]. LIB, i (46/7), 246.
R. O. Hummel, jr.

The 1631 quarto of *The Tragedy of Hoffman.* LIB, vi (51), 88-99.
H. Jenkins.

A note on variants in the dedication of Chettle's *Tragedy of Hoffman.* PBSA, xlii (48), 307-12.
E. J. Schlochauer.

The printing of *Greenes groatsworth of witte* and *Kind-harts dreame* [by H. Chettle]. SB, xix (66), 196-7.
S. Thomas.

CHETWIND, Philip
Philip Chetwind and the Allott copyrights. LIB, xv (34/5), 129-60.
H. Farr.

CHEWNING, Harris
The text of the *Envoy to Alison.* SB, v (52/3), 33-42.

CHEYNELL, Francis
Cheynell, Francis (1608-1665): *The Man of Honour.* London, J. R. for Samuel Gellibrand, 1645. PBSA, xxxv (41), 203.
H. R. Mead.

CHEYNEY, Reginald Evelyn Peter G.
Peter Cheyney's *Poems of love and war* and *To Corona and other Poems.* (Query, 192). BC, xiv (65), 367.
C. Woolf.

CHICAGO *Newberry libr.* The John M. Wing Foundation of the Newberry library. Illus. BC, viii (59), 157-62.
J. Wells.

CHILD, sir Josiah *bart.*
The published forms of Sir Josiah Child's *A New Discours of Trade.* LIB, xi (56), 95-102.
T. H. Bowyer.

CHILDREN'S BOOKS
Early children's books. (Query, 46). BC, iii (54), 73-4.
S. Roscoe.

—. BC, iii (54), 150-1.
W. B. Todd.

The use of the word 'lottery' in titles of 18th and 19th century children's books. (Query, 55). BC, iii (54), 310.
S. Roscoe.

The Children's books exhibition at the Pierpont Morgan Library. Illus. BC, iv (55), 34-44.
W. Schatzki.

Children's books in boxes. (Note, 59). BC, v (56), 76.
S. Roscoe.

An unrecorded children's book illustrated by Thomas Bewick. [A letter]. LIB, vii (52), 59-60.
S. Roscoe.

CHILDS, James Bennet
Bibliography the world over: some recent developments. PBSA, xlv (51), 257-64.

The story of the United States Senate documents, 1st Congress, 1st session, New York, 1789. PBSA, lvi (62), 175-94.

The authentic archetype of the United States Constitution. PBSA, lvi (62), 372-4.

"Disappeared in the wings of oblivion". The story of the U. S. House of Representatives printed documents at the first session of the first Congress, N.Y., 1789.
Illus. PBSA, lviii (64), 91-132.

CHILDS, James Rives
A clue to the mystery of Casanova's *Memoirs.* PBSA, xlvi (52), 287-326.

Further clues bearing on the mystery of Casanova's *Memoirs.* PBSA, xlviii (54), 248-62.

An unknown work of Casanova identified. PBSA, l (56), 264-78.

CHINANTEC INDIANS
Nicolás de la Barreda and his works on the Chinantec Indians of Mexico. PBSA, liii (59), 1-14.
H. F. Cline.

CHINKS *pseud.*
Chinks. *Mr. Hardy Lee, his yacht.* Boston, 1857. PBSA, xxxiv (40), 362.
R. W. Henderson.

CHIRM, Silvanus
Chirm's banded bindings. Illus. TCBS, i (49/53), 181-6.
A. N. L. Munby.

CHISWICK PRESS
'A contract of eternal bond of love, confirmed by . . .'? [The leaflet printed at the Chiswick press announcing the marriage of M. Lee and R. Le Gallienne]. BC, xv (66), 215.
M. Trevanion.

CHODERLOS DE LACLOS, Pierre Ambroise F.
The first editions of *Les Liaisons Dangereuses*.
(Query, 65). BC, iv (55), 331.
J. Haywood.

—. BC, vi (57), 74.
J. Haywood.

CHOREOGRAPHY
Chorégraphie. The dance notation of the
eighteenth century: Beauchamp or Feuillet
Illus. BC, xvi (67), 450-76.
F. Derra de Moroda.

Chorégraphie. F. Le Roussaü. BC, xvii (68),
216-7.
B. Brown.

CHRIST, Robert W.
[Edwards, Jonathan]. *Conversion of President
Edwards.* American Tract Society, 1825.
PBSA, xxxvii (43), 308-9.

Mather, Cotton. *Corderius Americanus . . .*
Boston, 1828. PBSA, xxxix (45), 163.

CHRISTIAANS, William
William Christiaans, Leyden, and his English
Books. LIB, x (55), 121-3.
A. F. Johnson.

CHRISTINA *queen of Sweden*
A manuscript from Queen Christina's library:
The *Amores* of Sigismondo Boldini. Illus.
LIB, xvii (62), 281-315.
J. Sparrow.

CHRISTOPHERS, Richard Albert *and*
O'DONOGHUE, Michael
Halkett and Laing continued. (Query, 186).
BC, xiii (64), 360.

CHURCHILL, Charles
Charles Churchill. (Some uncollected authors,
8). BC, iv (55), 316-23.
D. Grant.

CHURCHILL, Sir Winston Leonard S.
Churchilliana. (Note, 230). BC, xiii (64), 352-2.
P. Eaton.

—. BC, xiii (64), 497.
F. Woods.

Hemingway, Churchill, and the printed word.
'Dukedom large enough' II. PBSA, lvi (62),
346-53.
D. A. Randall.

CHURCH OF SCOTLAND
See SCOTLAND, Church of

CIARDI, John
Mr. Ciardi, Mr. Adams, and Mr. White.
PBSA, lv (61), 393.
C. E. Feinberg.

CICERO, Marcus Tullius
Cicero, Marcus Tullius. *Laelius de amictia.*
[Cologne, Ulrich Zell, 1467]. PBSA, xl (46),
160.
J. Fleming.

Aldine anchors, initials and the 'counterfeit'
Cicero [*Le Pistole ad Attico*]. Illus. PBSA, lx
(66), 413-7.
W. B. Todd.

CIRCULATING LIBRARIES
See LIBRARIES

CIRCULATION
See READING PUBLIC

CIVES *pseud.*
*The following publication . . . To William
Smith . . .* [by Cives]. [New York, Hugh Gaine?
1783.] PBSA, xxxiv (40), 359.
J. C. Wyllie.

CIVIL DISOBEDIENCE
'Civil disobedience': a bibliographical note.
BC, xviii (69). 295-6.
L. Lane.

CLAGHORN, George S.
Jonathan Edward MSS and books from his
library. (Query, 174). BC, xiii (64), 71.

CLAIR, Colin
Christopher Plantin *c.* 1520-1589. A quater-
centenary tribute. Illus. BC, iv (55), 200-7.

'An English *ABC* imitating handwriting'.
(Note, 56). BC, iv (55), 329-30.

Clement Perrett, calligrapher. LIB, xi (56),
50-2.

—. [A letter]. LIB, xi (56), 286.

CLAPHAM
An eighteenth-century book club at Clapham.
LIB, xxiv (69), 243-6.
D. H. Knott.

CLAPP, Sarah Lewis C.
Subscription publishers prior to Jacob Tonson.
LIB, xiii (32/3), 158-83.

CLARE, John
John Clare, 1793-1864. (English literary auto-
graphs 14). Illus. BC, iv (55), 146-7.
T. J. Brown.

CLARE, Robert
The reports of a press spy [Robert Clare] for
Robert Harley; new bibliographical data for
the reign of Queen Anne. LIB, xxii (67),
326-45.
H. L. Snyder.

CLAREMONT *coll., Honnold libr.*
An Oxford collection [the William W. Clary
Oxford collection, Honnold Library, Claremont
Colleges]. (Contemporary collectors, 44). Illus.
BC, xvii (68), 177-89.
W. W. Clary.

CLARK, Charles Edwin
The literature of the New England earthquake
of 1755. PBSA, lix (65), 295-305.

CLARK, George Thomas
Leland Stanford and H. H. Bancroft's *History* a bibliographical curiosity. Illus. PBSA, xxvii (33), 12-23.

CLARK, James
The writings and controversies of James Clark, minister at Glasgow, 1702-1724. GBSR, xi (33), 73-95.
W. J. Couper.

CLARK, Leonard
A handlist of the writings in book form, 1902-1953, of Walter de la Mare. SB, vi (54), 197-217.

—. Addendum. SB, viii (56), 269-70.

CLARKE, Adam
Adam Clarke's *Bibliographical Dictionary*, 1802-1806. SB, iv (51), 188-91.
F. Cordasco.

CLARKE, Derek Ashdown
A selective check-list of bibliographical scholarship for 1964. Part I: Incunabula and early Renaissance. SB, xix (66), 251-62.

CLARKE, Robert, *and Co.*
The publishing activities of Robert Clarke and Co., of Cinncinnati, 1858-1909. PBSA, xxxiv (40), 315-26.
C. H. McMullen.

CLARKSON, John W.
A bibliography of Franklin Benjamin Sanborn. PBSA, lx (66), 73-85.

CLARKSON, Paul S.
Letters of Junius. (Query, 8). BC, i (52), 57.

CLARY, William Webb
An Oxford collection [the William W. Clary Oxford collection. Honnold Library, Claremont Colleges]. (Contemporary collectors, 44). Illus. BC, xvii (68), 177-89.

CLASSICAL TRADITION
The classical tradition in colonial Virginia. PBSA, xxxiii (39), 85-97.
L. B. Wright.

CLASSICS
Printing the classics in the eighteenth century. BC, i (52), 98-111.
J. P. W. Gaskell.

Editions of the classics and English translations. [A letter]. LIB, viii (53), 204.
C. Blagden.

CLAVELL, Robert
See TERM CATALOGUES

CLEEVE, Alexander
A binding by Alexander Cleeve, *c.* 1690. (English bookbindings, 54). Illus. BC, xiv (65), 348.
H. M. Nixon.

CLELAND, John
John Cleland and the publication of the *Memoirs of a Woman of Pleasure*. Illus. BC, xii (63), 476-87.
D. F. Foxon.

The reappearance of two lost black sheep. [*Venus in the Cloister*, 1725; and Cleland's own abridgement of the *Memoirs of a Woman of Pleasure*, entitled *Memoirs of Fanny Hill*]. BC, xiv (65), 75-6.
D. F. Foxon.

CLEMENCE, Abel
'Abel Clémence' of 'Rouen': a sixteenth-century secret press. Illus. LIB, xx (39/40), 136-53.
G. Clutton.

CLEMENS, Samuel Langhorne
Samuel Clemens and John Camden Hotten. LIB, xx (65), 230-42.
D. Ganzel.

That *Gilded Age* again: an attempt to un-muddle the mystery of the fifty-seven variants. PBSA, xxxvii (43), 141-56.
F. C. Willson.

Marketing a best seller: Mark Twain's *Innocents Abroad*. Illus. PBSA, xli (47), 107-22.
L. T. Dickinson.

Kipling's *American Notes* and Mark Twain interview. PBSA, xliv (50), 69-73.
I. Kaplan.

The fake title-page of the *Gilded Age*: a solution. PBSA, i (56), 292-6.
D. Woodfield.

Mark Twain material in the *New York Weekly Review*. PBSA, lii (58), 56-62.
P. J. Carter.

An unrecorded Mark Twain. [A Russian transl. of *The Czar's Soliloquy*]. PBSA, lv (61), 236-9.
K. E. Carpenter.

King Leopold's Soliloquy. PBSA, lvii (63), 351-2.
J. F. Guido.

Mark Twain and the *Golden Era*. PBSA, lviii (64), 8-23.
L. E. Moberley.

Toward a critical text of *The gilded age*. PBSA, lix (65), 142-9.
H. Hill

BAL addendum 3479: Twain's *A dog's tale*. PBSA, lxii (68), 617.
J. Blanck.

CLEMENT, Francis
Francis Clement's *Petie school* at the Vautrollier press, 1587. LIB, xxii (67), 1-12.
R. D. Pepper.

CLEMENTS, H. J. B.
Armorial book-stamps and their owners. LIB, xx (39/40), 121-35.

CLEMENTS, Henry
See BENNET, Thomas and CLEMENTS, Henry

CLEMENTS, Jeff
Early editions of Bloomfield's poems. (Note, 179). BC, xi (62), 216-17.

Samuel Rogers's *Poems*, 1812. (Query, 169). BC, xiii (64), 353.

CLEMENTS, William C.
See MICHIGAN *univ., W.C. Clements libr.*

CLEVERDON, Douglas
Three booksellers and their catalogues. C. S. Millard: Everard Meynell: Douglas Cleverdon. BC, iv (55), 291-8.
G. Sims.

CLINE, Clarence Lee
The missing Meredith letters. (Note, 240). BC, xiv (65), 76-8.

Sir William Hardman's Journal. (Note, 267). BC, xv (66), 207-10.

CLINE, Howard Francis
Nicolás de la Barreda and his works on the Chinantec Indians of Mexico. PBSA, liii (59), 1-14.

CLOPPENBURG PRESS
The 'Cloppenburg' Press, 1640, 1641. Illus. LIB, xiii (58), 280-2.
A. F. Johnson.

CLOUGH, Arthur Hugh
Variant binding of Clough's *Poems*. (Note, 257). BC, xiv (65), 542.
D. A. Randall.

CLUBB, Merrel Darl
Census of extant copies of Junius's *Caedmon*, 1655. (Query, 147). BC, xi (62), 218.

Junius's edition of *Caedmon*. [A letter]. LIB, xvii (62), 157.

A request for assistance. [Junius's *Caedmon*.] PBSA, lvi (62), 116.

CLUTTON, George
Notes on two French devices. Illus. LIB, xviii (37/8), 456-60.

'Abel Clémence' of 'Rouen': a sixteenth-century secret press. Illus. LIB, xx (39/40), 136-53.

CLYDE, William McCallum
Parliament and the press, 1643-7. 2 pts. LIB, xiii (32/3), 399-424; xiv (33/4), 39-58.

COBBETT, James P.
A Sketch of the life of General Lafayette. Translated from the French by James P. Cobbett. Lond., 1830. PBSA, xxxv (41), 207.
E. B. Steere.

COBBETT, William
An introduction to a bibliography of William Cobbett. Illus. LIB, xx (39/40), 1-40.
A. M. Muirhead.

COBDEN-SANDERSON, Thomas James
See SANDERSON, Thomas James Cobden-

COBHAM *lord*
See OLDCASTLE, John *lord Cobham*

COCK LORELL
The date of *Cocke Lorelle's bote* [pr. by Wynkyn de Worde]. SB, xix (66), 175-81.
P. R. Baumgartner.

COCKER, Edward
Johnson and Cocker's *Arithmetic*. PBSA, lvi (62), 107-9.
S. O. Mitchell.

COCKERELL, Douglas
The development of bookbinding methods — Coptic influence. Illus. LIB, xiii (32/3), 1-19.

COCKERELL, sir Sydney Carlyle
Robert Proctor's diaries. [A letter]. LIB, vi (51/2), 219.

Signed manuscripts in my collection. 1. Illus. BH, i (47/51), 321-8.
—. 2. BH, i (47/51), 402-4.
—. 3. BH, i (47/51), 429-49.
—. 4. BH, ii (51/2), 13-25.
—. 5. Illus. BC, i (52), 77-91.
—. 6. Illus. BC, i (52), 219-25.

COCKFIGHTING
Books on cockfighting. BH, i (47/51), 405-12.
A. J. B. Kiddell.

COCKLE, Maurice James Draffen
A Newberry Library supplement to the foreign books in M. J. D. Cockle's *A bibliography of English military books up to 1642 and of contemporary foreign works*. PBSA, lv (61), 137-9.
J. R. Hale.

COCKX-INDESTEGE, Elly
Location of Denison-Gilbey copy [of *Dit boecxken leert hoe men mach voghelen vanghen metten handen*]. BC, xvii (68), 219.

CODLOCK, Roger
An unusual form of dating quires. (Query, 143). BC, x (61), 202.

COECKE, Pieter
An alphabet by Pieter Coecke van Aelst. LIB, xxiii (42/3), 195-7.
A. F. Johnson.

COHEN, B. Bernard
Hawthorne and *Parley's Universal History*. PBSA, xlviii (54), 77-90.

COHEN, Bertha Solis
An account of a voyage for the discovery of a north-west passage . . . London: Jonah Warens. 1748/1749. PBSA, xxxvii (43), 308.

The great probability of a north-west passage: . . . London: Thomas Jefferys, 1768. PBSA, xxxix (45), 319-20.

Opening up northern North America. PBSA, xliii (49), 340-4.

COHEN, Henry Hennig
Melville's copy of Broughton's *Popular poetry of the Hindoos*. PBSA, lxi (67), 266-7.

COHEN, Morton N. *and* GREEN, Roger Lancelyn
C. L. Dodgson's correspondence. (Query, 189). BC, xiii (64), 360.

COKE, Thomas *earl of Leicester*
Thomas Coke, earl of Leicester, 1697-1759. (Portrait of a bibliophile, 2). Illus. BC, viii (59), 249-61.
W. O. Hassall.

COLBECK, Norman
Sir William Watson. Additions and corrections. (Some uncollected authors, 12). BC, vi (57), 66-7.

Variant bindings on Moxon authors. (Query, 183). BC, xiii (64), 356-7.

COLBOURN, H. Trevor
The reading of Joseph Carrington Cabell: 'A list of books on various subjects recommended to a young man . . .' SB, xiii (60), 179-88.

COLBURN, Henry
Colburn-Bentley and the march of the intellect. SB, ix (57), 197-213.
R. A. Gettmann.

COLE, Francis Joseph
Bibliographical reflections of a biologist. Illus. OBSP, v (36/9), 167-86.

COLE, George Watson
Do you know your Lowndes? A bibliographical essay on William Thomas Lowndes and incidentally on Robert Watt and Henry G. Bohn. PBSA, xxxiii (39), 1-22.

George Watson Cole. PBSA, xxxiii (39), 22-4.
V. H. Paltsits.

COLEMAN, Dorothy *and* McGOWAN, Margaret M.
Cupid and the bees: an emblem in the Stirling-Maxwell collection. Illus. BTHK, iii (60/2), 3-14.

COLEMAN, Earle E.
Edward Everett Hale: preacher as publisher. PBSA, xlvi (52), 139-50.

Éphémérides du Citoyen, 1767-1772. PBSA, lvi (62), 17-45.

—. Addendum. PBSA, lvii (63), 95-6.

COLEMAN, Thomas
Coleman, Thomas (1598-1647). *Hopes deferred and dashed*. London, for Christopher Meredith, 1645. PBSA, xxxv (41), 204.
H. R. Mead.

COLERIDGE, Samuel Taylor
Samuel Taylor Coleridge, 1772-1834. (English literary autographs, 12). Illus. BC, iii (54), 300-1.
T. J. Brown.

Samuel Taylor Coleridge, 1772-1834. (Portrait of a bibliophile, 7). BC, x (61), 275-90.
G. Whalley.

Coleridge *Marginalia* lost. Illus. BC, xvii (68), 428-42.
G. Whalley.

—. (Note, 315). BC, xviii (69), 223.
G. Whalley.

A presentation copy of Coleridge's *Sibylline Leaves*, with manuscript notes, altered readings, and deletions by the author. LIB, xvii (36/7), 221-4.
N. Van Patten.

The Bristol Library borrowings of Southey and Coleridge, 1793-8. LIB, iv (49/50), 114-32.
G. Whalley.

The printing of *Lyrical Ballads*, 1798. Illus. LIB, ix (54), 221-41.
D. F. Foxon.

Poems, by S. T. Coleridge, Esq., PBSA, xxxix (45), 163-7.
R. F. Brinkley.

Unrecorded Coleridge variants. SB, xi (58), 143-62.
D. V. Erdman.

—. Additions and corrections. SB, xiv (61), 236-45.
D. V. Erdman, L. Werkmeister *and* R. S. Woof.

A Coleridge-Wordsworth manuscript and 'Sarah Hutchinson's poets'. SB, xix (66), 226-31.
R. S. Woof.

Coleridge's *Lines to Thelwall:* a corrected text and a first version. SB, xx (67), 254-7.
C. G. Martin.

COLES, William A.
Magazine and other contributions by Mary Russell Mitford and Thomas Noon Talfourd. SB, xii (59), 218-26.

COLGRAVE, Bertram *and* MASSON, sir James Irvine O.
The *editio princeps* of Bede's prose Life of St. Cuthbert, and its printer's XIIth-century 'copy'. Illus. LIB, xix (38/9), 289-303.

COLIN, Georges
A 'vernis sans odeur' binding. (Foreign bookbindings, 3). Illus. BC, xviii (69), 361.

COLKET, Meredith B.
Family records printed during the colonial period. Illus. PBSA, lvii (63), 61-7.

COLLABORATION
See JOINT AUTHORSHIP

COLLATERAL SUBSTANTIVE TEXTS
Collateral substantive texts, with special reference to *Hamlet*. SB, vii (55), 51-67.
A. Walker.

COLLATING MACHINE
Mechanized collation a preliminary report. PBSA, xli (47), 99-106.
C. Hinman.

The poor man's mark IV or ersatz Hinman collator. Illus. PBSA, lx (66), 149-58.
V. A. Dearing.

Collating machine, poor man's, mark VII. PBSA, lxi (67), 110-3.
G. A. Smith.

Standardization of photographic reproductions for mechanical collation. Illus. PBSA, lxii (68), 237-40.
G. R. Guffey.

Hinman collators: present locations. PBSA, lxiii (69), 119-20.
A. M. Johnson.

COLLECTION OF POEMS BY SEVERAL HANDS
A collection of poems by several hands, 1693. [Identity of two of the authors]. (Query, 227). BC, xvii (68), 353.
H. Bohem.

COLLECTIONS: America
Rare books in American state university libraries. BC, vi (57), 232-43.
R. B. Downs.

Special collections for the study of history and literature in the Southeast. PBSA, xxviii (34), 97-131.
R. B. Downs *and* L. R. Wilson.

COLLECTIONS: Scotland
Records of medical and scientific societies in Scotland. I. Early medical and scientific societies of North-east Scotland. BTHK,i/2 (57), 31-3.
H. J. H. Drummond.

—. II. Records of scientific and medical societies preserved in the University Library, Edinburgh. BTHK, i/3 (58), 14-9.
C. P. Finlayson.

—. Additions. BTHK, iv (63/6), 38-9.

—. III. The records of the Royal College of Physicians of Edinburgh. BTHK, i/3 (58), 20-7.
L. Jolley.

COLLES, Christopher
Christopher Colles and his two American map series. PBSA, xlviii (54), 170-82.
L. W. Griffin.

Christopher Colles and his two American map series. [A letter]. PBSA, xlix (55), 287.
E. L. Yonge.

COLLIER, Robert Ruffin
Original and miscellaneous essays. By a Virginian . . . [R. R. Collier]. Richmond, 1829. PBSA, xxxiv (40), 359.
J. C. Wyllie.

COLLIER LEAF
See MARLOWE, Christopher

COLLINS, Arthur Jefferies
The printer's copy for an apparently lost Limoges service-book. LIB, xxiv (43/4), 87.

COLLINS, Benjamin
Account books of Benjamin Collins of Salisbury. (Query, 232). BC, xvii (68), 492.
O. M. Brack *jr*.

COLLINS, Carvel
Spirit of the Times. PBSA, xl (46), 164-8.

An extra issue of the *Spirit of the Times*. PBSA, xlviii (54), 198.

— *and* HENDERSON, Robert W.
Eugene Sue's *The King of the Winds* [*The Godolphin Arabian*] translated for the *Spirit of the Times*. PBSA, xl (46), 162-4.

COLLINS, Rowland L.
How rare are Montagu Butler's translations of Tennyson? (Query, 162). BC, xii (63), 72-3.

COLLINS, Samuel
A Cambridge proof-sheet of 1617. [Samuel Collins's *Epphata to F. T.*]. (Note, 36). BC, iii (54), 226.
A. N. L. Munby.

COLLINS, William
William Collins's *Odes*, 1747. (Query, 17). BC, i (52), 195.
W. B. Todd.

The plate in Collins's *Odes*. (Query, 17). BC, ii (53), 157.
T. R. Francis.

COLLINS, William Wilkie
Collins, Wilkie (1824-1889). *The Woman in White*. New York, 1860. PBSA, xxxvi (42), 232.
H. S. Mott.

COLOGNE
Schoolmen and printers in Old Cologne. LIB, iv (49/50), 133-5.
J. V. Scholderer.

COLOMBO, Cristoforo
The textual relations of the Thacher manuscripts on Columbus and early Portuguese navigations. PBSA, xxxiv (40), 199-220.
W. J. Wilson.

COLOMBO, Fernando
Don Fernando Colón and his London book purchases, June 1522. PBSA, lii (58), 231-48.
D. E. Rhodes.

COLÓN, Fernando
See COLOMBO, Fernando

COLONNA, Francesco
Rebound in the 16th century? [F. Colonna's *Hypnerotomachia* of 1499]. (Query, 202). BC, xv (66), 214.
A. Ehrman.

COLONNA, Vittoria
The library of Vittoria Colonna, 1490-1547? (Query, 234). BC, xviii (69), 93.
D. E. Rhodes.

COLOPHONS
Arithmetic colophons in nineteenth-century books. SB, xix (66), 244-5.
W. B. Todd.

COLOUR IDENTIFICATION
A system of color identification for bibliographical description. SB, xx (67), 203-34.
G. T. Tanselle.

COLUMBIAN PRESS
The Columbian press. Illus. JPHS, v (69), 1-23.
J. Moran.

COLUMBUS, Christopher
See COLOMBO, Cristoforo

COLVERT, James B.
Agent and author: Ellen Glasgow's letters to Paul Revere Reynolds. SB, xiv (61), 177-96.

COMAS, Guillermus Petrus
A Spanish incunable? Comas. Guillermus Petrus. *Quaestio de sudore sanguinis Christi*, [Barcelona: Johann Luschner, *ca.* 1498]. PBSA, xliii (49), 191.
C. F. Bühler.

COMMENDATORY VERSES
An index of dedications and commendatory verse. Illus. LIB, xii (57), 11-22.
F. B. Williams, *jr.*

Commendatory verses: the rise of the art of puffing. SB, xix (66), 1-14.
F. B. Williams, *jr.*

COMMON PRAYER, Book of
See PRAYER, Book of common

COMPAGNIA DEL MANTELLACCIO
The second edition of the *Compagnia del Mantellaccio*. SB, xi (58), 225-7.
C. F. Bühler.

COMPOSING MACHINE
Kniaghininsky's tape-operated composing machine. JPHS, iii (67), 93-6.
J. Moran.

COMPOSITION
See also FILM SETTING

Principles governing the use of variant spellings as evidence of alternate setting by two compositors. LIB, xxi (40/1), 78-94.
C. Hinman.

A printer's error. LIB, xxiii (42/3), 132.
J. de M. Johnson.

Compositorial practices and the localization of printed books, 1530-1800. Illus. LIB, xxi (66), 1-45.
R. A. Sayce.

Compositors methods with two quartos reprinted by Augustine Matthewes. PBSA, xliv (50), 269-70.
G. R. Price.

The compositor of the 'Pied Bull' *Lear*. SB, i (48/9), 59-68.
P. Williams.

Author, compositor and metre: copy-spelling in *Titus Andronicus* and other Elizabethan printings. PBSA, liii (59), 160-87.
H. T. Price.

The composition and printing of Middleton's *A mad world, my masters*. SB, iii (50/1), 246-52.
G. J. Eberle.

The careless compositor for '*Christian Ethicks*'. PBSA, lxiii (69), 123-6.
L. Sauls.

Compositor determination in the first folio *King Lear*. SB, v (52), 73-80.
I. B. Cauthen.

The folio text of *1 Henry IV*. SB, vi (54), 45-59.
A. Walker.

The compositors of *Hamlet Q2* and *The Merchant of Venice*. SB, vii (55), 17-40.
J. R. Brown.

The two compositors in the first quarto of Peele's *Edward I*. SB, vii (55), 170-7.
F. S. Hook.

Compositor determination and other problems in Shakespearian texts. SB, vii (55), 3-15.
A. Walker.

New approaches to textual problems in Shakespeare. SB, viii (56), 3-14.
P. Williams.

Roberts' compositors in *Titus Andronicus*, Q2. SB, viii (56), 27-38.
P. L. Cantrell *and* G. W. Williams.

Some editorial principles, with special reference to *Henry V*. SB, viii (56), 95-111.
A. Walker.

The prentice hand in the tragedies of the Shakespeare first folio: Compositor E. SB, ix (57), 3-20.
C. Hinman.

Setting by formes in quarto printing. SB, xi (58), 39-53.
G. W. Williams.

Compositor B's role in *The Merchant of Venice*, Q2, 1619. SB, xii (59), 75-90.
D. F. McKenzie.

The compositors of *Henry IV, Part 2, Much Ado About Nothing, The Shoemakers' Holiday*, and *The First Part of the Contention*. SB, xiii (60), 19-29.
W. C. Ferguson.

The influence of justification on spelling in Jaggard's compositor B. SB, xx (67), 235-9.
W. S. Kable.

COMPOSITORS
See COMPOSITION

COMPOST ET CALENDRIER DES BERGIERS
Le compost et calendrier des bergiers 1529.
(Query, 64). BC, xviii (69), 93.
W. B. Todd.

COMPUTERS
Problems in the making of computer concordances. SB, xv (62), 1-14.
S. M. Parrish.

Electronic computers and Elizabethan texts.
SB, xv (62), 15-31.
E. G. Fogel.

A computer concordance to Middle English texts. SB, xvii (64), 55-75.
A. Markman.

Emily Dickinson and the machine. SB, xviii
(65), 207-27.
S. P. Rosenbaum.

CONCEALED EDITIONS
A concealed edition? (Query, 33). BC, ii (53),
158.
A. S. Weekly.

CONCORDANCES
Problems in the making of computer concordances. SB, xv (62), 1-14.
S. M. Parrish.

A computer concordance to Middle English
texts. SB, xvii (64), 55-75.
A. Markman.

CONDIT, Lester
Editions of Little and Smith's *Easy Instructor*.
PBSA, xl (46), 233-6.

CONE, Carl B.
Edmund Burke's library. PBSA, xliv (50),
153-72.

CONGRATULARY VERSES
Cambridge books of congratulatory verses,
1603-1640, and their binders. Illus. TCBS, i
(49/53), 395-421.
J. C. T. Oates.

CONGREVE, William
William Congreve, 1670-1729. (English literary
autographs, 21). Illus. BC, vi (57), 61.
T. J. Brown.

Congreve's library. LIB, xx (39/40), 41-2.
J. Isaacs.

The cancel leaf in Congreve's *Double Dealer*,
1694. PBSA, xliii (49), 78-82.
F. T. Bowers.

CONKWRIGHT, P. J. *and* VERNER, Coolie
The printing of Jefferson's *Notes*, 1793-94.
SB, v (52/3), 201-3.

CONNECTICUT
Some notes on early Connecticut printing.
PBSA, xxvii (33), 1-11.
A. C. Bates.

Early Connecticut laws. PBSA, xl (46), 151-8.
A. C. Bates.

CONRAD, Joseph
Copies of Conrad's *Chance*, dated 1913. (Query,
198). BC, xv (66), 68.
D. Randall.

—. BC, xv (66), 213.
G. Sims.

Conrad and T. J. Wise. (Note, 272). BC, xv
(66), 350-1.
M. L. Turner.

The publication of Joseph Conrad's *Chance*.
Illus. BC, xvi (67), 305-22.
W. R. Cagle.

Conrad, Joseph. *Suspense*. PBSA, xl (46),
237-8.
F. B. Johnson.

Imposition figures and plate gangs in *The
Rescue*. SB, xiv (61), 258-62.
M. J. Bruccoli *and* C. A. Rheault.

CONSOBRINUS, Johannes
Johannes Consobrinus and his English connections. PBSA, lvii (63), 211-2.
C. F. Bühler.

CONSTANCE MISSAL
See MISSAL

CONSTANTINOPLE
The Greek press at Constantinople in 1627 and
its antecedents. Illus. LIB, xxii (67), 13-43.
R. J. Roberts.

CONSULATE OF THE SEA
Some early editions of the *Consulate of the Sea*.
Illus. PBSA, li (57), 119-25.
J. M. Edelstein.

CONTINENTAL CONGRESS
Proposals of nine printers for a new edition of
the *Journals of the Continental Congress*, 1785.
SB, ii (49/50), 189-96.
E. P. Dandridge, *jr.*

The Continental Congress considers the publication of a Bible, 1711. SB, iii (50/1), 274-81.
W. H. Gaines.

COOK, D. F.
Inverted imposition. LIB, xii (57), 193-6.

'Register of books'. 1732 [from the *Monthly
Chronicle*]. (Note, 289). BC, xvi (67), 374-5.

— *and* RICKETTS, A. N.
Kenneth Povey, 1898-1965. [An obituary notice].
LIB, xxiii (68), 51-6.

COOK, sir Edward Tyas
Some errors in the bibliography of the library
edition of John Ruskin's works [by E. T. Cook
and A. Wedderburn. London, 1912]. PBSA,
lxii (68), 127-9.
J. Halladay.

COOK, James
Collecting Captain Cook. Illus. BC, i (52), 166-73.
Sir M. Holmes.

COOKE, Ebenezer
The papers of Ebenezer Cooke. (Query, 182). BC, xiv (65), 218.
A. E. Richardson.

COOKE, John Esten
John Esten Cooke on publishing, 1865. SB, viii (56), 239-41.
I. B. Cauthen.

COOKE, William
Shirley's publishers: the partnership of Crooke and Cooke. LIB, xxv (44/5), 140-61.
A. H. Stevenson.

COOLIDGE, Joseph
Lord Byron and Mr. Coolidge of Boston. BC, xiii (64), 211-3.
E. M. Oldham.

COOPER, Anthony Ashley *3rd earl of Shaftesbury*
The first edition of Shaftesbury's *Moralists*. LIB, vii (52), 235-41.
S. F. Whitaker.

English editions of Shaftesbury's *Characteristics*. PBSA, lxi (67), 315-34.
W. E. Alderman.

COOPER, Bertram E. *and* HASKER, Richard E.
The printer of Harvard's *Humble Proposal* 1659 [i.e. Thomas Newcombe]. SB, iv (51/3), 199-201.

COOPER, Charles Purton
Letters from Lincoln's Inn, 1846-9. [Correspondence between C. P. Cooper, Q.C., and Frederick William Halfpenny]. LIB, xii (57), 256-69.
E. Halfpenny.

COOPER, T. M.
The Berne legal manuscript. EBST, ii (38/45), 379-81.

COOTE, Edmund
The English Schoolmaster: Dexter v. Burby, 1602. LIB, xxiii (42/3), 90-3.
Sir W. W. Greg.

COPE, sir Zachary Vincent
Who was Sophia Sentiment? Was she Jane Austen? BC, xv (66), 143-51.

COPE'S TOBACCO PLANT
Cope's tobacco plant: an episode in Victorian journalism. Illus. PBSA, xlv (51), 333-50.
R. D. Altick.

COPELAND, Thomas Wellsted
Burke's *Vindication of Natural Society*. LIB, xviii (37/8), 461-2.

Edmund Burke's friends and *The Annual Register*. LIB, xviii (63), 29-39.

COPINGER, Walter Arthur
A correction to Copinger. Illus. LIB, xviii (37/8), 114-6.
G. Goddard.

A probable source of Copinger's *On the authorship of the first hundred numbers of the Edinburgh Review*. LIB, ix (54), 49-53.
F. W. Fetter.

COPLAND, Robert
Six tracts about women: a volume in the British Museum. [*The deceyte of women*. A. Vele, n.d.; *The scole house of women*. J. King, 1560; Edward More, *The defence of women*. J. King, 1560; *The proude wyues pater noster*. J. King, 1560; Robert Copland, *The seuen sorowes*. W. Copland, n.d.; and, *Frederyke of Iennen*. A Vele, n.d.] LIB, xv (34/5), 38-48.
H. Stein.

COPLESTON, Edward *bp. of Llandaff*
Copleston, *Advice to a Young Reviewer*. (Note, 85). BC, vi (53), 293.
W. B. Todd.

COPPER-PLATES
See ENGRAVING

COPYBOOKS
Writing masters and copybooks. (Note, 138). BC, ix (60), 326-7.
H. G. Pollard.

Undescribed copy-books in the Ekström collection, Svenska Skolmuseet, Stockholm. LIB, xiv (33/4), 107-13.
C. Björkbom.

Printers' 'Copybooks' and the black market in the Elizabethan book trade. LIB, i (46/7), 97-105.
F. R. Johnson.

COPYE OF A LETTER SENT BY BY JOHN BRADFORTH
See CAPSTOCKE, John

COPY MONEY
Printers' perks: paper windows and copy money. LIB, xv (60), 288-91.
D. F. McKenzie.

COPYRIGHT
See also LEGAL DEPOSIT

Philip Chetwind and the Allott copyrights. LIB, xv (34/5), 129-60.
H. Farr.

The copyright of *Hero and Leander*. LIB, xxiv (43/4), 165-74.
Sir W. W. Greg.

The copyright-holder of the second edition of the Rheims New Testament, Antwerp, 1600, Richard Gibbons, S. J. LIB, vi (51), 116-20.
H. R. Hoppe.

The copyright of Elizabethan plays. LIB, xiv (59), 231-50.
L. Kirschbaum.

The laws of Elizabethan copyright: the Stationers' view. LIB, xv (60), 8-20.
C. J. Sisson.

Records in the Copyright Office of the Library of Congress deposited by the United States District Courts, 1790-1870. Illus. PBSA, xxxi (37), 81-101.
M. A. Roberts.

Early copyright litigation and its bibliographical interest. PBSA, xxxvi (42), 81-96.
R. C. Bald.

Author's copyright in England before 1640. PBSA, xl (46), 43-80.
L. Kirschbaum.

Copyright and Andrew Law. PBSA, liii (59), 150-9.
I. Lowens.

The Putnams in copyright: the father, the son, and a ghost. [*An argument on behalf of international copyright, 1840*]. PBSA, lxiii (69), 15-22.
H. Ehrlich.

Prologue to copyright in America: 1772. SB, xi (58), 259-62.
R. G. Silver.

Copyright records and the bilbiographer. SB, xxii (69), 77-124.
G. T. Tanselle.

COPY TEXT
Pynson's manuscript of *Dives and Pauper*. Illus. LIB, viii (53), 217-28.
M. M. Morgan.

The rationale of copy text. SB, iii (50/1), 19-36.
Sir W. W. Greg.

The meaning of copy-text. SB, xxii (69), 311-18.
P. Baender.

CORANTOS
See NEWSPAPERS

CORDASCO, Francesco G. M.
The Letters of Junius. (Query, 8). BC, i (52), 194.

An eighteenth-century forgery of Robert Wilkinson's *Merchant Royall*, 1607. LIB, v (50/1), 274.

Edward Bocquet's illustrated edition of the *Letters of Junius.* PBSA, xlvi (52), 66-7.

Adam Clarke's *Bibliographical Dictionary*, 1802-1806. SB, iv (51/2), 188-91.

CORDIALE
Corrections in Caxton's *Cordiale.* PBSA, xlviii (54), 194-6.
C. F. Bühler.

CORDINGLEY, Nora E.
Extreme rarities in the published works of Theodore Roosevelt. Illus. PBSA, xxxix (45), 20-50.

CORNCOB, Jonathan
Adventures of Jonathan Corncob, loyal American refugee, 1787, a commentary. PBSA, l (56), 101-14.
R. W. G. Vail.

CORONATION
The Coronation. A Poem, 1727. (Query, 103). BC, vii (56), 417.
J. B. Shipley.

CORRECTIONS
See also PRESS CORRECTIONS

Pen and ink corrections in mid-seventeenth-century books. LIB, xiv (33/4), 59-72.
G. Tillotson *and* A. Tillotson.

—. LIB, ii (47/8), 59-60.
W. Peery.

Coleridge's *Lines to Thelwall*: a corrected text and a first version. SB, xx (67), 254-7.
C. G. Martin.

CORSON, James Clarkson
The *Border Antiquities.* BTHK, i/1 (56), 23-6.

A supplementary note on *The Border Antiquities.* BTHK, iii (60/2), 15-23.

Scott's boyhood collection of chapbooks. BTHK, iii (60/2), 202-18.

Some American books at Abbotsford. BTHK, iv (63/6), 44-65.

CORY, William
A hand-list of the printed works of William Johnson, afterwards Cory, fellow of King's College, Cambridge and assistant master at Eton. TCBS, i (49/53), 69-87.
J. W. Carter.

—. Addenda and corrigenda. TCBS, iv (64/8), 318-20.
J. W. Carter.

COSIN, John *bp. of Durham*
John Cosin's *Collection of Private Devotions*, 1627. Illus. LIB, xiii (58), 282-92.
L. W. Hanson.

COSTER, Laurens Janszoon
The invention of printing. LIB, xxi (40/1), 1-25.
J. V. Scholderer.

The 'Costerian' *Liber Precum*. [A letter]. LIB, iii (48/9), 65-6.
J. C. T. Oates.

A note on Zedler's Coster theory. PBSA, xxxvii (43), 61-8.
C. F. Bühler.

COTES' WEEKLY JOURNAL
Cotes' weekly journal; or *The English stage-player.* PBSA, lvi (62), 104-6.
C. J. Stratman.

COTTERSFORD, E. Thomas
Thomas Cottersford's *Two Letters.* LIB, xi (56), 44-7.
I. B. Horst.

COTTRELL, G. W.
Henry Bradley Martin. The ornithological collection. (Contemporary collectors, 35). Illus. BC, xii (63), 316-32.

COUCH, sir Arthur Thomas Quiller
Four 'O' rarities. Illus. BH, ii (51/2), 26-35.
F. Brittain.

COUPER, William James
The writings and controversies of James Clark, minister at Glasgow, 1702-1724. GBSR, xi (33), 73-95.

COURTNEY, William Prideaux
Johnsonian bibliography, a supplement to Courtney [*A bibliography of Samuel Johnson*]. OBSP, v (36/9), 117-66.
R. W. Chapman *and* A. T. Hazen.

COURT OF VENUS
Wyatt and the several editions of *The court of Venus*. SB, xix (66), 181-95.
C. A. Huttar.

COURTS OF FANCY
The Court of Fancy in England. PBSA, lix (65), 48-9.
R. D. Harlan.

COWEN, David Lawrence
The Edinburgh dispensatories. PBSA, xlv (51), 85-96.

COWLEY, Abraham
Cowley, Abraham (1618-1667). *Verses, lately written upon several occasions*. London, for Henry Herringham, 1663. PBSA, xxxv (41), 68.
H. R. Mead.

Two issues of Cowley's *Vision*. Illus. PBSA, xlv (51), 77-81.
H. R. Mead.

The order of stanzas in Cowley and Crashaw's 'On hope'. SB, xxii (69), 207-10.
G. W. Williams.

COWLEY, Hannah
Hannah Cowley, 1743-1809. (Some uncollected authors, 16). BC, vii (58), 68-76.
J. E. Norton.

Hannah Cowley: re-impressions, not reviews. (Note, 102). BC, vii (58), 301.
W. B. Todd.

COWPER, William
William Cowper, 1731-1800. (English literary autographs, 43). Illus. BC, xi (62), 331.
T. J. Brown.

MSS. by or relating to William Cowper. (Query, 214). BC, xvi (67), 225.
C. Ryskamp.

—. BC, xvii (68), 217.
J. D. Baird.

Cowper on the King's sea-bathing. LIB, xv (60), 208-9.
C. Ryskamp.

The library of William Cowper. Addendum. TCBS, iii (59/63), 47-69, 167.
Sir G. L. Keynes.

—. Addenda. TCBS, iii (59/63), 225-31.
N. H. Russell.

Hand-list of manuscripts in the Cowper and Newton museum, Olney, Bucks. TCBS, iv (64/8), 107-27.
K. Povey.

COWPER AND NEWTON MUSEUM
See OLNEY *Cowper mus.*

COX, Nicholas
Gerard Langbaine the younger and Nicholas Cox. LIB, xxv (44/5), 67-70.
Sir W. W. Greg.

—. LIB, xxv (44/5), 186.
H. MacDonald.

COXE, Campbell R.
The pre-publication printings of Tarkington's *Penrod*. SB, v (52/3), 153-7.

COXE, Daniel
Coxe's *A description of Carolana* (1722-1741). SB, ix (57), 252-5.
R. K. Turner.

COX-JOHNSON, Ann
See JOHNSON, Ann Cox-

COYKENDALL, Frederick
Haggard, Sir Rider (1856-1925). *King Solomon's Mines*. Lond., 1885. PBSA, xxxiv (40), 90.

—. Erratum. PBSA, xxxiv (40), 273-4.

COZZENS, James Gould
The English editions of James Gould Cozzens. SB, xv (62), 207-17.
J. B. Meriwether.

CRABBE, George
Crabbe's *Inebriety* 1775. (Query, 53). BC, iii (54), 309-10.
J. Aillevard *pseud.*

An unrecorded edition of Crabbe. PBSA, xliii (49), 349-50.
F. P. Batdorf.

Notes on three editions of George Crabbe's *Tales*. PBSA, xliv (50), 276-9.
F. P. Batdorf.

Two issues of Crabbe's *Works*, 1823. PBSA, xlv (51), 250-1.
W. B. Todd.

An unrecorded early anthology of Crabbe. SB, iii (50/1), 266-7.
F. P. Batdorf.

The Murray reprints of George Crabbe: a publisher's record. SB, iv (51/2), 192-9.
F. P. Batdorf.

CRACOW *univ, bibl. Jagiellońska.*
The Jagellonian Library, Cracow. (Unfamiliar libraries, 8). Illus. BC, xiii (64), 24-32.
J. Zathey.

CRADDOCK, Patricia B.
Gibbon's revision of the *Decline and fall.* SB, xxi (68), 191-204.

CRAFTSMAN
Reprinting *The Craftsman.* (Note, 27). BC, ii (53), 279-82.
H. J. Davis.

CRAIG, David M.
'First check list' of the works of Hugh MacDiarmid. [A letter]. BTHK, ii (59/60), 35.

CRAIG, Maurice
The Irish Parliamentary bindings. Illus. BC, ii (53), 24-37.

CRAIGHTON, William
An Ipswich master-stationer's [William Craighton] tiff with his journeyman. TCBS, ii (54/8), 381-4.
J. B. Oldham.

CRAIGIE, James
A sonnet by King James VI of Scotland. EBST, ii (38/45), 404-6.

The Latin folio of King James's prose works. EBST, iii (48/55), 17-30.

—. EBST, iii (48/55), 155.

Basilicon Doron: a late seventeenth-century edition. EBST, iii (48/55), 155-6.

The *Basilicon Doron* of King James I. LIB, iii (48/9), 22-32.

CRAMPTON, Hope
Charles de Spoelberch de Lovenjoul, 1836-1907. (Portrait of a bibliophile, 6). BC, x (61), 18-27.

CRANBROOK, *4th earl of*
See GATHORNE-HARDY, John David *4th earl of Cranbrook*

CRANE, Cora Ethel E.
Cora Crane and the poetry of Stephen Crane. PBSA, lviii (64), 469-76.
J. Katz.

Cora's mouse [Stephen Crane's gift of Kipling's *The seven seas* to Cora Taylor]. PBSA, lix (65), 188-9.
M. J. Bruccoli.

CRANE, Harold Hart
Three decades in periodical criticism of Hart Crane's *The Bridge.* PBSA, lvii (63), 360-71.
J. Bloomingdale.

A further note on Hart Crane's critics. PBSA, lviii (64), 180-1.
G. T. Tanselle.

CALM addendum no. 1: Hart Crane. PBSA, lxiii (69), 130.
J. Katz.

CRANE, Hart
See CRANE, Harold Hart

CRANE, Ralph
Some notes on Crane's manuscript of *The Witch.* LIB, xxii (41/2), 208-22.
Sir W. W. Greg.

CRANE, Stephen
Crane, Stephen (1871-1900). *The Famine of Hearts.* 1899. PBSA, xxxv (41), 297.
C. Honce.

The Red badge of courage: a collation of two pages of manuscript expunged from chapter XII. PBSA, xlix (55), 273-7.
R. W. Stallman.

Stephen Crane's English years: the legend corrected. PBSA, lvii (63), 340-9.
J. B. Stronks.

A bibliographical study of Stephen Crane's poem *In the Night.* PBSA, lviii (64), 173-9.
M. Bassan.

Cora Crane and the poetry of Stephen Crane. PBSA, lviii (64), 469-76.
J. Katz.

Toward a descriptive bibliography of Stephen Crane *The black riders.* PBSA, lix (65), 150-7.
J. Katz.

Cora's mouse [Stephen Crane's gift of Kipling's *The seven seas* to Cora Taylor]. PBSA, lix (65), 188-9.
M. J. Bruccoli.

Toward a descriptive bibliography of Stephen Crane: *Spanish-American war songs* [by S. A. Witherbee]. PBSA, lxi (67), 267-9.
M. J. Bruccoli *and* J. Katz.

Grand opera for the people: an unrecorded Stephen Crane printing. PBSA, lxiii (69), 29-30.
G. Monteiro.

The Red Badge of Courage manuscript: new evidence for a critical edition. SB, xviii (65), 229-47.
W. L. Howarth.

Some new Stephen Crane items. SB, xx (67), 263-6.
G. W. Hallam.

Crane's *Red badge of courage* and other advance copies. SB, xxii (69), 273-7.
F. T. Bowers.

Scholarship and mere artifacts: the British and Empire publications of Stephen Crane. SB, xxii (69), 277-87.
M. J. Bruccoli *and* J. Katz.

CRANE, Verner Winslow
Certain writings of Benjamin Franklin on the British Empire and the American colonies. PBSA, xxviii (34), 1-27.

CRANE, Walter
Dating of Walter Crane toy books. (Query, 228). BC, xvii (68), 353.
P. H. Muir.

—. BC, xviii (69), 223.
C. S. Bliss.

CRANFIELD, Geoffrey Alan
Handlist of English provincial newspapers and periodicals, 1700-1760. Additions and corrections. TCBS, ii (54/8), 269-74.

CRANMER, Thomas *abp. of Canterbury*
Nicholas Harpsfield's note of Cranmer's recantation. TCBS, iv (64/8), 310-12.
J. Fines *and* J. M. Fletcher

CRASHAW, Richard
Textual revision in Crashaw's *Upon the bleeding crucifix*. SB, i (48/9), 191-3.
G. W. Williams.

The order of stanzas in Cowley and Crawshaw's 'On hope'. SB, xxii (69), 207-10.
G. W. Williams.

CRASHAW, William
The fatal vesper [by W. Crashaw] and T. Goad's] *The doleful evensong*: claim-jumping in 1623. LIB, xxii (67), 128-35.
A. Freeman.

The library of William Crashaw. Illus. TCBS, ii (54/8), 213-28.
P. J. Wallis.

CRASTER, sir Herbert Henry Edmund
Co-operation between college libraries. OBSP, iv (50), 43-52.

CRAWFORD, *27th earl of*
See LINDSAY, David Alexander E. *27th earl of Crawford*

CRAWFORD, Ronald L.
A note on Robert Aitken, printer of the 'Bible of the Revolution'. BTHK, v (67/70), 36-7.

The enigma of John Fraser. BTHK, v (67/70), 106-10.

CREDENHILL
Traherne's hand in the Credenhill records. LIB, xxiv (69), 50.
L. Sauls.

CREE, Joseph
Verses addressed by Joseph Cree, To the Gentlemen and Ladies, To whom he carries The New-York Gazetteer. January 1, 1775. PBSA, xxxiv (40), 187.
O. Wegelin.

CREECH, William
Justice to William Creech. PBSA, lx (66), 453-64.
S. Parks.

Robert Burns and William Creech — a reply. PBSA, lxi (67), 357-9.
G. R. Roy.

CREMER, Robert Wyndham Ketton-
Johnson's last gifts to Windham. BC, v (56), 354-6.

Locker-Lampson's *Lyra Elegantium*, 1867. (Note, 113). BC, viii (59), 296.

CRESCENTINO
The brothers De Cregoriis at Crescentino? Illus. LIB, xvii (62), 316-17.
D. E. Rhodes.

CREVENNA
Crevenna and La Vallière. (Note, 35). BC, iii (54), 148-9.
D. M. Rogers.

CRICKET
Cricket in *The Matrimonial Magazine*. (Note, 71). BC, v (56), 276.
A. Rogers.

CRITICAL HISTORY OF CHILDREN'S LITERATURE
A Critical History of Children's Literature [by C. Meigs and others]: a second list of errata. PBSA, xlviii (54), 263-7.
E. F. Walbridge.

CRITICAL REVIEW OF THE . . . BUILDINGS.
A Critical Review of the . . . Buildings, 1734. (Query, 107). BC, viii (59), 72.
J. B. Shipley.

CROCHET BOOKS
English knitting and crochet books of the nineteenth century. 2 pts. Illus. LIB, x (55), 25-40, 103-19.
E. Potter.

CROKE, sir George
The printing of sir George Croke's *Reports*. SB, xi (58), 231-46.
L. Spencer.

CROLL, Robert Henderson
Australian book plates, some makers and owners. Illus. BH, i (47/51), 381-401.

CROM, Mathew
A misdated testament printed by Crom. LIB, xvii (62), 155-6.
C. Clair.

CROMEK, Robert Hartley
A slashed copy [in Wellesley College Library] of *Reliques of Robert Burns* [collected and published by R. H. Cromek], 1808. (Note, 265). BC, xv (66), 67.
H. D. French.

Cromek's *Reliques of Robert Burns* a footnote to Egerer 112 [J. W. Egerer's *A bibliography of Robert Burns*]. BTHK, v (67/70), 33-5.
H. D. French.

CROMWELL, Oliver
A binding by Lewis for Oliver Cromwell, 1656. (English bookbindings, 29). Illus. BC, viii (59), 168.
H. M. Nixon.

Another binding for Oliver Cromwell. (Note, 117). BC, viii (59), 299-300.
H. M. Nixon.

CRON, B. S.
Dr. Arthur Simony. (Query, 93). BC, vii (58), 188.

CRONE, Gerald Roe
Early atlases of the British Isles. Illus. BH, i (47/51), 340-4.

A note on Bradock Mead, alias John Green. LIB, v (50/1), 42-3.

CROOKE, Andrew
Shirley's publishers: the partnership of Crooke and Cooke. LIB, xxv (44/5), 140-61.
A. H. Stevenson.

CROSBY, James O'Hea
The poet Claudian in Francisco de Quevedo's *Sueño del Juicio final*. PBSA, lv (61), 183-91.

CROSS PETITION
The *Cross Petition*, 1643. Illus. EBSP, xv (30/5), 55-76.
J. D. Ogilvie.

CROSSE, Gordon
Charles Jennens as editor of Shakespeare. LIB, xvi (35/6), 236-40.

CROSSE, Henry
Henry Crosse's *Vertues Common-wealth*. PBSA, xliii (49), 196-9.
R. O. Hummel *jr*.

CROW, John William
A thing called *Adagia*. LIB, iv (49/50), 71-3.

Thomas Goad and *The dolefull euen-song*; an editorial experiment. Illus. TCBS, i (49/53), 238-59.

CROWLEY, Francis
Voltaire at Stationers' Hall. LIB, x (55), 126-7.

CROWLEY, Joseph Donald
A false edition of Hawthorne's *Twice-told tales*. PBSA, lix (65), 182-8.

CRUIKSHANK, George
Cruikshank's *Uncle Tom's Cabin,* 1851. (Note, 183). BC, xi (62), 345-7.
W. B. Todd.

Advertisements in Cruikshank's *The Bee and the Wasp*. (Query, 150). BC, xi (62), 352.
J. M. Shaw.

Two editions of 'Cruikshank's Grimm'. (Note, 286). BC, xvi (67), 82-3.
G. Wakeman.

Cruishank's *Sketch Book*: the 'Gold' question. Illus. PBSA, xl (46), 225-8.
J. P. Holbrook.

A Cruikshank catalogue raisonné. PBSA, xli (47), 144-7.
J. P. Holbrook.

CRUM, Margaret Campbell
Notes on the texts of William Lawes's songs in B.M. MS. Add. 31432. LIB, ix (54), 122-7.

A manuscript of John Wilson's songs. LIB, x (55), 55-7.

Notes on the physical characteristics of some manuscripts of the poems of Donne and of Henry King. LIB, xvi (61), 121-32.

CRUMP, Galbraith Miller
Thomas Stanley's manuscript of his poems and translations. TCBS, ii (53/8), 359-65.

CRUTCHLEY, Brooke
The Penguin achievement. (Penguin books: three short essays, 2). BC, i (52), 211-3.

CULLEN, William
Two inquiries about the bibliography of William Cullen. BTHK, i/1 (56), 28-9.
L. Jolley.

A note on the portraiture of William Cullen. Illus. BTHK, i/3 (58), 27-36.
L. Jolley.

The Beauties of Magazines and an engraving of William Cullen. BTHK, i/4 (58), 40-2.
R. H. Carnie.

CUMBERLAND, Richard
Press figures and book reviews as determinants of priority: a study of Home's *Douglas, 1757,* and Cumberland's *The Brothers*, 1770, PBSA, xlv (51), 72-6.
W. B. Todd.

CUMING, Agnes
Frankfurt book-fair catalogues. (Query, 106). BC, viii (59), 71.

CUNARD, Nancy
The Hours Press. Retrospect, catalogue, commentary. BC, xiii (64), 488-96.

CUNNINGHAM, John
John Cunningham's *Day: a pastoral:* illustrator of 1854 edition. (Query, 243). BC, xviii (69), 521.
J. M. Shaw.

CUNNINGHAM, Robert Newton
A bibliography of the writings of Peter Anthony Motteux. OBSP, iii (31/3), 317-37.

CURLING, Henry
The recollections of Rifleman Harris [by H. Curling]. BH, i (47/51), 450-4.
C. Ray.

CURLL, Edmund
Edmund Curll and the 'cursed blunders' in Fresnoy's *New Method of Studying History*, 1728. LIB, ix (54), 200-5.
B. J. Enright.

The Edward Young-Edmund Curll quarrel, a review. Illus. PBSA, lxii (68), 321-35.
H. Leek.

'The unspeakable Curll': prolegomena. SB, xiii (60), 220-3.
R. L. Haig.

CURRIER, Thomas Franklin
The Autocrat of the Breakfast-Table: a bibliographical study. PBSA, xxxviii (44), 284-311.

CURRY, Kenneth
The contributors to *The Annual Anthology*. PBSA, xlii (48), 50-65.

Two new works of Robert Southey. SB, v (52/3), 197-200.

CURTIS, Newton Mallory
Addenda to Wright [*American fiction 1774-1850*]: Burdett, Curtis, Judson, Weeks. PBSA, lxii (68), 452-3.
W. S. Kable.

CUTTS, John P.
British Museum Additional MS. 31432. William Lawes' writing for the theatre and the court. LIB, vii (52), 225-34.

CZECHOSLOVAKIA
Early Czech books. (Note, 41). BC, iv (55), 73-4.
A. Varadi.

CZERWINSKI, Roman
Robert Landor and *Guy's Porridge Pot*. LIB, xvi (61), 44-8.

D

DAHL, Folke
Short-title catalogue of English corantos and newsbooks, 1620-1642. Illus. LIB, xix (38/9), 44-99.

Amsterdam — cradle of English newspapers. Illus. LIB, iv (49/50), 166-78.

DAICHES, David
The centenary of *Leaves of Grass*. Two Whitman catalogues. BC, iv (55), 324-6.

DAILY JOURNAL
Two notes on Samuel Richardson. Richardson's chapel rules. The printer of the *Daily Journal*. LIB, xxiii (68), 242-7.
T. C. D. Eaves *and* B. D. Kimpel.

DALE, Donald
The 1680 'Antwerp' edition of Rochester's *Poems*. LIB, xx (39/40), 105-6.

DALRYMPLE, sir David *3rd bart., lord Hailes*
Bishop Percy's annotated copy of Lord Hailes's *Ancient Scottish Poems* [by G. Bannatyne]. EBST, ii (38/45), 432-7.
A. F. Falconer.

Lord Hailes's contributions to contemporary magazines. SB, ix (57), 233-44.
Robert Hay Carnie.

DALTON, Jack P.
A note on D. H. Lawrence. PBSA, lxi (67), 269.

DALTON, John
An unrecorded Dalton prospectus, 1808. (Note, 112). BC, viii (59), 295.
R. G. Neville.

DALY, Denis
An eighteenth-century Irish gentleman's library. (Rt. Hon. D. Daly, of Dunsdandle, Co. Galway). BC, ii (53), 173-6.
T. G. Sadleir.

Denis Daly's library. (Note, 28). BC, ii (53), 282.
G. D. Painter.

DAMON, Samuel Foster
The negro in early American songsters. PBSA, xxviii (34), 132-63.

DAMON AND ALEXIS
Damon and Alexis: nuptial satire or political squib? PBSA, xlix (55), 354-8.
N. Varga.

DANA, Henry Wadsworth Longfellow
and HAWTHORNE, Manning
The origin of Longfellow's *Evangeline*. Illus. PBSA, xli (47), 165-203.

DANDRIDGE, Edmund P.
Proposals of nine printers for a new edition of the *Journals of the Continental Congress*, 1785. SB, ii (49/50), 189-96.

DANIEL, Carter A.
West's revisions of *Miss Lonelyhearts*. SB, xvi (63), 232-43.

DANIEL, Petrus
A possible new source for Servius Danielis on *Aeneid* III-V. SB, iv (51), 129-41.
A. F. Stocker.

The Servius of Cassel for *Aeneid* III-V. SB, vi (54), 93-100.
A. F. Stocker.

DANIEL, Samuel
Some bibliographical notes on Samuel Daniel's *Civil Wars*. SB, iv (51), 31-9.
J. G. McManaway.

DANIEL PRESS
The Daniel Press. PBSA, lv (61), 40.
A. C. Berol.

DANSKIN, Henry
Henry Danskin's *De Remoris*: a bio-bibliographical note. BTHK, i/2 (57), 15-25.
R. Donaldson.

DANTE ALIGHIERI
A rediscovered Dante *Credo*. PBSA, i (56), 181-2.
T. R. Adams.

Cary: *Dante*. (Query, 1). BC, i (52), 54.
H. Marlow *pseud*.

—. BC, i (52), 127-8.
S. Roscoe.

DARBYSHIRE, Helen
The chronology of Milton's handwriting. Illus. LIB, xiv (33/4), 229-35.

DARLEY, George
George Darley, 1795-1846. (Some uncollected authors, 28). BC, x (61), 186-92.
C. Woolf.

Cancels in Darley's *Sylvia*, 1827. (Query, 146). BC, x (61), 337.
S. Nowell-Smith.

George Darley's *Poems* [1890]. (Note, 169). BC, x (61), 449.
J. S. G. Simmons.

DART, Thurston
Henry Loosemore's organ-book [now in New York Public Library, Drexel 5469]. TCBS, iii (59/63), 143-51.

A suppressed dedication for Morley's four-part madrigals of 1594. Illus. TCBS, iii (59/63) 401-5.

DARTMOUTH COLLEGE
The Dartmouth College library. (Unfamiliar libraries, 10). Illus. BC, xv (66), 175-82.
H. F. West.

Rastell fragments at Dartmouth. Illus. LIB, xxiv (43/4), 66-73.
R. Nash.

An American colonial calligraphic sheet of King Charles's Twelve good rules at Dartmouth College library. Illus. LIB, vii (52), 111-16.
R. Nash.

DARWIN, Charles Robert
The first edition of *On The Origin of Species*.
(Note, 130). BC, ix (60), 77-8.
E. A. Osborne.

—. BC, x (61), 446.

Variant issues of *On the Origin of Species*,
1859. (Note, 131). BC, ix (60), 78.
W. B. Todd.

Issues of the fifth thousand of *On the Origin
of Species*. (Note, 222). BC, xiii (64), 213-4.
R. B. Freeman.

Issues of the fifth edition of *On the Origin of
Species*. (Note, 225). BC, xiii (64), 350.
R. B. Freeman.

On the Origin of Species, 1859. Illus. BC, xvi
(67), 340-44.
R. B. Freeman.

—. (Note, 297). BC, xvii (68), 215.
W. Nethery.

DATES
Dates in English imprints, 1700-54. LIB, xii
(57), 190-3.
R. M. Wiles.

The dates in certain German incunabula.
PBSA, xxxiv (40), 17-67.
F. R. Goff.

DAVANZATI, Mariotto
Mariotto Davanzati and an unrecorded incun-
able. LIB, vii (52), 51-3.
D. E. Rhodes.

DAVENANT, Charles
The writings of Charles Davenant, 1656-1714.
LIB, xi (56), 206-12.
D. Waddell.

DAVENANT, sir William
The first edition of *Gondibert*: quarto or
octavo? LIB, xx (39/40), 167-79.
C. M. Dowlin.

The manuscript corrections and printed
variants in the quarto edition of *Gondibert*,
1651. LIB, xx (65), 298-309.
D. H. Woodward.

D'Avenant, Sir William (1608-1668). *Gondibert: an heroick poem*. London, John Holden,
1651. PBSA, xxxv (41), 68-9.
H. R. Mead.

DAVID, Charles Wendell
The correspondence of Admiral Du Pont.
[A letter]. LIB, xiv (59), 132.

The Longwood library. PBSA, li (57), 183-202.

DAVIDSON, Alexander
How Benson J. Lossing wrote his *Field Books*
of the Revolution, the War of 1812 and the
Civil War. PBSA, xxxii (38), 57-64.

French Policy Defeated . . . London, 1760.
PBSA, xxxiv (40), 86.

*A Memorial containing a Summary View of
Facts*. PBSA, xxxiv (40), 87.

Pownall, Thomas (1722-1805). *Considerations
towards a General Plan of Measures for the
English Provinces*. New-York printed, Edinburgh
reprinted, 1756. PBSA, xxxiv (40), 88.

Pownall, Thomas (1722-1805). *A Memorial
Addressed to the Sovereigns of America . . .*
London, 1783. PBSA, xxxiv (40), 88.

Ramsay, David (1749-1815). *The History of the
American Revolution . . .* London, 1791. PBSA,
xxxiv (40), 88.

Harvey, Edward (fl. 1750). *A New Manual;
and Platoon Exercise*. New-York: 1769.
PBSA, xxxiv (40), 359.

*An Impartial Relation of the Hail-Storm on the
Fifteenth of July and the Tornado on the
second of August, 1799*. Norwich: 1799.
PBSA, xxxiv (40), 359.

James Rivington and Silas Deane. PBSA, lii
(58), 173-8.

DAVIDSON, Thomas
Fragments of *The Palyce of honour* of Gawin
Douglas, printed by Thomas Davidson at
Edinburgh *c*. 1540. Illus. EBST, iii (48/55),
31-46.
W. Beattie.

DAVIES, John
Davies, John (1565?-1618). Wittes pilgrimage.
London [1605?]. PBSA, xxxvi (42), 63.
E. M. Sowerby.

DAVIES, John. *of Kidwelly*
John Davies of Kidwelly 1627?-1693, translator
from the French. With an annotated bibliography of his translations. PBSA, xliv (50),
119-52.
J. E. Tucker.

DAVIES, sir John
Some later editions of sir John Davies's *Nosce
Teipsum*. LIB, i (46/7), 136-42.
J. Sparrow.

Additional observations on the later editions of
Nosce Teipsum. LIB, ii (47/8), 61-3.
R. H. Perkinson.

Sir John Davies' *Nosce Teipsum*, 1599: a
bibliographical puzzle. SB, i (48/9), 133-48.
G. J. Eberle.

DAVIES, William Twiston
A bibliography of John Bale. Illus. OBSP, v
(36/9), 201-79.

DAVIN, Daniel Marcus
John Locke, (Query, 86). BC, vi (57), 292.

DAVIS, Curtis Carroll
Wise words from Virginia: the published
writings of John S. Wise, of the Eastern Shore
and New York City. PBSA, liv (60), 273-85.

Mr. Legaré inscribes some books. The literary
tenets, and the library, of a Carolina writer.
PBSA, lvi (62), 219-36.

DAVIS, Henry
See BRITISH MUSEUM Henry Davis collection.

DAVIS, Herbert John
Reprinting the *Craftsman*. (Note, 26). BC, ii (53), 279-82.

Notes on a cancel in *The Alchemist*. Illus. BC, xiii (58), 278-80.

Jonathan Swift and the *Four Last Years of the Queen*. [A letter]. LIB, xvi (35/6), 344-6.

Bowyer's paper stock ledger. Illus. LIB, vi (51), 73-87.

DAVIS, Irving
Tammaro de Marinis. (Contemporary collectors, 21). Illus. BC, viii (59), 262-70.

DAVIS, Richard Beale
George Sandys v. William Stansby: the 1632 edition of Ovid's *Metamorphosis*. LIB, iii (48), 193-212.

Early editions of George Sandys's *Ovid*: the circumstances of production. PBSA, xxxv (41), 255-76.

Two new manuscript items for a George Sandys bibliography. PBSA, xxxvii (43), 215-22.

Sandys' *Song of Solomon*: its manuscript versions and their circulation. PBSA, i (56), 328-41.

In re George Sandys' Ovid. SB, xiii (56), 226-30.

Jefferson as collector of Virginiana. SB, xiv (61), 117-44.

DAVIS, Richard Beale *and* LIEVSAY, John L.
A Cavalier library — 1643. [The library of Sir Thomas Bludder]. SB, vi (54), 141-60.

DAVIS, Robert G.
A reply [to W. B. Todd's 'Texts and Pretexts']. PBSA, xlvi (52), 165.

DAVIS, Robert Murray
Textual problems in the novels of Evelyn Waugh. PBSA, lxii (68), 259-63.

The text of Firbank's *Vainglory*. PBSA, lxiii (69), 36-41.

Textual problems in the novels of Evelyn Waugh. PBSA, lxiii (69), 41-6.

The anthologist: editor vs. compiler. [L. Trilling's *The experience of literature*]. PBSA, lxiii (69), 321-3.

DAVIS, Tom
J. D. Salinger: a checklist. PBSA, liii (59), 69-71.

DAVISON, Peter H.
The Fair Maid of the Exchange. Illus. LIB, xiii (58), 119-20.

The annotations to copies of Thomas Milles's books in the British Museum and Bodleian libraries. Illus. LIB, xvi (61), 133-9.

DAVISON, William
Bewick, Catnach, and William Davison. (Query, 161). BC, xii (63), 72.
P. C. G. Isaac.

William Davison of Alnwick, pharmacist and printer. LIB, xxiv (69), 1-32.
P. C. G. Isaac.

DAWSON, Giles E.
An early list of Elizabethan plays [in the commonplace book of Henry Oxinden]. LIB, xv (34/5), 445-56.

A bibliographical problem in the first folio of Shakespeare. LIB, xv (34/5), 445-56.

The Arlaud-Duchange portrait of Shakespeare. Illus. LIB, xvi (35/6), 290-4.

A note on the Arlaud-Duchange portrait of Shakespeare. LIB; xviii (37/8), 342-4.

Three Shakespeare piracies in the eighteenth century. [*Hamlet, Othello,* and *Macbeth*]. Illus. SB, i (48/9), 47-58.

Warburton, Hanmer and the 1745 edition of Shakespeare. SB, ii (49/50), 35-48.

Some bibliographical irregularities in the Shakespeare fourth folio. SB, iv (51/2), 93-103.

Guide-lines in small formats, about 1600. SB, xiv (61), 206-8.

DAWSON, John
Concerning two anonymous printings by John Dawson. PBSA, lvii (63), 218-9.
G. W. Stuart, *jr.*

Two more anonymous printings by John Dawson. PBSA, lvii (63), 445-6.
G. W. Stuart, *jr.*

DAWSON, Lawrence R.
A checklist of reviews by Charles Williams. PBSA, lv (61), 100-17.

DAWSON, Warren Royal
A bibliography of the printed works of Dawson Turner. TCBS, iii (59/63), 232-56.

DAY, Cyrus Lawrence *and* MURRIE, Eleanore Boswell
English song-books, 1651-1702, and their publishers. Illus. LIB, xvi (35/6), 355-401.

Playford *versus* Pearson. LIB, xvii (36/7), 427-47.

DAY, John *1522-1584*
The design of Day's Saxon. Illus. LIB, xxii (67), 283-98.
G. Wakeman.

DAY, John *1574-1640*
Correction at press in the quarto of *Law-Trickes*. LIB, ii (47/8), 186-90.
W. Peery.

Correction at press in *The blind-beggar of Bednal-Green*. PBSA, xli (47), 140-4.
W. Peery.

DAY, Robert Adam
Aphra Behn's first biography [*Life and memoirs . . . by one of the fair sex*]. SB, xxii (69), 227-40.

DEAN, Harold Lester
An identification of the *Gentleman of Virginia*. PBSA, xxxi (37), 10-20.

DEAN, Irene F. M.
The Scottish textile industries. GBSR, xi (33). 96-107.

DEANE, Edmund
Spadacrene Anglica. (Note, 47). BC, iv (55), 170-1.
R. G. Neville.

DEANE, Silas
James Rivington and Silas Deane. PBSA, lii (58), 173-8.
A. Davidson, *jr*.

DEARDEN, James Shackley
Thomas Gabitus. (Query, 20). BC, i (52), 197.

John Ruskin's bookplates. Illus. BC, xiii (64), 335-9.

John Ruskin's *Poems*, 1850. (Query, 201). BC, xv (66), 214.

The production and distribution of John Ruskin's *Poems* 1850. Illus. BC, xvii (68), 151-67.

Wise and Ruskin. I. BC, xviii (69), 45-56.

John Ruskin's bookplates. (Note, 303). Illus. BC, xviii (69), 88-9.

II, ii. Forgeries. iii. Binary editions. BC, xviii (69), 170-188.

Wise and Ruskin III, iv. Wise's editions of letters from John Ruskin. BC, xviii (69), 318-39.

John Ruskin, the collector, with a catalogue of the illuminated and other manuscripts formerly in his collection. Illus. LIB, xxi (66), 124-54.

DEARING, Vinton A.
New light on the first printing of the letters of Pope and Swift. LIB, xxiv (43/4), 74-80.

Some routines for textual criticism. LIB, xxi (66), 309-17.

Two notes on the copy for Pope's *Letters*. PBSA, li (57), 327-33.

The poor man's mark IV or ersatz Hinman collator. Illus. PBSA, lx 66), 149-58.

Abaco-textual criticism. PBSA, lxii (68), 547-78.

Dryden's *MacFlecknoe*: the case for authorial revision. SB, vii (55), 85-102.

DE BEER, Esmond Samuel
George Sandy's account of Campania. LIB, xvii (36/7), 458-65.

The correspondence between Sir Thomas Browne and John Evelyn. LIB, xix (38/9), 103-6.

François Schott's *Itinerario d'Italia*. LIB, xxiii (42/3), 57-83.

Robert Langton's *Pylgrimage*. LIB, x (55), 58-9.

DECEYTE OF WOMEN
Six tracts about women; a volume in the British Museum. [*The deceyte of women*. A. Vele, n.d.; *The scole house of women*. J. King, 156; Edward More, *The defence of women*. J. King, 1560; *The proude wyues pater noster*. J. King, 1560. Robert Copland, *The Seuen sorowes*. W. Copland, n.d.; and *Frederyke of Lennen*. A. Vele, n.d.]. LIB, xv (34/5), 38-48.
H. Stein.

DECLARATION OF INDEPENDENCE
French publications of the Declaration of Independence and the American Constitutions, 1776-1783. PBSA, xlvii (53), 313-38.
D. Echeverria.

Thomas Jefferson and the Declaration of Independence. (Dukedom large enough, 3). PBSA, lvi (62), 472-80.
D. A. Randall.

DECHERT, Robert
A new copy of the Paris 1660 Jesuit *Relation*, with notes on other editions. PBSA, lvi (62), 368-72.

DEDICATIONS
A collection of poems by several hands . . . 1693. Identity of authors. (Query, 227). BC, xvii (68), 353.
H. Bohem.

Special presentation epistles before 1641: a preliminary check-list. Illus. LIB, vii (52), 15-20.
F. B. Williams *jr*.

An index of dedications and commendatory verse. Illus. LIB, xii (57), 11-22.
F. B. Williams, *jr*.

A suppressed dedication for Morley's four-part madrigals of 1594. Illus. TCBS, iii (59/63), 143-51.
T. Dart.

DEE, John
An identification of some manuscripts owned by Dr. John Dee and Sir Simonds D'Ewes. LIB, xiii (58), 194-8.
A. G. Watson.

DEELEY, Ann *and* GIBSON, Strickland
Fragments of accounts relating to the Royal Works from Oxford bindings. LIB, xxv (44/5), 66-7.

DEFOE, Daniel
Daniel Defoe, 1661?-1731. (English literary autographs, 24). Illus. BC, vi (57), 387.
T. J. Brown.

A 'lost' edition, 1745, of Defoe's *Roxana*. (Query, 99). BC, vii (58), 295.
S. Peterson.

—. (Query, 99). BC, xi (62), 483-4.
W. R. Cagle.

Sale catalogue of Defoe's library. (Note, 147). BC, ix (60), 454-5.
A. O'Donovan.

The printers of *Robinson Crusoe*. LIB, vii (52), 124-31.
K. I. D. Maslen.

The canon of Defoe's writings. LIB, vi (56), 155-69.
J. R. Moore.

Defoe's *Proposals* for printing the *History of the Union*. Illus. LIB, xi (56), 202-6.
J. H. P. Pafford.

Defoe: a specimen of a catalogue of English verse, 1701-1750. LIB, xx (65), 277-97.
D. F. Foxon.

Edition quantities for *Robinson Crusoe*, 1719. LIB, xxiv (69), 145-50.
K. I. D. Maslen.

An Eskimo translation of Defoe's *Robinson Crusoe*. Godthaal, Greenland, 1862-1865. illus. PBSA, xxxvi (42), 56-8.
N. Van Patten.

DE FOREST, John William
A checklist of the writings of John William De Forest, 1826-1906. SB, viii (56), 185-94.
E. R. Hagemann.

DEGRUSON, Gene
An unlocated Bret Harte — Joaquin Miller book. [*Thompson's Prodigal and other sketches*]. PBSA, lxi (67), 60.

DEKKER, Thomas
The Honest Whore or *The converted Courtezan*. LIB, xv (34/5), 54-60.
Sir W. W. Greg.

The undated quarto of *1 Honest Whore*. [A letter]. LIB, xvi (35/6), 241-2.
H. Spencer.

Bibliographical problems in Dekker's *Magnificent Entertainment*. LIB, xvii (36/7), 333-9.
F. T. Bowers.

Dekker's *Magnificent Entertainment*. [A letter]. LIB, xvii (36/7), 476-8.
Sir W. W. Greg.

Thomas Dekker: two textual notes. [*The roaring girle*, 1601; *The honest whore*, 1605]. LIB, xviii (37), 338-41.
F. T. Bowers.

Thomas Dekker: further textual notes. LIB, xix (38/9), 176-9.
J. G. McManaway.

The manuscript and the quarto of the *Roaring Girl*. LIB, xi (56), 180-6.
G. R. Price

The collaboration of Dekker and Webster in *Northward Ho* and *Westward Ho*. PBSA, lvi (62), 482-6.
P. B. Murray.

The compositors of Henry IV, Pt. 2, *Much Ado About Nothing, The Shoemaker's holiday,* and *The First Part of the Contention*. SB, xiii (60), 19-29.
W. C. Ferguson.

—. *and* WEBSTER, John
If you know not me you know nobidie, and *The famous historie of sir Thomas Wyat*. LIB, xiii (32/3), 272-81.
M. F. Martin.

DE LA MARE, Walter John
A handlist of the writings in book form, 1902-1953, of Walter de la Mare. Addendum. SB, vi (54), 197-217; viii, 269-70.
L. Clark.

DELEON, Thomas Cooper
T. C. DeLeon's *The Rock or The Rye*. PBSA, lvii (63), 354-6.
B. W. Korn.

DELL, Floyd
Floyd Dell in the *Friday Literary Review*. PBSA, lvii (63), 371-6.

D'ELWES, sir Simonds *1st bart.*
See D'EWES, sir Simonds

DE L'OBEL
See L'OBEL, de

DE MORGAN, Augustus,
De Morgan's incorrect description of Maurolico's books. PBSA, li (57), 111-18.
E. Rosen.

DENISON-GILBEY
Location of Denison-Gilbey copy [of *Dit boecxken leert hoe men mach voghelen vanghen metten handen*]. BC, xvii (68), 219.
E. Cockx-Indestege.

DENNIS, Rodney G.
Attributions of critical notices in the *North American Review*. PBSA, lviii (64), 292-3.

DE QUINCEY, Thomas
Thomas de Quincey, 1785-1859. (English literary autographs, 34). Illus. BC, ix (60), 179.
T. J. Brown.

DERRA DE MORODA, Frederika
Chorégraphie. The dance notation of the eighteenth century: Beauchamp or Feuillet? Illus. BC, xvi (67), 450-76.

DE SAUTY, A.
A mosaic binding by A. de Sauty, c. 1904.
(English bookbindings, 18). Illus. BC, v (56),
248.
H. M. Nixon.

DES GRAZ, Charles Geoffrey
'The Doctor'. [Dr. Rosenbach]. Illus. BC, i
(52), 176-9.

Charles Geoffrey des Graz, 1893-1953. Illus.
BC, ii (53), 133-7.
A. N. L. Munby.

DETECTIVE FICTION
Hawkshaw rides again. BC, xii (63), 178-83.
J. W. Carter.

DE UTILITATE MISSAE
Missa. [De utilitate missae. Rome. Johann
Besicken, after 1500?]. PBSA, xxxvii (43),
158.
C. F. Bühler.

DEUTSCH, Otto Erich
The editions of Morley's Introduction. LIB,
xxiii (42/3), 127-9.

Music bibliography and catalogues. Illus. LIB,
xxiii (42/3), 151-70.

DEVAL, Laurie
The bibliography of Beatrix Potter. Illus.
BC, xv (66), 454-9.

DEVENTER
Printing at Deventer in the fifteenth century.
Illus. LIB, xxiv (43/4), 101-19.
L. A. Sheppard.

DEVEREUX, Edward James
The English editions of Erasmus's Catechismus.
LIB, xvii (62), 154-5.

Some lost English translations of Erasmus.
LIB, xvii (62), 255-9.

DEVEREUX, Robert 3rd earl of Essex
An inventory of the lord general's library, 1646.
LIB, xxi (66), 115-23.
V. F. Snow.

DEVICES
A bookseller's stamp. (Query, 37). BC, ii (53),
222-3.
J. C. T. Oates.

—. BC, ii (53), 223.
L. W. Hanson.

—. BC, ii (54), 149.
T. R. Francis.

—. BC, iv (55), 254.
H. E. Hammelmann.

Elliot Stock's devices. (Query, 76). BC, v (56),
384.
H. R. Page.

DE VOTO, Bernard Augustine
Typee and De Voto once more. PBSA, lxii
(68), 601-4.
G. T. Tanselle.

D'EWES, sir Simonds 1st bart.
An identification of some manuscripts owned
by Dr. John Dee and Sir Simonds D'Ewes.
LIB, xiii (58), 194-8.
A. G. Watson.

Sir Simonds [D'Ewes] buys a manuscript.
PBSA, i (56), 379-81.
R. H. Bowers.

DEWEY, Melvil
[Dewey, Melvil]. A Classification and Subject
Index for Cataloguing and Arranging the
Books and Pamphlets of a Library. Amherst,
Mass., 1876. PBSA, xl (46), 236-7.
M. W. Getchell.

DEXTER, Robert
The English Schoolmaster [by E. Coote]:
Dexter v. Burby, 1602. LIB, xxiii (42/3), 90-3.
Sir W. W. Greg.

DIBDIN, Thomas Frognall
Portraits of T. F. Dibdin. (Note, 46). Illus.
BC, iv (55), 168-70.
A. N. L. Munby.

W. A. Jackson's Dibdin: a revised entry.
BC, xv (66), 352-3.
W. H. Bond.

DICEY FAMILY
The Diceys and the chapbook trade. Illus. LIB,
xxiv (69), 219-31.
V. E. Neuburg.

DICK, Hugh G.
The authorship of Foure Great Lyers, 1585.
LIB, xix (38/9), 311-4.

DICKENS, Charles
See also HOUSEHOLD WORDS

Charles Dickens, 1812-1870. (English literary
autographs, 15). Illus. BC, iv (55), 237.
T. J. Brown.

The Tauchnitz David Copperfield, 1849. (Note,
53). BC, iv (55), 253-4.
P. H. Muir.

Dickens and Tauchnitz. (Note, 55). BC, iv (55),
329.
P. H. Muir.

Dickens's A Tale of Two Cities, 1859. (Note, 94)
BC, vii (58), 80.
W. B. Todd.

Dickens's Christmas Carol. (Note, 170). BC, x
(61), 449-54.
W. B. Todd.

Dicken's Battle of Life: round six. Illus. BC, xv
(66), 48-54.
W. B. Todd.

Boz's Memoirs of Joseph Grimaldi, 1838.
(Note, 277). BC, xv (66), 354-6.
R. T. Stott.

Boz's Memoirs of Joseph Grimaldi, 1838.
(Note, 277). BC, xvi (67), 80.
W. J. Smith.

A curious dance round a curious tree. (Note, 295). BC, xvii (68), 80-1.
P. H. Muir.

The Lea and Blanchard edition of Dickens's *American notes*, 1842. BC, xviii (69), 296-300.
P. Bracher.

Oliver Twist in three volumes. LIB, xviii (63), 113-32.
K. Tillotson.

The 'cheap edition' of Dickens's works [first series] 1847-1852. Illus. LIB, xxii (67), 245-51.
S. Nowell-Smith.

Dickens' *Christmas Carol* after a hundred years: a study in bibliographical evidence. PBSA, xxxix (45), 271-317.
P. Calhoun *and* H. J. Heaney.

Dickensiana in the rough. PBSA, xli (47), 293-320.
P. Calhoun *and* H. J. Heaney.

Some Dickens variants. PBSA, xli (47), 344.
H. R. Mead.

The chapter numbering in *Oliver Twist*. PBSA, lx (66), 337-43.
J. Schweitzer.

'Woodcuts dropped into the text': the illustrations in *The Old Curiosity Shop* and *Barnaby Rudge*. Illus. SB, xx (67), 113-34.
J. Stevens.

DICKIE, William M.
Richard de Bury and the *Philobiblon*. Illus. BH, i (47/51), 282-92.

DICKINS, Bruce
Thumbnail sketch of an Edinburgh scholar. [William Law Mathieson, 1868-1938]. EBST, ii (38/45), 450-1.

The Irish broadside of 1571 and Queen Elizabeth's types. Illus. TCBS, i (49/53), 48-60.

Stationers made free of the City in 1551/2 and 1552. TCBS, i (49/53), 194-5.

John Heaz, Elizabethan letter-founder to the printers. TCBS, i (49/53), 287.

Samuel Page Sidnall and his press at Grantchester, 1871-1892. Illus. TCBS, ii (54/8), 366-72.

—. Addenda. TCBS, iii (59/63), 95.

—. Further addenda. TCBS, iii (59/63), 176-8.

Henry Gostling's library. TCBS, iii (59/63), 216-24.

The U.L.C. copy of *Posthumous fragments of Margaret Nicholson*. TCBS, iii (59/63), 423-7.

Printed playbills in the Peninsular war. TCBS, iv (64/8), 314-17.

DICKINSON, Emily Elizabeth
Emily Dickinson: a check list of criticism, 1930-1966. PBSA, lxi (67), 359-85.
S. Freis.

Establishing a text: the Emily Dickinson papers. SB, v (52), 21-32.
T. H. Johnson.

Emily Dickinson and the machine. SB, xviii (65), 207-27.
S. P. Rosenbaum.

DICKINSON, Gladys
Fourquevaux and military art in the sixteenth century. EBST, ii (38/45), 397-8.

A work assigned to Bernault D'Aubigny. EBST, iii (48/55), 81.

DICKINSON, J. C. *and* BARNES, F.
A seventeenth-century Cambridge book and its cost. [John Armstrong's *Secret and family prayers* and *The souls worth and danger*]. TCBS, ii (54/8), 376-81.

DICKINSON, Leon T.
Marketing a best seller: Mark Twain's *Innocents Abroad*. Illus. PBSA, xli (47), 107-22.

DICKINSON, William Croft *and* PLANT, Marjorie
The Bray collection in the British Library of Political and Economic Science. EBST, ii (38/45), 440-3.

DICKSON, Alexander
Alexander Dickson and S.T.C. 6823. BTHK, iii (60/2), 183-90.
J. Durkan.

DICKSON, James K.
Lewis, Sinclair (1885-   ). *The Innocents*, 1917. PBSA, xxxix (45), 167-8.

DICKSON, Sarah
The *Humours* of Samuel Rowlands. Illus. PBSA, xliv (50), 101-18.

The Melancholy Cavalier. [by J. C., in relation to S. Rowlands' *The Melancholy Knight*]. A study in seventeenth-century plagiarism. SB, v (52/3), 161-3.

DICTES AND SAYINGS OF THE PHILOSOPHERS
The Dictes and Sayings of the Philosophers. LIB, xv (34/5), 295-329.
C. F. Bühler.

The Churl and the Bird and *The Dictes and Sayings of the Philosophers* — two notes. LIB, xxi (40/1), 279-90.
C. F. Bühler.

A word on Caxton's *Dictes*. Illus. LIB, iii (48/9), 155-85.
G. Legman.

Some observations of *The Dictes and Sayings of the Philosophers*. LIB, viii (53), 77-88.
C. F. Bühler.

DICTIONARIES
Two Estienne dictionaries. LIB, xvi (61), 48-50.
D. E. Rhodes.

DIDOT, Pierre
The Didot *Horace*, 1799. (Note, 182). BC, xi (62), 345.
A. N. L. Munby.

—. BC, xi (62),480.
H. D. Lyon.

DIGBY, Everard
Presentation copies of Everard Digby's *Theoria Analytica*. LIB, xii (57), 121-2.
J. Wilks.

DIGBY, John
Digby's *Philosophical account of Nature*, 1722. (Note, 92). BC, vii (58), 79.
R. G. Neville.

—. BC, vii (58), 189.
C. A. Gordon.

DILLARD, Richard Henry W.
The writer's best solace: textual revisions in Ellen Glasgow's *The past*. SB, xix (66), 245-50.

DILLEY, E and C.
The American interests of the firm of E. and C. Dilley, with their letters to Benjamin Rush, 1770-1795. PBSA, xlv (51), 283-332.
L. H. Butterfield.

DILLON, Richard H.
Bound for Bashan. [Rev. R. B. Stratton's *Captivity of the Oatman Girls, being an interesting narrative of Life among the Apache and Mohave Indians*]. PBSA, lvii (63), 449-53.

DILWORTH, Mark
Two Ratisbon manuscripts in the National Library of Scotland. [*Ratisbona religiosa* and *Index monasteriorum Scotorum extra Scotiam*]. BTHK, v (67/70), 24-32.

DIONYSIUS *Carthusianus*
The works of Dionysius Cartusianus. LIB, xiii (58), 51-4.
J. V. Scholderer.

DISRAELI, Benjamin *earl of Beaconsfield*
The production of Disraeli's trilogy. PBSA, lviii (64), 239-51.
B. R. Jerman.

DISSENTERS
The literature of dissent in Glasgow in the latter half of the eighteenth century. Illus. GBSR, xi ((33), 56-72.
R. Morton.

The exiled English Church at Amsterdam and its press. Illus. LIB, v (50/1), 219-42.
A. F. Johnson.

DISTRIBUTION
The case of the missing apostrophes [in Dwight's *Triumph of infidelity*, 1788]. (Note, 219). BC, xiii (64), 210-11.
G. T. Tanselle.

DISTRIBUTIONAL STUDY
Some postulates for distributional study of texts. SB, iii (50/1), 63-96.
A. A. Hill.

The text of the *Envoy to Alison*. SB, v (52/3), 33-42.
H. Chewning.

DIT BOECXKEN LEERT HOE MEN MACH VOGHELEN VANGHEN METTEN HANDEN
Location of Denison-Gilbey copy [of *Dit boecxken leert men mach voghelen vanghen metten handen*]. BC, xvii (68), 219.
E. Cockx-Indestege.

DIXON, Richard Watson
Richard Watson Dixon, 1833-1900. (Some uncollected authors, 29). BC, x (61), 322-8.
S. Nowell-Smith.

DOBELL, Robert J.
The bibliography of Gilbert Burnet. [A letter]. LIB, v (50/1), 61-3.

Cancels. (Note, 19). BC, ii (53), 73.

DOBIE, Marryat R.
The development of Scott's *Minstrelsy:* an attempt at a reconstruction. EBST, ii (38/46), 65-87.

— *and* BEATTIE, William
The first twenty years of the National Library of Scotland, 1925-1945. EBST, ii (38/45), 285-302.

DOBSON, Christopher
James Ralph. (Note, 44). BC, iv (55), 168.

L'Encyclopédie in contemporary morocco. (Note, 76). BC, v (56), 280.

By Lytton or Grenville Murray? (Query, 73). BC, v (56), 281-2.

DOBSON, Jessie *and* THOMAS, Bryn
Letters to William Hunter from his American pupils, John Morgan and William Shippen jr. Illus. BTHK, iii (60/2), 61-7.

DOCKWRA, William
Will Dockwra. (Note, 45). BC, iv (55), 168.
P. H. Muir.

DOCTRINAL OF SAPIENCE
A bibliographical curiosity. [Caxton's *Doctrinal of Sapience* and Duff's *Fifteenth century English books*]. PBSA, xxxv (41), 58-60.
C. F. Bühler.

DOCTRYNALL OF SYMPLE PEOPLE
Three English books of the sixteenth century. [*Opuscules or smale werkes of saynt bonaventure; The Pomander of prayer; The doctrynall of symple people*]. Illus. LIB, xvii (36), 184-9.
Sir F. C. Francis.

DODGSON, Charles Lutwidge
Alice, 1865. (Note, 6). BC, i (52), 127.
J. Hayward.

Alice in Wonderland: proof illustrations. (Query, 79). BC, vi (57), 181.
W. H. Bond.

The first edition of Carroll's *Phantasmagoria*, 1869. (Query, 116). BC, viii (59), 184.
H. Nathanson.

—. BC, viii (59), 309.
R. L. Green.

—. BC, viii (59), 309.
J. M. Shaw.

C. L. Dodgson ['Lewis Carroll's]' correspondence. (Query, 189). BC, xiii (64), 360.
M. N. Cohen *and* R. L. Green.

Lanrick — a game for two players, by Lewis Carroll. PBSA, liii (59), 74.
A. C. Berol.

DODGSON, John McNeal
A library at Pott Chapel, Pott Shrigley, Cheshire, *c.* 1493. LIB, xv (60), 47-53.

DODINGTON, John
John Dodington's translation of Quevedo's *Los Sueños*. (Query, 189). BC, xiv (65), 367.
T. Rodgers.

DODSLEY, Robert
Dodsley's *Collection of poems by several hands*. OBSP, iii (31/3), 269-316; NS i (47), 43-4, 46.

Concurrent printing: an analysis of Dodsley's *Collection of Poems by Several Hands*. PBSA, xlvi (52), 45-57.
W. B. Todd.

Burke's authorship of the historical articles in Dodsley's *Annual Register*. PBSA, li (52), 344-9.
J. C. Weston, *jr.*

Dodsley's *Collection of poems by several hands*, six volumes, 1758. Index of authors. PBSA, lx (66), 9-30.
D. D. Eddy.

Predecessors to Burke's and Dodsley's *Annual Register*. SB, xvii (64), 215-20.
J. C. Weston, *jr.*

DOGGART, James Hamilton
Gibbon's eyesight. Illus. TCBS, iii (59/63), 406-11.

DOHENY, mrs. Edward Laurence
Reminiscences of a California collector, Mrs. Edward Laurence Doheny, 1875-1958. Illus. BC, xiv (65), 49-59.
E. Shaffer.

DOIG, Ronald Paterson
George Paton's contributions to Herbert's *Typographical antiquities*. EBST, iii (48/55), 213-19.

A note on John Baine. EBST, iii (48/55), 222.

A bibliographical study of Gough's *British Topography*. EBST, iv (55), 103-36.

DOIG, Ronald Paterson *and* CARNIE, Robert Hay
Scottish printers and booksellers 1668-1775. A supplement. SB, xii (59), 131-59.

—. A second supplement. (1) SB, xiv (61), 81-96.
R. H. Carnie.

—. A second supplement. (2). SB, xv (62), 105-20.
R. H. Carnie.

DOLE, William
The works of William Dole, a judicial inquiry. Illus. BC, xv (66), 296-302.
N. Barker.

DOLL, Conrad
The tunebook of Conrad Doll. PBSA, xlii (48), 229-38.
F. Braun *and* R. B. Brown.

DOME
The Dome, an aesthetic periodical of the 1890's. BC, vi (57), 160-9.
P. West.

DONALDSON, Robert
Henry Danskin's *De remoris*: a bio-bibliographical note. BTHK, i/2 (57), 15-25.

Nine incunabula in the Cathcart White collection in Edinburgh University Library. BTHK, ii/2 (60), 66-9.

The engraved title-pages of the *Fabrica* of Vesalius, 1543 and 1555, and a drawing in the Hunterian Library, Glasgow University. Illus. BTHK, iii (60/2), 96-7.

Two block-books in the Hunterian Library, Glasgow University. BTHK, iii (60/2), 103-4.

A mixed edition of *De Verborum Significatione*. BTHK, iii (60/2), 219-20.

An early imprint of Andro Hart. Illus. BTHK, iv (63/6), 34-6.

William Ged and the invention of stereotype, a second postscript. Illus. LIB, xxii (67), 352-4.

DONATION LABELS
A bookseller's donation-label. (Note, 134). BC, ix (60), 192-5.
J. C. T. Oates.

DONNE, John
Erratum. [The date of the first edition of Donne's *Biathanatos*]. (Note, 4). BC, i (52), 127.
H. Edwards.

Fine paper copies of Donne's *Biathanatos* [?1646]. (Note, 250). BC, xiv (65), 362.
R. S. Pirie.

Notes on the physical characteristics of some manuscripts of the poems of Donne and of Henry King. LIB, xvi (61), 121-32.
M. C. Crum.

John Donne's dark lantern. PBSA, xlix (55), 181-6.
P. Elmen.

New texts of John Donne. SB, ix (57), 225-33.
C. F. Main.

Dr. Donne and the booksellers. SB, xviii (65), 69-80.
R. C. Bald.

Books from Donne's library. TCBS, i (49/53), 64-8.
Sir G. L. Keynes.

DONOVAN, Denis G.
Two corrected forme readings in the 1632 *The anatomy of melancholy*. (Note, 276). BC, xv (66), 353-4.

A note on the text of *The anatomy of melancholy*. PBSA, lx (66), 85-6.

DORAN, Madeleine
Manuscript notes in the Bodleian copy of Bright's *Characterie*. Illus. LIB, xvi (35/6), 418-24.

DOS PASSOS, John Roderigo
A textual note on John Dos Passos' *Journeys Between Wars*. PBSA, xliii (49), 346-8.
M. Kallich.

More Dos Passos: bibliographical addenda. PBSA, xlv (51), 156-8.
W. White.

John Dos Passos' textual revisions. PBSA, xlviii (54), 95-7.
C. W. Bernadin.

Mr. Kallich replies [to C. W. Bernardin's 'John Dos Passos' textual revisions']. PBSA, xlviii (54), 97-8.
M. Kallich.

DOUBLE PP
Richard Vennar and *The Double PP*. PBSA, xliii (49), 199-202.
P. Shaw.

DOUGAN, R. O.
E. Ph. Goldschmidt, 1887-1954. Illus. LIB, ix (54), 75-84.

DOUGHTY, Dennis William
Fracastor's *Syphilis*. An issue of which perhaps the only known copy is in the Library of Queen's College, Dundee. BTHK, i/l (56), 29-30.

A note on some old books found in the High School of Dundee. BTHK, i/4 (58), 42-6.

Notes on the provenance of books belonging to Lord James Stewart, afterwards the Regent Moray, other than those in the University of St. Andrews. Illus. BTHK, iii (60/2), 75-88.

DOUGHTY, George W.
The Shadows of Life. (Query, 92). BC, vii (58), 77.

DOUGLAS, lady Eleanor
A bibliography of the printed pamphlets and broadsides of the Lady Eleanor Douglas, the 17th-century prophetess. Illus. EBSP, xv (30/5), 35-54.
C. J. Hindle.

—. [Revised]. EBST, i (35/8), 65-98.

DOUGLAS, Gawin *bp. of Dunkeld*
Fragments of *The palyce of honour* of Gawin Douglas, printed by Thomas Davidson at Edinburgh *c.* 1540. Illus. EBST, iii (48/55), 31-46.
W. Beattie.

DOUGLAS, Norman
Norman Douglas (Query, 34). BC, ii (53), 158.
C. Woolf.

—. (Query, 34). BC, ii (53), 222.
H. E. James.

DOVES PRESS
Wise forgeries in Doves bindings. (Query, 226). BC, xvii (68), 352-3.
J. Carter.

DOW, Lorenzo Americano
The opinion of Dow . . . Windham, 1804. PBSA, xxxv (41), 1205.
J. C. Wyllie.

DOWLIN, Cornell March
The first edition of *Gondibert*: quarto or octavo? LIB, xx (39/40), 167-79.

DOWLING, Margaret
Nathaniel Ponder. [A letter]. LIB, xvii (36/7), 109-10.

DOWNS, Robert Bingham
Rare books in American State University libraries. BC, vi (57), 232-43.

DOWNS, Robert Bigham *and* WILSON, Louis R.
Special collections for the study of history and literature in the southeast. PBSA, xxxviii (34), 97-131.

DOYLE, Anthony Ian
A late use of a crested roll. (Note, 12). BC, ii (53), 154-5.

The Bamburgh library. (Unfamiliar libraries, 4). Illus. BC, viii (59), 14-24.

Date of a MS in Bibliotheca Bodmeriana. (Note, 105). BC, viii (59), 69.

Thomas Betson of Syon Abbey. LIB, xi (56), 115-18.

Two medieval calendars and other leaves removed by John Bowtell from University Library MSS. TCBS, i (49/53), 29-36.

The earliest printed statutes of Pembroke College. Illus. TCBS, i (49/53), 130-8.

DOYLE, sir Arthur Conan
Holmesiana. (Note, 84). BC, vi (57), 183.
R. A. Brimmell.

Sir Arthur Conan Doyle (1879-1928). *Memoirs of Sherlock Holmes*. New York, 1894. PBSA, xxxiv (40), 190-1.
D. A. Randall.

An additional note on *The Card-board Box*. PBSA, xlvii (53), 75-6.
E. F. Walbridge.

Sherlock Holmes: rare book collector. A study in book detection. PBSA, xlvii (53), 133-55.
M. B. Stern.

DOYLE, Joseph
A finding list of manuscript materials relating to George Edward Woodberry. PBSA, xlvi (52), 165-8.

DOYLE, Paul
Mary Lavin: a checklist. BC, xviii (69), 317-21.

DOYLE, Paul A.
A rare copy of John Stedman's *Laelius and Hortensia*. PBSA, li (57), 241-4.

DRAKE, Daniel
Daniel Drake and his contributions to education. PBSA, xxxiv (40), 303-14.
E. F. Horine.

DRAKE, sir Francis
The treatment of Drake's circumnavigation in Hakluyt's *Voyages*, 1589. PBSA, xxxiv (40), 281-302.
W. H. Kerr.

'DRAWBACK'
'Drawback' in the book trade. (Query, 168). BC, xii (63), 356.
A. Wesson.

—. BC, xii (63), 494-5.
C. B. Oldman.

DRAYTON, Michael
A Drayton collection. Illus. BC, iv (55), 133-43.
B. Juel-Jensen.

Three lost Drayton items. (Query, 122). BC, ix (60), 78-9.
B. Juel-Jensen.

Polyolbion, Poemes Lyrick and pastorall, Poems 1619, *The Owle*, and a few other books by Michael Drayton. Illus. LIB, viii (53), 145-62.
B. Juel-Jensen.

Isaac Oliver's portrait of Prince Henry and *Polyolbion*, a footnote. Illus. LIB, x (55), 206-7.
B. Juel-Jensen.

An Oxford variant of Drayton's *Polyolbion*. Illus. LIB, xvi (61), 53-4.
B. Juel-Jensen.

Michael Drayton and William Drummond of Hawthornden: a lost autograph letter rediscovered. Illus. LIB, xxi (66), 328-30.
B. Juel-Jensen.

DREIS, Hazel
Lancaster, Pennsylvania, bookbindings. An historical study. PBSA, xlii (48), 119-28.

DREW, Fraser Bragg
Some contributions to the bibliography of John Masefield. 2 pts. PBSA, liii (59), 188-96. 262-7.

DREYFUS, John Gustave
John Baskerville's books. BC, viii (59), 185-9.

George Friend 1881-1969: a memoir. Illus. JPHS, v (69), 81-6.

The Baskerville punches 1750-1950. Illus. LIB, v (50/1), 26-48.

Baskerville's ornaments. Illus. TCBS, i (49/53), 173-7.

—. and KINGSFORD, R. J. L.
John Baskerville, proposals for a revised edition of Straus and Dent's bibliography and memoir. TCBS, i (49/53), 191-2.

DRING, E. M.
An early blurb. (Query, 12). BC, i (52), 130.

DRUE, Thomas
Thomas Drue's *Duchess of Suffolk*: a Protestant drama. SB, iii (50), 241-6.
L. M. Oliver.

DRUMMOND, H. J. H.
Records of Medical and Scientific Societies in Scotland. 1. Early Medical and Scientific Societies of North-East Scotland. BTHK, i/2 (57), 31-3.

Aberdeen University Library special collections. (Printed books). BTHK, iii (60/2), 35-40.

DRUMMOND, William *1585-1649*
William Drummond of Hawthornden. (Query, 187). BC, xii (64), 360.
R. H. MacDonald.

Michael Drayton and William Drummond of Hawthornden: a lost autograph letter undiscovered. Illus. LIB, xxi (66), 328-30.
B. Juel-Jensen.

DRYDEN, John
John Dryden, 1631-1700. (English literary autographs, 3). Illus. BC, i (52), 180-1.
T. J. Brown.

Some unrecorded variants in the first edition of Dryden's *All for Love*, 1678. (Note, 232). BC, xiii (64), 498-500.
P. Caracciolo.

John Dryden's *All for Love*: unrecovered editions. PBSA, lvii (63), 77-9.
C. J. Stratman.

Dryden, Tonson, and subscriptions for the 1697 *Virgil*. PBSA, lvii (63), 129-51.
J. Barnhard.

Dryden's *Indian Emperour*: the early editions and their relation to the text. SB, ii (49/50), 139-52.
J. S. Steck.

The Dryden *Troilus and Cressida* imprint: another theory. [A sequel to F. T. Bowers 'Variants in early editions of Dryden's plays'. *Harvard Library Bulletin*, III, no 2 (1949), 280-3]. SB, ii (49/50), 185-9.
P. S. Dunkin.

A prompt copy of Dryden's *Tyrannic Love.*
SB, iv (51/2), 170-4.
H. H. Adams.

The early editions of Dryden's *State of Innocence.* SB, v (52/3), 163-6.
M. H. Hamilton.

The pirated quarto of Dryden's *State of Innocence.* SB, v (52/3), 166-9.
F. T. Bowers.

The manuscripts of Dryden's *The State of Innocence* and the relation of the Harvard Ms. to the first quarto. SB, vi (54), 237-46.
M. H. Hamilton.

Dryden's *MacFlecknoe*: the case for authorial revision. SB, vii (55), 85-102.
V. A. Dearing.

DUBLIN
Stephen Hero's bookshop. BC, xiv (65), 194-9.
A. Walbank.

DUBLIN, *Trinity coll., libr.*
The *Piers Plowman* manuscripts in Trinity College, Dublin. LIB, vi (51/2), 141-50.
E. St. J. Brooks.

DUCHANGE, G.
See ARLAUD-DUCHANGE PORTRAIT OF SHAKESPEARE

DUCK, Stephen
Duck and the Duchess of Newcastle. (Note, 14). BC, i (52), 265.
D. Grant.

DUDLEY, Robert *earl of Leicester*
A binding by the Dudley binder, *c.* 1558. (English bookbindings, 30). Illus. BC, viii (59), 282.
H. M. Nixon.

DUDLEY BINDER
A binding by the Dudley binder, *c.* 1558. (English bookbindings: 30). Illus. BC, viii (59), 282.
H. M. Nixon.

DÜRER, Albrecht
Books illustrated by Albert Dürer. LIB, xv (34/5), 385-7.
Sir. T. D. Barlow.

DUFF, Edward Gordon
The early London editions of the *Doctrinale* of Alexander Grammaticus: with a note on Duff 224. LIB, xxiv (69), 232-4.
D. E. Rhodes.

A bibliographical curiosity. [Caxton's *Doctrinal of Sapience* and Duff's *Fifteenth Century English Books*]. PBSA, xxxv (41), 58-60.
C. F. Bühler.

DUGARD, William
William Dugard, pedagogue and printer to the Commonwealth. PBSA, lii (58), 179-204.
L. Rostenberg.

Thomas Fuller, William Dugard, and the pseudonymous *Life of Sidney*, 1655. PBSA, lxii (68), 501-10.
D. H. Woodward.

DUMAS, Alexandre *1802-1870*
Dumas: some translation difficulties. (Query, 4). BC, i (52), 54-5.
F. W. Reed.

Dumas: *La Maison de Savoie.* (Query, 5). BC, i (52), 55-6.
F. W. Reed.

DUMFRIES MERCURY
The date of the *Dumfries Mercury.* GBST, iv (18), 61-4.
W. J. Couper.

DUNCAN, Archibald Alexander
An interim list of the heads of some Scottish monastic houses before *c.* 1300. Edited from the papers of the late D. W. Hunter Marshall. BTHK, ii (59/60), 4-27.

DUN COW
The authorship of *Guy's Porridge Pot* and *The Dun Cow.* LIB, v (50/1), 55-8.
R. H. Super.

DUNDEE *high sch.*
A note on some old books found in the High School of Dundee. BTHK, i/4 (58), 42-6.
D. W. Doughty.

DUNDEE *Queen's coll., libr.*
See DUNDEE *univ., libr.*

DUNDEE *univ., libr.*
Fracastor's *Syphilis.* An issue of which perhaps the only copy is in the Library of Queen's College, Dundee. BTHK, i/1 (56), 29-30.
D. W. Doughty.

DUNDEE *St. Paul's cathedral, libr.*
A note on *God's Judgement upon the Gentile Apostatized Church & A Treatise of the Three Evils of the Last Times,* with special reference to a volume in the library of St. Paul's Cathedral Dundee, which contains both title-pages. BTHK, iii (60/2), 31-4.
R. C. Rider.

DUNIWAY, David Cushing
A study of the Nuremberg Chronicle. PBSA, xxxv (41), 17-34.

DUNKIN, Paul S.
Issues of *The Fairy Queen*, 1692. [E. Settle's operatic adaptation of *A Midsummer Night's Dream*]. LIB, xxvi (45/6), 297-304.

Foxe's *Acts and Monuments*, 1570, and single-page imposition. Illus. LIB, ii (47/8), 159-70.

The 1613 editions of Bacon's *Essays.* LIB, iii (48/9), 122-4.

The Whole Works of Homer;... Translated... by Geo: Chapman. Lond., (1616). PBSA, xl (46), 230-1.

Two notes on Richard Hooker. PBSA, xli (47), 344-6.

A Warning for Tabacconists. PBSA, xlii (48), 148-50.

The state of the issue. PBSA, xlii (48), 239-55.

—. [A letter]. PBSA, xliii (49), 93.

The ghost of the turned sheet. PBSA, xlv (51), 246-50.

The Dryden *Troilus and Cressida* imprint: another theory. SB, ii (49/50), 185-9.

DUNLAP, Leslie Whittaker
United States. Inspector's Office. Washington, Feb. 19, 1812. *At a General Court-Martial, . . . Brigadier General James Wilkinson was tried...* PBSA, xxxiv (40), 189-90.

DUNLOP, Annie Isabella
Registers of supplications. Registra supplicationum. EBST, ii (38/45), 383-4.

DUNNE, Tom *and* WHITE, Norman
A Hopkins discovery [in L. Magnus's and C. Headlam's *Prayers from the poets: a calendar of devotion]*. LIB, xxiv (69), 56-8.

DUNSANY, lord
See PLUNKETT, Edward John M.D., 18th baron Dunsany.

DUNTON, John
John Dunton and *The Works of the Learned*. LIB, xxiii (68), 13-24.
S. Parks.

DU PONT, Samuel Francis
The correspondence of Admiral Du Pont. [A letter]. LIB, xiv (59), 132.
C. W. David.

DUPRE, Robert
MSS. of *The Life of Sir Thomas More*. (Query, 182). BC, xiii (64), 356.

DURANTUS, Gulielmus, *bp. of Mende*
A French version of Duranti's prescription on the presentation of Papal bulls. LIB, xxiii (42/3), 84-9.
S. H. Steinberg.

D'URFEY, Thomas
Thomas D'Urfey's *Comical History of Don Quixote*, 1694. PBSA, xliii (49), 191-5.
F. T. Bowers.

Thomas D'Urfey's *Richmond Heiress*, 1693: a bibliographical study. SB, v (52), 169-78.
R. A. Biswanger.

DURIE, John
Notes on John Durie's *Reformed Librarie-Keeper*. LIB, i (46/7), 64-7.
G. H. Turnbull.

DURING, Richard L. *and* DURING; Sheila M.
An Ulm unicum of 1501 [M. Puff von Schrick's *Ain guts nutzlichs büchlin von den auss geprenten wassern*] in the National Library of Medicine, Bethesda, Maryland. Illus. LIB, xx (65), 55-7.

DURING, Sheila M. *see* DURING, Richard L.

DURKAN, John
Henry Scrimgeour, Fugger librarian: a biographical note. BTHK, iii (60/2), 68-70.

The library of St. Salvator's College, St. Andrews. BTHK, iii (60/2), 97-100.

An Arbroath book inventory. BTHK, iii (60/2), 144-6.

Alexander Dickson and S.T.C. 6823. BTHK, iii (60/2), 183-90.

Andrew Leech, Scottish latinist. BTHK, iv (63/6), 24-34.

George Buchanan: some French connections. BTHK, iv (63/6), 66-72.

David Lauxius. EBST, iii (48/55), 78-80.

—. A further note. EBST, iii (48/55), 156-7.

Robertus Richardinus and S.T.C. 21021. EBST, iii (48/55), 83-4.

DURLING, Richard Jasper
Two unrecorded Edinburgh theses of 1676 and 1680. BTHK, ii (59/60), 63-6.

Unsigned editions of Galen and Hippocrates, 1527: further light on an elusive printer. LIB, xvi (61), 55-7.

DURRELL, Lawrence George
Recollections of a Durrell collector. (Some uncollected authors, 23). BC, ix (60), 56-63.
L. C. Rowell *and* A. G. Thomas.

Regarding a checklist of Lawrence Durrell. PBSA, lv (61), 142-52.
A. Knerr.

DU SEUIL, Abbé
The library of Louis-Henri de Loménie, Comte de Brienne, and the bindings of the Abbé Du Seuil. Illus. LIB, xvii (62), 105-31.
R. Birley.

DUST, Alvin I. *and* STANTON, Ralph G.
A defense of Innocencio [Francisco da Silva]. PBSA, lxi (67), 241-3.

DUSTIN, John E.
The 1735 Dublin edition of Swift's *Poems*. PBSA, liv (60), 57-60.

DUTHIE, George Ian
The text of Shakespeare's *Romeo and Juliet*. SB, iv (51/2), 3-29.

DUVEEN, Denis Ian
The Duveen alchemical and chemical collection. (Contemporary collectors, 11). Illus. BC, v (56), 331-42.

Conrad Gesner and his *Thesaurus Evonymi Philiatri*. Illus. BH, i (47/51) 422-8.

Two alchemical books. [Khunrath's *Amphitheatrum Sapientiae Solius Verae*; and Count Michael Maier's *Atalanta Fugiens*]. BH, ii (51/2), 51-5.

Notes on some alchemical books. Illus. LIB, i (46/7), 56-61.

—. *and* KLICKSTEIN, Herbert S.
Le Journal polytype des sciences et des arts. Illus. PBSA, xlviii (54), 402-10.

DUYN, Cornelius
English manuscripts owned by Johannes, Limmerius and Cornelius Duyn. LIB, xxii (41/2), 205-7.
N. R. Ker.

DWIGHT, Timothy
The case of the missing apostrophes in Dwight's *Triumph of infidelity*, 1788]. (Note, 219). BC, xiii (64), 210-1.
G. T. Tanselle.

DYSON, Gillian
The manuscripts and proof sheets of Scott's Waverley novels. EBST, iv (55), 13-42.

DYSON, Humphrey
Humphrey Dyson's library, or some observations on the survival of books. PBSA, xliii (49), 279-87.
W. A. Jackson.

E

E., J. M. *and* Metzdorf, Robert Frederic
Donald Frizell Hyde 1909-1966 [an obituary].
PBSA, lx (66), 101.

EAGLE, Roderick L.
The *Arcadia*, 1593, title-page border. LIB, iv
(49/50), 68-71.

EAMES, Wilberforce
The Lennox-Eames classification scheme at
the William L. Clements Library. PBSA, xliv
(50), 87-100.
R. B. Brown.

EARLE, John *bp. of Salisbury*
The 1628 editions of John Earle's *Micro-cosmographie*. LIB, xxi (66), 231-4.
B. Juel-Jensen.

EASTERLING, P. E.
Two Greek MSS. of Spanish provenance in
Bishop Moore's collection. TCBS, iii (59/63),
257-62.

Greek manuscripts in Cambridge: recent acquisitions by college libraries, the Fitzwilliam
museum and private collectors. TCBS, iv
(64/8), 179-91.

EATON, Peter
Shaw and Shaviana. (Note, 185.) BC, xi (62),
349-50.

Churchilliana. (Note, 230). BC, xiii (64), 352-3.

EAVES, Thomas Cary Duncan
The publication of the first translations of
Fielding's *Tom Jones*. LIB, xxvi (45/6),
189-90.

A note on Lord Byron's *Select Works*, 1823.
LIB, i (46/7), 70-2.

An unrecorded children's book illustrated by
Thomas Bewick. LIB, v (50/1), 272-3.

—. *and* KIMPEL, Ben D.
Two notes on Samuel Richardson. Richardson's
chapel rules. [*and*] the printer of the *Daily
Journal*. LIB, xxiii (68), 242-7.

Richardsoniana. SB, xiv (61), 232-4.

Samuel Richardson's London houses. Illus.
SB, xv (62), 135-48.

Richardson's revisions of *Pamela*. SB, xx
(67), 61-88.

EBEL, Julie G.
A numerical survey of Elizabethan translations.
illus. LIB, xxii (67), 104-27.

EBERLE, Gerald J.
Sir John Davies' *Nosce Teipsum*, 1599: a
bibliographical puzzle. SB, i (48/9), 133-48.

The composition and printing of Middleton's
A mad world, my masters. SB, iii (50/1),
246-52.

EBERSTADT, Charles
Nickerson, Freeman (fl. 1850). *Death of the
Prophets Joseph and Hyram Smith*. Boston:
1844. PBSA, xxxv (41), 160.

Leonard, H. L. W. *Oregon Territory*. Cleveland:
1846. PBSA, xxxvi (42), 66.

EBERSTADT, Lindley
The passing of a noble *Spirit*. PBSA, xliv (50),
372-3.

EBY, Cecil D.
Bryant's *The Prairies*: notes on date and text.
PBSA, lvi (62), 356-7.

ECCLES, Mark
Bynneman's books. LIB, xii (57), 81-92.

ECHEVERRIA, Durand
French publications of the Declaration of
Independence and the American Constitutions,
1776-1783. PBSA, xlvii (53), 313-38.

EDDISON, Eric Rücker
E. R. Eddison. BH, i (47/51), 53-7.
G. R. Hamilton.

EDDY, Donald D.
Samuel Johnson's editions of Shakespeare
(1765). PBSA, lvi (62), 428-44.

Dodsley's *Collection of poems by several
hands*, six volumes, 1758, index of authors.
PBSA, lx (66), 9-30.

The printing of Fielding's *Miscellanies*, 1743.
SB, xv (62), 247-56.

EDEL, Joseph Léon
Addendum to Edel and Laurence [*A bibliography of Henry James*]: Henry James's *Future
of the novel*. PBSA, lxiii (69), 130.
G. N. Monteiro.

EDELSTEIN, David Simeon
Joel Munsell: printer and bibliographer. PBSA,
xliii (49), 383-96.

Joel Munsell prints Lossing's *Memorial of
Alexander Anderson*. PBSA, xlv (51), 351-5.

EDELSTEIN, Jerome Melvin
Some early editions of the *Consulate of the Sea*.
Illus. PBSA, li (57), 119-25.

Two autographs of a ' Sienese Gentleman ' in
the Library of Congress. PBSA, liv (60), 291-3.

Another Bulgarini book. PBSA, lvi (62), 482.

Another Bulgarini volume. PBSA, lviii (64), 24.

EDES, Benjamin
Benjamin Edes, trumpeter of sedition. PBSA,
xlvii (53), 248-68.
R. G. Silver.

EDINBURGH
The Edinburgh Dispensatories. PBSA, xlv (51),
85-96.
-D. L. Cowen.

EDINBURGH *Advocates' libr.*
See NATIONAL LIBRARY OF SCOTLAND.

EDINBURGH *city, roy. coll. of physicians*
See ROYAL COLLEGE OF PHYSICIANS OF EDINBURGH.

EDINBURGH *nat. libr. of Scotland*
See NATIONAL LIBRARY OF SCOTLAND.

EDINBURGH *univ.*
Two unrecorded Edinburgh theses of 1676 and 1680. BTHK, ii (59/60), 63-6.
R. J. Durling.

EDINBURGH *univ. libr.*
Records of medical and scientific societies in Scotland. II. Records of scientific and medical -societies preserved in the University Library, Edinburgh. BTHK, i/3 (58), 14-9.
C. P. Finlayson.

—. Additions. BTHK, iv (63/9), 38-9.

Nine incunabula in the Cathcart White collection in Edinburgh University Library. BTHK, ii (59/60), 66-9.
R. Donaldson.

The Sarolea papers in Edinburgh University Library. BTHK, iii (60/2), 24-31.
D. F. Griffiths.

Notes on C. R. Borland's *A Descriptive Catalogue of Western Mediaeval Manuscripts in Edinburgh University Library*, 1916. BTHK, iii (60/2), 44-52.
C. P. Finlayson.

A note on the Edinburgh University Library MS. DK. 5-25, 'Brian Fairfax's Account'. BTHK, iii (60/2), 71-2.
W. Ferguson.

Thomas Carlyle's borrowings from Edinburgh University Library, 1819-1820. Illus. BTHK, iii (60/2), 138-43.
C. P. Finlayson.

Carlyle's borrowings from the Theological Library of Edinburgh university. BTHK, v (67/70), 165-8.
I. Campbell.

National Library of Scotland and Edinburgh University Library copies of plays in Greg's *Bibliography of the English Printed Drama*. SB, xvi (62), 91-104.
M. Linton.

EDINBURGH BIBLIOGRAPHICAL SOCIETY
The story of the Edinburgh Bibliographical Society. EBST, xv (32/5), 77-86.
G. P. Johnston.

EDINBURGH ENCYCLOPEDIA
The Edinburgh Encyclopedia, 1808-30. BC, x (61), 75.
C. Kruyskamp.

The Edinburgh Encyclopaedia, 1808-30. (Query, 141). BC, x (61), 201.
J. Fyfe.

EDINBURGH REVIEW
On some authors of *Edinburgh Review* articles, 1830-1849. LIB, vii (52), 38-50.
L. G. Johnson.

Edinburgh Review authors, 1830-49. LIB, vii (52), 212-4.
C. Blagden.

Sydney Smith's contributions to the *Edinburgh Review*. LIB, viii (53), 275-8.
J. Murphy.

A probable source of Copinger's *On the Authorship of the first hundred Numbers of the Edinburgh Review*. LIB, ix (54), 49-53.
F. W. Fetter.

EDITION
Early references to size of edition. (Note, 65). BC, v (56), 171.
A. Ehrman.

Designation of edition on the title-page. (Note, 200). BC, xii (63), 350.
A. Ehrman.

EDITORIAL PROBLEMS
The problem of the variant forme in a facsimile edition. LIB, vii (52), 262-72.
F. T. Bowers.

Textual problems in Restoration broadsheet prologues and epilogues. LIB, xii (57), 197-203.
R. Morton.

Henry James: some bibliographical and textual matters. Illus. LIB, xx (65), 108-23.
B. Birch.

Some routines for textual criticism. LIB, xxi (66), 309-17.
V. A. Dearing.

On the indifferent and one-way variants in Shakespeare. LIB, xxii (67), 189-204.
E. A. J. Honigmann.

A reply [to W. B. Todd's 'Texts and pretexts'] PBSA, xlvi (52), 165.
R. G. Davis.

Two unique copies of Stephen Gosson's *Schoole of Abuse*, 1579: criteria for judging nineteenth-century editing. PBSA, lix (65), 425-9.
A. F. Kinney.

Abaco-textual criticism. PBSA, lxi (68), 547-78.
V. A. Dearing.

Textual problems in the novels of Evelyn Waugh. PBSA, lxii (68), 259-63.
R. M. Davis.

Editorial problems — a preliminary survey. SB, iii (50), 3-17.
R. C. Bald.

The rationale of copy-text. SB, iii (50), 19-36.
Sir W. W. Greg.

Some relations of bibliography to editorial problems. SB, iii (50), 37-62.
F. T. Bowers.

Some postulates for distributional study of texts. SB, iii (50), 63-96.
A. A. Hill.

Bibliography and the editorial problem in the eighteenth century. SB, iv (51), 41-55.
W. B. Todd.

Compositor determination and other problems in Shakespearian texts. SB, vii (55), 3-15.
A. Walker.

Collateral substantive texts, with special reference to *Hamlet*. SB, vii (55), 51-67.
A. Walker.

New approaches to textual problems in Shakespeare. SB, viii (56), 3-14.
P. Williams.

Editorial problems in Shakespeare: semi-popular editions. SB, viii (56), 15-26.
A. Brown.

Some editorial principles, with special reference to *Henry V*. SB, viii (56), 95-111.
A. Walker.

Principles of annotation: some suggestions for editors of Shakespeare. SB, ix (57), 95-105.
A. Walker.

Editing the letters of letter-writers. SB, xi (58), 25-37.
R. Halsband.

The rationale of old-spelling editions of the plays of Shakespeare and his contemporaries. SB, xiii (60), 49-67.
J. R. Brown.

The rationale of old spelling editions of the plays of Shakespeare and his contemporaries: a rejoinder [to J. R. Brown's article]. SB, xiii (60), 69-76.
A. Brown.

Literary problems in seventeenth-century scientific manuscripts. SB, xiv (61), 69-80.
H. W. Jones.

Electronic computers and Elizabethan texts. SB, xv (62), 13-31.
E. G. Fogel.

Some principles for scholary editions of nineteenth-century American authors. SB, xvii (64), 223-8.
F. T. Bowers.

A quantitative solution to the ambiguity of three texts. SB, xviii (65), 147-82.
A. Hrubý.

Today's Shakespeare texts, and tomorrow's. SB, xix (66), 39-65.
F. T. Bowers.

EDMONDSON, Godfrey
See EMERSON, Godfrey

EDMONSTON, Elizabeth
Sion College. (Unfamiliar libraries, 9). Illus. BC, xiv (65), 165-77.

EDWARD VI *king of England*
London binding for King Edward VI, *c.* 1550. (English bookbindings, 4). Illus. BC, i (52), 244-5.
H. M. Nixon.

A binding presented to Edward VI, *c.* 1552. (English bookbindings, 2). Illus. BC, ii (53), 272-3.
H. M. Nixon.

EDWARDS *family*
Edwards of Halifax, bookbinders. Illus. BH, i (47/51), 329-38.
T. W. Hanson.

EDWARDS, H. W.
Erratum. [The date of the first edition of Donne's *Biathanatos*]. (Note, 4). BC, i (52), 127.

Mrs. Thomson and Miss Pigott. (Note, 86). BC, vi (57), 405.

EDWARDS, Harry Stillwell
Edwards, Harry Stillwell (1854-1938). *Eneas Africanus*. PBSA, xxxiv (40), 273.
J. Blanck.

EDWARDS, Jonathan
Jonathan Edwards MSS. and books from his library. (Query, 174). BC, xiii (64), 71.
G. S. Claghorn.

[Edwards, Jonathan.] *Conversion of President Edwards*. American Tract Society, 1825. PBSA, xxxvii (43), 308-9.
R. W. Christ.

EELES, F. C. *and* ARNOLD, J. H.
Some leaves of a thirteenth-century missal probably from Jedburgh Abbey. [*With*] Notes on the music. EBST, iii (48/55), 1-15.

EGERER, Joel Warren
Cromek's *Reliques of Robert Burns*, a footnote to Egerer 112 [J. W. Egerer *A Bibliography of Robert Burns*]. BTHK, v (67/70), 33-5.
H. D. French.

Thomas Stewart, Robert Burns and the law. PBSA, lvi (62), 46-55.

EHRENPREIS, Irvin
Swift's April Fool for a bibliophile. BC, ii (53), 205-8.

EHRLICH, Heyward
The Putnams on copyright: the father, the son, and a ghost. [*An argument in behalf of international copyright,* 1840]. PBSA, lxiii (69), 15-22.

EHRMAN, Albert
See also BROXBOURNE LIBRARY.

An English miscellany printed abroad. (Query, 32). BC, ii (53), 79-80.

The School Press. (Query, 44). BC, iii (54), 73.

The Broxbourne Library. (Contemporary collectors, 2). Illus. BC, iii (54), 190-7.

Castano psalter. (Note, 43). BC, iv (55), 168.

Beaulieu Abbey account book, XIII. (Note, 50). BC, iv (55), 252.

Book club in Huntingdon. (Query, 68). BC, v (56), 79.

Early references to size of edition. (Note, 65). BC, v (56), 171.

Incunable towns. (Note, 72). BC, v (56), 277.

The Garrison Press, Gibraltar. (Query, 75). BC, v (56), 384.

A Paris imprint. (Query, 83). BC, vi (57), 291.

The earliest dated woodcut book plate. (Note, 119). Illus. BC, viii (59), 426-7.

—. BC, ix (60), 326.

The private press and publishing activities of Prince Louis-Lucien Bonaparte. Illus. BC, ix (60), 31-7.

Early thumb-indexes. (Query, 131). BC, ix (60), 456.

Prince L.-L. Napoleon's first catalogue. (Note, 154). BC, x (61), 70-1.

To bind or not to bind. (Note, 166). BC, x (61), 336.

Broadsides concerning early printing. (Query, 147). BC, x (61), 337.

The private press of T. E. Williams. (Query, 160). BC, xii (63), 72.

Designation of edition on the title-page. (Note, 200). BC, xii (63), 350.

An admonition to borrowers. (Note, 220). BC, xiii (64), 211.

The earliest bookseller's catalogue of incunabula. (Query, 188). BC, xiv (65), 366.

Les reliures vernis sans odeur, autrement dit 'Vernis Martin'. Illus. BC, xiv (65), 523-7.

The earliest catalogue of incunabula. (Query, 196). BC, xiv (65), 546.

The disappearance of a famous collection [Von Klemperer of Dresden]. (Query, 194). BC, xiv (65), 546.

Rebound in the 16th century? [Hypnerotomachia of 1499]. (Query, 202). BC, xv (66), 214.

Priced copies of the La Valliere catalogue 1783. BC, xv (66), 357.

Authors' catalogues of the 16th century. (Note, 301). BC, xvii (68), 352.

Binding in Oxford in A.D. 1520. (Note, 311). BC, xviii (69), 220.

Italian broadside catalogues. [A letter]. LIB, iv (49/50), 281.

Early American bookbinders. PBSA, xxxv (41), 210-1.

EHRMAN, John
The Friends of the National Libraries. Illus. BC, iii (54), 55-60.

EHRSAM, Theodore G.
Major Byron. (Note, 31). BC, iii (54), 69-71.

The Wise Shelley letter. [A letter]. LIB, v (50/1), 63-4.

EISEMANN, H.
Brant's Narrenschiff, 1494. (Query, 117). BC, viii (59), 431.

ELDRIDGE, Herbert G.
The American republication of Thomas Moore's Epistles, Odes, and other poems: an early version of the reprinting 'game'. PBSA, lxii (68), 199-205.

ELIOT, George pseud.
See EVANS, Mary Ann

ELIOT, Thomas Stearns
An address to members of the London Library. BC, i (52), 139-44.

Unrecorded article by T. S. Eliot. (Note, 139). BC, ix (60), 198-9.
D. M. Walmsley.

An unrecorded article by T. S. Eliot. (Note, 186). BC, xi (62), 350.
B. C. Bloomfield.

John Quinn and T. S. Eliot's First Book of Criticism. PBSA, lvi (62), 259-65.
D. H. Woodward.

Notes on the publishing history and text of The Waste Land. PBSA, lviii (64), 252-69.
D. H. Woodward.

The text of T. S. Eliot's Gerontion. SB, iv (51), 213-17.
W. H. Marshall.

Notes on the text of T. S. Eliot: variants from Russell Square. SB, ix (57), 21-49.
R. L. Beare.

ELIZABETH queen of England
A binding for Elizabeth I by the Initial Binder, 1563. (English bookbindings, 35). Illus. BC, ix (60), 444.
H. M. Nixon.

Elstrack's portrait of Queen Elizabeth I. (Note, 205). BC, xii (63), 490.
A. W. G. Lowther.

A note on Queen Elizabeth's Godly Meditation. LIB, xv (34/5), 237-40.
R. Hughey.

The funeral procession of Queen Elizabeth. LIB, xxvi (45/6), 262-71.
W. A. Jackson.

ELKIN MATHEWS ltd.
A. H. Hallam's Poems, 1830. (Note, 123). BC, ix (60), 64-5.

J. A. Symonds and the 'peccant' pamphlets. (Note, 215). BC, xiii (64), 206-7.

ELKINS, William McIntire
Portrait of a Philadephia collector: . . . (1882-1947). PBSA, i (56), 115-67.
E. Shaffer.

ELLIOT, Thomas
A Harleian binding by Thomas Elliot, 1721. (English bookbindings, 49). Illus. BC, xiii (64), 194.
H. M. Nixon.

ELLIS, Frank H. and FOXON, David
Prior's *Simile*. Illus. PBSA, lvii (63), 337-9.

ELLIS, Ralph
A pair of bibliomanes for Kansas: Ralph Ellis and Thomas Jefferson Fitzpatrick. PBSA, lv (61), 207-25.
R. Vosper.

ELMEN, Paul
Richard Allestree and *The Whole Duty of Man*. LIB, vi (51/2), 19-27.

John Donne's dark lantern. PBSA, xlix (55), 181-6.

ELSTRACK, Renold
Elstrack's portrait of Queen Elizabeth I. (Note, 205). BC, xii (63), 490.
A. W. G. Lowther.

ELYOT, sir Thomas
On the identity of Papyrius Geminus Eleates, author of *Hermathena* [i.e. sir Thomas Elyot]. TCBS, ii (54/8), 352-8.
C. W. Bouck.

EMBLEM, Donal Lewis
The library of Peter Mark Roget. Illus. BC, xviii (69), 449-69.

Peter Mark Roget: a centenary bibliography. PBSA, lxii (68), 436-47.

EMBLEMS
Cupid and the bees: an emblem in the Stirling-Maxwell collection. Illus. BTHK, iii (60/2), 3-14.
D. Coleman *and* M. M. McGowan.

EMERSON, Godfrey
Godfrey Edmondson or Emerson. LIB, xxiv (43/4), 86.
Sir W. W. Greg.

EMERSON, Ralph Waldo
Ralph Waldo Emerson's trip to Europe in 1848. (Query, 203). BC, xv (66), 214-5.
B. Gallant.

BAL Addenda. Ralph Waldo Emerson entry no. 5272. PBSA, lxi (67), 124-5.
J. Blanck.

EMSLIE, Macdonald
Pepys's songs and songbooks in the diary period. LIB, xii (57), 240-55.

Two of Pepys's "very lewd songs" in print. LIB, xv (60), 291-3.

ENCYCLOPÉDIE
L'encyclopédie in contemporary morocco. (Note, 76). BC, v (56), 280.
C. S. A. Dobson.

—. BC, v (56), 383.
A. Rau.

END PAPERS
End papers. LIB, xxv (44/5), 79.
R. W. Chapman.

ENGELS, Friedrich
Karl Marx & Friedrich Engels. (Portrait of a bibliophile, 14). Illus. BC, xviii (69), 189-98.

ENGLAND, Sylvia Lennis
An unrecognized document in the history of French Renaissance staging. Illus. LIB, xvi (35/6), 232-5.

ENGLEY, Donald B.
James Hammond Trumbull, bibliographer of Connecticut. PBSA, xlviii (54), 239-47.

George Brinley, Americanist. PBSA, lx (66), 465-72.

ENGLISH BOOKS PRINTED ABROAD
English books printed abroad. LIB, iv (49/50), 273-6.
A. F. Johnson.

ENGLISH HISTORY
The literature of splendid occasions in English history. LIB, i (46/7), 184-96.
I. K. Fletcher.

ENGLISH STOCK
The English Stock of the Stationers' Company. LIB, x (55), 163-85.
C. Blagden.

The English Stock of the Stationers' Company. [A letter]. LIB, xi (56), 53.
Sir W. W. Greg.

The English Stock of the Stationers' Company in the time of the Stuarts. LIB, xii (57), 167-86.
C. Blagden.

ENRIGHT, Brian James
Edmund Curll and the "cursed blunders" in Fresnoy's *New Method of Studying History*, 1728. LIB, ix (54), 200-5.

The later auction sales of Thomas Rawlinson's library, 1727-34. 2 pts. LIB, xi (56), 23-40; 103-13.

ENVOY TO ALISON
The text of the *Envoy to Alison*. SB, v (52) 33-42.

EPHEMERA
Petits papiers. BH, ii (51/2), 91-5.

ÉPHÉMÉRIDES DU CITOYEN
Éphémérides du Citoyen, 1767-1772. Illus. PBSA, lvi (62), 17-45.
E. Coleman.

—. Addendum. PBSA, lvii (63), 95-6.
E. Coleman.

EPILOGUES
Textual problems in Restoration broadsheet prologues and epilogues. LIB, xii (57), 197-203.
R. Morton.

ERASMUS, Desiderius
Erasmus and his English patrons. LIB, iv (49/50), 1-13.
H. W. Garrod.

The English editions of Erasmus's *Catechismus*. LIB, xvii (62), 154-5.
E. J. Devereux.

Some lost translations of Erasmus. LIB, xvii (62), 255-9.
E. J. Devereux.

ERDMAN, David Vorse
Unrecorded Coleridge variants. SB, xi (58), 143-62.

The suppressed and altered passages in Blake's *Jerusalem*. Illus. SB, xvii (64), 1-54.

Blake's *Jerusalem*: Plate 3 fully restored. SB, xviii (65), 281-2.

ERDMAN, David Vorse, WERKMEISTER, Lucyle *and* WOOF, R. S.
Unrecorded Coleridge variants: additions and corrections. SB, xiv (61), 236-45.

EREVAN *Matenadaran*
The Matenadaran at Erevan. (Unfamiliar libraries, 6). Illus. BC, ix (60), 146-50.
G. Abgarian.

ERRATA
Notes on errata from books in the Chapin library. LIB, xiii (32/3), 259-71.
L. E. Osborne.

ESHER, *3rd viscount*
See BRETT, Oliver, *3rd viscount Esher*

ESPLIN, David G.
J. M. *Letters to a sick friend*. 1682. (Query, 132). BC, ix (60), 456-7.

ESSLINGEN-AM-NECKAR
An incunabulum of Esslingen. [Aquinas's *Catena aurea*]. LIB, xii (51), 270-1.
J. V. Scholderer.

ESTERQUEST, Ralph Theodore
L'Imprimerie Royale d'Hayti (1817-1819). A little known royal press of the western hemisphere. Illus. PBSA, xxxiv (40), 171-84.

ESTIENNE *family*
Two Estienne dictionaries. LIB, xvi (61), 48-50.
D. E. Rhodes.

ESTIENNE, Henri
Henry Stephanus and Thucydides. [A letter]. LIB, xvii (36/7), 361-2.
J. E. Powell.

ESTIENNE, Robert
The chronology of the Estienne editions, Paris, 1526-50: Old Style or New? LIB, iv (49/50), 64-8.
A. E. Tyler.

Robert Estienne and his privileges, 1526-1550. LIB, iv (49/50), 225-37.
A. E. Tyler.

ET AMICORUM
The earliest English 'Et Amicorum' inscription? (Note, 133). BC, ix (60), 192.
E. A. Osborne.

The earliest English 'Et Amicorum' inscription. (Note, 133). BC, ix (60), 326.
H. G. Pollard.

'Et Amicorum'. LIB, iv (49/50), 87-99.
G. D. Hobson.

ETON, *coll., libr.*
The Storer collection in Eton college library. Illus. BC, v (56), 115-26.
R. Birley.

An Eton binding by Roger Payne, 1764. (English bookbindings, 45). Illus. BC, xii (63), 194.
H. M. Nixon.

The history of Eton college library. LIB, xi (56), 231-61.
R. Birley.

Additions from Eton college library to the record of copies in sir W. W. Greg's *A Bibliography of the English printed Drama to the Restoration*. LIB, xviii (63), 228-9.
R. Birley.

Some unrecorded Cambridge books in the library of Eton college. TCBS, i (49/53), 441-3.
R. Birley.

EUING MUSIC COLLECTION
See GLASGOW *univ., libr.*

EULER, Leonhard
An example of eighteenth-century Swiss printer's copy: Euler on the calculus of variations. [*Methodus inveniendi lineas curvas*]. LIB, xxii (67), 147-9.
G. G. Barber.

EVANS, Charles
A note on *Carmen Becceriense*. Illus. BC, i (52), 215-8.

EVANS, D. D.
The Grovers, letter-founders. LIB, xviii (63), 61-3.

EVANS, D. Wyn
A note on the content of the Thorkelin collection in the National Library of Scotland. BTHK, iv (63/6), 79-80.

Andrew Robertson of Aberdeen. BTHK, iv (63/6), 81.

EVANS, Frank B.
The printing of Spenser's *Faerie Queene* in 1596. SB, xviii (65), 49-67.

EVANS, Gwynne Blakemore
Comedies, Tragi-Comedies, with other poems, by Mr. William Cartwright, 1651. A bibliographical study. LIB, xxiii (42/3), 12-22.

Notes on English retail book-prices, 1550-1640. [A letter]. LIB, v (50/1), 275-6.

The missing third edition of Wheble's *Junius,* 1771, SB, xiii (60), 235-8.

New evidence on the provenance of the Padua prompt-books of Shakespeare's *Macbeth, Measure for Measure,* and *Winter's Tale.* SB, xx (67), 239-42.

EVANS, Henry
A London binding by Henry Evans, *c.* 1665. (English bookbindings, 34). Illus. BC, ix (60), 316.
H. M. Nixon.

EVANS, Mary Ann
George Eliot's *Agatha* 1869- and after. BC, vi (57), 244-52.
J. W. Carter.

EVELYN, John
The correspondence between sir Thomas Browne and John Evelyn. LIB, xix (38/9), 103-6.
E. S. de Beer.

A note on John Evelyn's History of the *Three Late Famous Imposters.* LIB, ix (54), 267-8.
M. Fixler.

William Upcott and John Evelyn's papers. LIB, xx (65), 320-5.
W. G. Hiscock.

EWING, Douglas C.
A note on Mary Russell Mitford's *Bedford Regis.* PBSA, lx (66), 473.

The three-volume novel. PBSA, lxi (67), 201-7.

EWING, James Cameron
Brash and Reid, booksellers in Glasgow and their collection of *Poetry Original and Selected.* Illus. GBSR, xii (36), 1-20.

EXAMINER
The printing of eighteenth-century periodicals: with notes on the *Examiner* and the *World.* LIB, x (55), 49-54.
W. B. Todd.

EXCHEQUER, Court of
Some Exchequer cases involving members of the book-trade, 1534-1558. LIB, xvi (35/6), 402-17.
H. J. Byrom.

EXCISE
The paper-makers and the excise in the eighteenth century. illus. LIB, xiv (59), 100-16.
R. C. Jarvis.

EXECUTORSHIP
See LITERARY EXECUTORSHIP

EX LIBRIS
See BOOK PLATES

EXPORT LICENCES
[Export licences. A letter]. BC, v (56), 247.
A. Rogers.

—. BC, v (56), 113-4.
A. R. A. Hobson.

EXPOSITIO AUREA HYMNORUM
Expositio aurea hymnorum. Seville, Johann Pegnitzer and Magnus Herbst, 1500. PBSA, xxxv (41), 66.
H. R. Mead.

F

FABES, Gilbert H.
An encounter with G.B.S. BH, ii (51/52), 36-40.

FABIAN, Bernhard
David Skene and the Aberdeen Philosophical Society. BTHK, v (67/70), 81-99.

FABIAN, Bernhard *and* KLOTH, Karen
The manuscript background of James Beattie's *Elements of normal science*. BTHK, v (67/70), 181-9.

FABRICIUS, Johann Albert
Johann Albert Fabricius, eighteenth-century scholar and bibliographer. PBSA, lx (66), 282-326.
M. Verner.

FABULOUS FICTION
Fabulous fiction. PBSA, xlvii (53), 231-47.
R. S. Wormser.

FACSIMILES
J. Sturt, facsimilist. LIB, xxv (44/5), 72-9.
A. T. Hazen.

J. Sturt, facsimilist. LIB, xxvi (45/6), 307-8.
H. MacDonald.

The problem of the variant forme in a facsimile edition. LIB, vii (52), 262-72.
F. T. Bowers.

What is a facsimile? PBSA, xxxvii (43), 114-30.
F. Weitenkampf.

Photo-facsimiles of *STC* books: a cautionary check list. SB, xxi (68), 109-30.
F. B. Williams.

FAIGEL, M. J.
Two states of a Bodoni type specimen. (Note, 218). BC, xiii (64), 207-10.

FAIRFAX, Brian
A note on the Edinburgh University Library MS. DK. 5.25, 'Brian Fairfax's Account'. BTHK, iii (60/2), 71-2.
W. Ferguson.

FALCONER, A. F.
Bishop Percy's annotated copy of Lord Hailes's *Ancient Scottish Poems*. EBST, ii (38/45), 432-7.

FALKNER, John Meade
John Meade Falkner, 1858-1932. (Some uncollected authors, 25). BC, ix (60), 318-25.
H. G. Pollard.

FARMER, Bernard J.
Adventures of a bookseller's runner. BH, ii (51/2), 172-5.

FARMER, David
The American edition of Huxley's *Leda*. (Note, 312). BC, xviii (69), 220-1.

A note on the text of Huxley's *Crome Yellow*. PBSA, lxiii (69), 131-3.

Addenda to Keynes's *Bibliography of Siegfried Sassoon*. PBSA, lxiii (69), 310-17.

FARMER, Henry George
Two unrecorded items in the Euing Music Collection. BTHK, i/3 (58), 44-5.

The music to Allan Ramsay's songs. BTHK, ii (59/60), 34.

The source of Arabian music: a bibliography of Arabic MSS. which deal with the theory, practice and history of Arabian music. GBSR, xiii (39), 1-96 = whole vol.

FARR, Harry
Philip Chetwind and the Allott copyrights. LIB, xv (34/5), 129-60.

FASCICULUS TEMPORUM
See ROLEWINCK, Werner.

FAULKNER, George
When Swift first employed George Faulkner. PBSA, lvi (62), 354-6.
B. Slepian.

The publication history of Faulkner's edition of *Gulliver's Travels*. PBSA, lvii (63), 219-21.
B. Slepian.

FAULKNER, William
The writings of William Faulkner: a challenge to the bibliographer. PBSA, l (56), 229-42.
H. R. Archer.

Some notes on the text of Faulkner's *Sanctuary*. PBSA, lv (61), 192-206.
J. B. Meriwether.

Notes on the textual history of *The Sound and the Fury*. PBSA, lvi (62), 285-316.
J. B. Meriwether.

Notes on the unrevised galleys of Faulkner's *Sanctuary*. SB, viii (56), 195-208.
L. Massey.

The manuscript of *The Sound and the Fury*: the revisions in the first section. SB, xx (67), 189-202.
E. K. Izsak.

FAURE, Jacqueline
Two poems by Susanna Centlivre. (Note, 151). BC, x (61), 68-9.

FAUST, Johann
An account of the Faustus ballad. Illus. LIB, xvi (61), 176-89.
L. M. Goldstein.

The Faustus ballad. [A letter]. LIB, xviii (63), 64.
F. N. Lees.

FAUTEUX, Aegidius
Fleury Mesplet: une étude sur les commencements de l'imprimerie dans la ville de Montréal. PBSA, xxviii (34), 164-93.

FAWCETT, Trevor
An eighteenth-century book club at Norwich. LIB, xxiii (68), 47-50.

Some aspects of the Norfolk book-trade, 1800-24. TCBS, iv (64/8), 383-95.

FAWKES, Francis
Francis Fawkes: *The Brown Jug*. (Query, 11). Illus. BC, i (52), 58-9.
J. Hadfield.

Francis Fawkes: *The Brown Jug*. (Query 11). BC, i (52), 130.
W. N. H. Harding.

FAY, H.
Chapman's text corrections in his Iliads. LIB, vi (51/2), 275-81.

Critical marks in a copy of Chapman's *Twelve Bookes of Homers Iliades*. LIB, viii (53), 117-21.

FEILITZEN, Carl Olof von
Journal politique et littéraire d'Angleterre, 1784. LIB, i (46/7), 142-3.

FEINBERG, Charles E.
A Whitman collector destroys a Whitman myth. Illus. PBSA, lii (58), 73-92.

Mr. Ciardi, Mr. Adams, and Mr. White. PBSA, lv (61), 393.

FELIPPE, Bartolome
John Wolfe and a Spanish book [Bartolome Felippe's *Tractado del consejo y de los consejeros*]. LIB, iii (48/9), 214-16.
F. B. Benger.

FEMALE WANDERER
The female wanderer. Boston, (Mass) 1820. PBSA, xxxvi (42), 230-1.
E. C. Skarshaug.

FERGUSON, Frederic Sutherland
A bibliography of the works of Sir George Mackenzie, Lord Advocate, founder of the Advocates' Library. EBST, i (35/8), 1-60.

Additions to *Title-page Borders 1485-1640*. Illus. LIB, xvii (36/7), 264-311.

John Siberch of Cambridge: an unrecorded book from his press, new light on his material. Illus. TCBS, i (49/53), 41-5.

FERGUSON, John
A further bibliography of the writings of John Ferguson, M.A. LL.D., F.S.A., Regius Professor of Chemistry in the University of Glasgow, 1874-1915. Illus. GBST, xii (36), 82-127.
E. H. Alexander.

FERGUSON, W.
A note on the Edinburgh University Library MS. DK.5.25, 'Brian Fairfax's Account'. BTHK, iii (60/2), 71-2.

FERGUSON, W. Craig
Some additions to McKerrow's *Printers' and Publishers' Devices*. LIB, xiii (58), 201-3.

The compositors of *Henry iv, Part 2, Much Ado About Nothing, The Shoemakers' Holiday*, and *The First Part of the Contention*. SB, xiii (60), 19-29.

A note on printers' measures. SB, xv (62), 242-3.

FERGUSON COLLECTION
See GLASGOW *univ. libr., Ferguson coll.*

FERGUSSON, Robert
The inscribed copies of the first edition, 1773, of the poems of Robert Fergusson. EBST, iii (48/55), 125-35.
A. Law.

FERN, Alan M. *and* BERRY, W. Turner
Typographical specimen books. A checklist of the Broxbourne collection with an introduction. Illus. BC, v (56), 256-272.

FETTER, Frank Whitson
A probable source of Copinger's *On the Authorship of the First Hundred Numbers of the Edinburgh Review*. LIB, ix (54), 49-53.

FEUILLET, Raoul Auger
Chorégraphie. The dance notation of the eighteenth century: Beauchamp or Feuillet. BC, xvi (67), 450-76.

FICINUS, Marsilius
Traherne's Ficino notebook [MS. Burney 126]. PBSA, lxiii (69), 73-81.
C. M. Sicherman.

The first edition of Ficino's *De Christiana Religione*: a problem in bibliographical description. SB, xviii (65), 248-52.
C. F. Bühler.

FIELD, Nathan
The quarto of Field's *Weather-Cocke*. LIB, i (46/7), 62-4.
W. Peery.

The 1618 quarto of Field's *Amends for Ladies*. LIB, ii (47/8), 53-9.
W. Peery.

FIELD, W. S.
The techno-chemical receipt book. (Among my books, l). BH, i (47/51), 58-60.

FIELDING, Henry
Fielding's *The Modern Husband*, 1732. (Note, 61). BC, v (56), 76-7.
D. F. Foxon.

Fielding's The Modern Husband, 1732. (Note, 61). BC, v (56), 276.
W. B. Todd.

Proposals for a definitive edition of Fielding's *Tom Jones*. LIB, xviii (37/8), 314-30.
G. E. Jensen.

The publication of the first translations of Fielding's *Tom Jones*. LIB, xxvi (45/6), 189-90.
T. C. D. Eaves.

Fielding, Henry (1707-1764). *The Coffee-House Politician* London, 1730. PBSA, xxxv (41), 69.
H. R. Mead.

Three notes on Fielding. PBSA, xlvii (53), 70-5.
W. B. Todd.

A preliminary census of Henry Fielding's legal manuscripts. PBSA, lxii (68), 587-601.
H. Amory.

Variant forms of Fielding's *Coffee-House Politician*. SB, v (52), 178-83.
J. A. Masengill.

The printing of Fielding's *Miscellanies*, 1743. SB, xv (62), 247-56.
D. D. Eddy.

Fielding's revisions of *Joseph Andrews*. SB, xvi (63), 81-117.
M. C. Battestin.

FIERER, Charles
A printer soldier of fortune. [Charles Fierer and Thomas U. Fosdick]. PBSA, xxx (36), 91-103.
A. H. Lerch.

FIFTY BEST POEMS OF AMERICA
The Little Leather Library Corporation's *Fifty best poems of America*. PBSA, lxii (68), 604-7.
G. T. Tanselle.

FILDES, sir Paul
Phototransfer of drawings in wood-block engraving. Illus. JPHS, v (69), 87-97.

FILELFO, Francesco
A fifteenth-century humanist, Francesco Filelfo. Illus. LIB, xvi (35/6), 1-26.
L. A. Sheppard.

FILM SETTING
Filmsetting — bibliographical implications. LIB, xv (60), 231-45.
J. Moran.

FILOCOLO
A misprint in the Venetian *Filocolo*. PBSA, li (57), 319-22.
C. F. Bühler.

FINCH, Jeremiah S.
A newly discovered *Urn Burial*. Illus. LIB, xix (38/9), 347-53.

Sir Hans Sloane's printed books. LIB, xxii (41/2), 67-72.

Sir Thomas Browne: early biographical notices, and the disposition of his library and manuscripts. SB, ii (49/50), 196-201.

FINE PAPER COPIES
Fine paper copies of Donne's *Biathanatos*. [?1646]. (Note, 250). BC, xiv (65), 362.
R. S. Pirie.

Fine paper copies of Bacon's *Essays*, 1625. (Note, 263). BC, xiv (65), 545.
R. S. Pirie.

Fine and large-paper copies of *S.T.C.* books: a further note. LIB, xxiii (68), 239-40.
B. Juel-Jensen.

FINES, John *and* FLETCHER, John M.
Nicholas Harpsfield's note of Cranmer's recantation. TCBS, iv (64/8), 310-2.

FINES, John *and* VAUGHAN, Richard
A handlist of manuscripts in the Library of Corpus Christi College, Cambridge, not described by M. R. James. TCBS, iii (59/63), 113-23.

FINKELPEARL, Philip J.
Henry Walley of the Stationers' Company and John Marston. PBSA, lvi (62), 366-8.

FINLAYSON, C. P.
Records of Medical and Scientific Societies in Scotland. II. Records of Scientific and Medical Societies preserved in the University Library, Edinburgh. BTHK, i/3 (58), 14-9.

—. Additions. BTHK, iv (63/6), 38-9.

Notes on C. R. Borland's *A Descriptive Catalogue of Western Mediaeval Manuscripts in Edinburgh University Library*, 1916. BTHK, iii (60/2), 44-52.

Thomas Carlyle's borrowings from Edinburgh University Library, 1819-1820. Illus. BTHK, iii (60/2), 138-43.

An unpublished commentary by George Buchanan on Virgil. EBST, iii (48/55), 269-88.

FIORE DI VIRTÚ
Studies in the early editions of the *Fiore di virtú*. PBSA, xlix (55), 315-39.
C. F. Bühler.

FIORETI DELLA BIBBIA HISTORIATI IN LINGUA FIORENTINA
Fioreti della bibbia historiati in lingua fiorentina. Venice, Matteo Capcasa for Lucantonio Giunta, 1494. PBSA, xxxiv (40), 267.
H. R. Mead.

FIRBANK, Arthur Annesley Ronald
Ronald Firbank in periodicals. PBSA, liv (60), 295-7.
M. J. Benkovitz.

The text of Firbank's *Vainglory*. PBSA, lxiii (69), 36-41.
R. M. Davis.

FIRBANK, Ronald
See FIRBANK, Arthur Annesley Ronald

FIRMAN, Catherine K.
A collection of Oxford novels. (Note, 143). BC, ix (60), 331-2.

FIRTH, John
Harriet Weaver's letters to James Joyce, 1915-20. SB, xx (67), 151-88.

James Pinker to James Joyce, 1915-20. SB, xxi (68), 205-24.

FISCHER, Hans
Conrad Gessner, 1516-1565, as bibliographer and encyclopedist. Illus. LIB, xxi (66), 269-81.

FISHER, Harold Henry
The Hoover Library on war, revolution, and peace. PBSA, xxxiii (39), 107-15.

FISHER, John H.
Seven variants in *The Tretyse of Love*. PBSA, xliv (52), 393-6.

FISHER, Jonathan
Two elegies, on the Deaths of Mrs. Marianne Burr; and of Mrs. Rebekah Walker. Hanover, 1796. PBSA, xxxiv (40), 86.
L. M. Stark.

FISKE, John
John Fiske — bookman. Illus. PBSA, xxxv (41), 221-54.
L. C. Powell.

FITZALAN, Henry *12th earl of Arundel*
A binding for the earl of Arundel, *c.* 1555. (English bookbindings, 60). Illus. BC, xvi (67), 54.
H. M. Nixon.

FITZER, William
William Fitzer, the publisher of Harvey's *De Motu Cordis*, 1628. LIB, xxiv (43/4), 142-64.
E. Weil.

FITZGERALD, Edward
Edward Fitzgerald's *Six dramas of Calderon* 1854 edition? (Query, 229). BC, xvii (68), 491.
A. Bridge.

FITZGERALD, Francis Scott K.
F. Scott Fitzgerald's first book appearance. PBSA, lix (65), 58.
M. J. Bruccoli.

F. Scott Fitzgerald as book reviewer. PBSA, lx (66), 369-70.
J. R. Bryer.

Two versions of F. Scott Fitzgerald's *Babylon revisited*: a textual and bibliographical study. PBSA, lx (66), 439-52.
W. White.

A collation of F. Scott Fitzgerald's *This Side of Paradise*. SB, ix (57), 263-5.
M. J. Bruccoli.

Bibliographical note on F. Scott Fitzgerald's *The Beautiful and Damned*. SB, xiii (60), 258-61.
M. J. Bruccoli.

Material for a centenary edition of *Tender is the Night*. SB, xvii (64), 177-93.
M. J. Bruccoli.

FITZPATRICK, Thomas Jefferson
A pair of bibliomanes for Kansas: Ralph Ellis and Thomas Jefferson Fitzpatrick. PBSA, lv (61), 207-25.
R. Vosper.

FIXLER, Michael
A note on John Evelyn's *History of the Three Late Famous Imposters*. LIB, ix (54), 267-8.

FLAMBOYANT BINDER
A binding by the Flamboyant binder, *c.* 1540-45. (English bookbindings, 53). Illus. BC, xiv (65), 200.
H. M. Nixon.

FLAXMAN, John
Blake's engravings and his friendship with Flaxman. SB, xii (59), 161-88.
G. E. Bentley.

FLEEMAN, John David
Some proofs of Johnson's *Prefaces to the Poets*. LIB, xvii (62), 213-30.

The making of Johnson's *Life of Savage*, 1744. LIB, xxii (67), 346-52.

William Somervile's *The Chace*, 1735. PBSA, lviii (64), 1-7.

Johnson's *Journey*, 1775, and its cancels. Illus. PBSA, lviii (64), 232-8.

FLEMING, Ian Lancaster
Ian Fleming: a personal memoir. BC, xiv (65), 24-33.
P. H. Muir.

FLEMING, James
A signed binding by James Fleming, Newcastle, *c.* 1710. Illus. LIB, xv (60), 58-60.
W. S. Mitchell.

FLEMING, John
Cicero, Marcus Tullius. *Laelius de amicitia.* [Cologne, Ulrich Zell, 1467]. PBSA, xl (46), 160.

FLEMING, Thomas Paul
Bridges, Robert (1844-1930). *A case of Thickening of the Cranial Bones in an Infant, due to Congenital Syphilis. In Transactions of the Clinical Society of London.* London, 1897. PBSA, xxxv (41), 161.

FLETCHER, G.B.A.
A. E. Housman, an annotated check-list. [A letter]. LIB, xxiii (42/3), 133.

A. E. Housman bibliography. [A letter]. LIB, viii (53), 51.

FLETCHER, Giles
Giles Fletcher the Elder's *Licia.* LIB, xv (60), 133-4.
L. E. Berry.

Giles Fletcher, the elder: a bibliography. TCBS, iii (59/63), 200-15.
L. E. Berry.

FLETCHER, Harris Francis
A second (?) title-page of the second edition of *Paradise Lost.* Illus. PBSA, xliii (49), 173-8.

FLETCHER, Harris Francis
Fletcher's Milton: a first appraisal. PBSA, xli (47), 33-52.
W. Parker.

FLETCHER, Ifan Kyrle
Theatrical collecting. Illus. BC, i (52), 41-51.

The literature of splendid occasions in English history. LIB, i (46/7), 184-96.

FLETCHER, John *1579-1625*
See also BEAUMONT, Francis *and* FLETCHER, John

Rollo, duke of Normandy. Some bibliographical notes on the seventeenth-century editions. LIB, xviii (37/8), 279-86.
J. D. Jump.

—. *and* BETTERTON, Thomas
A bibliographical history of the Fletcher-Betterton play, *The Prophetess*, 1690. LIB, xvi (61), 169-75.
F. T. Bowers.

FLETCHER, John *binder*
A London binding by Fletcher, 1660. (English bookbindings, 16). Illus. BC, v (56), 53-4.
H. M. Nixon.

A London binding by Fletcher, *c.* 1662. (English bookbindings, 17). Illus. BC, v (56), 150.
H. M. Nixon.

FLETCHER, John *fl. 1968*
Athanasius Kircher and the distribution of his books. LIB, xxiii (68), 108-17.

FLETCHER, John M.
Addendum to 'Provost Argentine of King's and his books' by D. Rhodes. TCBS, iii (59/63), 263.

FLETCHER, John M. *and* FINES, John
Nicholas Harpsfield's note of Cranmer's recantation. TCBS, iv (64/8), 310-12.

FLETCHER, John M. *and* McCONICA, James K.
A sixteenth-century inventory of the library of Corpus Christi College, Cambridge. TCBS, iii (59/63), 187-99.

FLOOD, John L.
Some notes on German heroic poems in print. Illus. LIB, xxii (67), 228-42.

FLORA
A bibliography of the British Flora. [A notice]. LIB, xxv (44/5), 187.
J. S. L. Gilmour *and others*.

FLORA *fict. name*
Flora: or The deserted child: by the author of James Manners [Elizabeth Helme or Elizabeth Somerville]. BC, xvi (67), 83.
S. Roscoe.

Flora: or The deserted child. (Query, 213). BC, xvi (67), 377.
W. J. Smith.

Flora: or The deserted child. [Attributed to E. Somerville or E. Helme, jr.] (Query, 213). BC, xviii (68), 83.
S. Roscoe.

FLORENCE
An unknown Florentine incunabulum. [*Miracoli della gloriosa Vergine Maria*, 1495?]. Illus. LIB, xviii (37/8), 331-4.
J. V. Scholderer.

The flood of 4 November 1966. BC, xvi (67), 13-25.
M. M. Witt.

Return to Florence, January 1967. BC, xvi (67), 26-8.
N. Rubinstein.

British aid for Florence. Illus. BC, xvi (67), 29-35.
H. M. Nixon.

The principal libraries of Florence. BC, xvi (67), 36-43.
D. E. Rhodes.

FLORENCE, *bibl. naz. centrale*
The Biblioteca Nazionale at Florence. Illus. BC, xviii (69), 11-22.
N. Barker.

FLORISTS' MAGAZINE
The Florists' Magazine. (Query, 28). BC, ii (53), 79.
J. S. L. Gilmour.

FLOWER, Desmond John N.
A Hampshire library. (Contemporary collectors, 1). BC, iii (54), 5-10.

Voltaire's *La Henriade.* (Query, 47). BC, iii (54), 307-8.

Marivaux: *Le paysan parvenu.* (Note, 73). BC, v (56), 277.

Candide: a perennial problem. BC, viii (59), 284-8.

A Dashiell Hammett omnibus. (Note, 181). BC, xi (62), 217.

Le livre anglais. Illus. BH, ii (51/2), 163-71.

Some aspects of the bibliography of Voltaire. LIB, i (46/7), 223-36.

FLOWER, Margaret
Thomas Stanley, 1625-1678: a bibliography of his writings in prose and verse, 1647-1743. TCBS, i (49/53), 139-72.

FLYE
The Flye, 1569. Illus. LIB, xviii (37/8), 195-200.
E. F. Bosanquet.

FLYNN, Vincent Joseph
The grammatical writings of William Lily, ?1468-?1523. PBSA, xxxvii (43), 85-113.

FOAKES, Reginald Anthony
On the first folio text of *Henry VIII*. SB, xi (58), 55-60.

FOGEL, Ephim G.
Electronic computers and Elizabethan texts. SB, xv (62), 15-31.

FOGLIETTA, Uberto
The printing history of Uberto Foglietta's *De sacro foedere in Selimum*. Illus. PBSA, lxii (68), 77-80.
D. Brockway.

FOLEY, Patrick Kevin
Aldis, Foley and the collection of American literature at Yale. PBSA, xlii (48), 41-9.
D. C. Gallup.

FOLGER SHAKESPEARE LIBRARY
See WASHINGTON *D.C., Folger Shakespeare libr.*

FONTAINE, Jacques
Editions of Fontanus, *De bello Rhodio*. LIB, xxiv (69), 333-6.
A. Freeman.

FONTANUS
See FONTAINE, Jacques

FOOD AND WINE
Bibliotheca gastronomica. (Contemporary collectors, 30). Illus. BC, xi (62), 45-54.
A. C. Simon.

FORBES, Allyn B.
The Provisions Made by the Treaties of Utrecht, etc. London, 1762. PBSA, xxxv (41), 73.

FORBES, George Hay
The Pitsligo Press of George Hay Forbes. Illus. EBST, iv (55/71), 53-89.
J. B. Primrose.

FORBES, John
Forbes, John (1568?-1634). *Four Sermons.* [Amsterdam] 1635. PBSA, xxxiv (40), 85.
E. H. Willoughby.

FORCE, Peter
Peter Force. PBSA, xliv (50), 1-16.
F. R. Goff.

FORD, Brinsley
Richard Ford's articles and reviews. BH, i (47/51), 369-80.

FORD, Charles
The Ford changes and the text of *Gulliver's Travels*. PBSA, lxii (68), 1-23.
C. Jenkins.

FORD, Richard
Richard Ford and his *Hand-book for travellers in Spain*. Illus. BH, i (47/51), 349-68.
E. W. Gilbert.

Richard Ford's articles and reviews. BH, i (47/51), 369-80.
B. Ford.

FORD COUNTY JOURNAL
The Ford County Journal, 1859-1860: an unrecorded Illinois newspaper. PBSA, xlviii (54), 273-82.
I. Iben.

FORDUN, John
The debt of Bower to Fordun and Wyntoun. EBST, ii (38/45), 386-9.
E. W. M. Balfour-Melville.

FORDYCE, C. J. *and* BAXTER, J. H.
Books published abroad by Scotsmen before 1700. GBSP, xi (33), 1-55.

FORDYCE, C. J. *and* KNOX, T. M.
The library of Jesus College, Oxford, with an appendix on the books bequeathed thereto by Lord Herbert of Cherbury. Illus. OBSP, v (36/9), 49-115.

FORE-EDGES
Fore-edge titles in Cambridge Universtiy Library. Illus. TCBS, iii (59/63), 163-5.
J. C. T. Oates.

FORGERIES
The detection of faked literary MSS. Illus. BC, ii (53), 6-23.
T. J. Brown.

FORMAN, P.
Two rare books in the University Library, Glasgow [Michael Scott's *Mensa Philosophica* and the *Grammar of Sulpitius*]. BTHK, i/1 (56), 22-3.

FORMAT
Some notes on agenda format. Illus. LIB, viii (53), 163-73.
D. F. Foxon.

A modern instance [of an error in pagination in T. Besterman, *World Bibliography of bibliographies*, Vol. I, 2nd ed]. Illus. PBSA, l (56), 302-4.
J. D. Thomas.

Guide-lines in small formats, about 1600. SB, xiv (61), 206-8.
G. E. Dawson.

FORMES
The problem of the variant forme in a facsimile edition. LIB, vii (52), 262-72.
F. T. Bowers.

Variant formes in Elizabethan printing. Illus. LIB, x (55), 41-8.
K. Povey.

Setting by formes in quarto printing. SB, xi (58), 39-53.
G. W. Williams.

The optical identification of first formes. SB, xiii (60), 189-90.
K. Povey.

FORSTER, Edward Morgan
Additions to the E. M. Forster bibliography [by B. J. Kirkpatrick]. PBSA, lx (66), 224-5.
J. B. Shipley.

FOSDICK, Thomas U.
A printer soldier of fortune. [Charles Fierer and Thomas U. Fosdick]. PBSA, xxx (36), 91-103.
A. H. Lerch.

FOSS, Daniel
The Star Rover and Daniel Foss's Oar. PBSA, xliv (50), 182-5.
C. R. Toothaker.

FOSTER, I. J. C. *and* POVEY, K.
Turned chain-lines. Illus. LIB, v (50/1), 184-200.

FOSTER, Katherine *and* MITCHELL, Alison
Sir William Alexander's *Supplement* to book III of Sidney's *Arcadia*. Illus. LIB, xxiv (69), 234-41.

FOULIS *family*
See FOULIS PRESS.

FOULIS EXHIBITIONS
See FOULIS PRESS.

FOULIS PRESS
The early work of the Foulis Press and the Wilson Foundry. Illus. LIB, vii (52), 77-110, 149-77.
P. Gaskell.

FOUL PAPERS
The foul papers of a revision. LIB, xxvi (45/6), 37-50.
R. C. Bald.

FOURE GREAT LYERS
The authorship of *Foure great Lyers*, 1585. [Attributed to W. Perkins]. LIB, xix (38/9), 311-4.
H. G. Dick.

FOURQUEVAUX, Raimond, baron de
Fourquevaux and military art in the sixteenth century. EBST, ii (38/45), 397-8.
G. Dickinson.

FOXE, John
Single-page imposition in Foxe's *Acts and Monuments*, 1570. LIB, i (46/7), 49-56.
L. M. Oliver.

Foxe's *Acts and Monuments*, 1570, and single-page imposition. Illus. LIB, ii (47/8), 159-70.
P. S. Dunkin.

The seventh edition of John Foxe's *Acts and Monuments*. PBSA, xxxvii (43), 243-60.
L. M. Oliver.

FOXON, David Fairweather
Binding variants in the Brontes' *Poems*. (Note, 25). BC, ii (53), 219-21.

E typis Palgravianis. (Note, 51). BC, iv (55), 252.

The Golden Treasury, 1861. (Note, 52). BC, iv (55), 252-3.

—. BC, v (56), 75.

Fielding's *The Modern Husband*, 1732. (Note, 61). BC, v (56), 76-7.

Akenside's *The Pleasures of Imagination*. *(Note, 62)*.

Concealed Pope editions. (Note, 74). BC, v (56), 277-9.

The chapbook editions of the Lambs' *Tales from Shakespear*. Illus. BC, vi (57), 41-53.

Prior's *A new collection of Poems*, 1724 &c. (Note, 106). BC, viii (59), 69-70.

Libertine literature in England, 1660-1745. 3 pts. Illus. BC, xii (63), 21-36; 159-77; 294-307.

John Cleland and the publication of the *Memoirs of a Woman of Pleasure*. Illus. BC, xii (63), 476-87.

The reappearance of two lost black sheep. [*Venus in the Cloister*, 1725; and Cleland's own abridgement of the *Memoirs of a Woman of Pleasure*, entitled *Memoirs of Fanny Hill*]. (Note, 239). BC, xiv (65), 75-6.

Some notes on agenda format. Illus. LIB, viii (53), 163-73.

The printing of *Lyrical Ballads*, 1798. Illus. LIB, ix (54), 221-41.

A piracy of Steel's *The Lying Lover*. LIB, x (55), 127-9.

On printing 'at one pull', and distinguishing impressions by point-holes. LIB, xi (56), 284-5.

Monthly Catalogues of books published. LIB, xviii (63), 223-8.

Defoe: a specimen of a catalogue of English verse, 1701-1750. LIB, xx (65), 277-97.

'Oh! *Sophonisba*! *Sophonisba*! Oh!' SB, xii (59), 204-13.

FRACASTORO, Girolamo
Fracastor's *Syphilis*. An issue of which perhaps the only known copy is in the Library of Queen's College, Dundee. BTHK, i/1 (56), 29-30.
D. W. Doughty.

FRAGMENTS
A sixteenth-century fragment. (Query, 26). Illus. BC, i (52), 269.
J. Wellesley.

FRAGOSA
Fragosa, King of Aragon? 1618. (Query, 105). BC, viii (59), 70-1.
F. B. Williams.

FRANCE
News from France. BC, iv (55), 310-14.
A. Rau.

FRANCE, Anatole *pseud.*
See THIBAULT, Jacques Anatole

FRANCIS, sir Frank Chalton
Three unrecorded English books of the six-teenth-century. [ii *Opuscules or smale werkes of saynt bonaueture; The Pomander of prayer;* and *The doctrynall of symple people*]. Illus. LIB, xvii (36/7), 184-99.

The Earl of Crawford and Balcarres. [Obituary notice]. LIB, xxi (40/1, 229-63).

Recent bibliographical work. LIB, xxiii (42/3), 108-26.

A. W. Pollard, 1859-1944. LIB, xxv (44/5), 82-6.

A list of Dr. Greg's writings. LIB, xxvi (45/6), 72-97.

Booksellers' warranties. LIB, i (46/7), 244-5.

Drawback on paper. LIB, iv (49/50), 73.

J. Mirk's *Liber Festivalis* and *Quattuor Sermones*, Pynson, 1499. LIB, iv (49/50), 73.

William Alexander Jackson, obituary notice. Illus. LIB, xxi (66), 158-9.

— and BATEY, Charles
John Johnson. [Obituary notice]. LIB, xii (57), 55-7.

FRANCIS, T. R.
The plate in Collins's *Odes*. (Query, 17). BC, ii (53), 157.

A bookseller's stamp. (Query, 37). BC, iii (54), 149.

A variant issue of Thomson's *Summer*, 1727. (Note, 77). BC, v (56), 383.

Some Dublin editions of James Thomson's *Tancred and Sigismunda*. (Note, 96). BC, vii (58), 190.

James Thomson's *Tancred and Sigismuda*. (Note, 109). BC, viii (59), 181-2.

FRANCO, Matteo
An edition of the *Sonetti* by Matteo Franco and Luigi Pulci. PBSA, xlv (51), 356-7.
C. F. Bühler.

FRANKFURT-AM-MAIN
Frankfurt book fair catalogues. (Query, 106). BC, viii (59), 71.
A. Cuming.

FRANKLIN, Benjamin
Certain writings of Benjamin Franklin on the British Empire and the American Colonies. PBSA, xxviii (34), 1-27.
V. W. Crane.

The year after Franklin's year. PBSA, li (57), 227-35.
E. Wolf, *2nd*

The reconstruction of Benjamin Franklin's library: an unorthodox jigsaw puzzle. Illus. PBSA, lvi (62), 1-16. E. Wolf.

Benjamin Franklin's way to wealth. PBSA, lxiii (69), 231-46.
C. W. Miller.

Benjamin Franklin's Philadelphia type. SB, xi (58), 179-206.
C. W. Miller.

Franklin's *Poor Richard Almanacs*: their printing and publication. SB, xiv (61), 97-115.
C. W. Miller.

FRANKLIN, sir John
Sir John Franklin and the search for the North-West passage. Illus. BH, i (47/51), 37-46.
J. Gallatly.

Bibliography [of sir John Franklin]. BH, i (47/51) 46-9.
E. A. Osborne.

FRASER, John
The enigma of John Fraser. BTHK, v (67/70), 106-10.
R. L. Crawford.

FRASER, K. C.
The Beveridge collection in St. Andrews University Library. BTHK, v (67/70), 211-12.

FRASER'S MAGAZINE
Thackeray's contribution to *Fraser's magazine*. SB, xix (66), 67-84.
E. M. White.

FREDEMAN, William Evan
D. G. Rossetti's *Early Italian Poets*. (Note, 142). BC, x (61), 183-8.

FREDERIC, Harold
Harold Frederic: an unrecorded story. PBSA, lix (65), 327.
G. Monteiro.

Harold Frederic: an unrecorded review [of Gissing's *The whirlpool*]. PBSA, lxiii (69), 30-1.
G. Monteiro.

BAL addendum: Harold Frederic's *Gloria mundi* — entry 6293. The first four printings of Harold Frederic's *Gloria mundi*. PBSA, lxiii (69), 197-8.
J. Katz.

Harold Frederic: a bibliography. SB, xiii (60), 247-57.
R. H. Woodward.

A Harold Frederic first. SB, xv (62), 268-9.
S. B. Garner.

FREDERYKE OF IENNEN
Six tracts about women; a volume in the British Museum. [*The deceyte of women*. A. Vele, n.d.; *The Scole house of women*. J. King, 1560; Edward More, *The defence of women*. J. King, 1560; 5 Robert Copland, *The seuen sorowes*. W. Copland n.d.; 4 *The proude wyues pater noster*. J. King, 1560; and *Frederyke of Iennen*. A. Vele, n.d.]. LIB, xv (34/5), 38-48.
H. Stein.

FREEBAIRN, Robert
The rebel press at Perth in 1715 [i.e. that of Robert Freebairn]. GBST, viii (28), 44-56.
W. J. Couper.

FREEMAN
Charles A. Beard in the *Freeman*. PBSA, lvii (62), 226-9.
G. T. Tanselle.

Unsigned and initialed contributions to *The Freeman*. SB, xvii (64), 153-75.
G. T. Tanselle.

FREEMAN, Arthur
Octavo nonce collections of John Taylor. LIB, xviii (63), 51-7.

The fatal vesper [by W. C.] and [T. Goad's] *The doleful evensong*; claim-jumping in 1623. LIB, xxii (67), 128-35.

The printing of *The Spanish tragedy*. LIB, xxiv (69), 187-99.

Editions of Fontanus, *De bello Rhodio*. LIB, xxiv (69), 333-6.

FREEMAN, Gene
Biographical information concerning N. Bailey and John Kersey. (Query, 216). BC, xvi (67), 225.

FREEMAN, John Firley
Pirated editions of Schoolcraft's *Oneóta*. PBSA, liii (59), 252-61.

FREEMAN, Mary Eleanor Wilkins
BAL addenda. M. E. W. Freeman — entry no. 6380. PBSA, lxi (67), 127.
R. B. O'Connor.

FREEMAN, Richard Broke
Issues of the fifth thousand of *On the Origin of Species*. (Note, 222). BC, xiii (64), 213-14.

Issues of the fifth edition of *On the Origin of Species*. (Note, 225). BC, xiii (64), 350.

On the Origin of Species 1859. BC, xvi (67), 340-4.

FREEMASONS
Anti-Masonic newspapers, 1826-1834. PBSA, xxxii (38), 71-97.
M. W. Hamilton.

FREE THOUGHT
A free thought collection and its predecessors. (Contemporary collectors, 31). Illus. BC, xi (62), 184-96.
J. S. L. Gilmour.

FREIS, Susan
Emily Dickinson: a check list of criticism, 1930-66. PBSA, lxi (67), 359-85.

FRENCH, Hannah D.
Scottish-American bookbindings. Six examples from colonial North America. Illus. BC, vi (57), 150-9.

A slashed copy [in Wellesley College Library] of *Reliques of Robert Burns* [collected and published by R. H. Cromek] 1808. (Note, 265). BC, xv (66), 67-8.

Cromek's *Reliques of Robert Burns*, a footnote to Egerer 112 [J. W. Egerer *A bibliography of Robert Burns*]. BTHK, v (67/70), 33-5.

The amazing career of Andrew Barclay, Scottish bookbinder of Boston. SB, xiv (61), 145-62.

'Bound in Boston by Henry B. Legg.' Illus. SB, xvii (64), 135-9.

FRENCH, Joseph Milton
The date of Milton's first *Defense*. LIB, iii (48/9), 56-8.

An unrecorded edition of Milton's *Defensio Secunda*, 1654. PBSA, xlix (55), 262-8.

FRENCH POLICY DEFEATED
French policy defeated. London, 1760. PBSA, xxxiv (40), 86.
A. Davidson.

FRENCH TRANSLATIONS
Wing's *Short-title catalogue,* and translations from the French, 1641-1700. PBSA, xlix (55), 37-67.
J. E. Tucker.

FRESNOY, Nicolas Lenglet du
See LENGLET DU FRESNOY, Nicolas

FRICK, George Frederick
Mark Catesby: the discovery of a naturalist. PBSA, liv (60), 163-75.

FRIDAY LITERARY REVIEW
Floyd Dell in the *Friday Literary Review*. PBSA, lvii (63), 371-6.
G. T. Tanselle.

FRIED, Harvey
The early quartos of Brome's *Northern Lasse*. PBSA, liv (60), 179-81.

FRIEDLAND, Louis S.
Richard Hildreth's minor works. PBSA, xl (46), 127-50.

FRIEDMAN, Arthur
The first edition of *Essays by Mr. Goldsmith*, 1765. SB, v (52/3), 190-3.

The first edition of Goldsmith's *Bee,* no. 1. SB, xi (58), 255-9.

The problem of indifferent readings in the eighteenth century, with a solution from *The Deserted Village*. SB, xiii (60), 143-7.

Two notes on Goldsmith. 1. The first edition of Goldsmith's *Life of Bolingbroke*. 2. The 1772 edition of Goldsmith's *Traveller*. SB, xiii (60), 232-5.

FRIEND, George
George Friend 1881-1969; a memoir. Illus. JPHS, v (69), 81-6.
J. Dreyfus.

FRIENDS OF THE NATIONAL LIBRARIES
The Friends of the National Libraries. Illus. BC, iii (54), 55-60.
J. Ehrman.

FRITELLI, *abbé*
L'Abbé Fritelli. (Query, 31). BC, ii (53), 79.
P. Gaskell.

FROST, Maurice
More bee books. (Note, 10). BC, i (52), 193-4.

John Bishop, 1665-1737. (Query, 15). BC, i (52), 195.

Woodcuts for an almanac. (Query, 64). Illus. BC, iv (55), 254-5.

FÜSSLI, Johann Heinrich
Henry Fuseli. (Eighteenth-century English illustrators). Illus. BC, vi (57), 350-60.
H. A. Hammelmann.

Books with illustrations by Fuseli. (Note, 101). BC, vii (58), 299-300.
G. Schiff.

Where are Fuseli's letters? (Query, 199). BC, xv (66), 69.
M. Allentuck.

FUHRMANN, Otto Walter
The modern conception of Guttenburg. PBSA, xxxv (41), 1-16.

FULLER, Thomas
A bibliography of the works of Thomas Fuller. Illus. OBST, iv (36/48), 63-161.
S. Gibson *and* sir G. L. Keynes.

Thomas Fuller, William Dugard and the pseudonymous *Life of Sidney*, 1655. PBSA, lxii (68), 501-10.
D. H. Woodward.

Thomas Fuller, the Protestant divines, and plagiary yet speaking. [*Abel redevivus*]. TCBS, iv (64/8), 201-24.

FULLONIUS, Gulielmus
See GNAPHEUS Gulielmus

FULTON, John Farquhar
Bibliography of the Honourable Robert Boyle. Illus. OBSP, iii (31/3), 1-172.

A bibliography of two Oxford physiologists, Richard Lower, 1631-91, John Mayow, 1643-79. Illus. OBSP, iv (34/5), 1-62.

—. *and* PETERS, Charlotte H.
An introduction to a bibliography of the educational and scientific works of Joseph Priestley. PBSA, xxx (36), 150-67.

FUNERAL POEM TO . . . THE EARL OF LINCOLN
A Funeral Poem to . . . the Earl of Lincoln, 1728. (Query, 118). BC, viii (59), 431.
J. B. Shipley.

FURSTENBERG, Jean
Jean Furstenberg. (Contemporary collectors, 25). Illus. BC, ix (60), 423-34.

FUSELI, Henry
See FÜSSLI, Johann Heinrich

FUSSELL, George Edwin *and* ATWATER, V. G. B.
Travel and topography in seventeenth-century England. A bibliography of sources for social and economic history. LIB, xiii (32/3), 292-311.

FUST, Johann
The first pirate. [The priority of Fust or Mentelin's editions of St. Augustine's *De Arte Praedicandi*]. LIB, xxiv (43/4), 30-46.
F. W. Householder.

FYFE, Albert J. *and* HAGAN, John
John Stuart Mill. (Query, 127). BC, ix (60), 202-3.

FYFE, Janet
The Edinburgh Encyclopedia, 1808-30. (Query, 141). BC, x (61), 201.

G

GABEL, John Butler
Some notable errors in Parrott's edition of Chapman's Byron plays. PBSA, lviii (64), 465-8.

GABITUS, Thomas
Thomas Gabitus. (Query, 20). BC, i (52), 197.
J. S. Dearden.

Thomas Gabitus. (Query, 20). BC, i (52), 267-8.
J. C. T. Oates.

GAINES, William H.
The Continental Congress considers the publication of a Bible. Illus. SB, iii (50/1), 274-81.

GALBRAITH, Vivian Hunter
More about John Seward. EBST, ii (38/45), 385-6.

GALENUS, Claudius
An apparently unrecorded French translation of Galen's *De Simplicium Medicamentorum Facultatibus*, 1544. LIB, ii (47/8), 170-1.
S. Mitchell.

Unsigned editions of Galen and Hippocrates, (1527): further light on an elusive printer. LIB, xvi (61), 55-7.
R. J. Durling.

Galenus Claudius (Fl. 160 A.D.) *Galeni comitiali Puero consilium bisariam de græco in latinû coûersum.* 1533. PBSA, xxxiv (40), 270.
R. W. Henderson.

GALIGNANI *family*
Galignani's and the publication of English books in France from 1800 to 1852. LIB, xvi (61), 267-86.
G. G. Barber.

GALIS, Richard
Richard Galis and the witches of Windsor. LIB, xviii (37/8), 268-78.
E. Seaton.

GALLANT, Barbara
Ralph Waldo Emerson's trip to Europe in 1848. (Query, 203). BC, xv (66), 214-15.

GALLATLY, Jean
Sir John Franklin and the search for the North-West Passage. Illus. BH, i (47/51), 37-46.

GALLEYS
See PROOFS

GALLUCI, Giovanni Paolo
A special copy of Galluci's *Theatrum mundi*. (Note, 307). BC, xviii (69), 92-3.
H. Bohem.

GALLUP, Donald Clifford
(Some uncollected authors, 3). [John Hamilton Reynolds]. Additions & corrections. BC, iv (55), 156.

Aldis, Foley, and the collection of American literature at Yale. PBSA, xlii (48), 41-9.

GANDO, Nicolas
The type-specimen books of Claude Lamesle and Nicolas Gando. Illus. LIB, xviii (37/8), 201-11.
A. F. Johnson.

GANZEL, Dewey
Samuel Clemens and John Camden Hotten. LIB, xx (65), 230-42.

GARAMOND, Claude
The Garamond types of Christopher Plantin. Illus. JPHS, i (65), 14-20.
H. D. L. Vervliet.

GARDINER, Clinton Harvey
Promoting a book: Prescott to Bancroft, December 20, 1837. PBSA, li (57), 335-9.

GARDNER, Anthony
The ethics of book repairs. LIB, ix (54), 194-8.

GARNER, Stanton B.
A Harold Frederic first. SB, xv (62), 268-9.

GARRATT, K. B. *and* TRENCH, W. F.
On Swift's marginalia in copies of Macky's *Memoirs*. LIB, xix (38/9), 354-62.

GARRETT, Christina
The resurrection of the Masse, by Hugh Hilarie — or John Bale(?). LIB, xxi (40/1), 143-59.

GARROD, Heathcote William
Erasmus and his English patrons. LIB, iv (49/50), 1-13.

GARZONI, Tomaso
The Hospitall of Incurable Fooles. SB, xvi (63), 204-7.
W. E. Miller.

GASELEE, sir Stephen
The aims of bibliography. LIB, xiii (32/3), 225-58.

The Austrian post-incunabula. [A summary]. Illus. LIB, xix (38/9), 1-5.

GASKELL, John Philip W.
Dr. Johnson. An imaginary portrait. Illus. BC, i (52), 92-3.

—. BC, i (52), 192.

Printing the classics in the eighteenth century. Illus. BC, i (52), 98-111.

Pope: *One Thousand Seven Hundred and Thirty-eight*. (Note, 5). BC, i (52), 192.

Borrow, *The Death of Balder*, 1889. (Query, 6). BC, i (52), 266-7.

Inches v millimetres. (Query, 25). BC, ii (53), 78.

L'Abbé Fritelli. (Query, 31). BC, ii (53), 79.

Raymond Chandler. (Some uncollected authors 1). BC, ii (53), 209-11.

The Duke of Norfolk's press. (Query, 40). BC, ii (53), 224.

A plate from Ged's 'Sallust', Edinburgh, 1739, 1744. BTHK, iv (63/6), 76.

The bibliographical press movement. JPHS, i (65), 1-13.

Eighteenth-century press numbers. Illus. LIB, iv (49/50), 149-61.

The early work of the Foulis Press and the Wilson Foundry. Illus. 2 pts. LIB, vii (52), 77-110, 149-61.

Photographic reproduction versus quasi-facsimile transcription. [A letter]. LIB, vii (52), 135-7.

An early reference to press-figures. [A letter]. LIB, vii (52), 211.

Notes on eighteenth-century British paper. LIB, xii (57), 34-42.

Type sizes in the eighteenth century. SB, v (52), 147-51.

—. Addendum. SB, vi (54), 286.

The lay of the case. Illus. SB, xxii (69), 125-42.

Prolegomena to the revised edition of Straus and Dent's *John Baskerville*. TCBS, i (48/53), 288-95.

Henry Justice, a Cambridge book thief. TCBS, i (49/53), 348-57.

The first editions of William Mason. Addenda and corrigenda. TCBS, i (49/53), 360-1.

The meaning of 'impression' and 'issue'. TCBS, i (49/53), 361-2.

The first two years of the Water Lane press. [*With*] A check-list of . . . pamphlets, etc., printed. TCBS, ii (54/8), 170-84.

—. *and* BARBER, Giles Gaudard *and* WAR-RILOW, Alice Georgina
An annotated list of printers' manuals to 1850. Illus. JPHS, iv (68), 11-32.

—. *and* BLACK, Hester
Special collections in Glasgow University Library. Illus. BC, xvi (67), 161-8.

GASKELL, Philip
See GASKELL, John Philip W.

GATES, Payson G.
Leigh Hunt's review of Shelley's *Posthumous Poems*. PBSA, xlii (48), 1-40.

GATHORNE-HARDY, John David *4th earl of Cranbrook*
See HARDY, John David Gathorne *4th earl of Cranbrook.*

GATHORNE-HARDY, hon. Robert
See HARDY, hon. Robert Gathorne-

GAUDEN, John *bp. of Worcester*
John Gauden and the authorship of the *Eikon Basilike*. LIB, xx (65), 142-4.
H. A. Beecham.

A new bibliography of the *Eikon Basilike* of King Charles the first. OBSP, iii (50).
F. F. Madan.

GAUFFECOURT, Jean-Vincent Capronnier de
Windham and Gauffecourt. TCBS, i (49/53), 186-90.
A. N. L. Munby.

GAUSTAD, Edwin Scott
Charles Chauncy and the Great Awakening: a survey and bibliography. PBSA, xlv (51), 125-35.

GAWAIN, sir.
A bibliography paradox [*Re Gawain and the Green Knight*, MS. Cotton, Nero A.x.]. LIB, xiii (32/3), 188-91.
Sir W. W. Greg.

GAY, John
'That on Whiston' by John Gay. PBSA, lvi (62), 73-8.
J. M. Osborn.

GAYARRÉ, Charles Étienne A.
Charles Gayarré, 1805-95. PBSA, xxvii (33), 24-64.
E. L. Tinker.

GAZETTE FRANÇOISE
Gazette Françoise, Newport, R. I., 1780-81. PBSA, xxviii (34), 64-79.
A. J. Barthold.

GAZETTEER
The last years of the *Gazetteer*. LIB, vii (52), 242-61.
R. L. Haig.

GED, William
William Ged and the invention of stereotype. (Query, 102). BC, vii (58), 296-7.
J. W. Carter.

—. [A letter]. LIB, xiii (58), 141.

—. Illus. LIB, xv (60), 161-92.

— A postscript. Illus. LIB, xvi (61), 143-5.

A plate from Ged's 'Sallust', Edinburgh, 1739, 1744. BTHK, iv (63/6), 76.
J. P. W. Gaskell.

William Ged and the invention of stereotype, a second postscript. Illus. LIB, xxii (67), 352-4.
R. Donaldson.

GEESTELIJKE MINNEBRIEF
The creation of a ghost. [Stillwell, *Census* M504: *Een geestelijke Minnebrief. Die negen Couden. Die seven Banden.* (Schoonhoven: Fratres apud S. Michaelem in den Hem, c. 1500)]. PBSA, xlix (55), 249-52.
M. E. Kronenberg.

GEMINUS, Thomas
The Vesalian compendium [*De Humane Corporis Fabrica*] of Geminus and Nicholas Udall's translation; their relation to Vesalius, Caius, Vicary and De Mondeville. Illus. LIB, xiii (32/3), 367-94.
S. V. Larkey.

GEMMETT, Robert J.
An annotated checklist of the works of William Beckford. PBSA, lxi (67), 243-58.

GEMS FROM THE POETS
Gems from the poets, 1859. (Note, 199). BC, xii (63), 207-8.
G. Wakeman.

GENEALOGY
American genealogical research, its beginning and growth. PBSA, xxxvi (42), 305-14.
A. J. Wall.
Family records printed during the Colonial period. Illus. PBSA, lvii (63), 61-7.
M. B. Colket. *jr.*

GENERYDES
Notes on the manuscript of *Generydes*. [MS. Trinity College, Camb., 0.5.2]. LIB, xvi (61), 205-10.
D. A. Pearsall.

GENEVA
Geneva as a centre of early printing. Illus. LIB, ii (47/8), 213-23.
J. V. Scholderer.

GENNADIUS, Joannes
Joannes Gennadius, 1844-1932. (Portrait of a bibliophile, 12). Illus. BC, xiii (64), 305-26.
F. R. Walton.

GENNADIUS LIBRARY
See ATHENS *Gennadius libr.*

GENTLEMAN OF VIRGINIA
An identification of the *Gentleman of Virginia*. PBSA, xxxi (37), 10-20.
H. L. Dean.

GENTLEMAN'S MAGAZINE
First edition of the *Gentleman's Magazine*. (Query, 96). BC, vii (58), 188-9.
W. B. Todd.
Two notes on Johnson and the *Gentleman's Magazine*. PBSA, liv (60), 101-110.
J. Leed.
Some reprintings of the *Gentleman's Magazine*. SB, xvii (64), 210-4.
J. Leed.
A bibliographical account of the *Gentleman's Magazine*, 1731-1754. SB, xviii (65), 81-109.
W. B. Todd.

GEORGE III *king of Gt. Britain*
A George III binding, *c.* 1810-20. (English bookbindings, 15). Illus. BC, iv (55), 308-9.
H. M. Nixon.
Bookbinders to George II and his immediate descendants and collaterals. LIB, xiii (58), 186-93.
C. Ramsden.

GEORGE-A-GREENE
The *Locrine* and *George-a-Greene* title-page inscriptions. Illus. LIB, xv (34/5), 295-305.
R. C. Bald.

GEORGIA
The Journal of the Convention of the State of Georgia, on the Federal Constitution. Augusta, 1788. PBSA, xl (46), 161.
W. J. Van Schreeven.

GÉRARD DE RAYNEVAL, Joseph Mathias
[Gérard de Rayneval, Joseph Mathias] (1746-1812). Observations on the Justificative memorial of the court of London. Philadelphia, 1781. PBSA, xxxv (41), 159.
F. B. Bowe.

GERE, J. A.
A lost drawing of Taddeo Zuccaro. (Query, 166). BC, xii (63), 208.

GERMAN HEROIC POEMS
Some notes on German heroic poems in print. Illus. LIB, xxii (67), 228-42.
J. L. Flood.

GERMAN LITERATURE
Writers on German literature in *Blackwood's Magazine*, with a footnote on Thomas Carlyle. LIB, ix (54), 35-44.
A. L. Strout.

GERMANY
News from Germany. BC, iii (54), 65-7.
E. Hauswedell.
A survey of books printed in Germany between 1501 and 1530. The book production in the German speaking cultural area. PBSA, xxxiv (40), 117-36.
R. Hirsch.

GERRITSEN, Johan
The printing of the Beaumont and Fletcher folio of 1647. Illus. LIB, iii (48/9), 233-64.
The dramatic piracies of 1661: a comparative analysis. SB, xi (58), 117-31.
—; BOWERS, Fredson Thayer *and* LASLETT, Peter
Further observations on Locke's *Two Treatises of Government*. TCBS, ii (54/8), 53-87.

GERSON, J. H. C.
The 1796 edition of Walpole's *Anecdotes*: a fifth volume. (Note, 279). BC, xv (66), 484.

GERSON, Jean Charlier de
Gerson, Johannes (1363-1429). *De passionibus animae*. [Paris, Gaspard Philippe, about 1500]. PBSA, xxxv (41), 66-7.
H. R. Mead.

GERSON, Johannes
See GERSON, Jean Charlier de

GESNER, Conrad
Conrad Gesner and his *Thesaurus Evonymi Philiatri*. Illus. BH, i (47/51), 422-8.
D. I. Duveen.
Conrad Gesner as bibliographer and encyclopedist. Illus. LIB, xxi (66), 269-81.
H. Fischer.

Gesner, Petzholdt, et al. PBSA, liii (59), 15-20.
S. Pargellis.

GETCHELL, Myron Warren
[Dewey, Melvil]. *A Classification and Subject Index for Cataloguing and Arranging the Books and Pamphlets of a Library.* Amherst, 1876. PBSA, xl (46), 236-7.

GETTMANN, Royal Alfred
Colburn-Bentley and the march of the intellect. SB, ix (57), 197-213.

GHOST IN THE BANK OF ENGLAND
A ghost laid. [The *Ghost in the Bank of England*]. (Note, 226). BC, xiii (64), 350-1.
P. F. Hinton.

GHOSTS
A ghost of [Mary Tighe's] *Psyche*? (Query, 193). BC, xiv (65), 545.
S. Nowell-Smith.

Ghosts. (Query, 233). BC, xvii (68), 492.
J. Carter.

Three Scottish ghosts. EBST, ii (38/45), 429-32.
D. N. Smith'

GIBBINGS, Robert
Memories of Eric Gill. Illus. BC, ii (53), 95-103.

GIBBON, Edward
Edward Gibbon, 1737-1794. (English literary autographs, 9). Illus. BC, iii (54), 52-3.
T. J. Brown.

Gibbon's copy of Steele's *Dramatick Works*. (Note, 217). BC, xiii (64), 207.
C. C. Nickerson.

The man with the iron mask. [With] Bibliographical notes on Gibbon. [Followed by] Edward Gibbon: Bibliography. BH, i (47/51), 72-84.

The Library of Edward Gibbon. LIB, xix (38/9), 155.
Sir. G. L. Keynes.

A note on the bibliography of Gibbon, 1776-1802. LIB, xviii (63), 40-50.
N. Barker.

The costs of publishing Gibbon's *Vindication*. PBSA, xliii (49), 335-9.
G. K. Boyce.

Some notes on Edward Gibbon's *Mémoire Justificatif*. SB, v (52), 194-7.
R. Rea.

Gibbon's revision of the *Decline and fall*. SB, xxi (68), 191-204.
P. B. Craddock.

Gibbon's eyesight. Illus. TCBS, iii (59/63), 406-11.
J. H. Doggart.

GIBBON, Lewis Grassic *pseud.*
See MITCHELL James Leslie

GIBBONS, Richard
The copyright-holder of the second edition of the Rheims New Testament, Antwerp, 1600, Richard Gibbons, S. J. LIB, vi (51), 116-20.
H. R. Hoppe.

GIBRALTAR
The Garrison Press, Gibraltar. BC, v (56), 384.
A. Ehrman.

GIBSON, Reginald Walter
Thomas More: unlocated items. (Query, 94). BC, vii (58), 188.

St Thomas More's Book of Hours. (Query, 126). BC, ix (60), 202.

Pursuits, problems and pitfalls in sixteenth and seventeenth-century bibliography. PBSA, lix (65), 355-66.

GIBSON, Strickland
Thomas Bennet, a forgotten bibliographer. LIB, vi (51), 43-7.

The protocollum of Thomas Berthelet. Illus. LIB, i (46/7), 47-9.

A bibliography of Francis Kirkman, with his prefaces, dedications and commendations, 1652-80. Illus. OBSP, i (for 48/9), 47-148.

—. *and* DEELEY, Ann
Fragments of accounts relating to the Royal Works from Oxford bindings. LIB, xxv (44/5), 66-7.

—. *and* HINDLE C. J.
Philip Bliss, 1787-1857, editor and bibliographer. OBSP, iii (31/3), 173-260.

—. *and* KEYNES, sir Geoffrey Langdon
A bibliography of the works of Thomas Fuller. Illus. OBSP, iv (34/5), 63-161.

—. Additions and corrections. OBSP, i (47), 44.

GIFFARD, Henry
Giffard's *Pamela*. A comedy. (Note, 148). BC, ix (60), 455-6.
A. D. McKillop.

GIFT BOOKS
New Year's day gift books in the sixteenth century. SB, xv (62), 233-41.
E. H. Miller.

GIGEDO, Juan Vincente
Güenez, *count de Revilla*. Checklist of the official imprints of the administration of Revilla Gigedo the Younger, 1789-1794. PBSA, xlvi (52), 215-63.
E. H. Carpenter.

GILBERT, Edmund William
Richard Ford and his *Hand-book for travellers in Spain*. Illus. BH, i (47/51), 349-68.

GILBERT, sir William Schwenk
The Gondoliers. PBSA, lix (65), 193-8.
D. A. Randall.

Gilbert and Sullivan's *Princess Ida*. PBSA, lix (65), 322-6.
D. A. Randall.

The printing of *The Grand duke*: notes toward a Gilbert bibliography. PBSA, lxi (67), 335-42.
J. B. Jones.

GILBERTSON, Richardson
A variant spine label on Hawker's *Ecclesia*, 1840. (Note, 252). BC, xiv (65), 365.

GILDON, Charles
The Groans of Great Britain: an unassigned tract by Charles Gildon. PBSA, xl (46), 22-31.
J. R. Moore.

The authorship of *Cato examin'd*, 1713. [By C. Gildon?]. PBSA, li (57), 84-90.
G. L. Anderson.

GILES, Phyllis Margaret *and* SHIRE, Helena M.
Court song in Scotland after 1603: Aberdeenshire. Illus. EBST, iii (48/55), 159-68.

—. *and* WORMALD, Francis
A handlist of the additional manuscripts in the Fitzwilliam Museum, received since the publication of the catalogue of Dr. M. R. James in 1895, excluding the McClean bequests. Pt. 1. TCBS, i (49/53), 197-207.

—. Pt. 2. TCBS, i (49/53), 297-309.

—. Pt. 3. TCBS, i (49/53), 365-75.

—. Pt. 4. Index. TCBS, ii (54/8), 1-13.

—. Pt. 5. Accessions 1953-65. TCBS, iv (66), 173-8.

Description of Fitzwilliam Museum MS. 3-1954. Illus. TCBS, iv (63/6), 1-28.

GILES GINGERBREAD
See GINGERBREAD, Giles, *fict. name.*

GILL, Arthur Eric R.
A note on Eric Gill's *Pilgrim* type. BC, ii (53), 50-3.
W. Tracy.

Memories of Eric Gill. Illus. BC, ii (53), 95-102.
R. Gibbings.

GILL, Eric
See GILL, Arthur Eric R.

GILL, Evan Robertson
Napoleon's travelling library. (Query, 113). BC, viii (59), 308-9.

GILLESPIE, R. A.
The parentage of Robert Urie, printer in Glasgow. BTHK, v (67), 38-40.

GILLAM, Stanley George
Prince Louis-Lucien Bonaparte's publications. (Note, 137). BC, ix (60), 198.

GILMER, Francis Walker
See WYLLIE, John Cook

GILMOUR, John Scott L.
The Florists' Magazine. (Query, 28). BC, ii (53), 79.

Thomas Hood. (Some uncollected authors, 7). BC, iv (55), 239-48.

William Winwood Reade. (Some uncollected authors, 13). BC, vi (57), 62-6.

Charles Blount, 1654-1693. (Some uncollected authors, 17). BC, vii (58), 182-7.

Julian Hibbert, 1800-1834. (Some uncollected authors, 26). BC, ix (60), 446-51.

A Freethought collection and its predecessors. (Contemporary collectors, 31). Illus. BC, xi (62), 184-96.

The early editions of Rogers's *Italy*. LIB, iii (48/9), 137-40.

—. *and* McKENZIE, Donald F.
Untraced MSS. etc., relating to Cambridge institutions. (Query, 124). BC, ix (60), 79.

—. *and others*
A bibliography of the British flora. LIB, xxv (44/5), 187.

GILSON, David J.
Prince Louis-Lucien Bonaparte's publications. (Note, 224). BC, xiii (64), 348-50.

The first American edition of Jane Austen. (Query, 218). BC, xvi (67), 512.

The early American editions of Jane Austen. Illus. BC, xviii (69), 340-52.

GILT
The Gwynn family of edge gilders. BC, xi (62), 483.
B. C. Middleton.

Gilt. LIB, iii (48/9), 223.
R. W. Chapman.

GIMBEL, Richard
The history of the Sneyd-Gimbel and Pigott-British Museum copies of Dr. Johnson's *Dictionary*. PBSA, liv (60), 286-9.
G. L. Kolb and J. H. Sledd.

GINGERBREAD, Giles *fict. name*
The renowned history of Giles Gingerbread. Boston, 1768. PBSA, xxxvi (42), 320.
A. C. Bates.

GIORDANO-ORSINI, Gian Napoleone
See ORSINI, Gian Napoleone Giordano-

GIRAULT DE SAINVILLE
Girault de Sainville. (Note, 48). BC, iv (55), 171.
C. S. Austin.

GLAREANUS, Henricus Loritus
See LORITUS, Henricus

GLASGOW
The literature of dissent in Glasgow in the latter half of the eighteenth century. GBSR, xi (53), 56-72.
R. Morton.

GLASGOW *acad. of the fine arts*
Robert & Andrew Foulis and the Glasgow press, with some account of the Glasgow Academy of the fine arts. Illus. GBST, ii (13).
D. Murray.

GLASGOW *hosp.*
A short account of the Town's Hospital in Glasgow. BTHK, i/3 (58), 37-41.
I. Brown.

GLASGOW *univ.*
The archives of the University of Glasgow. BTHK, i/2 (57), 27-30.
D. J. W. Reid.

A 1731 copyright list from Glasgow University Archives. BTHK, ii (59/60), 30-2.
A. Nairn.

GLASGOW *univ., Hunterian Libr.*
The engraved title-page of the *Fabrica* of Vesalius, 1543 and 1555, and a drawing in the Hunterian Library, Glasgow University. Illus. BTHK, iii (60/2), 96-7.
R. Donaldson.

Two block-books in the Hunterian Library, Glasgow University. BTHK, iii (60/2), 103-4.
R. Donaldson.

Notes on the heraldry of the Hunterian Manuscripts in the University of Glasgow. BTHK, iii (60/2), 151-65.
D. Reid.

GLASGOW *univ., libr.*
Special collections in Glasgow University Library. Illus. BC, xvi (67), 161-8.
H. M. Black *and* J. P. W. Gaskell.

Two unrecorded items in the Euing music collection. BTHK, i/3 (58), 44-5.
H. G. Farmer.

Cupid and the bees: an emblem in the Stirling-Maxwell collection. BTHK, iii (60/2), 3-14.
D. Coleman and M. M. McGowan,

An Irish Parliamentary binding in Glasgow University Library. Illus. BTHK, iii (60/2), 101-2.
H. M. Black.

Archbishop Law's books in Glasgow University Library. Illus. BTHK, iii (60/2), 107-21.
H. M. Black.

—. Suppl. BTHK, v (68), 100-1.

A Strassburg incunable in the Euing collection in Glasgow University LIbrary. BTHK, iii (60/2), 165-73.
F. W. Ratcliffe.

Notes in the Euing collection of bibles in the Euing room in Glasgow University library. Illus. GBST, iv (18), 38-53.
G. Milligan.

GLASGOW *univ., libr., Ferguson coll.*
An error in the catalogue of the Ferguson Collection. BTHK, ii (59/60), 28-9.
L. Jolley.

GLASGOW UNIVERSITY PRESS
The work of a Glasgow University printer. BTHK, ii (59/60), 69-71.
A. Nairn.

GLASGOW, Ellen Anderson G.
Early impressions of Ellen Glasgow's *The Miller of Old Church*. LIB, xvi (61), 50-2.
O. L. Steele, *jr.*

A note on the early impressions of Ellen Glasgow's *They stooped to Folly*. PBSA, lii (58), 310-2.
O. L. Steele, *jr.*

Agent and author: Ellen Glasgow's letters to Paul Revere Reynolds. SB, xiv (61), 177-96.
J. B. Colvert.

Evidence of plate damage as applied to the first impressions of Ellen Glasgow's *The Wheel of Fire*. Illus. SB, xvi (63), 223-31.
O. L. Steele.

The writer's best solace: textual revisions in Ellen Glasgow's *The past*. SB, xix (66), 245-50.
R. H. W. Dillard.

GLASGOW MAGAZINE
The Glasgow Magazine, 1770. BTHK, v (67/70), 142-3.
R. H. Carnie.

GLAZIER, William Simon
A collection of illuminated MSS. (Contemporary collectors, 15). Illus. BC, vi (57), 361-8.

GLENDINNING, Oliver Nigel
Spanish books in England: 1800-1850. TCBS, iii (59/63), 70-92.

GLOBE *theatre*
Macbeth at the Globe. LIB, ii (47/8), 108-18.
J. M. Nosworthy.

GLOVER, Josse
Josse Glover breaks into print. PBSA, lv (61), 383-5.
F. B. Williams, *jr.*

GNAPHEUS, Gulielmus
John Palsgrave's translation of *Acolastius*. LIB, xiv (33/4), 433-46.
P. L. Carver.

GOAD, Thomas
The fatal vesper [by W. C.] and [T. Goad's] *The doleful evensong*; claim-jumping in 1623. LIB, xxii (67), 128-35.
A. Freeman.

Thomas Goad and *The dolefull even-song*; an editorial experiment. Illus. TCBS, i (51), 238-59.
J. Crow.

GODDARD, Geoffrey
A correction to Copinger. Illus. LIB, xviii (37/8), 114-16.

GODFREY, Garrett.
Cambridge binding by Garrett Godfrey, *c.* 1552. (English bookbindings, 71). Illus. BC, xviii (69), 490.
H. M. Nixon.

GODSHALK, William Leigh
A Sidney autograph. (Note, 211). BC, xiii (64), 65.

Prior's copy of Spenser's *Works*, 1679. PBSA, lxi (67), 52-5.

GOD'S JUDGEMENT
A note on *God's Judgement upon the Gentile Apostatized Church* and *A Treatise of the Three Evils of the Last Times* [By J. Hildrop and F. Lee?] with special reference to a volume in the library of St. Paul's Cathedral Dundee, which contains both title-pages. BTHK, iii (60/2), 31-4.
R. C. Rider.

GODWIN, Francis *bp. of Hereford*
The third edition of Francis Godwin's *The Man in the Moone*. LIB, xvii (36/7), 472-5.
G. McColley.

GOETHE, Johann Wolfgang von
Goethe's interest in the physical aspect of his works. BC, xiv (65), 178-84.
I. C. Loram.

GOFF, Frederick Richmond
The Rosenwald Library. (Contemporary collectors, 8). Illus. BC, v (56), 28-37.

A correction [to G. D. Painter's review of F. R. Goff's *Incunabula in American libraries, a third census*, 1964, in the Book Collector]. BC, xv (66), 68.
G. D. Painter.

The dates in certain German incunabula. PBSA, xxxiv (40), 17-67.

Bonaventura, S. *Meditationes vitae Christi*. [Paris], Jean Petit, [n.d.]. PBSA, xxxiv (40), 84.

Aesopus Moralisatus. Brescia, Jacobus Britannicus, 1485. PBSA, xxxiv (40), 84.

Pulci, Luigi (1431-1487). *Morgante Maggiore*. Venice, Capcasa (di Codeca). [1494?]. PBSA, xxxiv (40), 85.

Statius, Publius Papinius (*c*. 45-96 A.C.). *Opera*. PBSA, xxxiv (40), 85.

Michele da Milano. *Confessionale generale*. Venice, Peregrinus de Pasqualibus, Bononiensis, 1493. PBSA, xxxv (41), 203.

De Beau Chesne, John & Baildon, John. *A Book containing divers sortes of hands*. London, Thomas Vautrouillier, 1581. PBSA, xxxv (41), 293.

Terentius, Publius, *Afer* (*c*. 190 - *c*. 159 B.C.) *Flowers for latine speakinge*. London, 1572. PBSA, xxxv (41), 294.

Kipling, Rudyard (1865-1936). *Departmental Ditties*. 3rd edition. Calcutta, 1888. PBSA, xxxvi (42), 232.

The Athenian Oracle. 2nd edition. London, 1704. PBSA, xxxvi (42), 320.

Peter Force. PBSA, xliv (50), 1-16.

Bishop Kennett and South Carolina. PBSA, lix (65), 158-60.

GOLDBERG, Homer
The two 1692 editions of Otway's *Caius Marius*. SB, iii (50/1), 253-4.

GOLDEN, Arthur
A note on a Whitman holograph poem. PBSA, lv (61), 233-6.

A recovered Whitman fair copy of a *Drum-taps* poem, and a *Sequel to drum-taps* fragment. PBSA, lix (65), 439-41.

GOLDEN ERA
Mark Twain and the *Golden Era*. PBSA, lviii (64), 8-23.
L. E. Moberley.

GOLDSCHMIDT, Ernst Philip
Ernst Philip Goldschmidt, 1887-1954. The evolution of a great bookseller. Illus. BC, iii (54), 119-24.
J. Vellekoop.

Some cuir-ciselé bookbindings in English libraries. Illus. LIB, xiii (32/3), 337-65.

Seymour de Ricci, 1881-1942. LIB, xxiv (43/4), 187-94.

Austrian monastic libraries. LIB, xxv (44/5), 46-65.

Medieval texts and their first appearance in print. Two corrections. LIB, xxv (44/5), 79-80.

E. Ph. Goldschmidt, 1887-1954. Illus. LIB, ix (54), 75-84.
R. O. Dougan.

An Italian panel-stamped binding of the fifteenth century. Illus. TCBS, i (49/53), 37-40.

GOLDSMITH, Oliver
Goldsmith, *The Traveller*, 1770. (Note, 13). BC, i (52), 264-5.
W. B. Todd.

Goldsmith's *Millenium Hall*, 1762. (Note, 15). BC, i (52), 265-6.
P. H. Muir.

—. BC, ii (53), 72.
W. B. Todd.

Goldsmith's *Millenium Hall*, 1762. (Note, 15). BC, ii (53), 155-7.
T. G. Harmsen.

Bulmer's *Poems of Goldsmith and Parnell*. (Query, 109). BC, viii (59), 72.
S. Roscoe.

Oliver Goldsmith, 1730?-1774. (English literary autographs, 32). Illus. BC, viii (59), 417.
T. J. Brown.

Goldsmith's *A survey of experimental philosophy*, 1776. (Note, 324). BC, xviii (69),519-20.
O. M. Brack, *jr*.

Issues of the first edition of *The Vicar of Wakefield*. PBSA, xlii (48), 312-15.
J. Thorpe.

The first edition of *Essays by Mr. Goldsmith*, 1765. SB, v (52), 190-3.
A. Friedman.

The 'private issues' of *The Deserted Village*. [*And*] Addendum. SB, vi (54/55), 25-44; vii, 239.
W. B. Todd.

Quadruple imposition: an account of Goldsmith's *Traveller*. SB, vii (55), 103-11.
W. B. Todd.

The first editions of *The good natur'd man* and *She stoops to conquer*. SB, xi (58), 133-42.
W. B. Todd.

The first edition of Goldsmith's *Bee*, no. 1. SB, xi (58), 255-9.
A. Friedman.

The problem of indifferent readings in the eighteenth century, with a solution from *The Deserted Village*. SB, xiii (60), 143-7.
A. Friedman.

Two notes on Goldsmith — 1. The first edition of Goldsmith's *Life of Bolingbroke*. 2. The 1772 edition of Goldsmith's *Traveller*. SB, xiii (60), 232-5.
A. Friedman.

GOLDSTEIN, Leba M.
An account of the Faustus ballad. Illus. LIB, xvi (61), 176-89.

The Pepys ballads. Illus. LIB, xxi (66), 282-92.

GOLUBEVA, Olga Dmitrievna
The Saltykov-Shchedrin Library, Leningrad. Illus. BC, iv (55), 99-109.

GOMEZ DE QUEVEDO-VILLEGAS, Francisco
John Dodington's translation of Quevedo's *Los Sueños*. (Query, 189). BC, xiv (65), 367.
T. Rodgers.

Quevedo's *Buscón* as a chapbook. PBSA, xliv (50), 66-9.
E. H. Hespelt.

The poet Claudian in Francisco de Quevedo's *Sueño del Juicio final*. PBSA, lv (61), 183-91.
J. O. Crosby.

GOMME, G. J. L.
T. B. Aldrich and *Household Words*. PBSA, xlii (48), 70-2.

GOMME, Laurence James
The Laurence Gomme imprint. PBSA, lxi (67), 225-40.
G. T. Tanselle.

GONCALVES, Antonio Nogueira
An unknown impression by the printer of the first edition of the *Lusíades*. Illus. LIB, xxi (40/1), 309-19.
H. Thomas.

GONCOURT, Edmund Louis A. H. de *and* Jules Alfred H. de
The Goncourts and Frederick Hankey. (Note, 107). BC, x (61), 336-7.
G. D. Painter.

GOODALL, A. L.
The writings of William Hunter. BTHK, i/4 (58), 46-7.

GOODBODY, Olive C. *and* POLLARD, Michael
The first edition of William Penn's *Great Case of Liberty of Conscience*, 1670. LIB, xvi (61), 146-9.

GOODRICH, Samuel Griswold
Goodrich, S. G., Juvenile Histories, 1831-1852. PBSA, xl (46), 161-2.
C. S. Brigham.

Hawthorne and Parley's *Universal History*. PBSA, xlviii (54), 77-90.
B. B. Cohen.

GOODSPEED, George T.
The Home Library. Illus. PBSA, xlii (48), 110-8.

GOODWIN, Rutherford
The Williamsburg paper mill of William Parks the printer. Illus. PBSA, xxxi (37), 21-44.

GORDAN, John Dozier
The Rose and the Ring, 1855. (Query, 10). BC, ii (53), 77.

A doctor's benefaction: the Berg collection at the New York Public Library. PBSA, xlviii (54), 303-14.

Leonard's *Two lives*: addendum. PBSA, lv (61), 153.

In memoriam: John D. Gordan. PBSA, lxii (68), 175-6.
G. N. Ray.

GORDAN, Phyllis Walter G.
The medieval library at Bryn Mawr. PBSA, xlvi (52), 87-98.

GORDON, Cosmo Alexander
Digby's Philosophical Account of Nature, 1772. (Note, 92). BC, vii (58), 189.

Notes on the incunabula of Lucretius. TCBS, iii (59/63), 152-5.

GORDON, Douglas
The Charlecote House library. (Contemporary collectors, 20). BC, viii (59), 147-56.

18th-century French illustrated books. (Note, 162). BC, x (61), 333-4.

Books in pictures. Illus. BC, xi (62), 175-83.

GORGONZOLA, Nicolaus de
Further notes on a Milanese edition of Virgil [published by N. de Gorgonzola]. LIB, xxiv (69), 142.
D. E. Rhodes.

GORUS, Joannes *of S. Geminiano*
Some notes on the printing of the *Summa de Exemplis*, 1499. LIB, xxi (40/1), 192-8.
D. C. Bain.

GOSDEN, Thomas
An angling binding by Thomas Gosden, *c.* 1825. (English bookbindings, 21). Illus. BC, vi (57), 170.
H. M. Nixon.

GOSPELS
The Lichfield St. Chad's Gospels: repair and rebinding, 1961-1962. Illus. LIB, xx (65), 259-76.
R. Powell.

GOSSE, sir Edmund William
Gosse, Wise and Swinburne. (Note, 115). BC, viii (59), 297-9.
E. E. Bissell.

Gosse and Henry Patmore's *Poems*. (Note, 155). BC, x (61), 71-2.
A. C. Berol.

So Gosse was in it after all? (Note, 235). BC, xiii (64), 501-3.
N. Barker.

Edmund Gosse and the *Sonnets from the Portuguese*. PBSA, xliv (52), 67-70.
R. Hagedorn.

'A certain 4to *'Elegy'*. [Re T. J. Wise, Sir Edmund Gosse and editions of Gray's *Elegy*]. PBSA, lv (61), 229-31.
D. K. Adams.

GOSSON, Stephen
Two unique copies of Stephen Gosson's *Schoole of abuse*, 1579; criteria for judging nineteenth-century editing. PBSA, lix (65), 425-9.
A. F. Kinney.

GOSTLING, Henry
Henry Gostling's library, a young don's books in 1674. iii (59/63), 216-24.
B. Dickins.

GOTHIC NOVELS
Gothic romances and yellowbacks. (Contemporary collectors, 32). Illus. BC, xi (62), 313-22.
A. Walbank.

GOUDAR, Ange
[Goudar, Ange]. L'Espion chinois. PBSA, xxxvi (42), 319.
J. E. Alden.

GOUGH, Richard
A bibliographical study of Gough's *British Topography*. EBST, iv (55), 103-36.
R. P. Doig.

GOUGHER, Ronald L.
Isaac Habrecht's *Janua Linguarum quadrilinguis*, 1624. PBSA, lxii (68), 586-7.

GOUT HOLLANDOIS TYPES
See TYPE

GOVAN, John
Mr. John Govan, bibliothecary. EBST, ii (38/45), 419-20.
G. H. Bushnell.

GOVANE, Johne
See GOVAN, John

GOVE, Philip Babcock
Early numbers of *The Morning Chronicle* and *Owen's Weekly Chronicle*. LIB, xx (39/40), 412-24.

—. [A letter]. LIB, xxi (41/2), 95.

Notes on serialization and competitive publishing: Johnson's and Bailey's *Dictionaries*, 1755. OBSP. v (36/9), 305-22.

—. Bailey's folio *Dictionary*: a supplementary note. OBSP, i (47), 45-6.

GOVERNMENT PRINTING
Printing for the House of Commons in the eighteenth century. LIB, xxii (68), 25-46.
S. Lambert.

Some correspondence with Thomas Jefferson concerning the public printers, transcribed, with a foreword. SB, i (48/9), 25-37.
J. R. Lucke.

Proposals of nine printers for a new edition of *Journals of the Continental Congress*, 1785. SB, ii (49/50), 189-96.
E. P. Dandridge.

Government printing in Massachusetts, 1751-1801. SB, xvi (63), 161-200.
R. G. Silver.

GOW, Neil
Authorship of the biographical notice of Neil Gow in *Scots Magazine*, 1809. BTHK, i/3 (58), 42.
E. Jack.

GRAECAE LINGUAE SPICILEGIUM
Graecae Linguae Spicilegium, 1575. (Query, 146). BC, xi (62), 217-8.
J. S. Harvey.

GRAFTON, Richard
The clarification of some obscurities surrounding the imprisonment of Richard Grafton in 1541 and in 1543. PBSA, lii (58), 262-82.
E. G. Hamann.

GRAHAM, Dougal
Bibliography of the chapbooks attributed to Dougal Graham. Illus. GBST, i (14), 125-215.
J. A. Fairley.

GRAHAM, J. E.
The cataloguing of the Holkham manuscripts. Illus. TCBS, iv (64/8), 128-54.

GRAHAM, James, 1st marquis of Montrose
Memoirs of James, Marquis of Montrose. BTHK, i/1 (56), 27-8.
R. O. MacKenna.

GRAHAM, John
Lavater's *Physiognomy*; a checklist. PBSA, lv (61), 297-308.

GRAHAME, Kenneth
Grahamania. (Query, 30). BC, ii (53), 79.
E. E. Bissell.

GREEN, Ralph
Early American power printing presses. Illus.
SB, iv (51/2), 143-53.

GREEN, Roger Lancelyn
Jane Locker's *Greystoke Hall*. (Note, 111).
BC, viii (59), 294.

The first edition of Lewis Carroll's *Phantasmagoria*, 1869. (Query, 116). BC, viii (59), 309.

—. *and* Cohen, Morton N.
C. L. Dodgson ['Lewis Carroll']'s correspondence. (Query, 189). BC, xiii (64), 360.

GREENBERG, Robert A.
Swinburne's *Heptalogia* improved. SB, xxii (69), 258-66.

GREENE, Donald Johnson
The False Alarm and *Taxation no Tyranny*: some further observations. SB, xiii (60), 223-31.

GREENE, Robert
See also GEORGE-A-GREENE
A note on Robert Greene's *Planetomachia*, 1585. LIB, xvi (35/6), 444-7.
C. Sanders and W. A. Jackson.

The Spanish Masquerado: a problem in double-edition. LIB, ii (47/8), 14-9.
L. M. Oliver.

An unsuspected earlier edition of the *Defence of conny-catching*. Illus. LIB, xviii (63), 88-112.
I. A. Shapiro.

A best seller brought up to date: later printings of Robert Greene's *A Disputation between a He Cony-Catcher and a She Cony-Catcher*, 1592. PBSA, lii (58), 126-31.
E. H. Miller.

The editions of Robert Greene's *A quip for an upstart courtier*, 1592. SB, vi (54), 107-16.
E. H. Miller.

The first edition of Greene's *Quip for an upstart courtier*. SB, xiv (61), 212-18.
I. A. Shapiro.

The printing of *Greenes Groatsworth of witte* and *Kind-harts dreame* [by H. Chettle]. SB, xix (66), 196-7.
S. Thomas.

GREENLY, Albert Harry
Father Louis Hennepin: his travels and his books. PBSA, li (57), 38-60.

The Sweet Singer of Michigan. Bibliographically considered. Illus. PBSA, xxxix (45), 91-118.

Camels in America. PBSA, xlvi (52), 327-72.

Lahontan: an essay and bibliography. PBSA, xlviii (54), 334-89.

GREENWOOD, Robert
Fifty-two early California imprints in the Bancroft Library, a supplementary list to Greenwood's *California Imprints, 1833-1862*. PBSA, lviii (64), 181-9.
J. R. K. Kantor.

GREG, Sir Walter Wilson
Authorship attributions in the early play-lists, 1656-1671. EBST, ii (38/45), 303-29.

Bibliography — an apologia. LIB, xiii (32/3), 113-43.

A bibliographical paradox [re- *Gawain and the Green Knight*, MS. Cotton, Nero A.x]. LIB, xiii (32/3), 188-91.

A formulary of collation. LIB, xiv (33/4), 365-82.

The Honest Whore or *The Converted Courtezan*. LIB, xv (34/5), 54-60.

Was there a 1612 quarto of *Epicene*? LIB, xv (34/5), 306-15.

Alice [Norton] and the Stationers. LIB, xv (34/5), 499-500.

Books and bookmen in the correspondence of Archbishop Parker. LIB, xvi (35/6), 243-79.

Richard III — Q5, 1612. LIB, xvii (36/7), 88-97.

King Lear — mislineation and stenography. LIB, xvii (36/7), 172-83.

A proof-sheet of 1606. LIB, xvii (36/7), 454-7.

Dekker's *Magnificent Entertainment*. [A letter]. LIB, xvii (36/7), 476-8.

A fragment from Henslowe's diary. Illus. LIB, xix (38/9), 180-4.

The date of *King Lear* and Shakespeare's use of earlier versions of the story. LIB, xx (39/40), 377-400.

Some notes on Crane's manuscript of *The Witch*. LIB, xxii (41/2), 208-22.

The English Schoolmaster: Dexter v. Burby, 1602. LIB, xxiii (42/3), 90-3.

The two John Busby's LIB, xxiv (43/4), 81-6.

—. A correction. LIB, xxiv (43/4), 186.

—. A correction. LIB, xii (57), 203.

Godfrey Edmondson or Emerson. LIB, xxiv (43/4), 86.

The copyright of *Hero and Leander*. LIB, xxiv (43/4), 165-74.

Entrance, licence, and publication. LIB, xxv (44/5), 1-22.

—. [A letter]. LIB, xxvi (45/6), 308-10.

Gerard Langbaine the younger and Nicholas Cox. LIB, xxv (44/5), 67-70.

The Merry Devil of Edmonton. LIB, xxv (44/5), 122-39.

The Triumph of Peace, a bibliographer's nightmare. Illus. LIB, i (46/7), 113-26.

Paper-saving in 1639. LIB, ii (47/8), 61.

The date of the earliest play-catalogues. LIB, ii (47/8), 190-1.

Was the first edition of *Pierce Penniless* a piracy? LIB, vii (52), 122-4.

Ad imprimendum solum. LIB, ix (54), 242-7.

Samuel Harsnett and Hayward's *Henry IV*. LIB, xi (56), 1-10.

The English stock of the Stationers' Company. [A letter]. LIB, xi (56), 53.

Walter Wilson Greg, 9 July 1875-4 March 1959. Illus. LIB, xiv (59), 151-74.
J. C. T. Oates and others.

A list of Dr. Greg's writings. LIB, xxvi (45/6), 72-97.
F. C. Francis.

The writings of Sir Walter Greg, 1945-59. LIB, xv (60), 42-6.
D. F. McKenzie.

Greg's *English Literary Autographs*: a corrected reading. LIB, xvi (61), 214-15.
R. G. Howarth.

Additions from Eton College library to the record of copies in Sir W. W. Greg's *A Bibliography of the English Printed Drama to the Restoration*. LIB, xviii (63), 228-9.
R. Birley.

The printing of Shakespeare's *Troilus and Cressida* in the first folio. PBSA, xlv (51), 273-82.

The rationale of copy-text. SB, iii (50/1), 19-36.

National Library of Scotland and Edinburgh University Library copies of plays in Greg's *Bibliography of the English Printed Drama*. SB, xvi (62), 91-104.
M. Linton.

GREGORY, st. *of Nazianzus*
The errata list in the first Aldine editions of Caro's *Rime* and of the *Due Orationi* of St. Gregorius Nazianzenus. SB, xv (62), 2198-22.
C. F. Bühler.

GREY, sir George
See CAPETOWN, *S. African publ. libr., Grey collection.*

GREY, Jill E.
'S.S.' alias Mary Kilner: a biographical amendment. (Note, 323). BC, xviii (69), 519.

GREY, Zane
Gray, Zane (1872-1939). *Riders of the purple sage*. New York & London, 1912. PBSA, xxxvi (42), 68.
D. A. Randall.

GRIERSON, George
The New Testament 1611. (Dublin: George Grierson 1799). (Query, 242). BC, xviii (69), 520-1.
D. W. Adams.

GRIEVE, Christopher Murray
C. M. Grieve/Hugh McDiarmid. BTHK, i/4 (58), 3-23.
W. R. Aitken.

'First check list' of the works of Hugh MacDiarmid. [A letter]. BTHK, ii (59/60), 35.
D. M. Craig.

GRIFFIN, Lloyd W.
Christopher Colles and his two American map series. PBSA, xlviii (54), 170-82.

GRIFFITH, Elizabeth
Elizabeth Griffith, 1727-1793. (Some uncollected authors, 22). BC, viii (59), 418-24.
J. E. Norton.

GRIFFITHS, D. E.
The Sarolea papers in the Edinburgh University Library. BTHK, iii (60/2), 24-31.

GRIFFITHS, Ralph
Ralph Griffiths, author and publisher, 1746-50. LIB, xx (39/40), 197-213.
L. M. Knapp.

GRIMALDI, Joseph
Boz's *Memoirs of Joseph Grimaldi*, 1838. (Note, 277). BC, xvi (67), 80.
W. J. Smith.

GRIMM, Jakob Ludwig C. *and* Wilhelm Carl
Kinder- und Hausmärchen of the brothers Grimm. (Note, 258). BC, xiv (65), 342.
R. L. Beare.

Two editions of 'Cruishanks Grimm'. (Note, 286). BC, xvi (67), 82.
G. Wakeman.

GROLIER, Jean *vicomte d'Aguisy*
Grolier's binders. Notes on the Paris exhibition. 2 pts. BC, ix (60), 45-51, 165-70.
H. M. Nixon.

A dedication Grolier discovered recovered. (Note, 149). BC, x (61), 66-8.
D. A. Randall.

Grolier's *Chrysostom*. Illus. BC, xi (62), 64-70.
H. M. Nixon.

Grolier's binders. (Note, 171). BC, xi (62), 79.
H. M. Nixon.

—. BC, xi (62), 213-4.

GROSS, B. A.
Woodcuts for an almanac. (Query, 64). BC, v (56), 174-5.

GROSS, Seymour L.
Four possible additions to Hawthorne's *Story Teller*. PBSA, li (57), 90-5.

Hawthorne's income from *The Token*. SB, viii (56), 236-8.

—. *and* LEVY, Alfred J.
Some remarks on the extant manuscripts of Hawthorne's short stories. SB, xiv (61), 254-7.

GROVER *family*
The Grovers, letter-founders. LIB, xviii (63), 61-3.
D. D. Evans.

GRUBB, Gerald G.
The American edition of *All the Year Round*.
PBSA, xlvii (53), 301-4.

GRÜNINGER, Johann
A note on G. W. 5231. [Second edition of the
Premonstratensian Breviary, Johann Grüninger
at Strassburg]. PBSA, li (57), 236-7.
C. F. Bühler.

GRYMESTON, Elizabeth
Elizabeth Grymeston and her *Miscellanea*.
Illus. LIB, xv (34/5), 61-91.
R. Hughey *and* P. Hereford.

Jeremy Taylor and Elizabeth Grymeston. [A
letter]. LIB, xv (34/5), 247-8.
G. Bone.

Manuscript evidence for dates of two *Short-
title Catalogue books*: George Wilkin's *Three
Miseries of Barbary* and the third edition of
Elizabeth's Grymeston's *Miscellanea*. LIB,
xvi (61), 141-2.
R. Krueger.

GUARDIAN
Establishing Berkeley's authorship of *Guardian*
papers. PBSA, liv (60), 181-3.
P. Kaufman.

GUASP *family*
The House of Guasp. Illus. BC, ii (53), 265-9.
I. Quigley.

GUFFEY, George Robert
Standardization of photographic reproductions for mechanical collation. Illus. PBSA,
lxii (68), 237-40.

GUIBÉ, Robert *bp of Nantes*
Guibé, bp of Nantes (d. 1513). *Oratio ad
Innocentium VIII*. (Rome, Bartholomaeus
Guildinbeck, 1485). PBSA, xxxiv (40), 356.
H. R. Mead.

GUIDE-LINES
Guide-lines in small formats, about 1600.
SB, xiv (61), 206-8.
G. E. Dawson.

GUIDO, John Foote
King Leopold's soliloquy. PBSA, lvii (63),
351-2.

Melville's *Mardi*; Bentley's blunder? PBSA,
lxii (68), 361-71.

GUILD, William
Devices used by Raban in Guild's *Limbo's
Batterie*, 1630. BTHK, iv (63/6), 77-9.
W. R. McDonald.

GUILD OF WOMEN BINDERS
A Guild of Women-binders binding *c.* 1903.
(English bookbindings, 56). Illus. BC, xv (66),
46.
H. M. Nixon.

T. B. Mosher and the Guild of women binders.
(Note, 285). BC, xvi (67), 82.
B. C. Bloomfield.

GUILDS, John C.
Simm's first magazine: *The Album*. SB, viii
(56), 169-83.

William Gilmore Simms and the *Southern
literary gazette*. SB, xxi (68), 59-92.

The 'lost' number of The *Southern literary
gazette*. SB, xxii (69), 266-73.

GUILELMUS *Hentisberus*
Hentisberus, Guilelmus, (William Heytesbury
fl. 1340) . . . *Quaedam consequentiae subtiles*
[also] Blasius de Pelicanis. *De propositione*
[and] Appollinaris Offredus *De suppositione*.
[Venice, Peregrinus de Pasqualibus, *c.* 1500].
PBSA, xxxv (41), 155.
H. R. Mead.

GUILLEMEAU, Jacques
Notes on a late-sixteenth century opthalmic
work in English. [*A worthy treatise of the
eyes*]. LIB, ii (47/8), 173-9.
F. N. L. Poynter.

GUILLET, Urbain
Guillet, Urbain (1764-1817). *Extrait d'une
Lettre de Baltimore*. [Fribourg, Switzerland,
C. 1805]. PBSA, xxxiv (40), 86-7.

GULICK, Sidney Lewis
A Chesterfield bibliography to 1800. Illus.
PBSA, xxix (35), 3-114.

Issued in parts: the seventh edition of Chesterfield's *Letters to his son*. PBSA, lx (66), 159-65.

GULIELMUS, *Laurentius*.
An unrecorded Caxton at Ripon Cathedral.
LIB, viii (53), 37-42.
J. E. Mortimer.

GULLIBLE, Richard
See Jennings, Richard

GULLANS, Charles Bennet
Ralegh and Ayton: the disputed authorship of
'Wrong not sweete Empress of my heart.'
SB, xiii (60), 191-8.

GUMBERT, H. L.
Georg Christoph Lichtenberg, 1742-99. (Query,
138). BC, x (61), 73.

GUNN, Neil Miller
Neil Miller Gunn. BTHK, iii (60/2), 89-95.
W. R. Aitken.

GUTENBERG, Johann
Gutenberg Bible census. (Note, 1). BC, i (52),
53.
P. H. Muir.

Quincentenary [of the death of J. Gutenberg].
BC, xvii (68), 42-3.
G. D. Painter.

The invention of printing. LIB, xxi (40/1),
1-25.
J. V. Scholderer.

The modern conception of Gutenberg. PBSA, xxxv (41), 1-16.
O. W. Fuhrmann.

Changing the Gutenberg census. (Dukedom large enough, 1). PBSA, lvi (62), 157-74.
D. A. Randall.

Metal cuts at the Gutenberg workshop. [A review of *Gutenberg and the Master of the Playing Cards* by H. Lehmann-Haupt]. Illus. PBSA, lxii (68), 581-6.
K. R. Bauer.

GUTHKE, Karl Siegfried
Some bibliographical errors concerning the romantic age. PBSA, li (57), 159-62.

The Rowley myth in eighteenth-century Germany. PBSA, li (57), 238-41.

GUTHRIE, Douglas James
The literature of domestic medecine. EBST, ii (38/45), 445-7.

GUY'S PORRIDGE POT
The authorship of *Guy's Porridge Pot* and *The Dun Cow*. [R. E. or W. S. Landor?]. LIB, v (50/1), 55-8.
R. H. Super.

Robert Landor and *Guy's Porridge Pot*. LIB, xvi (61), 44-8.
R. Czerwinski.

GWYNN, Edward
Edward Gwynn. illus. LIB, xv (34/5), 92-6.
W. A. Jackson.

GWYNN *family*
The Gwynn family of edge-gilders. BC, xi (62), 483.
B. C. Middleton.

H

H., H. P. *and* P., H.
Moor's *De Analogia Contractionum Linguae Graecae.* BTHK, i/4 (58), 47-8.

HAACK, Peter R.
H. M. Tomlinson's *A Bluebell at Thiepval.* (Query, 149). BC, xi (62), 219.

HABER, Tom Burns
A. E. Housman's printer's copy of *Last Poems.* PBSA, xlvi (52), 70-7.

A. E. Housman's poetry in book-titles. PBSA, xlix (55), 69-77.

—. II. PBSA, lii (58), 62-4.

—. III. PBSA, lv (61), 239-41.

—. IV. PBSA, lxii (68), 447-51.

A unique *Shropshire Lad.* PBSA, i (56), 198-200.

The war memorial at Sudbury, Ontario. PBSA, liv (60), 186-8.

Three unreported letters of A. E. Housman. PBSA. lvii (63), 230-3.

HABERLY, Loyd
Loyd Haberly and the Seven Acres Press. BH, ii (51), 147-54.
A. L. Irvine.

HABRECHT, Isaac
Isaac Habrecht's *Janua linguarum quadrilinguis,* 1624. PBSA, lxii (68), 586-7.
R. L. Gougher.

HADFIELD, John
Francis Fawkes: *The Brown Jug.* (Query, 11). Illus. BC, i (52), 58-9.

—. *and* HARDY, John David Gathorne-4th earl of Cranbrook
Robert Bloomfield, 1766-1823. (Some uncollected authors, 20). BC, viii (59), 170-9.

HADDON, Walter
An octavo edition of *Poëmata* by Walter Haddon, 1567. PBSA, xlv (51), 166-9.
L. V. Ryan.

Walter Haddon's *Poëmata,* 1592. PBSA, xlix (55), 68-9.
L. V. Ryan.

HAEBLER, Konrad
Konrad Haebler: in memoriam. LIB, ii (47/8), 150-2.
J. V. Scholderer.

A portrait of John-George of Brandenburg on presentation bindings: a footnote to Haebler. Illus. LIB, xvii (62), 88-92.
D. M. Rogers.

HAGAN, John *and* FYFE, Albert J.
John Stuart Mill. (Query, 127). BC, ix (60), 202-3.

HAGEDORN, Ralph K.
The first edition of Switzer's *Brocoli.* LIB, vii (52), 58.

Bibliotheca Thordarsoniana: the sequel. PBSA, xliv (50), 29-54.

Edmund Gosse and the *Sonnets from the Portuguese.* PBSA, xlvi (52), 67-70.

HAGEMANN, Edward Robert
A checklist of the work of B. Traven and the critical estimates and biographical essays on him; together with a brief biography. PBSA, liii (59), 37-67.

Life buffets (and comforts) Henry James, 1883-1916: an introduction and an annotated checklist. PBSA, lxii (68), 207-25.

A checklist of the writings of John William De Forest, 1826-1906. SB, viii (56), 185-94.

HAGGARD, sir Henry Rider
Haggard, Sir Rider (1856-1925). *King Solomon's Mines.* London, 1885. PBSA, xxxiv (40), 90.
F. Coykendall.

—. Erratum. PBSA, xxxiv (40), 273-4.
F. Coykendall.

Haggard, Sir Rider (1856-1925). *King Solomon's Mines.* London, 1885. PBSA, xxxiv (40), 273.
M. L. Parrish.

The New South Africa. 'By H. Rider Haggard' [i.e. William Adolf Baillie-Grohman]. 1900. PBSA, xxxviii (44), 63-5.
J. E. Scott.

HAGGARD, sir Rider
See HAGGARD, sir Henry Rider

HAIG, Robert Louis
The last years of the *Gazetteer.* LIB, vii (52), 242-61.

The circulation of some London newspapers, 1806-1811: two documents. SB, vii (55), 190-4.

New light on the King's Printing Office, 1680-1730. SB, viii (56), 157-67.

'The Unspeakable Curll': prolegomena. SB, xiii (60), 220-3.

HAIGHT, Gordon S. Herman
The publication of Quarles' *Emblems.* LIB, xv (34/5), 97-109.

The sources of Quarles's *Emblems.* Illus. LIB, xvi (35/6), 188-209.

HAIKU
Haiku: an annotated checklist. PBSA, lvi (62), 488-94.
J. Bloomingdale.

—. Correction. PBSA, lvii (63), 96.

Haiku: an addendum. PBSA, lvii (63), 273.
W. White.

HAILES, *lord*
See DALRYMPLE, sir David

HAIN, Ludwig Friedrich T.
Imprint of an incunable, listed as Hain 14348. (Note, 270). BC, xv (66), 211-12.
S. V. Lenkey.

HAITI
L'Imprimerie Royale d'Hayti, 1817-1819. A little known royal press of the Western Hemisphere. Illus. PBSA, xxxiv (40), 171-84.
R. T. Esterquest.

HAKLUYT, Richard
The treatment of Drake's circumnavigation in Hakluyt's *Voyages*, 1589. PBSA, xxxiv (40), 281-302.
W. H. Ken.

The *Voyage to Cadiz* in the second edition of Hakluyt's *Voyages*. PBSA, xlix (55), 254-62.
C. E. Armstrong.

Richard Hakluyt and *Of the Russe Common Wealth*. PBSA, lvii (63), 312-27.
R. O. Lindsay.

Richard Hakluyt and Turberville's poems on Russia. PBSA, lxi (67), 350-1.
L. E. Berry.

HALE, Edward Everett
Edward Everett Hale: preacher as publisher. PBSA, xlvi (52), 139-50.
E. Coleman.

HALE, Richard Walden
A journey of bibliographical exploration. PBSA, lvii (63), 33-41.

HALES, John Rigby
A Newberry Library Supplement to the foreign books in M. J. D. Cockle's *A Bibliography of English Military Books up to 1642 and of contemporary Foreign Works*. PBSA, lv (61), 137-9.

HALFPENNY, Eric
Letters from Lincoln's Inn, 1846-9. [Correspondence between Charles Purton Cooper, Q.C. and Frederick William Halfpenny]. LIB, xii (57), 256-69.

HALFPENNY, Frederick William
Letters from Lincoln's Inn, 1846-9. [Correspondence between Charles Purton Cooper Q.C. and Frederick William Halfpenny]. LIB, xii (57), 256-69.
E. Halfpenny.

HALF-SHEET IMPOSITION
See IMPOSITION

HALIFAX. *1st marq.*
See SAVILE, George *1st marq. of Halifax.*

HALKETT, Samuel *and* LAING, John
Halkett and Laing [*Dictionary of anonymous and pseudonymous English literature*] continued. (Query, 186). BC, xiii (64), 360.
R. A. Christophers *and* M. O'Donoghue.

Additions to Halkett & Laing. [A letter]. LIB, viii (53), 204.
D. E. Rhodes *and* A. E. C. Simoni.

HALL, C. P.
Two licences granted to Cambridge stationers. TCBS, i (49/53), 443-4.

William Rysley's Catalogue of the Cambridge University muniments, compiled in 1420. TCBS, iv (63/6), 85-99.

HALL, David
David Hall and the Stamp Act. PBSA, lxi (67), 13-37.
R. D. Harlan.

HALL, Edward
Edward Halle's *The Union of the Two Noble and Illustre Famelies of Lancastre and Yorke*, and its place among English Americana. PBSA, xxxiii (39), 40-54.
E. Wolf, *2nd*

HALL, P. E.
An early example of remaindering? (Query, 97). BC, vii (58), 189.

—. BC, x (61), 454.

An unidentifiable English binder. (Query, 144). BC, xi (62), 86.

A Latin translation of Tennyson's *In Memoriam*. (Note, 207). BC, xii (63), 490-2.

A Latin translation of *In Memoriam*. (Note, 207). BC, xvii (68), 78.

Tennyson's *Idylls of the King* and *The Holy Grail*. (Query, 222). BC, xvii (68), 218.

HALL, Parry
The printing [by M. Carey and P. Hall] of Jefferson's *Notes*, 1793-94. SB, v (52), 201.
P. J. Conkwright *and* C. Verner.

HALLADAY, Jean
Some errors in the bibliography of the library edition of John Ruskin's works [by E. T. Cook and A. Wedderburn, London, 1912]. PBSA, lxi (68), 127-9.

HALLAM, Arthur Henry
A. H. Hallam's *Poems*, 1830. (Note, 123). BC, viii (59), 430-1.
S. Nowell-Smith.

A. H. Hallam's *Poems*, 1830. (Note, 123). BC, ix (60), 64-5.
Elkin Mathews *ltd.*

Hallam's *Poems* of 1830: a census of copies. PBSA, xxxv (41), 277-80.
T. H. V. Motter.

The Hallam-Tennyson *Poems*, 1830. SB, i (48), 193-9.
M. V. Bowman.

HALLAM, George W.
Some new Stephen Crane items. SB, xx (67), 263-6.

HALLAM, Henry
Henry Hallam, *The Times* newspaper, and the Halliwell Case. LIB, xviii (63), 133-40.
W. H. Bond.

HALLAM, Henry Adrian Newton
Lamport hall revisited (Unfamiliar libraries, 12). Illus. BC, xvi (67), 439-49.

HALLE, Edward
See HALL, Edward

HALLENBECK, Chester T.
Book-trade publicity before 1800. PBSA, xxxii (38), 47-56.

—. Correction. PBSA, xxxiv (40), 60.

HALLIWELL, James Orchard
See PHILLIPPS, James Orchard Halliwell-

HALSBAND, Robert
Two facts about Mary Astell. (Note, 163). BC, x (61), 334.

Editing the letters of letter-writers. SB, xi (58), 25-37.

HAMILL, Frances
Some unconventional women before 1800: printers, booksellers, and collectors. PBSA, xlix (55), 300-14.

HAMILTON, Eugene Lee-
A publishing history of the writings of Eugene Lee-Hamilton. PBSA, li (57), 141-59.
T. H. Lyon.

Eugene Lee-Hamilton. PBSA, lv (61), 231-2.
S. Pantazzi.

—. PBSA, lvii (63), 92-4.

HAMILTON, George Rostrevor
E. R. Eddison. BH, i (47/51), 53-7.

HAMILTON, Marion H.
The early editions of Dryden's *State of Innocence*. SB, v (52/3), 163-6.

The manuscripts of Dryden's *The State of Innocence* and the relation of the Harvard MS to the first quarto. SB, vi (54), 237-46.

HAMILTON, Milton Wheaton
Anti-Masonic newspapers, 1826-1834. PBSA, xxxii (38), 71-97.

HAMLYN, Hilda M.
Eighteenth-century circulating libraries in England. LIB, i (46/7), 197-222.

HAMMAN, Edmund G.
The clarification of some obscurities surrounding the imprisonment of Richard Grafton in 1541 and in 1543. PBSA, lii (58), 262-82.

HAMMELMANN, Hanns Andreas
Isaac Taylor the elder. (Eighteenth-century English illustrators). Illus. BC, i (52), 14-27.

Samuel Wale. (Eighteenth-century English illustrators). Illus. BC, i (52), 150-65.

Francis Hayman. (Eighteenth-century English illustrators). Illus. BC, ii (53), 116-32.

Anthony Walker. (Eighteenth-century English illustrators). Illus. BC, iii (54), 87-102.

A bookseller's stamp. (Query, 37). BC, iv (55), 254.

The Infant's library. (Query, 46). BC, v (56), 78.

Rousseau's *Dictionnaire de Musique*, 1768. (Query, 67). BC, v (56), 79.

Henri Fuseli R. A. (Eighteenth-century English illustrators). Illus. BC, vi (57), 350-60.

A cancel in the Boucher Molière, 1734. (Query, 190). BC, xiv (65), 367.

A coloured frontispiece to the *Spectator*. (Query, 195). BC, xiv (65), 546.

John Vanderbank, 1694-1739. (Eighteenth-century English illustrators). Illus. BC, xvii (68), 285-99.

Proposals for printing: 'Doctor Thomas Jackson's works compleat . . . 1672'. (Query, 230). BC, xvii (68), 491-2.

English eighteenth-century book illustrators. [including a list of 'English books illustrated by Gravelot']. Illus. BH, ii (51/2), 127-135.

Gravelot in England. Illus. BH, ii (51/2), 176-190.

HAMMETT, Dashiell
See HAMMETT, Samuel Dashiell

HAMMETT, Samuel Dashiell
Dashiell Hammett, 1894-1961. (Some uncollected authors, 31). BC, xi (62), 71-8.
R. E. Stoddard.

A Dashiell Hammett omnibus. (Note, 181). BC, xi (62), 217.
D. Flower.

HAMPSTEAD, *Keats house and mus.*
The Leigh Browne collection at the Keats Museum. LIB, xvii (62), 246-50.
P. Kaufman.

HANAWAY, William L.
The earliest extant French armorial ex-libris. (Note, 161). BC, xi (62), 212.

HANDEL, George Frederick
Handel in France: editions published there during his lifetime. Illus. EBST, iii (48/55), 223-48.
C. Hopkinson.

HANDLEY-TAYLOR, Geoffrey
Extinct societies. (Query, 39). BC, ii (53), 223-4.

Winifred Holtby. (Query, 50). BC, iii (54), 227.

Musical epitaphs. (Query, 81). BC, vi (57), 181-2.

HANDOVER, Phyllis Margaret
Talbot Baines Reed, 1852-1893. (Some uncollected authors, 35). BC, xii (63), 62-7.

HANDS, M. S. G. *and* SMITH, Margaret S.
The Cathedral Libraries catalogue. [*With*] An appendix: Printed catalogues of books and manuscripts in cathedral libraries — England and Wales. LIB, ii (47/8), 1-13.

HANDS, Rachel
Sources of the Boke of St. Albans. (Query, 220). BC, xvii (68), 83.

HANDWRITTEN BOOKS
Handwritten books. (Query, 70). BC, v (56), 281.
H. E. James.

HANEMANN, Lotte
Three early Dutch printings. PBSA, lxii (68), 427.

HANKEY, Frederick
The Goncourts and Frederick Hankey. (Note, 107). BC, x (61), 336-7.
G. D. Painter.

HANMER, sir Thomas *4th bart.*
Warburton, Hanmer and the 1745 edition of Shakespeare. SB, ii (49), 35-48.
G. E. Dawson.

HANNEMAN, Audre
Addenda to Hanneman: Hemingway's *The old man and the sea.* [Audre Hanneman's *Ernest Hemingway: a comprehensive bibliography*]. PBSA, lxii (68), 613-14.
W. White.

HANOVER PAMPHLETS
The number, order and authorship of the Hanover pamphlets attributed to Chesterfield. PBSA, xliv (50), 224-38.
W. B. Todd.

HANSE MERCHANTS
See LONDON HANSE MERCHANTS.

HANSON, Laurence William
A bookseller's stamp. (Query, 37). BC, ii (53), 223.

English newsbooks, 1620-1641. LIB, xviii (37/8), 355-84.

The King's printer at York and Shrewsbury, 1642-3. LIB, xxiii (42/3), 129-31.

Two Caslon specimens. LIB, ii (47/8), 199-200.

John Cosin's *Collection of Private Devotions*, 1627. LIB, xiii (58), 282-92.

John Baskerville: a bibliography. LIB, xv (60), 201-6.

HANSON, Thomas William
An international binding design. (Note, 198). BC, xii (63), 206-7.

Edwards of Halifax, bookbinders. Illus. BH, i (47/51), 329-38.

HANTONE, Bueve de
Bueve de Hantone. PBSA, l (56), 379.
R. Hirsch.

HANWAY, Jonas
A London binding for Jonas Hanway, 1783. (English bookbindings, 61). Illus. BC, xvi (67), 194.
H. M. Nixon.

HARDACRE, Paul H.
Edward Hyde, earl of Clarendon, 1609-74. (Portrait of a bibliophile, 1). BC, vii (58), 361-8.

HARDING, George Laban
Tahitian imprints, 1817-1833. PBSA, xxxv (41), 48-57.

HARDING, Walter N. H.
Francis Fawkes: *The Brown Jug.* (Query, 11). BC, i (52), 130.

British song books and kindred subjects. (Contemporary collectors, 33). Illus. BC, xi (62), 448-59.

HARDING, Walter Roy
A sheaf of Whitman letters. SB, v (52/3), 203-10.

HARDMAN, sir William
Sir William Hardman's Journal. (Note, 267). BC, xv (66), 207-10.
C. L. Cline.

HARDY, John David Gathorne-, *4th earl of Cranbrook, and* HADFIELD, John
Robert Bloomfield, 1766-1823. (Some uncollected authors, 20). BC, viii (59), 170-9.

HARDY, hon. Robert Gathorne-
Some notes on the bibliography of Jeremy Taylor. Illus. LIB, ii (47/8), 223-49.

Halifax's *The Character of a Trimmer*: some observations in the light of a manuscript from Ickworth. LIB, xiv (59), 117-23.

HARDY, Thomas
Thomas Hardy, 1840-1928. (English literary autographs, 19). BC, v (56), 249.
T. J. Brown.

The first publication of *The Spectre of the Real.* LIB, xv (60), 60-1.
D. B. Green.

Hardy's grim note in *The Return of the Native.* PBSA, xxxvi (42), 37-45.
C. S. Weber.

The manuscript of Hardy's *Two on a Tower.* Illus. PBSA, xl (46), 1-21.
C. J. Weber.

A query concerning the handwriting in Hardy's manuscripts. PBSA, lvii (63), 357-60.
D. Kramer.

Hardy's debut — how a literary 'career was determined' one hundred years ago. PBSA, lix (65), 319-22.
C. J. Weber.

The 'duplicate' manuscript of Hardy's *Two on a tower*: a correction and comment. PBSA, lx (66), 219-21.
R. C. Schweik.

Two 'new' texts of Thomas Hardy's *The Woodlanders*. SB, xx (67), 135-50.
D. Kramer.

HARE, John Ellis
A bibliography of the works of Leon Pamphile Lemay, 1837-1918. PBSA, lvii (63), 50-60.

HARINGTON MS.
The Harington Manuscript at Arundel Castle and related documents. Illus. LIB, xv (34/5), 388-444.
R. Hughey.

HARKNESS, Bruce
The precedence of the 1676 editions of Milton's *Literæ Pseudo-Senatûs Anglicani*. SB, vii (55), 181-5.

Bibliography and the novelistic fallacy. SB, xii (59), 59-73.

HARLAN, Robert D.
Sales of and profits on some early editions of Sir William Blackstone's *Commentaries*. PBSA, lviii (64), 156-63.

The Court of Fancy in England. PBSA, lix (65), 48-9.

Some additional figures of distribution of eighteenth-century English books. PBSA, lix (65), 160-70.

The publishing of *The grand magazine of universal intelligence and monthly chronicle of our own times*. PBSA, lix (65), 429-36.

David Hall and the Stamp Act. PBSA, lxi (67), 13-37.

HARLEIAN MISCELLANY
A note on the publication of Johnson's *Proposals for printing the Harleian Miscellany*. PBSA, xlviii (54), 196-8.
G. J. Kolb.

HARLEQUINADES
Harlequinades. (Note, 83). BC, vi (57), 182-3.
P. H. Muir.

HARLEY, Edward *2nd earl of Oxford*
Edward Harley, 2nd earl of Oxford, 1689-1741. (Portrait of a bibliophile, 8). Illus. BC, xi (62), 158-74.
C. E. Wright.

HARLEY, Robert *1st earl of Oxford*
A Harleian binding by Thomas Elliot, 1721. (English bookbindings, 49). Illus. BC, xiii (64), 194.
H. M. Nixon.

Harleian bindings by Chapman, 1721. (English bookbindings, 58). Illus. BC, xv (66), 321-2.
H. M. Nixon.

The reports of a press spy [Robert Clare] for Robert Harley: new bibliographical data for the reign of Queen Anne. LIB, xxii (67), 326-45.
H. L. Snyder.

HARLOW, Neal
The well-tempered bibliographer. PBSA, l (56), 28-39.

HARLOW, Thompson R.
Thomas Robbins, clergyman, book collector, and librarian. Illus. PBSA, lxi (67), 1-11.

HARLOW, Virginia
Addenda to Harlow [V. Harlow's *Thomas Sergeant Perry: a biography*]: two T. S. Perry essays. PBSA, lxii (68), 612-3.
G. Monteiro.

HARMAN, Marian
A newly discovered Oxford book. PBSA, xxxii (38), 98-101.

HARMSEN, Tyrus G.
Goldsmith's *Millenium Hall*, 1762. (Note, 15). BC, ii (53), 155-7.

HARMSWORTH COLLECTION
See WASHINGTON *D. C., Folger Shakespeare libr.*

HARPER, Lathrop C.
Guillet, Urbain (1764-1817). *Extrait d'une Lettre de Baltimore*. [Fribourg, Switzerland, *c.* 1805]. PBSA, xxxiv (40), 86-7.

A Memorial Containing A Summary View of Facts, with their Authorities, In Answer to the Observations sent by the English Ministry to the Courts of Europe. Philadelphia, James Chattin, 1757. PBSA, xxxiv (40), 272-3.

Lathrop Colgate Harper: a happy memory. PBSA, lii (58), 161-72.
L. C. Wroth.

HARPSFIELD, Nicholas
Nicholas Harpsfield's note of Cranmer's recantation. TCBS, iv (64/8), 310-312.
J. M. Fletcher *and* J. Fines.

HARRINGTON, sir John
Harrington's metrical paraphrases of the Seven Penitential Psalms: three manuscript versions. PBSA, liii (59), 240-51.
K. E. Schmutzler.

HARRIS, Bernard
An early ownership rhyme. (Query, 27). BC, ii (53), 222.

HARRIS, Caleb Fiske
C. Fiske Harris, collector of American poetry and plays. PBSA, lvii (63), 14-32.
R. E. Stoddard.

HARRIS, Elizabeth M.
Experimental graphic processes in England 1800-1859. Illus. JPHS, iv (68), 33-86.

Experimental graphic processes in England 1800-1859. Part III. Illus. JPHS, v (69), 41-80.

HARRIS, Joel Chandler
BAL addendum. Joel Chandler Harris — entry no. 7115. PBSA, lxi (67), 266.
J. Blanck.

HARRIS, John
The recollections of Rifleman Harris [by H. Curling]. BH, i (47/51), 450-4.
C. Ray.

HARRISON, Frank Mott
Nathaniel Ponder; the publisher of *The Pilgrim's Progress*. LIB, xv (34/5), 257-94.

Some illustrators of *The Pilgrim's Progress*, Pt. 1; John Bunyan. Illus. LIB, xvii (36/7), 241-63.

Editions of *The Pilgrim's Progress*. LIB, xxii (41/2), 73-81.

HARRISON, Frederick
The library of the Dean and Chapter of York. EBST, ii (38/45), 390-1.

HARRISON, George Bagshawe
Books and readers, 1599-1603. LIB, xiv (33/4), 1-33.

HARRISON, John
John Harrison's signed roll? Illus. LIB, viii (53), 123-4.
W. S. Mitchell.

HARRISON, K. P.
Katharine of Aragon's pomegranate. TCBS, ii (54/8), 88-92.

HARRY, *Blind*
See BLIND HARRY

HARSNETT, Samuel *abp. of York*
Samuel Harsnett and Hayward's *Henry IV*. LIB, xi (56), 1-10.
Sir W. W. Greg.

HARSY, Noël de
Two notes on fifteenth-century printing. I. Jacobus Ledelh. II. Jacques Le Forestier and Noël de Harsy, printers at Rouen, 1490. EBST, iii (48/55), 75-7.
W. Beattie.

HART, Andro
An early imprint of Andro Hart. Illus. BTHK, iv (63/6), 34-6.
R. Donaldson.

HART, E. F.
Caroline lyrics and contemporary song-books. LIB, viii (53), 89-110.

HART, Francis Russell
Proofreading Lockhart's *Scott*: the dynamics of biographical reticence. SB, xiv (61), 3-22.

HART, James A.
American poetry of the first World War and the book trade. PBSA, lxi (67), 209-24.

HARTE, Francis Bret
An unlocated Bret Harte-Joaquin Miller book [*Thompson's Prodigal and other sketches*]. PBSA, lxi (67), 60.
G. Degruson.

HARTHAN, John P.
Early trade bindings. (Query, 2). BC, i (52), 266.

HARTZOG, Martha
Nineteenth-century cloth bindings. PBSA, lxi (67), 114-19.

HARVARD UNIVERSITY
James Russell Lowell's *Ode recited at the Commemoration of the Living and Dead soldiers of Harvard University*, July 21, 1865. PBSA, xxxvii (43), 169-202.
H. V. Bail.

Harvard University. Pietas et Gratulatio Collegii Cantabrigiensis apud Novanglos. Bostoni-Mass., [1762]. PBSA, xxxix (45), 321-2.
J. E. Alden.

The printer of Harvard's *Humble Proposal*, 1659 [i.e. Thomas Newcombe, not the Cambridge (Mass.) Press]. SB, iv (51), 199-200.
B. E. Cooper *and* R. E. Hasker.

HARVARD UNIVERSITY *libr., Houghton libr.*
Milton and the Harvard Pindar. SB, xvii (64), 77-82.
M. Kelley *and* S. B. Atkins.

The Houghton library's vernis binding. [A revised description]. BC, xv (66), 352.
W. H. Bond.

HARVARD UNIVERSITY *libr., Widener libr.*
The proofs of *Gareth and Lynette* in the Widener collection. PBSA, xli (47), 321-40.
E. F. Shannon.

HARVEY, Edward
Harvey, Edward (fl. 1750). *A New Manual; and Platoon Exercise*. New York, 1769. PBSA, xxxiv (40), 359.
A. Davidson.

HARVEY, Gabriel
The first edition of Gabriel Harvey's *Foure Letters*. LIB, xv (34/5), 212-23.
F. R. Johnson.

Gabriel Harvey's *Three Letters*: a first issue of his *Foure Letters*. LIB, i (46/7), 134-6.
F. R. Johnson.

HARVEY, John S.
Graecae Linguae Spicilegium, 1575. (Query, 146). BC, xi (62), 217-18.

HARVEY, William
William Harvey, 1578-1657. (English scientific autographs, 3). Illus. BC, xiv (65), 61.
T. J. Brown.

William Fitzer, the publisher of Harvey's *De Motu Cordis*, 1628. LIB, xxiv (43/4), 142-64.
E. Weil.

Harvey manuscripts. PBSA, liv (60), 177-9.
F. G. Kilgour.

HASKER, Richard E.
The copy for the first folio *Richard II*. SB, v (52/3), 53-72.

— *and* COOPER, Bertram C.
The printer of Harvard's *Humble Proposal*, 1659. SB, iv (51/2), 199-201.

HASSALL, William Owen
Thomas Coke, earl of Leicester, 1697-1759. (Portrait of a bibliophile, 2). Illus. BC, viii (59), 249-61.

The books of Sir Christopher Hatton at Holkham. Illus. LIB, v (50/1), 1-13.

HATTAWAY, Michael
Marginalia by Henry VIII in his copy of *The bokes of Salomon*. TCBS, iv (64/8), 166-70.

HATTON, sir Christopher
The books of Sir Christopher Hatton at Holkham. Illus. LIB, v (50/1), 1-13.
W. O. Hassall.

Sir Christopher Hatton's book stamps. Illus. LIB, xii (57), 119-21.
R. J. Roberts.

HAUDENT, Guillaume
Guillaume Haudent and the first translation of Poliziano's *Rusticus*. LIB, viii (53), 111-17.
A. E. C. Simoni.

HAUPT, Hellmut Lehmann
See LEHMANN-HAUPT, Hellmut

HAUSWEDELL, Ernst L.
News from Germany. BC, iii (54), 65-7.

HAWAII
The first printing in Hawaii. PBSA, l (56), 313-27.
T. M. Spaulding.

HAWES, Stephen
The conuercyon of swerers: another edition. Illus. LIB, xxiv (69), 44-50.
A. Morgan.

HAWKER, Robert Stephen
Hawker of Morwenstow, 1803-1875. (Some uncollected authors, 39). [2 pts.] BC, xiv (65), 62-71; 202-11.
C. Woolf.

A variant spine label on Hawker's *Ecclesia*, 1840. (Note, 252). BC, xiv (65), 365.
G. Gilbertson.

HAWKINS, Dorothy Lawson
James Adams. The first printer of Delaware. PBSA, xxviii (34), 28-63.

HAWKSHAW
Hawkshaw rides again. BC, xii (63), 178-83.
J. Carter.

HAWTHORNE, Manning *and* DANA Henry Wadsworth Longfellow
The origin of Longfellow's *Evangeline*. Illus. PBSA, lxi (47), 165-203.

HAWTHORNE, Nathaniel
Hawthorne and William Henry Smith. An essay in Anglo-American bibliography. BC, v (56), 370-4.
J. E. Alden.

On the imposition of the first edition of Hawthorne's *The Scarlet Letter*. Illus. LIB, xvii (62), 250-5.
O. L. Steele.

The early projected works of Nathaniel Hawthorne. PBSA, xxxix (45), 119-155.
N. F. Adkins.

Hawthorne and *Parley's Universal History*. PBSA, xlviii (54), 77-90.
B. B. Cohen.

Hawthorne's income from *The Token*. SB, viii (56), 236-8.
S. L. Gross.

Four possible additions to Hawthorne's *Story Teller*. PBSA, li (57), 90-5.
S. L. Gross.

Concealed printings in Hawthorne. PBSA, lvii (63), 42-9.
M. J. Bruccoli.

States of *Fanshawe*. PBSA, lviii (64), 32.
M. J. Bruccoli.

Negative evidence about *The Celestial Rail-Road*. PBSA, lviii (64), 290-2.
M. J. Bruccoli.

A false edition of Hawthorne's *Twice-told tales*. PBSA, lix (65), 182-8.
J. D. Crowley.

A sophisticated copy of *The house of the seven gables*. PBSA, lix (65), 438-9.
M. J. Bruccoli.

Notes on the Hawthorne canon. PBSA, lx (66), 364-7.
N. F. Adkins.

Some remarks on the extant manuscripts of Hawthorne's short stories. SB, xiv (61), 254-7.
S. L. Gross *and* A. J. Levy.

Notes on the destruction of *The Scarlet letter* manuscript. SB, xx (67), 257-9.
M. J. Bruccoli.

HAZEN, Allen Tracy
Eighteenth-century quartos with vertical chain-lines. LIB, xvi (35/6), 337-42.

J. Sturt, facsimilist. LIB, xxv (44/5), 72-9.

Signatures in nineteenth-century American printing. [A letter]. LIB, iii (48/9), 224-9.

—. LIB, vii (52), 134.

One meaning of the imprint. LIB, vi (51/2), 120-3.

Great Britain. Parliament. *Directions of the Lords and Commons assembled in Parliament . . . for the electing and choosing of Ruling-Elders . . . for the speedy settling of the Presbyteriall-Government*. Lond., 1645. PBSA, xxxv (41), 204.

Eustace Burnaby's manufacture of white paper in England. Illus. PBSA, xlviii (54), 315-33.

Baskerville and James Whatman. SB, v (52/3), 187-9.

The booksellers' 'ring' at Strawberry Hill in 1842. SB, vii (55), 194-8.

—. *and* CHAPMAN, Robert William
Johnsonian bibliography, a supplement to Courtney. [*A Bibliography of Samuel Johnson*]. OBSP, v (36/9), 117-66.

HAY, John
William Dean Howells and *The Breadwinners* [by J. Hay]. SB, xv (62), 267-8.
G. Monteiro.

HAYCRAFT, Howard
Poe's *Purloined Letter*. PBSA, lvi (62), 486-7.

Poe and *The Musiad*. PBSA, lix (65), 437-8.

HAYDAY, James
A binding by James Hayday, *c.* 1845. (English bookbindings 24). Illus. BC, vii (58), 62.
H. M. Nixon.

HAYDN, Franz Joseph
Haydn's settings of Scottish songs in the collections of Napier and Whyte. Illus. EBST, iii (48/55), 85-120.
C. Hopkinson *and* C. B. Oldman.

Thomson's collections of national song with special reference to the contributions of Haydn and Beethoven. Illus. EBST, ii (38/45), 1-64.
C. Hopkinson *and* C. B. Oldman.

—. Addenda and Corrigenda. EBST, iii (48/55), 121-4.

HAYES, Richard James
The Chester Beatty Library. (Contemporary collectors, 18). Illus. BC, vii (58), 253-64.

HAYLEY, William
Some notes on the bibliography of William Hayley: Pt. I - II. TCBS, iii (59/63), 103-12; 167-76.
N. J. Barker.

—: Pt. III. Note on printers and publishers. Illus. TCBS, iii (59/63), 339-60.
N. J. Barker.

HAYMAN, Francis
Francis Hayman. (Eighteenth-century English illustrators). Illus. BC, ii (53), 116-32.
H. A. Hammelmann.

HAYMAN, Robert G.
Addendum to Shaw and Shoemaker [*American Bibliography*]: Smith's *Indian doctor's dispensatory*. PBSA, lxiii (69), 126-8.

HAYWARD, sir John
Samuel Harsnett and Hayward's *Henry IV*. LIB, xi (56), 1-10.
Sir W. W. Greg.

HAYWARD, John Davy
The Rosenbach-Bodmer Shakespeare collection. BC, i (52), 112-16.

Alice, 1865. (Note, 6). BC, i (52), 127.

Shakespeare's *Sonnets*, 1609. (Note, 16). BC, i (52), 266.

Rochester rarities. (Query, 41). BC, ii (53), 224.

John Taylor's *Booke of Martyrs*, 1633. (Note, 49). BC, iv (55), 171-2.

The first edition of *Les Liaisons dangereuses*. (Query, 65). BC, iv (55), 331.

—. BC, vi (57), 74.

The location of copies of the first editions of Giordano Bruno. Illus. BC, v (56), 152-7.

First editions of Giordano Bruno. BC, v (56), 381-2.

The *Infants' Library*. (Note, 75). BC, v (56), 383.

Gray's *Elegy*. (Query, 77). BC, v (56), 384-5.

The Shadows of Life. (Query, 92). BC, vii (58), 77.

Jane Locker's *Greystoke Hall* ?1886. (Note, 111). BC, viii (59), 183.

The first American edition of the Brontës' *Poems*. (Query, 121). BC, viii (59), 432.

John Hayward, C.B.E., 1904-1965: some memories. Illus. BC, xiv (65), 443-86.
J. Carter *and others*.

HAYWOOD, Thomas
See HEYWOOD, Thomas

HAZARD, Samuel
Cheap repository tracts: Hazard and Marshall edition. LIB, xx (39/40), 295-340.
G. H. Spinney.

HAZLITT, William
William Hazlitt's *The spirit of the age,* third edition, 1858. (Query, 206). BC, xv (66), 356.
P. L. Story.

Hazlitt's *Grammar* abridged. Illus. LIB, xiii (32/3), 97-9.
Sir G. L. Keynes.

An addition to the Hazlitt canon: arguments from external and internal evidence. PBSA, lv (61), 347-70.
W. M. Marshall.

HEADLAM, Cecil
A Hopkins discovery [in L. Magnus and C. Headlam, *Prayers from the poets: a calendar of devotion*]. LIB, xxiv (69), 56-8.
N. White *and* T. Dunne.

HEADLINES
See RUNNING-TITLES

HEANEY, Howell J.
In memoriam: Philo Clarke Calhoun, 1889-1964. PBSA, lxii (68), 421-5.

A selective check-list of bibliographical scholarship for 1964. Part II: Later Renaissance to the present. SB, xix (66), 262-75.

—. and CALHOUN, Philo
Dickens' *Christmas Carol* after a hundred years: a study in bibliographical evidence. PBSA, xxxix (45), 271-317.

Dickensiana in the rough. PBSA, xli (47), 293-320.

HEARTSILL, William Williston
Texans in leopard skin pants [Capt. Sam J. Richardson and W. W. Heartsill's *Fourteen Hundred and 91 days in the Confederate Army*]. PBSA, xliv (50), 373-8.
R. B. Brown.

HEAWOOD, Edward
Further notes on paper used in England after 1600. Illus. LIB; ii (47/8), 119-49.

—. [A letter]. LIB, iii (48/9), 141-2.

A critical study of Heawood's *Watermarks mainly of the 17th and 18th centuries.* PBSA, xlv (51), 23-36.
A. H. Stevenson.

HEAZ, John
John Heaz, Elizabethan letter-founder to the printers. TCBS, i (49/53), 287.
B. Dickins.

HEBER, Richard
A puzzle in the Heber Sale catalogue. (Query, 157). BC, xi (62), 486.
R. S. Pirie.

HEDONICUS *pseud.*
A writer of prose [E. R. Eddison]. BH, i (47/51), 50-3.

HEIDELBERG
Books printed at Heidelberg for Thomas Cartwright. LIB, ii (47/8), 284-6.
A. F. Johnson.

Samuel Browne, printer to the University of Heidelberg, 1655-1662. LIB, v (50/1), 14-25.
E. Weil.

HEILBRON, Bertha Lion
[Banard's Mississippi Panorama pamphlets]. [A letter]. PBSA, xliii (49), 245.

Henry Lewis' *Das illustrirte Mississippithal*: a contemporary advertisement. PBSA, xliii (49), 344-5.

Henry Lewis in English. Illus. PBSA, xlv (51), 359-62.

HELME, Elizabeth
Flora; or, The deserted child: by the author of James Manners [Elizabeth Helme or Elizabeth Somerville]. BC, xvi (67), 83.
S. Roscoe.

Flora; or, The deserted child [attributed to Elizabeth Somerville or Elizabeth Helme, jr.]. (Query, 213). BC, xvii (68), 83.
S. Roscoe.

HEMENWAY, Robert E. *and* KELLER, Dean H.
Charles Brockden Brown, America's first important novelist: a check list of biography and criticism. PBSA, lx (66), 349-62.

HEMINGE, John
A note on John Heminge. LIB, iii (48/9), 287-8.
J. M. Nosworthy.

HEMINGWAY, Ernest
Hemingway, Churchill and the printed word. (Dukedom large enough, 2). PBSA, lvi (62), 346-53.
D. A. Randall.

The text of Hemingway. PBSA, lvii (63), 403-21.
J. B. Meriwether.

The dashes in Hemingway's *A Farewell to Arms.* PBSA, lviii (64), 449-457.
J. B. Meriwether.

Addition to the Hemingway bibliography. PBSA, lix (65), 327.
Sister Richard Mary.

Hemingway in Korea. PBSA, lix (65), 190-2.
W. White.

The old man and the sea as a German text-book. PBSA, lx (66), 89-90.
W. White.

Addenda to Hanneman: Hemingway's *The old man and the sea.* [Audre Hanneman's *Ernest Hemingway: a comprehensive bibliography*]. PBSA, lxii (68), 613-14.
G. Monteiro.

HENCH, Atcheson L.
Printer's copy for Tyrwhitt's *Chaucer.* SB, iii (50/1), 265-6.

HENDERSON, Alexander
Alexander Henderson, book collector. EBST, ii (38/45), 452-3.
W. M. Parker.

HENDERSON, Isabel
A printed text of a portion of Macpherson's *Ossian.* [Specimen of the intended edition of Ossian's poems, pr. by T. Bensley, 1830]. BTHK, v (67/70), 111-13.

HENDERSON, Robert William
Galenus, Claudius (Fl. 160 A.D.). *Galeni comitiali Puero consilium bisariam de graeco in latinū coũersum.* Venetiis per Aurelium Pintium Venetum, 1533. PBSA, xxxiv (40), 270.

Chinks. *Mr. Hardy Lee, his yacht.* Boston, 1857. PBSA, xxxiv (40), 362.

—. and COLLINS, Carvel
Sue, Eugene. *The King of the Winds* [The *Godolphin Arabian*] translated for the *Spirit of the Times.* 1857, 1861. PBSA, xl (46), 162-4.

HENLEY, William Ernest
William Ernest Henley. (Some uncollected authors, 10). BC, v (56), 162-8.
M. Sadleir.

HENNEPIN, Father Louis
Father Louis Hennepin: his travels and his books. PBSA, li (57), 38-60.
A. H. Greenly.

HENNING, Standish
The printer of *Romeo and Juliet*, Q1. PBSA, lx (66), 363-4.

The printers and the Beaumont and Fletcher folio of 1647, sections 4 and 8D-F. SB, xxii (69), 165-78.

HENRI II
See HENRY II, *king of France*

HENRI *de Mondeville*
The Vesalian compendium [*De Humane Corporis Fabrica*] of Geminus and Nicholas Udall's translation; their relation to Vesalius, Caius, Vicary and De Mondeville. Illus. LIB, xiii (32/3), 367-94.
S. V. Larkey.

HENRIETTA'S HEARTACHES
Henrietta's Heartaches. (Query, 69). BC, v (56), 280-1.
H. E. James.

HENRY VI *king of England*
King Henry's claim to France in picture and poem. [Shrewsbury MS. Royal 15, E vi]. Illus. LIB, xiii (32/3), 77-88.
B. J. H. Rowe.

HENRY VIII *king of England*
A binding for King Henry VIII, *c.* 1540. (English bookbindings, 14), Illus. BC, iv (55), 236.
H. M. Nixon.

Marginalia by Henry VIII in his copy of *The bokes of Salomon*. TCBS, iv (64/8), 166-70.
M. Hattaway.

HENRY II *king of France*
A faked Henri II/Diane de Poitiers binding. (Note, 236). BC, xiv (65), 72.
F. R. Walton.

HENRY *Prince of Wales*
Isaac Oliver's portrait of Prince Henry and *Polyolbion*, a footnote. Illus. LIB, x (55), 206-7.
B. E. Juel-Jensen.

HENRY E. HUNTINGTON LIBRARY AND ART GALLERY
Identification of New York Public Library manuscript 'Suckling collection' and of Huntington manuscript 198. SB, xix (66), 215-16.
C. M. Armitage.

HENSLOWE, Philip
A fragment from Henslowe's diary. Illus. LIB, xix (38/9), 180-4.
Sir W. W. Greg.

Another fragment from Hensloe's diary. Illus. LIB, xx (39/40), 154-8.
J. Q. Adams.

The author-plot of an early seventeenth century play. LIB, xxvi (45/6), 17-27.
J. Q. Adams.

HEPBURN, James Gordon
D. H. Lawrence's plays: an annotated bibliography. (Note, 241). BC, xiv (65), 78-81.

HERALDRY
Notes on the heraldry of the Hunterian manuscripts in the University of Glasgow. BTHK, iii (60/2), 151-65.
D. Reid.

A critical view of the recent literature of British heraldry. PBSA, lvi (62), 445-53.
R. C. Sutherland.

HERBERT, Edward *1st baron*
A binding by Lord Herbert's binder, *c.* 1633. (English bookbindings, 52). Illus. BC, xiv (65), 60.
H. M. Nixon.

Herbert of Cherbury's *Religio Laici*: a bibliographical note. EBST, iv (55), 43-52.
M. M. Rossi.

The Osler manuscript of Herbert's *Religio Laici*. LIB, xi (56), 120-2.
S. E. Sprott.

The library of Jesus College, Oxford, with an appendix on the books bequeathed thereto by Lord Herbert of Cherbury. Illus. OBSP, v (36/9), 49-115.
C. J. Fordyce *and* T. M. Knox.

HERBERT, George
The first edition of Herbert's *Temple*. OBST, v (36/9), 187-97.
F. E. Hutchinson.

HERBERT, Mary *countess of Pembroke*
The Tixall manuscript of Sir Philip Sidney's and the Countess of Pembroke's paraphrase of The Psalms. (Note, 314). BC, xviii (69), 222-3.
B. E. Juel-Jensen.

HERBERT, William
George Paton's contributions to Herbert's *Typographical Antiquities*. EBST, iii (48/55), 213-19.
R. P. Doig.

HERBERT, William *3rd earl of Pembroke*
Two ghosts: Herbert's *Baripenthes* and the Vaughan-Holland portrait of Sidney. LIB, xxiv (43/4), 175-81.
W. H. Bond.

HERD, David
Some notes on the Herd manuscripts. EBST, iii (48/55), 289-98.
W. Montgomerie.

HEREFORD, Philip *and* HUGHEY, Ruth
Elizabeth Grymeston and her *Miscellanea*. Illus. LIB, xv (34/5), 61-91.

HERNLUND, Patricia
William Strahan's ledgers: standard charges for printing, 1738-1785. SB, xx (67), 89-111.

William Strahan's ledgers, II: charges for papers, 1738-1785. Illus. SB, xxii (69), 179-95.

HERON, Robert
Robert Heron and his writings, with a bibliography. EBSP, xv (30/5), 17-33.
J. Sinton.

HERRICK, Robert
Herrick's tercentenary. Illus. BH, i (47/51), 273-81.
O. Lodge.

HERRING, Phillip F.
Ulysses notebook VIII. A.5 at Buffalo. SB, xxii (69), 287-310.

HERRINGMAN, Henry
Henry Herringman, Restoration bookseller-publisher. PBSA, xlii (48), 292-306.
C. W. Miller.

HESIODUS
Blake's *Hesiod*. LIB, xx (65), 315-20.
G. E. Bentley, *jr.*

HESKETH, Christian
Marie Antoinette and Charlotte de Villette. (Note, 89). BC, vi (57), 408.

HESLIN, James J.
Historical research and bibliography. PBSA, lviii (64), 133-40.

In memoriam: Robert William Glenroie Vail, 1890-1966. PBSA, lxii (68), 579-80.

HESPELT, Ernest Herman
Quevedo's *Buscón* as a chapbook. PBSA, xliv (50), 66-9.

HESSE, Hermann
Additions to the bibliography of Hermann Hesse. PBSA, xlix (55), 358-60.
K. W. Jonas.

HETHERINGTON, John Rowland
Edward Reynolds: *Three treatises*, 1631. (Query, 72). BC, v (56), 281.

Robert Walker, printer, *c.* 1755. [A letter]. LIB xi (56), 286.

HEVENTHAL, Charles
Robert Burton's *Anatomy of Melancholy* in early America. PBSA, lxiii (69), 157-75.

HEYLYN, Peter
A table in Heylyn's *Observations*. (Query, 171). BC, xii (63), 495.
A. W. G. Lowther.

—. (Query, 171). BC, xiii (64), 354.
I. Williams.

HEYTESBURY, William.
See GULIELMUS *Hentisberus.*

HEYWOOD, John
Heywood, John (c. 1497- c. 1580). A dialogue conteining the nomber in effect of all the prouerbes in the Englishe tongue. PBSA, xxxiv (40), 358.
E. M. Sowerby.

Quarto editions of *Play of the wether*. PBSA, lxii (68), 313-9.
D. G. Ganzler.

HEYWOOD, Thomas
If you know not me you know nobodie, and *The famous historie of Sir Thomas Wyat*. LIB, xiii (32/3), 272-81.
M. F. Martin.

Thomas Heywood's play on *The Troubles of Queen Elizabeth*. LIB, xiv (33/4), 313-38.
G. N. Giordano-Orsini.

Some manuscripts of Heywood's *Art of Love*. LIB, i (46/7), 106-112.
S. Musgrove.

A proof sheet in Thomas Heywood's *The Iron Age*. Illus. LIB, x (55), 275-8.
A. Brown.

Hand B in *Sir Thomas More*. [Possibly T. Heywood]. LIB, xi (56), 47-50.
J. M. Nosworthy.

The Fair Maid of the Exchange. Illus. LIB, xiii (58), 119-20.
P. H. Davison.

The text of Heywood's *The fair maid of the West*. Illus. LIB, xxii (67), 299-325.
R. K. Turner, *jr.*

Two compositors in Heywood's *Londons ius honorarium* (1631). SB xxii (69), 223-6.
D. M. Bergeron.

HIBBERD, Lloyd
Physical and reference bibliography. LIB, xx (65), 124-34.

HIBBERT, Julian
Julian Hibbert, 1800-1834. (Some uncollected authors, 26). BC, ix (60), 446-51.
J. S. L. Gilmour.

HICKMOTT, Allerton C.
A collection of English literature of the 16th and 17th centuries. (Contemporary collectors, 17). Illus. BC, vii (58), 152-64.

HIERON, Samuel
A Helpe vnto Deuotion. The fifth edition. London, H. L[ownes], Samuel Macham, 1613. PBSA, xxxiv (40), 271.
E. M. Sowerby.

HIGGINS, Jesse
Higgins, Jesse. *Sampson against the Philistines.* Philadelphia, 1805. PBSA, xxxiv (40), 87.
J. P. Boyd.

HILARIE, Hugh
See BALE, John *bp. of Ossory.*

HILDRETH, Richard
Richard Hildreth's minor works. PBSA, xl (46), 127-50.
L. S. Friedland.

HILDROP, John
A note on *God's Judgement upon the Gentile Apostatized Church* and *A Treatise of the Three Evils of the Last times.* [By J. Hildrop or F. Lee?]. with special reference to a volume in the library of St. Paul's Cathedral, Dundee, which contains both title pages. BTHK, iii (60/2), 31-4.
R. C. Rider.

HILL, Abraham
Hill's list of early plays in manuscript. LIB, (39/40), 71-99.
J. Q. Adams.

HILL, Archibald Anderson
Some postulates for distributional study of texts. SB, iii (50/1), 63-95.

HILL, Betty
Trinity College Cambridge MS B.14.52, and William Patten. Illus. TCBS, iv (64/8), 192-200.

HILL, Cecil
The St. Andrews University Library copy of Glareanus and Barbarini. BTHK, iv (53), 72-5.

HILL, Hamilin Lewis
Toward a critical text of *The gilded age* [by Mark Twain and C. D. Warner]. PBSA, lix (65), 142-9.

HILL, Peter Murray
Numbered and signed. (Query, 43). BC, iii (54), 73.

HILL, Trevor Howard Howard-
Spelling and the bibliographer. LIB, xviii (63), 1-28.

The Oxford old-spelling Shakespeare concordances. SB, xxii (69), 143-64.

HILLACRE BOOKHOUSE
See BURSCH, Frederick Conrad

HILLS, Henry
A London printer's visit to India in the seventeenth century. LIB, xx (39/40), 100-4.
J. B. Primrose.

'Pirate Hills' and the quartos of *Julius Caesar.* PBSA, lxiii (69), 177-93.
J. W. Velz.

HINDLE, Christopher Joseph
A bibliography of the printed pamphlets and broadsides of Lady Eleanor Douglas, the 17th-century prophetess. Illus. Revised. EBST, i (35/8), 65-98.

— *and* GIBSON, Strickland
Philip Bliss, 1787-1857, editor and bibliographer. OBSP, iii (31/3), 173-260.

HINDMARSH, Joseph
Hindmarsh's *Collection of tracts.* Illus. BTHK, v (67/70), 73-4.
I. R. Grant.

HINMAN, Charlton Joseph K.
See also COLLATING MACHINES

Principles governing the use of variant spellings as evidence of alternate setting by two compositors. LIB, xxi (40/1), 78-94.

A proof-sheet in the first folio of Shakespeare. Illus. LIB, xxiii (42/3), 101-7.

Mechanized collation: a preliminary report. PBSA, xli (47), 99-106.

Mark III: New light on the proof-reading for the first folio of Shakespeare. Illus. SB, iii (50/1), 145-53.

The proof-reading of the first folio text of *Romeo and Juliet.* Illus. SB, vi (54), 61-70.

The prentice hand in the tragedies of the Shakespeare first folio: Compositor E. SB, ix (57), 3-20.

HINTON, Percival F.
Samuel Rogers's *Poems*, 1812. (Query, 169). BC, xiii (64), 70-1.

A ghost laid. [*The Ghost in the Bank of England*]. (Note, 226). BC, xiii (64), 350-1.

A forgotten indiscretion. (Note, 233). BC, xiii (64), 500.

The 'green' Tennysons. (Note, 246). BC, xiv (65), 215.

Richard Savage's *Various Poems*, 1761. (Note, 213). SB, xiii (64), 66-7.

HIPPOCRATES
Unsigned editions of Galen and Hippocrates 1522: further light on an elusive printer. LIB, xvi (61), 55-7.
R. J. Durling.

HIRSCH, Lester
A note on John Gray, 1724-1811. PBSA, xlvi (52), 275-6.

HIRSCH, Rudolf
A survey of books printed in Germany between 1501 and 1530. The book production in the German speaking cultural area. PBSA, xxxiv (40), 117-36.

An undescribed printed poster of 1516. PBSA, xlviii (54), 414-6.

Bueve de Hantone. PBSA, l (56), 379.

The art of selling books: notes on three Aldus catalogues, 1586-1592. SB, i (48/9), 83-101.

HISCOCK, Walter George
William Upcott and John Evelyn's papers. LIB, xx (65), 320-5.

HISTORICAL OCCASIONS
The literature of splendid occasions in English history. LIB, i (46/7), 184-96.
I. K. Fletcher.

HISTORICAL STUDIES
The bibliography of newspapers and the writing of history. LIB, ix (54), 153-75.
S. Morison.

Historical research and bibliography. PBSA, lviii (64), 133-40.
J. J. Heslin.

Bibliography and the collecting of historical material. PBSA, lviii (64), 141-5.
H. H. Peckham.

The bibliographer and the collecting of historical materials. PBSA, lviii (64), 148-53.
J. C. Wyllie.

HISTORY OF JASON
Caxton's *History of Jason*. PBSA, xxxiv (40), 254-61.
C. F. Bühler.

HISTORY OF LITTLE GOODY TWO-SHOES
The history of Little Goody Two-Shoes. (Query, 179). BC, xiii (64), 214.
S. Roscoe.

—. BC, xiii (64), 503.
J. Birkbeck.

HITZ, Benjamin D.
Cather, Willa Sibert (1876-   ). *O Pioneers!* Boston, 1913. PBSA, xxxv (41), 161.

HOBBES, Thomas
Annotated copies of Hobbes's *Leviathan*, 1651. (Query, 178). BC, xiii (64), 214.
R. H. Hopkins.

The '1651' editions of *Leviathan*. (Note, 29). BC, iii (54), 68-9.
W. B. Todd.

Hobbes and Talon's Ramist rhetoric in English. TCBS, i (49/53), 260-9.
W. J. Ong.

HOBHOUSE, Edmund
The library of a physician, *circa* 1700. [Claver Morris]. LIB, xiii (32/3), 89-96.

HOBSON, Anthony Robert A.
Early trade bindings. (Query, 2). Illus. BC, ii (53), 221-2.

[Export licences]. A letter. BC, v (56), 113-14.

The Pillone Library. Illus. BC, vii (58), 28-37.

Two Renaissance bindings. I. A binding presented to René of Anjou, 1459. II. A binding for Matthias Corvinus, King of Hungary and Bohemia, c. 1480-90. Illus. BC, vii (58), 265-8.

Waddesdon Manor. (Unfamiliar libraries, 5). Illus. BC, viii (59), 131-9.

Beckfordiana. (Query, 120). BC, viii (59), 432.

Bindings with a device of a pelican in its piety. (Note, 291). BC, xvi (67), 509.

—. *and* MUNBY, A. N. L.
John Roland Abbey. (Contemporary collectors, 26). Illus. BC, x (61), 40-8.

HOBSON, Geoffrey Dudley
German Renaissance patrons of bookbinding. Illus. 2 pts. BC, iii (54), 171-89; 251-71.

An early seventeenth-century Scottish binding. Illus. EBST, ii (38/45), 416-18.

Further notes on Romanesque bindings. Illus. LIB, xv (34/5), 161-211.

Some early bindings and binders' tools. Illus. LIB, xix (38/9), 202-49.

'Et Amicorum'. LIB, iv (49/50), 87-99.

A gift to the [Bibliographical] Society's library. [A letter about the gift, by Mr. A. R. A. Hobson, of the line-blocks for G. D. Hobson's *Les Reliures à la fanfare. Le Problème de l'S fermé*, 1935, and three sets of slides intended to illustrate lectures on binding]. LIB, xiii (58), 63.
C. Blagden.

HODGSON, Sidney
William A. Jackson and the Stationers' Company (Note, 281). BC, xv (66), 485.

Papers and documents recently found at Stationers' Hall. LIB, xxv (44/5), 23-36.

HÖLTGEN, Karl Josef *and* HORDEN, John
Arthur Warwick, 1603/4-1633: the author of *Spare minutes*. Illus. LIB, xxi (66), 223-30.

HOFER, Philip
On collecting Japanese manuscript scrolls. Illus. BC, vii (58), 369-80.

Philip Hofer. (Contemporary collectors, 24). Illus. 2 pts. BC, ix (60), 151-64, 292-300.
W. A. Jackson.

Notes on the Philip Hofer reference collection. (Contemporary collectors, 45). Illus. BC, xviii (69), 159-69.
J. E. Walsh.

HOGAN, Charles Beecher.
Austen, Jane (1775-1817). *Emma: A Novel.* Philadelphia, 1816. PBSA, xxxiv (40), 89-90.

Edwin Arlington Robinson: new bibliographical notes. PBSA, xxxv (41), 115-44.

HOGG, James
James Hogg's *Altrive tales*: an 1835 reissue. BTHK, v (67/70), 210-11.
D. S. Mack.

Notes on the bibliography of James Hogg, the Ettrick Shepherd. Illus. LIB, xvi (35/6), 309-26.
E. C. Batho.

HOGG, Thomas Jefferson
Thomas Jefferson Hogg. (Query, 7). BC, i (52), 56-7, 130.
J. T. Barb.

—. BC, i (52), 129.
W. S. Scott.

—. BC, i (52), 129.
D. Massey.

HOGREFE, Pearl
John More's translations. PBSA, xlix (55), 188-9.

HOLBROOK, John Pinckney
Cruikshank's *sketch book*: the 'Gold' question. Illus. PBSA, xl (46), 225-8.

A Cruikshank catalogue raisonné. PBSA, xli (47), 144-7.

HOLCROFT, Thomas
Holcroft's *Follies of a day*, 1785. (Note, 260). BC, xiv (65), 544.
W. B. Todd.

HOLINSHED, Raphael
The illustrations of the first edition of Holinshed. Illus. EBST, ii (38/45), 398-403.
J. V. Scholderer.

Three eighteenth-century reprints of the castrated sheets in Holinshed's *Chronicles*. Illus. LIB, xiii (58), 120-4.
K. I. Maslen.

HOLKHAM HALL
A list of the printed books recently acquired by the British Museum from the Earl of Leicester, Holkham Hall. 3 pts. BC, i (52), 120-6, 185-9, 259-63.
L. A. Sheppard *and others*.

The cataloguing of the Holkham manuscripts. TCBS, iv (64/8), 128-54.
J. E. Graham.

HOLLAND, David
The Rothschild Library. (Contemporary collectors, 4). BC, iv (55), 28-33.

HOLLAND, Henry
Two ghosts: Herbert's *Baripenthes* and the Vaughan-Holland portrait of Sidney. LIB, xxiv (43/4), 175-81.
W. H. Bond.

HOLLIS, Thomas
Binding by Richard Montagu for Thomas Hollis, 1758. (English bookbindings, 3). Illus. BC, i (52), 182-4.
H. M. Nixon.

The collection of Hollis bindings at Berne. Illus. BC, vii (58), 165-70.
C. Ramsden.

HOLME, Constance
Constance Holme. (Some uncollected authors, 11). BC, v (56), 250-5.
B. Rota.

HOLMES, sir Maurice Gerald
Collecting Captain Cook. Illus. BC, i (52), 166-73.

'London and New York' imprint, 1781. (Query, 56). BC, iv (55), 81.

HOLMES, Oliver Wendell
The Autocrat at the Breakfast Table: a bibliographical study. PBSA, xxxviii (44), 284-311.
T. F. Currier.

Literary Bantlings: addenda to the Holmes bibliography. PBSA, li (57), 1-18.
E. M. Tilton.

HOLMES, Thomas James
The Mather bibliography. PBSA, xxxi (37), 57-76.

HOLT, Lee Elbert
Samuel Butler's revisions of *Erewhon*. PBSA, xxxviii (44), 22-38.

HOLTBY, Winifred
Winifred Holtby. (Query, 50). BC, iii (34), 227.
G. Handley-Taylor.

HOME, John
John Home: a checklist of editions. BTHK, iii (60/2), 121-38.
J. M. Lefèvre.

Press figures and book reviews as determinants of priority: a study of Home's *Douglas*, 1751 and Cumberland's *The Brothers*, 1770. PBSA, xlv (51), 72-6.
W. B. Todd.

HOME LIBRARY
The *Home library* Illus. PBSA, xlii (48), 110-18.
G. T. Goodspeed.

HOMER
An unknown edition of the *Iliad* [Paris, Jean Vatel, 1520]. Illus. LIB, xvii (36/7), 448-53.
P. Auerbach.

Chapman's text corrections in his *Iliads*. LIB, vii (52), 275-81.
H. C. Fay.

Critical marks in a copy of Chapman's *Twelve Bookes of Homers Iliades*. LIB, viii (53), 117-21.
H. C. Fay.

The Whole Works of Homer. Translated . . . by Geo. Chapman. London for Nathaniell Butter. [1616?]. PBSA, xl (46), 230-1.
P. S. Dunkin.

HOMER, rev. Arthur
More data on a proposed 'Bibliotheca Americana' of the Rev. Arthur Homer, D.D., in 1799. PBSA, xxxvii (43), 158-60.
V. H. Paltsits.

HONCE, Charles
Crane, Stephen (1871-1900). *The Famine of Hearts*, 1899. PBSA, xxxv (41), 297.

HONEYMAN, Robert Broadhead
The manuscript alterations in the Honeyman first folio. PBSA, liii (59), 334-8.
F. S. Hook.

HONIGMANN, Ernest Anselm J.
Spelling tests and the first quarto of *King Lear*. LIB, xx (65), 310-15.

On the indifferent and one-way variants in Shakespeare. LIB, xxii (67), 189-204.

HOOD, Robin
The little gest of Robin Hood: a note on Pynson and lettersnijder editions. SB, xvi (63), 3-8.
J. C. T. Oates.

HOOD, Thomas
Thomas Hood. (Some uncollected authors, 7). BC, iv (55), 239-48.
J. S. L. Gilmour.

HOOK, Frank S.
The manuscript alterations in the Honeyman first folio. PBSA, liii (59), 334-8.

The two compositors in the first quarto of Peele's *Edward I*. SB, vii (55), 170-7.

HOOKER, Richard
Two notes on Richard Hooker. PBSA, xli (47), 344-6.
P. S. Dunkin.

HOOLE, Charles
An unrecorded edition of a Hoole schoolbook. PBSA, lv (61), 226-9.
G. W. Jones.

HOOVER LIBRARY
See STANFORD UNIVERSITY, *Hoover inst. and libr.*

HOPE, Thomas Charles
Manuscripts of Dr. T. C. Hope's chemical lectures. (Query, 139). BC, x (61), 73-5.
R. G. Neville.

HOPKINS, Gerard Manley
Gerard Manley Hopkins, 1884-1889. (English literary autographs, 39). Illus. BC, x (61), 321.
T. J. Brown.

G. M. Hopkins and the Silver jubilee album. Illus. LIB, xx (65), 148-52.
A. Thomas.

A Hopkins discovery [in L. Magnus and C. Headlam, *Prayers from the poets: a calendar of devotion*]. LIB, xxiv (69), 56-8.
N. White *and* T. Dunne.

HOPKINS, R. H.
Annotated copies of Hobbes's *Leviathan*, 1651. (Query, 178). BC, xiii (64), 214.

HOPKINSON, Cecil
Eighteenth-century editions of the keyboard compositions of Domenico Scarlatti, 1685-1757. EBST, iii (48/55), 47-71.

Handel and France: editions published there during his lifetime. Illus. EBST, iii (48/55), 223-48.

— *and* OLDMAN, C. B.
Thomson's collections of national song with special reference to the contributions of Haydn and Beethoven. Illus. EBST, ii (38/45), 1-64.

—. Addenda et corriegenda. EBST, iii (48/55), 121-4.

Haydn's settings of Scottish songs in the collections of Napier and Whyte. Illus. EBST, iii (48/55), 85-120.

HOPPE, Harry Reno
John Wolfe, printer and publisher, 1579-1601. Illus. LIB, xiv (33/4), 241-88.

An approximate printing date for the first quarto of *Romeo and Juliet*. LIB, xviii (37/8), 447-55.

The birth-year of Gillis van Diest I, Antwerp printer of English books. LIB, iii (48/9), 213.

The birthplace of Stephen Mierdman, Flemish printer in London *c.* 1549-*c.*1552. LIB, iii (48/9), 213-14.

HOPSON, William Fowler
Side lights on William James Linton, 1812-97. PBSA, xxvii (33), 74-82.

HOPTON, Susanna
Whereabouts of Hopton's *Collection of meditations*. (Query, 235). BC, xviii (69), 225.
L. Sauls.

Whereabouts of books owned by Traherne, Hopton, Bridgeman. (Query, 236). BC, xviii (69), 225-6.
L. Sauls.

HORATIUS FLACCUS Quintus
The Didot *Horace*, 1799. (Note, 182). BC, xi (62), 345.
A. N. L. Munby.

—. (Note, 182). BC, xi (62), 480.
H. D. Lyon.

An undescribed *Ars Poetica* printed at Paris about 1500. Illus. LIB, i (46/7), 127-31.
C. F. Bühler.

A Horatian ghost. LIB, xi (56), 278-82.
G. D. Painter.

A previously undescribed Horace. [*Sermones*. Paris, Gui Marchand, 1492]. Illus. PBSA, xlv (51), 70-2.
C. F. Bühler.

A previously undescribed Horace. Illus. PBSA, xlv (51), 70-6.
W. B. Todd.

HORDEN, John Robert B.
Quarles's *Enchiridion*, 1682. (Query, 95). BC, vii (58), 188.

Edmund Marmion's illustrations for Francis Quarles' *Argalus and Parthenia*. Illus. TCBS, ii (54/8), 55-62.

—. *and* HÖLTGEN, Karl Josef
Arthur Warwick, 1603/4-1633: the author of *Spare minutes*. Illus. LIB, xxi (66), 223-30.

HORINE, Emmet Field
Daniel Drake and his contributions to education. PBSA, xxxiv (40), 303-14.

HORMAN, William
The Virgin and Child Binder, LVL, and William Horman. Illus. LIB, xvii (62), 77-85.
N. R. Ker.

HORN, Robert D.
The early editions of Addison's *Campaign*. SB, iii (50/1), 256-61.

HORNE, Colin James
Dr. William King's *Miscellanies in Prose and Verse*. LIB, xxv (44/5), 37-45.

HORNE, John
Brief instructions for children, 1654. (Query, 57). BC, iv (55), 81.
W. C. Kimber.

HORNE, Richard Henry Hengist
Horne, *Orion: an epic poem*. 1843. (Note, 309). BC, xviii (69), 219.
W. B. Todd.

HORROX, Reginald
Tables for the identification and collation of the Shakespeare folios. Illus. BH, i (47/51), 105-76.

HORST, Irvin B.
Thomas Cottesford's *Two Letters*. LIB, xi (56), 44-57.

HORTULUS ANIMAE
The *Hortulus Animae* in English, 1530. LIB, vi (51), 109-15.
L. A. Sheppard.

HOSLEY, Richard
Quarto copy for Q2 *Romeo and Juliet*. SB, ix (57), 129-41.

HOTSON, John Leslie
The library of Elizabeth's embezzling teller [Richard Stonley]. SB, ii (49/50), 49-61.

HOTTEN, John Camden
The Hotten piracy, of Tennyson's *Poems MDCCCXXX-MDCCCXXXIII*. (Note, 208). BC, xii (63), 492-3.
J. R. Taylor.

Samuel Clemens and John Camden Hotten. LIB, xx (65)m 230-42.
D. Ganzel.

HOUGHTON, Arthur Amory
Arthur Amory Houghton *Jr*. (Contemporary collectors, 12). Illus. BC, vi (57), 28-40.
W. H. Bond.

HOUGHTON, Esther Rhodes
The British Critic and the Oxford Movement. SB, xvi (63), 119-37.

HOUGHTON-CREWE
The Houghton-Crewe draft of Keat's *Ode to a Nightingale*. PBSA, xlviii (54), 91-5.
R. N. Roth.

HOURS
Three French Books of Hours. (Note, 124). Illus. BC, ix (60), 65-7.
O. L. Shaw.

Three *Horae ad usum Sarum* printed by Philippe Pigouchet. LIB, xix (38/9), 304-10.
C. F. Bühler.

Horae ad usum Romanum. [Paris] Philippe Pigouchet, for Enguilbert, Jean, and Geofroy de Marnef [about 1489]. PBSA, xxxiv (40), 268.
H. R. Mead.

Horae ad usum Sarum. Paris, Philippe Pigouchet, for Simon Vostre, 1499. PBSA, xxxv (41), 156.
H. R. Mead.

Notes on two incunabula printed by Aldus Manutius. [*Brevissima Introductio ad Litteras Graecas* and *Horae ad Usum Romanum*]. Illus. PBSA, xxxvi (42), 18-26.
C. F. Bühler.

A Book of Hours for the use of Autun printed for Simon Vostre (*c.* 1507). A correction to the Stillwell census. PBSA, xli (47), 341-2.
H. Bober.

An unrecorded Sarum book of hours of 1526. Illus. TCBS, i (49/53), 178-9.
H. S. Bennett.

HOURS PRESS
The Hours Press Retrospect. Catalogue. Commentary. BC, xiii (64), 488-96.
N. Cunard.

HOUSEHOLDER, Fred W.
The first pirate. [The priority of Fust or Mentelin's editions of St. Augustine's *De Arte Praedicandi*]. LIB, xxiv (43/4), 30-46.

HOUSEHOLD WORDS
T. B. Aldrich and *Household Words*. PBSA, xlii (48), 70-2.
G. J. L. Gomme.

Household Words in America. PBSA, xlv (51), 160-6.
W. E. Buckler.

HOUSMAN, Alfred Edward
Variant readings in Housman's *More Poems*. (Note, 20). BC, ii (53), 73-7.
W. White.

A variant reading in Housman's *Collected Poems*. (Note, 80). BC, vi (53), 71.
W. White.

—. BC, vi (57), 182.
J. Carter.

Variant reading in Housman's *Collected Poems*. (Note, 34). BC, iii (54), 145-8.
W. White.

The A. E. Housman manuscripts in the Library of Congress. BC, iv (55), 110-4.
J. Carter.

Housman's *Epitaph on an army of mercenaries*. (Query, 63). BC, iv (55), 173.
W. White.

Housman presentation copies. (Note, 79). BC, v (56), 384.
H. Marlow *pseud*.

A. E. Housman's contributions to an Oxford magazine [*Ye Rounde Table*]. (Query, 90). BC, vi (57), 404.
J. Carter.

Alfred Edward Housman, 1859-1936. Illus. (English literary autographs, 31). BC, viii (59), 283.
T. J. Brown.

Housman manuscripts. (Query, 130). BC, ix (60), 204-5.
J. Carter.

—. BC, ix (60), 456.
D. A. Randall.

A Shropshire Lad with a variant title-page. (Query, 135). BC, ix (60), 458.
D. A. Randall.

Housmaniana. (Note, 174). BC, xi (62), 84.
J. Carter.

—. BC, xiv (65), 215-7.
J. Carter.

A. E. Housman's *Collected Poems*. (Note, 192). BC, xii (63), 71.
W. White.

Emendations in Housman. (Note, 234). BC, xiii (64), 500-1.
W. White.

Misprint in Housman's *Last Poems*. (Note, 255). BC, xiv (65), 540-1.
W. White.

Letters of A. E. Housman. (Query, 211). BC, xv (66), 488.
H. Maas.

A. E. Housman, an annotated check-list. Illus. 1 pl. LIB, xxi (40/1), 160-91.
J. Carter *and* J. Sparrow.

—. Additions and corrections. I-III. LIB, xxiii (42/3), 31-44.
W. White, J. Carter *and* R. C. Bald.

A. E. Housman, an annotated check-list. [A letter]. LIB, xxiii (42/3), 133.
G. B. A. Fletcher.

Additions and corrections: III. LIB, vii (52), 201-10.
W. White.

A. E. Housman bibliography. [A letter]. LIB, viii (53), 51.
G. B. A. Fletcher.

A Shropshire Lad in process: the textual evolution of some A. E. Housman poems. LIB, ix (54), 255-64.
W. White.

[Housman, A. E. (1859-1936)]. *Odes from the Greek Dramatists*. London, 1890. PBSA, xxxiv (40), 274.
W. White.

—. PBSA, xxxv (41), 397-8.

Housman, A. E. (1859-1936). *The Oracles*. PBSA, xxxvii (43), 78.
W. White.

Titles from Housman. PBSA, xliv (50), 190-2.
W. White.

Two problems in A. E. Housman's bibliography. PBSA, xlv (51), 358-9.
W. White.

A. E. Housman's printer's copy of *Last Poems*. PBSA, xlvi (52), 70-7.
T. B. Haber.

Abercrombie and Housman: a coincidence in parodies. PBSA, xlviii (54), 98-9.
W. White.

A. E. Housman's poetry in book-titles. PBSA, xlix (55), 69-78.
T. B. Haber.

—. II. PBSA, lii (58), 62-4.
T. B. Haber.

—. III. PBSA, lv (61), 239-41.
T. B. Haber.

—. IV. PBSA, lxii (68), 447-51.
T. B. Haber.

An unrecorded Housman MS item. PBSA, xlix (55), 78-9.
W. White.

A unique *Shropshire Lad*. PBSA, i (56), 198-200.
T. B. Haber.

Housman's Sydney address. PBSA, lii (58), 132-9.
W. White.

Dylan Thomas and A. E. Housman. PBSA, lii (58), 309-10.
W. White.

The War Memorial at Sudbury, Ontario. PBSA, liv (60), 186-8.
T. B. Haber.

A checklist of A. E. Housman's writings in Latin. PBSA, liv (60), 188-90.
W. White.

Housman in Sudbury, Ontario. PBSA, liv (60), 295.
W. White.

Housman in French and music. PBSA, lvi (62), 257-9.
W. White.

Three unreported letters of A. E. Housman. PBSA, lvii (63), 230-3.
T. B. Haber.

The text of A. E. Housman's *Collected Poems*. PBSA, lx (66), 221-3.
W. White.

HOWARD, Alison K.
Montesquieu, Voltaire and Rousseau in eighteenth century Scotland; a checklist of editions and translations of their works published in Scotland before 1801. BTHK, ii (59/60), 40-63.

HOWARD, Edward G.
The issue of Richard Parkinson's *Tour*, 1805. (Note, 202). BC, xii (63), 350-5.

An unnoticed first issue relating to the Baltimore Riot of 1812. PBSA, lvii (63), 222-4.

An unrecorded Baltimore imprint from Philadelphia. [*The romance of real life* by Mrs. Charlotte Turner Smith]. PBSA, lxi (67), 121-3.

An unknown Maryland imprint of the eighteenth century. [I. Campbell, *A rational enquiry into the origin . . . of civil government*, 1785?]. PBSA, lxii (69), 200-3.

HOWARD, Henry *earl of Surrey*
The poet Earl of Surrey's library. (Note, 67). BC, v (56), 172.
B. E. Juel-Jensen.

HOWARD, Robert
Robert Howard, Franciscan. LIB, iii (48/9), 288-91.
A. F. Allison.

HOWARD, William J.
Dr. Johnson on abridgement — a re-examination. PBSA, lx (66), 215-19.

HOWARTH, Robert Guy
Greg's *English Literary Autographs*: a corrected reading. LIB, xvi (61), 214-15.

HOWARTH, William L.
The Red Badge of Courage manuscript: new evidence for a critical edition. SB, xviii (65), 229-47.

HOWE, Ellic Paul
Petits papiers. BH, ii (51/2), 91-5.

The archives of the London journeymen bookbinders. LIB, xxv (44/5), 185-6.

London bookbinders: masters and men, 1780-1840. LIB, i (46/7), 28-38.

Typographical studies. [A letter]. LIB, i (46/7), 250-3.

French type specimen books. LIB, vi (51), 28-41.

HOWE, Parkman D.
[Longfellow's] *Outre-Mer*, Part 1: three variants of the first edition. Illus. PBSA, xli (47), 346-8.

New England authors. (Contemporary collectors, 36). Illus. BC, xii (63), 467-75.

HOWELLS, William Dean
William Dean Howells and his 'Library edition'. PBSA, lii (58), 283-94.
R. W. Walts.

William Dean Howells: two mistaken attributions. PBSA, lvi (62), 254-7.
G. Monteiro.

Howell's plans for two travel books. PBSA, lvii (63), 453-9.
R. W. Walts.

William Dean Howells: a bibliographical amendment. PBSA, lviii (64), 468-9.
G. Monteiro.

Howells and Salvini. PBSA, lx (66), 86-9.
M. E. Nickerson.

A concealed printing in W. D. Howells [*A traveller from Alturia*]. PBSA, lxi (67), 56-60.
S. Bennett.

A note on Lowell bibliography: the review [in the *North American Review*] of Howells' *Venetian Life* [wrongly attributed to C. E. Norton]. SB, iv (51), 210-1.
J. L. Woodress.

Howells bibliography: a 'find' and a clarification. SB, xii (59), 230-3.
E. H. Cady.

William Dean Howells and *The Breadwinners* [by J. Hay]. SB, xv (62), 267-8.
G. Monteiro.

A speech by W. D. Howells. SB, xx (67), 262-3.
G. Monteiro.

HOWES, Martin K.
Anderson, Maxwell (1876-   ). *Saturday's Children*. New York, 1927. PBSA, xxxiv (40), 89.

HOY, Cyrus
The shares of Fletcher and his collaborators in the Beaumont and Fletcher canon. 7 pts. SB, viii (56), 129-46; ix (57), 144-62; xi (58), 85-106; xii (59), 91-116; xiii (60), 77-108; xiv (61), 45-67; xv (62), 71-90.

HRUBY, Antonin
A quantitative solution of the ambiguity of three texts. SB, xviii (65), 147-82.

HUBBARD, William
William Hubbard's *Narrative*, 1677. A bibliographical study. PBSA, xxxiii (39), 25-39.
R. G. Adams.

HUBERMAN, Edward
Bibliographical note on James Shirley's *The Politician*. LIB, xviii (37/8), 104-8.

HUBLEY, Bernard
Title variants in Hubley's *American Revolution*. PBSA, xxx (36), 85-90.
R. G. Adams.

HUDLESTON, Christopher Roy
The infant Johnson. (Note, 7). BC, i (52), 192.

HUDSON, Richard B.
The publishing of Meredith's *Rhoda Fleming*. SB, vi (54), 254-7.

HUGHEY, Ruth
A note on Queen Elizabeth's *Godley Meditation*. LIB, xv (34/5), 237-40.

The Harington manuscript at Arundel Castle and related documents. Illus. LIB, xv (34/5), 388-444.

—. *and* HEREFORD, Philip
Elizabeth Grymeston and her *Miscellanea*. Illus. LIB, xv (34/5), 61-91.

HUMANISTIC SCRIPTS
See CALLIGRAPHY

HUME, David
George Berkeley, 1685-1753; David Hume, 1711-1776. (English literary autographs, 26). BC, vii (58), 181.
T. J. Brown.

Hume, exposé succinct. (Note, 97). BC, vii (58), 191.
W. B. Todd.

The first printing of Hume's *Life*, 1777. LIB, vi (51), 123-5.
W. B. Todd.

Hume's manuscript corrections in a copy of *A Treatise of Human Nature*. PBSA, lvii (63), 446-7.
W. Nethery.

HUMMEL, Ray O.
A further note on Southern's *The Disappointment*. LIB, i (46/7), 67-9.

Henry Chettle, *Englandes Mourning Garment*, 1603. [A letter]. LIB, i (46/7), 246.

Henry Crosse's *Vertues Common-wealth*. PBSA, xliii (49), 196-9.

HUMPHREY *duke of Gloucester*
Humphrey, duke of Gloucester, d.1447. (Portrait of a bibliophile, 11). Illus. BC, xiii (64), 161-9.
R. Weiss.

HUNGARY
Early printed books in Hungary. BC, vii (58), 15-27.
G. Borsa.

HUNT, Christopher John
Scottish ballads and music in the Robert White collection in the University library, Newcastle-upon-Tyne. BTHK, v (67/70), 138-41.

HUNT, James Henry Leigh
Leigh Hunt's *Feast of the poets*: Boston 1813 edition. (Note, 321). BC, xviii (69), 515-18.
E. L. Nicholes.

Leigh Hunt's *The Descent of Liberty*, 1815. LIB, xvii (62), 238-40.
S. Nowell-Smith.

Leigh Hunt's review of Shelley's *Posthumous poems*. PBSA, xlii (48), 1-40.
P. G. Gates.

The first publication of Leigh Hunt's *Love Letters Made of Flowers*. PBSA, lii (58), 52-5.
D. B. Green.

The publications of Leigh Hunt's *Imagination and Fancy*. SB, xii (59), 227-30.
D. B. Green.

HUNT, Richard William
Halliwell-Phillipps and Trinity College Library. An additional note. LIB, ii (47/8), 277-82.

Medieval inventories of Clare College Library. TCBS, i (49/53), 105-25.

HUNTER, George Kirkpatrick
The marking of *sententiae* in Elizabethan printed plays, poems, and romances. LIB, vi (51), 171-88.

HUNTER, J. V. B. Stewart
George Reynolds, sensational novelist and agitator. (Among my books, 4). Illus. BH, i (47/51), 225-36.

Captain of romance [Mayne Reid]. Illus. BH, i (47/51), 455-67.

HUNTER, Richard Alfred *and* MACALPINE, Ida
Alexander Boswell's copies of *The Anatomy of Melancholy*, 1621 and 1624. (Note, 88). BC, vi (57), 406-7.

HUNTER, William
The writings of William Hunter, F.R.S. BTHK, i/3 (58), 3-14.
W. R. Le Fanu.

The writings of William Hunter. BTHK, i/4 (58), 46-7.
A. L. Goodall.

Letters to William Hunter from his American pupils, John Morgan and William Shipper, *jnr*. Illus. BTHK, iii (60/2), 61-7.
J. Dobson *and* B. Thomas.

HUNTINGDON
Book club in Huntingdon. (Query, 68). BC, v (56), 79.
A. Ehrman.

HUNTLY, *Brander libr., George MacDonald collection.*
The George MacDonald collection, Brander Library, Huntly. (Unfamiliar libraries, 13). Illus. BC, xvii (68), 13-25.
M. Hutton.

HUSSEY, Maurice Percival H.
An addition to Northrup. [*On the Death of a Favourite Cat*, reprinted 1755]. (Note, 8). BC, i (52), 192.

Not in Wing. [*A Declaration written by John Ivie the elder*, 1661]. (Note, 21). BC, ii (53), 157.

HUTCHINSON, Sara
A Coleridge-Wordsworth manuscript and 'Sarah Hutchinson's poets'. SB, xix (66), 226-31.
R. S. Woof.

HUTCHINSON, William Thomas
The papers of James Madison. (Query, 87). BC, vi (57), 292-3.

HUTTAR, Charles Adolph
Wyatt and the several editions of *The court of Venus*. SB, xix (66), 181-95.

HUTTON, Catherine
The life of Robert Bage, paper-maker and novelist. Illus. BH, i (47/51), 18-30.

HUTTON, Muriel
The George Macdonald collection, Brander Library, Huntly. (Unfamiliar libraries, 13). Illus. BC, xvii (68), 13-25.

HUXLEY, Aldous Leonard
The American edition of Huxley's *Leda*. (Note, 312). BC, xviii (69), 220-1.
D. Farmer.

A note on the text of Huxley's *Crome Yellow*. PBSA, lxiii (69), 131-3.
D. Farmer.

HYDE, Donald Frizell
Donald Frizell Hyde 1909-1966. [An obituary]. PBSA, lx (66), 107.
R. F. Metzdorf *and* J. M. E.

—. *and* HYDE, Mary Morley Crapo.
The Hyde collection. (Contemporary collectors, 6). BC, iv (55), 208-16.

HYDE, Edward *1st earl of Clarendon*
Edward Hyde, Earl of Clarendon, 1609-74. (Portrait of a bibliophile, 1). BC, vii (58), 361-8.
P. H. Hardacre.

HYDE, Harford Montgomery
The Lamb House library of Henry James. Illus. BC, xvl (67), 477-80.

HYDE, Mary Morley Crapo
The history of the Johnson papers. PBSA, xlv (51), 103-16.

I

I., C.
A Pleasant Comedie, called The two merry milke-maids London, Bernard Alsop, for Lawrence Chapman, 1620. PBSA, xxxiv (40), 270.
E. M. Sowerby.

—. PBSA, xxxiv (40), 357.
E. M. Sowerby.

IBEN, Icko
The Ford County Journal, 1859-1860: an unrecorded Illinois newspaper. PBSA, xlviii (54), 273-82.

ICELANDIC
Icelandic translations of Maugham. PBSA, xlv (51), 158-9.
N. Van Patten.

ICKWORTH
Halifax's *The Character of a Trimmer*: some observations in the light of a manuscript from Ickworth. LIB, xiv (59), 117-23.
R. Gathorne-Hardy.

IGNATIUS *st., bp. of Antioch*
The letters of St. Ignatius, Bishop of Antioch: the *Fortuna* of their fifteenth-century editions. PBSA, lvii (63), 152-6.
D. E. Rhodes.

ILLINOIS *univ. libr.*
A newly discovered Oxford book [Theophrastus' *Characters*, Oxford, John Lichfield, 1628, in the University of Illinois Library]. PBSA, xxxii (38), 98-101.
M. Harman.

ILLUSTRATION
Eighteenth-century English illustrators: Isaac Taylor the elder. [*With* a list of] Books with illustrations designed and engraved by Isaac Taylor the elder. Illus. BC, i (52), 14-27.
H. A. Hammelmann.

French illustrations in English books of the Romantic period. (Note, 159). BC, x (61), 200-1.
G. G. Barber.

18th-century French illustrated books. (Note, 162). BC, x (61), 333-4.
D. Gordan.

The progress of wood-engraving in current book-illustration. Illus. BH, i (47/51), 254-62.
C. Sandford.

Some eighteenth-century French illustrated books. Illus. BH, ii (51/2), 56-74.
L. J. Lloyd.

English eighteenth-century book illustrators. [With a list of] English books illustrated by Gravelot. Illus. BH, ii (51/2), 127-35.
H. A. Hammelman.

English book-illustration, 1700-1775. Illus. LIB, xvii (36/7), 1-21.
I. A. Williams.

Copperplate engravings in early Spanish books. Illus. LIB, xxi (40/1), 109-42.
H. Thomas.

Copperplate engravings in Portuguese books of the late sixteenth century. Illus. LIB, xxii, 145-62.
H. Thomas.

Some illustrators of Milton's *Paradise Lost*, 1688-1850. Illus. 2 pts. LIB, iii (48/9), 1-21; 101-19.
C. H. Baker.

Some illustrators of Milton's *Paradise Lost*. [A letter]. LIB, iv (49/50), 146-7.
T. Balston.

IMITATIO CHRISTI
The G. U. Yule collection of the *Imitatio Christi* in the library of St. John's College. TCBS, i (49/53), 88-90.
J. C. T. Oates.

IMPARTIAL RELATION
An impartial relation of the Hail-Storm on the Fifteenth of July and the Tornado on the second of August, 1799. PBSA, xxxiv (40), 359.
A. Davidson.

IMPOSITION
Eighteenth-century quartos with vertical chain-lines. LIB, xvi (35/6), 337-42.
A. T. Hazen.

Imposition by half-sheets. Illus. LIB, xxii, 163-7.
W. H. Bond.

Single-page imposition in Foxe's *Acts and Monuments*, 1570, LIB, i (46/7), 49-56.
L. M. Oliver.

Imposition of a half-sheet in duodecimo. LIB, i (46/7), 242-4.
L. F. Norwood.

Foxe's *Acts and Monuments*, 1570, and single-page imposition. Illus. LIB, ii (47/8), 159-170.
P. S. Dunkin.

Turned chain-lines. Illus. LIB, v (50/1), 184-200.
K. Povey *and* I. J. C. Foster.

On the diagnosis of half-sheet impositions. Illus. LIB, vi (56), 268-72.
K. Povey.

Inverted imposition. LIB, xii (57), 193-6.
D. F. Cook.

On the imposition of the first edition of Hawthorne's *The Scarlet Letter*. Illus. LIB, xvii (62), 250-5.
O. L. Steele.

A misprinted sheet in the 1479 *Mammotrectus super Bibliam* [of Johannes Marchesinus] (Goff M-239). PBSA, lxi (67), 51-2.
D. M. Schullian *and* C. F. Bühler.

Running-title evidence for determining half-sheet imposition. SB, i (48), 199-202.
F. T. Bowers.

Quadruple imposition: an account of Goldsmith's *Traveller*. SB, vii (55), 103-11.
W. B. Todd.

Twenty-fours with three signatures. SB, ix (57), 215-6.
K. Povey.

Imposition figures and plate gangs in *The Rescue*. SB, xiv (61), 285-62.
M. J. Bruccoli *and* C. A. Rheault.

Half-sheet imposition of eight-leaf quires in formes of thirty-two and sixty-four pages. SB, xv (62), 274-8.
O. L. Steele.

IMPRESSIONS
On printing 'at one pull', and distinguishing impressions by point-holes. LIB, xi (56), 284-5.
D. F. Foxon.

The meaning of 'impression' and 'issue'. TCBS, i (49/53), 361-2.
J. P. W. Gaskell.

IMPRIMATURS
A manuscript imprimatur. (Query, 29). BC, ii (53), 79.
J. B. Oldham.

An author's imprimatur. (Query, 123). BC, ix (60), 79.
A. Muirhead.

—. BC, ix (60), 202.
C. Blagden.

The Laudian imprimatur. Illus. LIB, xv (60), 96-204.
F. B. Williams.

Molière's privilege of 18 March, 1671. LIB, xx (65), 57-63.
G. E. Reed.

IMPRINTS
'London and New York' imprint, 1781. (Query, 56). BC, iv (55), 81.
Sir M. Holmes.

Doctoring the date; two Glasgow examples. BTHK, v (67/70), 144-6.
P. J. Wallis.

English imprints after 1640. LIB, xiv (33/4), 157-77.
P. H. Muir.

'Printed For'. [A letter]. LIB, xvi (35/6), 455.
R. W. Chapman.

The meaning of the imprint in early printed books. LIB, xxiv (43/4), 120-41.
M. A. Shaaber.

Forged addresses in Low Country books in the period of the Reformation. LIB, ii (47/8), 81-94.
M. E. Kronenberg.

One meaning of the imprint. LIB, vi (51), 120-3.
A. T. Hazen.

The meaning of imprint. [A letter]. LIB, vii (52), 60.
R. S. Mortimer.

Dates in English imprints, 1700-52. LIB, xii (57), 190-3.
R. M. Wiles.

London printers' imprints, 1800-1848. LIB, xxi (66), 46-62.
W. B. Todd.

English provincial imprints. LIB, xxii (67), 70.
P. Morgan.

American imprints concerning King's College. PBSA, xliv (50), 301-39.
B. McAnear.

The first trans-Mississippi imprint. PBSA, lii (58), 306-9.
D. Kaser.

In the Savoy: a study in post-Restoration imprints. SB, i (48), 39-46.
C. W. Miller.

Deception in Dublin: problems in seventeenth century Irish printing. SB, vi (54), 232-7.
J. E. Alden.

Deception compounded: further problems in seventeenth-century Irish printing. SB, xi (58), 246-9.
J. E. Alden.

INCUNABULA
Incunabula in Cambridge University Library. BC, iv (55), 51-7.
G. D. Painter.

Incunabula in the Saltykov-Shchedrin library, Leningrad. Illus. BC, iv (55), 273-8.
N. V. Varbanets.

Incunable towns. (Note, 72). BC, v (56), 277.
A. Ehrman.

List of books acquired by the British Musuem from Chatsworth. BC, viii (58), 401-6.
G. D. Painter.

Chatsworth incunabula in the British Museum. Addenda and corrigenda. (Note, 108). BC, viii (59), 180-1.
G. D. Painter.

—. BC, viii (59), 294.

An unrecorded Spanish incunable in Moscow. [*Proverbios* by I. López de Mendoza, *c.* 1500]. BC, viii (59), 271-4.
N. P. Kiselev.

Incunabula in the USSR. I. Russia and the Ukraine. BC, xiv (65), 311-23.
J. S. G. Simmons.

The earliest bookseller's catalogue of incunabula. (Query, 188). BC, xiv (65), 366.
A. Ehrman.

The earliest catalogue of incunabula. (Query, 196). BC, xiv (65), 546.
A. Ehrman.

Incunabula in the USSR. II. The Baltic republics, addenda, and concordances. BC, xv (66), 19-34.
J. S. G. Simmons.

The earliest catalogue of incunabula. (Query, 196). BC, xv (66), 213.
G. Austin.

Incunabula in the USSR: supplementary notes. (Note, 287). BC, xvi (67), 223-4.
J. S. G. Simmons.

Nine incunabula in the Cathcart White collection in Edinburgh University Library. BTHK, ii/2 (60), 66-9.
R. Donaldson.

Supplement to the Handlist of incunabula in the National Library of Scotland. Illus. [And] Second supplement. EBST, ii (38/45), 151-251; 331-51.
W. Beattie.

The liturgical music incunabula in the British Museum. LIB, xx (39/40), 274-94.
K. Meyer.

An unidentified 'incunable' printed at Augsburg not before 1502. LIB, xiii (58), 54-6.
D. E. Rhodes.

The dates in certain German incunabula. PBSA, xxxiv (40), 17-67.
F. R. Goff.

Incunabula and fine printing in Argentina. PBSA, xxxvi (42), 315-18.
M. B. Stillwell.

Two undescribed incunabula. PBSA, xxix (45), 162-3.
C. F. Bühler.

Two unknown American incunabula. PBSA, xxxix (45), 318-9.
H. R. Wagner.

Dates in incunabular colophons. SB, xxii (69), 207-14.
C. F. Bühler.

INDEPENDENT
John Greenleaf Whittier in The Independent. PBSA, lx (66), 91.
G. Monteiro.

INDIA
A London printer's visit to India in the seventeenth century. LIB, xx (39/40), 100-4.
J. B. Primrose.

INDIANA
Manuscript copies and printed editions of the Indiana Constitution, 1816. PBSA, xlviii (54), 390-402.
C. K. Byrd.

INDULGENCES
A Mondovì indulgence and Pierre Sabran. LIB, vii (52), 117-20.
D. E. Rhodes.

Santiago de Compostela and its early indulgences. LIB, xi (56), 41-4.
D. E. Rhodes.

Two issues of an Indulgence of Alexander VI. LIB, xv (60), 206-7.
D. E. Rhodes.

INFANT MINSTREL
The Infant Minstrel, 1816. (Query, 177). BC, xiii (64), 72.
J. L. Shaw.

—. BC, xiii (64), 354-5.
R. J. F. Carnon.

INFANT'S LIBRARY
John Marshall and The Infant's Library. Illus. BC, iv (55), 148-57.
S. Roscoe.

The Infant's Library. (Note, 75). Illus. BC, v (56), 279-80.
S. Roscoe.

—. BC v (56), 383.
J. Hayward.

—. (Query, 46). BC, v (56), 78.
H. A. Hammelmann.

John Marshall and The Infant's Library. (Note, 180). BC, xi (62), 217.
M. Papantonio.

INFORMATION RETRIEVAL
An information retrieval system for modern language studies. PBSA, lviii (64), 270-8.
S. O. Mitchell and L. Sears.

INGLIS, Esther
Check-list, 1937, of the calligraphic MSS of Esther Inglis, 1571-1624. (Query, 210). BC, xv (66), 487-8.
D. J. Jackson.

INITIAL BINDER
A binding for Elizabeth I by the Initial binder, 1563. (English book-bindings, 35). Illus. BC, ix (60), 444.
H. M. Nixon.

A binding for William Bullein by the Initial binder, 1562. (English book-bindings, 37). Illus. BC, x (61), 184.
H. M. Nixon.

INITIALS
Some tell-tale initials in books of the 1550's. Illus. LIB, xii (57), 122-4.
V. Scholderer.

More tell-tale initials. LIB, xiii (58), 198-9.
V. Scholderer.

An initiation into initials. SB, ix (57), 163-78.
F. B. Williams.

INNES, sir Thomas
Sir David Lindsay of the Mount, Secundus. EBST, ii (38/45), 406-9.

INNOCENCIO
See SILVA, Innocencio Francisco da

INNOCENT VIII pope
An undescribed indulgence. Innocentius VIII. Indulgence. Antwerp, Thierry Martens, 1497. PBSA, xl (46), 229.
C. F. Bühler.

INSCRIPTIONS
The non-runic scripts of Anglo-Saxon inscriptions. Illus. TCBS, iv (64/8), 321-38.
E. Okasha.

INSECTS
Insect pests of books. Illus. BC, v (56), 57-62.
F. J. L. Kett.

INTERNATIONAL LEAGUE OF ANTIQUAR-
IAN BOOKSELLERS
The International League of Antiquarian
Booksellers. BC, ii (53), 147-9.
G. Blaizot.

INTERPOLATIONS
Playhouse interpolations in the folio text of
Hamlet. SB, xiii (60), 30-47.
H. Jenkins.

INVENTORIES
An Arbroath book inventory of 1473. BTHK,
iii (60/2), 144-6.
J. Durkan.

Roger Ward's Shrewsbury stock: an inventory
of 1585. LIB, xiii (58), 247-68.

An inventory of the Lord General's Library,
1646. LIB, xxi (66), 115-23.
S. F. Snow.

Two medieval book lists [the libraries of Simon
Burley and William de Walcote]. LIB, xxiii
(68), 236-9.
V. J. Scattergood.

The library of Elizabeth's embezzling teller
[i.e. Richard Stonley]. SB, ii (49), 49-61.

A Cavalier library — 1643 [i.e. that of sir
Thomas Bludder]. SB, vi (54), 141-60.
J. L. Lievsay.

Medieval inventories of Clare College library.
TCBS, i (49/53), 105-15.
R. W. Hunt.

Notes on King's College Library, 1500-1570, in
particular for the period of the Reformation.
[With an] Appendix — the inventory of 1556/
7. TCBS, ii (54/8), 38-54.
W. D. J. Cargill Thompson.

A sixteenth-century inventory of the library of
Corpus Christi College, Cambridge. TCBS,
iii, 187-99.
J. M. Fletcher *and* J. K. McConica.

IRELAND, William Henry
The Ireland Shakespeare forgeries. (Note, 17).
BC, ii (53), 72-3.
P. H. Muir.

IRISH, Wynot R.
Addenda to Irish [W. R. Irish's *The modern
American muse*]: Brown, North and Wild.
PBSA, lxii (68), 452.
G. T. Tanselle.

Addenda to Irish [W. R. Irish's *The modern
American muse*]: Theodora Taylor, Rixford J.
Lincoln, David Bailey, Lester S. Parker.
PBSA, lxiii (69), 198-200.
R. C. Johnson.

IRISH REVIEW
James Stephen's contributions to *The Irish
Review*. PBSA, xlvi (52), 398-9.
G. B. Saul.

IRVINE, A. L.
Lloyd Haberly and the Seven Acres Press.
BH, ii (51), 147-54.

IRVING, Washington
Washington Irving's *Life of Capt. James
Lawrence*. PBSA, liii (59), 338-40.
J. Blanck.

Another reprint of Irving's biography of James
Lawrence. PBSA, lvii (63), 448-9.
E. L. West.

Washington Irving: an unrecorded periodical
publication. SB, xx (67), 260-1.

ISAAC, Frank Swinton
Elizabethan Roman and Italic types. Illus.
2 pts. LIB, xiv (33/4), 85-100; 212-28.

Frank Swinton Isaac. [Obituary notice]. LIB,
xii (57), 54-5.
A. F. Johnson.

ISAAC, Peter Charles G.
Bulmer and the Roxburghe Catalogue. (Query,
82). BC, vi (57), 182.

Bulmer printed? (Query, 110). BC, viii (59), 73.

A Bewick prospectus. Query, 133). BC, ix (60),
457.

Bewick, Catnach, and William Davison. (Query,
161). BC, xii (63), 72.

William Bulmer, 1757-1830: an introductory
essay. Illus. LIB, xiii (58), 37-50.

The history of the book trade in the North: a
preliminary report on a group research project.
LIB, xxiii (68), 248-52.

William Davison of Alnwick, pharmacist and
printer. LIB, xxiv (69), 1-32.

—and WATSON, W. M.
The history of the book trade in the North: a
review of a research project. Illus. JPHS, iv
(68), 87-98.

ISAACS, Jacob
Congreve's library. [A Summary]. LIB, xx
(39/40), 41-2.

ISSUES
Criteria for classifying hand-printed books as
issues and variant states. PBSA, xli (47),
271-92.
F. T. Bowers.

—. [A letter]. PBSA, xlii (48), 341-3.

The state of the issue. PBSA, xlii (48), 239-55.
P. S. Dunkin.

—. [A letter]. PBSA, xliii (49), 83

The issues and states of the second folio and
Milton's *Epitaph on Shakespeare*. Illus. SB, v
(52), 81-108.
W. B. Todd.

The 'private issues' of *The Deserted Village*.
[*And*] Addendum. SB, vi (54), 25-44; vii, 239.
W. B. Todd.

The early editions and issues of Scott's *Border
Antiquities*. SB, ix (57), 244-51.
W. B. Todd.

The meaning of 'impression' and 'issue'.
TCBS, i (49/53), 361-2.
J. P. W. Gaskell.

ITALY
Italian sixteenth-century books. LIB, xiii (58),
161-74.
A. F. Johnson.

IVES, Sidney
A Melville ghost. PBSA, lix (65), 318.

IVIE, John
Not in Wing [*A Declaration written by John
Ivie the elder, London, 1661*]. (Note, 21). BC, ii
(53), 157.
M. Hussey.

IZSAK, Emily K.
The manuscript of *The Sound and the Fury*; the
revisions in the first section. SB, xx (67),
189-202.

J

JACK, E. G.
Authorship of the biographical notice of Niel Gow in *Scots Magazine,* 1809. BTHK, i/3 (56/8), 42.

John Bell's *A Discourse on Witchcraft* — a query. BTHK, ii/2 (59/60), 72.

JACKSON, Andrew
Footnote for Andrew Jackson bibliography. PBSA, lix (65), 437.
J. C. Wyllie.

JACKSON, Dorothy J.
Check-list, 1937, of the calligraphic MSS of Esther Inglis, 1571-1624. (Query, 210). BC, xv (66), 487-8.

JACKSON, Sara E.
Manuscript collections of British folk music, etc. [A letter]. LIB, xiii (58), 63.

JACKSON, Shirley
Shirley Jackson: a checklist. PBSA, lvi (62), 110-3.
R. S. Phillips.

Shirley Jackson: a chronology and a supplementary checklist. PBSA, lx (66), 203-13.
R. S. Phillips.

JACKSON, Stuart
The first printing of the Constitution in a book. PBSA, xlii (1948), 256-8.

JACKSON, Thomas
Proposals for printing: 'Doctor Thomas Jackson's works compleat . . . 1672'. (Query, 230). BC, xvii (68), 491-2.
H. Hammelmann.

Proposals for printing Jackson's *Works* 1672. (Query, 230). BC, xviii (69), 223.
H. G. Pollard.

Proposals for printing Jackson's *Works,* 1672. (Query, 230). BC, xviii (69), 224-5.
C. B. L. Barr.

JACKSON, William Alexander
Bewick's *Quadrupeds,* 1790. (Query, 14). BC, i (52), 195.

The revised STC. A progress report. BC, iv (55), 16-27.

John Taylor's *Booke of Martyrs,* 1633. (Note, 49). BC, iv (55), 327.

Philip Hofer. (Contemporary Collectors, 24). 2 pts. Illus. BC, ix (60), 151-64; 292-300.

'The Librarian's Library': the William A. Jackson bibliographical collection. I. Illus. BC, xiv (65), 499-510.
J. E. Walsh.

W. A. Jackson's *Dibdin*: a revised entry. BC, xv (66), 352-3.
W. H. Bond.

William A. Jackson and the Stationers' Company. (Note, 281). BC, xv (66), 485.
S. Hodgson.

Wayland's edition of *The Mirror for Magistrates.* Illus. LIB, xiii (32/3), 155-7.

Edward Gwynn. Illus. LIB, xv (34/5), 92-6.

Counterfeit printing in Jacobean times. Illus. LIB, xv (34/5), 364-76.

The funeral procession of Queen Elizabeth. LIB, xxvi (45/6), 262-71.

Signatures in nineteenth-century American printing. [A letter]. LIB, iii (48/9), 224.

Robert Waldegrave and the books he printed or published in 1603. Illus. LIB, xiii (58), 225-33.

An English printed sheet-number of 1579. Illus. LIB, xvi (61), 197-201.

William Alexander Jackson, obituary notice. Illus. LIB, xxi (66), 158-9.
Sir F. Francis.

Shirley James (1596-1666). *The Polititian.* London, 1655. PBSA, xxxiv (40), 86.

Some limitations of microfilm. PBSA, xxxv (41), 281-8.

Note on the Pforzheimer Catalogue. [A letter]. PBSA, xl (46), 159.

Humphrey Dyson's library, or Some observations on the survival of books. PBSA, xliii (49), 279-87.

Variant entry fees of the Stationers' Company. PBSA, li (57), 103-10.

William Alexander Jackson, 1905-1964. PBSA, lviii (64), 479-80.
H. W. Liebert.

—. and SANDERS, Chauncey
A note on Robert Greene's *Planetomachia,* 1585. LIB, xvi (35/6), 444-7.

JAGELLONIAN LIBRARY
See CRACOW *univ., bibl. Jagiellońska.*

JAGGARD, William
The influence of justification on spelling in Jaggard's compositor B. SB, xx (67), 235-9.
W. S. Kable.

JAMES I *king of Gt. Britain*
A binding supplied by John Bull to James I, *c* 1621. (English book-bindings, 40). Illus. BC, xi (62), 62.
H. M. Nixon.

A sonnet by King James VI of Scotland. EBST, ii (38/45), 404-6.
J. Craigie.

The Latin folio of King James's prose works. EBST, iii (48/55), 17-30, 155.
J. Craigie.

Basilicon Doron: a late seventeenth-century edition. EBST, iii (48/55), 155-6.
J. Craigie.

The *Basilicon Doron* of King James I. LIB, iii (48/9), 22-32.
J. Craigie.

JAMES II *king of Gt. Britain*
Some new editions from the reign of James II.
PBSA, lv (61), 118-30.
D. Brockway.

JAMES VI *king of Scotland*
See JAMES I *king of England*

JAMB, Harold E.
Norman Douglas. (Query, 34). BC, ii (53), 222.

Henrietta's heartaches. (Query, 69). BC, v (56), 280-1.

Handwritten books. (Query, 70). BC, v (56), 281.

The Long Lost Found. (Query, 88). BC, vi (57), 403-4.

JAMES, Henry
Without benefit of bibliography, some notes on Henry James. BC, vii (58), 64-7.
S. Nowell-Smith.

The Lamb House library of Henry James. Illus. BC, xvi (67), 477-80.
H. M. Hyde.

Henry James: some bibliographical and textual matters. Illus. LIB, xx (65), 108-23.
B. Birch.

A bibliographical novitiate: in search of Henry James. PBSA, lii (58), 23-33.
D. H. Laurence.

—. [A letter in reply]. PBSA, lii (58), 329-30.
R. T. Stott.

The Whole Family and Henry James. PBSA, lii (58), 144-5.
E. F. Walbridge.

Life buffets (and comforts) Henry James, 1883-1916: an introduction and an annotated checklist. PBSA, lxii (68), 207-25.
E. R. Hagemann.

Addendum to Edel and Laurence [*A bibliography of Henry James*]: Henry James's *Future of the novel*. PBSA, lxiii (69), 130.
G. N. Monteiro.

Henry James and his reviewers: some identifications. PBSA, xviii (69), 300-4.
G. Monteiro.

Texts of *The portrait of a lady 1881-1882*: the bibliographical evidence. PBSA, xviii (69), 304-10.
S. Nowell-Smith.

The spoils of Poynton: revisions and editions. SB, xix (66), 161-74.
S. P. Rosenbaum.

An unpublished review by Henry James [of E. Stoddard's *Two Men*]. SB, xx (67), 267-73.
J. Kraft.

James's *Pandora*: the mixed consequences of revision. SB, xxi (68), 93-108.
C. Vandersee.

JAMES, Montague Rhodes
The ghost stories of Montague Rhodes James. BH, i (47/51), 237-53.
L. J. Lloyd.

Bibliographical notes [on the *Ghost Stories* of M. R. James]. BH, i (47/51), 253.
E. A. Osborne.

The manuscripts of St. George's Chapel, Windsor. LIB, xiii (32/3), 55-76.

A handlist of the additional manuscripts in the Fitzwilliam Museum, received since the publication of the catalogue of dr. M. R. James in 1895, (excluding the McClean bequests). TCBS, i (51/4), 197-207; 297-309: 365-75; ii, 1-13.
P. M. Giles *and* F. Wormald.

Additions to a list of the writings of Dr. M. R. James [in S. G. Lubbock's *A Memoir of Montague Rhodes James*, 1939]. TCBS, ii (54/8), 95.
A. F. Scholfield.

The history of Lambeth Palace library. TCBS, iii (59/63), 1-31.

A handlist of manuscripts in the Library of Corpus Christi College, Cambridge, not described by M. R. James [in his *Descriptive Catalogue of the manuscripts in the Library of Corpus Christi College, Cambridge*]. TCBS, iii (59/63), 113-23.
J. Fines *and* R. Vaughan.

JAMIESON, H. D.
Watermark copying by an X-ray method. (Note, 248). Illus. BC, xiv (65), 217-18.

JAMMES, André
Louis XIV, sa bibliothèque et le *Cabinet du Roi*. LIB, xx (65), 1-12.

Académisme et typographie: the making of the romain du roi. Illus. JPHS, i (65), 71-95.

The Musée de l'Imprimerie, Lyons. JPHS, i (65), 96-7.

JANTZ, Harold Stein
Unrecorded verse broadsides of seventeenth-century New England. Illus. PBSA, xxxix (45), 1-19.

JARRY, Francois Théophile
M. de Jarry's project for an edition of the *Moniteur*. LIB, iv (49/50), 277-9.
J. F. Kerslake.

JARVIS, F. P.
A textual comparison of the first British and American editions of D. H. Lawrence's *Kangaroo*. PBSA, lix (65), 400-24.

JARVIS, Rupert Charles
The paper-makers and the excise in the eighteenth century. Illus. LIB, xiv (59), 100-16.

JEDBURGH ABBEY
Some leaves of a thirteenth-century missal probably from Jedburgh Abbey. [*With*] Notes on the music. EBST, iii (48/55), 1-15.
J. M. Arnold *and* F. C. Eeles.

JEFFERS, John Robinson
The Cardinal. Univ. of Southern California, November '05. PBSA, xxxiv (40), 362-3.
W. White.

A textual note on Robinson Jeffers' *The beginning and the end*. PBSA, lx (66), 344-8.
R. J. Brophy.

Robinson Jeffers' '*The beginning and the end*': another error. PBSA, lxi (67), 126.
W. White.

JEFFERSON, Thomas
Jefferson, Thomas (1743-1826). Observations sur la Virginie. Paris, 1786. PBSA, xxxv (41), 71.
J. C. Wyllie.

Thomas Jefferson and his library. PBSA, i (56), 213-28.
E. M. Sowerby.

Thomas Jefferson and the Declaration of Independence. (Dukedom large enough, 3). PBSA, lvi (62), 472-80.
D. A. Randall.

The manuscript of Jefferson's unpublished errata list for Abbé Morellet's translation of the *Notes on Virginia*. SB, i (48), 3-24.
J. M. Carrière.

Some correspondence with Thomas Jefferson concerning the public printers, transcribed, with a foreword. SB, i (48), 25-37.
J. R. Lucke, *ed.*

Some observations on the Philadelphia 1794 editions of Jefferson's *Notes*. SB, ii (49), 201-4.
C. Verner.

The printing [by M. Carey and P. Hall] of Jefferson's *Notes*, 1793-94. SB, v (52), 201.
P. J. Conkwright *and* C. Verner.

Jefferson as collector of Virginiana. SB, xiv (61), 117-44.
R. B. Davis.

JENKINS, Clauston
The Ford changes and the text of *Gulliver's Travels*. PBSA, lxii (68), 1-23.

JENKINS, Gladys
The Archpriest controversy and the printers, 1601-1603. LIB, ii (47/8), 180-6.

JENKINS, Harold
The 1631 quarto of *The Tragedy of Hoffman*. LIB, vi (51), 88-99.

The relation between the second quarto and the folio text of *Hamlet*. SB, vii (55), 69-83.

Playhouse interpolations in the folio text of *Hamlet*. SB, xiii (60), 31-47.

JENNENS, Charles
Charles Jennens as editor of Shakespeare. LIB, xvi (35/6), 236-40.
G. Crosse.

JENNINGS, John Melville
Note on the original library of the College of William and Mary in Virginia, 1693-1705. PBSA, xli (47), 239-67.

JENNINGS, Richard
Richard Jennings: 1881-1953. BC, ii (53), 144-6.
R. Senhouse.

Thomas J. Wise and 'Richard Gullible'. (Note, 110). BC, viii (59), 182-3.
J. Carter.

Richard Jennings, 1881-1952. (Portrait of a bibliophile, 3). BC, viii (59), 370-82.
C. H. B. Kitchin.

JENSEN, Bent Einer Juel-
See JUEL-JENSEN, Bent Einer

JENSEN, Gerard E.
Proposals for a definitive edition of Fielding's *Tom Jones*. LIB, xviii (37/8), 314-30.

JENSON, John R.
The author of *Jura Cleri*. [Ascribed to William Carpender]. PBSA, lxii (68), 241-5.

JERMAN, B. R.
The production of Disraeli's trilogy. PBSA, lviii (64), 239-51.

JEROME, st.
Hieronymus. *Vitae sanctorum, sive Vitae patrum*. [n.p., n.d.] PBSA, xxxix (45), 68-70.
H. R. Mead.

JESUITS
The Jesuit relations from New France. PBSA, xxx (36), 110-19
L. C. Wroth.

A new copy of the Paris 1660 Jesuit *Relation*, with notes on other editions. PBSA, lvi (62), 368-72.
R. Dechert.

Separated Jesuit letters. PBSA, lx (66), 91-9.
F. M. Rogers.

JEVON, Thomas
Another early edition of Thomas Jevon's *Devil of a Wife*. PBSA, xlix (55), 253-4.
F. T. Bowers.

Three 1695 editions of Jevon's *Devil of a Wife*. SB, iii (50), 255.
F. O. Waller.

JEWETT, Sarah Orne
Sarah Orne Jewett's *A Dark Night*. PBSA, liii (59), 331-4.
D. B. Green.

The Sarah Orne Jewett canon: additions and a correction. PBSA, lv (61), 141-2.
D. B. Green.

JOANNES PRESBYTER
See John (Prester)

JOBBING PRINTING
The development of printing, other than book-printing. LIB, xvii (36/7), 22-35.
J. Johnson.

JODRELL, Richard Paul
[Jodrell, Richard Paul] (1745-1831). *The knight and friars; an historical tale*. New York, 1786. PBSA, xxxv (41), 72.
J. C. Wyllie.

JOHN (Prester)
A Prêtre Jean from Poitiers. PBSA, xlvi (52), 151-4.
C. F. Bühler.

JOHN GEORGE *elector of Brandenburg*
A portrait of John-George of Brandenburg on presentation bindings: a footnote to Haebler. Illus. LIB, xvii (62), 88-92.
D. M. Rogers.

JOHN OF LANCASTER *duke of Bedford*
The books and patronage of learning of a 15th-century prince. [John, duke of Bedford, 1389-1435]. BC, xii (63), 308-15.
M. J. Barber.

The personal prayer-book of John of Lancaster, Duke of Bedford, K. G. Illus. LIB, xiii (32/3), 148/54.
E. F. Bosanquet.

JOHN O'LONDON'S WEEKLY
Dylan Thomas, Mr. Rolph, and *John O'London's Weekly*. PBSA, lx (66), 370-2.
W. White.

JOHNS, Francis Ashley T.
The privately printed *Chinese Poems*, 1916. (Query, 136). BC, ix (60), 458.

Arthur Waley's *Chinese Poems*, 1916. (Note, 210). BC, xii (63), 494.

JOHNS, James
James Johns, Vermont pen printer. Illus. PBSA, xxvii (33), 89-132.
R. W. G. Vail.

JOHNSON, Alfred Forbes
An unrecorded specimen sheet of a Scottish printing house. Illus. EBST, i (35/8), 61-4.

Sources of Roman and italic types used by English printers in the sixteenth century. Illus. LIB, xvii (36/7), 70-82.

The type-specimen books of Claude Lamesle and Nicolas Gando. Illus. LIB, xviii (37/8), 201-11.

Catalogue of Specimens of Printing Types by English and Scottish Printers and Founders, 1665-1830. [*A letter*]. LIB, xviii (37/8), 230-1.

Some types used by Paolo Manuzio. Illus. LIB, xix (38/9), 167-75.

Type-design and type-founding in Scotland. EBST, ii (38/45), 253-61.

The 'goût hollandois'. Illus. LIB, xx (39/40), 180-96.

The italic types of Robert Granjon. Illus. LIB, xxi (40/1), 291-308.

An alphabet by Pieter Coecke van Aelst. LIB, LIB, xxiii (42/3), 195-7.

The supply of types in the sixteenth century. LIB, xxiv (43/4), 47-65.

Books printed at Heidelberg for Thomas Cartwright. LIB, ii (47/8), 284-6.

English books printed abroad. LIB, iv (49/50), 273-6.

The exiled English Church at Amsterdam and its press. Illus. LIB, v (50/1), 219-42.

J. F. Stam, Amsterdam, and English bibles. Illus. LIB, ix (54), 185-93.

Willem Christiaans, Leyden, and his English books. LIB, x (55), 121-3.

Frank Swinton Isaac. [Obituary notice]. LIB, xii (57), 54-5.

Italian sixteenth-century books. LIB, xiii (58), 161-74.

The 'Cloppenburg' press, 1640, 1641. Illus. LIB, xiii (58), 280-2.

Cardinal Cervini and the printing of Greek. [A letter]. LIB, xiii (58), 299.

Devices of German printers, 1501-1540. Illus. LIB, xx (65), 81-107.

JOHNSON, Ann Cox-
Lambeth Palace Library, 1610-1664. TCBS, ii (54/8), 105-26.

JOHNSON, Arthur M.
Hinman collators: present locations. PBSA, lxiii (69), 119-20.

JOHNSON, Francis R.
The first editions of Gabriel Harvey's *Fovre Letters*. LIB, xv (34/5), 212-23.

Printers' copy-books' and the black market in the Elizabethan book trade. LIB, i (46/7), 97-105.

Gabriel Harvey's *Three Letters*: a first issue of his *Foure Letters*. LIB, i (46/7), 134-6.

Notes on English retail book-prices, 1550-1640. LIB, v (50/1), 83-112.

The editions of Robert Greene's three parts of *Conny-Catching*: a bibliographical analysis. LIB, ix (54), 17-24.

Press corrections and press-work in the Elizabethan printing shop. PBSA, xl (46), 276-86.

JOHNSON, Fred Bates
Conrad, Joseph. *Suspense*. PBSA, xl (46), 237-8.

JOHNSON, John de Molins
The development of printing other than book-printing. LIB, xvii (36/7), 22-35.

A printer's error [in *The Library*]. LIB, xxiii (42/3), 132.

John Johnson. [Obituary notice]. LIB, xii (57), 55-7.
C. Batey *and* sir F. Francis.

JOHNSON, L. G.
On some authors of *Edinburgh Review* articles, 1830-1849. LIB, vii (52), 38-50.

JOHNSON, Richard
Richard Johnson and the successors to John Newberry. LIB, iv (49/50), 25-63.
M. J. P. Weedon.

JOHNSON, Richard Colles
Copies of Melville's *John Marr* and *Timoleon*. (Query, 197). BC, xv (66), 68.

Addenda to Irish [*The modern American muse*]: Theodora Taylor, Rixford J. Lincoln, David Bailey, Lester S. Parker. PBSA, lxiii (69), 198-200.

Addendum to Byrd and Lincoln: Issac A. Pool. PBSA, lxiii (69), 295.

— *and* LOWMAN, Matthew P., II.
The California *Constitution* of 1849. PBSA, lxiii (69), 25-9.

JOHNSON, rev. Samuel
The Rev. Samuel Johnson's *Collection of Prayers*. (1759). PBSA, xlviii (54), 416-21.
M. H. Thomas.

JOHNSON, Samuel
Dr. Johnson, a[n] imaginary portrait. Illus. BC, i (52), 92-3.
J. P. W. Gaskell.

Johnson's *Lives*: an unrecorded variant and a new portrait. Illus. BC, i (52), 174-5.
D. F. Rowan.

The infant Johnson. (Note, 7). BC, i (52), 192.
C. R. Hudleston.

Concealed editions of Samuel Johnson. BC, ii (53), 59-65.
W. B. Todd.

Johnson's *Marmor Norfolciense*. (Note, 18). BC, ii (53), 73.
W. B. Todd.

Samuel Johnson, 1709-1784. (English literary autographs, 6). Illus. BC, ii (53), 142-3.
T. J. Brown.

Johnson's last gifts to Windham. BC, v (56), 354-6.
R. W. Ketton-Cremer.

Variants in Johnson's *Dictionary*, 1755. (Note, 242). BC, xiv (65), 212-13.
W. B. Todd.

Notes on Johnson's *Plan of a Dictionary*. LIB, xix (38/9), 198-201.
R. F. Metzdorf.

Supplementary note on Johnson's *Plan of a Dictionary*. LIB, xix (38/9), 363.
R. F. Metzdorf.

Some proofs of Johnson's *Prefaces to the Poets*. LIB, xvii (62), 213-30.
J. D. Fleeman.

The making of Johnson's *Life of Savage*, 1744. LIB, xxii (67), 346-52.
J. D. Fleeman.

Johnsonian bibliography, a supplement to Courtney. OBSP, v (36/9), 117-66.
R. W. Chapman *and* A. T. Hazen.

Notes on serialization and competitive publishing: Johnson's and Bailey's *Dictionaries*, 1755. OBSP, v (36/9), 305-22.
P. B. Gove.

—. A supplementary note. OBSP, i (48), 45-6.

An addition to the bibliography of Samuel Johnson. PBSA, xli (47), 231-8.
H. W. Liebert.

The history of the Johnson papers. PBSA, xlv (51), 103-16.
M. Hyde.

The first American *Rasselas* and its imprint. PBSA, xlvii (53), 374-6.
R. F. Metzdorf.

The cancels in Dr. Johnson's *Works*. (Oxford, 1825). PBSA, xlvii (53), 376-8.
A. Sherbo.

A note on the publishing of Johnson's *Proposals for Printing the Harleian Miscellany*. PBSA, xlviii (54), 196-8.
G. J. Kolb.

Two notes on Johnson and the *Gentleman's Magazine*. PBSA, liv (60), 101-10.
J. Leed.

The history of the Sneyd-Gimbel and Pigott-British Museum copies of Dr. Johnson's *Dictionary*. PBSA, liv (60), 286-9.
G. J. Kolb *and* J. H. Sledd.

Johnson and Cocker's *Arithmetic*. PBSA, lvi (62), 107-9.
S. O. Mitchell.

Samuel Johnson's editions of Shakespeare, 1765. PBSA, lvi (62), 428-44.
D. D. Eddy.

Johnson's *Journey*, 1775, and its cancels. Illus. PBSA, lviii (64), 232-8.
J. D. Fleeman.

A note on Johnson's *Journey*, 1775. PBSA, lix (65), 317-18.
L. H. Kendal, *jr*.

Variant readings in Johnson's *London*. PBSA, lx (66), 214-15.
R. R. Allen.

Dr. Johnson on abridgement — a re-examination. PBSA, lx (66), 215-9.
W. J. Howard.

Works by and about Samuel Johnson in eighteenth-century America. PBSA, lxii (68), 537-46.
R. B. Winans.

The preface to *A dictionary of the English language*: Johnson's revision and the establishment of the text. SB, v (52), 129-46.
W. R. Keast.

The printing of Johnson's *Journey*, 1775. SB, vi (54), 247-54.
W. B. Todd.

Dr. Johnson and the *Public Ledger*: a small addition to the canon. SB, xi (58), 252-5.
G. J. Kolb.

The False Alarm and *Taxation no Tyranny*: some further observations. SB, xiii (60), 223-31.
D. J. Greene.

Rasselas: purchase price, proprietors, and printings. SB, xv (62), 256-9.
G. J. Kolb.

JOHNSON, Thomas Herbert
Establishing a text: the Emily Dickinson papers. SB, v (52/3), 21-32.

JOHNSON [*afterwards CORY*] William
See CORY, William

JOHNSTON, Algernon Sidney
Memoirs of a Nullifier, by a native of South Columba [A. S. Johnston]. PBSA, xxxvi (42), 233.
M. B. Meriwether.

JOHNSTON, Brendan
Raymond Chandler. (Note, 30). BC, iii (54), 69.
—. (Query, 45). BC, iii (54), 73.

JOHNSTON, George P.
The story of the Edinburgh Bibliographical Society. EBSP, xv (32/5), 77-86.

JOINT AUTHORSHIP
Bibliographical clues in collaborate plays. LIB, xiii (32/3), 21-48.
M. St. C. Byrne.

JOLLEY, L. J.
Two inquiries about the bibliography of William Cullen. BTHK, i/1 (56), 28-9.

William Thomson's *Orpheus Caledonius*. BTHK, i/2 (57), 26-7.

Lewis Grassic Gibbon: an additional note. BTHK, i/2 (57), 35.

The records of medical and scientific societies in Scotland. 3. The records of the Royal College of Physicians of Edinburgh. BTHK, i/3 (58), 20-7.

A note on the portraiture of William Cullen. Illus. BTHK, i/3 (58), 27-36.

An error in the catalogue of the Ferguson Collection. BTHK, ii (59/60), 28-9.

JONAS, Klaus Werner
More Maughamiana. PBSA, xliv (50), 378-83.

Additions to the bibliography of Herman Hesse. PBSA, xlix (55), 358-60.

Additions to the bibliography of Carl Van Vechten. PBSA, lv (61), 42-5.

JONES *family*
Jones' *Nests and Eggs of the Birds of Ohio*. PBSA, xlvii (53), 218-30.
E. J. Wessen.

JONES, Claude
Christopher Smart, Richard Rolt, and *The Universal Visiter*. LIB, xviii (37/8), 212-14.

JONES, E. Alfred
Newcome's Academy and its plays. LIB, xiv (33/4), 339-47.

JONES, Gordon W.
An unrecorded edition of a Hoole schoolbook. PBSA, lv (61), 226-9.

A Virginia-owned shelf of early American medical imprints. PBSA, lviii (64), 281-90.

JONES, H. W.
Stubbe and Wotton. (Note, 63). BC, v (56), 78.

An unexplained 17th-century cancel. (Query, 129). BC, ix (60), 203-4.

Literary problems in seventeenth-century scientific manuscripts. SB, xiv (61), 69-80.

JONES, John Bush
The printing of *The Grand Duke*: notes toward a Gilbert bibliography. PBSA, lxi (67), 335-43.

JONSELMUS *de Canova*
Philippus de Monte Calerio. *Dominicale*. Abridged by Jonselmus de Canova. [Paris, P. Pigouchet, *c.* 1500]. PBSA, xxxvi (42), 62-3.
H. R. Mead.

JONSON, Ben
More books from Ben Jonson's library. (Note, 223). BC, xiii (64), 346-8.
C. B. L. Barr.

Was there a 1612 quarto of *Epicene*? LIB, xv (34/5), 306-15.
Sir W. W. Greg.

The press-corrections in Jonson's *The King's Entertainment*. LIB, xxiv (43/4), 181-6.
A. K. McIlwraith.

Notes on a cancel in *The Alchemist,* 1612. LIB, xiii (58), 278-80.
H. Davis.

Benson's alleged piracy of *Shake-speares Sonnets* and of some of Jonson's works. SB, xxi (68), 235-48.
J. W. Bennett.

JOURNAL POLITIQUE ET LITTÉRAIRE D'ANGLETERRE
Journal politique et littéraire d'Angleterre, 1784. LIB, i (46/7), 142-3.
O. von Feilitzen.

JOURNAL POLYTYPE DES SCIENCES ET DES ARTS
Le Journal polytype des sciences et des arts. Illus. PBSA, xlviii (54), 402-10.
D. I. Duveen *and* H. S. Klickstein.

JOURNALS OF THE CONTINENTAL CONGRESS
Proposals of nine printers for a new edition of the *Journals of the Continental Congress*, 1785. SB, ii (49), 189-96.
E. P. Dandridge.

JOYCE, James Augustine A.
Press copies of Joyce's *Ulysses*. (Note, 156).
BC, x (61), 72.
W. White.

James Joyce, 1882-1941. (English literary autographs, 40). Illus. BC, x (61), 441.
T. J. Brown.

Joyce's *Ulysses*, 1922. (Note, 175). BC, xi (62), 85-6.
W. Thornton.

Stephen Hero's bookshops. BC, xiv (65), 194-9.
A. Walbank.

Harriet Weaver and James Joyce. (Query, 212). BC, xv (66), 488-9.
J. H. Lidderdale.

Ulysses and the Attorney-General 1936. LIB, xxiv (69), 343-5.
D. Thomas.

James Joyce: Addenda to Alan Parker's bibliography. PBSA, xliii (49), 401-11.
W. White.

The Odyssey Press edition of James Joyce's *Ulysses*. PBSA, l (56), 195-8.
J. F. Spoerri.

Some observations on the text of *Dubliners: The Dead*. SB, xv (62), 191-205.
R. E. Scholes.

Grant Richards to James Joyce. SB, xvi (63), 139-60.
R. Scholes.

Light on Joyce's *Exiles*? A new MS, a curious analogue, and some speculations. SB, xvii (64), 83-105.
R. M. Adams.

Further observations on the text of *Dubliners*. SB, xvii (64), 107-22.
R. Scholes.

Harriet Weaver's letters to James Joyce, 1915-1920. SB, xx (67), 151-88.
J. Firth.

James Pinker to James Joyce, 1915-1920. SB, xxi (68), 205-24.
J. Firth.

Ulysses notebook VIII. A.5 at Buffalo. SB, xxii (69), 287-310.
P. F. Herring.

JUDSON, mrs. Emily Chubbuck
Addenda to Wright [*American fiction 1774-1850*]: Burdett, Curtis, Judson, Weeks. PBSA, lxii (68), 452-3.
W. S. Kable.

JUEL-JENSEN, Bent Einer
John Hamilton Reynolds. (Some uncollected authors, 3). BC, iii (54), 211-15.

—. (Note, 269). BC, xv (66), 210-11.

A Drayton collection. Illus. BC, iv (55), 133-43.

John Taylor's *Booke of Martyrs*, 1633. (Note, 49). BC, iv (55), 327.

The poet Earl of Surrey's library. (Note, 67). BC, v (56), 172.

Bulmer and the Roxburghe Club catalogue. (Query, 82). BC, vi (57), 290-1.

Sir Hugh Plat, ?1552-?1611. (Some uncollected authors, 19). BC, viii (59), 60-8.

—. Errata and addenda. BC, viii (59), 179.

—. (Note, 271). BC, xv (66), 212-13.

Three lost Drayton items. (Query, 122). BC, ix (60), 78-9.

Non est mortale quod opto. (Note, 141). BC, x (61), 446.

Sir Philip Sidney, 1554-1586. (Some uncollected authors, 34). 2 pts. BC, xi (62), 468-79; xii (63), 196-201.

Bent Juel-Jensen. (Contemporary collectors, 43). Illus. BC, xv (66), 152-74.
B. Juel-Jensen.

Sidney's *Arcadia*, 'London, 1599'. A distinguished 'ghost'. (Note, 283). BC, xvi (67), 80.

The Tixall manuscript of Sir Philip Sidney's and the Countess of Pembroke's paraphrase of the Psalms. (Note, 314). BC, xviii (69), 222-3.

Polyolbion, Poemes Lyrick and pastorall, Poems 1619, The Owle, and a few other books by Michael Drayton. Illus. LIB, viii (53), 145-62.

Isaac Oliver's portrait of Prince Henry and *Polyolbion*, a footnote. Illus. LIB, x (55), 206-7.

An Oxford variant of Drayton's *Polyolbion*. Illus. LIB, xvi (61), 53-4.

The 1628 editions of John Earle's *Microcosmographie*. LIB, xxi (66), 231-4.

Michael Drayton and William Drummond of Hawthornden: a lost autograph letter rediscovered. Illus. LIB, xxi (66), 328-30.

Fine and large-paper copies of S.T.C. books: a further note. LIB, xxiii (68), 239-40.

JUMP, John Davies
Rollo, Duke of Normandy. Some bibliographical notes on the seventeenth-century editions. LIB, xviii (37/8), 227-86.

JUNIUS, pseud.
The Letters of Junius. (Query, 8). BC, i (52), 194.
F. Cordasco.

Letters of Junius. (Query, 8). BC, i (52), 57.
P. S. Clarkson.

Edward Bocquet's illustrated edition of the *Letters of Junius*. PBSA, xlvi (52), 66-67.
F. Cordasco.

The missing third edition of Wheble's *Junius*, 1771. SB, xiii (60), 235-8.
G. B. Evans.

JUNIUS, Franciscus
Census of extant copies of Junius's *Caedmon*, 1655. (Query, 147). BC, xi (62), 218.
M. D. Clubb.

Junius's edition of Caedmon. [A letter]. LIB, xvii (62), 157.
M. D. Clubb.

A request for assistance. [Junius's *Caedmon*]. PBSA, lvi (62), 116.
M. D. Clubb.

JURA CLERI
The author of *Jura Cleri*. [Ascribed to William Carpender]. PBSA, lxii (68), 241-5.
J. R. Jenson.

JUSTICE, Henry
Henry Justice, a Cambridge book thief. TCBS, i (49/53), 348-57.
J. P. W. Gaskell.

JUSTIFICATION
Typographical justification and grammatical change in the eighteenth century. PBSA, lvi (62), 248-51.
M. A. Manzalaoui.

JUSTINIANO, Leonardo
Two undescribed incunabula. [Justiniano, Leonardo. *Sonetti d'amore. El desperato*. [Rome, Johann Besicken, c. 1500]: [*and*], *Strambotti d'ogni sorte e Sonetti alla Bergamasca*. [Rome: Eucharius Silber, c. 1500). PBSA, xxxix (45), 162-3.
C. F. Bühler.

JUVENALIS, Guido
Juvenalis, Guido (ca. 1460-1505). *In latinae linguae Elegantis interpretatio*. Paris, Jean Tréperel, 1497. PBSA, xxxiv (40), 269-70.
H. R. Mead.

K

K, E.
A note on the printing of E. K.'s glosses [to *The Shepheardes Calender*]. SB, xiv (61), 203-5.
J. Stillinger.

KABLE, William S.
Addenda to Wright [*American fiction 1774-1850*]: Burdett, Curtis, Judson, Weeks. PBSA, lxii (68), 452-3.

Addenda to Wright: Mancur, Pise, Tuthill, Weld. PBSA, lxiii (69), 294.

The influence of justification on spelling in Jaggard's compositor B. SB, xx (67), 235-9.

Compositor B, the Pavier quartos, and copy spellings. SB, xxi (68), 131-61.

KALLICH, Martin
A textual note on John Dos Passos' *Journeys Between Wars*. PBSA, xliii (49), 346-8.

Mr. Kallich replies [to C. W. Bernardin's "*John Dos Passos' textual revisions*"]. PBSA xlviii (54), 97-8.

KALTHOEBER, Christian
A new address for Christian Kalthoeber. 1962. LIB, xvii (62), 95.
D. G. Neill.

KANE, Norman
Artemus Ward His Book, 1862. PBSA, lv (61), 392.

Some Lardner variants. PBSA, lvi (62), 487.

Loguen's *Narrative*, 1859. PBSA, lvi (62), 488.

A further printing of *That Lass o'Lowrie's*. PBSA, lvii (63), 222.

KANTOR, J. R. K.
Fifty-two early California imprints in the Bancroft Library, a supplementary list to Greenwood's *California Imprints, 1833-1862*. PBSA, lviii (64), 181-9.

KAPLAN, Israel
Kipling's *American Notes* and Mark Twain interview. PBSA, xliv (50), 69-73.

KASER, David
The chronology of Carey imprints. PBSA, l (56), 190-3.

The origin of the book trade sales. PBSA, l (56), 296-302.

Waverley in America. PBSA, li (57), 163-7.

The first trans-Mississippi imprint. PBSA, lii (58), 306-9.

KATHERINE *of Aragon.*
See CATHERINE *of Aragon, consort of Henry VIII, King of England.*

KATZ, Joseph
Cora Crane and the poetry of Stephen Crane. PBSA, lviii (64), 469-76.

Toward a descriptive bibliography of Stephen Crane *The black riders*. PBSA, lix (65), 150-7.

CALM addendum no. 1: Hart Crane. PBSA, lxiii (69), 130.

BAL addendum: Harold Frederic's *Gloria Mundi?* — entry 6293. The first four printings of Harold Frederic's *Gloria mundi?*. PBSA, lxiii (69), 197-8.

— *and* BRUCCOLI, Matthew Joseph
Toward a descriptive bibliography of Stephen Crane: *Spanish-American war songs* [collected by S. A. Witherbee]. PBSA, lxi (67), 267-9.

Scholarship and mere artifacts: the British and empire publications of Stephen Crane. SB, xxii (69), 277-87.

—. *and* MANNING, John J.
Notes on Frank Norris's revisions of two novels. [*McTeague* and *A man's woman*]. Illus. PBSA, lxii (68), 256-9.

KATZ, William Armstrong
Tracing western territorial imprints through the National archives. PBSA, lix (65), 1-11.

KAUFMAN, Paul
Bunyan signatures in a copy of the Bible. (Note, 120). Illus. BC, viii (59), 427-8.

A bookseller's record of eighteenth-century Book Clubs. Illus. LIB, xv (60), 278-87.

The Leigh Browne collection at the Keats Museum. LIB, xvii (62), 246-50.

The Westminster library: history and mystery. LIB, xxi (66), 240-5.

The loan records of Shrewsbury school library. LIB, xxii (67), 252-6.

The eighteenth-century forerunner of the London Library. PBSA, liv (60), 89-100.

Establishing Berkeley's authorship of *Guardian* papers. PBSA, liv (60), 181-3.

Chatterton's brother-poet, William Roberts. PBSA, lvii (63), 184-90.

The rise of community libraries in Scotland. Illus. PBSA, lix (65), 233-94.

Zion's temple, Manchester: an introduction to libraries of dissent. PBSA, lxii (68), 337-49.

KEACH, Benjamin
Keach, Benjamin (1640-1704). Instructions for children. PBSA, xxxv (41), 72.
C. S. Brigham.

KEAST, William Rea
The preface to *A Dictionary of the English Language*: Johnson's revision and the establishment of the text. SB, v (52/3), 129-46.

KEATS, John
See also HAMPSTEAD, *Keats House and Mus.*

John Keats, 1795-1821. (English literary autographs, 36). Illus. BC, ix (60), 445.
T. J. Brown.

An early annotated edition of *The Eve of St. Agnes*. PBSA, xlvi (52), 269-73.
J. S. Stull.

The Houghton-Crewe draft of Keats' *Ode to a Nightingale*. PBSA, xlviii (54), 91-5.
R. N. Roth.

An early reprinting of three poems from Keats's 1820 volume. PBSA, lx (66), 363.
D. B. Green.

Notes on Keats's *Letters*. SB, ix (57), 179-95.
H. E. Rollins.

The text of *The Eve of St. Agnes*. SB, xvi (63), 207-12.
J. Stillinger.

The text of Keats's *Ode on indolence*. SB, xxii (69), 255-8.
J. Stillinger.

KEBABIAN, John S.
The Henry C. Taylor collection. (Contemporary collectors, 40). Illus. BC, xiv (65), 35-48.

KELLER, Dean Howard
A checklist of the writings of Albion W. Tourgée, 1838-1905. SB, xviii (65), 269-79.

— *and* HEMENWAY, Robert E.
Charles Brockden Brown, America's first important novelist: a check list of biography and criticism. PBSA, lx (66), 349-62.

KELLEY, Maurice Willyle
A note on Milton's *Pro Populo Anglicano Defensio*. LIB, xvii (36/7), 466-7.

Milton and the 'Notes on Paul Best'. Illus. LIB, v (50/1), 49-51.

Milton and Machiavelli's *Discorsi*. Illus. SB, iv (51/2), 123-7.

— *and* ATKINS, Samuel B.
Milton and the Harvard Pindar. SB, xvii (64), 77-82.

KEMPSON, E. G. H.
The Vicar's library, St. Mary's, Marlborough. LIB, xxvi (45/6), 192-3.

KENDALL, Lyle H.
George Wither's *Three Private Meditations*. (Note, 87). BC, vi (57), 405-6.

Locations of copies of Lang's *Lines on . . . the Shelley society*; Meredith's *Jump-to-glory Jane*. (Query, 237). BC, xviii (69), 226.

Two unrecorded editions of John Taylor's *Verbum Sempiternum*. LIB, xii (57), 46-8.

A note on Johnson's *Journey*, 1775. PBSA, lix (65), 317-8.

The first edition of *The Moon and Sixpence*. PBSA, lv (61), 242-3.

John Taylor's piracy of *The Packman's Paternoster*. PBSA, lvii (63), 201-10.

The not-so-gentle art of puffing: William G. Kingsland and Thomas J. Wise. PBSA, lxii (68), 25-37.

KENNERLEY, Mitchell
The Mitchell Kennerley imprint. BC, xiii (64), 185-93.
G. T. Tanselle.

KENNETT, White *bp. of Peterborough*
Bishop Kennett and South Carolina. PBSA, lix (65), 158-60.
F. R. Goff.

KENNEY, C. E.
William Leybourn, 1626-1716. LIB, v (50/1), 159-71.

KENNY, Shirley Strum
Two scenes by Addison in Steele's *Tender husband*. SB, xix (66), 217-26.

Eighteenth-century editions of Steele's *Conscious lovers*. SB, xxi (68), 253-61.

KENTUCKY GAZETTE
The *Kentucky Gazette* and John Bradford its founder. PBSA, xxxi (37), 102-32.
S. M. Wilson.

KENYON, Lloyd, *baron*
Mirk's *Liber Festivalis* and *Quattuor Sermones*. [A letter]. LIB, v (50/1), 59-60.

KER, Neil Ripley
A palimpsest in the National Library of Scotland: early fragments of Augustine *De Trinitate*, the *Passio S. Laurentii* and other texts. Illus. EBST, iii (48/55), 169-78.

English manuscripts owned by Johannes Vlimmerius and Cornelius Duyn. LIB, xxii (41/2), 205-7.

The migration of manuscripts from the English medieval libraries. LIB, xxiii (42/3), 1-11.

Sir John Price. Illus. LIB, x (55), 1-24.

The Virgin and Child binder, LVL, and William Horman. Illus. LIB, xvii (62), 77-85.

Fragments of medieval manuscripts used as pastedowns in Oxford bindings, with a survey of Oxford binding, c. 1515-1620. Illus. OBSP, v (54).

Medieval manuscripts from Norwich Cathedral priory. Illus. TCBS, i (49/53), 1-28.

KERLING, Nelly Johanna M.
Caxton and the trade in printed books. BC, iv (55), 190-9.

KERPNECK, Harvey
A shorn *Shagpat*. (Note, 173). BC, xi (62), 80-3.

KERR, Willis Holmes
The treatment of Drake's circumnavigation in Hakluyt's *Voyages*, 1589. PBSA, xxxiv (40), 281-302.

KERSEY, John
Biographical information concerning N. Bailey and John Kersey. (Query, 216). BC, xvi (67), 225.
G. Freeman.

KERSLAKE, John F.
M. de Jarry's project for an edition of the *Moniteur*. LIB, iv (49/50), 277-9.

KETT, F. J. L.
Insect pests of books. Illus. BC, v (56), 57-62.

KETTON-CREMER, Robert Wyndham
See CREMER, Robert Wyndham Ketton-

KEYNES, sir Geoffrey Langdon
Blake's *Holy Thursday* in Anne and Jane Taylor's *City Scenes*. (Note, 128). BC, ix (60), 75-6.

A Blake engraving in Bonnycastle's *Mensuration*, 1782. Illus. BC, xii (63), 205-6.

The first American edition of *1914 and other Poems*. (Query, 185). BC, xiii (64), 503.

Scott of Amwell's *Elegy*. (Note, 262). BC, xiv (65), 544-5.

Blake's *Little Tom the sailor*. Illus. BC, xvii (68), 421-7.

Sir Geoffrey Keynes. (Contemporary collectors, 39). Illus. BC, xiii (64), 473-80.
J. C. T. Oates.

Addenda to Keynes's *Bibliography of Siegfried Sassoon*. BC, xviii (69), 310-17.
D. Farmer.

Hazlitt's *Grammar* abridged. Illus. LIB, xiii (32/3), 97-9.

The library of Edward Gibbon. [A summary]. LIB, xix (38), 155.

Blake, Tulk, and Garth Wilkinson. LIB, xxvi (45/6), 190-2.

Religio Bibliographici. LIB, viii (53), 63-76.

Books from Donne's library. TCBS, i (49/53), 64-8.

The Library of William Cowper. TCBS, iii (59/63), 47-69.

—. Addendum. TCBS, iii (59/63), 167.

The hand of Thomas Thomas. Illus. TCBS, iv (64/8), 291-2.

A note on Locke's library. Illus. TCBS, iv (64/8), 312-13.

— *and* GIBSON, Strickland
A bibliography of the works of Thomas Fuller. Illus. OBSP, iv (34/5), 63-161.

—. Additions and corrections. OBSP, i (47), 44.

KHUNRATH, Heinrich
Two Alchemical books. [Khunrath's *Amphitheatrum Sapientiae Solius Verae*; and Count Michael Maier's *Atalanta Fugiens*]. BH, ii (51/2), 51-5.
D. I. Duveen.

KIDD, James
James Leslie Mitchell/ Lewis Grassic Gibbon: a chronological check list. Additions II. BTHK, v (67/70), 174-7.

KIDDELL, A. J. B.
Books on cockfighting. BH, i (47/51), 405-12.

KIEV
A unique *Provinciale Romanum* at Kiev. (Note, 118). BC, viii (59), 425.
J. V. Scholderer.

KILGOUR, Frederick Gridley
Harvey manuscripts. PBSA, liv (60), 177-9.

KILNER, Mary Jane
'S.S.' alias Mary Kilner: a biographical amendment. (Note, 323). BC, xviii (69), 519.
J. E. Grey.

KIMBER, Edward Isaac
The *Relation of a late expedition to St. Augustine*, with biographical and bibliographical notes on Isaac and Edward Kimber. Illus. PBSA, xxviii (34), 81-96.

KIMBER, W. C.
Brief instructions for children, 1654. (Query, 57). BC, iv (55), 81.

KIMPEL, Ben Drew *and* EAVES, Thomas Carey Duncan
Two notes on Samuel Richardson. Richardson's chapel rules. The printer of the *Daily Journal*. LIB, xxiii (68), 242-7.

Richardsoniana. SB, xiv (61), 232-4.

Samuel Richardson's London houses. Illus. SB, xv (62), 135-48.

Richardson's revisions of *Pamela*. SB, xx (67), 61-88.

KING, Alexander Hyatt
The Royal Music library. Some account of its provenance and associations. Illus. BC, vii (58), 241-52.

Frederick Nicolay, 1728/9-1809. (Portrait of a bibliophile, 5). Illus. BC, ix (60), 401-13.

Untraced auction sale-catalogues of music. (Query, 148). BC, xi (62), 219.

Recent work in music bibliography. LIB, xxvi (45/6), 122-48.

English pictorial music title-pages, 1820-1885. Illus. LIB, iv (49/50), 262-72.

A subscription list to Mozart's *Cosi fan tutte*. LIB, vii (52), 132-3.

William Barclay Squire, 1855-1927, music librarian. LIB, xii (57), 1-10.

KING, Henry *bp. of Chichester*
Notes on the physical characteristics of some manuscripts of the poems of Donne and of Henry King. LIB, xvi (61), 121-32.
M. C. Crum.

KING, Richard L.
Ursprung vnd Ordnungen der Bergwerge . . . (Leipzig 1616): location of copies. (Query, 223). BC, xvii (68), 219.

KING, T. J.
Shirley's *Coronation* and *Love Will Find out the Way;* erroneous title-pages. SB, xviii (65), 265-9.

KING, William
Dr. William King's *Miscellanies in Prose and Verse*. LIB, xxv (44/5), 37-45.
C. J. Horne.

KING LEOPOLD'S SOLILOQUY
King Leopold's soliloquy. PBSA, lvii (63), 351-2.
J. F. Guido.

KINGSALE, Gerald, *baron.*
A mosaic binding for Lord Kingsale, 1720. (English bookbindings, 20). Illus. BC, vi (57), 60.
H. M. Nixon.

KING'S COLLEGE
See CAMBRIDGE *King's College.*

and NEW YORK *King's College.*

KINGSFORD, Reginald John L. *and* DREYFUS, John Gustave
John Baskerville: proposals for a revised edition of Straus and Dent's bibliography and memoir. TCBS, i (49/53), 191-2.

KINGSLAND, William G.
The note-so-gentle art of puffing: William G. Kingsland and Thomas J. Wise. PBSA, lxii (68), 25-37.
L. H. Kendall, *jr.*

KING'S PRINTING OFFICE
The King's printer at York and Shrewsbury, 1642-3. LIB, xxiii (42), 129-31.
L. W. Hanson.

The King's Printers, 1660-1742. LIB, iii (48/9), 33-8.
A. F. Johnson.

In the Savoy: a study in post-Restoration imprints. SB, i (48), 39-46.
C. W. Miller.

New light on the King's Printing Office, 1680-1730. SB, viii (56), 157-67.
R. L. Haig.

KINIETZ, Vernon
Schoolcraft's manuscript magazines. PBSA, xxxv (41), 151-4.

KINNEY, Arthur F.
Two unique copies of Stephen Gosson's *Schoole of abuse*, 1579: criteria for judging nineteenth-century editing. PBSA, liv (65), 425-9.

KINSER, Samuel
The Sunderland copy of Jacques-Auguste De Thou's *History of his time*. BC, xv (66), 446-53.

An unknown manuscript catalogue of the library of J. A. De Thou. Illus. BC, xvii (68), 168-76.

KIPLING, Rudyard
Kipling, Rudyard (1865-1936). *Departmental Ditties*. Third ed. Calcutta, 1888. PBSA, xxxvi (42), 232.
F. R. Goff.

Kipling's *American Notes* and Mark Twain interview. PBSA, xliv (50), 69-73.
I. Kaplan.

Cora's mouse [Stephen Crane's gift of Kipling's *The seven seas* to Cora Taylor]. PBSA, lix (65), 188-9.
M. J. Bruccoli.

Rudyard Kipling: early printings in American periodicals. PBSA, lxi (67), 127-8.
G. Monteiro.

KIRCHER, Athanasius
Athanasius Kircher and the distribution of his books. LIB, xxiii (68), 108-17.
J. Fletcher.

KIRCHNERUS, Timotheus
[Latin commentary on Luther, with preface signed by Timotheus Kirchnerus, and dated December 29, 1565]. PBSA, xxxv (41), 68.
C. K. Shipton.

KIRKHAM, E. Bruce
The first English editions of John Lawson's *Voyage to Carolina*: a bibliographical study. PBSA, lxi (67), 258-65.

KIRKMAN, Francis
The first series of plays published by Francis Kirkman in 1661. LIB, ii (47/8), 289-91.
F. T. Bowers.

A bibliography of Francis Kirkman with his prefaces, dedications, and commendations, 1652-80. Illus. OBSP, i (49), 47-152.
S. Gibson.

KIRKPATRICK, Brownlee Jean
Additions to the bibliography of Virginia Woolf. (Note, 216). BC, xiii (64), 70.

Additions to the E. M. Forster bibliography [by B. J. Kirkpatrick]. PBSA, lx (66), 224-5.
J. B. Shipley.

KIRSCHBAUM, Leo
Walkley's supposed piracy of Wither's *Workes* in 1620. LIB, xix (38/9), 339-46.

Entrance, licence, and publication. [A letter]. LIB, xxvi (45/6), 195.

The good and bad quartos of *Doctor Faustus*. LIB, xxvi (45/6), 272-94.

The copyright of Elizabethan plays. LIB, xiv (59), 231-50.

Author's copyright in England before 1640. PBSA, xl (46), 43-80.

KISELEV, Nikolai Petrovich
An unrecorded Spanish incunable in Moscow. BC, viii (59), 271-4.

KITCHIN, C. H. B.
Richard Jennings, 1881-1952. (Portrait of a bibliophile, 3). BC, viii (59), 370-82.

KLEPIKOV, Sokrat Aleksandrovich
Russian bookbinding from the 11th to the middle of the 17th century. Illus. BC, x (61), 408-22.

Russian bookbinding from the middle of the 17th to the end of the 19th century. Illus. BC, xi (62), 437-47.

Historical notes on Ukrainian bookbinding. Illus. BC, xv (66), 135-42.

Russian watermarks and embossed paper-stamps of the eighteenth and nineteenth centuries. Illus. PBSA, lvii (63), 121-8.

KLICKSTEIN, Herbert S. and DUVEEN, Denis Ian
Le Journal polytype des sciences et des arts. Illus. PBSA, xlviii (54), 402-10.

KLINEFELTER, Ralph A.
Lydgate's LIfe of Our Lady and the Chetham MS. 6709. PBSA, xlvi (52), 396-7.

KLOTH, Karen and FABIAN, Bernhard
The manuscript background of James Beattie's Elements of moral science. BTHK, v (67/70), 181-9.

KNAPP, Lewis Mansfield
Smollett's works as printed by William Strahan, with an unpublished letter of Smollett to Strahan. LIB, xiii (32/3), 282-91.

The publication of Smollett's Complete History . . . and Continuation. LIB, xvi (35/6), 295-308.

Ralph Griffiths, author and publisher, 1746-1750. LIB, xx (39/40), 197-213.

KNEPPER, Adrian W.
Obadiah Rich: bibliopole. PBSA, xlix (55), 112-30.

KNERR, Anthony
Regarding a checklist of Lawrence Durrell. PBSA, lv (61), 142-52.

KNIAGHININSKY, Petr Pavlovich
Kniaghininsky's tape-operated composing machine. JPHS, iii (67), 93-6.
J. Moran.

KNIGHT, Sarah Kemble
The editing and publication of The Journal of Madam Knight. PBSA, lviii (64), 25-32.
A. Margolies.

KNITTING BOOKS
English knitting and crochet books of the nineteenth century. Illus. 2 pts. LIB, x (55), 25-40; 103-19.
E. Potter.

KNOTT, David H.
Unpublished second volume of Edward Burrow's A new and compleat book of rates 1774. (Note, 290). BC, xvi (67), 375-7.

An eighteenth-century book club at Clapham. LIB, xxiv (69), 243-6.

KNOWLES, Edwin B.
Some textual peculiarities of the first English Don Quixote. Illus. PBSA, xxxvii (43), 203-14.

Don Quixote abridged. Illus. PBSA, xlix (55), 19-36.

KNOX, T. M. and FORDYCE, C. J.
The library of Jesus College, Oxford, with an appendix on the books bequeathed thereto by Lord Herbert of Cherbury. Illus. OBSP, v (36/9), 49-115.

KNOX, Ronald Arbuthnott
Knox's Absolute and Abitofhell. (Query, 21). BC, i (52), 268.
J. Carter.

KOLB, Gwin Jackson
A note on the publication of Johnson's Proposals for Printing the Harleian Miscellany. PBSA, xlviii (54), 196-8.

John Newbery, projector of the Universal Chronicle: a study of the advertisements. SB, xi (58), 249-51.

Dr. Johnson and the Public Ledger: a small addition to the canon. SB, xi (58), 252-5.

Rasselas: purchase price, proprietors, and printings. SB, xv (62), 256-9.

— and SLEDD, James H.
The history of the Sneyd-Gimbel and Piggott-British Museum copies of Dr. Johnson's Dictionary. PBSA, liv (60), 286-9.

KONIGSBERG, I.
Dr. Griffith Roberts and his Welsh Grammar (Milan, 1567). (Note, 237). BC, xiv (65), 73-4.

KORN, Bertram Wallace
Benjamin Levy: New Orleans printer and publisher. Illus. PBSA, liv (60), 221-64.

T. C. DeLeon's The Rock or The Rye. PBSA, lvii (63), 354-6.

Additional Benjamin and Alexander Levy imprints. PBSA, lxii (68), 245-52.

KRAFT, James
An unpublished review by Henry James [of E. Stoddard's Two Men]. SB, xx (67), 267-73.

KRAMER, Dale
Two 'new' texts of Thomas Hardy's The Woodlanders. SB, xx (67), 135-50.

KRAMER, Sidney
There was a Little Girl: its first printing, its authorship, its variants. PBSA, xl (46), 287-310.

Some Stone & Kimball addenda. [S. Kramer's A history of Stone & Kimball and Herbert S. Stone & company]. PBSA, lx (66), 476-8.
G. T. Tanselle.

Stone and Kimball addendum: Blossom's *Checkers.* PBSA, lxii (68), 451-2.
G. T. Tanselle.

KRAUS, H. P.
Rebound in the 16th century? [An answer to Query 202]. BC, xv (66), 487.

KRAUSE, Jacob
Bindings by Jacob Krause and his school in English collections. Illus. BC, viii (59), 25-30. I. Schunke.

KRONENBERG, Marie Elizabeth
Forged addresses in Low Country books in the period of the Reformation. LIB, ii (47/8), 81-94.

A printed letter of the London Hanse Merchants, 3 March 1526. Illus. OBSP, i (48), 25-32.

The creation of a ghost. [Stillwell, *Census* M 504: *Een geestelijke Minnebrief. Die Negen Couden. Die seven Banden.* Schoonhoven: Fratres apud S. Michaelem in den Hem, about 1500]. PBSA, xlix (55), 249-52.

Fragment of a book-seller's list, probably Antwerp, about 1533-35. Illus. TCBS, ii (54/8), 14-37.

KRONICK, David A.
Scientific journal publication in the eighteenth century. PBSA, lix (65), 28-44.

KRUEGER, Robert
Manuscript evidence for dates of two *Short-title Catalogue* books: George Wilkins's *Three Miseries of Barbary* and the third edition of Elizabeth Grymeston's *Miscelanea.* LIB, xvi (61), 141-2.

KRUYSKAMP, C.
The *Edinburgh Encyclopedia,* 1808-30. (Query, 141). BC, x (61), 75.

KÜP, Karl
The illustrations for Ulrich von Richenthal's *Chronicle of the Council of Constance* in manuscripts and books. Illus. PBSA, xxxiv (40), 1-16.

KYD, Thomas
The printing of *The Spanish tragedy.* LIB, xxiv (69), 187-99.
A. Freeman.

KYRISS, Ernst
Notes on bindings from English collections at Stuttgart. BC, v (56), 158-61.

An Erfurt binding of the 15th century. (Foreign bookbindings, 1). BC, xviii (69), 63.

A Bavarian monastic binding *c.* 1480. (Foreign bookbindings, 4). Illus. BC, xviii (69), 491.

Notes on Nuremberg panel stamps before the Reformation. Illus. PBSA, xliv (50), 59-62.

Bookbindings in the libraries of Prague. Illus. SB, iii (50/1), 105-30.

Addendum [to E. Wead's *Early binding stamps of religious significance in certain American libraries: a supplemental report*]. SB, v (52/3), 210.

Parisian panel stamps between 1480 and 1530. Illus. SB, vii (55), 113-24.

L

LA BARREDA, Nicolás de
Nicolás de la Barreda and his works on the Chinantec Indians of Mexico. PBSA, liii (59), 1-14.
H. F. Cline.

LA BAUME LE BLANC, Louise François, *duchesse de La Vallière*
Crevenna and La Vallière. (Note 35). BC, iii (54), 148-9.
D. M. Rogers.

Priced copies of the La Vallière catalogue 1783. (Query, 209). BC, xv (66), 357.
A. Ehrman.

LA CAVA
La Cava; or Recollections of the Neapolitans. (Query, 19). BC, i (52), 197.
R. White.

LACLOS, Choderlos de
See Choderlos de Laclos, Pierre Ambroise F.

LADBOROUGH, Richard William
A discovery in the Pepys Library. BC, ii (53), 278-9.

A lost Pepys-library book recovered. Illus. TCBS, iii (59/63), 292-4.

LAFAUEUR, Jacques Matte
See Matte Lafaueur, Jacques

LAFAYETTE, Marie Joseph Gilbert du Motier, *marquis de*
A sketch of the life of General Lafayette. Translated from the French by James P. Cobbett. London, 1830. PBSA, xxxv (41), 207.
E. B. Steere.

LAHONTAN, Louis Armand de Lom d'Arce, *baron de*
Lahontan: an essay and bibliography. PBSA, xlviii (54), 334-89.
A. H. Greenly.

LAING, Catherine
Additions to Halkett & Laing. [A letter]. LIB, viii (53), 204.
D. E. Rhodes *and* A. E. C. Simoni.

LAMACRAFT, C. T.
Early book-bindings from a Coptic monastery. Illus. LIB, xx (39/40), 214-33.

LAMB, Charles
C. and M. Lamb's *Mrs. Leicester's School.* (Query 59). BC, iv (55), 81-2.
H. G. Smith.

The chapbook edition of the Lambs' *Tales from Shakespear.* BC, vi (57), 41-53.
D. F. Foxon.

An irregular copy of Lamb's *Tales from Shakespeare*, 1807. (Query 155). BC, xi (62), 485-6.
W. R. N. Payne.

Southey, Lamb and Joan of Arc. (Query 186). BC, xiv (65), 82.
S. Nowell-Smith.

LAMB, Lynton
The binding of the Coronation Bible. Illus. BC, ii (53), 139.

LAMB, Mary Ann
See LAMB, Charles

LAMBERT, Sheila
Printing for the House of Commons in the eighteenth century. LIB, xxiii (68), 25-46.

LAMBETH PALACE *libr.*
Lambeth Palace library. LIB, xxi (66), 192-206.
E. G. W. Bill.

Lambeth Palace Library, 1610-1664. TCBS, ii (54/8), 105-26.
A. Cox-Johnson.

The history of Lambeth Palace library. TCBS, iii (59/63), 1-31.
M. R. James.

LAMBORN, Peter Spendelow
A check-list of prints made at Cambridge by Peter Spendelow Lamborn, 1722-1774. Illus. TCBS, iii (59/63), 295-312.
J. M. Morris.

LAMESLE, Claude
The type-specimen books of Claude Lamesle and Nicolas Gando. Illus. LIB, xviii (37/8), 201-12.
A. F. Johnson.

LAMPORT HALL
Lamport Hall revisited. (Unfamiliar libraries, 12). Illus. BC, xvi (67), 439-49.
H. A. N. Hallam.

LAMPSON, Frederick Locker
Locker-Lampson's *Lyra Elegantium*, 1867. (Note, 113). BC, viii (59), 296.
R. W. Ketton-Cremer.

LANCASTER *Pa.*
Lancaster, Pennsylvania, bookbindings: an historical study. PBSA, xlii (48), 119-28.
H. Dreis.

LANDOR, Robert
Robert Landon and *Guy's Porridge Pot.* LIB, xvi (61), 44-8.
R. Czerwinski.

LANDOR, Robert *and* LANDOR, Walter Savage
The authorship of *Guy's Porridge Pot* and *The Dun Cow.* LIB, v (50/1), 55-8.
R. H. Super.

LANDOR, Walter Savage
Landor's *Sponsalia Polyxenae.* LIB, iv (49), 211-12.
R. C. Bald.

LANSDOWNE, lord
A letter with a character of Mr. Wycherly. BH, i (47/51), 177-83.

LANE, Lauriat
Civil disobedience: a bibliographical note. PBSA, lxiii (69), 295-6.

LANE, Robert Frederick
Two untraced Bodoni items. (Query, 100). BC, vii (58), 295-6.

—. (Query, 100). BC, viii (59), 300.

Mac Carthy-Reagh and Bodoni. (Note, 104). BC, vii (58), 418.

Count Mac Carthy-Reagh and Bodoni. (Note, 127). BC, ix (60), 72-5.

Bodoni's *Manuale Tipografico* and the recent facsimile. LIB, xvii (62), 132-8.

Bodoni's first hundred printing commissions. PBSA, liii (59), 21-36.

LANG, Andrew
Location of copies of Lang's *Lines on . . . the Shelley society*; Meredith's *Jump-to-Glory Jane*. (Query, 237). BC, xviii (69), 226.
L. H. Kendall, *jr*.

LANGBAINE, Gerard *the younger*
Gerard Langbaine the younger and Nicholas Cox. LIB, xxv (44/5), 67-70.
Sir W. W. Greg.

—. LIB, xxv (44/5), 186.
H. Macdonald.

LANGLAND, William
The Piers Plowman manuscripts in Trinity College, Dublin. LIB, vi (51), 141-53.
E. St.J. Brooks.

LANGLOIS, André
André Langlois. (Contemporary collectors, 13). Illus. BC, vi (57), 129-42.
A. Rau.

LANGTON, Robert
Robert Langton's *Pylgrimage*. LIB, viii (53), 42-5.
R. J. Mitchell.

—. LIB, x (55), 58-9.
E. S. de Beer.

LANIER, Sidney
Sidney Lanier's *Tiger-Lilies*: a bibliographical mystery. PBSA, liv (60), 265-72.

LA RAMÉE, Pierre de
Hobbes and Talon's Ramist rhetoric in England. TCBS, i (49/53), 260-9.
J. W. Ong.

LARDNER, Dionysius
Dr. Lardner's Cabinet Cyclopaedia. PBSA, xlv (51), 37-58.
M. Beckham.

LARDNER, Ring Wilmer
Some Lardner variants. PBSA, lvi (62), 487.
N. Kane.

Notes on Ring Lardner's *What of It?* PBSA, lvii (63), 88-90.
M. J. Bruccoli.

A further note on Lardner's *What of It?* PBSA, lvii (63), 377.
M. J. Bruccoli.

Ring Lardner's first book. PBSA, lviii (64), 34-5.
M. J. Bruccoli.

Five notes on Ring Lardner. PBSA, lviii (64), 297-8.
M. J. Bruccoli.

LARKEY, Sandford V.
The Vesalian compendium [*De Humane Corporis Fabrica*] of Geminus and Nicholas Udall's translation; their relation to Vesalius, Caius, Vicary and De Mondeville. Illus. LIB, xiii (32/3), 367-94.

LARREMORE, Thomas A.
An American typographic tragedy — the imprints of Frederick Conrad Bursch. 2 pts. PBSA, xliii (49), 1-38, 111-72.

—. [A letter]. PBSA, xliii (49), 425-6.

LASLETT, Peter
The 1690 edition of Locke's *Two Treatises of Government*: two states. TCBS, i (49/53), 341-7.

—. BOWERS, Fredson Thayer *and* GERRITSEN, Johann
Further observations on Locke's *Two Treatises of Government*. TCBS, ii (54/8), 63-87.

LATIFI, K.
T. Osborne's retirement. [A letter]. LIB, xvii (36/7), 363-4.

LATIMER, Nigel
Trade card as frontispiece. (Query, 49). BC, iii (54), 227.

LAUD, William *abp. of Canterbury*
The Laudian imprimatur. Illus. LIB, xv (60), 96-104.
F. B. Williams.

The authorship of *The Life and Death of William Laud*, 1645. LIB, xvi (61), 140-1.
D. E. Rhodes.

LAURENCE, Dan H.
A bibliographical novitiate: in search of Henry James. PBSA, lii (58), 23-33.

Addendum to Edel and Laurence [*A Bibliography of Henry James*]: Henry James's *Future of the novel*. PBSA, lxiii (69), 130.
G. N. Monteiro.

LAURENS, Henry
Laurens, Henry (1724-1792). *Extracts from the proceedings of the High Court of Vice-Admiralty, in Charlestown, South-Carolina . . . in the years 1767 and 1768.* Charlestown, 1769. PBSA, xxxv (41), 294-7.
V. H. Paltsits.

LAUTERBACH, Charles E. *and* Edward S.
The nineteenth-century three-volume novel.
PBSA, li (57), 263-302.

LAUTERBACH, Edward S. *and* Charles E.
The nineteenth-century three-volume novel.
PBSA, li (57), 263-302.

LAUXIUS, David
David Lauxius. EBST, iii (48/55), 78-80.

—. a further note. EBST, iii (48/55), 156-7.
J. Durkan.

LA VALLIÈRE, Louis Françoise La Baume Le
Blanc *duchesse de*
See LA BAUME LE BLANC, Louise Françoise,
duchesse de La Vallière.

LAVATER, Johann Caspar
Lavater's *Physiognomy*: a checklist. PBSA, lv
(61), 297-308.
J. Graham.

LAVIN, J. S.
Three 'owl' blocks: 1590-1640. Illus. LIB, xxii
(67), 143-7.

Additions to McKerrow's *Devices*. LIB, xxiii
(68), 191-205.

William Barley, draper and stationer. SB, xxii
(69), 214-23.

LAVIN, Mary
Mary Lavin: a checklist. BC, xviii (69), 317-21.
P. Doyle.

LAVOISIER, Antoine Laurent
[Lavoisier, Antoine Laurent] (1743-1794). *The
art of manufacturing alkaline salts and pot-
ashes*, Tr. from the French. [Philadelphia,
1820?]. PBSA, xxxiv (40), 359; xxxv, (41), 72.
F. B. Bowe.

LAW, Alexander
The first edition of [Allan Ramsey's] *The tea-
table miscellany*. BTHK, v (67/70), 198-203.

The inscribed copies of the first edition, 1773
of the poems of Robert Fergusson. EBST, iii
(48/55), 125-35.

William Perry, his academy and printing press
in Edinburgh, and his publications. EBST, iv
(55/71). 91-102.

LAW, Andrew
Copyright and Andrew Law. PBSA, liii (59),
150-9.
I. Lowens.

LAW, James *abp. of Glasgow*
Archbishop Law's books in Glasgow University
Library. Illus. BTHK, iii (60/2), 107-21.
H. M. Black.

LAW BOOKS
Some early law books in Aberdeen University
Library. Illus. EBST, xv (32/5), 1-16.
W. Menzies.

Prices of some second-hand law books in 1620.
PBSA, lvii (63), 212-17.
A. G. Watson.

LAWES, William
British Museum Additional MS.31432. William
Lawes' writing for the theatre and the court.
LIB, vii (52), 225-34.
J. P. Cutts.

Notes on the texts of William Lawes's Songs
in B.M. MS. Add. 31432. LIB, ix (54), 122-7.
M. C. Crum.

LAWRENCE *st.*
A palimpsest in the National Library of Scot-
land: Early fragments of Augustine *De Trini-
tate*, the *Passio S. Laurentii* and other texts.
Illus. EBST, iii (48/55), 169-78.
N. R. Ker.

LAWRENCE, David Herbert
D. H. Lawrence's plays: an annotated biblio-
graphy. (Note, 241). BC, xiv (65), 78-81.
J. G. Hepburn.

A textual comparison of the first British and
American editions of D. H. Lawrence's
Kangaroo. PBSA, lix (65), 400-24.
E. P. Jarvis.

A note on D. H. Lawrence. PBSA, lxi (67),
269.
J. P. Dalton.

LAWRENCE, James
Another reprint of Irving's biography of James
Lawrence. PBSA, lvii (63), 448-9.
E. L. West.

LAWSON, John
The first English editions of John Lawson's
Voyage to Carolina: a bibliographical study.
PBSA, lxi (67), 258-65.
E. B. Kirkham.

LAZARUS, George
The George Lazarus library. (Contemporary
collectors, 7). Illus. BC, iv (55), 278-84.
B. Rota.

LEAR, Edward
Early American editions of Lear's *A Book of
Nonsense*. (Query, 151). BC, xi (62), 353.
J. M. Shaw.

LEDELH, Jacobus
Two notes on fifteenth-century printing.
I. Jacobus Ledelh. II. Jacques Le Forestier and
Noel de Harsy, printers at Rouen, 1490. EBST,
iii (48/55), 75-7.
W. Beattie.

LEE, Francis *1661-1719*
A note on *God's judgement upon the Gentile
apostatized Church & A treatise of the three
evils of the last times* [by J. Hildrop or F. Lee?]
with special reference to a volume in the library
of St. Paul's Cathedral, Dundee, which contains
both title-pages. BTHK, iii (60/2), 31-4.
R. C. Rider.

LEE, Nathaniel
Nathaniel Lee: three probable seventeenth-century piracies. PBSA, xliv (50), 62-6.
F. T. Bowers.

The prologue to Nathaniel Lee's *Mithridates*, 1678. PBSA, xliv (50), 173-5.
F. T. Bowers.

LEECH, Andrew
Andrew Leech, Scottish Latinist.. BTHK, iv (63/6), 24-34.
J. Durkan.

LEECH, Clifford
A cancel in Southerne's *The Disappointment*, 1684. LIB, xiii (32/3), 395-8.

Southerne's *The Disappointment*. [A letter]. LIB, ii (47/8), 64.

LEED, Jacob
Two notes on Johnson and the *Gentleman's Magazine*. PBSA, liv (60), 101-10.

Some reprintings of the *Gentleman's Magazine*. SB, xvii (64), 210-14.

LEE-HAMILTON, Eugene
See HAMILTON, Eugene Lee-

LEEK, Helen
The Edward Young-Edmund Curll quarrel: a review. Illus. PBSA, lxii (68), 321-35.

LEES, Francis Noel
The Faustus Ballad. [A letter]. LIB, xviii (63), 64.

LE FANU, Joseph Sheridan
Le Fanu's *Ghost stories* Dublin 1851. (Note, 293). BC, xvii (68), 78.
W. J. Smith.

LE FANU, William Richard
A. Read's *Manuall of Anatomy*, 1634. LIB, viii (53), 201.

The writings of William Hunter, F.R.S. BTHK, i/3 (58), 3-14.

LEFÈVRE, Jean M.
John Home: a checklist of editions. BTHK, iii (60/2), 121-38.

LE FORESTIER, Jacques
Two notes on fifteenth-century printing. I. Jacobus Ledell. II. Jacques Le Forestier and Noel de Harsy, printers at Rouen, 1490. EBST, iii (48/55), 75-7.
W. Beattie.

LEFROY, Edward Cracroft
Edward Cracroft Lefroy, 1855-1891. (Some uncollected authors, 30). BC, x (61), 442-5.
T. d'A. Smith.

LEGAL DEPOSIT
A 1731 copyright list from Glasgow University Archives. BTHK, ii (59/60), 30-2.
A. Nairn.

St. Andrews University Library and the copyright acts. EBST, iii (48/55), 179-211.
P. Ardagh.

Copyright renewal deposit copies. PBSA, lx (66), 473-4.
K. E. Carpenter.

The deposit of books at Cambridge under the Licensing Acts, 1662-79. 1685-95. TCBS, ii (54/8), 290-304.
J. C. T. Oates.

LE GALLIENNE, Richard
'A contract of eternall bond of love, confirmed by . . .'? [The leaflet printed at the Chiswick press announcing the marriage of M. Lee and R. Le Gallienne]. BC, xv (66), 215.
M. Trevanion.

Richard le Gallienne's *Perseus and Andromeda*. PBSA, xliii (49), 399-401.
H. R. Mead.

LEGARÉ, James Matthews
Mr. Legaré inscribes some books: the literary tenets, and the library, of a Carolina writer. PBSA, lvi (62), 219-36.
C. C. Davis.

LEGG, Henry B.
'Bound in Boston by Henry B. Legg'. Illus. SB, xvii (64), 135-9.
H. D. French.

LEGGETT, William
William Leggett, 1801-1839: journalist and literator. PBSA, xliv (50), 239-53.
P. S. Proctor, *jr.*

LEGMAN, Gershon
A word on Caxton's *Dictes*. Illus. LIB, iii (48/9), 155-85.

LEHMANN-HAUPT, Hellmut
The first edition of the New Testament in French. PBSA, li (57), 61-7.

Metal cuts at the Gutenberg workshop. [A review of *Gutenberg and the Master of the Playing cards* by H. Lehmann-Haupt]. Illus. PBSA. lxii (68), 581-6.
K. F. Bauer.

LEIDEN *univ., libr.*
Notes on a manuscript now at Leyden, from the library of St. James's Palace. TCBS, i (49/53), 358-9.
K. A. de Meyier.

LEIDEN *univ., libr.*
The *Psalterium Hebraycum* from St. Augustine's Canterbury rediscovered in the Scaliger bequest at Leyden. Illus. TCBS, ii (54/8), 97-104.
G. I. Lieftinck.

LEIGH, Ralph Alexander
D'Alembert's copy of Rousseau's first *Discours*. LIB, xxii (67), 243-5.

LEIGHTON, Douglas
Canvas and bookcloth, an essay on beginnings. Illus. LIB, iii (48/9), 39-49.

LEISHMAN, James Blair
You meaner beauties of the night, a study in transmission and transmogrification. LIB, xxvi (45/6), 99-121.

LEMAY, Léon Pamphile
A bibliography of the works of Léon Pamphile Lemay, 1837-1918. PBSA, lvii (63), 50-60.
J. E. Hare.

LENAGHAN, Robert Thomas
The variants in Caxton's *Esope*. PBSA, lv (61), 34-6.

LENFEST, David S.
A checklist of illustrated editions of *Gulliver's Travels*, 1727-1914. PBSA, lxii (68), 85-123.

LENGLET DU FRESNOY, Nicolas
Edmund Curll and the 'cursed blunders' in Fresnoy's *New Method of Studying History*, 1728. LIB, ix (54), 200-5.
B. J. Enright.

LENINGRAD *gosud. publ. bibl.*
The Saltykov-Shchedrin library, Leningrad. Illus. BC, iv (55), 99-109.
O. D. Golubeva.

Incunabula in the Saltykov-Shchedrin library, Leningrad. Illus. BC, iv (55), 273-8.
N. V. Varbanets.

Western MSS. in the Saltykov-Shchedrin library, Leningrad. Illus. BC, v (56), 12-18.
T. P. Voronova.

LENKEY, Susan V.
A misprinted title in a *Prudentius* of 1499. (Note, 256). BC, xiv (65) 541.

Imprint of an incunable, listed as Hain 14348. (Note, 270). BC, xv (66), 211.

LENOX, James
The bibliophilic transactions of James Lenox with Bernard Quaritch, 1874-1880. PBSA, xl (46), 181-204.
V. H. Paltsits.

The Lenox-Eames classification scheme at the William L. Clements Library. PBSA, xliv (50), 87-100.
R. B. Brown.

LEO I *st., pope.*
The printer of Leo 1, *Sermones* (Proctor 3248). PBSA, liv (60), 111-13.
J. V. Scholderer.

LEONARD, H. L. W.
Leonard, H. L. W. *Oregon Territory*. Cleveland, 1846. PBSA, xxxvi (42), 66.
C. Eberstadt.

LEONARD, William Ellery
Two states of *Two lives*. PBSA, liv (60), 295.
D. A. Randall.

Leonard's *Two lives*: addendum. PBSA, lv (61), 153.
J. D. Gordan.

LERCH, Alice H.
A printer soldier of fortune. [Charles Fierer and Thomas U. Fosdick]. PBSA, xxx (36), 91-103.

LE ROUSSAÜ, F.
Chorégraphie. F. Le Roussaü. (Note, 298). BC, xvii (68), 216-7.
B. Brown.

LE SAGE, Alain René
[Le Sage, Alain René] 1668-1747. The comical adventures of Gil Blas of Santillane. Philadelphia, 1790. PBSA, xxxv (41), 205-6.
F. B. Bowe.

LESLIE, Charles
An old error once more corrected. [A letter about the attribution of Charles Leslie's *The New Association* to Sacheverell]. LIB, xiii (58), 207.
F. F. Madan.

LETTERS
Editing the letters of letter-writers. SB, xi (58), 25-37.
R. Halsband.

LETTERSNIJDER
The little gest of Robin Hood: a note on the Pynson and lettersnijder editions. SB, xvi (63), 3-8.
J. C. T. Oates.

LETTOU, John
Lettou's address: a correction. LIB, xviii (37/8), 335-7.
H. G. Pollard.

LETTS, Malcolm Henry I.
The source of the woodcuts in Wynkyn de Worde's edition of Mandeville's *Travels*, 1499. LIB, vi (51), 154-61.

LEVER, Charles James
Lever, Charles (1806-1872). *Our Mess*. Dublin, 1843-4. PBSA, xxxiv (40), 274-6.
D. A. Randall.

LEVINSON, Harry A.
Mayne's *Part of Lucian made English* 1663. (Note, 305). BC, xviii (69), 90.

LEVY *family*
Additional Benjamin and Alexander Levy imprints. PBSA, lxii (68), 245-52.
B. W. Korn.

LEVY, Alexander
See LEVY *family*

LEVY, Alfred J. *and* GROSS, Seymour L.
Some remarks on the extant manuscripts of Hawthorne's short stories. SB, xiv (61), 254-7.

LEVY, Benjamin
See also LEVY *family*

LEVY, Benjamin
Benjamin Levy: New Orleans printer and publisher. Illus. PBSA, liv (60), 221-64.
B. W. Korn.

Benjamin Levy imprints in the Boston Public Library. PBSA, lv (61), 48-50.
J. E. Alden.

LEWIS *family*
A binding by Lewis for Oliver Cromwell, 1656. (English bookbindings, 29). Illus. BC, viii (59), 168.
H. M. Nixon.

LEWIS, Charles
A London binding by Charles Lewis, 1812. (English bookbindings, 10). Illus. BC, iii (54), 134-5.
H. M. Nixon.

LEWIS, Clarissa O.
A further note on Milton's *Pro Populo Anglicano Defensio*. LIB, xxiii (42/3), 45-7.

LEWIS, Henry
Henry Lewis's *Das illustrirte Mississippithal.* contemporary advertisement. PBSA, xliii (49), 344-5.
B. L. Heilbron.

Henry Lewis's *Das illustrirte Mississippithal.* PBSA, xlv (51), 152-5.
J. F. Mcdermott.

Henry Lewis in English. Illus. PBSA, xlv (51), 359-62.
B. L. Heilbron.

LEWIS, Matthew Gregory
The early editions and issues of *The Monk*, with a bibliography. SB, ii (49), 3-24.
W. B. Todd.

Some bibliographical errors concerning the Romantic age. PBSA, li (57), 159-62.
K. S. Guthke.

An early copy of *The Monk*. PBSA, lvii (63), 350-1.
L. F. Peck.

The manuscript of M. G. Lewis's *The Monk*: some preliminary notes. PBSA, lxii (68), 427-34.
H. Anderson.

LEWIS, Sinclair
Lewis, Sinclair (1885-). *The Innocents,* 1917. PBSA, xxxix (45), 167-8.
J. K. Dickson.

Textual variants in Sinclair Lewis's *Babbitt.* SB, xi (58), 263-3.
M. J. Bruccoli.

LEWIS, Wilmarth Sheldon
Horace Walpole's library. LIB, ii (47/8), 45-52.

LEYBOURN, William
William Leybourn, 1626-1716. LIB, v (50/1), 159-71).
C. E. Kenney.

LEYDEN
See LEIDEN

LIBER CHRONICARUM
Liber chronicarum, 1493. (Note, 231). BC, xiii, (64), 497-8.
W. B. Todd.

LIBERTINE LITERATURE
Libertine literature in England, 1600-1745. Illus. 3 pts. BC, xii (63), 21-36, 159-77, 294-307.
D. F. Foxon.

LIBRARIES
Circulating libraries in the north-east of Scotland in the eighteenth century. BTHK, v (67/70), 119-37.
W. R. Mcdonald.

English circulating libraries, 1785-50. LIB, xiv (33/4), 477-85.
A. D. McKillop.

The migration of manuscripts from the English medieval libraries. LIB, xxiii (42/3), 1-11.
N. R. Ker.

Austrian monastic libraries. LIB, xxv (44/5), 46-65.
E. P. Goldschmidt.

Libraries under the German occupation. LIB, i (46/7). 45-6.
A. N. L. Munby.

Eighteenth-century circulating libraries in England. LIB, i (46/7), 197-222.
H. M. Hamlyn.

The Cathedral Libraries Catalogue. LIB, ii (47/8), 1-13.
M. S. G. Hands.

Early lending libraries. LIB, xiii (58), 204-5.
R. P. Bond.

The Westminster library: history and mystery. LIB, xxi (66), 240-5.
P. Kaufman.

An eighteenth-century book club at Norwich. LIB, xxiii 668), 47-50.
T. Fawcett.

An eighteenth-century book club at Clapham. LIB, xxiv (69), 243-6.
D. H. Knott.

Thoughts on books and libraries. PBSA, lvii (63), 438-44.
E. Wolf, *2nd.*

The rise of community libraries in Scotland. Illus. PBSA, lix (65), 233-94.
P. Kaufman.

Zion's temple, Manchester: an introduction to libraries of dissent. PBSA, lxii (68), 337-49.
P. Kaufman.

LIBRARY COMPANY OF PHILADELPHIA
Some books of early English provenance in the Library Company of Philadelphia. BC, ix (60), 275-84.
E. Wolf, *2nd.*

LIBRARY CO-OPERATION
Co-operation between college libraries. OBSP, iv (52), 42-52.
Sir H. H. E. Craster.

LIBRARY OF CONGRESS
See WASHINGTON *D.C., libr. of Congress*

LICENSES
Privilege to print SB, xvi (63), 201-3.
J. G. McManaway.

LICENSING ACTS, 1662-79, 1685-95.
The deposit of books at Cambridge under the Licensing Acts, 1662-79, 1685-95. TCBS, ii (54/8), 290-304.
J. C. T. Oates.

LICHFIELD *cathedral, libr.*
The Lichfield St. Chad's gospels: repair and rebinding, 1961-1962. Illus. LIB, xx (65), 259-76.
R. Powell.

LICHTENBERG, Georg Christoph
George Christoph Lichtenberg, 1742-99. (Query, 138). BC, x (61), 73.
H. L. Gumbert.

LIDDELL, J. R.
The library of Corpus Christi College, Oxford, in the sixteenth century. LIB, xviii (37/8), 385-416.

LIDDERDALE, J. H.
Harriet Weaver and James Joyce. (Query, 212). BC, xv (66), 488-9.

LIEBERT, Herman W.
An addition to the bibliography of Samuel Johnson. PBSA, xli (47), 231-8.

William Alexander Jackson, 1905-1964. PBSA, lviii (64), 479-80.

LIEFTINCK, Gerard Isaac
The *Psalterium Hebraycum* from St. Augustine's Canterbury rediscovered in the Scaliger bequest at Leyden. Illus. TCBS, ii (54/8), 97-104.

LIEVSAY, John Leon
William Barley: Elizabethan printer and bookseller. SB, viii (56), 218-25.

—. *and* DAVIS, Richard Beale
A Cavalier library — 1643. [The library of Sir Thomas Bludder]. SB, vi (54), 141-60.

LIFE
Life buffets (and comforts) Henry James, 1883-1916: an introduction and an annotated checklist. PBSA, lxii (68), 207-25.
E. R. Hagemann.

LILY, Josiah Kirby
Josiah Kirby Lilly. (Contemporary collectors, 14). Illus. BC, vi (57), 263-77.
D. A. Randall.

LILY, William 1468?-1522
The sources of 'Lily's Latin Grammar': a review of the facts and some further suggestions. LIB, ix (54), 85-100.
C. G. Allen

Certayne Briefe Rules and 'Lily's Latin Grammar'. LIB, xiv (59), 49-53.
C. G. Allen.

The grammatical writings of William Lily, ?1468-?1523. PBSA, xxxvii (43), 85-113.
V. J. Flynn.

LILY, William, 1602-1681
[Wm Lily's *Catastrophe Mundi: or, Merlin reviv'd . . . With Mr. Lily's Hieroglyphicks.*] (Query, 62). BC, iv (55), 172.
S. Roscoe.

LIMITED EDITIONS
Limited editions. (Note, 38). BC, iii (54), 226-7.
A. Noel.

LIMOGES
The printer's copy for an apparently lost Limoges service-book. LIB, xxiv (43/4), 87.
A. J. Collins.

LINACRE, Thomas
Thomas Linacre, 1460?-1534. (English scientific autographs, 1). Illus. BC, xiii (64), 341.
T. J. Brown.

Andrew Boorde's *Dyetary of Helth* and its attribution to Thomas Linacre. LIB, ii (47/8), 172-3.
J. L. Thornton.

LINCOLN *diocese*
'Vetus repertorium', an early memorandum book of the diocese of Lincoln. TCBS, iv (64/8), 100-6.
D. M. Owen.

LINCOLN, Abraham
Lincoln bibliography — its present status and needs. PBSA, xxxiv (40), 327-48.
E. J. Wessen.

Four Lincoln firsts. PBSA, xxxvi (42), 1-17.
P. M. Angle.

LINCOLN, Rixford Joseph
Addenda to Irish: [*The modern American muse*]: Theodora Taylor, Rixford J. Lincoln, David Bailey, Lester S. Parker. PBSA, lxiii (69), 198-200.
R. C. Johnson.

LINCOLN, Waldo
Bibliography of American cookery books, 1742-1860. Additions. PBSA, xxxiv (40), 360.
R. S. Wormser.

LINDER, Leslie
Peter Rabbit. (Query, 18). BC, ii (53), 77.

LINDHOLTZ, Johann
A folio with a strange device. Johann Lindholtz's *Arbores consanguinitatis et affinitatis,* etc., completed by Johann Schott at Strasburg in 1516. Illus. LIB, vii (52), 273-5.
J. V. Scholderer.

LINDSAY, Sir David
Sir David Lindsay of the Mount, *Secundus.*
EBST, ii (38/45), 406-9.
T. Innes.

LINDSAY, Robert O.
Richard Hakluyt and *Of the Russe Common Wealth.* PBSA, lvii (63), 312-27.

LINGUISTICS
Bibliography and historical linguistics. LIB, xxi (66), 181-91.
R. C. Alston.

LINTON, Marion P.
Special catalogues in the Department of Printed Books in the National Library of Scotland. BTHK, iii (60/2), 173-82.

National Library of Scotland and Edinburgh University Library copies of plays in Greg's *Bibliography of the English Printed Drama.* SB, xvi (62), 91-104.

LINTON, William James
Side lights on William James Linton, 1812-97. PBSA, xxvii (33), 74-82.
W. F. Hopson.

LIT DE JUSTICE
An undescribed incunable: *Le lit de justice,* [Paris, *circa* 1488]. PBSA, lvi (62), 481-2.
C. F. Bühler.

LITERARY AGENTS
Agent and author: Ellen Glasgow's letters to Paul Revere Reynolds. SB, xiv (61), 177-96.
J. B. Colvert.

LITERARY CRITICISM
The first anthologies of English literary criticism, Warton to Haslewood. SB, iii (50), 262-5.
R. M. Baine.

LITERARY EXECUTORSHIP
Problems of literary executorship. SB, v (52), 3-20.
N. H. Pearson.

LITERARY SOCIETIES
Extinct societies. (Query, 39). BC, ii (53), 223-4.
G. Handley-Taylor.

LITHOGRAPHY
The tinted lithograph. JPHS, i (65), 39-56.
M. Twyman.

LITTLE, William
Editions of Little & Smith's *Easy Instructor.* PBSA, xl (46), 233-6.
L. Condit.

LITTLE GEST OF ROBIN HOOD
See HOOD, Robin

LITTLE GIDDING
A little Gidding binding, *c.* 1635-40. (English bookbindings, 42). Illus. BC, xi (62), 330.
H. M. Nixon.

LITTLE LEATHER LIBRARY CORPORATION
The Little Leather Library Corporation's *Fifty best poems of America.* PBSA, lxii (68), 604-7.
G. T. Tanselle.

LITTLETON, Sir Thomas
Notes on a Pynson volume [comprising *Old Tenures; Natura Brevium*; Littleton, *Tenures Novelli*]. LIB, xviii, (37/8), 261-7.
C. F. Bühler.

LIVERMORE, Ann
Gil Vicente and Shakespeare. Illus. BH, ii (51/2), 1-12.

LLOYD, D. M.
A hitherto unrecorded Wreittoun pamphlet. BTHK, i/3 (58), 42-4.

LLOYD, Leslie John
Books from the library of Jacques Auguste de Thou. Illus. BH, i (47/51), 1-17.

The ghost stories of Montague Rhodes James. Illus. BH, i (47/51), 237-53.

Some eighteenth-century French illustrated books. Illus. BH, ii (51/2), 56-74.

Adventures in book-collecting. BH, ii (51/2), 105-10.

LOADES, David Michael
The authorship and publication of *The copye of a letter sent by John Bradforth to the right honorable lordes the erles of Arundel, Darbie, Shrewsbury and Pembroke,* [John Capstocke]. TCBS, iii (59/63), 155-60.

The press under the early Tudors: a study in censorship and sedition. TCBS, iv (64/8), 29-50.

L'OBEL, Matthias de
Persistent remaindering. (Pena and de l'Obel's *Adversaria,* 1570-1618). PBSA, lii (58), 295-9.
A. E. Lownes.

LOCKE, John
John Locke, 1632-1704. (English literary autographs, 22). Illus. BC, vi (57), 171.
T. J. Brown.

John Locke. (Query, 86). BC, vi (57), 292.
D. M. Davin.

Locke's reading during his stay in France, 1675-79. LIB, viii (53), 229-58.
J. Lough.

Locke, John: *Some thoughts concerning education.* PBSA, xxxvii (43), 309.
J. E. Alden.

The 1690 edition of Locke's *Two treatises of government*: two states. TCBS, i (49/53), 341-7.
P. Laslett.

Further observations on Locke's *Two Treatises of* government. TCBS, ii (54/8), 63-87.
F. Bowers, J. Gerritsen and P. Laslett.

A note on Locke's library. Illus. TCBS, iv (64/8), 312-13.
Sir G. L. Keynes.

LOCKER, Jane
Jane Locker's *Greystoke Hall* ?1886. (Note, 111), BC, viii (59), 183.
J. Hayward.

Jane Locker's *Greystoke Hall.* (Note, 111). BC, viii (59), 294.
R. L. Green.

LOCKER-LAMPSON, Frederick
See LAMPSON, Frederick Locker-

LOCKHART, John Gibson
Whereabouts of correspondence of J. G. Lockhart. (Query, 238). BC, xviii (69), 226.
J. Cameron *and* F. A. Pottle.

Proofreading Lockhart's *Scott*: the dynamics of biographical reticence. SB, xiv (61), 3-22.
F. R. Hart.

LOCKMAN, John
The cancels in Lockman's *Travels of the Jesuits*, 1743. SB, ii (49), 205-7.
J. R.Lucke.

LOCRINE
The *Locrine* and *George-a-Greene* title-page inscriptions. Illus. LIB, xv (34/5), 295-305.
R. C. Bald.

LODGE, Oliver
Herrick's tercentenary. Illus. BH, i (47/51), 273-81.

LOEWENSTEIN, Fritz Erwin
The autograph manuscripts of George Bernard Shaw. Illus. BH, i (47/51), 85-92.

LOFTHOUSE, Hilda
Chetham's library. (Unfamiliar libraries, 1). Illus. BC, v (56), 323-30.

LOGUEN, J. W.
Loguen's *Narrative*, 1859. PBSA, lvi (62), 488.
N. Kane.

LOMÉNIE, Louis-Henri de, *Comte de Brienne*
The library of Louis-Henri de Loménie, Comte de Brienne, and the bindings of the Abbé Du Seuil. Illus. LIB, xviii (62), 105-31.
R. Birley.

LONCLE, Maurice
Maurice Loncle. (Contemporary collectors, 23). Illus. BC, ix (60), 38-44.
A. Rau.

LONDON
London printers' imprints, 1800-1848. LIB, xxi (66), 46-62.
W. B. Todd.

LONDON *London libr.*
An address to members of the London Library. BC, i (52), 139-44.
T. S. Eliot.

The eighteenth-century forerunner of the London Library. PBSA, liv (60), 89-100.
P. Kaufman.

LONDON *London Oratory libr.*
Early English books at the London Oratory, a supplement to S.T.C. LIB, ii (47/8), 95-107.
A. F. Allison.

LONDON *univ., Lond. sch. of econ., Brit. libr. of pol. and econ. sci. .*
See BRITISH LIBRARY OF POLITICAL AND ECONOMIC SCIENCE

LONDON *St. Giles Cripplegate*
Printers and stationers in the parish of St. Giles Cripplegate, 1561-1640. SB, xix (66), 15-38.
W. E. Miller.

LONDON HANSE MERCHANTS
A printed letter of the London Hanse Merchants, 3 March 1526. Illus. OBSP, i (48), 25-32.
M. E. Kronenberg.

LONDON JOURNEYMEN BOOKBINDERS
The archives of the London Journeymen Bookbinders. LIB, xxv (44/5), 185-6.
E. Howe.

LONDON SCHOOL OF ECONOMICS LIBRARY
See BRITISH LIBRARY OF POLITICAL AND ECONOMIC SCIENCE

LONDON SOCIETY OF MASTER LETTER-FOUNDERS
The London Society of Master Letter-founders, 1793-1820. LIB, x (55), 86-102.
A. E. Musson.

LONGFELLOW, Henry Wadsworth
Longfellow's income from his writings, 1840-1852. PBSA, xxxviii (44), 9-21.
W. Charvat.

The origin of Longfellow's *Evangeline*. Illus. PBSA, lxi (47), 165-203.
M. Hawthorne *and* H. W. L. Dana.

A bibliographical footnote: 'Long' and 'Lo'. [In Longfellow: *Evangeline*]. PBSA, li (47), 204-9.
L. A. Wilson.

Outre-Mer, Pt. I: Three variants of the first edition. Illus. PBSA, xli (47), 346-8.
P. D. Howe.

American printings of Longfellow's *The Golden Legend*, 1851-1855. PBSA, lvii (63), 81-8.
J. E. Walsh.

LONG LOST FOUND
The Long Lost Found. (Query, 88). BC, vi (57), 403-4.
H. E. James.

LONGMAN
See LONGMANS, GREEN AND CO.

LONGMANS, GREEN AND CO.
Letters of Longman & Co. to Wordsworth, 1814-36. LIB, ix (54), 25-34.
W. J. B. Owen.

Costs, sales, and profits of Longman's editions of Wordsworth. LIB, xii (57), 93-107.
W. J. B. Owen.

LONSDALE, Roger Harrison
Dr. Burney and the integrity of Boswell's quotations. PBSA, liii (59), 327-31.

William Bewley and *The Monthly Review*: a problem of attribution. PBSA, lv (61), 309-18.

LOOKING GLASSE FOR LONDON AND ENGLAND
A date and a printer for *A looking glasse for London and England*, Q4. SB, xxi (68), 248-53.
B. Sturman.

LOOMIE, Albert Joseph
Philip II and the printing of *Andreas Philopater*. [R. Versteghen's abridged translation of R. Parsons's *Elizabethae . . . edictum promulgatum Londini 29 Nouemb. anni MDXCI Andreas Philopatris . . . responsio*]. LIB, xxiv (69), 143-5.

LOOSEMORE, Henry
Henry Loosemore's organ-book [now in New York Public Library, Drexel 5469]. TCBS, iii (59/63), 143-51.
T. Dart.

LÓPEZ DE MENDOZA, Inigo, *mar. de Santillana*
An unrecorded Spanish incunable in Moscow [the *Proverbios* of I. López de Mendoza]. BC, viii (59), 271-4.
N. P. Kiselev.

LORAM, Ian C.
Goethe's interest in the physical aspect of his works. BC, xiv (65), 178-84.

LORITUS, Henricus
The St. Andrews University copy of Glareanus and Barbarini. BTHK, iv (63/6), 72-5.
C. Hill.

LOSSING, Benson John
How Benson J. Lossing wrote his *Field Books* of the Revolution, the War of 1812 and the Civil War. PBSA, xxxiii (38), 57-64.
A. J. Davidson.

Joel Munsell prints Lossing's *Memorial of Alexander Anderson*. PBSA, xlv (51), 351-5.
D. S. Edelstein.

LOTTERY
The use of the word 'lottery' in titles of 18th and 19th century children's books]. (Query, 55). BC, iii (54), 310.
S. Roscoe.

LOUDEN, James Hamilton
Sir George Mackenzie's speech at the formal opening of the Advocates' library, Edinburgh, 15th March, 1689. EBST, ii (38/45), 273-84.

LOUGH, John
Locke's reading during his stay in France, 1675-79. LIB, viii (53), 229-58.

LOUIS XIV *king of France*
Louis XIV, sa bibliothèque et le *Cabinet du roi*. LIB, xx (65), 1-12.
A. Jammes.

LOVELL, Arthur
Raymond Chandler. (Note, 30). BC, iii (54), 69.

LOW, Donald A.
Scott's criticism of *The jolly beggars* [by R. Burns]. BTHK, v (67/70), 207-9.

LOWE, G. Burnham
Early book labels. (Query, 48). BC, iv (55), 172.

Aleyn's *The Historie of that Wise Prince, Henrie the Seventh*. (Query, 80). BC, vi (57), 181.

LOWE, Robert Liddell
Matthew Arnold and Percy William Bunting: some new letters, 1884-1887. SB, vii (55), 199-207.

LOWELL, James Russell
James Russell Lowell's *Ode*, recited at the commemoration of the living and dead soldiers of Harvard University, July 21, 1865. PBSA, xxxvii (43), 169-202.
H. V. Bail.

James Russell Lowell *On democracy*. PBSA, lix (65), 385-99.
J. C. Armstrong *and* K. E. Carpenter.

Twenty-eight additions to the canon of Lowell's criticism [from the *North American Review*]. SB, iv (51), 205-10.
F. de W. Miller.

A note on Lowell bibliography: the review [in the *North American Review*] of Howells' *Venetian Life* [wrongly attributed to C. E. Norton]. SB, iv (51), 210-11.
J. L. Woodress.

Identification of contributors to the *North American Review* under Lowell. SB, vi (54), 219-29.
F. de W. Miller.

LOWENS, Irving
Copyright and Andrew Law. PBSA, liii (59), 150-9.

The American songster before 1821, a list of incomplete and unlocated titles. PBSA, liv (60), 61-9.

— *and* BRITTON, Allen P.
Daniel Bayley's *The American Harmony*: a bibliographical study. PBSA, xlix (55), 340-54.

LOWER, Richard
A bibliography of two Oxford physiologists, Richard Lower, 1631-91, John Mayow, 1643-79. Illus. OBSP, iv (35), 1-62.
J. F. Fulton.

LOWERY, Margaret Ruth
A census of copies of William Blake's *Poetical Sketches*, 1783. LIB, xvii (36/7), 354-60.

LOWMAN, Matt. P., II, *and* JOHNSON, Richard Colles
The California *Constitution* of 1849. PBSA, lxiii (69), 25-9.

LOWNDES, William Thomas
Do you know your Lowndes? A bibliographical essay on William Thomas Lowndes and incidentally on Robert Watt and Henry G. Bohn. PBSA, xxxiii (39), 1-22.
G. W. Cole.

LOWNES, Albert E.
Two editions of John Wilkins's *Mathematicall Magick*, London, 1648. PBSA, xliii (49), 195..

Persistent remaindering (Pena and de l'Obel's *Adversaria*, 1570-1618). PBSA, lii (58), 295-9.

LOWNES, Irving *and* BRITTON, Allen P.
Daniel Bayley's *The American Harmony*: a bibliographical study. PBSA, xlix (55), 340-54.

LOWTHER, Anthony W. G.
A trade binding. (Note, 70). BC, v (56), 383.

Titling slips in 17th-century books. (Query, 128). BC, ix (60), 203.

Elstrack's portrait of Queen Elizabeth I. (Note, 205). BC, xii (63), 490.

'A table' in Heylyn's *Observations*. (Query, 171). BC, xii (63), 495.

LUBBOCK, Samuel Gurney
Additions to a list of the writings of dr. M. R. James [in S. G. Lubbock's a *Memoir of Montague Rhodes James*, 1939]. TCBS, ii (54/8), 95.
A. F. Scholfield.

LUBBOCK, William
A Newcastle binding by Lubbock, c. 1820. (English bookbindings, 3). Illus. BC, viii (59), 416.
H. M. Nixon.

LUBLINSKY, Vladimir Sergeevich
Voltaire and his library. Illus. BC, vii (58), 139-51.

LUCAS, R. Charles
Book-collecting in the eighteenth century; the library of James West. LIB, iii (48/9), 265-78.

LUCE, Samuel Slayton
Signatures on versos: Luce's *The woodman* 1887. (Note, 316). BC, xviii (69), 384.
G. T. Tanselle.

LUCIAN *of Samosata*
Mayne's *Part of Lucian made English* 1663. (Note, 305). BC, xviii (69), 90.
H. A. Levinson.

LUCKE, Jessie Ryon
Some correspondence with Thomas Jefferson concerning the public printers, transcribed, with a foreword. SB, i (48/9), 25-37.

The cancels in Lockman's *Travels of the Jesuits*, 1743. SB, ii (49/50), 205-7.

LUCRETIUS CARUS, Titus
Notes on the incunabula of Lucretius. TCBS, iii (59/63), 152-65.
C. Gordon.

LULLIN DE CHÂTEAUVIEUX, Frédéric
See LULLIN DE CHÂTEAUVIEUX, Jacob-Frédéric

LULLIN DE CHÂTEAUVIEUX, Jacob-Frédéric
[Lullin de Châteauvieux, Frédéric] 1772-1841.
Napoleon's own memoirs printed from a manuscript . . . from Saint Helena. Tr. from the French. Pittsburgh, 1817. PBSA, xxxiv (40), 188-9.
F. B. Bowe.

LUSCHNER, Johann
A Spanish incunable. [Comas, Guillermus Petrus. *Quaestio de sudore sanguinis Christi*. [Barcelona: Johann Luschner, *ca.* 1498]. PBSA, xliii (49), 191.
C. F. Bühler.

LUTHER, Martin
[Latin commentary on Luther, with preface signed by Timotheus Kirchnerus, dated December 29, 1565]. PBSA, xxxv (41), 68.
C. K. Shipton.

LUTTRELL, Narcissus
Reflections on Narcissus Luttrell, 1657-1732. Illus. BC, vi (57), 15-27.
J. M. Osborn.

LUTZ, Earle
Soldier newspapers of the Civil War. Illus. PBSA, xlvi (52), 373-86.

LYDENBERG, Harry Miller
Americanum Nauticum. PBSA, xli (47), 343-4.

George Philes: bookman. PBSA, xlviii (54), 1-48.

The problem of the pre-1776 American *Bible*. PBSA, xlviii (54), 183-94.

LYDGATE, John
The Lyf of our Lady. Fragments of the so-called second edition. [A letter]. LIB, xvii (36/7), 362-3.
E. F. Bosanquet.

Two Caxton problems. [*Morte Darthur: Lyf of our Lady*]. LIB, xx (39/40), 241-66.
C. F. Bühler.

The Churl and the Bird and *The Dictes and Sayings of the Philosophers* — two notes. LIB, xxi (40/1), 279-90.
C. F. Bühler.

The British Museum's fragment of Lydgate's *Horse, Sheep and Goose* printed by William Caxton. PBSA, xliv (49), 397-8.
C. F. Bühler.

Wynkyn de Worde's printing of Lydgate's *Horse, Sheep and Goose*. PBSA, xlvi (52), 392-3.
C. F. Bühler.

Lydgate's *Life of Our Lady* and the Chetham MS. 6709. PBSA, xlvi (52), 396-7.
R. A. Klinefelter.

The fragments *Virtue* and *The Assemble of Goddes*. S.T.C. 24844a and 17005-17007a. PBSA, xlvii (53), 378-80.
W. Ringler.

Observations on two Caxton variants [i.e. in Lydgate's *The Pilgrimage of the Soul*, 1483; Christine de Pisan's *The Book of the Fayettes of Armes and of Chyvalrye*, 1489]. SB, iii (50), 97-104.
C. F. Bühler.

Lydgate's *Serpent of Division*, 1559, edited by John Stow. SB, xiv (61), 201-3.
W. Ringler.

LYON, H. D.
Writing masters and copybooks. (Note, 138). BC, ix (60), 198.

Ink smudge as a mark of ownership. (Query, 134). BC, ix (60), 458.

More light required. [Ownership of a copy of Newton's *Opticks*]. (Query, 137). BC, x (61), 73.

An unidentifiable English binder. (Query, 144). BC, x (61), 202.

The Didot *Horace*, 1799. (Note, 182). BC, xi (62), 480.

LYON, Harvey T.
The publishing history of the writings of Eugene Lee-Hamilton. PBSA, li (57), 141-59.

LYONS, *mus. de l'imprimerie et de la banque*
The Musée de l'imprimerie, Lyons. JPHS, i (65), 96-7.
A. Jammes.

LYRICAL BALLADS
See WORDSWORTH, William

LYRIC YEAR
The Lyric Year: a bibliographical study. PBSA, lvi (62), 454-71. G. T. Tanselle.

LYSONS, Daniel
The theatrical collectanea of Daniel Lysons. PBSA, li (57), 333-4.
J. G. McManaway.

LYTTELTON, George *1st baron*
Variant editions of Lyttelton's *To the Memory of a Lady lately deceased*. PBSA, xliv (50), 274-5.
W. B. Todd.

Multiple editions of Lyttelton's *The Court-Secret*, 1741. PBSA, xlvii (53), 380-1.
W. B. Todd.

Patterns in press figures: a study of Lyttelton's *Dialogues of the Dead*. SB, viii (56), 230-5.
W. B. Todd.

LYTTON, Edward George E. L. Bulwer- , *1st baron*
By Lytton or Grenville Murray? (Query, 73). BC, v (56), 281-2.
C. S. A. Dobson.

Bulwer Lytton and George Stevenson, (Query, 84). BC, vi (57), 291-2.

M

M., J.
J. M. Letters to a rich friend, 1682. (Query, 132).
BC, ix (60), 456-7.
D. G. Esplin.

*The most famous and renowned Historie, of
that woorthie and illustrious Knight Meruine...*
By I. M. Gent. London, R. Blower and Val.
Sims, 1612. PBSA, xxxv (41), 157.
E. M. Sowerby.

M., R. F.
See METZDORF, Robert Frederic

MAAS, Henry Julius P.
Letters of A. E. Housman. (Query, 211). BC,
xv (66), 488.

MABBUT, George
The author of *Tables for purchasing leases*
attributed to Sir Isaac Newton [i.e. George
Mabbut]. TCBS, iii (59/63), 165-6.
D. F. McKenzie.

MACALPINE, Ida *and* HUNTER, Richard Alfred
Alexander Boswell's copies of *The Anatomy of
Melancholy,* 1621 and 1624. (Note, 88). BC, vi
(57), 406-7.

McANEAR, Beverly
William Bradford and *The Book of Common
Prayer.* PBSA, xliii (49), 101-10.

American imprints concerning King's College.
PBSA, xliv (50), 301-39.

MACAREE, David
Three early 18th-century prose romances. (Note,
177). BC, xi (62), 215-6.

McARTHUR, Herbert
Unrecorded type specimens at the University
of Vermont. PBSA, li (57), 162-3.

McCARTHY, William H.
The earliest extant French armorial ex-libris.
(Note, 161). BC, xi (62), 212-13.

McCOLLEY, Grant
The third edition of Francis Godwin's *The Man
in the Moone.* LIB, xvii (36/7), 472-5.

McCONICA, James K. *and* FLETCHER, John M.
A sixteenth-century inventory of the library of
Corpus Christi College, Cambridge. TCBS, iii
(59/63), 187-99.

McCORISON, Marcus Allen
A bibliography of Vermont bibliography and
printing. PBSA, lv (61), 17-33.

McCOY, Isaac
A frontier library: the books of Isaac McCoy.
PBSA, lii (58), 140-3.
J. F. McDermott.

McCOY, James Comly
J. C. McCoy's *Jesuit Relations of Canada.* [A
letter]. LIB, xviii (37/8), 464.
F. D. Cooper.

McCREERY, John
John McCreery: a radical printer, 1768-1832.
Illus. LIB, xvi (61), 81-103.
J. R. Barker.

McCUSKER, Honor
Books and manuscripts formerly in the possession of John Bale. LIB, xvi (35/6), 144-65.

Some ornamental initials used by Plateanus of
Wesel. LIB, xvi (35/6), 452-4.

McDERMOTT, John Francis
Louis Richard Cortambert and the first French
newspapers in Saint Louis, 1809-1854. PBSA,
xxxiv (40), 221-53.

Banvard's Mississippi Panorama pamphlets.
Illus. PBSA, xliii (49), 48-62.

Banvard's Mississippi Panorama pamphlets. [A
letter on an article by J. F. McDermott]. PBSA,
xliii (49), 245.
B. L. Heilbron.

French publications in Saint Louis. PBSA, xlv
(51), 83-4.

Henry Lewis's *Das illustrirte Mississippithal.*
PBSA, xlv (51), 152-5.

Baldwin's *Flush Times of Alabama and Mississippi* — a bibliographical note. PBSA, xlv (51),
251-6.

A lost poet of Louisiana [Louis de Badinsse].
Illus. PBSA, xlvi (52), 387-91.

An unrecorded Sealsfield publication. PBSA, l
(56), 193-4.

Private libraries in frontier St. Louis. PBSA, li
(57), 19-37.

A frontier library: the books of Isaac McCoy.
PBSA, lii (58), 140-3.

MacDIARMID, Hugh *pseud.*
See GRIEVE, Christopher Murray

MACDONALD, George
See HUNTLY *Brander libr., George Macdonald
collection.*

McDONALD, Gerald D.
New York (Colony). Statues. ... *At a Session of
the General Assembly of the Colony of New-
York, held at the City-Hall in the City of New-
York; began the 4th April, 1769, and continued
... to the 20th of May following, ...* New-York,
1769. PBSA, xxxiv (40), 87-8.

Smith, Sarah Pogson. *Daughters of Eve.*
Schenectady, 1826. PBSA, xxxiv (40) 361.

McDONALD, Hugh
Gerard Langbaine the younger and Nicholas
Cox. LIB, xxv (44/5), 186.

J. Sturt, facsimilist. LIB, xxvi (45/6), 307-8.

MACDONALD, Kenneth I.
William Minto, 1845-1893: a checklist. BTHK,
v (67/70), 152-64.

MacDONALD, Robert H.
William Drummond of Hawthornden. (Query,
187). BC, xiii (64), 360.

McDONALD, William R.
Devices used by Raban in Guild's *Limbo's
Batterie*, 1630. Illus. BTHK, iv (63/6), 77-9.

Circulating libraries in the north-east of Scotland
in the eighteenth century. BTHK, v (67/70),
119-37.

The *Aberdeen Journal* and the *Aberdeen Intelligencer* 1752-7: a further note on a Raban
device. BTHK, v (67/70), 204-6.

MACDURNAN GOSPELS BINDER
A binding by the Macdurnan gospels binder, *c.*
1570. (English bookbindings, 69). Illus. BC,
xviii (69), 200.
H. M. Nixon.

MACE, Herbert
Old bee books. BH, ii (51/2), 206-10.

McFARLANE, I. D.
George Buchanan's Latin poems from script to
print: a preliminary survey. Illus. LIB, xxiv (69),
277-332.

McFATE, Patricia
A holograph notebook and the publication of
its contents: a bibliographical note on James
Stephens. PBSA, lvii (63), 226.

The publication of James Stephens's short
stories in *The Nation*. PBSA, lviii (64), 476-7.

MACHIAVELLI, Niccolò
Milton and Machiavelli's *Discorsi*. Illus. SB, iv
(51), 123-7.
M. Kelley.

MACHLINIA, William de
See WILLIAM *of Mechlin*

McILWRAITH, Archibald Kennedy
The press-corrections in Jonson's *The King's
Entertainment*. LIB, xxiv (43/4), 181-6.

Marginalia on press-corrections in books of the
early seventeeth century. LIB, iv (49/50), 238-48.

The manuscript corrections in Massinger's plays.
LIB, vi (51/2), 213-16.

MACK, Douglas S.
James Hogg's *Altrive tales*: an 1835 reissue.
BTHK, v (67/70), 210-11.

MACK, Maynard
The first printing of the letters of Pope and Swift.
LIB, xix (38/9), 465-85.

Two variant copies of Pope's *Works ... Volume
II*: further light on some problems of authorship,
bibliography, and text. LIB, xii (57), 48-53.

MacKENNA, R. O.
Memoirs of James, Marquis of Montrose.
BTHK, i/1 (56), 27-8.

MACKENZIE, sir Alexander
Mackenzie, Alexander (1763-1820). *Voyages
from Montreal ... to the frozen and Pacific
ocean, 1789 & 1793*. London, 1802. PBSA,
xxxiv (40), 360.
A. W. Paine.

MACKENZIE, D. G.
Loose plates in *Modern Fortification*, 1673.
(Query, 115). BC, viii (59), 183-4.

McKENZIE, Donald Francis
Apprenticeship in the Stationers' Company,
1555-1640. LIB, xiii (58), 292-9.

The writings of Sir Walter Greg, 1945-59. LIB,
xv (60), 42-6.

Two bills for printing, 1620-2. LIB, xv (60),
128-32.

Printers' perks: paper windows and copy money.
LIB, xv (60), 288-91.

Compositor B's role in *The Merchant of
Venice*, Q2, 1619. SB, xii (59), 75-90.

A list of printers' apprentices, 1605-1640. SB,
xiii (60), 109-41.

Printers of the mind: some notes on bibliographical theories and printing-house practices.
SB, xxii (69), 1-75.

Press-figures: a case-history of 1701-1703.
[*Suidae Lexicon*, 1705]. TCBS, iii (59/63), 32-
44.

Notes on printing at Cambridge *c*.1590. TCBS,
iii (59/63), 96-103.

The author of *Tables for purchasing leases*
attributed to Sir Isaac Newton [i.e. George
Mabbut]. TCBS, iii (59/63), 165-6.

— *and* GILMOUR, J. S. L.
Untraced MSS. etc. relating to Cambridge institutions. (Query, 124). BC, ix (60), 79.

MACKENZIE, Sir George
A bibliography of the works of Sir George
Mackenzie, Lord Advocate, founder of the
Advocates' Library. EBST, i (35/8), 3-60.
F. S. Ferguson.

Sir George Mackenzie's speech at the formal
opening of the Advocates' Library, Edinburgh,
15th March, 1689, tr. by J. H. Loudon. EBST.
ii (38/45), 273-84.

MACKENZIE, Robert Shelton
Elizabeth Barrett and R. Shelton Mackenzie. SB,
xiv (61), 245-50.
D. B. Green.

McKERROW, Ronald Brunlees
A publishing agreement of the late seventeenth
century. [Re *Henrici Mori Cantabrigiensis
Theologica*, 1675]. LIB, xiii (32/3), 184-7.

A note on *Titus Andronicus*. LIB, xv (34/5),
49-53.

Robert Brunlees McKerrow, 12 December, 1872-
20 January, 1940. Illus. LIB, xx (39/40), 345-9.
H. Williams

A list of the writings of Ronald Brunlees Mc-
Kerrow. LIB, xxi (40/1), 229-63.
F. C. Francis.

Some additions to McKerrow's *Printers' and
Publishers' Devices*. LIB, xiii (58), 201-3.
W. C. Ferguson.

Additions to McKerrow's *Devices*. LIB, xxiii (68), 191-205.
J. A. Lavin.

MACKIE, Alexander
An assessment of Mackie's steam type-composing machine. JPHS, i (65), 57-67.
J. Moran.

McKILLOP, Alan Dugald
Mrs. Centlivre's *The Wonder*: a variant imprint. (Note, 93). BC, vii (58), 79-80.

Ornaments bearing printers' names. (Note, 100). BC, vii (58), 299.

Giffard's *Pamela*. A comedy. (Note, 148). BC, ix (60), 455-6.

English circulating libraries, 1725-50. LIB, xiv (33/4), 477-85.

Supplementary notes on Samuel Richardson as a printer. SB, xii (59), 214-18.

MACKINLAY, John
A London binding by John Mackinlay, *c*.1810. (English bookbindings, 51). Illus. BC, xiii (64), 486.
H. M. Nixon.

MACKY, John
On Swift's marginalia in copies of Macky's *Memoirs*. LIB, xix (38/9), 354-62.
W. F. Trench *and* K. B. Garratt.

McLENDON, Will L.
Misshelved Americana: *The post boy*. PBSA, lxi (67), 343-7.

McMAHON, Dorothy
Some observations on the Spanish and foreign editions of Zárate's *Historia del descubrimiento y conquista del Perú*. Illus. PBSA, xlix (55), 95-111.

McMANAWAY, James Gilmer
Thomas Dekker: further textual notes. LIB, xix (38/9), 176-9.

Latin title-page mottoes as a clue to dramatic authorship. LIB, xxvi (45/6), 28-36.

An unrecorded English coranto. LIB, viii (53), 125-6.

A miscalculation in the printing of the third folio. LIB, ix (54), 129-33.

The colophon of the second folio of Shakespeare. LIB, ix (54), 199-200.

A bibliography of John Bale. Additions and corrections. OBSP, i (47), 44-5.

The two earliest prompt books of *Hamlet*. Illus. PBSA, xliii (49), 288-320.

The *Theatrical Collectanea* of Daniel Lysons. PBSA, li (57), 333-4.

The first Five Bookes of Ovid's Metamorphosis, 1621, englished by Master George Sandys. SB, i (48/9), 69-82.

Some bibliographical notes on Samuel Daniel's *Civil Wars*. SB, iv (51/2), 31-9.

Privilege to print. SB, xvi (63), 201-3.

McMULLEN, Charles H.
The publishing activities of Robert Clarke and Co., of Cincinnati, 1858-1909. PBSA, xxxiv (40), 315-26.

McMURTRIE, Douglas Crawford
The first decade of printing in the royal province of South Carolina. Illus. LIB, xiii (32/3), 425-52.

The beginnings of printing in New Hampshire. Illus. LIB, xv (34/5), 340-63.

Early printing in Wyoming. PBSA, xxxvi (42), 267-304.

Printing in the Black Hills. PBSA, xxxvii (43), 37-60.

Trinidad Weekly Courant. PBSA, xxxvii (43), 235.

MACOMBER, Henry P.
A census of the owners of copies of the 1687 first edition of Newton's *Principia* [and] ... the 1726 presentation issue ... Illus. PBSA, xlvii (53), 269-300.

MACPHERSON, James
Macpherson's *Fingal* and *Temora*. (Note, 122). BC, viii (59), 429-30.
W. B. Todd.

A printed text of a portion of Macpherson's *Ossian*. [*Specimen of the intended edition of Ossian's poems*, pr. by T. Bensley, 1803]. BTHK, v (67/70), 111-13.
I. Henderson.

MACQUER, Pierre Joseph
Macquer's *Dictionnaire de chymie*, 1766. (Note, 280). BC, xv (66), 484-5.
R. G. Neville.

MADAN, Falconer
Not in Madan. BC, x (61), 448.
D. H. Woodward.

MADAN, Francis Falconer
A bibliography of George Bate's *Elenchus Motuum Nuperorum in Anglia*. LIB, vi (51/2), 189-99.

A revised bibliography of Salmasius's *Defensio Regia* and Milton's *Pro Populo Anglicano Defensio*. Illus. LIB, ix (54), 101-21.

A new bibliography of the *Eikon Basilike* of King Charles the first. OBSP, iii (49).

Some notes on the bibliography of Francis Osborne. OBSP, iv (50), 53-60.

An old error once more corrected. [A letter re the attribution of Charles Leslie's *The New Association*, to Sacheverell.]. LIB, xiii (58), 207.

MADDEN, Sir Frederic
Sir Frederic Madden at Cambridge. BC, x (61), 156-63.
A. N. L. Munby.

MADISON, James
The papers of James Madison. (Query, 87). BC,
vi (57), 292-3.
W. T. Hutchinson.

MAGAW, Barbara Louise
The work of John Shirley, an early hack writer.
PBSA, lvi (62), 332-45.

MAGNUS, Laurie
A Hopkins discovery [in L. Magnus and C.
Headlam, *Prayers from the poets: a calendar of
devotion*]. LIB, xxiv (69), 56-8.
N. White *and* T. Dunne.

MAIDENS OF THE UNITED KINGDOM.
A gift from the maidens of the United Kingdom,
1874. (English bookbindings, 41). Illus. BC, xi
(62), 204.
H. M. Nixon.

MAIER, Michael
Two alchemical books. (Khunrath's *Amphi-
theatrum Sapientiae Solius Verae* and Count
Michael Maier's *Atalanta Fugiens*]. BH, ii
(51/2), 51-5.
D. I. Duveen.

MAIN, C. F.
Wotton's *The Character of a Happy Life*. LIB,
x (55), 270-4.

New texts of John Donne. SB, ix (57), 225-33.

MALLET, David
The authorship of *William and Margaret*. LIB,
viii (53), 121-3.
G. F. Sleigh.

MALLOCH, David
See MALLET, David

MALONE, Edmond
Cancels in Malone's *Dryden*. LIB, xxiii (42/3),
131.
R. W. Chapman.

MALONE SOCIETY
Notes on the Malone Society reprint of *The
Cobler's Prophecy*. LIB, xxvi (45/6), 181-9.
I. Mann.

MAN WHOLLY MORTAL
See OVERTON, Richard

MANCHESTER *Chetham's libr.*
Chetham's Library. (Unfamiliar libraries, 1).
Illus. BC, v (56), 323-30.
H. Lofthouse.

MANCHESTER *Zion's temple libr.*
Zion's temple, Manchester: an introduction to
libraries of dissent. PBSA, lxii (68), 337-49.
P. Kaufman.

MANCUR, John Henry
Addenda to Wright [*American fiction 1774-
1850*]: Mancur, Pise, Tuthill, Weld. PBSA, lxiii
(69), 294.
W. S. Kable.

MANDEVILLE, Sir John *pseud.*
The source of the woodcuts in Wynkyn de
Worde's edition of Mandeville's *Travels*, 1499.
LIB, vi (51/2), 154-61.
M. Letts.

The woodcut illustrations in the English editions
of Mandeville's *Travels*. PBSA, xlvii (53), 59-69.
J. W. Bennett.

MANGNALL, Richmal
The early editions of Mangnall's *Questions*.
LIB, ix (54), 53-5.
W. G. Briggs.

MANIERRE, William R.
A 'Mather' of dates. SB, xvi (63), 217-20.

A description of *Paterna*; the unpublished
autobiography of Cotton Mather. SB, xviii (65),
183-205.

MANN, Irene
A political cancel in *The Coblers Prophesie*.
LIB, xxiii (42/3), 94-100.

Notes on the Malone Society reprint of *The
Cobler's Prophecy*. LIB, xxvi (45/6), 181-9.

MANN, Thomas
Concerning the affair *Wälsungenblut*. BC, xiii
(64), 463-72.
M. Walter.

MANNING, John J. *and* KATZ, Joseph
Notes on Frank Norris's revisions of two novels
[*McTeague* and *A man's woman*]. Illus. PBSA,
lxii (68), 256-9.

MANS MORTALLITIE
The authorship of *Mans Mortallitie*. LIB, v
(50/1), 179-83.
P. Zagorin.

MANUSCRIPT CORRECTIONS
Stop-press and manuscript corrections in the
Aldine edition of Benedetti's *Diaria de bello
Carolino*. PBSA, xliii (49), 365-73.
C. F. Bühler.

MANUSCRIPTS
The history of a manuscript [Bodleian MS.
Junius 11]. Illus. BC, i (52), 6-13.
B. J. Timmer.

Western MSS in the Saltykov-Shchedrin library
Leningrad. Illus. BC, v (56), 12-18.
T. P. Voronova.

A collection of illuminated MSS. (Contemporary
collectors, 15). Illus. BC, vi (57), 361-8.
W. S. Glazier.

Untraced MSS etc. relating to Cambridge institutions. (Query, 124). BC, ix (60), 79.
J. S. L. Gilmour *and* D. F. McKenzie.

Music manuscripts lost during World War II.
BC, xvii (68), 26-36.
C. Smith.

Signed manuscripts in my collection-I. Illus.
BH, i (47/51), 321-8.
Sir S. C. Cockerell.

— II BH, i (47/51), 402-4.

— III Illus. BH, i (47/51), 429-49.

— IV Illus. BH, ii (51/2), 13-25.

— V Illus. BC, i (52), 77-91.

— VI Illus. BC, i (52), 219-25.

The sources of Arabian music: a bibliography of Arabic MSS. which deal with the theory, practice and history of Arabian music. GBSR, xiii (39).
H. G. Farmer.

The manuscripts in St. George's Chapel, Windsor. LIB, xiii (32/3), 55-76.
M. R. James.

A list of printed catalogues of Greek manuscripts in Italy. LIB, xvii (36/7), 200-13.
J. E. Powell.

The migration of manuscripts from the English medieval libraries. LIB, xxiii (42/3), 1-11.
N. R. Ker.

English manuscripts owned by Johannes Vlimmerius and Cornelius Duyn. LIB, xxii (41/2), 205/7.
N. R. Ker.

The production and dissemination of vernacular manuscripts in the fifteenth century. LIB, i (46/7), 167-78.
H. S. Bennett.

An identification of some manuscripts owned by Dr. John Dee and Sir Simonds D'Ewes. LIB, xiii (58), 194-8.
A. G. Watson.

The Lichfield St. Chad's gospels; repair and rebinding, 1961-1962. Illus. LIB, xx (65), 259-76.
R. Powell.

Fragments of medieval manuscripts used as pastedowns in Oxford bindings, with a survey of Oxford binding c.1515-1620. Illus. OBSP, v (51/2).
N. R. Ker.

The acquisition of manuscripts by institutional libraries. PBSA, liv (60), 1-15.
A. N. L. Munby.

Medieval manuscripts from Norwich Cathedral priory. Illus. TCBS, i (49/53), 1-28.
N. R. Ker.

A handlist of the additional manuscripts in the Fitzwilliam museum, received since the publication of the catalogue by Dr. M. R. James in 1895 excluding the McClean bequest. TCBS, i (49/53), 197-207, 297-309, 365-75; ii (54/8), 1-13.
P. M. Giles and F. Wormald.

Notes on Cambridge manuscripts. Illus. TCBS, i (49/53), 432-41; ii (54/8), 185/99, 323-36; iii (59/63), 93-5.
T. A. M. Bishop.

A handlist of manuscripts in the library of Corpus Christi College, Cambridge, not described by M. R. James [in his *Descriptive catalogue of the manuscripts in the library of Corpus Christi College, Cambridge*]. TCBS, iii (59/63), 113-23.
J. Fines and R. Vaughan.

Two Greek MSS. of Spanish provenance in bishop Moore's collection. TCBS, iii (59/63), 257-62.
P. E. Easterling.

Greek manuscripts in Cambridge: recent acquisitions by college libraries, the Fitzwilliam museum and private collectors. TCBS, iv (64/8), 179-91.
P. E. Easterling.

MANUTIUS *family*
Some types used by Paolo Manuzio. Illus. LIB, xix (38/9), 167-75.
A. F. Johnson.

Two Strasburg reprints of Aldine classics. LIB, viii (53), 274-5.
J. V. Scholderer.

Paulus Manutius and his first Roman printings. PBSA, xlvi (52), 209-14.
C. F. Bühler.

MANUZIO *family*
See MANUTIUS *family*

MANZALAOUI, M.A.
Typographical justification and grammatical change in the eighteenth century. PBSA, lvi (62), 248-51.

MAPS
Early atlases of the British Isles. Illus. BH, i (47/51), 340-4.
G. R. Crone.

The early cartography of the Pacific. Illus. PBSA, xxxviii (44), 87-268.
L. C. Wroth.

Concerning the dating of Rust's and Sporer's world maps. PBSA, xlviii (53), 156-8.
E. Rosenthal.

Christopher Colles and his two American map series. PBSA, xlviii (54), 170-82.
L. W. Griffin.

Christopher Colles and his two American map series. [A letter]. PBSA, xlix (55), 287.
E. L. Yonge.

Mapping the American West. PBSA, i (56), 1-16.
C. I. Wheat.

A stone thrown at the map maker. PBSA, lv (61), 283-8.
K. Nebenzahl.

Nineteenth-century cadastral maps in Ohio [based on a paper by H. F. Walling]. PBSA, lix (65), 306-15.
W. W. Ristow.

The several states of the Farrer map of Virginia. SB, iii (50), 281-4.
C. Verner.

MARCELLUS II pope
Cardinal Cervini and the printing of Greek. [A letter]. LIB, xiii (58), 299.
A. F. Johnson.

MARCHESINUS, Johannes
A misprinted sheet in the 1479 *Mammotrectus super Bibliam* [of Johannes Marchesinus] (Goff M-239). PBSA, lxi (67), 51-2.
D. M. Schullian *and* C. F. Bühler.

MARGARET *consort of Henry II, king of Navarre*
A note on Queen Elizabeth's *Godly Meditation*. [Tr. from *Le miroir de l'âme pecheresse*, by Margaret of Angoulême]. LIB, xv (34/5), 237-40.
R. Hughey.

MARGINS
The margins in mediaeval books. Illus. PBSA, xl (46), 32-42.
C. F. Bühler.

MARGOLIES, Alan
The editing and publication of *The Journal of Madam Knight*. PBSA, lviii (64), 25-32.

MARIE *duchess of Edinburgh*
A gift [to the duchess of Edinburgh] from the maidens of the United Kingdom, 1874. (English bookbindings, 41). Illus. BC, xi (62), 204.
H. M. Nixon.

MARIE ANTOINETTE *consort of Louis xvi, king of France*
Marie Antoinette and Charlotte de Villette. (Note, 89). BC, vi (57), 408.
C. Hesketh.

MARINIS, Tammaro de
Tammaro de Marinis. (Contemporary collectors, 21). Illus. BC, viii (59), 262-70.
I. Davis.

MARIVAUX, Pierre Carlet de Chamblain de
Le paysan parvenu. (Note, 73). BC, v (56), 277.
D. Flower.

MARKMAN, Alan Mouns
A computer concordance to Middle English Texts. SB, xvii (64), 55-75.

MARKS, Carol L.
Thomas Traherne's commonplace book. PBSA, lviii (64), 458-65.

Traherne's *Church's year-book*. [MS. Bodl. Eng. th. e. 51]. PBSA, lx (66), 31-72.

Thomas Traherne's early studies. PBSA, lxii (68), 511-36.

MARKS, John L.
Some pamphlets connected with the early history of the Birmingham library. (Note, 294). BC, xvii (68), 78-80.

MARLBOROUGH *St. Mary's ch., Vicar's libr.*
The vicar's library, St. Mary's, Marlborough. LIB, xxvi (45/6), 192-3.
E. G. H. Kempson.

MARLOW, Harriet *pseud.*
Cary: *Dante*. (Query, 1). BC, i (52), 54.

Housman presentation copies. (Note, 79). BC, v (56), 384.

Beckford's *Vathek*, "Londres 1791". (Note, 99). BC, xi (62), 211.

MARLOWE, Christopher
The *Massacre at Paris* leaf. Illus. LIB, xiv (33/4), 447-69.
J. Q. Adams.

The copyright of *Hero and Leander*. LIB, xxiv (43/4), 165-74.
Sir W. W. Greg.

The Marlowe manuscript. LIB, xxvi (45/6), 158-71.
J. M. Nosworthy.

The good and bad Quartos of *Doctor Faustus*. LIB, xxvi (45/6), 272-94.
L. Kirschbaum.

The printer of the 1594 octavo of Marlowe's *Edward II*. SB, xvii (64), 197-8.
R. F. Welsh.

MARMION, Edmund
Edmund Marmion's illustrations for Francis Quarles' *Argalus and Parthenia*. Illus. TCBS, ii (54/8), 55-62.
J. Horden.

MARRANO TYPOGRAPHY
The Marrano typography in England. LIB, xv (60), 118-28.
C. Roth.

MARRIOT, John
Marriot's two editions of Randolph's *Aristippus*. Illus. LIB, xx (39/40), 163-6.
F. T. Bowers.

MARRYAT, capt. Frederick
Captain Marryat and the American pirates. LIB, xvi (35/6), 327-36.
A. L. Bader.

MARSHALL, David William Hunter
An interim list of the heads of some Scottish monastic houses before *c*.1300. Edited from the papers of the late D. W. Hunter Marshall. BTHK, ii (59/60), 4-27.
A. A. M. Duncan.

MARSHALL, John
Cheap Repository Tracts: Hazard and Marshall edition. LIB, xx (39/40), 295-340.
G. H. Spinney.

John Marshall and *The Infants' Library*. Illus. BC, iv (55), 148-57.
S. Roscoe.

John Marshall and *The Infants' Library*. (Note, 180). BC, xi (62), 217.
M. Papantonio.

MARSHALL, William
William Marshall and his books, 1533-1537. PBSA, lviii (64), 219-31.
D. E. Rhodes.

MARSHALL, William Harvey
The text of T. S. Eliot's *Gerontion*. SB, iv (51/2), 213-17.

An addition to the Hazlitt canon: arguments from external and internal evidence. PBSA, lv (61), 347-70.

MARSTON, John
Marston bibliography; a correction. LIB, xv (34/5), 241-2.
R. E. Brettle.

Henry Walley of the Stationers' Company and John Marston. PBSA, lvi (62), 366-8.
P. J. Finkelpearl.

The composition of *The Insatiate Countess*, Q2. SB, xii (59), 198-203.
R. K. Turner.

MARTAINVILLE, Alphonse
Louis Dieudonné [Martainville, Alphonse Louis Dieudonné] (1776-1830). *The life of Lamoignon Malesherbes*. Tr. by E. Mangin. New York, for Brisban & Brannan, by D. & G. Bruce, 1806. PBSA, xxxv (41), 159-60.
F. B. Bowe.

MARTIN, C. G.
Coleridge's *Lines to Thelwall*: a corrected text and a first version. SB, xx (67), 254-7.

MARTIN, Henry Bradley
Henry Bradley Martin. (Contemporary collectors, 35). Illus. BC, xii (63), 184-93.
R. H. Taylor.

Henry Bradley Martin. The ornithological collection. (Contemporary collectors, 35). Illus. BC, xii (63), 316-32.
G. W. Cottrell.

MARTIN, John
John Martin, 1789-1854, illustrator and pamphleteer. LIB, xiv (33/4), 383-432.
T. Balston.

MARTIN, Mary Forster
If you know not me you know nobodie, and *The famous historie of sir Thomas Wyat*. LIB, xiii (32/3), 272-81.

MARTYN, John
John Martyn, 'Printer to the Royal Society'. PBSA, xlvi (52), 1-32.
L. Rostenberg.

The will of John Martyn, printer to the Royal Society. PBSA, l (56), 279-84.
L. Rostenberg.

MARX, Karl
Karl Marx & Friedrich Engels. (Portrait of a bibliophile, 14). Illus. BC, xviii (69), 189-98.

Das Kapital and Marxism. BH, i (47/51), 263-5.
G. B. Shaw.

Early editions of Karl Marx's *Das Kapital*. BH, i (47/51), 265-6.
E. A. Osborne.

MARY, the virgin
An unknown Florentine incunabulum. [*Miracoli della gloriosa Vergine Maria*, 1495?]. LIB, xviii (37/8) 331-4.
J. V. Scholderer.

MARYLAND
A short account of the first settlement of the Provinces of Virginia, Maryland, New-York, New-Jersey and Pennsylvania, by the English. London, 1735. PBSA, xxxvi (42), 231.
N. B. Wainwright.

An unknown Maryland imprint of the eighteenth century. I. Campbell's *A rational enquiry into the origin ... of civil government*, 1785? PBSA, lxiii (69), 200-3.
E. G. Howard.

MASEFIELD, John
Three unrecorded issues of Masefield's *Tragedy of Nan*. LIB, xxiii (68), 145-7.
G. T. Tanselle.

Some contributions to the bibliography of John Masefield. 2 pts. PBSA, liii (58), 188-96; 262-7.
F. B. Howard.

MASENGILL, Jeanne Addison
Variant forms of Fielding's *Coffee-House Politician*. SB, v (52/3), 178-83.

MASLEN, Keith I. D.
Samuel Richardson and Smith's *Printer's grammar*. (Note, 322). BC, xviii (69), 518-19.

The printers of *Robinson Crusoe*. LIB, vii (52), 124-31.

Three eighteenth-century reprints of the castrated sheets in Holinshed's *Chronicles*. Illus. LIB, xiii (58), 120-4.

Some early editions of Voltaire printed in London. LIB, xiv (59), 287-93.

Point-holes as bibliographical evidence. LIB, xxiii (68), 240-1.

Edition quantities for *Robinson Crusoe*, 1719. LIB, xxiv (69), 145-50.

New editions of Pope's *Essay on man* 1745-48. Illus. PBSA, lxii (68), 177-88.

MASON, William
Duplicate editions of Mason's *Musaeus* (1747). PBSA, xlvi (52), 397-8.
W. B. Todd.

The first editions of William Mason, 1951. Cambr. bibliogr. soc., monogr., 1 Addenda and corrigenda. TCBS, i (49/53), 360-1.
J. P. W. Gaskell.

MASSACHUSETTS
Government printing in Massachusetts, 1751-1801. SB, xvi (63), 161-200.
R. G. Silver.

MASSEY, Dudley
Thomas Jefferson Hogg. (Query, 7). BC, i (52), 129.

MASSEY, Linton R.
Notes on the unrevised galleys of Faulkner's *Sanctuary*. SB, viii (56), 195-208.

MASSINGER, Philip
    See also BEAUMONT, Francis; FLETCHER, John; *and* MASSINGER, Philip.

    Still more Massinger corrections. LIB, v (50/1), 132-9.
    J. E. Gray.

    The manuscript corrections in Massinger's plays. LIB, vi (51/2), 213-6.
    A. K. McIlwraith.

MASSON, David I.
    The bibliography of Gilbert Burnet. [A letter]. LIB, v (50/1), 151.

MASSON, Sir James Irvine O.
    The bibliography of a small incunable. [Andreas Brentius's *C. Iul. Cesaris oratio Vesontione belgice ad milites habita*]. Illus. LIB, xvii (36/7), 36-61.

    Canon Missae [1457/8]. LIB, xii (57), 43-4.

    The dating of the *Missale Speciale Constantiense*. Illus. LIB, xiii (58), 81-101.

    — *and* COLGRAVE, Bertram. The *editio princeps* of Bede's prose Life of St. Cuthbert, and its printer's xiith century 'copy'. Illus. LIB, xix (38/9), 289-303.

MATHER, Cotton
    The Mather bibliography. PBSA, xxxi (37), 57-76.
    T. J. Holmes.

    Mather, Cotton. *Corderius Americanus . . .* Boston, 1828. PBSA, xxxix (45), 163.
    R. W. Christ.

    A 'Mather' of dates. SB, xvi (63), 217-20.
    W. R. Manierre.

    A description of *Paterna*: the unpublished autobiography of Cotton Mather. SB, xviii (65), 183-205.
    W. R. Manierre.

MATHEWS, Cornelius
    [Mathews, Cornelius (1817-1889)]. *Money penny, or, The Heart of the World*. New York, De Witt & Davenport, 1849. PBSA, xxxiv (40), 276.
    H. S. Mott.

MATHEWS, Elkin *ltd*.
    Elkin Mathews in the 'nineties. Illus. BC, i (52), 28-40.
    P. H. Muir.

    Elkin Mathews: III: Evans takes over. BC, i (52), 145-9.

    Elkin Mathews: IV: The background in Cork Street. BC, i (52), 228-39.

    Elkin Mathews: V: A new recruit. Illus BC, ii (53), 38-49.

    Elkin Mathews: VI: Worthington. Illus. BC, ii (53), 104-15.

    Elkin Mathews: VII: The team is completed. BC, ii (53), 194-204.

    Elkin Mathews: VIII: Sherry and shibboleths. Illus. BC, iii (54), 11-27.

    Elkin Mathews: IX: The depression. BC, iii (54), 125-33.

    A personal chapter. BH, ii (51/2), 75-90.
    P. H. Muir.

MATHIAS, Thomas James
    Thomas James Mathias' *The Pursuits of Literature*. PBSA, lxii (68), 123-7.
    O. M. Brack.

MATHIESON, William Law
    Thumbail sketch of an Edinburgh scholar [W. L. Mathieson]. EBST, ii (38/45), 450-1.
    B. Dickins.

MATRIMONIAL MAGAZINE
    Cricket in *The Matrimonial Magazine*. (Note, 71). BC, v (56), 276.
    A. Rogers.

MATTE LAFAVEUR, Jacques
    Matte Lafaveur's *Pratique de Chymie*, 1671. (Note, 57). BC, iv (55), 330-1.
    R. G. Neville.

MATTHEWS, William
    Shakespeare and the reporters. LIB, xv (34/5), 481-98.

    — [A letter]. LIB, xvii (36/7), 227-30.

MAUD, Ralph
    The date of Brian Melbancke's *Philotimus*. LIB, xi (56), 118-20.

MAUGHAM, William Somerset
    More Maughamiana. PBSA, xliv (50), 378-83.
    K. W. Jonas.

    Icelandic translations of Maugham. PBSA, xlv (51), 158-9.
    N. Van Patten.

    The first edition of *The Moon & Sixpence*. PBSA, lv (61), 242-3.
    L. H. Kendall.

MAURER, Oscar
    'My squeamish public': some problems of Victorian magazine publishers and editors. SB, xii (59), 21-40.

MAURITIUS
    An American printing equipment in Mauritius in the eighteenth century. Illus. PBSA, xliv (50), 175-81.
    A. Toussaint.

MAUS, Edmée
    Edmée Maus. (Contemporary collectors, 16). Illus. BC, vii (58), 38-50.
    A. Rau.

MAYBOLE PRINTS
    Three west country bibliographical problems. [The ancestry of Robert Sanders, printer in Glasgow; Was Prynne's *Newes from Ipswich* printed in Glasgow? An alleged Maybole print of 1694]. GBSR, vii (23), 13-26.
    W. J. Couper.

MAYER, Charles
The Shadows of Life. (Query, 92). BC, vii (58), 77.
G. W. Doughty.

MAYFIELD, John S.
Swinburne's *Atalanta in Calydon.* (Note, 39). BC, iii (54), 307.

A Swinburne puzzle. (Note, 42). Illus. BC, iv (55), 74-8.

Two presentation copies of Swinburne's *Atalanta in Calydon.* PBSA, xlix (55), 360-5.

Sidney Lanier's *Tiger-Lilies:* a bibliographical mystery. PBSA, liv (60), 265-72.

MAYNE, Jasper
Mayne's *Part of Lucian made English* 1663. BC, xviii (69), 90.
H. S. Levinson.

The printing of Mayne's plays [i.e. *The Citye Match* and *The Amorous Warre*]. OBSP, i (22/6), 255-62.
Sir W. W. Greg.

MAYNYAL, George
George Maynyal: a Parisian printer of the fifteenth century? LIB, xviii (37/8), 84-8.
C. F. Bühler.

MAYOR, Andreas
A suspected Shelley letter. LIB, iv (49/50), 141-5.

MAYOW, John
A bibliography of two Oxford physiologists, Richard Lower, 1631-91, John Mayow, 1643-79. Illus. OBSP, iv (34/5), 1-62.
J. F. Fulton.

MEAD, Bradock
See GREEN, John

MEAD, Herman Ralph
Three issues of *A Buckler against the Fear of Death.* LIB, xxi (40/1), 199-206.

A new title from De Worde's press. Illus. LIB, ix (54), 45-9.

Fioreti della bibbia historiati in lingua fiorentina. Venice, Matteo Capcasa, for Lucantonio Giunta, 1494. PBSA, xxxiv (40), 267.

Horae ad usum Romanum. [Paris] Philippe Pigouchet, for Enguilbert, Jean, and Geofroy de Marnef [about 1489]. PBSA, xxxiv (40), 268.

Juvenalis, Guido (ca.1460-1505). *In latinae linguae Elegantis interpretatio.* Paris, Jean Tréperel, 1497. PBSA, xxxiv (40), 269-70.

Guibé, Robert, bp. of Nantes (d.1513). *Oratio ad Innocentium VIII.* [Rome, Bartholomaeus Guldinbeck, 1485]. PBSA, xxxiv (40), 356.

Missale Ebroicense. Paris [Jean Dupré] 1492. PBSA, xxxiv (40), 356-7.

Natura verborum. [Paris] Pierre Levet [about 1488]. PBSA, xxxiv (40), 357.

Expositio aurea hymnorum. Seville, Johann Pegnitzer and Magnus Herbst, 1500. PBSA, xxxv (41), 66.

Gerson, Johannes (1363-1429). *De passionibus animae.* [Paris, Gaspard Philippe, about 1500]. PBSA, xxxv (41), 66-7.

Masparrautha, Stephanus. *Regulae gramaticales.* Valencia [Nicolaus Spindeler] 1498. PBSA, xxxv (41), 67-8.

Cowley, Abraham (1618-1667). *Verses, lately written upon several occasions.* London, for Henry Herringham, 1663. PBSA, xxxv (41), 68.

D'Avenant, Sir William (1608-1668). *Gondibert: an heroick poem.* London, John Holden, 1651. PBSA, xxxv (41), 68-9.

Fielding, Henry (1707-1754). *The Coffee-House Politician.* London, for J. Watts, 1730. PBSA, xxxv (41), 69.

Quarles, Francis (1592-1644). *Solomons Recantation.* London, M. F. for Richard Royston, 1645. PBSA, xxxv (41), 70.

Hentisberus, Guilelmus (William Heytesbury, fl. 1340). *Quaedam consequentiae subtiles.* [also] Blasius de Pelicanis. *De propositione* [and] Apollinaris Offredus. *De suppositione.* [Venice, Peregrinus de Pasqualibus, about 1500]. PBSA, xxxv (41), 155.

Horae ad usum Sarum. Paris, Philippe Pigouchet for Simon Vostre, 1499. PBSA, xxxv (41), 156.

Puteo, Paris de (d.1493). *Tractatus in materia ludi.* [Pavia, Christophorus de Canibus, about 1495]. PBSA, xxxv (41), 156.

Sulpitius Verulanus, Johannes (15th cent.). *De versuum scansione.* [Milan, Johannes Angelus Scinzenzeler, about 1500]. PBSA, xxxv (41), 156-7.

Cheynell, Francis (1608-1665). *The Man of Honour.* London, J. R. for Samuel Gellibrand, 1645. PBSA, xxxv (41), 203.

Coleman, Thomas (1598-1647). *Hopes Deferred and Dashed.* London, for Christopher Meredith, 1645. PBSA, xxxv (41), 204.

Ailly, Pierre d', *cardinal* (1350-1420?). *Destructiones modorum significandi.* [Lyons] Janon Carcain [about 1492]. PBSA, xxxv (41), 293.

Offredus, Apollinaris. *De primo et ultimo instanti adversus Petrum Mantuanum.* (Pavia, Antonius Carcanus, 1482]. PBSA, xxxvi (42), 62.

Philippus de Monte Calerio. *Dominicale.* Abridged by Jonselmus de Canova. [Paris, Philippe Pigouchet, about 1500]. PBSA, xxxvi (42), 62-3.

Recollectio epistolarum et prophetiarum. [Salamanca, Printer of Nebrissensis *Introductiones,* 1st roman group, about 1485]. PBSA, xxxvi (42), 63.

Great Britain. Parliament. *Directions ... for the electing and choosing of Ruling-Elders ... for the speedy setling of the Presbyteriall-Government.* London, 1645. PBSA, xxxvi (42), 63-4.

Mirabilia urbis Romae. [Rome, Stephan Plannck, about 1486]. PBSA, xxxvi (42), 229.

Tardivus, Guilelmus. *Grammatica, elegantia et rhetorica.* [Poitiers, Jean Bouyer, about 1488]. PBSA, xxxvi (42), 229-30.

Tardivus, Guilelmus. *In invidiosam falsamque detractionem ubicunque gentium responsio ac defensio.* [Paris, Atelier du Soufflet Vert (Louis Simonel and associates), about 1480]. PBSA, xxxvi (42), 230.

Ubertino da Busti. *Compendio devotissimo* [and other tracts]. Milan, Jacobus de Sancto Nazario and Philippus de Mantegatius, 1496. PBSA, xxxvi (42), 318-9.

Hieronymus. *Vitae sanctorum, sive Vitae patrum.* [n.p., n.d.]. PBSA, xxxix (45), 68-70.

Some Dickens variations. PBSA, xli (47), 344.

Richard Le Gallienne's *Perseus and Andromeda.* PBSA, xliii (49), 399-401.

Two issues of Cowley's *Vision.* Illus. PBSA, xlv (51), 77-81.

MEARES, John
Meares, John (1756-1809). *Voyages made in the years 1788 and 1789 from China to the northwest coast of America.* London, 1790. PBSA, xxxiv (40), 361.
A. W. Paine.

MEARNE, Charles
See MEARNE BINDERY

MEARNE, Samuel
See MEARNE BINDERY

MEARNE BINDERY
A binding from the Mearne shop, c. 1680. (English bookbindings, 32). Illus. BC, ix (60), 52.
H. M. Nixon.

A binding from Charles Mearne's shop, 1685. (English bookbindings, 38). Illus. BC, x (61), 320.
H. M. Nixon.

A binding from the Samuel Mearne bindery, c.1669. (English bookbindings, 39). Illus. BC, x (61), 440.
H. M. Nixon.

MEASUREMENTS
Inches versus millimetres. (Query, 25). BC, i (52), 269.
Radical *pseud.*

Inches *v.* millimetres. (Query, 25). BC, ii (53), 77-8.
R. G. Silver and J. P. W. Gaskell.

MEDALLION BINDER
A London binding by the Medallion binder, c.1545. (English bookbindings, 44). Illus. BC, xii (63), 60.
H. M. Nixon.

MEDICAL BOOKS
A Virginia-owned shelf of early American medical imprints. PBSA, lviii (64), 281-90.
G. W. Jones.

MEDICINE
The literature of domestic medicine. EBST, ii (38/45), 445-7.
D. Guthrie.

MEDIEVAL TEXTS
Medieval texts and their first appearance in print. Two corrections. LIB, xxv (44/5), 79-80.
E. P. Goldschmidt.

MEGAW, Robert N. E.
The two 1695 editions of Wycherley's *Country-wife.* SB, iii (50/1), 252-3.

MEIGS, Cornelia
A Critical history of Children's Literature [by C. Meigs and others]: a second list of errata. PBSA, xlviii (54), 263-7.
E. F. Walbridge.

MEIN, John
John Mein, publisher: an essay in bibliographic detection. PBSA, xxxvi (42), 199-214.
J. E. Alden.

MEISS, Millard
French painting in the time of Jean de Berry [by M. Meiss]: a review [article]. BC, xviii (69), 470-88.
T. J. Brown.

MELBANCKE, Brian
The date of Brian Melbancke's *Philotimus.* LIB, xi (56), 118-20.

MELVILLE, E. W. M. Balfour-
The debt of Bower to Fordun and Wyntoun. EBST, ii (38/45), 386-9.

MELVILLE, Herman
Books from Melville's library. (Query, 167). BC, xii (63), 208.
M. M. Sealts, *jr.*

Copies of Melville's *John Marr* and *Timoleon.* (Query, 197). BC, xv (66), 68.
R. C. Johnson.

A Melville ghost. PBSA, lix (65), 318.
S. Ives.

Melville's copy of Broughton's *Popular poetry of the Hindoos.* PBSA, lxi (67), 266-7.
H. Cohen.

The edition of Montaigne read by Melville. PBSA, lxii (68), 130-4.
A. J. Stevens.

Melville's *Mardi*; Bentley's blunder? PBSA, lxii (68), 361-71.
J. F. Guido.

'Typee' and De Voto once more. PBSA, lxii (68), 601-4.
G. T. Tanselle.

Melville and the Shakers. SB, ii (49), 105-14.
M. M. Sealts.

Melville and the common reader. SB, xii (59), 41-57.
W. Charvat.

MEMOIRS OF A NULLIFIER
Memoirs of a Nullifier: by a native of South Carolina. [? By A. S. Johnston]. PBSA, xxxvi (42), 233.
M. B. Meriwether.

MEMORIAL CONTAINING A SUMMARY VIEW
A Memorial containing a summary view of Facts. PBSA, xxxiv (40), 87.
A. Davidson.

A Memorial containing a summary view of facts, with their Authorities, in answer to the Observations sent by the English Ministry to the Courts of Europe. Philadelphia, James Chattin, 1757. PBSA, xxxiv (40), 272-3.
L. C. Harper.

MEMORIAL OF ALEXANDER ANDERSON
Joel Munsell prints Lossing's Memorial of Alexander Anderson. PBSA, xlv (51), 351-5.
D. S. Edelstein.

MENNONS, John
John Mennons, an early Glasgow journalist. Illus. GBSR, ix (31), 58-72.
J. Gourlay.

MENTELIN, Johann
The first pirate. [The priority of Fust or Mentelin's editions of St. Augustine De Arte Praedicandi]. LIB, xxiv (43/4), 30-46.
F. W. Householder.

MENZIES, Walter B.
Some early law books in Aberdeen University Library. Illus. EBSP, xv (30/5), 1-16.

MERCATOR, Gerard
A letter of Mercator concerning his Ptolemy. PBSA, xlii (48), 129-29.
G. K. Boyce.

MERCER, T. S.
Amanda M'Kittrick Ros. (Query, 38). BC, ii (53), 223.

MERCERS' COMPANY
Some observations on William Caxton and the Mercers' Company. Illus. BC, xv (68), 283-95.
N. F. Blake.

MERCHANT TAYLORS' SCHOOL libr.
Annals of Merchant Taylors' School library. Illus. LIB, xv (34/5), 457-80.
R. T. D. Sayle.

MEREDITH, George
A shorn Shagpat. (Note, 173). BC, xi (62). 80-3.
H. Kerpneck.

The missing Meredith letters. (Note, 240). BC, xiv (65), 76-8.
C. L. Cline.

A copy of Meredith's Poems, 1851. (Query, 208). BC, xv (66), 357.
P. Bartlett.

Location of copies of: Lang's Lines on . . . the Shelley society; Meredith's Jump-to-glory-Jane. (Query, 237). BC, xviii (69), 226.
L. H. Kendall.

The printing of George Meredith's The amazing marriage. Illus. LIB, xxi (66), 300-8.
S. H. Nowell-Smith.

MERIE AND PLEASANT PROGNOSTICATION
A Merie and Pleasant Prognostication, 1577. LIB, iv (49/50), 135-6.
F. P. Wilson.

MERIWETHER, James B.
Some notes on the text of Faulkner's Sanctuary. PBSA, lv (61), 192-206.

Notes on the textual history of The Sound and the Fury. Illus. PBSA, lvi (62), 285-316.

The text of Ernest Hemingway. PBSA, lvii (63), 403-21.

The dashes in Hemingway's A Farewell to Arms. PBSA, lviii (64), 449-57.

The English editions of James Gould Cozzens. SB, xv (62), 207-17.

MERIWETHER, M. B.
Memoirs of a Nullifier; by a native of South Columbia [? A. S. Johnston]. PBSA, xxxvi (42), 233.

MERRY DEVIL OF EDMONTON
The Merry Devil of Edmonton. LIB, xxv (44/5), 122-39.
Sir W. W. Greg.

MERVIN
The most famous and renowned Historie, of that woorthie and illustrious Knight Meruine . . . By I. M. Gent. London, R. Blower and Val. Sims, 1612. PBSA, xxxv (41), 157.
E. M. Sowerby.

MERVINE
See MERVIN

MERWIN, Walter S.
An imp with Uncle Sam. PBSA, xl (46), 247-58.

MESEROLE, Harrison T.
W. T. Sherwin: a little-known Paine biographer. PBSA, xlix (55), 268-72.

The 'Famous Boston Post List': mid-nineteenth century American best-sellers. PBSA, lii (58), 93-110.

MESPLET, Fleury
Fleury Mesplet: une étude sur les commencements de l'imprimerie dans la ville de Montréal. PBSA, xxviii (34), 164-93.
A. Fauteux.

METAL CUTS
Metal cuts at the Gutenberg workshop. [A review of *Gutenberg and the Master of the playing cards* by H. Lehmann-Haupt]. Illus. PBSA, lxii (68), 581-6.
K. F. Bauer.

METCALF, Keyes DeWitt
Microphotography and bibliography. PBSA, xxxii (38), 65-70.

METHODISM
Origins of Methodist publishing in America. Illus. PBSA, lix (65), 12-27.
L. D. Case.

METZDORF, Robert Frederic
Notes on Johnson's *Plan of a Dictionary*. LIB, xix (38/9), 198-201.

Supplementary note on Johnson's *Plan of a Dictionary*. LIB, xix (38/9), 363.

Three states of *The Revolter*. PBSA, xlv (51), 362.

The first American *Rasselas* and its imprint. PBSA, xlvii (53), 374-6.

—. *and* E., J. M.
Donald Frizell Hyde 1909-1966 [an obituary]. PBSA, lx (66), 101.

MEXICO
Sepan quantos esta carta vieren como yo: . . . Mexico. [Legal form]: Mexico Pedro Ocharte, before Oct. 25, 1565). PBSA, xxxiv (40), 87.
L. M. Stark.

Mexico. [Legal form]: *(S)Epan quantos esta carta vieren como yo* . . . [Mexico: Pedro Ocharte, 156-?]. PBSA, xxxiv (40), 87.
L. M. Stark.

Mexico. [Legal form]: *(E)Nla ciudad de Mexico a [diezeocho] dias del mes de [Abrill] de Mil y quinientos y ochenta y [seys] años* . . . [Mexico, 158-?]. PBSA, xxxiv (40), 87.
L. M. Stark.

Government publication in late eighteenth-century Mexico. PBSA, xlvi (52), 121-38.
E. H. Carpenter.

MEYER, Kathi
The liturgical music incunabula in the British Museum. LIB, xx (39/40), 274-94.

MEYER, Samuel
Spenser's *Colin Clout*: the poem and the book. PBSA, lvi (62), 397-413.

MEYIER, K. A. de
Note on a manuscript now at Leyden, from the library of St. James's Palace. TCBS, i (49/53), 359-9.

MEYNELL, Everard
Three booksellers and their catalogues. C. S. Millard: Everard Meynell: Douglas Cleverdon. BC, iv (55), 291-8.
G. Sims.

MICROBIBLIOGRAPHY
Microbibliography. (Note, 24). BC, ii (53), 219.
J. Wellesley.

MICROFILM
Some limitations of microfilm. PBSA, xxxv (41), 281-8.
W. A. Jackson.

An error in microfilms. LIB, viii (53), 126-7.
G. H. Blayney.

A journey of bibliographical exploration. PBSA, lvii (63), 33-41.
R. W. Hale.

MICROPHOTOGRAPHY
Microphotography and bibliography. PBSA, xxxii (38), 65-70.
K. D. Metcalf.

MICRONESIA
A press in paradise. The beginnings of printing in Micronesia. PBSA, xxxviii (44), 269-83.
J. E. Alden.

MIDDLE ENGLISH TEXTS
A computer concordance to Middle English texts. SB, xvii (64), 55-75.
A. Markman.

MIDDLETON, Bernard C.
The Gwynn family of edge-gilders. (Note, 190). BC, xi (62), 483.

The Bookbinders Case Unfolded. Illus. LIB, xvii (62), 66-76.

MIDDLETON, Thomas
Some notes on Crane's manuscript of *The Witch*. LIB, xxii (41/2), 208-22.
Sir W. W. Greg.

The first edition of *A Faire Quarrell*. LIB, iv (49/50), 137-41.
G. R. Price.

The first edition of *Your five gallants* and of *Michaelmas Term*. LIB, viii (53), 23-9.
G. R. Price.

The manuscript and the quarto of the *Roaring Girl*. LIB, xi (56), 180-6.
G. R. Price.

A bibliographical study of Middleton and Rowley's *The Changeling*. LIB, xvi (61), 37-43.
R. G. Lawrence.

The early editions of *A trick to catch the old one*. LIB, xxii (67), 205-27.
G. R. Price.

The quartos of *The Spanish Gypsy* and their relation to *The Changeling*. PBSA, lii (58), 111-25.
G. R. Price.

Dividing the copy for *Michaelmas term* [by T. Middleton]. PBSA, lx (66), 327-36.
G. R. Price.

The composition and printing of Middleton's *A mad world, my masters*. SB, iii (50), 246-52. G. J. Eberle.

MIDELFORT, H. C. Erik
Recent witch hunting research, or Where do we go from here? [With a bibliography]. PBSA, lxii (68), 373-420.

MIERDMAN, Stephen
The birthplace of Stephen Mierdman, Flemish printer in London, *c*. 1549 - *c*. 1552. LIB, iii (48/9), 213-14.
H. R. Hoppe.

MILFORD, Robert Theodore *and* SUTHERLAND, Donald Martell
A catalogue of English newspapers and periodicals in the Bodleian Library, 1622-1800. OBSP, iv (34/5), 163-346.

MILITARY DISCIPLINE
The military discipline, 1623. PBSA, xxxv (41), 157.
P. G. W. Skarshaug.

MILITARY PRINTING
Papers from an army press, 1650. EBST, ii (38/45), 420-3.
J. D. Ogilvie.

MILL, John Stuart
John Stuart Mill. (Query, 127). BC, ix (60), 202-3.
A. J. Fyfe *and* J. Hagan.

MILLAIS, Sir John Everett
Ruskin, Millais and Effie Gray. (Query, 22). BC, i (52), 268.
H. G. Viljoen.

MILLARD, Christopher Sclater
Three booksellers and their catalogues. C. S. Millard: Everard Meynell: Douglas Cleverdon. BC, iv (55), 291-8.
G. Sims.

MILLE, Thomas
The annotations to copies of Thomas Mille's books in the British Museum and Bodleian Libraries. Illus. LIB, xvi (61), 133-9.
P. H. Davison.

MILLER, A. T.
Trends in modern first edition collecting since 1939. BC, iv (55), 58-62.

MILLER, Cincinnatus Hiner
An unlocated Bret Harte-Joaquin Miller book. [*Thompson's Prodigal and other sketches*]. PBSA, lxi (67), 60.
G. DeGruson.

MILLER, Clarence H.
The order of stanzas in Cowley and Crawshaw's 'On hope' [by C. H. Miller, in *Studies in Philology* . . . lxi, 1964]. SB, xxii (69), 207-10.
G. W. Williams.

MILLER, Clarence William
Henry Herringman, Restoration bookseller-publisher. PBSA, xlii (48), 292-306.

Benjamin Franklin's way to wealth. PBSA, lxiii (69), 231-46.

In the Savoy: a study in post-Restoration imprints. SB, i (48/9), 39-46.

A bibliographical study of *Parthenissa* by Roger Boyle, Earl of Orrery. SB, ii (49/40), 115-37.

Thomas Newcomb: a Restoration printer's ornament stock. Illus. SB, iii (50/1), 155-70.

A London ornament stock: 1598-1683. Illus. SB, vii (55), 121-51.

Benjamin Franklin's Philadelphia type. Illus. SB, xi (58), 179-206.

Franklin's *Poor Richard Almanacs*: their printing and publication. SB, xiv (61), 97-115.

MILLER, Edwin Haviland
A best-seller brought up to date: later printings of Robert Greene's *A Disputation between a He Cony-Catcher and a She Cony-Catcher* 1592. PBSA, lii (58), 126-31.

The editions of Robert Greene's *A Quip for an Upstart Courtier*, 1592. SB, vi (54), 107-16.

Walt Whitman's correspondence with Whitelaw Reid, editor of the New York *Tribune*. SB, viii (56), 242-9.

New Year's day gift books in the sixteenth century. SB, xv (62), 233-41.

MILLER, Frederick DeWolfe
Twenty-eight additions to the canon of Lowell's criticism. [From the *North American Review*]. SB, iv (51/2), 205-10.

Identification of contributors to the *North American Review* under Lowell. SB, vi (54), 219-29.

MILLER, George J.
David A. Borrenstein, a printer and publisher at Princeton, N. J., 1824-28. Illus. PBSA, xxx (36), 1-56.

MILLER, James
A bibliographical contribution to biography: James Miller's *Seasonable Reproof*. LIB, iii (48/9), 295-8.
P. Stewart.

MILLER, Joaquin *pseud.*
See MILLER, Cincinnatus Hiner

MILLER, Robert Henry
The publication of Raymond Chandler's *The long goodbye*. BC, xviii (69), 279-90.

MILLER, William E.
The Hospitall of Incurable Fooles. SB, xvi (63), 204-7.

Printers and stationers in the parish of St. Giles Cripplegate, 1561-1640. SB, xix (66), 15-38.

MILTON, John
A forgotten indiscretion. [Pickersgill illustrations to Milton's *Comus*, Routledge, 1858]. (Note, 233). BC, xiii (64), 500.
P. F. Hinton.

Milton autographs established. Illus. LIB, xiii (32), 192-200.
H. C. H. Candy.

The chronology of Milton's handwriting. Illus. LIB, xiv (33/4), 229-35.
H. Darbishire.

Milton, N.LL, and Sir Tho. Urquhart. Illus. LIB, xiv (33/4), 470-6.
H. C. H. Candy.

— [A letter]. LIB, xv (34/5), 249-50.
J. W. Pendleton.

—. [A letter]. LIB, xv (34/5), 377-8.
H. C. H. Candy.

A cancel in an early Milton tract. [*Animadversions upon the Remonstrant's Defence against Smectymnuus*, 1641]. LIB, xv (34/5), 243-4.
W. R. Parker.

Milton's *Prolusio* script. Illus. LIB, xv (34/5), 330-9.
H. C. H. Candy.

A cancel in an early Milton tract. [*Animadversions upon the Remonstrant's Defence against Smectymnuus*. A letter]. LIB, xvi (35/6), 118.
H. C. H. Candy.

Contributions toward a Milton bibliography. LIB, xvi (35/6), 425-38.
W. R. Parker.

A note on Milton's *Pro Populo Anglicano Defensio*. LIB, xvii (36/7), 466-7.
M. Kelley.

Milton, Rothwell, and Simmons. LIB, xviii (37/8), 89-103.
W. R. Parker.

The different states of the first edition of *Paradise Lost*. Illus. LIB, xxii (41/2), 34-66.
J. Pershing.

A further note on Milton's *Pro Populo Anglicano Defensio*. LIB, xxiii (42/3), 45-7.
C. O. Lewis

Some illustrators of Milton's *Paradise Lost*, 1688-1850. 2 pts. Illus. LIB, iii (48/9), 1-21, 101-19.
C. H. C. Baker.

The date of Milton's first *Defense*. LIB, iii (48/9), 56-8.
J. M. French.

Some illustrators of Milton's *Paradise Lost*. [A letter]. LIB, iv (49/50), 146-7.
T. Balston.

Milton and the 'notes on Paul Best'. Illus. LIB, v (50/1), 49-51.
M. Kelley.

A revised bibliography of Salmasius's *Defensio Regia* and Milton's *Pro Populo Anglicano Defensio*. Illus. LIB, ix (54), 101-21.
F. F. Madan.

Fletcher's Milton: a first appraisal. PBSA, xli (47), 35-52.
W. Parker.

The box rule pattern in the first edition of *Paradise Lost*. PBSA, xlii (48), 315-21.
G. A. Battle.

A second (?) title-page of the second edition of *Paradise Lost*. Illus. PBSA, xliii (49), 173-8.
H. Fletcher.

An unrecorded edition of Milton's *Defensio Secunda* (1654). PBSA, xlix (55), 262-8.
J. M. French.

Wood's life of Milton: its sources and significance. PBSA, lii (58), 1-22.
W. Parker.

Certain relationships of the manuscripts of *Comus*. PBSA, liv (60), 38-56.
J. T. Shawcross.

—. An addendum. PBSA, liv (60), 293-4.

A suppressed edition of Milton's *Defensio Secunda* (1654). PBSA, lv (61), 75-87.
R. W. Ayers.

The John Phillips — John Milton *Angli Responsio*: editions and relations. PBSA, lvi (62), 66-72.
R. W. Ayers.

Establishment of a text of Milton's poems through a study of *Lycidas*. PBSA, lvi (62), 317 - 31.
J. T. Shawcross.

Milton's *Tenure of kings and magistrates*: date of composition, editions, and issues. PBSA, lx (66), 1-8.
J. T. Shawcross.

Milton and Machiavelli's *Discorsi*. Illus. SB, iv (51), 123-7.
M. Kelley.

The issues and states of the second folio and Milton's *Epitaph on Shakespeare*. Illus. SB, v (52), 81-108.
W. B. Todd.

The precedence of the 1676 editions of Milton's *Literae Pseudo-Senatus Anglicani*. SB, vii (55), 181-5.
B. Harkness.

Milton and the Harvard Pindar. Illus. SB, xvii (64), 77-82.
S. B. Atkins *and* M. Kelley.

The date of the separate edition of Milton's *Epitaphium Damonis*. SB, xviii (65), 262-5.
J. T. Shawcross.

MINER, Dorothy E.
The collection of manuscripts and rare books in the Walters Art Gallery. PBSA, xxx (36), 104-9.

The publishing ventures of a Victorian connoisseur: a sidelight on William T. Walters. Illus. PBSA, lvii (63), 271-311.

MINERVA PRESS
'Minerva Press' publicity — a publisher's
advertisement of 1794. LIB, xxi (40/1), 207-15.
M. Sadleir.

MINIATURE BOOKS
Collections of miniature books. (Query, 114).
BC, viii (59), 74.
P. E. Spielmann.

MINING COMPANIES
Bibliographical notes on certain Eastern mining
companies of the California Gold Rush, 1849-
1850. Illus. PBSA, xliii (49), 247-8.
R. W. G. Vail.

MINNS, Sir Ellis H.
A Byzantine silver binding. Illus. LIB, xvii
(46/7), 295-7.

MINTO, William
William Minto, 1845-1893: a checklist. BTHK,
v (67/70), 152-64.
K. I. Macdonald.

MIRABILIA URBIS ROMAE
Mirabilia urbis Romae. [Rome, Stephen Plannck,
about 1486]. PBSA, xxxvi (42), 229.
H. R. Mead.

MIRK, John
J. Mirk's Liber Festivalis and Quattuor Ser-
mones, Pynson, 1499. LIB, iv (49/50), 73.
Sir F. C. Francis.

Mirk's Liber Festivalis and Quattuor Sermones.
[A letter]. LIB, v (50/1), 59-60.
Kenyon, L. Tyrell-, 5th baron.

MIRROR FOR MAGISTRATES
Wayland's edition of The Mirror for Magi-
strates. Illus. LIB, xiii (32/3), 155-7.
W. A. Jackson.

MISCELLANEOUS PIECES
Gray's Elegy in Miscellaneous pieces, 1752.
LIB, xx (65), 144-8.
A. Anderson.

MISERIES OF INFORST MARIAGE
Variants in the first quarto of The Miseries of
Inforst Mariage. LIB, ix (54), 176-84.
G. H. Blayney.

MISH, Charles Caroll
Best sellers in seventeenth-century fiction.
PBSA, xlvii (53), 56-73.

MISPRINTS
A bibliographical misprint. (Note, 243). BC,
xiv (65), 214.
W. B. Todd.

A binder's misprint. (Note, 244). BC, xiv (65),
214.
W. B. Todd.

A misprinted title in a Prudentius of 1499.
(Note, 256). BC, xiv (65), 541.
S. V. Lenkey.

MISSAL
Missale speciale Constantiense. Illus. BC, iv
(55), 8-15.
J. V. Scholderer.

Who printed the Missale Speciale Constantiense?
BC, vi (57), 253-8.
C. F. Bühler.

Some leaves of a thirteenth-century missal
probably from Jedburgh Abbey. [With] Notes
on the music. EBST, iii (48/55), 1-15.
F. C. Eeles and J. H. Arnold.

The dating of the Missale Speciale Constantiense.
Illus. LIB, xiii (58), 81-101.
Sir I. Masson.

Another view on the dating of the Missale
Speciale Constantiense. LIB, xiv (59), 1-10.
C. F. Bühler.

Missale Ebroicense. Paris [Jean Dupré] 1492.
PBSA, xxxiv (40), 356-7.
H. R. Mead.

The Constance Missal and two documents from
the Constance diocese. PBSA, l (56), 370-5.
C. F. Bühler.

MISSALE SPECIALE CONSTANTIENSE
See MISSAL

MITCHELL, Alison and FOSTER, Katherine
Sir William Alexander's Supplement to book
III of Sidney's Arcadia. Illus. LIB, xxiv (69),
234-41.

MITCHELL, James Leslie
Further notes on the bibliography of James
Leslie Mitchell/Lewis Grassic Gibbon. BTHK,
i/2 (57), 34-5.
W. R. Aitken.

Lewis Grassic Gibbon: an additional note.
BTHK, i/2 (57), 35.
L. Jolley.

James Leslie Mitchell/Lewis Grassic Gibbon:
a chronological checklist. [G. Wagner in BTHK
i, no. 1]. Additions I. BTHK, v (67/70), 169-73.
D. F. Young.

James Leslie Mitchell/Lewis Grassic Gibbon:
a chronological checklist. Additions II. BTHK,
v (67/70), 174-7.
J. Kidd.

MITCHELL, Rosamond Joscelyne
A Renaissance library: the collection of John
Tiptoft, Earl of Worcester. LIB, xviii (37/8),
67-83.

Robert Langton's Pylgrimage. LIB, viii (53),
42-5.

MITCHELL, Stephen O.
Johnson and Cocker's Arithmetic. PBSA, lvi
(62), 107-9.

—. and SEARS, Loren
An information retrieval system for modern
language studies. PBSA, lviii (64), 270-8.

MITCHELL, William Smith
The earliest Newcastle binder's ticket. (Note, 296). BC, xvii (68), 81-2.

An apparently unrecorded French translation of Galen's *De Simplicium Medicamentorum Facultatibus*, 1544. LIB, ii (47/8), 170-1.

John Harrison's signed roll? Illus. LIB, viii (53), 123-4.

A signed binding by James Fleming, Newcastle, *c.* 1740. Illus. LIB, xv (60), 58-60.

German bindings in Aberdeen University Library: iconographic index, and indices of initials, binders and dates. LIB, xvii (62), 46-55.

MITCHNER, Robert W.
Wynkyn de Worde's use of the Plimpton manuscript of *De Proprietatibus Rerum*. Illus. LIB, vi (51/2), 7-18.

MITFORD, Mary Russell
A note on Mary Russell Mitford's *Belford Regis*. PBSA, lx (66), 473.
D. C. Ewing.

Magazine and other contributions by Mary Russell Mitford and Thomas Noon Talfourd. SB, xii (59), 218-26.
W. A. Coles.

MITHAL, H. S. D.
The variants in Robert Wilson's *The Three Lords of London*. LIB, xviii (63), 142-4.

MOBLEY, Lawrence E.
Mark Twain and the *Golden Era*. PBSA, lviii (64), 8-23.

MODERN LANGUAGE STUDIES
An information retrieval system for modern language studies. PBSA, lviii (64), 270-8.
S. O. Mitchell *and* L. Sears.

MOGG, William Rees-
A collection of 18th-century literature. (Contemporary collecters, 29). Illus. BC, x (61), 423-34.

Book prices past. [*A critical and historical account of the celebrated libraries in foreign countries*, ascribed to W. Oldys]. (Note, 278). BC, xv (66), 356.

Some reflections on the bibliography of Gilbert Burnet. Illus. LIB, iv (49/50), 100-13.

MOLIÈRE, Jean Baptiste Poquelin de
The first edition of Molière's *Sganarelle*. (Note, 126). BC, ix (60), 68-71.
A. Rau.

A cancel in the Boucher Molière, 1734. (Query, 190). BC, xiv (65), 367.
H. A. Hammelmann.

Molière's privilege of 18 March 1671. LIB, xx (65), 57-63.
G. E. Reed.

MONASTIC HOUSES
An interim list of the heads of some Scottish monastic houses before *c.* 1300. Edited from the papers of the late D. W. Hunter Marshall. BTHK, ii (59/60), 4-27.
A. A. M. Duncan.

MONASTIC LIBRARIES
Austrian monastic libraries. LIB, xxv (44/5), 46/65.
E. P. Goldschmidt.

The dispersal of the monastic libraries and the beginning of Anglo-Saxon studies; Matthew Parker and his circle: a preliminary study. TCBS, i (49/53), 208-37.
C. E. Wright.

MONDOVÌ
A Mondovì indulgence and Pierre Sabran. LIB, vii (52), 117-20.
D. E. Rhodes.

MONITEUR UNIVERSAL
M. de Jarry's project for an edition of the *Moniteur*. LIB, iv (49/50), 277-9.
J. F. Kerslake.

MONKMAN, Kenneth
Early editions of *Tristram Shandy*. (Query, 217). BC, xvi (67), 377.

MONOTYPE RECORDER
The Monotype recorder 'xxi no. 246'. (Note, 254). BC, xiv (65), 366.
J. Moran.

MONTAGU, Richard
Binding by Richard Montagu for Thomas Hollis, 1758. (English bookbindings, 3). Illus. BC, i (52), 182-4.
H. M. Nixon.

Richard Mountague, bookbinder. Illus. LIB, viii (53), 124-5.
J. W. Phillips.

MONTAIGNE, Michel Eyquem de
The edition of Montaigne read by Melville. PBSA, lxii (68), 130-4.
A. J. Stevens.

MONTE CALERIO, Philippus de
Philippus de Monte Calerio. *Dominicale*. Abridged by Joneselmus de Canova. [Paris, Philippe Pigouchet, about 1500]. PBSA, xxxvi (42), 62-3.
H. R. Mead.

MONTEIRO, George
Henry James and his reviewers: some identifications. BC, xviii (69), 300-4.

William Dean Howells: two mistaken attributions. PBSA, lvi (62), 254-7.

Snodgrass peoples his universe. PBSA, lvi (62), 494-5.

William Dean Howells: a bibliographical amendment. PBSA, lviii (64), 468-9.

Thomas Sergeant Perry: four attributions. PBSA, lix (65), 57.

Harold Frederic: an unrecorded story. PBSA, lix (65), 327.

John Greenleaf Whittier in *The Independent*. PBSA, lx (66), 91.

Unrecorded variants in two Yeats poems. PBSA, lx (66), 367-8.

Rudyard Kipling: early printings in American periodicals. PBSA, lxi (67), 127-8.

Addenda to Harlow [V. Harlow's *Thomas Sergeant Perry: a biography*]: two T. S. Perry essays. PBSA, lxii (68), 612-3.

Grand opera for the people : an unrecorded Stephen Crane printing. PBSA, lxiii (69), 29-30.

Harold Frederic: an unrecorded review [of Gissing's *The whirlpool*]. PBSA, lxiii (69), 30-1.

Addendum to Edel and Laurence [*A bibliography of Henry James*]. Henry James's *Future of the novel*. PBSA, lxiii (69), 130.

William Dean Howells, and *The Breadwinners* [by J. Hay]. SB, xv (62), 267-8.

A speech by W. D. Howells. SB, xx (67), 262-3.

MONTESQUIEU, Charles de Secondat *baron de*
Montesquieu, Voltaire, and Rousseau in eighteenth century Scotland; a check list of editions and translations of their works published in Scotland before 1801. BTHK, ii (59/60), 40-63.
A. K. Howard.

MONTGOMERIE, William
Some notes on the Herd manuscripts. EBST, iii (48/55), 289-98.

MONTGOMERY, John Warwick
The colonial parish library of Wilhelm Christoph Berkenmeyer. PBSA, liii (51), 114-49.

MONTHLY CATALOGUE OF BOOKS
Monthly catalogue of books published. LIB, xviii (63), 223-8.
D. F. Foxon.

MONTHLY CHRONICLE
'Register of books', 1732 [from the *Monthly chronicle*]. (Note, 289). BC, xvi (67), 374-5.
D. F. Cook.

MONTHLY MERCURY
Henry Rhodes and the *Monthly Mercury*, 1702-1720. BC, v (56), 343-53.
C. C. Blagden.

MONTHLY REVIEW
William Bewley and *The Monthly Review*: a problem of attribution. PBSA, lv (61), 309-18.
R. Lonsdale.

MONTREAL
Fleury Mesplet: une étude sur les commencements de l'imprimerie dans la ville de Montréal. PBSA, xxviii (34), 164-93.
A. Fauteux.

MONTROSE, James *marquis of*
See GRAHAM, James *1st marquis of Montrose*

MONUMENTA ORDINIS FRATRUM MINORUM
Monumenta ordinis Fratrum Minorum. (Lugd., J. Cleyn, 1504). PBSA, i (56), 375-8.
D. E. Rhodes.

MOODY, G. C.
Wise, Smart and Moody. (Note, 319). BC, xviii (69), 386-7.
S. Nowell-Smith.

MOOR, James
Moor's *De Analogia contractionum linguae Graecae*. BTHK, i/4 (58), 47-8.
A. P. H. *and* H. P.

MOORE, Dugald
Bibliography of Dugald Moore, poet and bookseller, 1805-1841. GBSR, iii (15), 109-14.
W. Sinclair.

MOORE, Edward
A Cambridge binding by Ed. Moore, *c*. 1748. (English bookbindings, 63). Illus. BC, xvi (67), 481.
H. M. Nixon.

MOORE, George
Moore, George (1852-1933). *Confessions of a Young Man*. London, 1888. PBSA, xxxvi (42), 68.
H. S. Mott.

The survival of wickedness [i.e. of copies of *Flowers of passion*, 1878 by George Moore]. PBSA, lvii (63), 356-7.
J. M. Munro.

MOORE, Sir Jonas
Loose plates in *Modern Fortification*, 1673. (Query, 115). BC, viii (59), 183-4.
D. G. Mackenzie.

MOORE, John Robert
On the use of advertisements as bibliographical evidence. [A letter]. LIB, ix (54), 134-5.

The canon of Defoe's writings. LIB, xi (56), 155-69.

The Groans of Great Britain: an unassigned tract by Charles Gildon. PBSA, xl (46), 22-31.

'Robin Hog' Stephens: Messenger of the press. PBSA, l (56), 381-7.

MOORE, Julia A.
The Sweet Singer of Michigan bibliographically considered. PBSA, xxxix (45), 91-118.
A. H. Greenly.

MOORE, Philip
Three little Tudor books [Xenophon's *Treatise of Household*, tr. G. Hervet. T. Berthelet, 1532; Philip Moore's *The Hope of Health*. J. Kingston, 1564; *The Viniard of Devotion*. Newly corrected for Edw. White, 1599]. Illus. LIB, xiv (33/4), 178-206.
E. F. Bosanquet.

MOORE, Thomas
The American republication of Thomas Moore's *Epistles, odes and other poems*: an early version of the reprinting 'game'. PBSA, lxii (68), 199-205.
H. G. Eldridge.

Chronological annotations to 250 letters of Thomas Moore. PBSA, lxiii (69), 105-17.
R. B. Pearsall.

MORAN, James
The Monotype recorder 'xxi, no. 246'. (Note, 254). BC, xiv (65), 366.

An assessment of Mackie's steam type-composing machine. JPHS, i (65), 57-76.

Kniaghininsky's tape-operated composing machine. JPHS, iii (67), 93-6.

The Columbian press. Illus. JPHS, v (69), 1-23.

Filmsetting — bibliographical implications. LIB, xv (60), 231-45.

William Blades. LIB, xvi (61), 251-66.

MORAY
See STEWART, lord James

MORE, Edward
Six tracts about women: a volume in the British Museum. [*The deceyte of women*. A. Vele, n.d.; *The scole house of women*. J. King, 1560; Edward More, *The defence of women*. J. King, 1560; *The proude wyues pater noster*. J. King, 1560; Robert Copland, *The seuen sorowes*. W. Copland, n.d.; and *Frederyke of Iennen*. A. Vele, n.d.]. LIB, xv (34/5), 38-48.
H. Stein.

MORE, Henry
A publishing agreement of the late seventeenth century. [Re *Henrici Mori Cantabrigiensis Opera Theologica*, 1675]. LIB, xiii (32/3), 184-7.
R. B. McKerrow.

MORE, John
John More's translations. PBSA, xlix (55), 188-9.
P. Hogrefe.

MORE, Sir Thomas
Thomas More: unlocated items. (Query, 94). BC, vii (58), 188.
R. W. Gibson.

St. Thomas More's book of hours. (Query, 126). BC, ix (60), 202.
R. W. Gibson.

MSS of the *Life of Sir Thomas More*. (Query, 182). BC, xiii (64), 356.
R. Dupré.

Printing evidence in Wynkyn de Worde's edition of *The Life of Johan Picus* by St. Thomas More. PBSA, xliii (49), 398-9.
F. T. Bowers.

MORELLET, André
The manuscript of Jefferson's unpublished errata list for Abbé Morellet's translation of the *Notes on Virginia*. SB, i (48/9), 3-24.
J. M. Carrière.

MORES, Edward Rowe
A dissertation upon English typographical founders and founderies (1778), with A catalogue and specimen of the typefoundry of John James (1782). Illus. OBSP, ix (61).
H. Carter *and* C. Ricks, ed.

MORGAN, Alice
The conuercyon of swerers [by S. Hawes]: another edition. Illus. LIB, xxiv (69), 44-50.

MORGAN, John
Letters to William Hunter from his American pupils, John Morgan and William Shippen jnr. Illus. BTHK, iii (60/2), 61-7.
J. Dobson *and* B. Thomas.

MORGAN, Margery Mary
Pynson's manuscript of *Dives and Pauper*. LIB, viii (53), 217-28.

MORGAN, Paul
Non est mortale quod opto. (Note, 141). BC, xi (62), 211.

Non est mortale quod opto. (Note, 141). BC, xvi (67), 507-8.

Some bibliographical aspects of the Scottish Prayer Book of 1637. BTHK, v (67/70), 1-23.

A bookseller's subscription in 1669. LIB, vii (52), 281-2.

English provincial imprints. LIB, xxii (67), 70.

—. *and* PAINTER, George Duncan
The Caxton *Legenda* at St. Mary's, Warwick. Illus. LIB, xii (57), 225-39.

MORICE, James
'English bokes concernyng [i.e. belonging] to James Morice'. TCBS, iii (59/63), 124-32.
J. C. T. Oates.

MORISON, Sir Richard
Sir Richard Morison as the author of two anonymous tracts on sedition [i.e. *A Lamentation in whiche is shewed what Ruyne and destruction cometh of seditious rebellyon*; and *A Remedy for Sedition*]. LIB, xvii (36/7), 83-7.
C. R. Baskervill.

MORISON, Stanley Arthur
Officina Bodoni exhibition. Illus. BC, iii (54), 244-50.

The adoption of the Latin uncial: a suggestion. EBST, ii (38/45), 375-9.

Early humanistic script and the first roman type. Illus. LIB, xxiv (43/4), 1-29.

The bibliography of newspapers and the writing of history. LIB, ix (54), 153-75.

Morisonianum. (Note, 253)., BC, xiv (65), 365.
J. Carter.

MORLEY, Thomas
The editions of Morley's *Introduction*. LIB, xxiii (42/3), 127-9.
O. E. Deutsch.

A suppressed dedication for Morley's four-part madrigals of 1594. Illus. TCBS, iii (59/63), 401-5.
T. Dart.

MORNING CHRONICLE
Early numbers of *The Morning Chronicle* and *Owen's Weekly Chronicle*. LIB, xx (39/40), 412-24.
P. B. Gove.

—. [A letter]. LIB, xxi (40/1), 95.
P. B. Gove.

MOROCCO BINDER
A binding by the Morocco Binder, *c.* 1563. (English bookbindings 22). Illus. BC, vi (57), 278.
H. M. Nixon.

MORRIS, Charles
Charles Morris. [An obituary]. BTHK, iv (63/6), 43.
R. Donaldson.

MORRIS, Claver
The library of a physician, circa 1700 [i.e. Claver Morris]. LIB, xiii (32/3), 89-96.
E. Hobhouse.

MORRIS, J. M.
A check-list of prints made at Cambridge by Peter Spendelow Lamborn, 1722-1774. Illus. TCBS, iii (59/63), 295-312.

MORRIS, John
A note on the first stereotyping in England. JPHS, i (65), 97-8.

Restrictive practices in the Elizabethan book trade: the Stationers' Company *v.* Thomas Thomas 1583-8. TCBS, iv (64/8), 276-90.

Thomas Thomas, printer to the university of Cambridge 1583-8. Part II: Some account of his materials and bookbindings with a short-title list of his printing. Illus. TCBS, iv (64/8), 339-62.

MORRIS, William
William Morris, 1834-1896. (English literary autographs, 18). Illus. BC, v (56), 151.
T. J. Brown.

MORTE DARTHUR
Two Caxton problems. [*Morte Darthur* and Lydgate's *Lyf of our Lady*]. LIB, xx (39/40), 266-71.
C. F. Bühler.

MORTENSON, Robert
The copyright of Byron's *Cain*. PBSA, lxiii (69), 5-13.

Yeats's *Vision* and "The Two Trees". SB, xvii (64), 220-2.

MORTIMER, Jean E.
An unrecorded Caxton at Ripon Cathedral. LIB, viii (53), 37-42.

MORTIMER, R. S.
The meaning of the imprint. [A letter]. LIB, vii (52), 60.

MORTIMER, Ruth
The earliest extant French armorial ex-libris. (Note, 161). BC, xi (62), 212.

MORTON, Richard
Textual problems in Restoration broadsheet prologues and epilogues. LIB, xii (57), 197-203.

MORTON, Robert
The literature of dissent in Glasgow in the latter half of the eighteenth century. Illus. GBSR, xi (33), 56-72.

MOSELEY, Humphrey
Humphrey Moseley, publisher. OBSP, ii (27/30), 57-142; i (47), 39.
J. C. Reed.

MOSLEY, James
Nineteenth-century decorated types at Oxford. Illus. JPHS, ii (66), inset.

The early career of William Caslon. Illus. JPHS, iii (67), 66-81.

MOSHER, Thomas Bird
Thomas Bird Mosher, publisher and pirate. Illus. BC, xi (62), 295-312.
J. D. Van Trump *and* A. P. Ziegler, *jr.*

Mosher and Bridges. (Note, 189). BC, xi (62), 482-3.
S. H. Nowell-Smith.

T. B. Mosher and the Guild of women-binders. (Note, 285). BC, xvi (67), 82.
B. C. Bloomfield.

MOTHER GOOSE'S MELODY
Mother Goose's Melody. LIB, vi (51), 216-8.
M. J. P. Weedon.

MOTT, Howard S.
Alcott, Louisa May (1832-1888). *Hospital Sketches*. Boston, James Redpath, 1863. PBSA, xxxiv (40), 190.

[Matthews Cornelius (1817-1889)]. *Moneypenny, or, The Heart of the World*. New York, DeWitt & Davenport, 1849. PBSA, xxxiv (40), 276.

[Prince, Oliver Hillhouse (1787-1837)]. *The Ghost of Baron Steuben.* N.p., n.d. PBSA, xxxv (41), 206.

Beebe, William (1877-). *Edge of the Jungle.* New York, 1921. PBSA, xxxv (41), 207.

The Blackwater Chronicle. New York, 1853. PBSA, xxxvi (42), 67-8.

Moore, George (1852-1933). *Confessions of a Young Man.* London, 1888. PBSA, xxxvi (42), 68.

Collins, Wilkie (1824-1889). *The Woman in White.* New York, 1860. PBSA, xxxvi (42), 232.

MOTTER, Thomas Hubbard Vail
Hallam's *Poems* of 1830: a census of copies. PBSA, xxxv (41), 277-80.

MOTTEUX, Pierre Antoine
A bibliography of the writings of Peter Anthony Motteux. OBSP, iii (31/3), 317-37.
R. N. Cunningham.

Motteux's *Love's a Jest,* 1696: a running-title and presswork problem. PBSA, xlviii (54), 268-73.
F. T. Bowers.

MOTTOES
Latin title-page mottoes as a clue to dramatic authorship. Illus. LIB, xxvi (45/6), 28-36.
J. G. McManaway.

MOXON, Edward
Variant bindings on Moxon authors. (Query, 183). BC, xiii (64), 356-7.
N. Colbeck.

MOXON, Joseph
Pepys's copy of Moxon's *Mechanick Exercises.* LIB, xiv (59), 124-6.
H. Carter *and* B. Wolpe.

MOYES, James
James Moyes and his Temple printing office of 1825. Illus. JPHS, iv (68), 1-10.
I. Bain.

MOZART, Wolfgang Amadeus
On the ascription of a Mozart aria. (Note, 201). BC, xii (63), 350.
C. B. Oldman.

A subscription list to Mozart's *Cosi fan tutte.* LIB, vii (52), 132-3.
A. H. King.

MUDIE'S CIRCULATING LIBRARY
Mudie's circulating library. (Note, 22). BC, ii (53), 157.
P. H. Muir.

MUIR, Kenneth Arthur
Elizabethan remainders. LIB, xiii (58), 56-7.

MUIR, Percival Horace
Elkin Matthews in the nineties. Illus. BC, i (52), 28-40.

Elkin Matthews. III Evans takes over. BC, i (52), 145-9.

Elkin Matthews. IV The background in Cork Street. BC, i (52), 228-39.

Elkin Matthews V A New recruit. Illus. BC, ii (53), 38-49.

Elkin Mathews. VI Worthington. Illus. BC, ii (53), 104-15.

Elkin Matthews. VII The team is completed. Illus. BC, ii (53), 194-204.

Elkin Mathews. VIII Sherry and shibboleths. Illus. BC, iii (54), 11-27.

Elkin Mathews. IX The depression. BC, iii (54), 125-33.

Gutenberg Bible census. (Note, 1). BC, i (52), 53.

The first edition of Rousseau's *Emile,* 1762. BC, i (52), 67-76.

Goldsmith's *Millenium Hall,* 1762. (Note, 15). BC, i (52), 265-6.

The Ireland Shakespeare forgeries. (Note, 17). BC, ii (53), 72-3.

Mudie's circulating library. (Note, 22). BC, ii (53), 157.

A. J. A. Symons. (Bibliomanes, 1). 3 pt. illus. BC, iii (54), 198-210; 279-92; iv (55), 122-32.

Hans Anderson. (Query, 52). BC, iii (54), 308-9.

Will Dockwra. (Note, 45). BC, iv (55), 168.

Sir Hugh Walpole. (Bibliomanes, 2). 3 pts. Illus. BC, iv (55), 217-28; 299-307; v (56), 38-47.

The Tauchnitz *David Copperfield,* 1849. (Note, 53). BC, iv (55), 253-4.

Jules Verne. (Note, 54). BC, iv (55), 327-9.

Dickens and Tauchnitz. (Note, 55). BC, iv (55), 329.

Further reminiscences. BC, v (56), 239-47.

—. BC, vi (57), 388-94.

—. BC, vii (58), 171-9.

—. BC, vii (58), 278-83.

—. BC, viii (59), 46-9.

—. BC, viii (59), 163-7.

—. BC, viii (59), 275-81.

—. BC, viii (59), 411-15.

—. BC, ix (60), 171-7.

—. BC, ix (60), 308-15.

—. BC, ix (60), 435-443.

—. BC, x (61), 49-55.

—. BC, x (61), 177-83.

—. BC, x (61), 311-19.

—. BC, x (61), 435-9.

—. BC, xi (62), 55-61.

—. BC, xi (62), 197-203.

—. BC, xi (62), 323-9.

—. BC, xi (62), 460-5.

—. BC, xii (63), 55-9.

—. BC, xii (63), 333-7.

—. BC, xiii (64), 45-51.

Harlequinades. (Note, 83). BC, vi (57), 182-3.

First edition of *L'Ile des Pingouins*. (Note, 144). BC, ix (60), 332-3.

Mr. Muir and Gabriel Wells: a rejoinder. BC, x (61), 53-5.

Ian Fleming: a personal memoir. BC, xiv (65), 24-33.

Printing and the mind of man, the inside story [of the exhibition]. BC, xvi (67), 47-53.

A curious dance round a curious tree. (Note, 295). BC, xvii (68), 80-1.

Dating of Walter Crane toy books. (Query, 228). BC, xvii (68), 353.

Friedrich Nietzsche. *Also sprach Zarathustra.* (Note, 313). BC, xviii (69), 221-2.

A personal chapter. BH, ii (51/2), 75-90.

English imprints after 1640. LIB, xiv (33/4), 157-77.

The Bickmans and their *Universal Penman.* Illus. LIB, xxv (44/5), 162-84.

—. [A letter]. LIB, i (46/7), 247-8.

The Kehl edition of Voltaire. LIB, iii (48/9), 85-100.

—. [A letter]. LIB, iv (49/50), 74.

MUIRHEAD, Arnold Meadowcroft
The School-Press. (Query, 44). BC, iii (54), 149-50.

An author's imprimatur. (Query, 123). BC, ix (60), 79.

John Farquhar Fulton, 1899-1960. (Portrait of a bibliophile, 9). BC, xi (62), 427-36.

An introduction to a bibliography of William Cobbett. Illus. LIB, xx (39/40), 1-40.

A Jeremy Bentham collection. Illus. LIB, i (46/7), 6-27.

MULHERN, James
Manuscript school-books. PBSA, xxxii (38), 17-37.

MULKEARN, Louis
The biography of a forgotten book — Pownall's *Topographical Description of . . . North America.* PBSA, xliii (49), 63-74.

MUM
A note on *Mum,* an eighteenth-century political ballad. EBST, iii (48/55), 249-52. D. N. Smith.

MUNBY, Alan Noel L.
Early trade bindings. (Query, 2). BC, i (52), 128-9.

—. BC, i (52), 194.

A late use of a crested roll. (Note, 12). BC, i (52), 264.

Sales talk in 1823. (Query, 24). Illus. BC, i (52), 269.

Charles Geoffrey des Graz 1893-1953. Illus. BC, ii (53), 133-7.

Collecting English signed bindings. Illus. BC, ii (53), 177-93.

The publication of *Camilla.* (Note, 23). BC, ii (53), 219.

A Cambridge proof-sheet of 1617. [Samuel Collins's *Epphata to F.T.*]. (Note, 36). BC, iii (54), 226.

Early book labels. (Query, 48). BC, iii (54), 227.

Fragment of a bookseller's day-book of 1622. BC, iii (54), 302-6.

Portraits of T. F. Dibdin. (Note, 46). Illus. BC, iv (55), 168-70.

Sir Thomas Phillipps and the disposal of his library. BC, v (56), 137-49.

The library of George Thackeray, Provost of King's College, Cambridge. Illus. BC, vi (57), 143-9.

The origin of offprints. (Query, 85). BC, vi (57), 292.

The comte de Marnay, a short story. BC, vii (58), 51-7.

Sir Frederic Madden at Cambridge. BC, x (61), 156-63.

The Didot *Horace*, 1799. (Note, 182). BC, xi (62), 345.

Joseph Hunter and Sir Thomas Phillipps. BC, xii (63), 37-43.

Three opportunities. [in book collecting]. BC, xv (66), 437-45.

Libraries under the German occupation. [A summary]. LIB, i (46/7), 45-6.

Jacob Bryant and the Sunderland Library. Illus. LIB, ii (47/8), 192-9.

The gifts of Elizabethan printers to the library of King's College, Cambridge. Illus. LIB, ii (47/8), 224-32.

Jacob Bryant's Caxtons. Some additions to De Ricci's *Census.* LIB, iii (48/9), 218-22.

The acquisition of manuscripts by institutional libraries. PBSA, liv (60), 1-15.

Elias Burling, *A Call to Back-sliding Israel,* New York, 1694: an unrecorded tract printed by William Bradford. Illus. SB, xiv (61), 251-3.

Chirm's banded bindings. Illus. TCBS, i (49/53), 181-6.

Windham and Gauffecourt. TCBS, i (49/53), 186-90.

Notes on King's College library in the fifteenth century. TCBS, i (49/53), 280-6.

—. *and* HOBSON, Anthony Robert A.
John Roland Abbey. (Contemporary collectors, 26). Illus. BC, x (61), 40-8.

—. *and* POLLARD, M.
Did Mr. Cavendish burn his Caxtons? Illus. BC, xii (63), 449-66.

MUNDUM ASTRAEA RELIQUIT
'Mundum Astraea Reliquit'. (Query, 158). BC, xii (63), 71-2.
J. S. G. Simmons.

MUNRO, Ion Smeaton
Books and Henry Stuart, Cardinal Duke of York. Illus. BH, ii (51/2), 191-205.

MUNRO, John M.
The survival of wickedness [i.e. of copies of *Flowers of passion*, 1878 by George Moore]. PBSA, lvii (63), 356-7.

MUNSELL, Joel
Joel Munsell: printer and bibliographer. PBSA, xliii (49), 383-96.
D. S. Edelstein.

Joel Munsell prints Lossing's *Memorial of Alexander Anderson*. PBSA, xlv (51), 351-5.
D. S. Edelstein.

MURPHY, James
Sydney Smith's contributions to the *Edinburgh Review*. LIB, viii (53), 275-8.

MURRAY, David
David Murray: a bibliographical memoir. GBSR, xii (36), 41-81.
S. W. Murray.

MURRAY, Eustace Clare Grenville
By Lytton or Grenville Murray? (Query, 73), BC, v (56), 281-2.
C. S. A. Dobson.

MURRAY, Judith (Sargent) Stevens
[Murray, Judith (Sargent) Stevens]: *Some deductions from the system promulgated in the page of Divine Revelation*. PBSA, xl (46), 232-3.
J. E. Alden.

MURRAY, John
The Murray reprints of George Crabbe: a publisher's record. SB, iv (51), 192-9.
F. P. Batdorf.

MURRAY, Peter B.
The authorship of *The Revenger's Tragedy*. PBSA, lvi (62), 195-218.

The collaboration of Dekker and Webster in *Northward Ho* and *Westward Ho*. PBSA, lvi (62), 482-6.

MURRAY, Sylvia W.
David Murray, a bibliographical memoir. GBSR, xii (36), 41-81.

MURRIE, Eleanore Boswell
Notes on the printers and publishers of English song-books, 1651-1702. EBST, i (35/8), 241-76.

Playford *versus* Pearson. LIB, xvii (36/7), 427-47.

—. *and* DAY, Cyrus Lawrence
English song-books, 1651-1702, and their publishers. Illus. LIB, xvi (35/6), 355-401.

MUSAE ANGLICANAE
Musae Anglicanae: a supplemental list. LIB, xxii (67), 93-103.
L. Bradner.

MUSARUM PANAGYRIS
The first Aldine. [*Musarum Panagyris*]. PBSA, xlii (48), 269-80.
C. F. Bühler.

MUSGROVE, Sydney
Some manuscripts of Heywood's *Art of Love*. LIB, i (46/7), 106-12.

MUSIAD
Poe and *The Musiad*. PBSA, lix (65), 437-8.
H. Haycraft.

MUSIC
Musical epitaphs. (Query, 81). BC, vi (57), 181-2.
G. Handley-Taylor.

Untraced auction sale-catalogues of music. (Query, 148). BC, xi (62), 219.
A. H. King.

Music manuscripts lost during World War II. BC, xvii (68), 26-36.
C. Smith.

Two unrecorded items in the Euing Music Collection. BTHK, i/3 (58), 44-5.
H. G. Farmer.

The music to Allan Ramsey's songs. BTHK, ii (59/60), 34.
H. G. Farmer.

Some leaves of a thirteenth-century missal probably from Jedburgh Abbey. [*With*] Notes on the music. EBST, iii (48/55), 1-15.
F. C. Eeles *and* J. H. Arnold.

The sources of Arabian music: a bibliography of Arabic MSS. which deal with the theory, practice and history of Arabian music. GBSR, xiii (39).
H. G. Farmer.

New music types. Invention in the eighteenth century: I. Illus. JPHS, i (65), 21-38.
H. E. Poole.

New music types. Invention in the eighteenth century: II. Illus. JPHS, ii (66), 23-44.
H. E. Poole.

Notes on early music printing. Illus. LIB, xix (38/9), 389-421.
B. Pattison.

The liturgical music incunabula in the British Museum. LIB, xx (39/40), 274-94.
K. Meyer.

Music bibliography and catalogues. Illus. LIB, xxiii (42/3), 151-70.
O. E. Deutsch.

Recent work in music bibliography. LIB, xxvi (45/6), 122-48.
A. H. King.

English pictorial music title-pages, 1820-1885. Illus. LIB, iv (49/50), 262-72.
A. H. King.

Manuscript collections of British folk music, etc. [A letter]. LIB, xiii (58), 63.
S. E. Jackson.

A collection of musical manuscripts in the autograph of Henry Purcell and other English composers, c. 1665-85. LIB, xiv (59), 126-31.
H. W. Shaw.

Early music publishing in the United States. PBSA, xxxi (37), 176-9.
O. Strunk.

MUSSON, Albert Edward
The London Society of Master Letter-Founders, 1793-1820. LIB, x (55), 86-102.

MYER, Charles
See MAYER, Charles

MYNORS, Sir Roger Aubrey B.
A fifteenth century scribe: T. Werken. [With] List of manuscripts written by T. Werken. Illus. TCBS, i (49/53), 97-104.

N

N.LL.
Milton, N.LL, and Sir Tho. Urquhart. Illus. LIB, xiv (33/4), 470-6.
H. C. H. Candy.

—. [A letter]. LIB, xv (34/5), 249-50.
D. W. Pendleton.

NAIRN, Audrey
A 1731 copyright list from Glasgow University archives. BTHK, ii (59/60), 30-2.

The work of a Glasgow University printer. BTHK, ii (60), 69-71.

NAPIER, William
Haydn's settings of Scottish songs in the collections of Napier and Whyte. Illus. EBST, iii (48/55), 85-120.
C. Hopkinson *and* C. B. Oldman.

NAPOLEON I *emperor of the French*
Napoleon's travelling library. (Query, 113). BC, vii (59), 308-9.
P. E. Spielmann.

(Query, 113). BC, viii (59), 308-9.
E. R. Gill.

NASH, Ray
Rastell fragments at Dartmouth. Illus. LIB, xxiv (43/4), 66-73.

An American colonial calligraphic sheet of King Charles's Twelve Good Rules at Dartmouth College Library. Illus. LIB, vii (52), 111-16.

NASH, Thomas
Was the first edition of *Pierce Penniless* a piracy? LIB, vii (52), 122-4.
Sir W. W. Greg.

NATHANSON, H.
The first edition of Carroll's *Phantasmagoria,* 1869. (Query, 116). BC, viii (59), 184.

NATHANSON, Leonard
Variants in Robert Wilson's *The Three Lords.* LIB, xiii (58), 57-9.

NATION
The publication of James Stephens's short stories in *The Nation*. PBSA, lviii (64), 476-7.
P. McFate.

NATIONAL LIBRARY OF IRELAND
Manuscript versions of Yeats's *The Shadowy Waters*, an abbreviated description and chronology of the papers relating to the play in the National Library of Ireland. PBSA, lxii (68), 39-57.
M. J. Sidnell.

NATIONAL LIBRARY OF MEDICINE
See UNITED STATES *nat. libr. of medicine.*

NATIONAL LIBRARY OF SCOTLAND
Special catalogues in the Department of Printed Books in the National Library of Scotland. BTHK, iii (60/2), 173-82.
M. P. Linton.

A note on the content of the Thorkelin collection in the National Library of Scotland. BTHK, iv (63/6), 79-80.
D. W. Evans.

Two Ratisbon manuscripts in the *National Library of Scotland*. BTHK, v (67/70), 24-32.
M. Dilworth.

Supplement to the Handlist of incunabula in the National Library of Scotland. Illus. [*and*] Second supplement. EBST, ii (38/45), 151-251, 331-51.
W. Beattie.

Sir George Mackenzie's speech at the formal opening of the advocates' Library, Edinburgh, 15th March 1689, EBST, ii (38/45), 273-84.
J. H. Loudon.

The first twenty years of the National Library of Scotland, 1925-1945. I. Manuscripts. II. Printed books. EBST, ii (38/45), 285-302.
M. R. Dobie *and* W. Beattie.

A palimpsest in the National Library of Scotland: early fragments of Augustine *De Trinitate*, the *Passio S. Laurentii* and other texts. Illus. EBST, iii (48/55), 169-78.
N. R. Ker.

National Library of Scotland and Edinburgh University Library copies of plays in Greg's *Bibliography of the English Printed Drama.* SB, xvi (62), 91-104.
M. P. Linton.

NATURA BREVIUM
Notes on a Pynson volume [comprising *Old Tenures*; *Natura Brevium*; and Littleton, *Tenures Novelli*]. LIB, xviii (37/8), 261-7.
C. F. Bühler.

NATURAL HISTORY
America — a hunting ground for eighteenth-century naturalists with special reference to their publications about trees. PBSA, xxxii (38), 1-16.
J. R. Butler.

NATURA VERBORUM
Natura verborum. [Paris] Pierre Levet [about 1488]. PBSA, xxxiv (40), 357.
H. R. Mead.

NATURE PRINTING
Henry Bradbury's nature printed books. Illus. LIB, xxi (66), 63-7.
G. Wakeman.

NAVAL BINDER
A binding by the Naval binder, *c.* 1675. (English bookbindings, 12). Illus. BC, iv (55), 45-7.
H. M. Nixon.

NEBENZAHL, Kenneth
A stone thrown at the map maker. PBSA, lv (61), 283-8.

NEGRO WRITING
Early American Negro writings: a bibliographical study. PBSA, xxxix (45), 192-268.
D. B. Porter.

NEILL, Desmond George
A poem by Mrs. Centlivre. (Note, 95). BC, vii (58), 189-90.

Samuel Parr's *Notes on Rapin's Dissertation on Whigs and Tories*. (Note, 158). BC, x (61), 199-200.

A new address for Christian Kalthoeber. LIB, xvii (62), 95.

John Case, *The Praise of Musicke*. PBSA, liv (60), 293.

NEKTARIOS *patriarch of Jerusalem*
Nektarios, patriarch of Jerusalem. (1605-1685). PBSA, xxxvii (43), 233-5.
E. C. Skarshaug.

NESMITH, James W.
Addendum to Belknap, Oregon imprints, No. 7: Nesmith's *To the world!!* PBSA, lxiii (69), 128-9.
G. N. Belknap.

NETHERY, Wallace
Early editions of Giordano Bruno at the University of Southern California. (Note, 238). BC, xiv (65), 74-5.

On the origin of species, 1859. (Note, 297). BC, xvii (68), 215.

Hume's manuscript corrections in a copy of *A Treatise of Human Nature*. PBSA, lvii (63), 446-7.

NEUBURG, Victor Edward R.P.
The Diceys and the chapbook trade. Illus. LIB, xxiv (69), 219-31.

NEUDOERFFER, Norma C.
The function of a nineteenth-century catalogue belonging to the Cambridge Philosophical Library. TCBS, iv (64/8). 293-301.

NEVILLE, Roy G.
Spadacrene Anglica. (Note, 47). BC, iv (55), 170-1.

Matte Lafaveur's *Pratique de Chymie*, 1671. (Note, 57). BC, iv (55), 330-1.

Digby's *Philosophical account of Nature*, 1722. (Note, 92). BC, vii (58), 79.

An unrecorded Dalton prospectus, 1808. (Note, 112). BC, viii (59), 295.

Boerhaave's *Elementa Chemiae*, 1732. (Note, 121). BC, viii (59), 428-9.

Manuscripts of Dr. T. C. Hope's chemical lectures. (Query, 139). BC, x (61), 73-5.

Macquer's *Dictionnaire de chymie* 1766. (Note, 280). BC, xv (66), 484-5.

NEWBERRY LIBRARY
See also CHICAGO *Newberry libr.*

NEWBERRY LIBRARY
A Newberry Library Supplement to the foreign books in M. J. D. Cockle's *A Bibliography of English Military Books up to 1642 and of contemporary Foreign Works*. PBSA, lv (61), 137-9.
J. R. Hale.

NEWBERY, Francis
Francis Newbery: a question of identity. (Query, 172). BC, xii (63), 495-6.
S. Roscoe.

NEWBERY, John
The ghost of Newbery's Smart's Pope's *Ode on St. Cecilia's day*. BC, xv (66), 215.
S. Roscoe.

Richard Johnson and the successors to John Newbery. LIB, iv (49/50), 25-63.
M. J. P. Weedon.

John Newbery, projector of the *Universal Chronicle*: a study of the advertisements. SB, xi (58), 249-51.
G. J. Kolb.

NEWCASTLE-UPON-TYNE
The earliest Newcastle binder's ticket. (Note, 296). BC, xvii (68), 81-2.
W. S. Mitchell.

NEWCASTLE-UPON-TYNE *univ. libr.*
'A Newcastle collection of wood blocks' [in the University Library, Newcastle-upon-Tyne]. Illus. BC, xvii (68), 443-57.
F. M. Thomson.

A Newcastle collection of wood blocks [by F. M. Thomson]. BC, xviii (69), 384-5.
S. Roscoe.

Chapbooks with Scottish imprints in the Robert White collection, the University Library, Newcastle-upon-Tyne. BTHK, iv (63/6), 88-174.
F. W. Ratcliffe.

Scottish ballads and music in the Robert White collection in the University Library, Newcastle-upon-Tyne. BTHK, v (67/70), 138-41.
C. Hunt.

NEWCOMB, Thomas
Thomas Newcomb: a Restoration printer's ornament stock. Illus. SB, iii (50), 155-70.
C. W. Miller.

The printer of Harvard's *Humble Proposal*, 1659 [i.e. Thomas Newcombe, not the Cambridge, Mass., Press]. SB, iv (51), 199-201.
B. C. Cooper *and* R. E. Hasker.

NEWCOME, Henry
Newcome's Academy and its plays. LIB, xiv (33/4), 339-47.
E. A. Jones.

NEWCOME'S ACADEMY
See NEWCOME, Henry

NEW ENGLAND
New England authors. (Contemporary collectors, 36). Illus. BC, xii (63), 467-75.
P. D. Howe.

Unrecorded verse broadsides of seventeenth-century New England. Illus. PBSA, xxxix (45), 1-19.
H. S. Jantz.

The literature of the New England earthquake of 1755. PBSA, lix (65), 295-305.
C. E. Clark.

Financing the publication of early New England sermons. SB, xi (58), 163-78.
R. G. Silver.

NEW ENGLAND PRIMER IMPROVED
The New-England Primer, improved. Litchfield, 1792. [&c.]. PBSA, xxxiv (40), 189.
A. C. Bates.

NEW FRANCE
The Jesuit relations from New France. PBSA, xxx (36), 110-49.
L. C. Wroth.

NEW HAMPSHIRE
The beginnings of printing in New Hampshire. Illus. LIB, xv (34/5), 340-63.
D. C. McMurtrie.

NEW JERSEY
The first testaments printed in New Jersey. PBSA, xlv (51), 148-51.
G. C. Rockefeller.

A short account of the first settlement of the Provinces of Virginia, Maryland, New-York, New-Jersey, and Pennsylvania, by the English. London, 1735. PBSA, xxxvi (42), 231.
N. B. Wainwright.

NEWMAN, Franklin B.
A consideration of the bibliographical problems connected with the first edition of Humphry Clinker. PBSA, xliv (50), 340-71.

NEWMAN, John Henry card.
J. H. Newman. The Dream of Gerontius, 1866. (Note, 64). BC, v (56), 171.
J. Carter.

NEWMYER, R. Kent
John Andrews's History of the War with America: a further note on eighteenth-century plagiarism. PBSA, lv (61), 385-92.

A nineteenth-century view of the historiography of American Revolution: a footnote on plagiarism. PBSA, lviii (64), 164-9.

NEWSBOOKS
See NEWSPAPERS

NEW SPAIN
The frontier presidios of New Spain: books, maps and a selection of manuscripts relating to the Rivera expedition of 1724-1728. PBSA, xlv (51). 191-218.
L. C. Wroth.

NEWSPAPERS
The circulation of newspapers and literary periodicals, 1700-30. LIB, xv (34/5), 110-24.
J. R. Sutherland.

English newsbooks, 1620-1641. LIB, xviii (37/8), 355-84.
L. W. Hanson.

Short-title catalogue of English corantos and newsbooks, 1620-1642. Illus. LIB, xix (38/9), 44-98.
F. Dahl.

Amsterdam — cradle of English newspapers. Illus. LIB, (49/50), 166-78.
F. Dahl.

An unrecorded English coranto. LIB, viii (53), 125-6.
J. G. McManaway.

The bibliography of newspapers and the writing of history. LIB, ix (54), 153-75.
S. Morison.

The circulation of newspapers in the reign of Queen Anne. LIB, xxiii (68), 206-35.
H. L. Snyder.

Anti-masonic newspapers, 1826-1834. PBSA, xxxii (38), 71-97.
M. W. Hamilton.

Louis Richard Certambert and the first French newspapers in Saint Louis, 1809-1854. PBSA, xxxiv (40), 221-53.
J. F. McDermott.

Soldier newspapers of the Civil War. Illus. PBSA, xlvi (52), 373-86.
E. Lutz.

The circulation of some London newspapers, 1806-1811: two documents. SB, vii (55), 190-4.
R. L. Haig.

A hand-list of English provincial newspapers and periodicals 1700-1760. Additions and corrections. Monogr. 2. TCBS, ii (54/8), 269-74.
G. A. Cranfield.

—. Further additions and corrections by R. Wiles. TCBS, ii (54/8), 385-9.

Early provincial newspapers in Reading university library. TCBS, iv (64/8), 256.
D. T. O'Rourke.

NEWTON, Sir Isaac
See also MABBUT, George, Tables for purchasing leases.

More light required [on the Ownership of a copy of Newton's Opticks 1704]. (Query, 137). BC, x (61), 73.
H. D. Lyon.

A census of the owners of copies of the 1687 first edition of Newton's Principia. Illus. PBSA, xlvii (53), 269-300.
H. P. Macomber.

NEWTON, John
Hand-list of manuscripts in the Cowper and Newton museum, Olney, Bucks. TCBS, iv (64/8), 107-27.
K. Povey.

NEW YORK city, Carl H. Pforzheimer libr.
Note on the Pforzheimer Catalogue. [A letter]. PBSA, xl (46), 159.
W. A. Jackson.

NEW YORK *city, Pierpont Morgan libr.*
The children's books exhibition at the Pierpont Morgan library. Illus. BC, iv (55), 34-44.
W. Schatzki.

The Morgan copy of Machlinia's *Speculum Christiani.* SB, v (52), 159-60.

NEW YORK *city, public libr.*
A doctor's benefaction: the Berg collection at the New York Public Library. PBSA, xlviii (54), 303-14.
J. D. Gordan.

Identification of New York Public Library manuscript 'Suckling collection' and of Huntington manuscript 198. SB, xix (66), 215-16.
C. M. Armitage.

Henry Loosemore's organ-book [now in New York Public Library, Drexel 5469]. TCBS, iii (59/63), 143-51.
T. Dart.

NEW YORK *city, univ., King's Coll.*
American imprints concerning King's College. PBSA, xliv (50), 301-39.
B. McAnear.

NEW YORK *colony*
New York (Colony). Statutes. *At a Session of the General Assembly of the Colony of New-York, held at the City-Hall in the City of New-York; began the 4th April, 1769, . . . and continued . . . to the 20th of May following.* New-York, 1769. PBSA, xxxiv (40), 87-8.
G. D. McDonald.

A short account of the first settlement of the Provinces of Virginia, Maryland, New-York, New-Jersey, and Pennsylvania, by the English. London, 1735. PBSA, xxxvi (42), 231.
N. B. Wainwright.

NEW YORK *state, univ., Buffalo, Lockwood Memorial libr.*
Ulysses notebook VIII. A.5 at Buffalo. SB, xxii (69), 287-310.
P. F. Herring.

NEW YORK WEEKLY REVIEW
Mark Twain material in the *New York Weekly Review.* PBSA, lii (58), 56-62.
P. J. Carter.

NICHOLES, Eleanor Louise
Leigh Hunt's *Feast of the poets*: Boston 1813 edition. (Note, 321). BC, xviii (69), 515-18.

NICHOLS, John
John Nichols and Hutchins's *History and Antiquities of Dorset.* LIB, xv (60), 81-95.
A. H. Smith.

NICHOLS, Philip
The case of Philip Nichols, 1731. TCBS, i (49/53), 422-31.
O. Chadwick.

NICHOLSON, Margaret
The U.L.C. copy of *Posthumous fragments of Margaret Nicholson.* TCBS, iii (59/63), 423-7.
B. Dickins.

NICHOLSON, Meredith
The ABA issue of Meredith Nicholson's *A Hoosier chronicle*, 1912. PBSA, lx (66), 223-4.
G. T. Tanselle.

NICKERSON, Charles C.
Gibbon's copy of Steele's *Dramatick Works.* (Note, 217). BC, xiii (64), 207.

NICKERSON, Charles Freeman
Nickerson, Freeman (fl. 1850). *Death of the prophets Joseph and Hyram Smith.* Boston, 1844. PBSA, xxxv (41), 160.
C. Eberstadt.

NICKERSON, Mildred E.
Howells and Salvini. PBSA, lx (66), 86-9.

NICOLAY, Frederick
Frederick Nicolay, 1728/9-1809. (Portrait of a bibliophile, 5). Illus. BC, ix (60), 401-13.
A. H. King.

NIETZSCHE, Friedrich
Friedrich Nietzsche *Also sprach Zarathustra.* (Note, 313). BC, xviii (69), 221-2.
P. H. Muir.

NIMS, John Frederick
The greatest English lyric? — A new reading of Joe E. Skilmer's *Therese.* Illus. SB, xx (67), 1-14.

NINEHAM, Ruth
K. Pellens' edition of the tracts of the *Norman Anonymous.* TCBS, iv (64/8), 302-9.

NIXON, Howard Millar
Restoration binding, circa 1680. (English bookbindings, 1). Illus. BC, i (52), 2-3.

Gilt binding by John Reynes. *c.* 1521-4. (English bookbindings, 2). Illus. BC, i (52), 94-5.

Binding by Richard Montagu for Thomas Hollis, 1758. (English bookbindings, 3). Illus. BC, i (52), 182-4.

London binding for King Edward VI, *c.* 1550. (English bookbindings, 4). Illus. BC, i (52), 244-5.

An eighteenth century London binding, *c.* 1764. (English bookbindings, 5). Illus. BC, ii (53), 66-7.

An early English panel-stamped binding. (English bookbindings, 6). Illus. BC, ii (53), 140-1.

Binding by T. J. Cobden-Sanderson, 1888. (English bookbindings, 7). Illus. BC, ii (53), 212-13.

A binding presented to Edward VI, c. 1552. (English bookbindings, 8). Illus. BC, ii (53), 272-3.

A Cambridge binding, perhaps by Daniel Boyse, c. 1627, (English bookbindings, 9). Illus. BC, iii (54), 50-1.

A London binding by Charles Lewis, 1812. (English bookbindings, 10). Illus. BC, iii (54), 134-5.

An Irish bookbinding probably bound for Lord Carteret, c. 1725-30. Illus. BC, iii (54), 216-17.

A binding from Southey's 'Cottonian' Library. (English bookbindings, 11). Illus. BC, iii (54), 298-9.

A binding by the Naval binder, c. 1675. (English bookbindings, 12). Illus. BC, iv (55), 45-7.

A London binding by Richard Balley, 1700. (English bookbindings, 13). Illus. BC, iv (55), 144-5.

A binding for King Henry VIII, c. 1540. (English bookbindings, 14). Illus. BC, iv (55), 236.

A George III binding, c. 1810-20. (English bookbindings, 15). Illus. BC, iv (55), 308.

A London, binding by Fletcher, 1660. (English bookbindings, 16). Illus. BC, v (56), 53-4.

A London binding by Fletcher, c. 1662. (English bookbindings, 17). Illus. BC, v (56), 150.

A mosaic binding by A. de Sauty, c. 1904. (English bookbindings, 18). Illus. BC, v (56), 248.

A binding for John Carteret, 2nd Earl Granville, 1741. (English bookbindings, 19). Illus. BC, v (56), 368.

A mosaic binding for Lord Kingsale, 1720. (English bookbindings, 20). Illus. BC, vi (57), 60.

An angling binding by Thomas Gosden, c. 1825. (English bookbindings, 21). Illus. BC, vi (57), 170.

A binding by the Morocco binder, c. 1563. (English bookbindings, 22). Illus. BC, vi (57), 278.

A binding for Archbishop Parker, c. 1574. (English bookbindings, 23). Illus. BC, vi (57), 386.

A binding by James Hayday, c. 1845. (English bookbindings, 24). Illus. BC, vii (58), 62.

A binding by the Settle bindery, 1704. (English bookbindings, 25). Illus. BC, vii (58), 180.

An illuminated vellum binding for the Prince Consort, 1843. (English bookbindings, 26). Illus. BC, vii (58), 284.

A Cambridge binding by Titus Tillet, 1677. (English bookbindings, 27). Illus. BC, vii (58), 396.

The Baltimore binding exhibition. BC, vii (58), 419-26.

A London binding by Queens' binder B, c. 1675. (English bookbindings, 28). Illus. BC, viii (59), 50.

A binding by Lewis for Oliver Cromwell, 1656. (English bookbindings, 29). Illus. BC, viii (59), 168.

A binding by Daniel Search. (Query, 117). BC, viii (59), 184.

A binding by the Dudley binder, c. 1558. (English bookbindings, 30). Illus. BC, viii (59), 282.

Another binding for Oliver Cromwell. (Note, 117). BC, viii (59), 299-300.

A Newcastle binding by Lubbock, c. 1820. (English bookbindings, 31). Illus. BC, viii (59), 416.

Grolier's binders. Notes on the Paris Exhibition. 2 pts. Illus. BC, ix (60), 45-51; 165-70.

A binding from the Mearne shop, c. 1680. (English bookbindings, 32). Illus. BC, ix (60), 52.

A London binding by Francis Bedford, 1866. (English bookbindings, 33). Illus. BC, ix (60), 178.

A London binding by Henry Evans, c 1665. (English bookbindings, 34). Illus. BC, ix (60), 316.

A binding for Elizabeth I by the Initial binder, 1563. (English bookbindings, 35). Illus. BC, ix (60), 444.

A binding by the Small Carnation binder, c. 1680. (English bookbindings, 36). Illus. BC, x (61), 56.

A binding for William Bullein by the Initial binder, 1562. (English bookbindings, 37). Illus. BC, x (61), 184.

A binding from Charles Mearne's shop, 1685. (English bookbindings, 38). Illus. BC, x (61), 320.

A binding from the Samuel Mearne bindery, c. 1669. (English bookbindings, 39). Illus. BC, x (61), 440.

A binding supplied by John Bill to James I, c. 1621. (English bookbindings, 40). Illus. BC, xi (62), 62.

Grolier's Chrysostom. Illus. BC, xi (62), 64-70.

Grolier's binders. (Note, 171). BC, xi (62), 79, 213-4.

A gift from the maidens of the United Kingdom, 1874. (English bookbindings, 41). Illus. BC, xi (62), 204.

A Little Gidding binding, c. 1635-40. (English bookbindings, 42). Illus. BC, xi (62), 330.

A binding by John Brindley, 1743. (English bookbindings, 43). Illus. BC, xi (62), 466.

A London binding by the Medallion binder, c. 1545. (English bookbindings, 44). Illus. BC, xii (63), 60.

An Eton binding by Roger Payne, 1764. (English bookbindings, 45). Illus. BC, xii (63), 194.

A Pyramus and Thisbe binding, c. 1616. (English bookbindings, 46). Illus. BC, xii (63), 338.

A London binding by Queens' binder A, c. 1670. (English bookbindings, 47). Illus. BC, xii (63), 488.

A binding from the Caxton bindery, c. 1490. (English bookbindings, 48). Illus. BC, xiii (64), 52.

A Harleian binding by Thomas Elliot, 1721. (English bookbindings, 49). Illus. BC, xiii (64), 194.

A binding attributed to John de Planche, c. 1572. (English bookbindings, 50). Illus. BC, xiii (64). 340.

A London binding by John Mackinlay, c. 1810. (English bookbindings, 51). Illus. BC, xiii (64), 486.

A binding by Lord Herbert's binder, c. 1633. (English bookbindings, 52). Illus. BC, xiv (65), 60.

A binding by the Flamboyant binder, c. 1540-45. (English bookbindings, 53). Illus. BC, xiv (65), 200.

A binding by Alexander Cleeve, c. 1690. (English bookbindings, 54). Illus. BC, xiv (65), 348.

A binding designed by James Stuart, 1762. (English bookbindings, 55). Illus. BC, xiv (65), 538.

A Guild of Women-Binders binding, c. 1903. (English bookbindings, 56). Illus. BC, xv (66), 46.

An Adam binding, 1764 [for R. Adam's *Ruins of the palace of the emperor Diocletian at Spalatro*]. (English bookbindings, 57). Illus. BC, xv (66), 184.

Harleian bindings by Chapman, 1721. (English bookbindings, 58). Illus. BC, xv (66), 321-2.

A London panel-stamped binding, c. 1530, rebacked for James West, c. 1755. (English bookbindings, 59). Illus. BC, xv (66), 460.

British aid for Florence. Illus. BC, xvi (67), 29-35.

A binding for the Earl of Arundel, c. 1555. (English bookbindings, 60). Illus. BC, xvi (67), 54.

A London binding for Jonas Hanway, 1783. (English bookbindings, 61). Illus. BC, xvi (67), 194.

A binding by the centre-rectangle binder. (English bookbindings, 62). Illus. BC, xvi (67), 345.

A Cambridge binding by Ed. Moore, c. 1748. (English bookbindings, 63). BC, xvi (67), 481.

A binding by the Royal Heads binder, c. 1665. (English bookbindings, 64). Illus. BC, xvii (68), 44.

A binding by S. T. Prideaux, 1901. (English bookbindings, 65). Illus. BC, xvii (68), 190.

A binding by Katharine Adams. (English bookbindings, 66). Illus. BC, xvii (68), 331.

An Oxford binding by Roger Bartlett, c. 1670. (English bookbindings, 67). Illus. BC, xvii (68), 463.

An Oxford binding by Richard Sedgley, 1699. (English bookbindings, 68). Illus. BC, xviii (69), 62.

A binding by the MacDurnan gospels binder, c. 1570. (English bookbindings, 69). Illus. BC, xviii (69), 200.

An emblematic rococo binding, 1781. (English bookbindings, 70). Illus. BC, xviii (69), 360.

Cambridge binding by Garrett Godfrey, c. 1522. (English bookbindings, 71). Illus. BC, xviii (69), 490.

Roger Bartlett's bookbindings. Illus. LIB, xvii (62), 56-65.

The gilt binding of the Whittinton *Epigrams*, MS. Bodley 523. LIB, vii (52), 120-1.

NOCTES AMBROSIANAE
The first twenty-three numbers of the *Noctes Ambrosianae*. LIB, xii (57), 108-18.
A. L. Strout.

NOEL, Adrian
Limited editions. (Note, 38). BC, iii (54), 226-7.

NOLTE, Eugene A.
Michael Scott and *Blackwood's Magazine*: some unpublished letters. LIB, viii (53), 188-96.

NON EST MORTALE QUOD OPTO
'Non est mortale quod opto'. (Note, 141). BC, ix (60), 327-9.

—. (Note, 141). BC, x (61), 66.

—. (Note, 141). BC, x (61), 446.
J. B. Oldham.

—. (Note, 141). BC, x (61), 446.
B. Juel-Jensen.

—. (Note, 141). BC, xi (62), 211.
P. Morgan.

—. (Note, 141). BC, xvi (67), 507-8.
P. Morgan.

NORFLEET, Fillmore
A St. Memin plate, with some notes on other St. Memin portraits. Illus. SB, i (48/9), 185-7.

NORFOLK
Some aspects of the Norfolk book-trade, 1800-24. TCBS, iv (64/8), 383-95.
T. Fawcett.

NORFOLK, *Duke of*
The Duke of Norfolk's press. (Query, 40). BC, ii (53), 224.
J. P. W. Gaskell.

—. (Query, 40). BC, ii (53), 283.
W. B. Todd.

NORLAND, Howard B.
The text of *The maid's tragedy* [by F. Beaumont and J. Fletcher]. PBSA, lxi (67), 173-200.

NORMAN ANONYMOUS
The tracts of the *Norman Anonymous*: C.C.C.C. MS. 415. TCBS, iv (64/8), 155-65.
K. Pellens.

K. Pellens' edition of the tracts of the *Norman Anonymous*. TCBS, iv (64/8), 302-9.
R. Nineham.

NORRIS, Frank
Notes on Frank Norris's revisions of two novels. [*McTeague* and *A man's woman*]. Illus. PBSA, lxii (68), 256-9.
J. Katz *and* J. J. Manning.

NORTH, Luke
Addenda to Irish [W. R. Irish's *The modern American muse*]: Brown, North and Wild. PBSA, lxii (68), 452.
G. T. Tanselle.

NORTH AMERICA
Opening up northern North America. PBSA, xliii (49), 340-4.
B. Solis-Cohen.

NORTH AMERICAN REVIEW
Attribution of critical notices in the *North American Review*. PBSA, lviii (64), 292-3.
R. G. Dennis.

Twenty-eight additions to the canon of Lowell's criticism [from the *North American Review*]. SB, iv (51), 205-10.
F. de W. Miller.

A note on Lowell bibliography: the review [in the *North American Review*] of Howells' *Venetian Life* [wrongly attributed to G. E. Norton]. SB, iv (51), 210-1.
J. L. Woodress.

Identification of contributors to the *North American Review* under Lowell. SB, vi (54), 219-29.
F. De W. Miller.

NORTHUP, Clark Sutherland
An addition to Northup. [*On the Death of a Favourite Cat* reprinted]. (Note, 8). BC, i (52), 192.
M. Hussey.

NORTH-WEST PASSAGE
An Account of a voyage for the discovery of a North-West Passage. London, 1748-1749. PBSA, xxxvii (43), 308.
B. Solis-Cohen.

The Great Probability of a North West Passage: . . . , London, Thomas Jefferys, 1768. PBSA, xxxix (45), 319-20.
B. Solis-Cohen.

Opening up northern North America. PBSA, xliii (49), 340-4.
B. Solis-Cohen.

NORTON, Alice
Alice [Norton] and the Stationers. LIB, xv (34/5), 499-500.
Sir W. W. Greg.

NORTON, Charles Eliot
A note on Lowell bibliography: the review [in the *North American Review*] of Howells' *Venetian Life* [wrongly attributed to C. E. Norton]. SB, iv (51), 210-11.
J. L. Woodress.

NORTON, Frederick John
The library of Bryan Rowe, Vice-Provost of King's College, d. 1521. TCBS, ii (54/8), 339-51.

Italian printers 1501-1520. An annotated list, with an introduction. Illus. TCBS, Monog. 3 (58).

NORTON, Jane Elizabeth
Susanna Centlivre. (Some uncollected authors, 14). 2 pts. BC, vi (57), 172-8; 280-5.

Hannah Cowley, 1743-1809. (Some uncollected authors, 16). BC, vii (58), 68-76.

A travelling library. (Query, 91). BC, vii (58), 188.

Elizabeth Griffith, 1727-1793. (Some uncollected authors, 22). BC, viii (59), 418-24.

Mary Astell, 1666-1731. (Some uncollected authors, 27). BC, x (61), 58-65.

Mary Astell's *Serious Proposal to the Ladies,* 1694. (Note, 164). BC, x (61), 448.

The *Post Office London directory.* LIB, xxi (66), 293-9.

NORTON, Thomas *and* SACKVILLE, Thomas
Gorboduc, Ferrex and Porrex: the first two quartos. SB, xv (62), 231-3.
I. B. Cauthen.

NORWICH
An eighteenth-century book club at Norwich. LIB, xxiii (68), 47-50.
T. Fawcett.

NORWICH *cathedral priory libr.*
Medieval manuscripts from Norwich Cathedral priory. Illus. TCBS, i (49/53), 1-28.
N. R. Ker.

NORWOOD, Luella F.
Imposition of a half-sheet in duodecimo. LIB, i (46/7), 242-4.

NOSWORTHY, James Mansfield
The Marlowe manuscript. LIB, xxvi (45/6), 158-71.

Macbeth at the Globe. LIB, ii (47/8), 108-18.

A note on John Heminge. LIB, iii (48/9), 287-8.

The Southouse text of *Arden of Feversham.* LIB, v (50/1), 113-29.

Hand B in *Sir Thomas More.* LIB, xi (56), 47-50.

NOTARY, Julian
Julian Notary and Andrew Rose: two contemporary records. LIB, xi (56), 277-8.
C. E. Welch.

NOVEL
The three-volume novel. PBSA, lxi (67), 201-7.
D. C. Ewing.

NOWICKI, Andrzej
Early editions of Giordano Bruno in Poland. BC, xiii (64), 342-5.

NOYCE, Frank
Tod's *Annals of Rajast'han*. Illus. BH, i (47/51), 293-303.

NUMBERED AND SIGNED
Numbered and signed. (Query, 43). BC, ii (53), 283-4.
J. B. Oldham.

—. (Query, 43). BC, iii (54), 73.
P. M. Hill.

NUREMBERG CHRONICLE
A study of the *Nuremberg Chronicle*, PBSA, xxxv (41), 17-34.
D. C. Duniway.

O

OAKDEN, James Parker
The scribal errors of the MS. Cotton Nero A. x. LIB, xiv (33/4), 353-8.

OAKESHOTT, Sir Walter Fraser
Imago mundi. [Sir Walter Raleigh's copy of the work by Pierre d'Ailly]. (Collector's piece, 1). Illus. BC, xv (66), 12-18.

Winchester College library before 1750. Illus. LIB, ix (54), 1-16.

Sir Walter Raleigh's library. [A catalogue]. Illus. LIB, xxiii (68), 285-327.

OATES, John Claude T.
On collecting Sterne. Illus. BC, i (52), 246-58.

Seventeenth-century briefs at Cambridge. (Note, 11). BC, i (52), 264.

Thomas Gabitus. (Query, 20). BC, i (52), 267-8.

An early ownership rhyme. (Query, 27). BC, ii (53), 78.

A bookseller's stamp. (Query, 37). BC, ii (53), 222-3.

—. LIB, x (55), 125-6.

Cancel slips. (Note, 33). BC, iii (54), 145.

A bookseller's donation-label. (Note, 134). BC, ix (60), 192-5.

'Non est mortale quod opto'. (Note, 141). BC, ix (60), 327-9.

—. BC, x (61), 66.

An old boot at Cambridge. Illus. BC, x (61), 291-300.

Sir Geoffrey Keynes. (Contemporary collectors, 39). Illus. BC, xiii (64), 473-80.

The 'Costerian' *Liber precum*. [A letter]. LIB, iii (48/9), 65-6.

Booksellers' guarantees. LIB, vi (51), 212-13.

Richard Pynson and the Holy Blood of Hayles. Illus. LIB, xiii (58), 269-77.

Hot air from Cambridge. LIB, xviii (63), 140-2.

The little gest of Robin Hood: a note on the Pynson and Lettersnijder editions. SB, xvi (63), 3-8.

The G.U. Yule collection of the *Imitatio Christi* in the library of St. John's College. TCBS, i (49/53), 88-90.

The trewe encountre: a pamphlet on Flodden Field. Illus. TCBS, i (49/53), 126-9.

Cambridge books of congratulatory verses, 1603-1640, and their binders. Illus. TCBS, i (49/53), 395-421.

Notes on the bibliography of Sterne. I *Letters from Eliza to Yorick, 1775*. TCBS, ii (54/8), 155-69.

The deposit of books at Cambridge under the Licensing Acts, 1662-79, 1685-95. TCBS, ii (54/8), 290-304.

'English bokes concernying [i.e. belonging] to James Morice'. TCBS, iii (59/63), 124-32.

Fore-edge title in Cambridge University Library. Illus. TCBS, iii (59/63), 163-5.

Charles Burney's theft of books at Cambridge. TCBS, iii (59/63), 324-6.

The University Library catalogue of 1556: an addendum. TCBS, iv (64/8), 77-9.

—. *and* PINK, Harold Leslie
The sixteenth-century catalogues of the University Library. Illus. TCBS, i (49/53), 310-40.

—. *and others*
Walter Wilson Greg. 9 July 1875-4 March 1959. Illus. LIB, xiv (59), 151-74.

OBSERVATIONS SUR LE MÉMOIRE DE LA FRANCE
Observations sur le Mémoire de la France, envoyées dans les cours de l'Europe, par le ministère Britannique, pour justifier la réponse faite à la réquisition de S.M.T.C. du 21 décembre 1755. [Paris, 1756?]. PBSA, xxxiv (40), 361. E. B. Steere.

OCKHAM, William of
See WILLIAM *of Ockham*

O'CONNOR, Roger B.
BAL addenda. M. E. W. Freeman — entry No. 6380. PBSA, lxi (67), 127.

O'DONOGHUE, Michael *and* CHRISTOPHERS Richard Albert
Halkett and Laing [*Dictionary of anonymous and pseudonymous English literature*], continued. (Query, 186). BC, xiii (64), 360.

O'DONOVAN, Anne
Sale catalogue of Defoe's library. (Note, 147). BC, ix (60), 454-5.

OFFENBACHER, E.
An annotated MacCarthy-Reagh catalogue. (Note, 136). BC, ix (60), 452.

OFFICINA BODONI
Officina Bodoni exhibition Illus. BC, iii (54), 245-50. S. Morison.

OFFPRINTS
The origin of offprints. (Query, 85). BC, vi (57), 292. A. N. L. Munby.

—. BC, vi (57), 403. B. H. Breslauer.

OFFREDUS, Apollinaris
Hentisberus, Guilelmus. *Quaedam consequentiae subtiles* [Also] Blasius de Pelicanis, *De propositione* [and] Apollinaris Offredus *De suppositione* [Venice, Peregrinus de Pasqualibus, *c.* 1500]. PBSA, xxxv (41), 155. H. R. Mead.

Offredus, Apollinaris *De primo et ultimo instanti adversus Petrum Mantuanum*. [Pavia, Antonius Carcanus, 1482]. PBDS, xxxvi (42), 62. H. R. Mead.

OGILBY, John
Ogilby's coronation *Entertainment*, 1661-1689: editions and issues. PBSA, xlvii (53), 339-55.
F. T. Bowers.

OGILVIE, James D.
The *Cross Petition*, 1643. Illus. EBSP. Illus. EBSP, xv 30/5), 55-76.

Papers from an army press, 1650. EBST, ii (38/45), 420-3.

A bibliography of the Bishops' wars, 1639-40. GBSR, xii (36), 21-40.

OHIO
Nineteenth-century cadastral maps in Ohio [Based on a paper by H. F. Walling]. PBSA, lix (65), 306-15.
W. W. Ristow.

OKASHA, Elizabeth
The non-runic scripts of Anglo-Saxon inscriptions. Illus. TCBS, iv (64/8), 321-38.

OKELL, Benjamin
An abstract of the Patent Granted by His Majesty King George to Benjamin Okell, the Inventor of a Medicine. PBSA, xxxiv (40), 186.
G. L. Annan.

OKES, Nicholas
A proof-sheet from Nicholas Okes' printing-shop. Illus. SB, xi (58), 228-31.
J. R. Brown.

OLDCASTLE, John *lord Cobham*
Sir John Oldcastle: legend or literature? LIB, i (46/7), 179-83.
L. M. Oliver.

OLDHAM, Ellen M.
Lord Byron and Mr. Coolidge of Boston. (Note, 221). BC, xiii (64), 211-13.

OLDHAM, James Basil
A manuscript imprimatur. (Query, 29). BC, ii (53), 79.

Numbered and signed. (Query, 43). BC, ii (53), 283-4.

'Non est mortale quod opto'. (Note, 141). BC, x (61), 446.

Shrewsbury School library: its earlier history and organization. LIB, xvi (35/6), 49-60.

Note on some new tools used by the 'Unicorn binder'. Illus. LIB, ii (47/8), 283-4.

Shrewsbury School library. Illus. LIB, xiv (59), 81-99.

Note on the binding of Ushaw College XVIII c. 9b. TCBS, i (49/53), 46-7.

An unrecorded Cambridge panel. Illus. TCBS, i (49/53), 179-80.

An Ipswich master-stationer's tiff with his journeyman. [William Craighton]. TCBS, ii (54/8), 381-4.

OLDHAM, John
A bibliography of John Oldham, the Restoration satirist, b. 1653, d. 1863. OBSP, v (36), 1-38.
H. F. Brooks.

OLDMAN, Cecil Bernard
On the ascription of a Mozart aria. (Note, 201). BC, xii (63), 350.

'Drawback' in the book trade. (Query, 168). BC, xii (63), 494-5.

Haydn's settings of Scottish songs in the collections of Napier and Whyte. Illus. EBST, ii (48/55), 85-120.

Watermark dates in English paper. LIB, xxv (44/5), 70-1.

—. *and* HOPKINSON, Cecil
Thomson's collections of national song, with special reference to the contributions of Haydn and Beethoven. Illus. EBST, ii (38/45), 1-64.

—. Addenda et corrigenda. EBST, iii (48/55), 121-4.

OLDMIXON, John
A lost poem by Oldmixon. BC, xviii (69), 291-4.
J. P. W. Rogers.

The printing of Oldmixon's *Histories*. LIB, xxiv (69), 150-4.
J. P. W. Rogers.

OLD TENURES
Notes on a Pynson volume [comprising *Old Tenures; Natura Brevium;* and Littleton, *Tenures Novelli*]. LIB, xviii (37/8), 261-7.
C. F. Bühler.

OLDYS, William
Book prices past. [*A critical and historical account of the celebrated libraries in foreign countries*, ascribed to W. Oldys]. (Note, 278). BC, xv (66), 356.
W. Rees-Mogg.

OLIVER, Isaac
Isaac Oliver's portrait of Prince Henry and *Polyolbion*, a footnote. Illus. LIB, x (55), 206-7.
B. Juel-Jensen.

OLIVER, Leslie Mahin
Single-page imposition in Foxe's *Acts and Monuments*, 1570. LIB, i (46/7), 49-56.

Sir John Oldcastle: legend or literature? LIB, i (46/7), 179-83.

The Spanish Masquerado: a problem in double-edition. LIB, ii (47/8), 14-9.

The seventh edition of John Foxe's *Acts and Monuments*. PBSA, xxxvii (43), 243-60.

Thomas Drue's *Duchess of Suffolk*: a Protestant drama. SB, iii (50/1), 241-6.

OLIVI, Petrus Joannis
The *Quodlibeta* of Petrus Joannes Olivi. PBSA, l (56), 85-7.
D. E. Rhodes.

OLNEY *Cowper and Newton mus.*
Hand-list of manuscripts in the Cowper and Newton museum, Olney, Bucks. TCBS, iv (64/8), 107-27.
K. Povey.

ONG, Walter Jackson
Hobbes and Talon's Ramist rhetoric in English. TCBS, i (49/53), 260-9.

OPHTHALMIC STUDIES
Notes on a late-sixteenth century opthalmic work in English. [*A worthy treatise of the eyes*]. LIB, iii (47/8), 173-9.
F. N. L. Poynter.

OREGON
An Oregon miscellany. PBSA, lvii (63), 191-200.
G. N. Belknap.

Oregon printing before the *Spectator*. PBSA, lix (65), 50-5.
G. N. Belknap.

ORNAMENTS
Ornaments bearing printers' names. (Note, 100). BC, vii (58), 299.
A. D. McKillop.

John Wolfe, printer and publisher, 1579-1601. Illus. LIB, xiv (33/4), 241-88.
H. R. Hoppe.

The printers of the Coverdale Bible, 1535. Illus. LIB, xvi (35/6), 280-9.
L. A. Sheppard.

Some ornamental initials used by Plateanus of Wesel. LIB, xvi (35/6), 452-4.
H. McCusker.

Three 'owl' blocks: 1590-1640. Illus. LIB, xxii (67), 143-7.
J. A. Lavin.

Thomas Newcomb: a Restoration printer's ornament stock. Illus. SB, iii (50/1), 155-70.
C. W. Miller.

A London ornament stock 1598-1683. Illus. SB, vii (55), 125-51.
C. W. Miller.

Baskerville's ornaments. Illus. TCBS, i (49/53), 173-7.
J. Dreyfus.

ORNITHOLOGICAL STUDIES
Henry Bradley Martin. The ornithological collection. (Contemporary collectors, 35). Illus. BC, xii (63), 316-32.
G. W. Cottrell.

O'ROURKE, D. T.
Early provincial newspapers in Reading University library. TCBS, iv (64/8), 256.

ORRERY *1st earl of*
See BOYLE, Roger *1st earl of Orrery*

ORSINI, Gian Napoleone G.
Thomas Heywood's play on *The Troubles of Queen Elizabeth*. LIB, xvi (33/4), 313-38.

OSBORN, James Marshall
Reflections on Narcissus Luttrell, 1657-1732. Illus.

'That on Whiston' by John Gay. PBSA. lvi (62), 73-8.

James Marshall Osborn (Contemporary Collectors, 23). Illus. BC, viii (59), 383-96.
L. Witten.

OSBORNE, Edgar A
The first edition of *On the Origin of Species*. (Note, 130). BC, ix (60), 77-8.

—. BC, x (61), 446.

The earliest English 'Et Amicorum' inscription? (Note, 133). BC, ix (60), 192.

Cancellandum R2 in Boyle's *Sceptical Chymist* 1661. (Note, 176). BC, xi (62), 215.

A preliminary survey for a bibliography of the novels of Robert Bage. BH, i (47/51), 30-6.

Bibliography [of Sir John Franklin]. BH, i (47/51), 46-9.

Bibliographical notes [on the *Ghost Stories* of M. R. James]. BH, i (47/51), 253.

Early editions of Karl Marx's *Das Kapital*. BH, i (47/51), 265-6.

OSBORNE, Francis
Some notes on the bibliography of Francis Osborne. OBST, iv (52), 53-60.
F. F. Madan.

OSBORNE, Lucy Eugenia
Notes on errata from books in the Chapin library. LIB, xiii (32/3), 259-71.

Congress of the United States. *Acts of the First Congress.* New York, Francis Childs and John Swaine. [And] *Acts passed at a Congress . . . begun . . . On Wednesday the fourth of March, In the year M,DCC, LXXXIX.* Philadelphia, Francis Childs and John Swaine. PBSA, xxxv (41), 158.

OSBORNE, Thomas
T. Osborne's retirement. [A letter]. LIB, xvii (36/7), 363-4.
K. Latifi.

OSLER, Sir William
The Osler manuscript of Herbert's *Religio Laici*. LIB, xi (56), 120-2.
S. E. Sprott.

Osler, Sir William (1849-1919). *The principles and practice of medicine.* New York, 1892. PBSA, xxxv (41), 162.
W. White.

—. PBSA, xxxvi (42), 233.
W. White.

OSTERLEY PARK
The birds at Osterley Park. Illus. BH, i (47/52), 193-7.
P. J. Thomas.

O'SULLIVAN, Vincent James
Vincent O'Sullivan. (Some uncollected authors, 15). BC, vi (57), 395-402.
G. Sims.

O THE TWELFE DAY OF DECEMBER
The twelfth day of December: *Twelfth Night*, II, iii 91. [O the twelfe day of December]. SB, ii (49), 182-5.
I. B. Cauthen.

OTWAY, Thomas
The two 1692 editions of Otway's *Caius Marius*. SB, iii (50), 253-4.
H. Goldberg.

OUGHTRED, William
William Oughtred's *Arithmeticæ in numeris* or *Clavis Mathematicæ,* 1647; an unrecorded (unique) edition in Aberdeen university library. BTHK, v, 147-50.
P. J. Wallis.

William Oughtred's *Circles of proportion* and *Trigonometries*. TCBS, iv (64/8), 372-82.
P. J. Wallis.

OVENELL, Ronald Francis
Brian Twyne's library. OBSP, iv (50), 1-42.

OVERBURY, sir Thomas
The editions of the 'Overburian' characters. LIB, xvii (36/7), 340-8.
W. J. Paylor.

OVIDIUS NASO, Publius
Some manuscripts of Heywood's *Art of Love*. [A transl. of Ovid's work]. LIB, i (46/7), 106-12.
S. Musgrove.

George Sandys *v.* William Stansby: the 1632 edition of Ovid's *Metamorphosis*. LIB, iii (48/9), 193-212.
R. B. Davis.

Early editions of George Sandys's *Ovid*: the circumstances of production. PBSA, xxxv (41), 255-76.
R. B. Davis.

Two notes on running-titles as bibliographical evidence. [George Sandys, *Ovid's Metamorphosis*, 1632; and *Christ's Passion*, 1640]. PBSA, xlii (48), 143-8.
F. T. Bowers.

The first five bookes of *Ovids Metamorphosis*, 1621, Englished by master George Sandys. SB, i (48), 69-82.
J. G. McManaway.

A volume from the library of Sebald Pirckheimer? [Ovid's *Metamorphoses*. Parma, 1480]. SB, viii (56), 212-15.
C. F. Bühler.

In re George Sandys *Ovid*. SB, viii (56), 226-30.
R. B. Davis.

OVIEDO Y VALDES, Gonzalo Fernández
See FERNÁNDEZ de OVIEDO y VALDES, Gonzalo.

Biblioteca Ovetense: a speculative reconstruction of the library of the first chronicler of the Indies. PBSA, lvii (63), 157-83.
D. Turner.

OWEN, Dorothy Mary
'Vetus Repertorium', an early memorandum book of the diocese of Lincoln. TCBS, iv (64/8), 100-6.

OWEN, Warwick Jack B.
Letters of Longman & Co. to Wordsworth, 1814-36. LIB, ix (54), 25-34.

Costs, sales, and profits of Longman's editions of Wordsworth. LIB, xii (57), 93-107.

OWEN, Wilfred Edward S.
Wilfred Owen, 1893-1918. (English literary autographs, 48). Illus. BC, xii (63), 489.
T. J. Brown.

OWEN'S WEEKLY CHRONICLE
Early numbers of *The Morning Chronicle* and *Owen's Weekly Chronicle*. LIB, xx (39/40), 412-24.
P. B. Gove.

—. [A letter]. LIB, xxi (40/1), 95.
P. B. Gove.

OWNERSHIP MARKS
Ink smudge as a mark of ownership. (Query, 134). BC, ix (60), 458.
H. D. Lyon.

OWNERSHIP RHYMES
An early ownership rhyme. (Query, 27). BC, ii (53), 78.
J. C. T. Oates.

—.BC, ii (53), 222.
B. Harris.

OXFORD
An unrecorded Oxford *Quæstiones*, 1617. (Note, 284). BC, xvi (67), 81-2.
D. H. Woodward.

An Oxford collection [the William W. Clary collection, Honnold library, Claremont Colleges]. (Contemporary collectors, 44). Illus. BC, xvii (68), 177-89.
W. W. Clary.

Nineteenth-century decorated types at Oxford. Illus. JPHS, ii (66), inset.
J. Mosley.

Fragments of accounts relating to the Royal works from Oxford bindings, LIB, xxv (44/5), 66-7.
A. Deeley *and* S. Gibson.

Library co-operation in Oxford. OBSP, ii (29), 201-5.
S. Gibson.

Co-operation between college libraries. OBSP, iv (52), 43-52.
Sir H. H. E. Craster.

Fragments of medieval manuscript used as paste-downs in Oxford bindings, with a survey of Oxford binding, *c*. 1515-1620. Illus. OBSP, v (54).
N. R. Ker.

OXFORD *univ., Bodleian libr.*
The history of a manuscript [Bodleian MS. Junius 11]. Illus. BC, i (52), 6-13.
B. J. Timmer.

Manuscript notes in the Bodleian copy of Bright's *Characterie*. Illus. LIB, xvi (36), 418-24.
M. Doran.

The gilt binding of the Whittinton *Epigrams*, MS. Bodley 523. LIB, vii (52), 120-1.
H. M. Nixon.

Traherne's *Church's year-book* [Bodleian MS. Eng.th.e.51]. PBSA, lx (66), 31-72.
C. L. Marks.

OXFORD *univ., Christ Church, libr.*
Lists of Burton's library. Two lists of Robert Burton's library as distributed between (a) the Bodleian Library, (b) the library of his college, Christ Church, Oxford. Illus. OBSP, i (26), 222-46.
S. Gibson *and* F. R. Needham, *ed.*

OXFORD *univ., Corpus Christi coll., libr.*
The Library of Corpus Christi College, Oxford, in the sixteenth century. LIB, xviii (38), 385-416.
J. R. Liddell.

OXFORD *univ., Jesus coll., libr.*
The library of Jesus College, Oxford, with an appendix on the books bequeathed thereto by lord Herbert of Cherbury. Illus. OBSP, v (37), 49-115.
C. J. Fordyce *and* T. M. Knox.

OXFORD MOVEMENT
The British Critic and the Oxford Movement. SB, xvi (63), 119-37.
E. R. Houghton.

OXFORD NOVELS
A collection of Oxford novels. (Note, 143). BC, ix (60), 331-2.
C. K. Firman.

OXFORD UNIVERSITY PRESS
Specimens of printing types before 1850 in the typographical library at the University Press, Oxford. BC, viii (59), 397-410.
J. S. G. Simmons.

The Oxford partners: some notes on the administration of the University Press 1780-1881. JPHS, iii (67), 51-65.
C. Batey.

The undated Oxford broadsheet *Specimen*. Illus. LIB, xi (56), 11-17.
J. S. G. Simmons.

The first minute book of the Delegates of the Oxford University Press, 1668-1756. OBSP, vi (43).
S. Gibson *and* J. Johnson, *ed.*

Print and privilege at Oxford to the year 1700. Illus. OBSP, vii (46).
J. Johnson *and* S. Gibson.

OXINDEN, Henry
An early list of Elizabethan plays [in the commonplace book of Henry Oxinden]. LIB, xv (35), 445-56.
G. E. Dawson.

P

Φ *pseud.*
[The Bickhams and their *Universal Penman.*]
[A letter]. LIB, xxvi (45/6), 196.

P., H., *and* H., A. P.
Moor's *De Analogia Contractionum Linguae
Graecae.* BTHK, i/4 (58), 47-8.

P., W.
See PERKINS, William.

PACE, George B.
The text of Chaucer's *Purse.* SB, i (48/9),
103-21.

Chaucer's *Lak of Stedfastnesse.* SB, iv (51/2),
105-22.

The Chaucerian *Proverbs.* SB, xviii (65), 41-8.

Speght's Chaucer and MS. GG.4.27 [a *Canterbury Tales* MS. in Cambridge University Lib-
rary]. SB, xxi (68), 225-35.

PACIFIC
The early cartography of the Pacific. Illus.
PBSA, xxxviii (44), 87-268.
L. C. Wroth.

PACKMAN'S PATERNOSTER
John Taylor's piracy of *The Packman's Pater-
noster.* PBSA, lvii (63), 201-10.
L. H. Kendall, *jr.*

PADEN, William Doremus
A note on the variants of *In Memoriam* and
Lucretius. LIB, viii (53), 259-73.

Tennyson's *The Lover's Tale*, R. H. Shepherd,
and T. J. Wise. SB, xviii (65), 111-45.

PADUA
Three rare Paduan catalogues [in the Broxbourne library]. (Note, 249). BC, xiv (65),
361-2.
D. E. Rhodes.

PAFFORD, John Henry P.
Terms of the trade. (Note, 194). BC, xii (63),
203-4.

Binding costs, 1735. LIB, iii (48/9), 222-3.

The bibliography of Gilbert Burnet. [A letter].
LIB, vi (51/2), 126.

Defoe's *Proposals* for printing the *History of
the Union.* Illus. LIB, xi (56), 202-6.

PAFORT, Eloise
A group of early Tudor schoolbooks. LIB, xxvi
(45/6), 227-61.

Notes on the Wynkyn de Worde editions of the
Boke of St. Albans and its separates. SB, v
(52/3), 43-52.

PAGE, H. R.
Elliot Stock's devices. (Query, 76). BC, v (56),
384.

PAGE, Thomas Nelson
The manuscript of Page's *Marse Chan.* SB, ix
(57), 259-62.
J. R. Roberson.

PAIGE, Donald
An additional letter and booklist of Thomas
Chard, stationer of London. LIB, xxi (40/1),
26-43.

PAINE, Alfred W.
Mackenzie, Alexander (1763-1820). *Voyages
from Montreal . . . to the frozen Pacific ocean,
1789 & 1793.* London, 1802. PBSA, xxxiv (40),
360.

Meares, John (1756-1809). *Voyages made in the
years 1788 and 1789 from China to the north-
west coast of America.* London, 1790. PBSA,
xxxiv (40), 361.

Truxton, Thomas (1755-1822). *Remarks, instructions, and examples relating to latitude &
longitude.* Philadelphia, 1794. PBSA, xxxiv
(40), 362.

PAINE, J.
Chronicles of the 'Cherry Pickers'. BH, ii (51/2),
119-26.

PAINE, Thomas
W. T. Sherwin: a little-known Paine biblio-
grapher. PBSA, xlix (55), 268-72.
H. T. Meserole.

PAINTER, George Duncan
Denis Daly's library. (Note, 28). BC, ii (53),
282.

Incunabula in Cambridge University Library.
BC, iv (55), 51-7.

List of books acquired by the British Museum
from Chatsworth. Part I: Incunabula. BC, vii
(58), 401-6.

Chatsworth incunabula in the British Museum.
Addenda & corrigenda. (Note, 108). BC, viii
(59), 180-1.

The Goncourts and Frederick Hankey. (Note,
107 [really 167]. BC, x (61), 336-7.

A correction [to G. D. Painter's review of
F. R. Goff's *Incunabula in American libraries,
a third census,* 1964, in the *Book Collector,*
autumn 1965]. (Note, 266). BC, xv (66), 68.

Quincentenary [of the death of J. Gutenberg].
BC, xvii (68), 42-3.

A Horatian ghost. LIB, xi (56), 278-82.

—. *and* MORGAN, Paul, 1915-
The Caxton *Legenda* at St. Mary's, Warwick.
Illus. LIB, xii (57), 225-39.

PAINTINGS
Books in pictures. Illus. BC, xi (62), 175-83.
D. Gordon.

PALAEOGRAPHY
Latin palaeography since Traube. TCBS, iii (59/63), 361-81.
T. J. Brown.

PALGRAVE, Francis Turner
E typis Palgravianis. (Note, 51). BC, iv (55), 252.
D. F. Foxon.

The Golden Treasury, 1861. (Note, 52). BC, iv (55), 252-3.
D. F. Foxon.

—. (Note, 52). BC, v (56), 75.
D. F. Foxon.

PALL MALL GAZETTE
H. G. Wells's dramatic criticism for the *Pall Mall Gazette*. LIB, xvii (62), 138-45.
M. Timko.

PALSGRAVE, John
John Palsgrave's translation of *Acolastus*. LIB, xiv (33/4), 433-46.
P. L. Carver.

PALTSITS, Victor Hugo
George Watson Cole. PBSA, xxxiii (39), 22-4.

In memoriam: Augustus Hunt Shearer. PBSA, xxxv (41), 172-5.

Laurens, Henry (1724-1792). *Extracts from the proceedings of The High Court of Vice-Admiralty, in Charlestown, South-Carolina.* Charlestown, 1769. PBSA, xxxv (41), 294-7.

Proposals of Henry Stevens for a *Bibliographia Americana* to the year 1700, to be published by the Smithsonian Institution. Illus. PBSA, xxxvi (42), 245-66.

More data on a proposed *Bibliotheca Americana* of the Rev. Arthur Homer, D.D., in 1799. PBSA, xxxvii (43), 158-60.

The bibliophilic transactions of James Lenox with Bernard Quaritch, 1874-1880. PBSA, xl (46), 181-204.

PANEL STAMPS
See BOOKBINDERS' TOOLS

PANTAZZI, Sybille
Eugene Lee-Hamilton. PBSA, lv (61), 231-2.

—. PBSA, lvii (63), 92-4.

Four designers of English publishers' bindings, 1850-1880, and their signatures. Illus. PBSA, lv (61), 88-99.

PANTZER, Katharine F.
The serpentine progress of the *STC* revision. Illus. PBSA, lxii (68), 297-311.

PAPANTONIO, Michael
John Marshall and *The Infant's Library*. (Note, 180). BC, xi (62), 217.

PAPER
See also WATERMARKS

Whatman paper in a book dated 1757. (Query, 68). BC, viii (59), 72.
E. Wolf 2nd.

Notes on the size of the sheet. LIB, xxii (41), 105-37.
H. G. Pollard.

Paper saving in 1639. LIB, ii (47/8), 61.
Sir W. W. Greg.

Further notes on paper used in England after 1600. Illus. LIB, ii (47/8), 119-49.
E. Heawood.

Paper used in England after 1600. LIB, iii (48/9), 141-2.
E. Heawood.

Gilt. LIB, iii (48/9), 223.
R. W. Chapman.

Drawback on paper. LIB, iv (49/50), 73.
Sir F. C. Francis.

Bowyer's paper stock ledger. Illus. LIB, vi (51), 73-87.
H. Davis.

Note on eighteenth-century British paper. LIB, xii (57), 34-42.
J. P. W. Gaskell.

A trial list of Irish papermakers, 1690-1800. LIB, xiii (58), 59-62.
J. W. Phillips.

The paper-makers and the excise in the eighteenth century. Illus. LIB, xiv (59), 100-16.
R. C. Jarvis.

Paper as bibliographical evidence. Illus. LIB, xvii (62), 197-212.
A. H. Stevenson.

The Williamsburg paper mill of William Parks the printer. Illus. PBSA, xlviii (54), 315-33.
R. Goodwin.

Eustace Burnaby's manufacture of white paper in England. Illus. PBSA, xlviii (54), 315-33.
A. T. Hazen.

Russian watermarks and embossed paper-stamps of the eighteenth and nineteenth centuries. [Transl. by J. S. G. Simmons]. PBSA, lvii (63), 121-8.
S. A. Klepikov.

Baskerville and James Whatman. SB, v (52), 187-9.
A. T. Hazen.

PAPER WINDOWS
Printers' perks: paper windows and copy money. LIB, xv (60), 288-91.
D. F. McKenzie.

PAPYRIUS GEMINUS ELEATES.
See ELYOT, sir Thomas.

PARCHMENT
Medieval parchment-making. LIB, xvi (35/6), 113-7.
D. V. Thompson.

'Parchment' and 'vellum'. LIB, xvi (35/6), 439-43.
W. L. Ustick.

PARENTI, Marino
An Italian book printed in Soho. BH, i (47/51), 345-8.

PARGELLIS, Stanley
Gesner, Petzholdt, et al. PBSA, liii (59), 15-20.

PARIKIAN, Diana
Was Mr. Spooner advertising? (Note, 195). BC, xii (63), 204.

PARIS
A Paris imprint. (Query, 83). BC, vi (57), 291.
A. Ehrman.

PARIS bibl. nat.
Louix XIV, sa bibliothèque et le Cabinet du roi. LIB, xx (65), 1-12.
A. Jammes.

PARIS, Matthew
The handwriting of Matthew Paris. [Together with a] List of MSS. containing the handwriting of Matthew Paris. Illus. TCBS, i (49/53), 376-94.
R. Vaughan.

PARISER, Sir Maurice Philip
Thomas J. Wise's Verses, 1882 & 1883. (Query, 36). BC, ii (53), 283.

PARK, Julian
Tales of the Wild and the Wonderful. 1825. (Query, 104). BC, vii (58), 417.

PARKER, Alan Dean
James Joyce: addenda to Alan Parkes's bibliography. PBSA, xliii (49), 401-11.
W. White.

PARKER, Henry
Dives et Pauper. LIB, xiv (33/4), 299-312.
H. G. Pfander.

Dives and Pauper. LIB, xv (34/5), 31-7.
H. G. Richardson.

Pynson's manuscript of Dives and Pauper. LIB, viii (53), 217-28.
M. M. Morgan.

PARKER, Lester S.
Milton, Rothwell, and Simmons. LIB, xviii (37/8), 89-103.

Henry Vaughan and his publishers. LIB, xx (39/40), 401-11.

Fletcher's Milton: A first appraisal. PBSA, xli (47), 33-52.

Principles and standards of bibliographical description. PBSA, xliv (50), 216-23.

Wood's Life of Milton: Its sources and significance. PBSA, lii (58), 1-22.

Addenda to Irish [The modern American muse]: Theodora Taylor, Rixford J. Lincoln, David Bailey, Lester S. Parker. PBSA, lxiii (69), 198-200.
R. C. Johnson.

PARKER, Matthew abp. of Canterbury
A binding for Archbishop Parker, c. 1574. (English bookbindings, 23). Illus. BC, vi (57), 386.
H. M. Nixon.

Books and bookmen in the correspondence of Archbishop Parker. LIB, xvi (35/6), 243-79.
Sir W. W. Greg.

The dispersal of the monastic libraries and the beginnings of Anglo-Saxon studies. Matthew Parker and his circle: a preliminary study. Illus. TCBS, i (49/53), 208-37.
C. E. Wright.

PARKER, Stephen
Stephen Parker's fount of Irish type. LIB, x (55), 278-80.
J. W. Phillips.

PARKER, W. M.
Alexander Henderson, book-collector. EBST, ii (38/45), 452-3.

PARKER, William Riley
A cancel in an early Milton tract. [Animadversions upon the Remonstrant's Defence against Smectymnuus, 1641]. LIB, xv (34/5), 243-6.

Contributions toward a Milton bibliography. LIB, xvi (35/6), 425-38.

PARKER, Wyman W.
Henry Stevens: the making of a bookseller. PBSA, xlviii (54), 149-69.

Henry Stevens sweeps the states. PBSA, lii (58), 249-61.

PARKINSON, Richard
The issues of Richard Parkinson's Tour, 1805. (Note, 202). BC, xii (63), 350-5.
E. G. Howard.

PARKMAN, Francis
The sources and revisions of Parkman's Pontiac. PBSA, xxxvii (43), 293-307.
H. H. Peckham.

PARKS, George Bruner
William Barker, Tudor translator. PBSA, li (57), 126-40.

PARKS, Stephen
John Dunton and The works of the learned. LIB, xxiii (68), 13-24.

Booksellers' trade sales. LIB, xxiv (69), 241-3.

Justice to William Creech. PBSA, lx (66), 453-64.

PARKS, William
The Williamsburg paper mill of William Parks the printer. Illus. PBSA, xxxi (37), 21-44.
R. Goodwin.

William Parks' errata. PBSA, xlvi (52), 275.
J. C. Wyllie.

PARLEY, Peter *pseud.*
See GOODRICH, Samuel Griswold

PARLIAMENT
Parliament and the press, 1643-7. 2 pts. LIB, xiii (32/3), 399-424.
W. M. Clyde.

—. LIB, xiv (33/4), 39-58.

Great Britain. Parliament. *Anno regni Georgii II . . . At the Parliament begun and holden at Westminster, the tenth day of November, anno Dom. 1747. . . .* Reprinted by Timothy Green, Connecticut, 1752. [An act for regulating the commencement of the year . . .]. PBSA, xxxiv (40), 271-2.
A. C. Bates.

Great Britain. Parliament. *Directions of the Lords and Commons assembled in Parliament . . . for the electing and choosing of Ruling Elders . . . for the speedy settling of the Presbyteriall Government.* London, 1645. PBSA, xxxv (41), 204.
A. T. Hazen.

Great Britain. Parliament. *Directions . . . for the electing and choosing of Ruling-Elders . . . for the speedy settling of the Presbyteriall Government.* London, 1645. PBSA, xxxvi (42), 63-4.
H. R. Mead.

PARLIAMENTARY REPORTING
Anglo-American parliamentary reporting: a study in historical bibliography. PBSA, xlix (55), 212-29.
R. R. Rea.

PARMA, Blasius de, *de Pelicanis.*
Hentisberus, Guilelmus. *Quaedam consequentiae subtiles* (also) Blasius de Pelicanis, *De propositione* (and) Appollinaris Offredus *De suppositione* (Venice, Peregrinus de Pasqualibus, c. 1500). PBSA, xxxv (41), 155.
H. R. Mead.

PARNELL, Thomas
Bulmer's *Poems of Goldsmith and Parnell.* (Query, 109). BC, viii (59), 72.
S. Roscoe.

Parnell on Whiston. PBSA, lvii (63), 91-2.
C. J. Rawson.

PARR, Samuel
Samuel Parr, 1747-1825. (Some uncollected authors, 9). BC, v (56), 63-72.
J. Sparrow.

Samuel Parr's *Notes on Rapin's Dissertation on Whigs and Tories.* (Note, 158), BC, x 661), 199-200.
D. G. Neill.

PARREAUX, André
Beckford's *Vathek,* 'Londres 1791'. (Note, 99). BC, vii (58), 297-9.

PARRISH, Morris Longstreth
Haggard, Sir Rider (1856-1925). *King Solomon's Mines.* Lond., 1885. PBSA, xxxiv (40), 273.

PARRISH, Stephen Maxfield
Problems in the making of computer concordances. SB, xv (62), 1-14.

PARROTT, Thomas Marc
'Shakespeare and the new bibliography'. [A letter]. LIB, iii (48/9), 63-5.

Some notable errors in Parrott's edition of Chapman's Byron plays. PBSA, lviii (64), 465-8.
J. B. Gabel.

PARSONAGE, Douglas G.
An unrecorded German translation. [*Die Brittische Apocalypse*, London, 1784]. PBSA, liv (60), 69.

PARSONS, Coleman Oscar
Serial publication of *Traditions of Edinburgh.* LIB, xiv (33/4), 207-11.

PARSONS, Robert
Philip II and the printing of 'Andreas Philopater'. [R. Versteghen's abridged translation of R. Parsons's *Elizabethae edictum promulgatum Londini 29 Nouemb. Anno MDXCI, Andreae Philopatris . . . responsio*]. LIB, xxiv (69), 143-5.
A. J. Loomie.

PARSONS, Wilfrid
Researches in early Catholic Americana. PBSA, xxxiii (39), 55-68.

PART-ISSUES
Part-issues of Bell's *History of the British Crustacea,* 1844-53. (Query, 112). BC, viii (59), 73-4.
H. O. Bull.

PARTRIDGE, John
John Partridge and the Company of Stationers. SB, xvi (63), 61-80.
R. P. Bond.

PASTEDOWNS
See BOOKBINDING FRAGMENTS

PASTON, Edward
Edward Paston, 1550-1630: a Norfolk gentleman and his musical collection. TCBS, iv (64/8), 51-69.
P. Brett.

PATMORE, Henry John
Gosse and Henry Patmore's *Poems.* (Note, 155). BC, x (61), 71-2.
A. C. Berol.

PATON, George
George Paton's contributions to Herbert's *Typographical Antiquities.* EBST, iii (48/55), 213-9.
R. P. Doig.

PATON, Henry M.
Two Scottish literary ventures of the early eighteenth century. [Petitions of J. Adair and C. Slezer in the Register House archives]. EBST, ii (38/45), 423-6.

PATRONAGE
German Renaissance patrons of bookbinding. Illus. 2 pts. BC, iii (54), 171-89, 251-71.
G. D. Hobson.

Erasmus and his English patrons. LIB, iv (49/50), 1-13.
H. W. Garrod.

PATTEN, William
Trinity College, Cambridge, MS. B. 14. 52, and William Patten. Illus. TCBS, iv (64/8), 192-200.
B. Hill.

PATTERSON, Jerry E. and STANTON, William R.
The Ephraim George Squier manuscripts in the Library of Congress: a checklist. PBSA, liii (59), 309-26.

PATTISON, Bruce
Notes on early music printing. Illus. LIB, xix (38/9), 389-421.

PAUL IV pope
Binding for Pope Paul IV. PBSA, liii (59), 68-9.
A. H. Bonnell.

PAULDING, James Kirke
Publication dates of three early works by James Kirke Paulding. PBSA, lix (65), 49-50.
R. M. Aderman.

Some unrecorded poems of James Kirke Paulding: an annotated check-list. SB, iii (50), 229-40.
J. A. Robbins.

James Kirke Paulding's contributions to American magazines. SB, xvii (64), 141-51.
R. M. Aderman.

PAVIER, Thomas
Compositor B, the Pavier quartos, and copy spellings. SB, xxi (68), 131-61.
W. S. Kable.

PAYLOR, Wilfrid James
The editions of the 'Overburian' characters. LIB, xvii (36/7), 340-8.

PAYNE family
Roger and Thomas Payne: with some account of their earlier bindings. LIB, xv (60), 33-41.
R. Birley.

PAYNE, L. M.
A. Read's Manuall of Anatomy, 1634. [A letter]. LIB, ix (54), 58.

PAYNE, Roger
An Eton binding by Roger Payne, 1764. (English bookbindings, 45). Illus. BC, xii (63), 194.
H. M. Nixon.

PAYNE, Waveney R. N.
An irregular copy of Lamb's Tales from Shakespeare, 1807. (Query, 155). BC, xi (62), 485-6.

PEARSALL, Derek A.
Notes on the manuscript of Generydes. LIB, xvi (61), 205-10.

PEARSALL, Robert Brainard
Chronological annotations to 250 letters of Thomas Moore. PBSA, lxiii (69), 105-17.

PEARSON, Norman Holmes
Problems of literary executorship. SB, v (52/3), 3-20.

PEARSON, William
Playford versus Pearson. LIB, xvii (36/7), 427-47.
C. L. Day and E. B. Murrie.

PECCANT PAMPHLETS
See SYMONDS, John Addington

PECK, Louis Francis
An early copy of The Monk. PBSA, lvii (63), 350-1.

PECKHAM, Howard Henry
The sources and revisions of Parkman's Pontiac. PBSA, xxxvii (43), 293-307.

Bibliography and the collection of historical material. PBSA, lviii (64), 141-5.

PECKHAM, Morse
English editions of Philip James Bailey's Festus. PBSA, xliv (50), 55-8.

Dr. Lardner's Cabinet Cyclopaedia. PBSA, xlv (51), 37-58.

PEELE, George
The text of Peele's Edward I. SB, vii (55), 133-70.
D. J. Ashe.

The two compositors in the first quarto of Peele's Edward I. SB, vii (55), 170-7.
F. S. Hook.

PÉLADEAU, Marius B.
Some additional facts about Royall Tyler. (Note, 292). BC, xvi (67), 511-12.

PELICANIS, Blasius de Parma de.
See PARMA, Blasius de, de Pelicanis.

PELLENS, Karl
The tracts of the Norman Anonymous: C.C.C.C. MS. 415. Illus. TCBS, iv (64/8), 155-65.

K. Pellens's edition of the tracts of the Norman Anonymous. TCBS, iv (64/8), 302-9.
R. Nineham.

PENA, Petrus
Persistent remaindering (Pena and de L'Obels Adversaria, 1570-1618). PBSA, lii (58), 295-9.
A. E. Lownes.

PENDLETON, John W.
Milton, N.LL., and Sir Tho. Urquhart. [A letter]. LIB, xv (34/5), 249-50.

PENGUIN BOOKS
The Penguin collector. (Penguin books: three short essays). BC, i (52), 213-14.
J. Wellesley.

The Penguin achievement. (Penguin books: three short essays). BC, i (52), 211-13.
B. Crutchley.

PENINSULAR WAR
Printed playbills in the Peninsular war. TCBS, iv (64/8), 314-17.
B. Dickins.

PENN, William
The first edition of William Penn's *Great Case of Liberty of Conscience*, 1670. LIB, xvi (61), 146-9.
O. C. Goodbody *and* M. Pollard.

PENNANT, Thomas
The *Tours* of Thomas Pennant. Illus. LIB, xix (38/9), 131-54.
L. F. Powell.

PENNSYLVANIA
A short account of the first settlement of the Provinces of Virginia, Maryland, New-York, New-Jersey, and Pennsylvania, by the English. London, 1735. PBSA, xxxvi (42), 231.
N. B. Wainwright.

PENNSYLVANIA *Devon, Barbados Hill*
The library at Barbados Hill, Devon, Pennsylvania. (Contemporary collectors, 28). Illus. BC, x (61), 301-10.
B. Penrose.

PENROSE, Boies
The library at Barbados Hill, Devon, Pennsylvania. (Contemporary collectors, 28). Illus. BC, x (61), 301-10.

PEPPER, Robert D.
Francis Clement's *Petie schole* at the Vautrollier press, 1587. LIB, xxii (67), 1-12.

PEPYS, Samuel
Samuel Pepys: his shorthand books. LIB, xiv (33/4), 71-84.
W. J. Carlton.

Pepys's songs and songbooks in the diary period. LIB, xii (57), 240-55.
M. Emslie.

Pepys's copy of Moxon's *Mechanick Exercises*. LIB, xiv (59), 124-6.
H. Carter *and* B. Wolpe.

Two of Pepys's 'very lewd songs' in print. LIB, xv (60), 291-3.
M. Emslie.

The Pepys ballads. Illus. LIB, xxi (66), 282-92.
L. M. Goldstein.

Samuel Pepys's Spanish chap-books. 3 pts. TCBS, ii (54/8), 127-54, 229-68, 305-22.
E. M. Wilson.

A lost Pepys-Library book recovered. Illus. TCBS, iii (59/63), 292-4.
R. W. Ladborough.

PERALTA GRANT
The Peralta Grant: A lost Arizona story. PBSA, l (56), 40-52.
D. M. Powell.

PERCY, Henry *9th earl of Northumberland*
The library of the 'Wizard' Earl: Henry Percy, ninth Earl of Northumberland, 1564-1632. Illus. LIB, xv (60), 246-61.
G. Batho.

PERCY, Thomas *bp of Dromore*
Percy's relations with Cadell and Davies. LIB, xv (34/5), 224-36.
T. Shearer *and* A. Tillotson.

Bishop Percy's annotated copy of Lord Hailes's *Ancient Scottish Poems*. EBST, ii (38/45), 432-7.
A. F. Falconer.

The country parson as research scholar: Thomas Percy, 1760-1770. PBSA, liii (59). 219-39.
C. Brooks.

PERIODICALS
The circulation of newspapers and literary periodicals, 1700-30. LIB, xv (34/5), 110-24.
J. R. Sutherland.

A bibliography of Wordsworth in American periodicals through 1825. PBSA, lii (58), 205-19.
J. C. Barnes.

Fees paid to authors by certain American periodicals, 1840-1850. SB, ii (49), 95-104.
J. A. Robbins.

Lord Hailes's contributions to contemporary magazines. SB, ix (57), 233-44.
R. H. Carnie.

'My squeamish public': some problems of Victorian magazine publishers and editors. SB, xii (59), 21-40.
O. Maurer.

Magazine and other contributions by Mary Russell Mitford and Thomas Noon Talfourd. SB, xii (59), 218-26.
W. A. Coles.

A hand-list of English provincial newspapers and periodicals, 1700-1760. TCBS, Monog. 2. (52).
G. A. Cranfield.

—. Additions and corrections. TCBS, ii (54/8), 269-74.

—. Further additions and corrections. TCBS, ii (54/8), 385-9.
R. M. Wiles.

PERKINS, William
The authorship of *Foure Great Lyers*, 1585. LIB, xix (38/9), 311-14.
H. G. Dick.

PERKINSON, Richard H.
Additional observations on the later editions of *Nosce Teipsum*. LIB, ii (47/8), 61-3.

PERRET, Clément
Clément Perret, calligrapher. LIB, xi (56), 50-2.
C. Clair.

—. [A letter]. LIB, xi (56), 286.
C. Clair.

—. An addendum. LIB, xiii 58), 127-8.
C. Clair.

PERRINS, Charles William Dyson
C. W. Dyson Perrins. [Obituary notice]. LIB, xiii (58), 129.
H. G. Pollard.

PERRY, Thomas Sergeant
Thomas Sergeant Perry: four attributions. PBSA, lix 665), 57.
G. Monteiro.

Addenda to Harlow [V. Harlow's *Thomas Sergeant Perry: a biography:* two T. S. Perry essays. PBSA, lxii (68), 612-13.
G. Monteiro.

PERRY, William
William Perry, his academy and printing press in Edinburgh, and his publications. EBST, iv (55/71), 91-102.
A. Law.

PERRY, William Wallace
The quarto of Field's *Weather-Cocke*. LIB, i (46/7), 62-4.

The 1618 quarto of Field's *Amends for Ladies*. LIB, ii (47/8), 53-9.

Pen-and-ink corrections in seventeenth-century books. LIB, ii (47/8), 59-60.

Correction at press in the quarto of *Law-Trickes*. LIB, ii (47/8), 186-90.

Correction at press in *The Blind-Beggar of Bednal-Green*. PBSA, xli (47), 140-4.

PERSHING, James
Storage of printed sheets in the seventeenth century. LIB, xvii (36/7), 468-71.

The different states of the first edition of *Paradise Lost*. Illus. LIB, xxii (41/2), 34-66.

PERTH
Perth booksellers and bookbinders in the records of the Wright calling, 1538-1864. BTHK, i/4 (58), 24-39.
R. H. Carnie.

PETERS, Charlotte H. *and* FULTON, John Farquhar
An introduction to a bibliography of the educational and scientific works of Joseph Priestley. PBSA, xxx (36), 150-67.

PETERSON, Spiro
A 'lost' edition, 1745, of Defoe's Roxana. (Query, 99). BC, vii (58), 295.

PETRIE, James A.
Association copies. EBST, ii (38/45), 447-8.

PETTIT, Henry
Young's *Night-Thoughts* re-examined. LIB, iii (48/9), 299-301.

A check-list of Young's *Night-Thoughts* in America. PBSA, xlii (48), 150-6.

Further additions to the check-list of Young's *Night-Thoughts* in America. PBSA, xliv (50), 192-5.

PETZHOLDT, Julius
Gesner, Petzholdt, et al. PBSA, liii (59), 15-20.
S. Pargellis.

PFANDER, Homer G.
Dives et Pauper. LIB, xiv (33/4), 299-312.

PFORZHEIM, Jakob Wolff de
See WOLFF, Jakob *de Pforzheim*.

PFORZHEIMER, Carl Howard
See NEW YORK *city, Carl H. Pforzheimer libr.*

PHILADELPHIA
Philadelphia contributions to the book arts and book trade, 1769-1810. PBSA, xxxvii (43), 275-92.
H. G. Brown.

John Bioren: printer to Philadelphia publishers. PBSA, xliii (49), 321-34.
M. S. Carson *and* M. W. S. Swan.

PHILADELPHIA *libr. co.*
See LIBRARY COMPANY OF PHILADELPHIA.

PHILBRICK, Thomas L.
British authorship of ballads in the Isaiah Thomas collection. SB, ix (57), 255-8.

PHILES, George
George Philes: bookman. PBSA, xlviii (54), 1-48.
H. M. Lydenberg.

PHILIP, Ian Gilbert
Sir William Pickering and his books. BC, v (56), 231-8.

Roger Bartlett, bookbinder. Illus. LIB, x (55), 233-43.

Philip Bliss, 1787-1857, editor and bibliographer. Additions and corrections. OBSP, i (47), 40-2.

PHILIP II *king of Spain*
Philip II and the printing of 'Andreas Philopater'. LIB, xxiv (69), 143-5.
A. J. Loomie.

PHILIPS, John
Philip's *Cyder*, 1708. (Note, 150). BC, x (61), 68.
W. B. Todd.

PHILLIPPE, Jean
The devices of J. Phillippe and G. Wolf. (Note, 193). BC, xii (63), 203.
O. L. Shaw.

PHILLIPPS, James Orchard Halliwell-
Halliwell Phillipps and Trinity College Library. LIB, ii (48), 250-77.
D. A. Winstanley.

—. Additional note to — Halliwell Phillipps and Trinity College LIbrary. LIB, ii (48) 277-82.
R. W. Hunt.

Henry Hallam, *The Times* newspaper, and the Halliwell case. LIB, xviii (63), 133-40.
W. H. Bond.

PHILLIPPS, Sir Thomas *bart.*
Sir Thomas Phillipps and the disposal of his library. BC, v (56), 137-49.
A. N. L. Munby.

Phillipps manuscripts in Australia. BC, xi (62), 332-7.
K. V. Sinclair.

Joseph Hunter and Sir Thomas Phillipps. BC, xii (63), 37-43.
A. N. L. Munby.

Anastatic printing for Sir Thomas Phillipps. Illus. JPHS, v (69), 24-40.
G. Wakeman.

PHILLIPS, James W.
Richard Mountague, bookbinder. Illus. LIB, viii (53), 124-5.

Stephen Parker's fount of Irish type. LIB, x (55), 278-80.

A trial list of Irish papermakers, 1690-1800. LIB, xiii (58), 59-62.

The origin of the publisher's binding in Dublin. TCBS, ii (54/8), 92-4.

PHILLIPS, John
The John Phillips — John Milton *Angli Responsio*: editions and relations. PBSA, lvi (62), 66-72.
R. W. Ayers.

PHILLIPS, Robert S.
Shirley Jackson: a checklist. PBSA, lvi (62), 110-13.

Shirley Jackson: a chronology and a supplementary checklist. PBSA, lx (66), 203-13.

PHILLIPS, William L.
The first printing of Sherwood Anderson's *Winesburg, Ohio*. SB, iv (51/2), 211-13.

PHILLPOTTS, Eden
A ghost laid. [*The Ghost in the Bank of England*]. (Note, 226). BC, xiii (64), 350-1.
P. F. Hinton.

PHILOPATER, Andreas *pseud.*
See PARSONS, Robert

PHOTOGRAPHY
Phototransfer of drawings in wood-block engraving. Illus. JPHS, v (69), 87-97.
Sir P. Fildes.

Photographic reproduction versus quasi-facsimile transcription. [A letter]. LIB, vii (52), 135-7.
J. P. W. Gaskell.

PICKERING, Basil Montagu
The date of Blake's Pickering manuscript or the way of a poet with paper. SB, xix (66), 232-43.
G. E. Bentley, *jr.*

PICKERING, Sir William
Sir William Pickering and his books. BC, v (56), 231-8.
I. G. Philip.

PICKERSGILL, Frederick Richard
A forgotten indiscretion. [Pickersgill's illustrations to Milton's *Comus*, Routledge, 1858]. BC, xiii (64), 500.
P. F. Hinton.

'PIED BULL' *LEAR.*
See SHAKESPEARE, William, *King Lear.*

PIERPONT MORGAN LIBRARY
See NEW YORK *city, Pierpont Morgan libr.*

PIERRES, Philippe-Denis
An improved printing press by Philippe-Denis Pierres. Illus. JPHS, iii (67), 82-92.
D. Chambers.

PIERSON, Robert Craig
The revisions of Richardson's *Sir Charles Grandison*. SB, xxi (68), 163-89.

PIGOTT, John Hugh Smyth
The history of the Sneyd-Gimbel and Pigott-British Museum copies of Dr. Johnson's *Dictionary*. PBSA, liv (60), 286-9.
G. J. Kolb *and* J. H. Sledd.

PIGOTT, Harriet
Mrs. Thomson and Miss Pigott. (Note, 86). BC, vi (57), 293-6.
D. E. Rhodes.

—. BC, vii (58), 77-8.

—. BC, vi (57), 405.
H. W. Edwards.

PIGOUCHET, Philippe
Three *Horae ad usum Sarum* printed by Philippe Pigouchet. Illus. LIB, xix (38/9), 304/10.
C. F. Bühler.

PILLONE, *family*
The Pillone Library. Illus. BC, vii (58), 28-37.
A. R. A. Hobson.

PINDAR
Milton and the Harvard Pindar. Illus. SB, xvii (64), 77-82.
S. D. Atkins *and* M. Kelley.

PINEAS, Rainer
The authorship of the *Resurreccion of the Masse*. LIB, xvi (61), 210-13.

PINHOLES
Pinholes in the 1457 Psalter. Illus. LIB, xi (56), 18-22.
K. Povey.

PINHORN, Malcolm
Ernest Bramah's dates (Note, 228). BC, xiii (64), 352.

PINK, H. L. *and* OATES, John Claud T.
The sixteenth-century catalogues of the University Library. Illus. TCBS, i (49/53), 310-40.

PINKER, James
James Pinker to James Joyce, 1915-1920. SB, xxi (68), 205-24.
J. Firth.

PINNEY, Thomas
Letters of Thomas Babington Macaulay. (Query, 221). BC, xvii (68), 83.

PINTO, Vivian de Sola
The 1680 'Antwerp' edition of Rochester's *Poems*. LIB, xx (39/40), 105.

PIO, Leonello
Aldus's *Paraenesis* to his pupil, Leonello Pio. LIB, xvii (62), 240-2.
C. F. Bühler.

PIPER, Alfred Cecil
The booksellers and printers of Richmond, Surrey. LIB, xiii (32/3), 201-7.

PIRACY
Counterfeit printing in Jacobean times. Illus. LIB, xv (34/5), 364-76.
W. A. Jackson.

Captain Marryat and the American pirates. LIB, xvi (35/6), 327-36.
A. L. Bader.

Walkley's supposed piracy of Wither's *Workes* in 1620. LIB, xix (38/9), 339-46.
L. Kirschbaum.

The first pirate. [The priority of Fust or Mentelin's editions of St. Augustine *De Arte Praedicandi*]. LIB, xxiv (43/4), 30-46.
F. W. Householder.

A piracy of Steele's *The lying lover*. LIB, x (55), 127-9.
D. F. Foxon.

The fatal vesper [by W. Crashaw] and [T. Goad's] *The dolefull evenson*: claim-jumping in 1623. LIB, xxi (67), 128-35.
A. Freeman.

Literary piracy in the Elizabethan age. OPSB, i (48), 1-23.
P. Simpson.

John Taylor's piracy of *The Packmans Paternoster*. PBSA, lvii (63), 201-10.
L. H. Kendall, *jr*.

Three Shakespeare piracies in the eighteenth century. [*Hamlet; Othello; Macbeth*]. Illus. SB, i, 47-58.
G. E. Dawson.

The pirated quarto of Dryden's *State of Innocence*. SB, v (52), 166-9.
F. T. Bowers.

The dramatic piracies of 1661: a comparative analysis. SB, xi (58), 117.
J. Gerritsen.

Benson's alleged piracy of *Shakespeares sonnets* and of some of Jonson's works. SB, xxi (68), 235-48.
J. W. Bennett.

PIRCKHEIMER, Bilibald
A letter of Petrus Savorgnanus to Bilibald Pirckheimer. LIB, ii (47/8), 153-8.
J. G. Birch.

PIRCKHEIMER, Sebald
A volume from the library of Sebald Pirckheimer [i.e. Ovid's *Metamorphosis*, Parma, 1480]. SB, viii (56), 212-15.
C. F. Bühler.

PIRIE, Robert S.
A puzzle in the Heber Sale catalogue. (Query, 157). BC, xi (62), 486.

Two editions of *Iter Boreale*, 1668. (Note, 196). BC, xii (63), 204-5.

Fine paper copies of Donne's *Biathanatos* [?1646]. (Note, 250). BC, xiv (65), 362.

Fine paper copies of Bacon's *Essays*, 1625. (Note, 263). BC, xiv (65), 545.

PISAN, Christine de
Observations on two Caxton variants [i.e. in Lydgate's *The Pilgrimage of the Soul*, 1483 and de Pisan's *The Book of the Fayttes of Armes and of Chyvalrye*, 1489]. SB, iii (50/1), 97-104.
C. F. Bühler.

PISE, Charles Constantine
Addenda to Wright [*American fiction, 1774-1850*]. Mancur, Pisc, Tuthill, Weld. PBSA, lxiii (69), 294.
W. S. Kable.

PITCAIRNE, Archibald
An anonymous and updated Edinburgh tract. [*Archimedis Epistola ad regem Gelonem, Albae Graecae reperta anno aerae Christianae 1688*, by A. Pitcairne]. (Note, 264). BC, xv (66), 67.
S. M. Simpson.

PITSLIGO
The Pitsligo Press of George Hay Forbes. Illus. EBST, iv (55/71), 53-89.
J. B. Primrose.

PITTS, John
John Pitts, printer in Seven Dials. (Query, 188). BC, xiii (64), 360.
L. Shepard.

PIX, Mary
Underprinting in Mary Pix, *The Spanish Wives*, 1696. LIB, ix (54), 248-54).
F. T. Bowers.

PLAGIARISM
Thomas Anburey's *Travels through America*: a note on eighteenth-century plagiarism. PBSA, xxxvii (43), 23-36.
W. J. Bell, *jr*.

John Andrew's *History of the War with America:* a further note on eighteenth-century plagiarism. PBSA, lvi (61), 385-92.
R. K. Newmyer.

The Melancholy Cavalier [by J. C., in relation to S. Rowlands' *The Melancholy Knight*]: a study in seventeenth-century plagiarism. SB, v (52), 161-3.
S. Dixon.

PLANCHE, John de
A binding attributed to John de Planche, *c.* 1572. (English bookbindings, 50). Illus. BC, xiii (64), 340.
H. M. Nixon.

PLANT, Marjorie *and* DICKINSON, William Croft
The Bray collection in the British Library of Political and Economic Science. EBST, ii (38/45), 440-3.

PLANTIN, Christopher
Christopher Plantin *c.* 1520-1589. A quarter-centenary tribute. Illus. BC, iv (55), 200-7.

The types of Christopher Plantin. Illus. LIB, xi (56), 170-9.
H. Carter.

Christopher Plantin's trade connexions with England and Scotland. LIB, xiv (59), 28-45.
C. Clair.

The printers' chapel in the Plantinian House. LIB, xvi (61), 1-14.
L. Voet.

The Garamond types of Christopher Plantin. Illus. JPHS, i (65), 14-20.
H. D. L. Vervliet.

PLAT, Sir Hugh
See PLATT, Sir Hugh

PLATEANUS *of Wesel*
Some ornamental initials used by Plateanus of Wesel. LIB, xvi (35/6), 452-4.
H. McCusker.

PLATE GANGS
Imposition figures and plate gangs in *The Rescue*. SB, xiv (61), 258-62.
M. J. Bruccoli *and* G. A. Rheault.

PLATES
See STEREOTYPE

PLATFORM OF CHURCH DISCIPLINE
The printing by the Cambridge [Mass.] press of *A platform of Church discipline*, 1649. SB, ii (49), 79-93.
L. G. Starkey.

PLATO
The 1472 Paris edition of Plato's letters. LIB, viii (73), 197-201.
D. E. Rhodes.

PLATT, Sir Hugh
Sir Hugh Plat ?1552-?1611. (Some uncollected authors, 19). BC, viii (59), 60-8.
B. Juel-Jensen.

—. Errata and addenda. BC, viii (59), 179.

Sir Hugh Plat. (Note, 271). BC, xv (66), 212-13.
B. Juel-Jensen.

PLAYBILLS
Printed playbills in the Peninsula war. TCBS, iv (64/8), 314-17.
B. Dickins.

PLAYFORD, Henry
Playford *versus* Pearson. LIB, xvii (36/7), 427-47.
C. L. Day *and* E. B. Murrie.

PLAYS
Authorship attributions in the early play-lists, 1656-1671. EBST, ii (38/45), 303-29.
Sir W. W. Greg.

Bibliographical clues in collaborate plays. LIB, xiii (32/3), 21-48.
M. St. C. Byrne.

Newcome's Academy and its plays. LIB, xiv (33/4), 339-47.
E. A. Jones.

An early list of Elizabethan plays [in the commonplace book of Henry Oxinden]. LIB, xv (34/5), 445-56.
G. E. Dawson.

The early nineteenth-century drama. Illus. LIB, xvi (35/6), 91-112, 210-231.
R. C. Rhodes.

Hill's list of early plays in manuscript. LIB, xx (39/40), 71-99.
J. Q. Adams.

Latin title-page mottoes as a clue to dramatic authorship. Illus. LIB, xxvi (45/6), 28-36.
J. G. McManaway.

The date of the earliest play-catalogues. LIB, ii (47/8), 190-1.
Sir W. W. Greg.

The copyright of Elizabethan plays. LIB, xiv ·(59), 231-50.
L. Kirschbaum.

Problems in *The Prompter*, a guide to plays. PBSA, iv (61), 36-40.
C. J. Stratman.

The dramatic piracies of 1661: a comparative analysis. SB, xi (58), 117.
J. Gerritsen.

Some Folger academic drama manuscripts. SB, xii (59), 117-30.
R. H. Bowers.

PLEASANT AND COMPENDIOUS HISTORY
A pleasant and compendious history of the first inventors — the 1685 edition a 'ghost'. (Note, 288). BC, xvi (67), 224.
S. M. Simpson.

PLESCH, Arpad
Arpad Plesh. (Contemporary collectors, 27). Illus. BC, x (61), 164-76.
J. Pley.

PLEY, Jacques
Arpard Plesh. (Contemporary collectors, 27). Illus. BC, x (61), 164-76.

PLIMPTON MANUSCRIPT
Wynkyn de Worde's use of the Plimpton manuscript of *De proprietatibus rerum*. Illus. LIB, vi (51), 7-18.
R. W. Mitchner.

PLINIUS CAECILIUS SECUNDUS, Gaius
More about the Aldine Pliny of 1508. LIB, xvi (35/6), 173-87.
A. E. Case.

PLOCH, Richard A.
Abbé Nicholas de Montfaucon de Villars' *The Count de Gabalis*, 1714. PBSA, lviii (64), 279-81.

PLUNKETT, Edward John M.D. *18th baron Dunsany*
'Future' and 'Fortune' and *A Night at an Inn*. PBSA, lviii (64), 477-8.
W. Wilson.

POE, Edgar Allan
Poe and Sarah Helen Whitman. BC, xii (63), 490.
C. S. Bliss.

'Chapter on American Cribbage': Poe and plagiarism. PBSA, xlii (48), 169-210.
N. F. Adkins.

Swinburne's letter concerning Poe. PBSA, xliv (50), 185-90.
I. B. Cauthen, *jr*.

Unrecorded early reprintings of two Poe tales. PBSA, lvi (62), 252.
G. T. Tanselle.

Poe's *Purloined Letter*. PBSA, lvi (62), 486-7.
H. Haycraft.

Two appearances of *The Raven*. PBSA, lvii (63), 229-30.
G. T. Tanselle.

Poe and *The Musiad*. PBSA, lix (65), 437-8.
H. Haycraft.

Poe's *Alone*: its background, source and manuscript. SB, iii (50), 284.
I. B. Cauthen, *jr*.

An unknown early appearance of *The Raven*. SB, xvi (63), 220-3.
G. T. Tanselle.

Poe and *Young America*. SB, xxi (68), 25-58.
C. Richard.

POEM, ADDRESSED TO A YOUNG LADY
Authorship of *A Poem, addressed to a young lady*, Antigua, 1757 and Boston, 1773. PBSA, lii (58), 155-6.
L. M. Stark.

POEMS SELECTED AND PRINTED
An English miscellany printed abroad. [*Poems selected and printed by a small party of English*, 1792]. (Query, 32). BC, ii (53), 79-80.
A. Ehrman.

POGO, Alexander
Early editions and translations of Xerez: *Verdadera relacion de la conquista del Peru*. Illus. PBSA, xxx (36), 57-84.

POINT-HOLES
On printing 'at one pull', and distinguishing impressions by point-holes. LIB, xi (56), 284-5.
D. F. Foxon.

Point-holes as bibliographical evidence. LIB, xxiii (68), 240-1.
K. I. D. Maslen.

POITIERS, Diane de.
See BRÉZÉ Diane de, *duchesse de Valentinois*.

POLIDORI, John William
The printings in America of Polidori's *The Vampyre* in 1819. PBSA, lxii (68), 434-5.
H. R. Viets.

The London editions of Polidori's *The Vampyre*. PBSA, lxiii (69), 83-103.
H. R. Viets.

POLITIANUS, Angelus
Guillaume Haudent and the first translation of Poliziano's *Rusticus*. LIB, viii (53), 111-17.
A. E. C. Simoni.

POLIZIANO, Angelo
See POLITIANUS, Angelus.

POLLARD, Alfred William
The bibliographical approach to Shakespeare. Notes on new contributions. LIB, xiv (33/4), 348-52.

A. W. Pollard, 1859-1944. LIB, xxv (44/5), 82-6.
Sir F. C. Francis.

POLLARD, Alfred William *and* REDGRAVE, Gilbert Richard
>The revised STC. A progress report. BC, iv (55), 16-27.
>W. A. Jackson.

>List of books acquired by the British Museum from Chatsworth. Part II. English books 1501-1640. Part III. Bindings. BC, viii (59), 52-9.
>A. F. Allison *and others.*

>Early English books at the London Oratory. Supplement to STC. LIB, ii (47/8), 95-107.
>A. F. Allison.

>Fine and large-paper copies of STC books: a further note. LIB, xxiii (68), 239-40.
>B. Juel-Jensen.

>The fragment *Virtue* and *The Assemble of Goddes.* STC 24844a and 17005-17007a. PBSA, xlvii (53), 378-80.
>W. Ringler.

>The serpentine progress of the STC revision. Illus. PBSA, lxii (68), 297-311.
>K. F. Pantzer.

>Photo-facsimiles of STC books; a cautionary check list. SB, xxi (68), 109-30.
>F. B. Williams, *jr.*

POLLARD, Henry Graham
>John Meade Falkner, 1858-1932. (Some uncollected authors, 25). BC, ix (60), 318-25.

>The earliest English 'Et Amicorum' inscription. (Note, 133). BC, ix (60), 326.

>Writing masters and copy books. (Note, 138). BC, ix (60), 326-7.

>Titling slips in 17th-century books. (Query, 128). BC, ix (60), 333.

>Proposals for printing Jackson's *Works* 1672. (Query, 230). BC, xviii (69), 223.

>The Company of Stationers before 1551. LIB, xviii (37/8), 1-38.

>The early constitution of the Stationers' Company. LIB, xviii (37/8), 235-60.

>Lettou's address: a correction. LIB, xviii (37/8), 335-7.

>Notes on the size of the sheet. LIB, xxii (41/2), 105-37.

>Changes in the style of bookbinding, 1550-1830. Illus. LIB, xi (56), 71-94.

>C. W. Dyson Perrins. [Obituary notice]. LIB, xiii (58), 129.

>Michael Sadleir. [Obituary notice]. LIB, xiii (58), 129-31.

>The construction of English twelfth-century bindings. Illus. LIB, xvii (62), 1-22.

POLLARD, Mary *and* BARR, C. B. L.
>The *Historia Plantarum* of John Ray. TCBS, iii (59/63), 335-8.

>—. *and* GOODBODY, Olive C.
>The first edition of William Penn's *Great Case of Liberty of Conscience,* 1670. LIB, xvi (61), 146-9.

>—. *and* MUNBY, Alan Noel L.
>Did Mr. Cavendish burn his Caxtons? Illus. BC, xii (63), 449-66.

POMANDER OF PRAYER
>Three English books of the sixteenth century [*Opuscules or smale werkes of saynt bonaventure; The Pomander of prayer; The doctrynall of symple people*]. Illus. LIB, xvii (36/7), 184-9.
>Sir F. C. Francis.

POMPEII
>*Pompeii* the fourth. (Query, 145). BC, xi (62), 86.
>M. Trevanion.

PONDER, Nathaniel
>Nathaniel Ponder; the publisher of *The Pilgrim's Progress.* LIB, xv (34/5), 257-94.
>F. M. Harrison.

>Nathaniel Ponder. [A letter]. LIB, xvii (36/7), 109-10.
>M. Dowling.

PONTANUS, Joannes Jovianus
>A printer's manuscript of 1508. [British Museum Add. MS. 12,027 of Pontanus, *De Prudentia*]. SB, viii (56), 147-56.
>W. H. Bond.

POOL, Isaac A.
>Addendum to Byrd [*Bibliography of Illinois imprints*] and Lincoln [*American cookery books 1742-1860*]: Isaac A. Pool [*The cake baker,* 1857]. PBSA, lxiii (69), 295.
>R. C. Johnson.

POOLE, Herbert Edmund
>New music types: invention in the eighteenth century. Illus. 2 pts. JPHS, i (65), 21-38; ii (66), 23-44.

POPE, Alexander
>Pope: *One thousand seven hundred and eight,* Dialogue II. (Note, 5). BC, i (52), 127.
>W. B. Todd.

>Pope: *One thousand seven hundred and thirty-eight.* (Note, 5). BC, i (52), 192.
>J. P. W. Gaskell.

>Alexander Pope, 1668-1744. (English literary autographs, 4). Illus. BC, i (52), 240-1.
>T. J. Brown.

>Concealed Pope editions. BC, v (56), 48-52.
>W. B. Todd.

>—. (Note, 74). BC, v (56), 277-9.
>D. F. Foxon.

>The ghost of Newbery's Smart's Pope's *Ode on St Cecilia's Day.* BC, xv (66), 215.
>S. Roscoe.

>The first printing of the letters of Pope and Swift. LIB, xix (38/9), 465-85.
>M. Mack.

New light on the first printing of letters of Pope and Swift. LIB, xxiv (43), 74-80.
V. A. Dearing.

Two variant copies of Pope's *Works . . . Volume II*: further light on some problems of authorship, bibliography, and text. LIB, xii (57), 48-53.
M. Mack.

Two notes on the copy for Pope's letters. PBSA, li (57), 327-33.
V. A. Dearing.

Swift, Pope and 'The sin of wit'. PBSA, lxii (68), 80-5.
J. M. Aden.

New editions of Pope's *Essay on man*, 1745-48. Illus. PBSA, lxii (68), 177-88.
K. I. D. Maslen.

POPE, Hugh
A brief history of the English version of the *New Testament* first published at Rheims in 1582, continued down to the present day. 2 pts. LIB, xx (39/40), 351-76; xxi (40/1), 44-77.

PORTER, Dorothy Burnett
Early American negro writings: a bibliographical study. PBSA, xxxix (45), 192-268.

PORTER, William T.
See also SPIRIT OF THE TIMES

POST BOY
Misshelved Americana: *The post boy*. PBSA, lxi (67), 343-7.
W. L. McLendon.

POSTERS
An undescribed printed poster of 1516. PBSA, xlviii (54), 414-16.
R. Hirsch.

POST OFFICE LONDON DIRECTORY
The *Post office London directory*. LIB, xxi (66), 293-9.
J. E. Norton.

POSTON, M. L.
The *Medleys* of 1712. LIB, xiii (58), 205-7.

Bibliotheca Medici. (Contemporary collectors, 34). Illus. BC, xii (63), 44-54.

POTE, Joseph
Joseph Pote of Eton and Bartlet's *Farriery*. LIB, xvii (36/7), 131-54.
R. A. Austen-Leigh.

POTT CHAPEL
See SHRIGLEY Pott chapel

POTTER, Beatrix
See POTTER, Helen Beatrix

POTTER, Esther
English knitting and crochet books of the nineteenth century. Illus. 2 pts. LIB, x (55), 25-40, 103-19.

POTTER, Helen Beatrix
Beatrix Potter: *Peter Rabbit,* 1900-1902. (Query, 18). BC, i (52), 196.
J. Carter.

Peter Rabbit. (Query, 18). BC, ii (53), 77.
E. E. Bissell.

—. BC, ii (53), 77.
L. Linder.

The bibliography of Beatrix Potter. Illus. BC, xv (66), 454-9.
L. Deval.

POTTER, Lee H.
The text of Scott's edition of Swift [*The works of Jonathan Swift, D.D.*, Dublin, 1814]. SB, xxii (69), 240-55.

POTTER, W. A.
Ayscough's *Weekly Courant*. [*A letter*]. LIB, xxv (44/5), 80-1.

POTTLE, Frederick Albert
Printer's copy in the eighteenth century. PBSA, xxvii (33), 65-73.

—. *and* CAMERON, John
Whereabouts of correspondence of J. G. Lockhart? (Query, 238). BC, xviii (69), 226.

POTTS, Denys C.
Saint Evremond. (Some uncollected authors, 3). BC, iii (54), 293-7.

POTT SHRIGLEY
See SHRIGLEY Pott chapel

POVEY, Kenneth
The Caxton Indulgence of 1476. LIB, xix (38/9), 462-4.

Variant formes in Elizabethan printing. Illus. LIB, x (55), 41-8.

Pinholes in the 1457 Psalter. Illus. LIB, xi (56), 18-22.

On the diagnosis of half-sheet impositions. Illus. LIB, xi (56), 268-72.

A century of press-figures. LIB, xiv (59), 251-73.

Working to rule, 1600-1800: a study of pressmen's practice. LIB, xx (65), 13-54.

Twenty-fours with three signatures. SB, ix (57), 215-16.

The optical identification of first formes. SB, xiii (60), 189-90.

Hand-list of manuscripts in the Cowper and Newton museum, Olney. Bucks. TCBS, iv (64/8), 107-27.

—. *and* FOSTER, I. J. C.
Turned chain-lines. Illus. LIB, v (50/1), 184-200.

Kenneth Povey, 1898-1965. [Obituary notice]. LIB, xxviii (68), 51-6.
D. F. Cook *and* A. N. Ricketts.

POWELL, Donald Moore
The Peralta Grant: a lost Arizona story. PBSA, l (56), 40-52.

POWELL, F. R.
Orley Farm. (Query, 16). BC, i (52), 267.

POWELL, John Enoch
A list of printed catalogues of Greek manuscripts in Italy. LIB, xvii (36/7), 200-13.

Henry Stephanus and Thucydides. [A letter]. LIB, xvii (36/7), 361-2.

POWELL, Lawrence Clark
The Western American — an early California newspaper. PBSA, xxxiv (40), 349-55.

John Fiske—bookman. Illus. PBSA, xxxv (41), 221-54.

—. *and* THOMAS, Alan Gradon
Recollections of a Durrell collector. (Some uncollected authors, 23). BC, ix (60), 56-63.

POWELL, Lawrence Fitzroy
The *Tours* of Thomas Pennant. Illus. LIB, xix (38/9), 131-54.

The anonymous designations in Boswell's *Journal of a Tour to the Hebrides* and their identification. EBST, ii (38/45), 353-71.

POWELL, Roger
Some early bindings from Egypt in the Chester Beatty Library: additional notes. LIB, xviii (63), 218-23.

The Lichfield St. Chad's gospels: repair and rebinding. 1961-1962. Illus. LIB, xx (65), 259-76.

POWNALL, Thomas
Pownall, Thomas (1722-1805). *Considerations towards a General Plan of Measures for the English Provinces*, N.Y., Edinb. repr, 1756. PBSA, xxxiv (40), 88.
A. Davidson, *jr*.

Pownall, Thomas (1722-1805). *A Memorial Addressed to the Sovereigns of America*. London, 1783. PBSA, xxxiv (40), 88.
A. Davidson, *jr*.

The biography of a forgotten book — Pownall's *Topographical Description of . . . North America*. PBSA, xliii (49), 63-74.
L. Mulkearn.

POYNTER, Frederick Noël L.
The Wellcome Historical Medical library. Illus. BC, iv (55), 285-90.

Elementa Chemiae, 1732. (Note, 121). BC, ix (60), 64.

Notes on a late-sixteenth century opthalmic work in English. LIB, ii (47/8), 173-9.

PRAGUE
Bookbindings in the libraries of Prague. Illus. SB, iii (50), 105-30.
E. Kyriss.

PRANCE, Claude Annett
Gilbert White 1720-1793. (Some uncollected authors, 43). BC, xvii (68), 300-21.

An ancient Whitaker. BH, i (47/51), 417-21.

PRAYER, Book of Common
Some bibliographical aspects of three Scottish Prayer Books of 1637. BTHK, v (67/70), 1-23.
P. Morgan.

Tables for the identification of octavo books of Common Prayer, 1553-1640. LIB, xiii (58), after 284.
H. M. Adams.

William Bradford and *The Book of Common Prayer*. PBSA, xliii (49), 101-10.
B. McAnear.

Tables for identifying the edition of imperfect copies of the Book of Common Prayer 1600-1640. TCBS, i (49/53), 61-3.
H. M. Adams.

Note on a copy of the Book of Common Prayer in the library of Emmanuel College, Cambridge. TCBS, iv (64/8), 79-83.
E. C. Ratcliff.

PRAYER BOOK
See PRAYER, Book of Common.

PRESCOTT, William Hickling
Promoting a book: Prescott to Bancroft, December 20, 1837. PBSA, li (57), 335-9.
C. H. Gardiner.

PRESENTATION EPISTLES
Special presentation epistles before 1641: a preliminary check-list. Illus. LIB, vii (52), 15-20.
F. B. Williams.

PRESS-CORRECTIONS
See also CORRECTIONS

The press corrections in Jonson's *The King's Entertainment*. LIB, xxiv (43/4), 181-6.
A. K. McIlwraith.

Correction at press in the quarto of *Law-Trickes*. LIB, ii (47/8), 186-90.
W. Peery.

Marginalia on press-correction in books of the early seventeenth century. LIB, iv (50), 238-48.
A. K. McIlwraith.

Press corrections in sixteenth and seventeenth-century quartos. PBSA, xxxvi (42), 187-98.

Press corrections and presswork in the Elizabethan printing shop. PBSA, xl (46), 276-86.
F. R. Johnson.

Stop press and manuscript corrections in the Aldine edition of Benedetti's *Diaria de bello Carolino*. PBSA, xliii (49), 365-73.
C. F. Bühler.

Mark III: New light on the proof-reading for the first folio of Shakespeare. Illus. SB, iii (50), 147-53.
C. Hinman.

PRESSES
Early American power printing presses. Illus.
SB, iv (51/2), 143-53.
R. Green.

PRESS FIGURES
Catch words and press figures at home and
abroad. BC, ix (60), 301-7.
G. G. Barber.

Eighteenth-century press numbers. Illus. LIB,
iv (50/1), 149-61.
J. P. W. Gaskell.

An early reference to press-figures. [A letter].
LIB, vii (52), 211.
J. P. W. Gaskell.

A century of press-figures. LIB, xiv (59), 251-73.
K. Povey.

The recording of press figures. Illus. LIB, xxi
(66), 318-25.
G. T. Tanselle.

Press figures and book reviews as determinants
of priority. A study of Home's *Douglas*, 1751,
and Cumberland's *The Brothers*, 1770. PBSA,
xlv (51), 72-6.
W. B. Todd.

Observations on the incidence and interpretation
of press figures. SB, iii (50), 171-205.
W. B. Todd.

Patterns in press figures: a study of Lyttelton's
Dialogues of the Dead. SB, viii (56), 230-5.
W. B. Todd.

Press figures in America: some preliminary
observations. SB, xix (66), 123-60.
G. T. Tanselle.

Press-figures: a case-history of 1701-1703.
[*Suidae Lexicon*, Cambridge Univ. Press, 1705].
TCBS, iii (59/63), 32-46.
D. F. McKenzie.

PRESSMEN
Working to rule, 1600-1800: a study of press-
men's practice. LIB, xx (65), 13-54.
K. Povey.

PRESTER JOHN
A Prêtre Jean from Poitiers. PBSA, xlvi (52),
151-4.
C. F. Bühler.

PRÊTRE, Jean
See PRESTER JOHN

PRICE, Cecil John L.
The Edinburgh edition of Chesterfield's *Letters
to his Son*. LIB, v (51), 271-2.

The text of the first performance of *The Duenna*.
PBSA, liii (59), 268-70.

Another Crewe MS. of *The School for Scandal?*
PBSA, lvii (63), 79-81.

The second Crewe MS. of *The School for
Scandal?* PBSA, lxi (67), 351-6.

PRICE, George R.
The first edition of *A Faire Quarrell*. LIB, iv
(49/50), 137-41.

The first edition of *Your five gallants* and of
Michaelmas Term. LIB, viii (53), 23-9.

The manuscript and the quarto of the *Roaring
Girl*. LIB, xi (56), 180-6.

The authorship and the bibliography of *The
Revenger's Tragedy*. LIB, xv (60), 262-77.

The early editions of *A trick to catch the old
one*. LIB, xxii (67), 205-27.

The early editions of *The Ant and the Nightingale*. PBSA, xliii (49), 179-90.

Compositors' methods with two quartos reprinted by Augustine Mathewes. PBSA, xliv
(50), 269-74.

The quartos of *The Spanish Gypsy* and their
relation to *The Changeling*. PBSA, lii (58),
111-25.

Setting by formes in the first edition of *The
Phoenix*. PBSA, lvi (62), 414-27.

Dividing the copy for *Michaelmas Term* [by T.
Middleton]. PBSA, lx (66), 327-36.

PRICE, Hereward Thimbleby
Shakespeare and the reporters. [A letter].
LIB, xvii (36/7), 225-7.

Author, compositor, and metre: copy-spelling
in *Titus Andronicus* and other Elizabethan
printings. PBSA, liii (59), 160-87.

PRICE, Sir John
Sir John Prise. Illus. LIB, x (55), 1-24.
N. R. Ker.

PRICK OF CONSCIENCE
Manuscript printer's copy for a lost early
English book, [i.e. the *Prick of Conscience*].
LIB, xxii (41/2), 138-44.
H. C. Schulz.

PRIDEAUX, Sarah Treverbian
A binding by S. T. Prideaux, 1901. (English
bookbindings, 65). Illus. BC, xvii (68), 190.
H. M. Nixon.

PRIESTLEY, Joseph
Joseph Priestley, 1733-1804. (English scientific
autographs, 6). Illus. BC, xiv (65), 539.
T. J. Brown.

An introduction to a bibliography of the
educational and scientific works of Joseph
Priestley. PBSA, xxx (36), 150-67.
C. H. Peters *and* J. F. Fulton.

PRIMERS
The prymer in English. LIB, xviii (37/8), 177-94.
E. Birchenough.

Early primers for the use of children. PBSA,
xliii (49), 374-82.
C. C. Butterworth.

PRIMROSE, Eve *Countess of Rosebery*
Barnbougle Castle. (Unfamiliar libraries, 7).
Illus. BC, xi (62), 35-44.

Books from Beckford's library now at Barnbougle. Illus. BC, xiv (65), 324-34.

PRIMROSE, J. B.
The Pitsligo Press of George Hay Forbes. Illus.
EBST, iv (55/71), 53-89.

A London printer's visit to India in the seventeenth century. LIB, xx (39/40), 100-4.

The first press in India and its printers. Illus.
LIB, xx (39/40), 241-65.

PRINCE, Oliver Hillhouse
[Prince, Oliver Hillhouse (1787-1837)]. *The
Ghost of Baron Steuben*. n.p., n.d. PBSA,
xxxv (41), 206.
H. S. Mott.

PRINCE, Thomas
Prince, Thomas (1687-1758). *The case of Herman
considered*. Boston, 1756. PBSA, xxvi (41), 73.
G. P. Winship.

PRINTERS
See also GOVERNMENT PRINTERS

See also KING'S PRINTING OFFICE

The printers of the Coverdale Bible, 1535. Illus.
LIB, xvi (35/6), 280-9.
L. A. Sheppard.

Working to rule, 1600-1800: a study of pressmen's practice. Illus. LIB, xx (65), 13-54.
K. Povey.

The roots of organization among journeymen
printers. Illus. JPHS, iv (68), 99-107.
I. C. Cannon.

Some unconventional women before 1800:
printers, book-sellers, and collectors. PBSA,
xlix (55), 300-14.
F. Hamill.

Printer's lobby: model 1802. SB, iii (50), 207-28.
R. G. Silver.

A London ornament stock: 1598-1683. Illus.
SB. vii (55), 125-51.
C. W. Miller.

Abstracts from the wills and estates of Boston
printers, 1800-1825. SB, vii (55), 212-18.
F. Hamill.

A list of printers' apprentices, 1605-1640. SB,
xiii (60), 109-41.
D. F. McKenzie.

Italian printers 1501-1520. An annotated list,
with an introd. Illus. TCBS, Monog. 3 (58).
F. J. Norton.

PRINTERS' CHAPEL
The printers' Chapel in the Plantinian House.
LIB, xvi (61), 1-14.
L. Voet.

Two notes on Samuel Richardson: Richardson's
chapel rules. The printer of the *Daily journal*.
LIB, xxiii (68), 242-7.
T. C. D. Eaves *and* B. D. Kimpel.

PRINTERS' COPY
The *editio princeps* of Bede's life of St. Cuthbert,
and its printer's XIIth century 'copy'. Illus.
LIB, xix (38/9) 289-303.
B. Colgrave *and* I. Masson.

Manuscript printer's copy for a lost early English
book [i.e. the *Prick of Conscience*]. LIB, xxii
(41/2), 138-44.
H. C. Schulz.

The printer's copy for an apparently lost
Limoges service-book. LIB, xxiv (43/4), 87.
A. J. Collins.

An example of eighteenth-century Swiss printer's
copy: Euler on the calculus of variations
[*Methodus inveniendi lineas curvas*]. LIB, xxii
(67), 147-9.
G. G. Barber.

Printer's copy in the eighteenth century. PBSA,
xxvii (33), 65-73.
F. A. Pottle.

Casting off copy by Elizabethan printers: a
theory. PBSA, xlii (48), 281-91.
W. H. Bond.

A. E. Housman's printer's copy of *Last poems*,
PBSA, xlvi (52), 70-7.
T. B. Haber.

Dividing the copy for *Michaelmas Term* [by T.
Middleton]. PBSA, lx (66), 327-36.
G. R. Price.

Printer's copy for Tyrwhitt's *Chaucer*. SB, iii
(50), 265-6.
A. L. Hench.

The copy for the first folio *Richard II*. SB, v
(52), 53-72.
R. E. Hasker.

Quarto copy for folio *Henry V*. Illus. SB, viii
(56), 67-93.
A. S. Cairncross.

A printer's manuscript of 1508. [J. J. Pontanus's
De Prudentia — B.M. Add. MS. 12,027]. Illus.
SB, viii (56), 147-56.
W. H. Bond.

The printing of the second quarto of *Romeo
and Juliet*, 1599. SB, ix (57), 107-28.
P. L. Cantrell *and* G. W. Williams.

Quarto copy for Q2 *Romeo and Juliet*. SB, ix
(57), 129-41.
R. Hosley.

Printer's copy for *The Two Noble Kinsmen*.
SB, xi (58), 61-84.
F. O. Waller.

PRINTERS' DEVICES
Notes on two French devices. Illus. LIB, xviii
(37/8), 456-60.
G. Clutton.

A folio with a strange device. Johann Lindholtz's *Arbores consanguinitatis et affinitatis, etc.*, completed by Johann Schott at Strasburg in 1516. Illus. LIB, vii (52), 273-5.
J. V. Scholderer.

Some additions to McKerrow's *Printers' and Publishers' Devices*. LIB, xii (58), 201-3.
W. C. Ferguson.

Devices of German printers, 1501-1540. Illus. LIB, xx (65), 81-107.
A. F. Johnson.

Additions to McKerrow's *Devices*. LIB, xxiii (68), 191-205.
J. A. Lavin.

PRINTERS' FLOWERS
Printers' flowers. Some notes on a few selected examples. BC, v (56), 19-27.
J. Ryder.

PRINTERS' MANUALS
An annotated list of printers' manuals to 1850. Illus. JPHS, iv (68), 11-32.
J. P. W. Gaskell, G. G. Barber *and* A. G. Warrilow.

PRINTER'S MEASURE
Bibliographical evidence from the printer's measure. SB, ii (49), 153-67.
F. T. Bowers.

A note on printers' measures. SB, xv (62), 242-3.
W. C. Ferguson.

PRINTERS' WILLS
Abstract from the wills and estates of Boston printers, 1800-1825. SB, vii (55), 212-18.
R. G. Silver.

PRINTING
Printing press in Malta in the sixteenth century? (Query, 60). BC, iv (55), 82.
D. E. Rhodes.

Printing in Italy in the seventeenth century. BC, viii (59), 140-6.
D. E. Rhodes.

Broadsides concerning early printing. (Query, 147). BC, x (61), 337.
A. Ehrman.

The first power-printed sheet. (Query, 176). BC, xiii (64), 71-2.
W. B. Todd.

Early Scottish editions of *The seven sages of Rome*. Illus. BTHK, v (67/70), 62-72.
C. B. L. Barr.

The Austrian post-incunabula. Illus. LIB, xix (38/9), 1-5.
Sir S. Gaselee.

A piety of printers. LIB, xix (38/9), 156-66.
J. V. Scholderer.

The first press in India and its printers. Illus. LIB, xx (39/40), 241-65.
J. B. Primrose.

The invention of printing. LIB, xxi (40/1), 1-25.
J. V. Scholderer.

Two Strasburg reprints of Aldine classics. LIB, viii (53), 274-5.
J. V. Scholderer.

The printing of eighteenth-century periodicals: with notes on the *Examiner* and the *World*. LIB, x (55), 49-54.
W. B. Todd.

On printing 'at one pull', and distinguishing impressions by point-holes. LIB, xi (56), 284-5.
D. F. Foxon.

Italian sixteenth-century books. LIB, xiii (58), 161-74.
A. F. Johnson.

The printing of Spanish books in Elizabethan England. LIB, xx (65), 177-229.
G. Ungerer.

London printers' imprints, 1800-1848. LIB, xxi (66), 46-62.
W. B. Todd.

The Greek press at Constantinople in 1627 and its antecedents. Illus. LIB, xxii (67), 13-43.
R. J. Roberts.

English provincial imprints. LIB, xxii (67), 70.
P. Morgan.

Press corrections and presswork in the Elizabethan printing shop. PBSA, xl (46), 276-86.
F. R. Johnson.

Three early Dutch printings. PBSA, lxii (68), 427.
L. Hanemann.

Metal cuts at the Gutenberg workshop. Illus. PBSA, lxii (68), 581-6.
K. F. Bauer.

Setting by formes in quarto printing. SB, xi (58), 39-53.
G. W. Williams.

Scottish printers and booksellers 1668-1778: a supplement. SB, xii (59), 131-59.
R. H. Carnie *and* R. P. Doig.

Recurrent printing. SB, xii (59), 189-98.
W. B. Todd.

Scottish printers and booksellers 1668-1775: a second supplement (I). SB, xiv (61), 81-96; —(II). SB, xv (62), 105-20.
R. H. Carnie.

Penny-pinching printers and tampered titles. SB, xiv (61), 209-11.
F. B. Williams.

Printers of the mind: some notes on bibliographical theories, and printing-house practices. SB, xxii (69), 1-75.
D. F. McKenzie.

The lay of the case. Illus. SB, xxii (69), 125-42.
J. P. W. Gaskell.

The Irish broadside of 1571 and Queen Elizabeth's types. Illus. TCBS, i (49/53), 48-60.
B. Dickins.

Italian printers 1501-1520. An annotated list, with an introduction. Illus. TCBS, Monog. 3 (58).
F. J. Norton.

Some notes on the bibliography of William Hayley. Pt. III. Note on printers and publishers. Illus. TCBS, iii (59/63), 339-60.
N. J. Barker.

PRINTING AND THE MIND OF MAN
Printing and the mind of man: the inside story [of the exhibition]. BC, xvi (67), 47-53.
P. H. Muir.

PRINTING COSTS
Costs of printing *c*. 1700. [A letter]. LIB, viii (53), 203.
C. C. Blagden.

Two bills for printing, 1620-2. LIB, xv (60), 128-32.
D. F. McKenzie.

The cost of Mathew Carey's printing equipment. SB, xix (66), 85-122.
R. G. Silver.

William Strahan's ledgers: standard charges for printing, 1733-1785. SB, xx (67), 89-111.
P. Hernlund.

PRINTING EQUIPMENT
An American printing equipment in Mauritius in the eighteenth century. Illus. PBSA, xliv (50), 175-81.
A. Toussaint.

PRINTING TECHNIQUES
Some contemporary accounts of Renaissance printing methods. LIB, xvii (36/7), 167-71.
D. C. Allen.

Experimental graphic processes in England, 1800-1859. Parts I—II. Illus. JPHS, iv (68), 33-86.
E. M. Harris.

Anastatic printing for Sir Thomas Phillipps. Illus. JPHS, v (69), 24-40.
G. Wakeman.

Experimental graphic processes in England 1800-1859. Part III. Illus. JPHS, v (69), 41-80.
E. M. Harris.

PRIOR, Matthew
Matthew Prior, 1664-1721. (English literary autographs, 23). Illus. BC, vi (57), 279.
T. J. Brown.

Prior's *A new collection of poems*, 1724, etc. (Note, 106). BC, viii (59), 69-70.
D. F. Foxon.

Prior's *Simile*. Illus. PBSA, lvii (63), 337-9.
F. M. Ellis *and* D. F. Foxon.

Prior's copy of Spenser's *Works*, 1679. PBSA, lxi (67), 52-5.
W. L. Godshalk.

PRISE, Sir John
See PRICE, Sir John

PRITCHARD, Allan
George Wither's quarrel with the stationers: an anonymous reply to *The Schollers Purgatory*. SB, xvi (63), 27-42.

PRIVATE PRESSES
Private presses. (Query, 89). BC, vi (57), 404.
T. Rae.

PRIVILEGE
See IMPRIMATUR

PROCLAMATIONS
Two unrecorded Jacobean proclamations. LIB, iii (48/9), 121.
C. F. Bühler.

PROCTER, Page S.
William Leggett, 1801-1839: journalist and literator. PBSA, xliv (50), 239-53.

PROCTOR, Robert George C.
The private diary of Robert Proctor. LIB, v (50/1), 261-9.
J. V. Scholderer.

Robert Proctor's diaries. [A letter]. LIB, vi (51), 219.
Sir S. Cockerell.

PROGNOSTICATIONS
The astrological prognostications of 1583. LIB, xiv (33/4), 101-6.
R. Pruvost.

PROLOGUES
Textual problems in Restoration broadsheet prologues and epilogues. LIB, xii (57), 197
R. Morton.

PROMPT COPIES
The two earliest prompt books of *Hamlet*. Illus. PBSA, xliii (49), 288-320.
J. G. McManaway.

A prompt copy of Dryden's *Tyrannic Love*. SB, iv (51), 170-4.
H. H. Adams.

Playhouse interpolations in the folio text of *Hamlet*. SB, xiii (60), 31-47.
H. Jenkins.

New evidence on the provenance of the Padua prompt-books of Shakespeare's *Macbeth, Measure for Measure* and *Winters Tale*. SB, xx (67), 239-42.
G. B. Evans.

PROMPTER
Problems in *The Prompter*, a guide to plays. PBSA, lv (61), 36-40.
C. J. Stratman.

PROOF READING
See PROOFS

PROOFS
A Cambridge proof-sheet of 1617. [Samuel Collins's *Epphata to F.T.*, 1617]. (Note, 36). BC, iii (54), 226.
A. N. L. Munby.

The manuscripts and proof sheets of Scott's Waverley novels. EBST, iv (55), 13-42.
G. Dyson.

A proof-sheet of 1606. LIB, xvii (36/7), 454-7.
Sir W. W. Greg.

A proof-sheet in the first folio of Shakespeare. Illus. LIB, xxiii (42/3), 101-7.
C. Hinman.

An examination of the method of proof correction in *Lear*. LIB, ii (47/8), 20-44.
F. T. Bowers.

A proof-sheet in Thomas Heywood's *The Iron Age*. Illus. LIB, x (55), 275-8.
A. Brown.

Some proofs of Johnson's *Preface to the Poets*. LIB, xvii (62), 213-30.
J. D. Fleeman.

A proof-sheet in *An humorous day's mirth,* 1599, printed by Valentine Simmes. Illus. LIB, xxi (66), 155-7.
A. Yamada.

Mark III: New light on the proof-reading for the first folio of Shakespeare. Illus. SB, iii (50), 145-53.
C. Hinman.

The proof-reading of the first folio text of *Romeo and Juliet.* Illus. SB, vi (54), 61-70.
C. Hinman.

Notes on the unrevised galleys of Faulkner's *Sanctuary*. SB, viii (56), 195-208.
L. Massey.

A proof-sheet from Nicholas Okes' printing-shop. Illus. SB, xi (58), 228-31.
J. R. Brown.

Proof reading Lockhart's *Scott*: the dynamics of biographical reticence. SB, xiv (61), 3-22.
F. R. Hart.

Mathew Carey's proof readers. SB, xvii (64), 123-33.
R. G. Silver.

PROPAGANDA
Propaganda in early American fiction. PBSA, xxxiii (39), 98-106.
L. H. Wright.

PROPOSITION FOR THE SAFETY AND HAPPINESS OF THE KING
The authorship of *A Proposition for the Safety and Happiness of the King . . .* (1667). PBSA, l (56), 182-3.
F. B. Whiting.

PROSE ROMANCES
Three early 18th century prose romances. (Note, 177). BC, xi (62), 215-16.
D. Macaree.

PROUDE WYUES PATER NOSTER
Six tracts about women; a volume in the British Museum. [*The deceyte of women.* A. Vele, n.d.; *The schole house of women,* J. King, 1560; Edward More; *The defence of women,* J. King, 1560; *The proude wyues pater noster,* J. King, 1560; Robert Copland. *The seven sorowes.* W. Copland, n.d.; and, *Frederyke of lennen.* A. Vele, n.d.]. LIB, xv (34/5), 38-48.
H. Stein.

PRUVOST, René
The astrological prognostications of 1583. LIB, xiv (33/4), 101-6.

PRYMERS
See PRIMERS

PSALMS
Castano Psalter, 1486. (Note, 43). BC, iv (55), 78.
D. E. Rhodes.

A 15th-century MS of *Les sept psaumes allégorisés.* (Query, 154). BC, xi (62), 485.
R. R. Rains.

Pinholes in the 1457 Psalter. Illus. LIB, xi (56), 18-22.
K. Povey.

Harington's metrical paraphrases of the seven penitential psalms: three manuscript versions. PBSA, liii (59), 240-51.
K. E. Schmutzler.

The 'Psalterium Hebraycum' from St. Augustine's Canterbury rediscovered in the Scaliger bequest at Leyden. Illus. TCBS, ii (54/8), 97-104.
G. I. Lieftinck.

PSALTERIUM HEBRAYCUM
The 'Psalterium Hebraycum' from St. Augustine's Canterbury rediscovered in the Scaliger bequest at Leyden. Illus. TCBS, ii (54/8), 97-104.
G. I. Lieftinck.

PSEUDO-XENOPHON
Two anonymous translations of Pseudo-Xenophon [*Xenophon's Defence of the Athenian democracy,* translated by H. J. Pye]. (Query, 219). BC, xvii (68), 218.
R. J. F. Carnon.

PUBLICATION ABROAD
Books published abroad by Scotsmen before 1700. GBST, xi (33), 1-55.
J. H. Baxter *and* C. J. Fordyce.

PUBLIC LEDGER
Dr. Johnson and the *Public Ledger*: a small addition to the canon. SB, xi (58), 252-5.
G. J. Kolb.

PUBLIC PRINTERS
See GOVERNMENT PRINTERS

PUBLISHING
For particular localities, e.g. Oxford *see* OXFORD

See also the names of individual publishers

See also BOOKSELLING

See also BOOKTRADE

Subscription publishers prior to Jacob Tonson. LIB, xiii (32/3), 158-83.
S. L. C. Clapp.

A publishing agreement of the late seventeenth century. [Re *Henrici Mori Cantabrigiensis Opera Theologica,* 1675]. LIB, xiii (32/3), 184-7.
R. B. McKerrow.

English song-books, 1651-1702, and their publishers. Illus. LIB, xvi (35/6), 355-401.
C. L. Day *and* E. B. Murrie.

Origins of Methodist publishing in America. Illus. PBSA, lix (65), 12-27.
L. D. Case.

The three-volume novel. PBSA, lxi (67), 201-7.
D. C. Ewing.

English publishing and the mass audience in 1852. SB, vi (54), 3-24.
R. D. Altick.

John Esten Cooke on publishing, 1865. SB, xiii (56), 239-41.
I. B. Cauthen, *jr.*

Colburn-Bentley and the march of the intellect. SB, ix (57), 197-213.
R. A. Gettmann.

From Aldine to Everyman: cheap reprint series of the English classics, 1830-1906. SB, xi (58), 3-24.
R. D. Altick.

The distribution of almanacks in the second half of the seventeenth century. SB, xi (58), 107-16.
C. C. Blagden.

Financing the publication of early New England sermons. SB, xi (58), 163-78.
R. G. Silver.

Publishers and sinners: the Augustan view. SB, xii (59), 3-20.
I. Watt.

The historiography of American literary publishing. SB, xviii (65), 3-39.
G. T. Tanselle.

The origin of the publisher's binding in Dublin. TCBS, ii (54/8), 92-4.
J. W. Phillips.

PUERTO RICO
The first non-serial Puerto Rican imprint. PBSA, xliv (50), 181-2.
L. S. Thompson.

PUFF VON SCHRICK, M.
An Ulm unicum of 1501 [M. Puff von Schrick's *Ain guts nutzlichs büchlin von den auss geprenten wassern*] in the National Library of Medicine, Bethesda, Maryland. Illus. LIB, xx (65), 55-7.
R. J. *and* S. M. Durling.

PULCI, Luigi
Pulci, Luigi (1431-1487), *Morgante Maggiore*. Venice, Matteo Capcasa (di Codeca), [1494]. PBSA, xxxiv (40), 85.
F. R. Goff.

On the earliest editions of the *Morgante* of Luigi Pulci. PBSA, xlv (51), 1-22.
E. H. Wilkins.

An edition of the *Sonetti* by Matteo Franco and Luigi Pulci. PBSA, xlv (51), 356-7.
C. F. Bühler.

PURCELL, Henry
A collection of musical manuscripts in the autograph of Henry Purcell and other English composers, *c.* 1665-85. LIB, xiv (59), 126-31.
W. Shaw.

PURVES, John
Some notes on the public library, Valletta. EBST, ii (38/45), 437-40.

PUTEO, Paris de
Puteo, Paris de (d. 1439). *Tractatus in materia ludi.* [Pavia, Christophorus de Canibus, *c.* 1495]. PBSA, xxxv (41), 156.
H. R. Mead.

PUTNAM *family*
The Putnams in copyright: the father, the son, and a ghost. [*An argument in behalf of international copyright, 1840*]. PBSA, lxiii (69), 15-22.
H. Ehrlich.

PYE, Henry James
Two anonymous translations of Pseudo-Xenophon [Xenophon's *Defence of the Athenian democracy,* translated by H. J. Pye.]. (Query, 219). BC, xvii (68), 218.
R. J. F. Carnon.

PYNSON, Richard
Notes on a Pynson volume. [*Old Tenures; Natura Brevium*; and Littleton, *Tenures Novelli*]. LIB, xviii (37/8), 261-7.
C. F. Bühler.

Pynson's manuscript of *Dives and Pauper*. Illus. LIB, viii (53), 217-28.
M. M. Morgan.

Richard Pynson and the Holy Blood of Hayles. Illus. LIB, xiii (58), 269-77.
J. C. T. Oates.

Some documents printed by Pynson for St. Botolph's, Boston, Lincs. LIB, xv (60), 53-7.
D. E. Rhodes.

A little gest of Robin Hood: a note on Pynson and Lettersnijder editions. SB, xvi (63), 3-8.
J. C. T. Oates.

PYRAMUS AND THISBE
A Pyramus and Thisbe binding, *c.* 1616. (English bookbindings, 46). Illus. BC, i (52), 2-3.
H. M. Nixon.

Q

'Q' *pseud.*
See COUCH, Sir Arthur Thomas Quiller-

QUAKER PARTISANS
The Quaker-Partisans. *A Story of the Revolution.* By the author of *The Scout.* Philadelphia, 1869. PBSA, xxxv (41), 208-9.
J. E. Alden.

QUARITCH, Bernard
The bibliophilic transactions of James Lenox with Bernard Quaritch, 1874-1880. PBSA, xl (46), 181-204.
V. H. Paltsits.

QUARLES, Francis
Quarles's *Enchiridion*, 1682. (Query, 95). BC, vii (58), 188.
J. Horden.

The publication of Quarles' *Emblems*. LIB, xv (34/5), 97-109.
G. S. Haight.

The sources of Quarles's *Emblems*. Illus. LIB, xvi (35/6), 188-209.
G. S. Haight.

Quarles, Francis (1592-1644). *Solomons Recantation* London, M.F. for Richard Royston, 1645. PBSA, xxxv (41), 70.
H. R. Mead.

Edmund Marmion's illustrations for Francis Quarles's *Argalus and Parthenia*. TCBS, ii (54/8), 55-62.
J. Horden.

QUEDLINBURG, Jordanus de
The printer of Jordanus de Quedlinburg, Strasburg, 1481-1502. PBSA, xlvi (52), 179-85.
J. V. Scholderer.

QUEEN'S BINDER 'A'
A London binding by Queen's binder A, *c.* 1670. (English bookbindings, 47). Illus. BC, xii (63), 488.
H. M. Nixon.

QUEEN'S BINDER 'B'
A London binding by Queen's binder B, *c.* 1675. (English bookbindings, 28). Illus. BC, viii (59), 50.
H. M. Nixon.

QUESNAY DE BEAUREPAIRE, Alexandre Marie
Quesnay de Beaurepaire, Alexandre Marie, (fl. 1780). *Mémoire et prospectus, concernant l'Académie des Sciences et Beaux Arts des États-Unis de l'Amérique*, Paris 1788. PBSA, xxxv (41), 73-4.
J. C. Wyllie.

Quesnay de Beaurepaire, Alexandre Marie (fl. 1780). *Mémoire et prospectus, concernant l'Académie des Sciences et Beaux Arts de États-Unis de l' Amérique.* Paris, 1788. PBSA, xxxvii (43), 75-7.
J. G. Roberts.

QUEVEDO VILLEGAS, Francisco Gomez de
See GOMEZ DE QUEVEDO VILLEGAS, Francisco

QUIGLY, Elizabeth Madeleine
The House of Guasp. Illus. BC, ii (53), 264-9.

QUIGLY, Isabel *pseud.*
See QUIGLY, Elizabeth Madeleine

QUILLER-COUCH, Sir Arthur Thomas
See COUCH, Sir Arthur Thomas Quiller-

QUIN, Henry George
Henry George Quin, 1760-1805. (Portrait of a bibliophile, 13). Illus. BC, xiii (64), 449-62.
A. Rau.

QUINN, John
John Quinn and T. S. Eliot's first book of criticism. PBSA, lvi (62), 259-65.
D. H. Woodward.

QUIRES
An unusual form of dating quires. (Query, 143). BC, x (61), 202.
R. Codlock.

QUYNN, Dorothy Mackay
Bartgis' lost newspaper. PBSA, lv (61), 133-7.

R

RABAN, Edward
Devices used by Raban in Guild's *Limbo's Balterie*, 1630. BTHK, iv (63/6), 77-9.
W. R. McDonald.

The *Aberdeen Journal* and the *Aberdeen Intelligencer*, 1752-7: a further note on a Raban device. BTHK, v (67/70), 204-6.
W. R. McDonald.

RABELAIS, François
A Rabelais discovery. Illus. BC, iii (54), 41-4.
L. Scheler.

RACIN, John
The early editions of Sir Walter Ralegh's *The History of the World*. SB, xvii (64), 199-209.

RACINE, Jean Baptiste
Racine, Jean Baptiste (1639-1699). *The suitors: a comedy in three acts.* PBSA, xxxiv (40), 361.
F. B. Bowe.

Racine, Jean (1639-1699). *The distrest mother: a tragedy.* PBSA, xxxv (41), 160.
F. B. Bowe.

RADICAL *pseud.*
Inches versus millimetres. (Query, 25). BC, i (52), 269.

RAE, Thomas
Private presses. (Query, 89). BC, vi (57), 404.

RAHIR, Édouard
Edouard Rahir, 1862-1924 Illus. BC, xvi (67), 169-76.
A. Rau.

RAILWAY READING
Railway reading. BC, ix (60), 285-91.
A. Walbank.

RAINS, Ruth R.
A 15th-century MS. of *Les sept psaumes allegorisés*. (Query, 154). BC, xi (62), 485.

RALEGH, Sir Walter
Imago mundi. [Sir Walter Ralegh's copy of the work by Pierre d'Ailly]. (Collector's piece, 1). Illus. BC, xv (66), 12-18.
W. Oakeshott.

The printing of *A declaration of the demeanor and cariage of Sir Walter Raleigh*, 1618. LIB, iii (48/9), 124-34.
P. Ropp *and* L. G. Starkey.

Sir Walter Ralegh's library. [A catalogue]. Illus. LIB, xxiii (68), 285-327.
W. Oakeshott.

Raleigh, Sir Walter (1552-1618). *A declaration of the demeanor and cariage of sir W. Raleigh, 1618.* PBSA, xxxiv (40), 358.
E. M. Sowerby.

Ralegh and Ayton: the disputed authorship of *Wrong Not Sweete Empress of my Heart.* SB, xiii (60), 191-8.
C. B. Gullans.

The early editions of sir Walter Ralegh's *The History of the World.* SB, xvii 664), 199-209.
J. Racin.

RALPH, James
James Ralph. (Note, 44). BC, iv (55), 168.
C. Dobson.

The authorship of *The Touch-stone*, 1728. [Attributed to J. Ralph]. PBSA, lxii (68), 189-98.
J. B. Shipley.

RAMBLER
Bibliographical note on *The Rambler*, 1848-62. PBSA, lvi (62), 113-44.
G. L. Altholz.

RAMSAY, Allan
The music of Allan Ramsay's songs. BTHK, ii (59/60), 34.
H. G. Farmer.

An edition of Allan Ramsay. BTHK, iii (60/2), 220-1.
G. R. Roy.

Ther first edition of [Allan Ramsay's] *The tea-table miscellany.* BTHK, v (67/70), 198-203.
A. Law.

RAMSAY, David
Ramsay, David (1749-1815). *The History of the American Revolution.* Lond., 1791. PBSA, xxxiv (40), 88.
A. Davidson.

David Ramsay's publication problems 1784-1808. PBSA, xxxix (45), 51-67.
R. L. Brunhouse.

RAMSDEN, Charles Frederick
French bookbinders, 1789-1848. [Summary of a paper]. LIB, v (50/1), 258-60.

—. (Note, 78). BC, v (56), 383-4.

Richard Wier and Count MacCarthy-Reagh. Illus. BC, ii (53), 247-57.

A waterproof binding (Query, 42). BC, ii (53), 283.

The collection of Hollis bindings at Berne. Illus. BC, vii (58), 165-70.

Bindings in the M. Wodhull library. [A letter] LIB, viii (53), 279.

Bookbinders to George III and his immediate descendants and collaterals. LIB, xiii (58), 186-93.

RAMUS, Petrus
See LA RAMÉE, Pierre de

RANDALL, David Anton
Josiah Kirby Lilly. (Contemporary collectors, 14). Illus. BC, vi (57), 263-77.

The first American edition of the Brontës' *Poems.* (Query, 121). BC, ix (60), 199-201.

Housman manuscripts. (Query, 130). BC, ix (60), 456.

A Shropshire Lad with a variant title-page. (Query, 135). Illus. BC, ix (60), 458.

Mr. Muir and Gabriel Wells: a rejoinder. BC, x (61), 53-5.

A dedication Grolier discovered recovered. (Note, 149). BC, x (61), 66-8.

The first American edition of *1914 and other poems*. (Query, 185). BC, xiii (64), 359.

Variant binding of Clough's *Poems*. (Note, 257). BC,. xiv (65), 542.

Copies of Conrad's *Chance*, dated '1913'. (Query, 198). BC, xv (66), 68.

Doyle, A. Conan (1879-1928). *Memoirs of Sherlock Holmes*. New York, 1894. PBSA, xxxiv (40), 190-1.

Lever, Charles (1806-1872). *Our Mess*. Dublin, 1843-4. PBSA, xxxiv (40), 274-6.

Thackeray, W. M. (1811-1863). *Vanity Fair*. 20 parts in 19. London, 1847-1848. PBSA, xxxiv (40), 191-2; 276-8.

Brooke, Rupert (1887-1915). *The Collected Poems*. New York, 1915. PBSA, xxxvi (42), 68.

Grey, Zane (1872-1939). *Riders of the Purple Sage*. New York & London, 1912. PBSA, xxxvi (42), 68.

A plea for a more consistent policy of cataloguing by auction galleries. PBSA, xl (46), 107-26.

Notes towards a correct collation of the first edition of *Vanity Fair*. Illus. PBSA, xlii (48), 95-109.

Two states of *Two Lives*. PBSA, liv (60), 295.

Bruce Rogers's first decorated book. PBSA, lv (61), 40-2.

Changing the Gutenberg Census. (Dukedom large enough, 1). PBSA, lvi (62), 157-74.

Hemingway, Churchill, and the printed word. (Dukedom large enough, 2). PBSA, lvi (62), 346-53.

Thomas Jefferson and the Declaration of Independence. (Dukedom large enough, 3). PBSA, lvi (62), 472-80.

The permanent questionnaire (Dukedom large enough, 4). PBSA, lvii (63), 68-76.

The Gondoliers. PBSA, lix (65), 193-8.

Gilbert and Sullivan's *Princess Ida*. PBSA, lix (65), 322-6.

RANDOLPH, Thomas
A possible Randolph holograph. LIB, xx (39/40), 159-62.
F. T. Bowers.

Marriot's two editions of Randolph's *Aristippus*. Illus. LIB, xx (39/40), 163-6.
F. T. Bowers.

RANSOME, Arthur Mitchell
Arthur Ransome, b. 1884. (Some uncollected authors, 21). BC, viii (59), 289-93.
A. Rota.

RAPIN-THOYRAS, Paul de
[Rapin-Thoyras, Paul de] (1661-1725). *A dissertation on the rise, progress, views, strength, interests and characters, of the two parties of the Whigs and Tories*. Boston, 1773. PBSA, xxxv (41), 161.
F. B. Bowe.

RATCHFORD, Fannie Elizabeth
Thomas J. Wise to John Henry Wrenn on nineteenth-century bibliography. PBSA, xxxvi (42), 215-28.

RATCLIFF, Edward Craddock
Note on a copy of the *Book of Common Prayer* in the library of Emmanuel College, Cambridge. TCBS, iv (64/8), 79-83.

RATCLIFFE, Frederick William
A Strassburg incunable in the Euing collection in Glasgow University Library. BTHK, iii (60/2), 165-73.

Chapbooks with Scottish imprints in the Robert White collection, the University Library, Newcastle upon Tyne. BTHK, iv (63/6), 88-174.

RATDOLT, Erhard
Erhard Ratdolt's vanity. PBSA, xlix (55), 186-8.
C. F. Bühler.

The laying of a ghost? Observations on the 1483 Ratdolt edition of the *Fasciculus Temporum*. SB, iv (51), 155-9.
C. F. Bühler.

RATH, Erich von
Bibliographical work in Germany, 1939-1945. LIB, xxvi (45/6), 193-4.

Erich von Rath. LIB, iv (49/50), 280.
J. V. Scholderer.

RATISBON
See REGENSBURG

RATTEY, Clifford C.
Ausonius, Decimus Magnus. *Opera*. Venice: [Epon. Press] 1472. LIB, v (50/1), 270-1.

The undated Aesop attributed to Jakob Wolff de Pforzheim (Hain-Copinger 327). LIB, xii (57), 119-21.

RAU, Arthur
News from France. BC, iv (55), 310-14.

L'Encyclopédie in contemporary morocco. (Note, 76). BC, v (56), 383.

André Langlois. (Contemporary collectors, 13). Illus. BC, vi (57), 129-42.

Edmée Maus. (Contemporary collectors, 16). Illus. BC, vii (58), 38-50.

Gilt tooling on macabre bindings. (Query, 98). BC, vii (58), 295.

Bibliotheca Bodmeriana. (Contemporary collectors, 19). Part I: Manuscripts. Part II. Printed books. Illus. BC, vii (58), 386-95; viii (59), 31-45.

Maurice Loncle. (Contemporary collectors, 23). Illus. BC, ix (60), 38-44.

The first edition of Molière's *Sganarelle*. (Note, 126). BC, ix (60), 68-71.

An annotated MacCarthy-Reagh catalogue. (Note, 136). BC, ix (60), 196-8.

The earliest extant French armorial ex-libris. (Note, 161). Illus. BC, x (61), 331-2.

Henry George Quin, 1760-1805. (Portrait of a bibliophile, 13). Illus. BC, xiii (64), 449-62.

Les reliures vernis sans odeur. [An addition]. (Note, 273). BC, xv (66), 484.

Édouard Rahir, 1862-1924. Illus. BC, xvi (67), 169-76.

Venice revisited. BC, xvii (68), 37-41.

Bibliotheca Parisina. Illus. BC, xviii (69), 307-17.

A 'vernis sans odeur' binding. (Note, 325). BC, xviii (69), 520.

RAWLINSON, Thomas
The later auction sales of Thomas Rawlinson's library, 1727-34. 2 pts. LIB, xi (56), 23-40; 103-13.
B. J. Enright.

RAWSON, Claude Julien
Parnell on Whiston. PBSA, lvii (63), 91-2.

RAY, Cyril
The Recollections of Rifleman Harris [by H. Curling]. BH, i (47/51), 450-4.

RAY, Gordon Norton
The Tom Turner library. Illus. BC, ii (53), 258-63.

A 19th-century collection. (Contemporary collectors, 37). English first editions. Part 2. A museum of the book. Illus. BC, xiii (64), 33-44; 171-84.

The Bentley papers. LIB, vii (52), 178-200.

H. G. Wells's contributions to the *Saturday Review*. LIB, xvi (61), 29-36.

The changing world of rare books. PBSA, lix (65), 103-41.

In memoriam: John D. Gordan. PBSA, lxii (68), 175-6.

RAY, John
The *Historia Plantarum* of John Ray. TCBS, iii (59/63), 335-8.
C. B. L. Barr *and* M. Pollard.

REA, Robert Right
Anglo-American parliamentary reporting: a case study in historical bibliography. PBSA, xlix (55), 212-29.

Some notes on Edward Gibbon's *Mémoire Justificatif*. SB, v (52/3), 194-7.

READ, Alexander
A. Read's *Manuall of Anatomy,* 1634,. LIB, viii (53), 201.
W. R. LeFanu.

A. Read's *Manuall of Anatomy*, 1634. [A letter]. LIB, ix (54), 58.
L. M. Payne.

READE, William Winwood
William Winwood Reade. (Some uncollected authors, 13). BC, vi (57), 62-6.
J. S. L. Gilmour.

READING *Berks, univ., libr.*
Early provincial newspapers in Reading university library. TCBS, iv (64/8), 256.
D. T. O'Rourke.

READING PUBLIC
Medieval English manuscripts and contemporary taste. EBST, ii (38/45), 382-3.
H. S. Bennett.

Translation for the Elizabethan middle class. LIB, xiii (32/3), 312-31.
L. B. Wright.

Books and readers, 1599-1603. LIB, xiv (33/4), 1-33.
G. B. Harrison.

The circulation of newspapers and literary periodicals, 1700-30. LIB, xv (34/5), 110-24.
J. R. Sutherland.

A London bookseller's bill, 1635-1639. LIB, xviii (37/8), 416-46.
M. E. Bohannon.

The production and dissemination of vernacular manuscripts in the fifteenth century. LIB, (46/7), 167-78.
H. S. Bennett.

Printers, authors, and readers, 1475-1557. LIB, iv (49/50), 155-65.
H. S. Bennett.

The reading of Shakespeare in colonial America. PBSA, xxxi (37), 45-56.
E. E. Willoughby.

Walt Whitman's reception in Scandinavia. PBSA, xl (46), 259-75.
G. W. Allen.

Best sellers in seventeenth-century fiction. PBSA, xlvii (53), 356-73.
C. C. Mish.

The *Famous Boston Post List*: mid-nineteenth century American best-sellers. PBSA, lii (58), 93-110.
H. T. Meserole.

English publishing and the mass audience in 1853. SB, vi (54), 3-24.
R. D. Altick.

The circulation of some London newspapers, 1806-1811; two documents. SB, vii (55), 190-4.
R. L. Haig.

Colburn-Bentley and the march of the intellect. SB, ix (57), 197-213.
R. A. Gettmann.

'My squeamish public': some problems of Victorian magazine publishers and editors. SB, xii (59), 21-40.
O. Maurer.

Melville and the common reader. SB, xii (59), 41-57.
W. Charvat.

Nineteenth-century English best-sellers: a further list. SB, xxii (69), 197-206.
R. D. Altick.

RECOLLECTIO EPISTOLARUM
Recollectio epistolarum et prophetiarum [Salamanca, Printer of Nebrissensis *Introductiones,* 1st roman group, *c.* 1485]. PBSA, xxxvi (42), 63.
H. R. Mead.

RECUYELL OF THE HISTORIES OF TROY
The early ownership of the British Museum copy of Caxton's *Recuyell of the Histories of Troy.* LIB, iii (48/9), 216-18.
L. A. Sheppard.

REDMAN, Robert
Robert Redman's *Prayers of the Byble.* LIB, iii (48/9), 279-86.
C. C. Butterworth.

—. [A letter]. LIB, v (50/1), 60.

REED, F. W.
Dumas: some translation difficulties. (Query, 4). BC, i (52), 54-5.

Dumas, *La Maison de Savoie.* (Query, 5). BC, i (52), 55-6.

REED, Gervais E.
Molière's privilege of 18 March 1671. LIB, xx (65), 57-63.

REED, John Curtis
Humphrey Moseley, publisher. [Addition]. — OBSP, i (47), 39. OBSP, ii (27/30), 57-142.

REED, Talbot Baines
Talbot Baines Reed, 1852-1893. (Some uncollected authors, 35). BC, xii (63), 62-67.
P. M. Handover.

REED, Thomas Mayne
See REID, Mayne

REES, Eiluned
Developments in the book trade in eighteenth-century Wales. LIB, xxiv (69), 33-43.

REES-MOGG, William
See MOGG, William Rees-

REFERENCE BOOKS
Some reference books in the sixteenth and seventeenth centuries: a finding-list. PBSA, xxxi (37), 133-75.
J. W. Spargo.

REGEMORTER, Berthe van
See VAN REGEMORTER, Berthe

REGENSBURG
Two Ratisbon manuscripts in the National library of Scotland. [*Ratisbona religosa* and *Index monasteriorum Scotarum extra Scotiam*]. BTHK, v (67/70), 24-32.
M. Dilworth.

REGIMEN SANITATIS
Regimen Sanitatis. Strassburg: Matthias Hupfuff. [14] 99. PBSA, xxxiv (40), 185.
G. L. Annan.

REGIOMONTANUS, Joannes
A note on the astrolable of Regiomontanus. LIB, xv (60), 209.
J. V. Scholderer.

REGIONAL BIBLIOGRAPHIES
Notes on North American regional bibliographies. PBSA, xxxvi (42), 171-86.
T. W. Streeter.

REID, D. J. Wilson
The archive of the University of Glasgow. BTHK, i/2 (57), 27-30.

An unusual seal of King Charles I. Illus. BTHK, ii (59/60), 33.

REID, David
Notes on the heraldry of the Hunterian manuscripts in the University of Glasgow. BTHK, iii (60/2), 151-65.

REID, Mayne
Captain of romance. [M. Reid]. Illus. BH, i (47/51), 455-67.
J. V. B. S. Hunter.

REID, Whitelaw
Walt Whitman's correspondence with Whitelaw Reid, editor of the New York *Tribune.* SB, viii (56), 242-9.
E. H. Miller.

REID, William
Brush and Reid, book-sellers in Glasgow and their collection of *Poetry Original and Selected.* Illus. GBSR, xii (36), 1-20.
J. C. Ewing.

REINGOLD, Nathan
A Russian bookstore catalogue of the eighteenth century. PBSA, lvi (62), 106-7.

REINKE, Edgar C.
A classical debate of the Charleston, South Carolina, Library Society. PBSA, lxi (67), 83-99.

RELATION
A new copy of the Paris 1600 Jesuit Relation, with notes on other editions. PBSA, lvi (62), 368-72.
R. Dechert.

REMAINDERING
An early example of remaindering? (Query, 97).
BC, vii (58), 189.
P. E. Hall.

—. BC, x (61), 454.

Elizabethan remainders. LIB, xii (58), 56-7.
K. Muir.

Persistent remaindering: Pena and de l'Obel's
Adversaria, 1570-1618. PBSA, lii (58), 295-9.
A. E. Lownes.

REMEDY FOR SEDITION
See MORISON, Sir Richard

REMORSE OF CONSCIENCE
The remorse of conscience. LIB, xiii (58), 199-200.
D. E. Rhodes.

RENSTROM, Arthur George
The earliest Swedish imprints in the United
States. Illus. PBSA, xxxix (45), 181-91.

REPORTING
Shakespeare and the reporters. [A letter]. LIB,
xvii (36/7), 225-7.
H. T. Price.

REPRINTS
Cheap reprints before the first World War.
BH, ii (51/2), 111-18.
E. Shanks.

The American republication of Thomas Moore's
Epistles, odes, and other poems: an early version
of the reprinting game. PBSA, lxii (68), 199-205.
H. G. Eldridge.

From Aldine to Everyman: cheap reprint series
of the English classics, 1830-1906. SB, xi (58),
3-24.
R. D. Altick.

RESURRECCION OF THE MASSE
The authorship of the *Resurreccion of the Masse.*
LIB, xvi (61), 210-13.
R. Pineas.

REVIEWS
Press figures and book reviews as determinants
of priority: A study of Home's *Douglas*, 1751,
and Cumberland's *The Brothers,* 1770. PBSA,
xlv (51), 72-6.
W. B. Todd.

REVILLA GIGEDO
See GIGEDO, Juan Vicente — Guërnez, *conde
de Revilla.*

REVOLTER
Three states of *The Revolter.* PBSA, xlv (51),
362.
R. F. Metzdorf.

REYNES. John
Gilt binding by John Reynes, *c.* 1521-4.
(English bookbindings, 2). Illus. BC, i (52),
94-5.
H. M. Nixon.

REYNOLDS, Edward *bp. of Norwich*
Edward Reynolds, *Three treatises,* 1631. (Query,
72). BC, v (56), 281.
J. R. Hetherington.

REYNOLDS, George William M.
Bibliography of G. W. M. Reynolds. (Query,
170). BC, xii (63), 357.
I. Stickland.

George Reynolds, sensational novelist and
agitator. (Among my books, 4). Illus. BH, i
(47/51), 225-36.
J. V. B. S. Hunter.

REYNOLDS, John
John Reynolds of Exeter and his canon. LIB,
xv (60), 105-17.
J. H. Bryant.

REYNOLDS, John Hamilton
John Hamilton Reynolds. (Some uncollected
authors, 3). BC, iii (54), 211-5.
B. Juel-Jensen.

—. Additions and corrections. BC, iv (55), 156.
D. G. Gallup.

—. (Note, 269). BC, xv (66), 210-11.
B. Juel-Jensen.

REYNOLDS, Sir Joshua
Reynolds's *Discourses.* 1769-1791. (Note, 103).
BC, vii (58), 417-18.
W. B. Todd.

REYNOLDS, Paul Revere
Agent and author: Ellen Glasgow's letters to
Paul Revere Reynolds. SB, xiv (61), 177-96.
J. B. Colvert.

RENAULT, Charles A. *and* BRUCCOLI, Matthew
Joseph
Imposition figures and plate gangs in *The Rescue.*
Illus. SB, xiv (61), 258-62.

RHODES, Dennis Everard
Francesco Villani. A forgotten poet of the
Lunigiana. (Some uncollected authors, 2). BC,
iii (54), 45-9.

Castano Psalter 1486. (Note, 43). BC, iv (55), 78.

Printing press in Malta in the sixteenth century?
(Query, 60). BC, iv (55), 82.

Mrs. Thomson and Miss Pigott. (Note, 86).
BC, vi (57), 293-6.

—. BC, vii (58), 77-8.

Printing in Italy in the seventeenth century.
BC, viii (59), 140-6.

Three rare Paduan catalogues [in the Broxbourne library]. (Note, 249). BC, xiv (65), 361-2.

The principal libraries of Florence. BC, xvi
(67), 36-43.

The library of Vittoria Colonna? (Query, 234).
BC, xviii (69), 93.

Mariotto Davanzati and an unrecorded incunable. LIB, vii (52), 51-3.

A Mondovi indulgence and Pierre Sabran.
LIB, vii (52), 117-20.

A note on some fragments of Vegetius from Augsburg. LIB, viii (53), 36-7.

The 1472 Paris edition of Plato's letters. LIB, viii (53), 197-201.

Provost Argentine of King's and his books. Illus. TCBS, ii (54/8), 205-12.

A volcano for the *S.T.C.* LIB; ix (54), 265-7.

A new line for the *Angler*, 1577. LIB, x (55), 123-5.

Santiago de Compostela and its early indulgences. LIB, xi (56), 41-4.

Volcanoes, variants and the *S.T.C.* LIB, xi (56), 282-3.

An unidentified 'incunable' printed at Augsburg not before 1502. LIB, xiii (58), 54-6.

The Remorse of Conscience. LIB, xiii (58), 199-200.

A post-incunable edition of Aesop. LIB, xiv (59), 281-2.

Some documents printed by Pynson for St. Botolph's, Boston, Lincs. LIB, xv (60), 53-7.

Two issues of an indulgence of Alexander VI. LIB, xv (60), 206-7.

Two Estienne dictionaries. LIB, xvi (61), 48-50.

The authorship of *The Life and Death of William Laud*, 1645. LIB, xvi (61), 140-1.

The brothers De Gregoriis at Crescentino? Illus. LIB, xvii (62), 316-7.

Further notes on a Milanese edition of Virgil [published by N. de Gorgonzola]. LIB, xxiv (69), 142.

The early London editions of the *Doctrinale* of Alexander Grammaticus: with a note on Duff 224. LIB, xxiv (69), 232-4.

The *Quodlibeta* of Petrus Joannes Olivi. PBSA, l (56), 85-7.

Monumenta Ordinis Fratrum Minorum. PBSA, l (56), 375-8.

Don Fernando Colón and his London book purchases, June 1522. PBSA, lii (58), 231-48.

The second edition of Celio Bichi's *Decisiones.* PBSA, liii (59), 196-7.

The letters of St. Ignatius, Bishop of Antioch: the *Fortuna* of their fifteenth-century editions. PBSA, lvii (63), 152-7.

William Marshall and his books, 1533-1537. PBSA, lviii (64), 219-31.

The British Museum's copy of a rare book from Brescia [G. Ruffo's *Arte de cognoscere la natura d'cavael*]: a problem in dating. SB, vi (54), 231-2.

The first book printed at Bari. Illus. [N. A. Carmignano's *Operette*]. SB, vii (55), 208-11.

—. Additional notes. SB, xi (58), 227-8.

Variants in the 1479 Oxford edition of Aristotle's *Ethics.* SB, viii (56), 209-12.

—. *and* SIMONI, Anna E. C.
Additions to Halkett & Laing. [*A dictionary of anonymous and pseudonymous English literature*]. [A letter]. LIB, viii (53), 204.

RHODES, Henry
The memorandum book of Henry Rhodes, 1695-1720. Illus. [2 pts.] BC, iii (54), 28-39; 103-17.
C. Blagden.

Henry Rhodes and the *Monthly Mercury*, 1702-1720. BC, v (56), 343-53.
C. Blagden.

RHODES, Raymond Crompton
The early nineteenth-century drama. Illus. 2 pts. LIB, xvi (35/6), 91-112; 210-31.

RICCI, Michele
See RITIUS, Michael

RICCI, Seymour Montefiore R.R. de
Seymour de Ricci, 1881-1942. LIB, xxiv (43/4), 187-94.
E. P. Goldschmidt.

Jacob Bryant's Caxtons: some additions to De Ricci's *Census.* LIB, iii (48/9), 218-22.
A. N. L. Munby.

RICH, Obadiah
Obadiah Rich: bibliopole. PBSA, xlix (55), 112-30.
A. W. Knepper.

RICHARD II *king of England*
King Richard II's books. LIB, xiii (32/3), 144-7.
M. E. Rickert.

RICHARD, Claude
Poe and 'Young America'. SB, xxi (68), 25-28.

RICHARD MARY *sister*
Addition to the Hemingway bibliography. PBSA, lix (65), 327.

RICHARDINUS, Robertus
See RICHARDSON, Robert *fl. 1543.*

RICHARDS, Franklin Thomas Grant
Grant Richards to James Joyce. SB, xvi (63), 139-60.
R. Scholes.

RICHARDS, William
The Christmas Ordinary: manuscripts and authorship. PBSA, l (56), 184-90.
T. B. Stroup.

RICHARDSON, Mrs. A. E.
The papers of Ebenezer Cooke. (Query, 187). BC, xiv (65), 218.

RICHARDSON, Robert, *fl.* 1543
Robertus Richardinus and S.T.C. 21021. EBST, iii (48/55), 83-4.
J. Durkan.

RICHARDSON, Sam J.
Texans in leopard-skin pants. [Capt. Sam J. Richardson and W. W. Heartsill's *Fourteen hundred and 91 days in the Confederate Army*]. PBSA, xlix (50), 373-8.
R. B. Brown.

RICHARDSON, Samuel
Samuel Richardson and Smith's *Printer's Grammar*. (Note, 322). BC, xviii (69), 518-19.
K. Maslen.

A bibliographical note on Richardson's *Clarissa*. LIB, xvi (35/6), 448-51.
W. M. Sale.

Two notes on Samuel Richardson. Richardson's chapel rules [*and*] The printer of the *Daily journal*. LIB, xxiii (68), 242-7.
T. C. D. Eaves *and* B. D. Kimpel.

Supplementary notes on Samuel Richardson as a printer. [An addition to W. M. Sales's *Samuel Richardson: Master Printer*]. SB, xii (59), 214-18.
A. D. McKillop.
Richardsoniana. SB, xiv (61), 232-4.
T. C. D. Eaves *and* B. D. Kimpel.

Samuel Richardson's London houses. SB, xv (62), 135-48.
T. C. D. Eaves *and* B. D. Kimpel.

Richardson's revisions of *Pamela*. SB, xx (67), 61-88.
T. C. D. Eaves *and* B. D. Kimpel.

The revisions of Richardson's *Sir Charles Grandison*. SB, xxi (68), 163-89.
R. C. Pierson.

RICHENTHAL, Ulrich von
The illustrations for Ulrich von Richenthal's *Chronicle of the Council of Constance* in manuscripts and books. Illus. PBSA, xxxiv (40), 1-16.
K. Küp.

RICHMOND
The booksellers and printers of Richmond, Surrey. LIB, xiii (32/3), 210-17.
A. C. Piper.

RICKERT, Edith
See RICKERT, Martha Edith

RICKERT, Martha Edith
King Richard II's books. LIB, xiii (32/3), 144-7.

RICKETTS, A. N. *and* COOK, D. F.
Kenneth Povey, 1898-1965. [An obituary notice]. LIB, xxviii (68), 51-6.

RICKS, Christopher Bruce
The variants of *In Memoriam*. [A letter]. LIB, xviii (63), 64.

Tennyson's *Lucretius*. LIB, xx (65), 63-4.

A note on Tennyson's *Ode on the Death of the Duke of Wellington*. SB, xviii (65), 282.

—. *and* CARTER, Harry Graham *eds*.
Mores, Edward Rowe: *A dissertation upon English typographical founders and founderies (1778), and A Catalogue and specimen of the typefoundry of John James (1782)*. Illus. OBSP, ix (61).

RIDER, R. C.
A note on *God's Judgements upon the Gentile Apostatized Church & A Treatise of the Three Evils of the Last Times* with special reference to a volume in the Library of St. Paul's Cathedral, Dundee, which contains both title-pages. BTHK, iii (60/2), 31-4.

RIGHTS OF THE ENGLISH COLONIES
The Rights of the English Colonies established in America stated and defended. London, 1774. PBSA, xl (46), 232.
S. T. Riley.

RIHEL, Josias
Two Strasburg reprints [by W. and J. Rihel] of Aldine classics. LIB, viii (53), 274-5.
J. V. Scholderer.

RIHEL, Wendelin
Two Strasburg reprints [by W. and J. Rihel] of Aldine classics. LIB, viii (53), 274-5.
J. V. Scholderer.

RILEY, Lyman W.
The French prose Alexander romance. LIB, xx (65), 243-4.

A variant edition of Ockham's *Summa Logicae*. PBSA, liv (60), 176.

RILEY, Stephen T.
The Rights of the English Colonies established in America Stated and Defended. London, 1774. PBSA, xl (46), 232.

RINGLER, William Andrew
The fragment *Virtue* and *The Assemble of Goddes*. S.T.C. 24844a and 17005-17007a. PBSA, xlvii (53), 378-80.

A bibliography and first-line index of English verse printed through 1500. A supplement to Brown and Robbins' *Index of Middle English Verse*. PBSA, xlix (55), 153-80.

The Praise of Musicke, by John Case. PBSA, liv (60), 119-21.

John Stow's editions of Skelton's *Workes* and of *Certaine Worthye Manuscript Poems*. SB, viii (56), 215-17.

Lydgate's *Serpent of Division*, 1559, edited by John Stow. SB, xiv (61), 201-3.

RIPON *cath., libr.*
An unrecorded Caxton at Ripon cathedral. LIB, viii (53), 37-42.
J. E. Mortimer.

RISTOW, Walter William
Nineteenth-century cadastral maps in Ohio. [Based on a paper by H. F. Walling]. PBSA, lix (65), 306-15.

RITIUS, Michael
The date of Michele Ricci's *Oratio ad Julium II*.
PBSA, lxi (67), 349.
C. F. Bühler.

RITSON, Joseph
Ritson's *Observations on . . . the history of English poetry*, 1782. (Note, 90). BC, vi (57), 408.
W. B. Todd.

RIVERA, Pedro de
The frontier presidios of New Spain: books, maps, and a selection of manuscripts relating to the Rivera expedition of 1724-1728. PBSA, xlv (51), 191-218.
L. C. Wroth.

RIVINGTON, James
James Rivington and Silas Deane. PBSA, lii (58), 173-8.
A. Davidson.

ROATEN, Darnell
Denis Brands: some imprints in the Bancroft library. PBSA, lxii (68), 252-4.

ROBBINS, J. Albert
Fees paid to authors by certain American periodicals, 1840-1850. SB, ii (49/50), 95-104.

Some unrecorded poems of James Kirke Paulding: an annotated check-list. SB, iii (50/1), 229-40.

ROBBINS, Russell H. *and* BROWN, Carleton F.
A bibliography and first-line index of English verse printed through 1500. A supplement to Brown and Robbins's *Index to Middle English Verse*. PBSA, xlix (55), 153-80.
W. A. Ringler.

ROBBINS, Thomas
Thomas Robbins, clergyman, book collector, and librarian. Illus. PBSA, lxi (67), 1-11.
T. R. Harlow.

ROBERSON, John R.
The manuscript of Page's *Marse Chan*. SB, ix (57), 259-62.

ROBERTS, Griffith
Dr. Griffith Roberts and his Welsh Grammar, Milan, 1567. (Note, 237). BC, xiv (65), 73-4.
I. Königsberg.

ROBERTS, James
The printing of *Hamlet* Q2 [and] Addendum. SB, vii (55/56), 41-50: viii, 267-9.
F. T. Bowers.

Roberts's compositors in *Titus Andronicus* Q2. SB, viii (56), 27-38.
G. W. Williams *and* P. L. Cantrell.

ROBERTS, John G.
Quesnay de Beaurepaire, Alexandre Marie (fl. 1780). *Mémoire et prospectus, concernant l'Académie des Sciences et Beaux Arts des États-Unis de l'Amérique*. Paris, 1788. PBSA, xxxvii (43), 75-7.

ROBERTS, Martin A.
Records in the Copyright Office of the Library of Congress deposited by the United States District Courts, 1790-1870. Illus. PBSA, xxxi (37), 81-101.

ROBERTS, R. F.
Saunders, Margaret Marshall. (1861-). *Beautiful Joe*. Philadelphia, 1894. PBSA, xxxv (41), 74-5.

ROBERTS, Richard Julian
An unrecorded Sassoon item. (Query, 165). BC, xii (63), 74.

The Tongue combatants . . . 1684. (Note, 299). BC, xvii (68), 217.

Sir Christopher Hatton's book-stamps. Illus. LIB, xii (57), 119-21.

The Greek press at Constantinople in 1627 and its antecedents. Illus. LIB, xxii (67), 13-43.

ROBERTS, Sir Sydney Castle
Association copies. Illus. BC, ii (53), 241-6.

'Estimate' Brown, 1715-1776. (Some uncollected authors, 24). BC, ix (60), 180-7.

A curious form of cancellation. (Query, 140). BC, x (61), 75.

Bibliography of 'Estimate' Brown. (Note, 157). BC, x (61), 198.

ROBERTS, William *poet*
Chatterton's brother-poet, William Roberts. PBSA, lvii (63), 184-90.
P. Kaufman.

ROBERTS, William *fl. 1963*
Sir William Temple on Orinda: neglected publications. Illus. PBSA, lvii (63), 328-36.

The Rogers editions of Sir Robert Aytoun. PBSA, lviii (64), 32-4.

ROBERTSON, Andrew
Andrew Robertson of Aberdeen. BTHK, iv (63/6), 81.
D. W. Evans.

ROBERTSON, Jean
Some additional poems by George Chapman. Illus. LIB, xxii (41/2), 168-76.

Sidney and Bandello. Illus. LIB, xxi (66), 326-8.

ROBINSON, Bartholomew
See ADAGIA

ROBINSON, Edwin Arlington
Letters of Edwin Arlington Robinson. [A proposed edition]. (Query, 224). BC, xvii (68), 219.
W. L. Anderson.

Edwin Arlington Robinson: new bibliographical notes. PBSA, xxxv (41), 115-44.
C. B. Hogan.

ROBINSON, Robert
The printer of the 1594 octavo of Marlowe's *Edward II*. [R. Robinson]. SB, xvii (64), 197-8.
R. F. Welsh.

ROCHESTER *earl of*
See WILMOT, John *earl of Rochester*

ROCKEFELLER, George C.
The first Testaments printed in New Jersey. Illus. PBSA, (51), 148-51.

RODGER, Alexander
Roger Ward's Shrewsbury stock: an inventory of 1585. LIB, xiii (58), 247-68.

RODGERS, Tobias
John Dodington's translation of Quevedo's *Los Sueños*. (Query, 189). BC, xiv (65), 367.

ROGERS, Arthur
[Export licences]. A letter. BC, v (56), 247.

Cricket in *The Matrimonal Magazine*. (Note 71). BC, v (56), 276.

A trade binding. (Note, 70). BC, v (56), 276.

The first edition of *Atalanta in Calydon*. (Query, 71). BC, v (56), 281.

ROGERS, Bruce
Bruce Rogers's first decorated book. PBSA, lv (61), 40-2.
D. A. Randall.

ROGERS, Charles
The Rogers editions of Sir Robert Aytoun. PBSA, lviii (64), 32-4.
W. Roberts.

ROGERS, David MacGregor
Crevenna and La Vallière. (Note, 35). BC, iii (54), 148-9.

A portrait of John-George of Brandenburg on presentation bindings: a footnote to Haebler. Illus. LIB, xvii (62), 88-92.

ROGERS, Francis Millet
Separated Jesuit letters. PBSA, lx (66). 91-9.

ROGERS, John Patrick W.
A lost poem by Oldmixon. BC, xviii (69), 291-4.

The printing of Oldmixon's *Histories*. LIB, xxiv (69), 150-4.

ROGERS, Samuel
Samuel Rogers's *Poems*, 1812. (Query, 169). BC, xii (63), 356-7.
T. Yonge.

Samuel Rogers. *Human life,* 1819. (Note, 251). BC, xiv (65), 365.
S. Nowell-Smith.

Samuel Rogers, his illustrators, J. M. W. Turner and Thomas Stothard, and other friends. (Among my books, 3). BH, i (47/51), 198-218.
H. Rycroft.

The early editions of Rogers's *Italy*. LIB, iii (48/9), 137-40.
J. S. L. Gilmour.

—. BC, xiii (64), 70-71.
P. F. Hinton.

—. BC, xiii (64), 353.
J. Clements.

ROGET, Peter Mark
The library of Peter Mark Roget. Illus. BC, xviii (69), 449-69.
D. L. Emblem.

Peter Mark Roget: a centenary bibliography. PBSA, lxii (68), 436-47.
D. L. Emblem.

ROLEWINCK, Werner
Adam Alamanus. Illus. LIB, i (46/7), 237-42.
J. V. Scholderer.

The laying of a ghost? Observations on the 1483 Ratdolt edition of the *Fasciculus Temporum*. SB, iv (51), 155-9.
C. F. Bühler.

ROLFE, Frederick William S.A.L.M.
Frederick Rolfe. (Some uncollected authors, 5). BC, iv (55), 63-8.
C. Woolf.

ROLLINS, Hyder Edward
Notes on Keats's *Letters*. [The O.U.P. ed., 1952]. SB, ix (57), 179-95.

ROLPH, John Alexander
Dylan Thomas, Mr. Rolph, and *John O'London's weekly*. PBSA, lx (66), 370-2.
W. White.

ROLT, Richard
Christopher Smart, Richard Rolt, and *The Universal Visiter*. LIB, xviii (37/8), 212-14.
C. Jones.

ROMAIN DU ROI
Académisme et typographie. The making of the Romain du roi. JPHS, i (65), 71-95.
A. Jammes.

ROMME, Mirjam M.
The Henry Davis collection. I. The British Museum gift. (Contemporary collectors, 44). Illus. BC, xviii (69), 23-44.

ROOSEVELT, Franklin Delano
Mr. Roosevelt continues, as President and author. PBSA, xxxvii (43), 223-32.
F. B. Adams, *jr.*

ROOSEVELT, Theodore
Extreme rarities in the published works of Theodore Roosevelt. Illus. PBSA, xxxix (45), 20-50.
N. E. Cordingley.

ROPP, Philip *and* STARKEY, Lawrence Granville
The printing of *A Declaration of the Demeanor and Cariage of Sir Walter Raleigh*, 1618. LIB, iii (48/9), 124-34.

ROS, Amanda M'Kittrick
Amanda M'Kittrick Ros. (Query, 38). BC, ii (53), 223.
T. S. Mercer.

ROSCOE, Sydney
Cary: *Dante*. (Query, 1). BC, i (52), 127-8.

Bewick: *Quadrupeds*, 1st edition, 1790. (Query, 14). BC, i (52), 130-1.

Early children's books. (Query, 46). BC, iii (54), 73-4.

[The use of the word 'lottery' in titles of 18th- and 19th-century children's books]. (Query, 55). BC, iii (54), 310.

Bibliography of Thomas Bewick. (Note, 40). Illus. BC, iv (55), 73.

John Marshall and *The Infant's Library*. Illus. BC, iv (55), 148-55.

[Wm. Lilly's *Catastrophe Mundi: or Merlin reviv'd* . . . *with Mr. Lily's Hieroglyphicks*]. (Query, 62). BC, iv (55), 172.

Children's books in boxes. (Note, 59). BC, v (56), 76.

The Infants Library. (Note, 75). Illus. BC, v (56), 279-80.

Bulmer's *Poems of Goldsmith and Parnell*. (Query, 109). BC, viii (59), 72.

The history of Little Goody Two-Shoes. (Query, 179). BC, xiii (64), 214.

Francis Newbery: a question of identity. (Query, 172). BC, xii (63), 495-6.

The ghost of Newbery's Smart's Pope's *Ode on St Cecilia's day*. BC, xv (66), 215.

Flora; or, The deserted child: by the author of 'James Manners' [Elizabeth Helme or Elizabeth Somerville]. BC, xvi (67), 83.

Flora; or, The deserted child [attributed to E. Somerville or E. Helme, *jr*.]. (Query, 213). BC, xvii (68), 83.

A Newcastle collection of wood blocks [by F. M. Thomson]. BC, xviii (69), 384-5.

An unrecorded children's book illustrated by Thomas Bewick. [A letter]. LIB, vii (52), 59-60.

ROSEN, Edward
De Morgan's incorrect description of Maurolico's books. PBSA, li (57), 111-18.

ROSENBACH, Abraham Simon Wolf.
The Rosenbach-Bodmer Shakespeare collection. BC, i (52), 112-16.
J. Hayward.

'The Doctor' [i.e. A. S. W. Rosenbach]. Illus. BC, i (52), 176-9.
C. G. des Graz.

ROSENBAUM, Stanford Patrick
Emily Dickinson and the machine. SB, xviii (65), 207-27.

The spoils of Poynton: revisions and editions. SB, xix (66), 161-74.

ROSENKILDE, Volmer
Printing at Tranquebar, 1712-1845. LIB, iv (49/50), 179-95.

ROSENTHAL, Erwin
Concerning the dating of Rüst's and Sporer's world maps. PBSA, xlvii (53), 156-8.

ROSENWALD, Lessing Julius
The Rosenwald Library. (Contemporary collectors, 8). Illus. BC, v (56), 28-37.
F. R. Goff.

ROSS, David John A.
A ghost edition of the *Historia Alexandri Magni*. (Note, 125). BC, ix (60), 67-8.

The printed editions of the French prose Alexander Romance. LIB, vii (52), 54-7.

ROSS, Thomas *and son*
Thomas Ross & Son: copper- and steel-plate printers since 1833. Illus. JPHS, ii (66), 3-22.
I. Bain.

ROSSETTI, Christina Georgina
Dante Gabriel Rossetti, 1828-1882. Christina Georgina Rossetti, 1830-1894. (English literary autographs, 16). Illus. BC, iv (55), 309.
T. J. Brown.

ROSSETTI, Dante Gabriel
Dante Gabriel Rossetti, 1828-1882. Christina Georgina Rossetti, 1830-1894. (English literary autographs, 16). Illus. BC, iv (55), 309.
T. J. Brown.

D. G. Rossetti's *Early Italian Poets*, 1861. (Note, 142). BC, ix (60), 329-31.
W. B. Todd.

(Note, 142). BC, x (61), 193-8.
W. E. Fredeman.

—. BC, x (61), 447.
W. B. Todd.

ROSSI, Mario Manlio
Herbert of Cherbury's *Religio Laici*: a bibliographical note. EBST, iv (55/71), 43-52.

ROSTENBERG, Leona
Nathaniel Thompson, Catholic printer and publisher of the Restoration. LIB, x (55), 186-202.

Nathaniel Butter and Nicholas Bourne, first 'Masters of the Staple'. LIB, xii (57), 23-33.

The printers of Strassburg and humanism, from 1501 until the advent of the Reformation. PBSA, xxxiv (40), 68-77.

Some anonymous and pseudonymous thrillers of Louisa M. Alcott. PBSA, xxxvii (43), 131-40.

John Martyn, 'Printer to the Royal Society'. PBSA, xlvi (52), 1-32.

Richard and Anne Baldwin, Whig patriot publishers. PBSA, xlvii (53), 1-42.

Robert Scott, Restoration stationer and importer. PBSA, xlviii (54), 49-76.

Robert Stephens, Messenger of the Press: an episode in 17th-century censorship. PBSA, xlix (55), 131-52.

The will of John Martyn, printer to the Royal Society. PBSA, l (56), 279-84.

John Bellamy: 'Pilgrim' publishers of London. PBSA, l (56), 342-69.

William Dugard, pedagogue and printer to the Commonwealth. PBSA, lii (58), 179-204.

Thomas Thorpe, publisher of *Shake-Speares Sonnets*. PBSA, liv (60), 16-37.

ROTA, Anthony
Arthur Ransome, b. 1884. (Some uncollected authors, 21). BC, viii (59), 289-93.

ROTA, Bertram
The George Lazarus library. (Contemporary collectors, 7). Illus. BC, iv (55), 278-84.

Constance Holme. (Some uncollected authors, 11). BC, v (56), 250-5.

ROTH, Cecil
The Marrano typography in England. LIB, xv (60), 118-28.

ROTH, Robert N.
The Houghton-Crewe draft of Keats's *Ode to a Nightingale*. PBSA, xlviii (54), 91-5.

ROTH, Samuel
Samuel Roth's *Love secrets*, 1927. (Note, 282). BC, xv (66), 486-7.
G. Tanselle.

ROTHSCHILD, Nathaniel Mayer Victor *3rd baron*
The publication of the first Drapier letter. LIB, xix (38/9), 107-15.

The Rothschild library. (Contemporary collectors, 4). BC, iv (55), 28-33.
D. Holland.

ROTHWELL, John
Milton, Rothwell, and Simmons. LIB, xviii (37/8), 89-103.
W. R. Parker.

ROUEN
'Abel Clemence' of 'Rouen': a sixteenth-century secret press. Illus. LIB, xx (39/40), 136-53.
G. Clutton.

ROUNDE TABLE
A. E. Housman's contributions to an Oxford magazine. [*Ye Rounde Table*]. (Query, 90). BC, vi (15), 404.
J. Carter.

ROUSSEAU, Jean Jacques
The first edition of Rousseau's *Émile*, 1762. BC, i (52), 67-76.
P. H. Muir.

Rousseau's *Dictionnaire de Musique*, 1786. (Query, 67). BC, v (56), 79.
H. A. Hammelmann.

Montesquieu, Voltaire and Rousseau in eighteenth century Scotland; a checklist of editions and translations of their works published in Scotland before 1801. BTHK, ii (59/60), 40-63.
A. K. Howard.

D'Alembert's copy of Rousseau's first *Discours*. LIB, xxii (67), 243-5.
R. A. Leigh.

ROWAN, D. F.
Johnson's *Lives*: an unrecorded variant and a new portrait. Illus. BC, i (52), 174-5.

ROWE, A.
Julian Notary and A. Rowe: two contemporary records. LIB, xi (56), 277-8.
C. E. Welch.

ROWE, B. J. H.
King Henry VI's claim to France in picture and poem, [in British Library MS. Royal 15, E vi]. Illus. LIB, xiii (32/3), 77-88.

ROWE, Bryan
The library of Bryan Rowe, vice-provost of King's college, d. 1521. Addendum by F. B. Williams. TCBS, ii (58/60), 339-51; iii, 167.
F. J. Norton.

ROWLANDS, Richard
Philip II and the printing of 'Andreas Philopater'. [R. Versteghen's abridged translation of R. Parsons's *Elizabethae Reginae Angliae edictum promulgatum Londini 29 Nouemb. Anni MDXCI, Andreae Philopatris . . . responsio*]. LIB, xxiv (69), 143-5.
A. J. Loomie.

ROWLANDS, Samuel
The *Humours* of Samuel Rowlands. Illus. PBSA, xliv (50), 101-18.
S. Dickson.

The Melancholy Cavalier [by 'J. C.' in relation to S. Rowlands' *The Melancholy Knight*]: a study in seventeenth-century plagiarism. SB, v (52), 161-3.

ROWLEY, William
The first edition of *A Faire Quarell*. LIB, iv (49/50), 137-41.
G. R. Price.

A bibliographical study of Middleton and Rowley's *The Changeling*. LIB, xvi (61), 37-43.
R. G. Lawrence.

The quartos of *The Spanish Gypsy* and their relation to *The Changeling*. PBSA, lii (58), 111-25.
G. R. Price.

ROXBURGHE SALE CATALOGUE
Bulmer and the Roxburghe Catalogue. (Query, 82). BC, vi (57), 182.
P. C. G. Isaac.

—. BC, vi (57), 290-1.
B. Juel-Jensen.

—. BC, vi (57), 291.
C. S. Bliss.

ROY, George Ross
An edition of Allan Ramsay. BTHK, iii (60/2), 220-1.

Robert Burns and the *Aberdeen magazine*. BTHK, v (67/70), 102-5.

ROYAL COLLEGE OF PHYSICIANS OF EDIN-BURGH
The records of medical and scientific societies in Scotland. 3. The Records of the Royal College of Physicians of Edinburgh. BTHK, i/3 (58), 20-7.
L. Jolley.

ROYAL HEADS BINDER
A binding by the Royal heads binder, *c.* 1665. (English bookbindings, 64). Illus. BC, xvii (68), 44.
H. M. Nixon.

ROYAL MUSIC LIBRARY
The Royal Music Library [in the British Library]. Some account of its provenance and associations. Illus. BC, vii (58), 241-52.
A. H. King.

ROYAL WORKS
Fragments of accounts relating to the Royal works from Oxford bindings. LIB, xxv (44/5), 66-7.
A. Deeley *and* S. Gibson.

RUBINSTEIN, Joseph
Borrow, *The Death of Balder*, 1889. (Query, 6). BC, iv (55), 78-81.

T. J. Wise and *Tales of the Wild and the Wonderful.* (Query, 104). BC, viii (59), 300-6.

RUBINSTEIN, Nicolai
Return to Florence, January 1967. BC, xvi (67), 26-8.

RÜST, Hans
Concerning the dating of Rüst's and Sporer's world maps. PBSA, xlviii (53), 156-8.
E. Rosenthal.

RUFF, William
A bibliography of the poetical works of Sir Walter Scott. 1796-1832. Illus. EBST, i (35/8), 99-239.

—. Additions and corrections. EBST, i (35/8), 276-81.

Cancels in Sir Walter Scott's *Life of Napoleon.* EBST, iii (48/55), 137-51.

RUFFO, Giordano
The British Museum's copy of a rare book from Brescia [G. Ruffo's *Arte de cognoscere la natura d'cavael*]: a problem in dating. SB, vi (54), 231-2.
D. E. Rhodes.

RUNNING-TITLES
Notes on running-titles as bibliographical evidence. LIB, xix (38/9), 315-38.
F. T. Bowers.

Two notes on running-titles as bibliographical evidence. [George Sandys: *Ovid's Metamorphosis*, 1632, and *Christ's Passion*, 1640]. PBSA, xlii (48), 143-8.
F. T. Bowers.

Motteux's *Love's a jest*, 1696. A running-title and press work problem. PBSA, xlviii (54), 268-73.
F. T. Bowers.

The headlines of William de Machlinia's *Year Book, 37 Henry VI.* SB, i (48), 123-32.
C. F. Bühler.

Running-title evidence for determining half-sheet imposition. SB, i (48), 199-202.
F. T. Bowers.

RUPPEL, Berthold
Berthold Ruppel, Printer of the *Sermones Meffreth.* Illus. LIB, xv (60), 1-7.
J. V. Scholderer *and* C. A. Webb.

RUSCH, Adolf
Adolf Rusch and the earliest roman types. Illus. LIB, xx (39/40), 43-50.
J. V. Scholderer.

RUSH, Benjamin
The American interests of the firm of E. and C. Dilley, with their letters to Benjamin Rush, 1770-1795. PBSA, xlv (51), 283-332.
L. H. Butterfield.

RUSH, Nixon Orwin
Fifty years of *The Virginian.* Illus. PBSA, xlvi (52), 99-120.

RUSKIN, John
Ruskin, Millais and Effie Gray. (Query, 22). BC, i (52), 268.
H. G. Viljoen.

John Ruskin, 1819-1900. (English literary autographs, 38). Illus. BC, x (61), 185.
T. J. Brown.

John Ruskin's bookplates. BC, xiii (64), 335-9.
J. S. Dearden.

John Ruskin's *Poems*, 1850. (Query, 201). BC, xv (66), 214.
J. S. Dearden.

The production and distribution of John Ruskin's *Poems* 1850. Illus. BC, xvii (68), 151-67.
J. S. Dearden.

Wise and Ruskin, I. BC, xviii (69), 45-56.

—. II (II Forgeries. III Binary editions). Illus. BC, xviii (69), 170-88.
J. S. Dearden.

—. III. (IV Wise's editions of letters from John Ruskin. V Miscellanea). BC, xviii (69), 318-39.
J. S. Dearden.

John Ruskin's bookplates. (Note, 303). BC, xviii (69), 88-9.
J. S. Dearden.

John Ruskin, the collector, with a catalogue of the illuminated and other manuscripts formerly in his collection. Illus. LIB, xxi (66), 124-54.
J. S. Dearden.

Some errors in the bibliography of the library edition of John Ruskin's works [by E. T. Cook and A. Wedderburn. London, 1912]. PBSA, lxii (68), 127-9.
J. Halladay.

RUSSELL, G. H.
Philip Woodward; Elizabethan pamphleteer and translator. LIB, iv (49/50), 14-24.

RUSSELL, Norma Hull
Frances Sheridan, 1724-1766. (Some uncollected authors, 38). BC, xiii (64), 196-205.

A bibliography of William Cowper to 1837. Illus. OBSP, xii (63).

The library of William Cowper. Addenda. TCBS, iii (59/63), 225-31.

John Scott of Amwell, 1710-1782. (Some uncollected authors, 40). BC, xiv (65), 350-60.

— and BLAGDEN, Cyprian Claude
The notebook of Thomas Bennet and Henry Clements, 1686-1719, with some aspects of book trade practice. OBSP, vi (53).

RUYSCH, Joannes
The Ruysch map of the world. PBSA, lv (51), 219-36.
B. F. Swan.

RYALS, Claude de L.
A nonexistent variant in Tennyson's *Poems, chiefly lyrical,* 1830. (Note, 245). BC, xiv (65), 214-15.

RYAN, Lawrence Vincent
An octavo edition of *Poëmata* by Walter Haddon, 1567. PBSA. xlv (51), 166-9.

Walter Haddon's *Poëmata,* 1592. PBSA, xlix (55), 68-9.

RYCROFT, Harry
Samuel Rogers, his illustrators, J. M. W. Turner and Thomas Stothard, and other friends. (Among my books, 3). Illus. BH, i (47/51), 198-218.

RYDER, Herta
Joyce's *Ulysses,* 1922. (Note, 175). BC, xi (62), 214.

RYDER, John Stanley
Printer's flowers. Some notes on a few selected examples. BC, v (56), 19-27.

RYGHT PROFYTABLE TREATYSE
Notes on two incunables: *The Abbey of the Holy Ghost* and *A Ryght Profytable Treatyse.* LIB, x (55), 120-1.
H. S. Bennett.

RYPINS, Stanley
The Ferrara Bible at press. Illus. LIB, x (55), 244-69.

—. [A letter]. LIB, xi (56), 124.

The Ferrara Bible: an addition to the census. LIB, xiii (58), 128.

RYSKAMP, Charles Andrew
MSS. by or relating to William Cowper. (Query, 214). BC, xvi (67), 225.

Problems in the text of Smart. LIB, xiv (59), 293-8.

Cowper on the King's sea-bathing. LIB, xv (60), 208-9.

RYSLEY, William
William Rysley's catalogue of the Cambridge university muniments, compiled in 1420. TCBS, iv (64/8), 85-99.
C. P. Hall.

S

S., S. *pseud.*
See KILNER, Mary

S.T.C.
See POLLARD, Alfred William *and* RED-GRAVE, Gilbert Richard

SABIN, Joseph
Sabin's *Dictionary*, PBSA, xxxi (37), 1-9.
R. W. G. Vail.

SABRAN, Pierre
A Mondovì indulgence and Pierre Sabran. LIB, vii (52), 117-20.
D. E. Rhodes.

SACHEVERELL, Henry
An old error once more corrected. [A letter re the attribution of Charles Leslie's *The New Association* to Sacheverell]. LIB, xiii (58), 207.
F. F. Madan.

SACKVILLE, Thomas *1st earl of Dorset*
Gorboduc, Ferrex and Porrex; the first two quartos. SB, xv (62), 231-3.
I. B. Cauthen.

SADLEIR. Michael Thomas H.
Orley Farm: an underline variant. (Query, 16). BC, i (52), 195.

The Sadleir library. (Contemporary collectors, 5). BC, iv (55), 115-21.

William Ernest Henley. (Some uncollected authors, 10). BC, v (56), 162-8.

Michael Sadleir: a valediction. BC, vii (58), 58-61.
J. W. Carter.

Tales from Blackwood. EBST, ii (38/45), 443-5.

Archdeacon Francis Wrangham, 1769-1842, and his books. LIB, xvii (36/7). 129-30.

—. A supplement. LIB, xix (38/9), 422-61.

'Minerva Press' publicity — a publisher's advertisement of 1794. LIB, xxi (40/1), 207-15.

Mr. Michael Sadleir's collection of XIXth century fiction. LIB, xxv (44/5), 105-10.

Michael Sadleir. [An obituary notice]. LIB, xiii (58), 129-31.
H. G. Pollard.

—. *and* CARTER, John Waynflete
The nomenclature of nineteenth-century cloth grains. Illus. BC, ii (53), 54-8.

SADLEIR, Thomas Ulick
An eighteenth-century Irish gentleman's library. [i.e. that of the Rt. Hon. Denis Daly of Dunsdale, Co. Galway.] BC, ii (53), 173-6.

SÄLLSKAPET BOKVÄNNERNA
Sällskapet Bokvännerna and its publications. PBSA, xlvi (52), 263-9.
L. S. Thompson.

ST. ALBANS *King Edward VI grammar sch.*
Three notes on Caxton. [Concerning the recovery by W. Blades of fragments from the *Boethius* in the King Edward VI grammar school at St. Albans]. LIB, xvii (36/7), 155-66.
C. F. Bühler.

ST. ANDREWS
Stationers and bookbinders in the records of the Hammermen of St. Andrews. Illus. BTHK, iii (60/2), 53-60.
R. H. Carnie.

The library of St. Salvator's College, St. Andrews. BTHK, iii (60/2), 97-100.
J. Durkan.

The St. Andrews University theses, 1579-1749: a bibliographical introduction. Illus. EBST, iii (38/45), 105-50.
R. G. Cant.

—. Supplement. EBST, ii (38/45), 263-72.
R. G. Cant.

ST. ANDREWS *univ., libr.*
St. Andrews University Library. (Unfamiliar libraries, 3). BC, vii (58), 128-38.
G. H. Bushnell.

The St. Andrews University copy of Glareanus and Barbarini. BTHK, iv (63/6), 72-5.
C. Hill.

The Beveridge collection in St. Andrews University Library. BTHK, v (67/70), 211-12.
K. C. Fraser.

St. Andrews University Library and the copyright acts. EBST, iii (48/55), 179-211.
P. Ardagh.

ST. CHAD'S GOSPELS
See GOSPELS

SAINT-EVREMOND, Charles Marguetel de Saint-Denis, *Seigneur de*
Saint Evremond. (Some uncollected authors, 3). BC, iii (54), 293-7.
D. C. Potts.

ST. GILES, *Cripplegate*
See LONDON *St. Giles Cripplegate*

ST. JAMES'S PALACE *libr.*
Note on a manuscript now at Leyden, from the library of St. James's Palace. TCBS, i (49/53), 358-9.
K. A. de Meyier.

ST. JOHN, Henry *1st visct. Bolingbroke*
Henry Saint John, viscount Bolingbroke, 1678-1751. (Some uncollected authors, 41). BC, xiv (65), 528-37.
G. G. Barber.

Bolingbroke's *Letters on history* 1738: a special copy. (Note, 300). BC, xvii (68), 351.
J. Carswell.

SAINT LOUIS
Louis Richard Certambert and the first French newspapers in Saint Louis, 1809-1854. PBSA, xxxiv (40), 221-53.
J. F. McDermott.

French publications in Saint Louis. PBSA, xlv (51), 83-4.
J. F. McDermott.

Private libraries in frontier St. Louis. PBSA, li (57), 19-37.
J. F. McDermott.

St. MEMIN
A St. Memin plate, with some notes on other St. Memin portraits. SB, i (48/9), 185-7.
F. Norfleet.

SALE, William Merritt
A bibliographical note on Richardson's *Clarissa*. LIB, xvi (35/6), 448-51.

Supplementary notes on Samuel Richardson as a printer. [An addition to W. M. Sale's *Samuel Richardson: Master Printer*]. SB, xii (59), 214-18.
A. D. McKillop.

SALE CATALOGUES
A plea for a more consistent policy of cataloguing by auction galleries. PBSA, xl (46), 107-26.
D. A. Randall.

Untraced auction sale catalogues of music. (Query, 148). BC, xi (62), 219.
A. H. King.

The art of selling books: notes on three Aldus catalogues, 1586-1592. SB, i (48/9), 83-101.
R. Hirsch.

SALINGER, Jerome David
J. D. Salinger: a checklist. PBSA, liii (59), 69-71.
T. Davis.

SALISBURY
Hymns and sequences of the Use of Salisbury. *Hymnorum cum notis opusculum*. [Wynkyn de Worde, 1530]. PBSA, xxxv (41), 157.
E. M. Sowerby.

SALMAGUNDI
Salmagundi and its publisher. PBSA, xli (47), 1-32.
J. Blanck.

SALMASIUS
See SAUMAISE, Claude de

SALMON, Vivian
An ambitious printing project of the early seventeenth century. [Joseph Webbe's works]. LIB, xvi (61), 190-6.

SALTYKOV-SHCHEDRIN LIBRARY
See LENINGRAD *gosud. publ. bibl.*

SALVINI, Tommaso
Howells and Salvini. PBSA, lx (66), 86-9.
M. E. Nickerson.

SAMPSON, Ezra
Who shall be governor, Strong or Sullivan? N.P., 1806. [Repr. of E. Sampson's *The sham-patriot unmasked*, 1801.] PBSA, xxxv (41), 74.
E. B. Steere.

SANBORN, Franklin Benjamin
A bibliography of Franklin Benjamin Sanborn. PBSA, lx (66), 73-85.
J. W. Clarkson, *jr.*

SANDARS, Samuel
See SANDARS READERSHIP IN BIBLIO-GRAPHY

SANDARS READERSHIP IN BIBLIOGRAPHY
[List of Readers with the subjects of their lectures, 1895-1950]. LIB, v (50/1), 149-50.

SANDEEN, E. R.
The origin of Sir Nicholas Bacon's book-plate. TCBS, ii (54/8), 373-6.

SANDERS, Chauncey *and* JACKSON, William Alexander
A note on Robert Greene's *Planetomachia*, 1585. LIB, xvi (35/6), 444-7.

SANDERSON, James L.
Thomas Bastard's disclaimer of an Oxford libel. LIB, xvii (62), 145-9.

SANDERSON, Thomas James Cobden-
Binding by T. J. Cobden-Sanderson, 1888. (English bookbindings, 7). Illus. BC, ii (53), 212-13.
H. M. Nixon.

Cobden-Sanderson pattern books. (Note, 308). BC, xviii (69), 93.
C. S. Bliss.

SANDFORD, Christopher
The progress of wood-engraving in current book-illustration. Illus. BH, i (47/51), 254-62.

SANDS, Donald Belshaw
Caxton as a literary critic. PBSA, li (57), 312-18.

SANDYS, George
George Sandys's account of Campania. LIB, xvii (36/7), 458-65.
E. S. de Beer.

George Sandys *v.* William Stansby: the 1632 editor of Ovid's *Metamorphosis*. LIB, iii (48/9), 193-212.
R. B. Davis.

Early editions of George Sandys's *Ovid*: the circumstances of production. PBSA, xxxv (41), 255-76.
R. B. Davis.

Two new manuscripts items for a George Sandys bibliography. PBSA, xxxvii (43), 215-22.
D. R. Beale.

Two notes on running-titles as bibliographical evidence. (1) George Sandys: *Ovid's Metamorphosis*, 1632. (2) George Sandys: *Christ's Passion*, 1640. PBSA, xlii (48), 143-8.
F. T. Bowers.

Sandys' *Song of Solomon*: its manuscript versions and their circulation. PBSA, l (56), 328-41.
R. B. Davis.

Another manuscript version of Sandys' *Song of Solomon*. PBSA, liii (59), 71-4.
K. E. Schmutzler.

The *First five bookes of Ovids Metamorphosis*, 1621, Englished by master George Sandys. SB, i (48/9), 69-82.
J. G. McManaway.

In re George Sandys' *Ovid*. SB, viii (56), 226-30.
R. B. Davis.

SAN FRANCISCO
Commercial printers of San Francisco from 1851 to 1880. PBSA, xxxiii (39), 68-84.
H. R. Wagner.

Some unrecorded San Francisco imprints. PBSA, lvii (63), 225.
J. E. Alden.

SAN MARINO, *Henry E. Huntington libr. and art gall.*
See *HENRY E. HUNTINGTON LIBRARY AND ART GALLERY.*

SANTIAGO DE COMPOSTELA
Santiago de Compostela and its early indulgences. LIB, xi (56), 41-4.
D. E. Rhodes.

SARASON, Bertram D.
Editorial mannerisms in the early *Annual Register*. PBSA, lii (58), 131-7.

SAROLEA, Charles
The Sarolea papers in Edinburgh University Library. BTHK, iii (60/2), 24-31.
D. F. Griffiths.

SASSOON, Siegfried Loraine
An unrecorded Sassoon item. (Query, 165). BC, xii (63), 74.
R. J. Roberts.

Addenda to Keynes's *Bibliography of Siegfried Sassoon*. BC, xviii (69), 310-17.
D. Farmer.

SATURDAY REVIEW
H. G. Wells's contributions to the *Saturday Review*. LIB, xvi (61), 29-36.
G. N. Ray.

SAUL, George Brandon
James Stephens' contributions to *The Irish Review*. PBSA, xlvi (52), 398-9.

SAULS, Lynn
Whereabouts of Hopton's *Collection of meditations*. (Query, 235). BC, xviii (69), 225.

Whereabouts of books owned by Traherne, Hopton, Bridgemon. (Query, 236). BC, xviii (69), 225-6.

Traherne's hand in the Credenhill records. LIB, xxiv (69), 50.

The careless compositor for *Christian ethicks*. PBSA, lxiii (69), 123-6.

SAUMAISE, Claude de
A revised bibliography of Salmasius's *Defensio Regia* and Milton's *Pro Populo Anglicano Defensio*. Illus. LIB, ix (54), 101-21.
F. F. Madan.

SAUNDERS, Charles Coleman
A journey to Philadelphia: or, Memoirs of Charles Coleman Saunders. PBSA, xxxv (41), 205.
C. S. Brigham.

SAUNDERS, Margaret Marshall
Saunders, (Margaret), Marshall (1861-). *Beautiful Joe*. Philadelphia, 1894. PBSA, xxxv (41), 74-5.
R. F. Roberts.

SAVAGE, Richard
Richard Savage, d. 1743. (Some uncollected authors, 36). Illus. BC, xii (63), 340-9.
C. Tracy.

Richard Savage's *Various Poems*, 1761. (Note, 213). BC, xiii (64), 66-7.
P. E. Hinton.

SAVONAROLA, Girolamo
Savonarola's *Expositions* on the fifty-first and thirty-first Psalms. LIB, vi (51), 162-70.
C. C. Butterworth.

SAVILE, George *1st marquess of Halifax*
Halifax's *The Character of a Trimmer*: some observations in the light of a manuscript from Ickworth. LIB, xiv (59), 117-23.
R. Gathorne-Hardy.

SAVORGNANUS, Petrus
A letter of Petrus Savorgnanus to Bilibald Pirckheimer. LIB, ii (47/8), 153-8.
J. G. Birch.

SAVOY
In the Savoy: a study in post-Restoration imprints. SB, i (48/9), 39-46.
C. W. Miller.

SAYCE, Richard Anthony
Compositorial practices and the localization of printed books, 1530-1800. Illus. LIB, xxi (66), 1-45.

SAYLE, Robert Theophily D.
Annals of Merchant Taylors' School library. Illus. LIB, xv (34/5), 457-80.

SCALIGER, Joseph Justus
The 'Psalterium Hebraycum' from St Augustine's Canterbury rediscovered in the Scaliger bequest at Leyden. Illus. TCBS, ii (54/8), 97-104.
G. I. Lieftinck.

SCARLATTI, Domenico
Eighteenth-century editions of the keyboard compositons of Domenico Scarlatti, 1685-1757. EBST, iii (48/55), 47-71.
C. Hopkinson.

SCATTERGOOD, V. J.
Two medieval book lists. [The libraries of Simon Burley and William de Walcote]. LIB, xxiii (68), 236-9.

SCHATZKI, Walter
The Children's Books Exhibition at the Pierpont Morgan Library. Illus. BC, iv (55), 34-44.

SCHEIDE, William H.
Love for the printed word as expressed in the Scheide Library. PBSA, li (57), 214-26.

SCHELER, Lucien
A Rabelais discovery. Illus. BC, iii (54), 40-4.

SCHEVEZ, William abp. of St. Andrews
William Schevez, Archbishop of St. Andrews, d. 1497. (Portrait of a bibliophile, 4). BC, ix (60), 19-29.
G. H. Bushnell.

SCHIFF, Gert
Books with illustrations by Fuseli. (Note, 101). BC, vii (58), 299-300.

SCHLENGEMANN, E.
Borrow: *The Death of Balder*. London, Jarrold, 1889. (Query, 6). BC, i (52), 129.

SCHLOUCHAUER, Ernst J.
A note on variants in the dedication of Chettle's *Tragedy of Hoffman*. PBSA, xlii (48), 307-12.

SCHMUTZLER, Karl E.
Another manuscript version of Sandys' *Song of Solomon*. PBSA, liii (59), 71-4.

Harrington's metrical paraphrases of the Seven Penitential Psalms: three manuscript versions. PBSA, liii (59), 240-51.

SCHOLDERER, Julius Victor
Missale speciale Constantiense. Illus. BC, iv (55), 8-15.

A unique *Provinciale Romanum* at Kiev. (Note, 118). BC, viii (59), 425.

The illustrations of the first edition of Holinshed. Illus. EBST, ii (38/45), 398-403.

An unknown Florentine incunabulum. [*Miracoli della gloriosa Vergine Maria*, 1495?]. Illus. LIB, xviii (37/8), 331-4.

An almanac for the year 1487. LIB, xix (38/9), 99-102.

A piety of printers. LIB, xix (38/9), 156-66.

Adolf Rusch and the earliest roman types. Illus. LIB, xx (39/40), 43-50.

The invention of printing. LIB, xxi (40/1), 1-25.

Adam Alamanus. Illus. LIB, i (46/7), 237-42.

Konrad Haebler: in memoriam. LIB, ii (47/8), 150-2.

Geneva as a centre of early printing. Illus. LIB, ii (47/8), 213-23.

The beginnings of printing at Basel. LIB, iii (48/9), 50-4.

Schoolmen and printers in Old Cologne. LIB, iv (49/50), 133-5.

Hilprand Brandenburg and his books. Illus. LIB, iv (49/50), 196-201.

Erich von Rath. [An obituary]. LIB, iv (49/50), 280.

The private diary of Robert Proctor. LIB, v (50/1), 261-9.

Notes on early Augsburg printing. Illus. LIB, vi (51), 1-6.

A folio with a strange device. Johann Lindholtz's *Arbores consanguinitatis et affinitatis, etc.*, completed by Johann Schott at Strasburg in 1516. Illus. LIB, vii (52), 273-5.

An unrecorded early printing centre. [Castano Primo]. Illus. LIB, viii (53), 128-9.

Two Strasburg reprints of Aldine classics. LIB, viii (53), 274-5.

Two unrecorded early book advertisements. LIB, xi (56), 114-15.

The Strasbourg *Speculum Iudiciale*, 1473: with a note on the career of Johann Bekenhub. LIB, xi (56), 273-7.

Some tell-tale initials in books of the 1550's. Illus. LIB, xii (57), 122-4.

An incunabulum of Esslingen. [Aquinas's *Catena aurea*]. LIB, xii (57), 270-1.

The works of Dionysius Cartusianus. LIB, xiii (58), 51-4.

More tell-tale initials. LIB, xiii (58), 198-9.

The first collected edition of Saint Augustine. LIB, xiv (59), 46-9.

A note on the astrolabe of Regiomontanus. LIB, xv (60), 209.

The printer of Jordanus de Quedlinburg, Strasburg, 1481-1502. PBSA, xlvi (52), 179-85.

The printer of Leo I, *Sermones*. (Proctor 3824). PBSA, liv (60), 111-13.

—. and WEBB, C. A.
Berthold Ruppel, printer of the *Sermones Meffreth*. Illus. LIB, xv (60), 1-7.

SCHOLDERER, Victor
See SCHOLDERER, Julius Victor

SCHOLE HOUSE OF WOMEN
Six tracts about women; a volume in the British Museum. [*The deceyte of women*. A. Vele, n.d.; *The schole house of women*, J. King, 1560; Edward More. *The defence of women*, J. King, 1560; *The proude wyues pater noster*, J. King, 1560; Robert Copland. *The Seuen sorowes*, W. Copland, n.d.; and, *Frederyke of Iennen*. A. Vele, n.d.]. LIB, xv (34/5), 38-48.
H. Stein.

SCHOLES, Robert Edward
Some observations on the text of *Dubliners*: *The Dead*. SB, xv (62), 191-205.

Grant Richards to James Joyce. SB, xvi (63), 139-60.

Further observations on the text of *Dubliners*. SB, xvii (64), 107-22.

SCHOLFIELD, Alwyn Faber
Additions to a list of the writings of Dr. M. R. James [appended to S. G. Lubbock's *Memoir of Montague Rhodes James*, 1939]. TCBS, ii (54/8), 95.

SCHOOL BOOKS
Manuscript school-books. PBSA, xxxii (38), 17-37.
J. Mulhern.

A group of early Tudor school-books. LIB, xxvi (45/6), 227-61.
E. Pafort.

SCHOOLCRAFT, Henry Rowe
Schoolcraft's manuscript magazines. PBSA, xxxv (41), 151-4.
V. Kinietz.

Pirated editions of Schoolcraft's *Oneota*. PBSA, liii (59), 252-61.
J. F. Freeman.

SCHOOL PRESS
See WHITECHAPEL *School Press*

SCHOTTUS, Franciscus
François Schott's *Itinerario d'Italia*. LIB, xxiii (42/3), 57-83.
E. S. de Beer.

SCHULLIAN, Dorothy May
Here the frailest leaves. PBSA, xlvii (53), 201-17.

—. *and* BÜHLER, Curt Ferdinand
A misprinted sheet in the 1479 *Mammotrectus super Bibliam* [of Johannes Marchesinus] (Goff M-239). PBSA, lxi (67), 51-2.

SCHULZ, H. C.
Manuscript printer's copy for a lost early English book [*The Pricke of Conscience*]. LIB, xxii (41/2), 138-44.

SCHUNKE, Ilse
Bindings by Jacob Krause and his school in English collections. Illus. BC, viii (59), 25-30.

Italian Renaissance bookbindings: i. Bologna 1519. (Foreign bookbindings, 2). Illus. BC, xviii (69), 201.

SCHWEIK, Robert C.
The 'duplicate' manuscript of Hardy's *Two on a tower*: a correction and a comment. PBSA, lx (66), 219-21.

SCHWEITZER, Joan
The chapter numbering in *Oliver Twist*. PBSA, lx (66), 337-43.

SCIENTIFIC JOURNALS
Scientific journal publication in the eighteenth century. PBSA, lix (65), 28-44.
D. A. Kronick.

SCIENTIFIC MANUSCRIPTS
Literary problems in seventeenth-century scientific manuscripts. SB, xiv (61), 69-80.
H. W. Jones.

SCOT, Sir Michael
See SCOTT, Sir Michael

SCOTLAND
Records of medical and scientific societies in Scotland. 1. Early medical and scientific societies of north-east Scotland. BTHK, i/2 (57), 31-3.
H. J. H. Drummond.

Records of medical and scientific societies in Scotland. 2. Records of scientific and medical societies preserved in the University Library, Edinburgh. BTHK, i/3 (58), 14-19.
C. P. Finlayson.

—. Additions. BTHK, iv (63/6), 38-9.

Montesquieu, Voltaire and Rousseau in eighteenth century Scotland; a checklist of editions and translations of their works published in Scotland before 1801. BTHK, ii (59/60), 40-63.
A. K. Howard.

An eighteenth-century social and economic survey of the Highlands. EBST, ii (38/45), 426.
W. Angus.

SCOTLAND *nat. libr.*
See NATIONAL LIBRARY OF SCOTLAND

SCOTS MAGAZINE
Authorship of the biographical notice of Neil Gow in *Scots Magazine*, 1809. BTHK, i/3 (58), 42.
E. Jack.

SCOTSMEN
Books published abroad by Scotsmen before 1700. GBSR, xi (33), 1-55.
J. H. Baxter *and* C. J. Fordyce.

SCOTT, J. E.
The New South Africa. By H. Rider Haggard. [i.e. William Adolf Baillie-Grohman]. 1900. PBSA, xxxviii (44), 63-5.

SCOTT, John
John Scott of Amwell, 1710-1782, (Some uncollected authors, 40). BC, xiv (65), 350-60.
N. H. Russell.

Scott of Amwell's elegy. (Note, 262). BC, xiv (65), 544-5.
Sir G. L. Keynes.

SCOTT, Michael
Michael Scott and *Blackwood's Magazine*: some unpublished letters. LIB, vii (53), 188-96.
E. A. Nolte.

SCOTT, Sir Michael
Two rare books in the University Library, Glasgow. [Michael Scott's *Mensa Philosophica;* and the *Grammar of Sulpitius*] BTHK, i/1 (56), 22-3.
P. Forman.

A problem as to incunabula of the *Phisionomia* of Michael Scot. PBSA, xlviii (54), 411-13.
L. Thorndike.

SCOTT, Robert
Robert Scott, Restoration stationer and importer. PBSA, xlviii (54), 49-76.
L. Rostenberg.

SCOTT, Sir Walter *bart.*
A Scott facsimile. (Query, 78). BC, vi (57), 74.
H. Cahoon.

Scott's *Vision of Don Roderick*, 1811. (Note, 261). BC, xiv (65), 544.
W. B. Todd.

The Border Antiquities. BTHK, i/1 (56), 23-6.
J. C. Corson.

A supplementary note on *The Border Antiquities.* BTHK, iii (60/2), 15-23.
J. C. Corson.

Scott's boyhood collection of chapbooks. BTHK, iii (60/2), 202-18.
J. C. Corson.

Some American books at Abbotsford. BTHK, iv (63/6), 44-65.
J. C. Corson.

Scott's criticism of *The jolly beggars* [by R. Burns]. BTHK, v (67/70), 207-9.
D. A. Low.

A bibliography of the poetical works of Sir Walter Scott, 1796-1832. Illus. EBST, i (35/8), 99-239.
W. Ruff.

—. Additions and corrections. EBST, i (35/8), 276-81.

The development of Scott's *Minstrelsy*: an attempt at a reconstruction. EBST, ii (38/45), 65-87.
M. R. Dobie.

Cancels in Sir Walter Scott's *Life of Napoleon.* EBST, iii (48/55), 137-51.
W. Ruff.

The manuscripts and proof sheets of Scott's Waverley novels. EBST, iv (55/71), 13-42.
G. Dyson.

A newly discovered issue of Scott's *The Vision of Don Roderick.* LIB, xviii (37/8), 109-13.
N. Van Patten.

Cancels in Scott's *Minstrelsy.* LIB, xxiii (42/3), 198.
R. W. Chapman.

Twin titles in Scott's *Woodstock.* (1826). PBSA, xlv (51), 256.
W. B. Todd.

Waverley in America. PBSA, li (57), 163-7.
D. Kaser.

The early editions and issues of Scott's *Border Antiquities.* SB, ix (57), 244-51.
W. B. Todd.

The text of Scott's edition of Swift. [*The Works of Jonathan Swift, D.D.*, Dublin, 1814]. SB, xxii (69), 240-55.
L. H. Potter.

SCOTT, Walter Sidney
Thomas Jefferson Hogg. (Query, 7). BC, i (52), 129.

Gilbert White's *The natural history of Selborne.* (Note 304). BC, xviii (69), 89-90.

SCOUTEN, A. H.
The earliest London printings of *Verses on the Death of Doctor Swift.* SB, xv (62), 243-7.

SCRIBAL ERRORS
The scribal errors of the MS. Cotton, Nero A.x. LIB, xiv (33/4), 353-8.
J. P. Oakden.

SCRIBES
Signed manuscripts in my collection. Illus.
I. BH, i (47/51), 321-8.
II. BH, i (47/51), 402-4.
3. BH i (47/51), 429-49.
4. BH, ii (51/2), 13-25.
5. BC, i (52), 79-91.
6. BC, i (52), 219-25.
Sir S. C. Cockerell.

SCRIMGEOUR, Henry
Henry Scrimgeour, Fugger Librarian; a bibliographical note. BTHK, iii (60/2), 68-70.
J. Durkan.

SCROLLS
On collecting Japanese manuscript scrolls. BC, vii (58), 396-80.
P. Hofer.

SEALS
An unusual seal of King Charles I. Illus. BTHK, ii (59/60), 33.
D. J. W. Reid.

SEALSFIED, Charles
An unrecorded Sealsfield publication. PBSA, l (56), 193-4.
J. F. McDermott.

SEALTS, Merton M.
Books from Melville's library. (Query, 167). BC, xii (63), 208.

Melville and the Shakers. SB, ii (49/50), 105-14.

SEARCH, Daniel
A binding by Daniel Search. (Query, 117). BC, viii (59), 184.
H. M. Nixon.

SEARS, Loren *and* MITCHELL, Stephen O.
An information retrieval system for modern language studies. PBSA, lviii (64), 270-8.

SEATON, Ethel
See SEATON, Mary Ethel

SEATON, Mary Ethel
Richard Galis and the Witches of Windsor. LIB, xviii (37/8), 268-78.

SEDGLEY, Richard
An Oxford binding by Richard Sedgley, 1699. (English bookbindings, 68). Illus. BC, xviii (69), 62.
H. M. Nixon.

SEEBER, Edward D.
The authenticity of the voyage of Richard Castelman, 1726. PBSA, xxxvii (43), 261-74.

SELTZER, Thomas
The Thomas Seltzer imprint. Illus. PBSA, lviii (64), 380-448.
G. T. Tanselle.

SENECA, Lucius Annaeus
A correction to Copinger. Illus. LIB, xviii (37/8), 114-16.
G. Goddard.

A Paris incunable. Seneca, Lucius Annaeus. *Proverbia De Moribus*. [Paris: Ulrich Gering c. 1483]. PBSA, xli (47), 342-3.
C. F. Bühler.

SENHOUSE, Roger
Richard Jennings: 1881-1953. BC, ii (53), 144-6.

SENTENTIAE
The marking of *Sententiae* in Elizabethan printed plays, poems, and romances. LIB, vi (51), 171-88.
G. K. Hunter.

SENTIMENT, Sophia *pseud.*
Who was Sophia Sentiment? Was she Jane Austen? BC, xv (66), 143-51.
Sir V. Z. Cope.

SEPT PSAUMES ALLÉGORISÉS
A 15th century MS. of *Les sept psaumes allégorisés*. (Query, 154). BC, xi (62), 485.
R. R. Rains.

SERIAL PUBLICATION
Serial publication of *Traditions of Edinburgh* [by R. Chambers]. LIB, xiv (33/4), 207-11.
C. O. Parsons.

Notes on serialization and competitive publishing: Johnson's and Bailey's dictionaries, 1795. OBST, v (40), 305-22; N.S. i (48), 45-6.
P. B. Gove.

SERMONES MEFFRETH
Berthold Ruppel, printer of the *Sermones Meffreth*. Illus. LIB, xv (60), 1-7.
J. V. Scholderer *and* C. A. Webb.

SERMONES THESAURI NOVI DE TEMPORE
A West Baden incunabulum [*Sermones thesauri novi de tempore*, 1486]. PBSA, xli (47), 147-8.
E. R. Smothers.

SERMONS
A note on the reporting of Elizabethan sermons. LIB, iii (48/9), 120-1.
S. Thomas.

SERVIUS *of Cassel*
See DANIEL, Pierre

SERVIUS DANIELIS
See DANIEL, Pierre

SETTLE, Elkanah
A binding by the Settle Bindery, 1704. (English bookbindings, 25). Illus. BC, vii (58), 180.
H. M. Nixon.

Issues of *The Fairy Queen*, 1692. [E. Settle's operatic adaptation of a *Midsummer Night's Dream*]. LIB, xxvi (45/6), 297-304.
P. S. Dunkin.

SEVEN ACRES PRESS
Loyd Haberly and the Seven Acres Press. BH, ii (51/2), 147-54.
A. L. Irvine.

SEVEN SAGES OF ROME
Early Scottish editions of *The seven sages of Rome*. Illus. BTHK, v (67/70), 62-72.
C. B. L. Barr.

SEVERNE, Cecily
Michael Wodhull. (Note, 60). BC, v (56), 76.

SEWARD, John
More about John Seward. EBST, ii (38/45), 385-6.
V. H. Galbraith.

SHAABER, Matthias Adam
The meaning of the imprint in early printed books. LIB, xxiv (43/4), 120-41.

SHAFFER, Ellen
Mrs. Edward Laurence Doheny, 1875-1958. Reminiscences of a California collector. Illus. BC, xiv (65), 49-59.

Portrait of a Philadelphia collector: William McIntire Elkins, 1882-1947. PBSA, l (56), 115-68.

SHAKERS
Melville and the Shakers. SB, ii (49), 105-14.
M. M. Sealts.

SHAKESPEARE, William
The Rosenbach-Bodmer Shakespeare collection. BC, i (52), 112-16.
J. Hayward.

The Ireland Shakespeare forgeries. (Note, 17). BC, ii (53), 72-3.
P. H. Muir.

Gil Vicente and Shakespeare. Illus. BH, ii (51/2), 1-12.
A. Livermore.

The bibliographical approach to Shakespeare. Notes on new contributions. LIB, xiv (33/4), 348-52.
A. W. Pollard.

Shakespeare and the reporters. LIB, xv (34/5), 481-98.
W. Matthews.

—. [A letter]. LIB, xvii (36/7), 225-7.
H. T. Price.

—. [A letter]. LIB, xvii (36/7), 227-30.
W. Matthews.

Charles Jennens as editor of Shakespeare. LIB, xvi (35/6), 236-40.
G. Crosse.

The Arlaud-Duchange portrait of Shakespeare. Illus. LIB, xvi (35/6), 290-4.
G. E. Dawson.

[A note on the Arlaud-Duchange portrait]. LIB, xviii (37/8), 342-4.
G. E. Dawson.

'Shakespeare and the new bibliography'. [A letter]. LIB, iii (48/9), 63-5.
T. M. Parrott.

On the indifferent and one-way variants in Shakespeare. LIB, xxii (67), 189-204.
E. A. J. Honigmann.

The reading of Shakespeare in colonial America. PBSA, xxxi (37), 45-56.
E. E. Willoughby.

America's first Shakespeare collection. PBSA, lviii (64), 169-73.
J. E. Alden.

Shakespearian dated watermarks. Illus. SB, iv (51/2), 150-64.
A. H. Stevenson.

A supplement to the bibliography of *Shakespeare idolatry* [by R. W. Babcock]. SB, iv (51/2), 164-6.
M. L. Wiley.

Shakespeare's text and the bibliographical method. SB, vi (54), 71-91.
F. T. Bowers.

Compositor determination and other problems in Shakespearian texts. SB, vii (55), 3-15.
A. Walker.

New approaches to textual problems in Shakespeare. SB, viii (56), 3-14.
P. Williams.

Editorial problems in Shakespeare: semi-popular editions. SB, viii (56), 15-26.
A. Brown.

Principles of annotation: some suggestions for editors of Shakespeare. SB, ix (57), 95-105.
A. Walker.

The rationale of old-spelling editions of the plays of Shakespeare and his contemporaries. SB, xiii (60), 49-67.
J. R. Brown.

The rationale of old-spelling editions of the plays of Shakespeare and his contemporaries: a rejoinder [to J. R. Brown's article]. SB, xiii (60), 69-76.
A. Brown.

Today's Shakespeare texts, and tomorrow's. SB, xix (66), 39-65.
F. T. Bowers.

The influence of justification on spelling in Jaggard's compositor B. SB, xx (67), 235-9.
W. S. Kable.

—. *The Folios* The Shakespeare folios. BH, i (47/51), 100-5.
R. C. Bald.

Tables for the identification and collation of the Shakespeare folios. Illus. BH, i (47/51), 105-76.
R. Horrox.

—. *1st Folio* A bibliographical problem in the first folio of Shakespeare. LIB, xxii (41/2), 23-33.
G. E. Dawson.

A proof-sheet in the first folio of Shakespeare. Illus. LIB, xxiii (42/3), 101-7.
C. Hinman.

Publications of 1623. LIB, xxi (66), 207-22.
J. Simmons.

The manuscript alterations in the Honeyman first folio. PBSA, liii (59), 334-8.
F. S. Hook.

The Fl *Othello* copy-text. PBSA, lxiii (69), 23-5.
W. P. Williams.

Mark III: new light on the proof-reading for the first folio of Shakespeare. Illus. SB, iii (50/1), 145-57.
C. Hinman.

The prentice hand in the tragedies of the Shakespeare first folio: compositor E. SB, ix (57), 3-20.
C. Hinman.

— *2nd Folio* The colophon of the second folio of Shakespeare. LIB, ix (54), 199-200.
J. G. McManaway.

The issues and states of the second folio and Milton's *Epitaph on Shakespeare*. Illus. SB, v (52/3), 81-108.
W. B. Todd.

—. *3rd Folio* A miscalculation in the printing of the third folio. LIB, ix (54), 129-33.
J. G. McManaway.

—. *4th Folio* Some bibliographical irregularities in the Shakespeare fourth folio. SB, iv (51/2), 93-103.
G. E. Dawson.

—. *The Quartos* First editions of Shakespeare's quortos. LIB, xvi (35/6), 166-72.
H. C. Bartlett.

Compositor B, the Pavier quartos, and copy spellings. SB, xxi (68), 131-61.
W. S. Kable.

—. *18th century editions* Samuel Johnson's editions of Shakespeare, 1765. PBSA, lvi (62), 428-44.
D. D. Eddy.

—. *Individual Plays* — *Hamlet* The two earliest prompt books of Hamlet. Illus. PBSA, xliii (49), 288-320.
J. G. McManaway.

Three Shakespeare piracies in the eighteenth century. [*Hamlet; Othello; Macbeth*]. Illus. SB, i (48/9), 47-58.
G. E. Dawson.

The compositors of *Hamlet* Q2 and *The Merchant of Venice*. SB, vii (55), 17-40.
J. R. Brown.

The printing of *Hamlet* Q2. [And] Addendum. SB, vii (55/56), 41-50; viii (56), 267-9.
F. T. Bowers.

Collateral substantive texts, with special reference to *Hamlet*. SB, vii (55), 51-67.
A. Walker.

The relation between the second quarto and the folio text of *Hamlet*. SB, vii (55), 69-83.
H. Jenkins.

The textual relation of Q2 to Q1 *Hamlet* (1). SB, viii (56), 39-66.
F. T. Bowers.

Playhouse interpolations in the folio text of *Hamlet*. SB, xiii (60), 30-47.
H. Jenkins.

—. *Henry IV* The origins and development of Shakespeare's *Henry IV*. LIB, xxvi (45/6), 2-16.
J. D. Wilson.

— *1 Henry IV* The folio text of *1 Henry IV*. SB, vi (54), 45-59.
A. Walker.

—. *2 Henry IV* The cancelled lines in *2 Henry IV*, IV.i.93, 95. LIB, vi (51), 115-16.
A. Walker.

The compositors of *Henry IV, Pt. 2., Much Ado About Nothing. The Shoemaker's Holiday,* and *The First Part of the Contention*. SB, xiii (60), 19-20.
W. C. Ferguson.

—. *Henry V* Quarto copy for folio *Henry V*. Illus. SB, viii (56), 67-93.
A. S. Cairncross.

Some editorial principles, with special reference to *Henry V*. SB, viii (56), 95-111.
A. Walker.

—. *Henry VIII* The first folio text of *Henry VIII*. SB, xi (58), 55-60.
R. A. Foakes.

— *Julius Caesar* 'Pirate Hills' and the quartos of *Julius Caesar*. PBSA, lxiii (69), 177-93.
J. W. Velz.

—. *King Lear King Lear* — mislineation and stenography. LIB, xvii (36/7), 172-83.
Sir W. W. Greg.

The date of *King Lear* and Shakespeare's use of earlier versions of the story. LIB, xx (39/40), 377-400.
Sir W. W. Greg.

An examination of the method of proof correction in *Lear*. LIB, ii (47/8), 20-44.
F. T. Bowers.

Spelling tests and the first quarto of *King Lear*. LIB, xx (65), 310-15.
E. A. J. Honigmann.

The compositor of the 'Pied Bull' *Lear*. SB, i (48/9), 59-68.
P. Williams.

A note on *King Lear*, III, ii, 1-3. SB, ii (49/50), 175-82.
G. W. Williams.

Compositor determination in the first folio *King Lear*. SB, v (52/3), 73-80.
I. B. Cauthen.

—. *Macbeth*. A note on the porter in *Macbeth*. EBST, ii (38/45), 413-16.
J. D. Wilson.

Macbeth at the Globe. LIB, ii (47/8), 108-18.
J. M. Nosworthy.

Three Shakespeare piracies in the eighteenth century. [*Hamlet; Othello; Macbeth*]. Illus. SB, i (48/9), 47-58.
G. E. Dawson.

New evidence on the provenance of the Padua prompt-books of Shakespeare's *Macbeth, Measure for Measure,* and *Winter's Tale*. SB, xx (67), 239-42.
G. B. Evans.

—. *Merchant of Venice*. The compositors of *Hamlet* Q2 and *The Merchant of Venice*. SB, vii (55), 17-40.
J. R. Brown.

Compositor B's role in *The Merchant of Venice*, Q2, 1619. SB, xii (59), 75-90.
D. F. McKenzie.

—. *Merry Wives of Windsor* Two notes on the text of Shakespeare. [*A Midsummer Night's Dream*, Act II, Sc. 1, 1.77; *The Merry Wives of Windsor*, Act II, Sc. ii]. EBST, ii (38/45), 409-13.
P. Alexander.

—. *Midsummer Night's Dream* Two notes on the text of Shakespeare. [*A Midsummer Night's Dream*, Act II, Sc. 1, 1.77; *The Merry Wives of Windsor*, Act II, Sc. ii]. EBST, ii (38/45), 409-13.
P. Alexander.

Issues of *The Fairy Queen*, 1692. [E. Settle's operatic adaptation of *A Midsummer Night's Dream*]. LIB, xxvi (45/6), 297-304.
P. S. Dunkin.

Printing methods and textual problems in *A Midsummer Night's Dream*, Q1. SB, xv (62), 33-55.
R. K. Turner.

—. *Much Ado About Nothing* The Compositors of Henry IV, Pt. 2., *Much Ado About Nothing, The Shoemaker's Holiday,* and *The First Part of the Contention*. SB, xiii (60), 19-29.
W. C. Ferguson.

Warburton, Hanmer and the 1745 edition of Shakespeare. SB, ii (49/50), 35-48.
G. E. Dawson.

The composition of the quarto of *Much Ado About Nothing*. SB, xvi (63), 9-26.
J. H. Smith.

—. *Othello* The Fl *Othello* copy-text. PBSA, lxiii (69), 23-5.
W. P. Williams.

Three Shakespeare piracies in the eighteenth century. (*Hamlet; Othello; Macbeth*). Illus. SB, i (48/9), 47-58.
G. E. Dawson.

— *Richard II* The copy for the first folio *Richard II*. SB, v (52/3), 53-72.
R. E. Hasker.

—. *Richard III Richard III* — Q5, 1612. LIB, xvii (36/7), 88-97.
Sir W. W. Greg.

Coincidental variants in *Richard III*. LIB, xii (57), 187-90.
A. S. Cairncross.

—. *Romeo and Juliet* An approximate printing date for the first quarto of *Romeo and Juliet*. LIB, xviii (37/8), 447-55.
H. R. Hoppe.

The printer of *Romeo and Juliet*, Q1. PBSA, lx (66), 363-4.
S. Henning.

The text of Shakespeare's *Romeo and Juliet*. SB, iv (51/2), 3-29.
G. I. Duthie.

The proof-reading of the first folio text of *Romeo and Juliet*. Illus. SB, vi (54), 61-70.
C. Hinman.

The printing of the second quarto of *Romeo and Juliet*, 1599. SB, ix (57), 107-28.
P. L. Cantrell *and* G. W. Williams.

Quarto copy for Q2 *Romeo and Juliet*. SB, ix (57), 129-41.
R. Hosley.

The printer and the date of *Romeo and Juliet*, Q4. SB, xviii (65), 253-4.
G. W. Williams.

—. *Sonnets and Poems* Shakespeare's *Sonnets*, 1609. (Note, 16). BC, i (52), 266.
J. D. Hayward.

Shakespeare's *Poems*: the first three Boston editions. PBSA, xxxvi (42), 27-36.
M. W. S. Swan.

Benson's alleged piracy of *Shakespeare's Sonnets* and of some of Johnson's works. SB, xxi (68), 235-48.
J. W. Bennett.

—. *Titus Andronicus* A note on *Titus Andronicus*. LIB, xv (34/5), 49-53.
R. B. McKerrow.

Author, compositor and metre: copy-spelling in *Titus Andronicus* and other Elizabethan printings. PBSA, liii (59), 160-87.
H. T. Price.

Roberts' compositors in *Titus Andronicus* Q2. SB, viii (56), 27-38.
P. L. Cantrell *and* G. W. Williams.

—. *Troilus and Cressida* The printing of Shakespeare's *Troilus and Cressida* in the first folio. PBSA, xlv (51), 273-82.
Sir W. W. Greg.

The 'second issue' of Shakespeare's *Troilus and Cressida*, 1609. SB, ii (49/50), 25-33.
P. Williams.

Shakespeare's *Troilus and Cressida*: the relationship of quarto and folio. SB, iii (50/1), 131-43.
P. Williams.

—. *Twelfth Night* The twelfth day of December: *Twelfth Night*, II, iii, 91. [O the twelfe day of December]. SB, ii (49/50), 182-5.
I. B. Cauthen.

—. *Two Noble Kinsmen* Printer's copy for *The two noble kinsmen*. SB, xi (58), 61-84.
F. O. Waller.

—. *Winter's Tale* New evidence on the provenance of the Padua prompt-books of Shakespeare's *Macbeth, Measure for Measure,* and *Winter's Tale*. SB, xx (67), 239-42.
G. B. Evans.

—. *Concordances* The Oxford old-spelling Shakespeare concordances. SB, xxiii (69), 143-64.
T. H. Howard-Hill.

SHANKS, Edward
Cheap reprints before the First World War. BH, ii (51/2), 111-18.

SHANNON, Edgar Finley
The proofs of *Gareth and Lynette* in the Widener collection. PBSA, xli (47), 321-40.

The history of a poem: Tennyson's *Ode on the Death of the Duke of Wellington*. SB, xiii (60), 149-77

SHAPIRO, Issac Aby
An unsuspected earlier edition of the *Defence of Conny-catching*. Illus. LIB, xviii (63), 88-112.

The first edition of Greene's *Quip for an Upstart Courtier*. SB, xiv (61), 212-18.

SHARPLES, Edward
A missing MS. section of Carlyle's *Reminiscences*. (Query, 173). BC, xii (63), 496.

SHAW, George Bernard
Shaw and Shavian. (Note, 185). BC, xi (62), 349-50).
P. Eaton.

George Bernard Shaw, 1856-1950. (English literary autographs, 50). Illus. BC, xiii (64), 195.
T. J. Brown.

Das Kapital and Marxism. BH, i (47/51), 263-6.

The autograph manuscripts of George Bernard Shaw. Illus. BH, i (47/51), 85-92.
F. E. Loewenstein.

An encounter with G.B.S. BH, ii (51/2), 36-40.
G. H. Fabes.

SHAW, Harold Watkins
A collection of musical manuscripts in the autograph of Henry Purcell and other English composers, *c.* 1665-85. LIB, xiv (59), 126-31.

SHAW, John Mackay
The first edition of Lewis Carroll's *Phantasmagoria*, 1869. (Query, 116). BC, viii (59), 309.

Advertisements in Cruikshank's *The Bee and the Wasp*. (Query, 150). BC, xi (62), 352.

Early American editions of Lear's *A Book of Nonsense*. (Query, 151). BC, xi (62), 353.

The Infant Minstrel, 1816. (Query, 177). BC, xiii (64), 72.

SHAW, Otto L.
Three French Books of Hours. (Note, 124). Illus. BC, ix (60), 65-7.

'An essay in bibliometry'. [A letter in reply to N. J. Barker's 'An essay in bibliometry']. BC, x (61), 48.

The devices of J. Phillippe and G. Wolf. (Note, 193). BC, xii (63), 203.

Early Parisian printing &c. (Contemporary collectors, 38). Illus. BC, xiii (64), 327-34.

SHAW, Phillip
Richard Vennar and *The Double PP*. PBSA, xliii (49), 199-202.

SHAW, Ralph Robert
Addendum to Shaw and Shoemaker [*American Bibliography*]: Smith's *Indian doctor's dispensatory*. PBSA, lxiii (69), 126-8.
R. G. Hayman.

SHAW, Watkins
See SHAW, Harold Watkins

SHAWANGUNK
Sketch of an Indian irruption into the town of Shawangunk, in the year 1780. PBSA, xxxvii (43), 77-8.
R. W. G. Vail.

SHAWCROSS, John Thomas
Certain relationships of the manuscripts of *Comus*. PBSA, liv (60), 38-56.

The manuscript of *Comus*: an addendum. PBSA, liv (60), 293-4.

Establishment of a text of Milton's Poems through a study of *Lycidas*. PBSA, lvi (62), 317-31.

Milton's *Tenure of kings and magistrates*. date of composition, editions and issues. PBSA, lx (66), 1-8.

The date of the separate edition of Milton's *Epitaphium Damonis*. SB, xviii (65), 262-5.

SHEARER, Augustus Hunt
In memoriam: Augustus Hunt Shearer. PBSA, xxxv (41), 172-5.
V. H. Paltsits.

SHEARER, James F.
French and Spanish works printed in Charleston, South Carolina. Illus. PBSA, xxxiv (40), 137-70.

SHEARER, Thomas *and* TILLOTSON, Arthur
Percy's relations with Cadell and Davies. LIB, xv (34/5), 224-36.

SHEET-NUMBERS
An English printed sheet-number of 1579. Illus. LIB, xvi (61), 197-201.
W. A. Jackson.

SHEETS
Storage of printed sheets in the seventeenth century. LIB, xvii (36/7), 468-71.
H. Pershing.

Wormholes in stored sheets. [A letter]. LIB, xvii (37/8), 463-4.
F. B. Williams, *jr*.

SHEET-SIZE
See PAPER

SHELLEY, Mary Wollstonecraft
A chapter in the Shelley legend. The letter to Mary Shelley of December 16, 1816. Illus. PBSA, xxxviii (44), 312-34.
R. M. Smith.

SHELLEY, Percy Bysshe
Percy Bysshe Shelley, 1792-1822. (English literary autographs, 1). Illus. BC, i (52), 4-5.
T. J. Brown.

A suspected Shelley letter. LIB, iv (49/50), 141-5.
A. Mayor.

The Wise Shelley letter. [A letter]. LIB, v (50/1), 63-4.
T. G. Ehrsam.

A chapter in the Shelley legend. The letter to Mary Shelley of December 16, 1816. Illus. PBSA, xxxviii (44), 312-34.
R. M. Smith.

Leigh Hunt's review of Shelley's *Posthumous Poems*. PBSA, xlii (48), 1-40.
P. G. Gates.

SHELLEY, Philip Allison
Archdeacon Wrangham's *Poems*. LIB, iv (49/50), 205-11.

SHEPARD, Leslie
John Pitts, printer in Seven Dials. (Query, 188). BC, xiii (64), 360.

SHEPHERD, Richard Herne
Tennyson's *The Lover's Tale*, R. H. Shepherd, and T. J. Wise. SB, xviii (65), 111-45.
W. D. Paden.

SHEPPARD, Leslie Alfred
A fifteenth-century humanist, Francesco Filelfo. Illus. LIB, xvi (35/6), 1-26.

The printers of the Coverdale Bible, 1535, Illus. LIB, xvi (35/6), 280-9.

Printing at Deventer in the fifteenth century. Illus. LIB, xxiv (43/4), 101-19.

Fragments from a binding. LIB, xxvi (45/6), 172-5.

Albertus Trottus and Albertus de Ferrariis. LIB, ii (47/8), 158-9.

The early ownership of the British Museum copy of Caxton's *Recuyell of the Histories of Troy*. LIB, iii (48/9), 216-18.

The *Hortulus Animae* in English, 1530. LIB, vi (51), 109-15.

Two benefactions of Ulrich Zel. LIB, xii (57), 271-3.

—. *and others* A list of the printed books recently acquired by the British Museum from the Earl of Leicester, Holkham Hall. 3 pts. BC, i (52), 120-6, 185-9, 259-63.

SHERBO, Arthur
Christopher Smart and *The Universal Visiter*. LIB, x (55), 203-5.

The cancels in Dr. Johnson's *Works* Oxford, 1825. PBSA, xlvii (53), 376-8.

SHERIDAN, Frances
Frances Sheridan, 1724-1766. (Some uncollected authors, 38). BC, xiii (64), 196-205.
N. H. Russell.

SHERIDAN, Richard Brinsley B.
The text of the first performance of *The Duenna*. PBSA, liii (59), 268-70.
C. Price.

Another Crewe MS. of *The School for Scandal*? PBSA, lviii (63), 79-81.
C. Price.

The second Crewe MS. of *The School for Scandal*. PBSA, lxi (67), 351-6.
C. Price.

Sheridan's *The Critic*. (Note, 68). SB, v (56), 172-3.
W. B. Todd.

SHERWIN, William Thomas
W. T. Sherwin: a little-known Paine bibliographer. PBSA, xlix (55), 268-72.
H. T. Meserole.

SHINE, Hill
See SHINE, Wesley Hill P.

SHINE, Wesley Hill P.
The authorship of poems in *The Anti-Jacobin*. (Query, 180). BC, xiii (64), 214.

SHIP, John
An admonition to borrowers. (Note, 220). BC, xiii (64), 211.
A. Ehrman.

SHIPLEY, John B.
The Champion. (Query, 61). BC, iv (55), 172.

The Coronation. A poem, 1727. (Query, 103). BC, vii (58), 417.

A Critical Review of the . . . Buildings, 1734. (Query, 107). BC, viii (59), 72.

A funeral poem to . . . the Earl of Lincoln, 1728. (Query, 112). BC, viii (59), 431.

The Touch-stone, London, 1728. (Query, 145). BC, x (61), 337.

Evidence of authorship. (Query, 175). BC, xiii (64), 71.

Additions to the E. M. Forster bibliography. [by B. J. Kirkpatrick]. PBSA, lx (66), 224-5.

The authorship of *The Touch-stone*, 1728. [Attributed to James Ralph]. PBSA, lxii (68), 189-98.

SHIPPEN, William
Letters to William Hunter from his American pupils, John Morgan and William Shippen jnr. Illus. BTHK, iii (60/2), 61-7.
T. Dobson *and* B. Thomas.

SHIPTON, Clifford K.
[Latin commentary on Luther, with preface signed by Timotheus Kirchnerus, dated December 29, 1565]. PBSA, xxxv (41), 68.

SHIRE, Helena Mennie
Court song in Scotland after 1603: Aberdeenshire. III. EBST, iv (55/71), 1-12.

—. *and* GILES, Phyllis Margaret
Court song in Scotland after 1603: Aberdeenshire. I, II. Illus. EBST, iii (48/55), 159-68.

SHIRLEY, James
Bibliographical note on James Shirley's *The Politician*. LIB, xviii (37/8), 104-8.
E. Huberman.

Shirley's publishers: the partnership of Crooke and Cooke. LIB, xxv (44/5), 140-61.
A. H. Stevenson.

The Triumph of Peace, a bibliographer's nightmare. Illus. LIB, i (46/7), 113-26.
Sir W. W. Greg.

Shirley, James (1596-1666). *The politician*. London, 1655. PBSA, xxxiv (40), 86.
W. A. Jackson.

Shirley's *Coronation* and *Love Will Find a Way*, erroneous title-pages. SB, xviii (65), 265-9.
T. J. King.

SHIRLEY, John
The work of John Shirley, an early hack writer. PBSA, lvi (62), 332-45.
B. L. Magaw.

SHOEMAKER, Richard H.
Addendum to Shaw and Shoemaker [*American bibliography*]: Smith's *Indian doctor's dispensatory*. PBSA, lxiii (69), 126-8.
R. G. Hayman.

SHORT ACCOUNT OF THE FIRST SETTLEMENT
A short account of the first settlement of the provinces of Virginia [&c]. London, 1735. PBSA, xxxvi (42), 231.
N. B. Wainwright.

SHORTHAND
Shakespeare and the reporters. LIB, xv (34/5), 481-98.
W. Matthews.

SHORT-TITLE CATALOGUE
See POLLARD, Alfred William *and* RED-GRAVE, Gilbert Richard

SHREWSBURY
The King's printer at York and Shrewsbury, 1642-3. LIB, xxiii (42/3), 129-31.
L. W. Hanson.

SHREWSBURY *sch. libr.*
Shrewsbury School library: its earlier history and organization. LIB, xvi, 49-60.
J. B. Oldham.

Shrewsbury School library. Illus. LIB, xiv (59), 81-99.
J. B. Oldham.

The loan records of Shrewsbury School library. LIB, xxii (67), 252-6.
P. Kaufman.

SHRIGLEY *Pott chapel*
A library at Pott Chapel, Pott Shrigley, Cheshire, *c.* 1493. LIB, xv (60), 47-53.
J. McN. Dodgson.

SIBERCH, John
John Siberch of Cambridge: an unrecorded book from his press, new light on his material. Illus. TCBS, i (49/53), 41-5.
F. S. Ferguson.

SIBTHORPE, Henry
The library of Lady Southwell and Captain Sibthorpe. SB, xx (67), 234-54.
J. C. Cavanaugh.

SICHERMAN, Carol Marks
Traherne's Ficino notebook. [MS. Burney 126]. PBSA, lxiii (69), 73-81.

SIDNELL, M. J.
Manuscript versions of Yeats's *The Countess Cathleen*. PBSA, lvi (62), 79-103.

Manuscript versions of Yeats's *The Shadowy Waters,* an abbreviated description and chronology of the papers relating to the play in the National Library of Ireland. PBSA, lxii (68), 39-57.

SIDNEY, Sir Philip
Sir Philip Sidney, 1554-1586. (Some uncollected authors, 34). 2 pts. BC, xi (62), 468-79; xii (63), 196-201.
B. Juel-Jensen.

A Sidney autograph. (Note, 211). BC, xiii (64), 65.
W. L. Godshalk.

Sidney's *Arcadia*, London, 1599. A distinguished 'ghost'. (Note, 283). BC, xvi (67), 80.
B. Juel-Jensen.

The Tixall manuscript of Sir Philip Sidney's and the Countess of Pembroke's paraphrase of the Psalms. (Note, 314). BC, xviii (69), 222-3.
B. Juel-Jensen.

Two ghosts: Herbert's *Baripenthes* and the Vaughan-Holland portrait of Sidney. LIB, xxiv (43/4), 175-81.
W. H. Bond.

The *Arcadia*, 1593, title-page border. LIB, iv (49/50), 68-71.
R. L. Eagle.

The printer of the first folio of Sidney's *Arcadia*. LIB, xii (57), 274-5.
G. W. Williams.

Sidney and Bandello. Illus. LIB, xxi (66), 326-8.
J. Robertson.

Sir Philip Sidney's *Arcadia*, 1638: an unrecorded issue. LIB, xxii (67), 67-70.
D. H. Woodward.

Sir William Alexander's *Supplement* to book III of Sidney's *Arcadia*. Illus. LIB, xxiv (69), 234-41.
K. Foster *and* A. Mitchell.

The date of publication and composition of Sir William Alexander's supplement to Sidney's *Arcadia*. PBSA, l (56), 387-92.
A. G. D. Wiles.

Thomas Fuller, William Dugard, and the pseudonymous *Life of Sidney*, 1655. PBSA, lxii (68), 501-10.
D. H. Woodward.

SIGNATURES
An unusual form of dating quires. (Query, 143). BC, x (61), 202.
R. Codlock.

Signatures on versos: Luce's *The woodman* 1887. (Note, 316). BC, xviii (69), 304.
G. T. Tanselle.

Signatures on some nineteenth-century Massachussets duodecimos: a query, LIB, iii (48/9), 58-62.
S. H. Nowell-Smith.

Signatures in nineteenth-century American printing [A letter]. LIB, iii (48/9), 224.
W. A. Jackson.

Signatures in nineteenth-century American printing. [A letter]. LIB, iii (48/9), 224-9.
A. T. Hazen.

-—. [A letter]. LIB, vii (52), 134.
A. T. Hazen.

SILVA, Innocencio Francisco da
A defense of Innocencio [Francisco da Silva]. PBSA, lxi (67), 241-3.
R. G. Stanton *and* A. I. Dust.

SILVER, Rollo Gabriel
Inches *v.* millimetres. (Query, 25). BC, ii (53), 77-8.

Problems in nineteenth-century American bibliography. PBSA, xxxv (41), 35-47.

The book trade and the protective tariff: 1800-1804. PBSA, xlvi (52), 33-44.

Benjamin Edes, trumpeter of sedition. PBSA, xlvii (53), 248-68.

Three eighteenth-century American book contracts. PBSA, xlvii (53), 381-7.

The costs of Mathew Carey's printing equipment. SB, xix (66), 85-122.

Printer's lobby: model 1802. SB, iii (50/1), 207-28.

Belcher and Armstrong set up shop: 1805. SB, iv (51/2), 201-4.

Abstracts from the wills and estates of Boston printers, 1800-1825. SB, vii (55), 212-18.

Financing the publication of early New England sermons. SB, xi (58), 163-78.

Prologue to copyright in America: 1772. SB, xi (58), 259-62.

Government printing in Massachusetts, 1751-1801. SB, xvi (63), 161-200.

Mathew Carey's proofreaders. SB, xvii (64), 123-33.

SILVIUS, Willem
Willem Silvius. LIB, xiv (59), 192-205.
C. Clair.

SIMMES, Valentine
A proof-sheet in *An Humorous day's mirth*, 1599, printed by Valentine Simmes. Illus. LIB, xxi (66), 155-7.
A. Yamada.

SIMMONS, John Simon G.
Specimens of printing types before 1850 in the typographical library at the University Press, Oxford. BC, viii (59), 397-410.

Early editions of Giordano Bruno in Leningrad. (Note, 145). BC, ix (60), 453.

The Leningrad method of watermark reproduction. (Note, 160). Illus. BC, x (61), 329-30.

George Darley's *Poems* '[1890]'. (Note, 169). BC, x (61), 449.

'Mundum Astraea Reliquit'. (Query, 158). BC, xii (63), 71-2.

Incunabula in the USSR I. BC, xiv (65), 311-23.

USSR II. BC, xv (66), 19-34.

USSR: Supplementary notes. (Note, 287). BC, xvi (67), 223-4.

Breviarium Coloniense (Cologne: Petrus in Altis, de Olpe, 1478; GW 5305). (Note, 287). BC, xvi (67), 508.

The Delft method of watermark reproduction. (Note, 320). BC, xviii (69), 514-15.

The undated Oxford broadsheet *Specimen*. Illus. LIB, xi (56), 11-7.

—. *and* TYRRELL, E. P.
Slavonic books before 1700 in Cambridge libraries. Illus. TCBS, iii (59/62), 382-400.

—. —. Slavonic books of the eighteenth century in Cambridge libraries. TCBS, iv (64/8), 225-45.

SIMMONS, Judith
Publications of 1623. LIB, xxi (66), 207-22.

SIMMONS, Mathew
Milton, Rothwell, and Simmons. LIB, xviii (37/8), 89-103.
W. R. Parker.

SIMMS, William Gilmore
Simms's first magazine; *The Album*. SB, vii (56), 169-83.
J. C. Guilds, *jr*.

William Gilmore Simms and the *Southern literary gazette*. SB, xxi (68), 59-92.
J. C. Guilds.

SIMON, André Louis
Bibliotheca gastronomica. (Contemporary collectors, 30). Illus. BC, xi (62), 45-54.

SIMONI, Anna E. C.
Guillaume Haudent and the first translation of Poliziano's *Rusticus*. LIB, viii (53), 111-17.

Additions to Halkett and Laing [*Dictionary of annonymous and pseudonymous English literature*]. LIB, viii (53), 204.
D. E. Rhodes *and* A. E. C. Simoni.

SIMONY, Arthur
Dr. Arthur Simony. (Query, 93). BC, vii (58), 188.
B. S. Cron.

SIMPSON, Percy
Literary piracy in the Elizabethan age. OBSP, i (48), 1-23.

SIMPSON, S. M.
An anonymous and undated Edinburgh tract. [*Archimedis Epistola ad regem Gelonem, Albae Graecae reperta anno aerae Christianae 1688*, by A. Pitcairne]. (Note, 264). BC, xv (66), 67.

A pleasant and compendious history of the first inventers — the 1685 edition a 'ghost'. (Note, 288). BC, xvi (67), 224.

SIMS, George
Three booksellers and their catalogues. C. S. Millard: Everard Meynell: Douglas Cleverdon. BC, iv (55), 291-8.

Vincent O'Sullivan. (Some uncollected authors, 15). BC, vi (57), 395-402.

Who wrote *For Love of the King*? Oscar Wilde or Mrs. Chan Toon? BC, vii (58), 269-77.

The privately printed *Chinese Poems*, 1916. (Query, 136). BC, x (61), 72.

Copies of Conrad's *Chance*, dated '1913'. (Query, 198). BC, xv (66), 213-14.

SIMSON, Patrick
See SYMSON, Patrick

SINCLAIR, Henry *bp. of Ross*
The library of Henry Sinclair, bishop of Ross, 1560-1565. BTHK, iv (63/6), 13-24.
T. A. F. Cherry.

SINCLAIR, Keith Val
Phillipps manuscripts in Australia. BC, xi (62), 332-7.

A Boccaccio manuscript in Australia. PBSA, lvi (62), 56-65.

SINGER, George Chapman
T. J. Wise and the technique of promotion. (Note, 184). BC, xi (62), 347-8.

Who was Mr. Y. Z.? (Query, 152). BC, xi (62), 353.

A unique copy of *The Runaway Slave*, 1849. (Note, 191). BC, xii (63), 68-71.

SINGLETON, Hugh
Edmund Spenser's first printer, Hugh Singleton. LIB, xiv (33/4), 121-56.
H. J. Byrom.

SINTON, James
Robert Heron and his writings, with a bibliography. EBSP, xv (30/5), 17-33.

SION ABBEY
Thomas Betson of Sion Abbey. LIB, xi (56), 115-18.
A. I. Doyle.

SION COLLEGE *libr.*
Sion College. (Unfamiliar libraries, 9). Illus. BC, xiv (65), 165-77.
E. Edmonston.

SIR THOMAS MORE
Hand B. in *Sir Thomas More*. [Possibly that of T. Heywood]. LIB, xi (56), 47-50.
J. M. Nosworthy.

SISSON, Charles Jasper
The laws of Elizabethan copyright: the Stationers' view. LIB, xv (60), 8-20.

SIXTEENTH AND SEVENTEENTH CENTURY STUDIES
Some reference books of the sixteenth and seventeenth centuries: a finding-list. PBSA, xxxi (33), 133-75.
J. W. Spargo.

SKARSHAUG, Pauline Grant Waite
The Military Discipline 1623. PBSA, xxxv (41), 157.

The female wanderer. Boston, (Mass), 1820. PBSA, xxxvi (42), 230-1.

Bernard Perger von Stanz. PBSA, xxxvii (43), 69-74.

Nektarios, patriarch of Jerusalem, 1605-1685. PBSA, xxxvii (43), 233-5.

SKEEL, Mrs. Roswell *jr.*
Salesmanship of an early American best seller. [Noah Webster jr's, *Grammatical Institute*]. PBSA, xxxii (38), 38-46.
W. Ringler.

SKELTON, John
John Stow's editions of Skelton's *Workes* and of *Certaine Worthye Manuscript Poems*. SB, viii (56), 215-17.

SKELTON, Raleigh Ashlin
Pieter van den Keere. LIB, v (50/1), 130-2.

SKENE, David
David Skene and the Aberdeen Philosophical society. BTHK, v (67/70), 81-99.
B. Fabian.

SKENE, sir John
A mixed edition of *De Verborum Significatione*. BTHK, iii (60/2), 219-20.
R. Donaldson.

SKIPP, Francis E.
The first editing of *Look Homeward, Angel*. PBSA, lvii (63), 1-12.

SLAVONIC BOOKS
Slavonic books before 1700 in Cambridge libraries. Illus. TCBS, iii (59/62), 382-400.
J. S. G. Simmons *and* E. P. Tyrrell.

Slavonic books of the eighteenth century in Cambridge libraries. TCBS, iv (64/8), 225-35.
J. S. G. Simmons *and* E. P. Tyrrell.

SLEDD, James Hinton *and* KOLB, Gwin Jackson
The history of the Sneyd-Gimbel and Pigott-British Museum copies of Dr. Johnson's *Dictionary*. PBSA, liv (60), 286-9.

SLEIGH, Gordon F.
The authorship of *William and Margaret*. LIB, viii (53), 121-3.

SLEPIAN, Barry
When Swift first employed George Faulkner. PBSA, lvi (62), 345-6.

The publication history of Faulkner's editions *Gulliver's Travels*. PBSA, lvii (63), 219-21.

SLOANE, Sir Hans *bart.*
Sir Hans Sloane, 1660-1753. (English scientific autographs, 14). BC, xiv (65), 201.
T. J. Brown.

Sir Hans Sloane's printed books. LIB, xxii (41/2), 67-72.
J. S. Finch.

SMALL CARNATION BINDER
A binding by the Small Carnation binder, *c.* 1680. (English bookbindings, 36). Illus. BC, x (61), 56.
H. M. Nixon.

SMART, Christopher
The ghost of Newbery's Smart's Pope's *Ode on St. Cecilia's day*. BC, xv (66), 215.
S. Roscoe.

Christopher Smart, Richard Rolt, and *The Universal Visiter*. LIB, xviii (37/8), 212-14.
C. Jones.

Christopher Smart in the magazines. LIB, xxi (40/1), 320-36.
R. E. Brittain.

Christopher Smart and *The Universal Visiter*. LIB, x (55), 203-5.
A. Sherbo.

Another edition of Smart's *Hymns for the Amusement of Children*. LIB, x (55), 280-2.
K. Williamson.

Problems in the text of Smart. LIB, xiv (59), 293-8.
C. Ryskamp.

Christopher Smart's *Hymns for the Amusement of Children*. PBSA, xxxv (41), 61-5.
R. E. Brittain.

SMART, James P.
Wise, Smart and Moody. (Note, 319). BC, xviii (69), 386-7.
S. H. Nowell-Smith.

SMITH, Albert Hugh
John Nichols and Hutchins's *History and Antiquities of Dorset*. LIB, xv (60), 81-95.

SMITH, Carleton
Music manuscripts lost during World War II. BC, xvii (68), 26-36.

SMITH, Charlotte
An unrecorded Baltimore imprint from Philadelphia [*The romance of real life* by Mrs. Charlotte Turner Smith]. PBSA, lxi (67), 121-3.
E. G. Howard.

SMITH, David Nichol
Three Scottish ghosts. EBST, ii (38/45), 429-32.

A note on *Mum*, an eighteenth-century political ballad. EBST, iii (48/55), 249-52.

SMITH, Ernest Bramah
Ernest Bramah, 1869?-1942. (Some uncollected authors, 37). BC, xiii (64), 54-63.
W. White.

Ernest Bramah's dates. (Note, 228). BC, xiii (64), 352.
M. Pinhorn.

—. (Note, 228). BC, xiv (65), 72.
W. White.

Two Bramah variants. [*A little flutter* and *The moon of much gladness*]. PBSA, lxii (68), 254-6.
W. White.

SMITH, Gerald A.
Collating machine, poor man's, mark vii. PBSA, lxi (67), 110-13.

SMITH, H. G.
C. and M. Lamb's *Mrs. Leicester's School*. (Query, 59). BC, iv (55), 81-2.

SMITH, John *1580-1631*
Smith, John (1580-1631). *The True Travels*. Richmond, 1819. PBSA, xxxiv (40), 88.
J. C. Wyllie.

SMITH, John *printer*
Samuel Richardson and Smith's *Printer's grammar*. (Note, 322). BC, xviii (69), 518-19.
K. Maslen.

SMITH, John Hazel
The composition of the quarto of *Much Ado About Nothing*. SB, xvi (63), 9-26.

SMITH, Margaret S. *and* HANDS, M. S. G.
The Cathedral Libraries catalogue. [*With*] Appendix: Printed catalogues of books and manuscripts in cathedral libraries: England and Wales. LIB, ii (47/8), 1-13.

SMITH, Peter
Addendum to Shaw and Shoemaker [*American bibliography*]: Smith's *Indian doctor's dispensatory*. PBSA, lxiii (69), 126-8.
R. G. Hayman.

SMITH, Richard
Richard Smith: 'foreign to the Company'. LIB, iii (48/9), 186-92.
S. Thomas.

SMITH, Robert Metcalf
A chapter in the Shelley legend. The letter to Mary Shelley of December 16, 1816. Illus. PBSA, xxxviii (44), 312-34.

SMITH, Sarah Pogson
Smith, Sarah Pogson. *Daughters of Eve*. Schenectady, 1826. PBSA, xxiv (40), 361.
G. D. McDonald.

SMITH, Simon Harcourt Nowell-
With benefit of bibliography. Some notes on Henry James. BC, vii (58), 64-7.

A. H. Hallam's *Poems*, 1830. (Note, 123). BC, viii (59) 430-1.

Tennyson's *In Memoriam* 1850. (Note, 129). BC, ix (60), 76-7.

Richard Watson Dixon, 1833-1900. (Some uncollected authors, 29). BC, x (61), 322-8.

Cancels in Darley's *Sylvia*, 1827. (Query, 146). BC, x (61), 337.

[Tennyson, A., C., & F.] *Poems by Two Brothers*, 1827. (Note, 172). BC, xi (62), 80.

Southey's *Poems*, Bristol 1797. (Note, 178). BC, xi (62), 216.

Thomas Edward Brown, 1830-1897. (Some uncollected authors, 33). BC, xi (62), 338-44.

Mosher and Bridges. (Note, 189). BC, xi (62), 482-3.

The Warwickshire Talents, 1809. (Query, 156). BC, xi (62), 486.

The Tennysons' *Poems by Two Brothers*, 1827. (Note, 172). BC, xii (63), 68.

John Gray's *Silverpoints*, 1893. (Query, 163). BC, xii (63), 73.

The *Abinger Chronicle*. 1939-44. (Note, 229). BC, xiii (64), 352.

Swinburne's *The Queen-Mother* [and] *Rosamond*, 1860. (Query, 184). BC, xiii (64), 357-9.

Southey, Lamb and *Joan of Arc*. (Query, 186). BC, xiv (65), 82.

Samuel Rogers. *Human Life*, 1819. (Note, 251). BC, xiv (65), 365.

A ghost of [Mary Tighe's] *Psyche*? (Query, 193). BC, xiv (65), 545.

Firma Tauchnitz 1837-1900. Illus. BC, xv (66), 423-6.

Tennyson's *In memoriam* 1850. (Note, 129). BC, xvii (68), 350-1.

Texts of *The portrait of a lady* 1881-1882: the bibliographical evidence. BC, xviii (69), 304-10.

Wise, Smart & Moody. (Note, 319). BC, xviii (69), 386-7.

Signatures in some nineteenth-century Massachusetts duodecimos: a query. LIB, iii (48/9), 58-62.

[Walter Savage Landor]. *Gebir; A Poem* 1798. Illus. LIB, xvii (62), 149-52.

Leigh Hunt's *The Descent of Liberty* 1815. LIB, xvii (62), 238-40.

The printing of George Meredith's *The amazing marriage*. Illus. LIB, xxi (66), 300-8.

The 'cheap edition' of Dickens's *Works* [first series] 1847-1852. Illus. LIB, xxii (67), 245-51.

Tennyson's *Tiresias*, 1885 LIB, xxiv (69), 55-6.

T. J. Wise as bibliographer. LIB, xxiv (69), 129-41.

SMITH, Sydney
Sydney Smith's contributions to the *Edinburgh Review*. LIB, viii (53), 275-8.
J. Murphy.

SMITH, Timothy d'Arch
Edward Cracroft Lefroy, 1855-1891. (Some uncollected authors, 30). BC, x (61), 442-5.

John Addington Symonds: the 'peccant' pamphlets. (Note, 215). BC, xiii (64), 68-70.

The second edition of Dylan Thomas's *18 Poems*. (Note, 227). BC, xiii (64), 351-2.

Theodore Wratislaw's *Caprices* 1893. (Note, 306). BC, xviii (69), 90-2.

SMITH, Warren Hunting
Architectural design on English title-pages. LIB, xiv (33/4), 289-98.

SMITH, Wilbur J.
Boz's *Memoirs of Joseph Grimaldi* 1838. (Note, 277). BC, xvi (67), 80.

Flora; or, The deserted child. (Query, 213). BC, xvi (67), 377.

Le Fanu's *Ghost stories*, Dublin, 1851. (Note, 293). BC, xvii (68), 78.

SMITH, William
Editions of Little and Smith's *Easy Instructor*. PBSA, xl (46), 233-6.
L. Condit.

SMITH, William Charles
John Walsh, music publisher: the first twenty-five years. LIB, i (46/7), 1-5.

John Walsh and his successors. LIB, iii (48/9), 291-5.

SMITH, William Henry
Hawthorne and William Henry Smith. An essay in Anglo-American bibliography. BC v (56), 370-4.
J. E. Alden.

SMOLLETT, Tobias George
Smollett's *Roderick Random*, 1754. (Query, 215). BC, xvi (67), 225.
O. M. Brack, *jr*.

The publication of Smollett's *Complete History . . . and Continuation*. LIB, xvi (35/6), 295-308.
L. M. Knapp.

A consideration of the bibliographical problems connected with the first edition of *Humphrey Clinker*. PBSA, xliv (50), 340-71.
F. B. Newman.

SMOTHERS, Edgar R.
A West Baden incunabulum. [*Sermones Thesauri novi de tempore*, Strassburg, 1486]. PBSA, xli (47), 147-8.

SMYTH, Mrs. A. Gillespie
The anonymous works of Mrs. A. Gillespie Smyth. LIB, x (55), 208-9.
A. L. Strout.

SMYTHE, Sir John
A manuscript of sir John Smythe's *Certain Discourses*. PBSA, xxxi (33), 18004.
T. M. Spaulding.

SNEYD *family*
The history of the Sneyd-Gimbel and Piggot-British Museum copies of Dr. Johnson's *Dictionary*. PBSA, liv (60), 286-9.
G. J. Kolb *and* J. H. Sledd.

SNODGRASS, W. D.
Snodgrass peoples his universe. PBSA, lvi (62), 494-5.
G. Monteiro.

—. PBSA, lvii (63), 94.
W. White.

SNOW, Vernon F.
An inventory of the Lord General's library, 1646 [i.e. that of Robert Devereux, 3rd earl of Essex]. LIB, xxi (66), 115-23.

SNYDER, Henry L.
The reports of a press spy [Robert Clare] for Robert Harley; new bibliographical data for the reign of Queen Anne. LIB, xxii (67), 326-45.

The circulation of newspapers in the reign of Queen Anne. LIB, xxiii (68), 206-35.

SOCIETY FOR THE ENCOURAGEMENT OF LEARNING
The Society for the Encouragement of Learning. LIB, xix (38/9), 263-88.
C. Atto.

SOHO
An Italian book printed in Soho. BH, i (47/51), 345-8.
M. Parenti.

SOLORZANO, Alonso de Castillo
See CASTILLO SOLORZANO, Alonso de

SOMERVILE, William
William Somervile's *The Chase*, 1735. PBSA, lviii (64), 1-7.
J. D. Fleeman.

SOMERVILLE, Elizabeth
Flora; or, the deserted child . . . [Attributed to Elizabeth Helme, jr. or Elizabeth Somerville]. (Query, 213). BC, xvi (67), 83.
S. Roscoe.

Flora; or, The deserted child [The question of authorship pursued]. (Query, 83). BC, xvii (68), 83.
S. Roscoe.

SONGS AND SONG BOOKS
British song books and kindred subjects. (Contemporary collectors, 32). Illus. BC, xi (62), 448-59.
W. N. Harding.

The music of Alan Ramsay's songs. BTHK, ii (59/60), 34; EBST i (35/8) 241-76.

Thomson's collections of national song with special reference to the contributions of Haydn and Beethoven. Illus. EBST, ii (38/45), 1-64.
C. Hopkinson *and* C. B. Oldman.

—. Addenda and corrigenda. EBST, iii (48/55), 121-4.

Notes on the printers and publishers of English song-books, 1651-1702. EBST, i (35/8), 241-76.
E. B. Murrie.

Haydn's settings of Scottish songs in the collections of Napier and Whyte. Illus. EBST, iii (48/55), 85-120.
C. Hopkinson *and* C. B. Oldman.

Court song in Scotland after 1603: Aberdeenshire. I, II. Illus. EBST, iii (48/55), 159-68.
P. M. Giles *and* H. M. Shire.

—. III. EBST, iv (55/71), 1-12.
H. M. Shire.

English song-books, 1651-1702, and their publishers. Illus. LIB, xvi (35/6), 355-401.
C. L. Day *and* E. B. Murrie.

Caroline lyrics and contemporary song-books. LIB, viii (53), 89-110.
E. F. Hart.

Pepys's songs and songbooks in the diary period. LIB, xii (57), 240-55.
M. Emslie.

Two of Pepys's 'very lewd songs' in print. LIB, xv (60), 291-3.
M. Emslie.

Rump songs, and index with notes. OBSP, v (40), 281-304.
H. F. Brooks.

The negro in early American songsters. PBSA, xxxviii (34), 132-63.
S. F. Damon.

The American songster before 1821. A list of incomplete and unlocated titles. PBSA, liv (60), 61-9.
I. Lowens.

SORG, Anton
A variant specimen of Anton Sorg's *Bücheranzeige* of 1483-1484. PBSA, vii (58), 48-52.
S. F. Anderson.

SOUTAR, William
William Soutar, bibliographical notes and a checklist. BTHK, i/2 (57), 3-14.
W. R. Aitken.

SOUTH CAROLINA
The first decade of printing in the Royal Province of South Carolina. Illus. LIB, xiii (32/3), 425-52.
D. C. McMurtrie.

Bishop Kennet and South Carolina. PBSA, lix (65), 158-60.
F. R. Goff.

SOUTHAM, Brian Charles
The manuscript of Jane Austen's *Volume the First*. LIB, xvii (62), 231-7.

SOUTHERN LITERARY GAZETTE
William Gilmore Simms and the *Southern Literary Gazette*. SB, xxi (68), 59-92.
J. C. Guilds.

The 'lost' number of the *Southern Literary Gazette*. SB, xxii (69), 266-73.
J. C. Guilds.

SOUTHERNE, Thomas
A cancel in Southerne's *The Disappointment*, 1684. LIB, xiii (32/3), 395-8.
C. Leech.

A further note on Southerne's *The Disappointment*. LIB, i (46/7), 67-9.
R. O. Hummel.

Southerne's *The Disappointment*. [A letter]. LIB, ii (47/8), 64.
C. Leech.

The supposed cancel in Southerne's *The Disappointment* reconsidered. LIB, v (50/1), 140-9.
F. T. Bowers.

SOUTHEY, Robert
A binding from Southey's 'Cottonian' library. (English bookbindings, 11). Illus. BC, iii (54), 298-9.
H. M. Nixon.

Southey's *Poems*, Bristol, 1797. (Note, 178). BC, xi (62), 216.
S. H. Nowell-Smith.

Southey, Lamb and Joan of Arc. (Query, 186). BC, xiv (65), 82.
S. H. Nowell-Smith.

The Bristol Library borrowings of Southey and Coleridge, 1793-8. LIB, iv (49/50), 114-32.
G. Whalley.

Two new works of Robert Southey. [An edition of I. Molina's *The geographical, natural, and civil history of Chile* and *An exposure of the misrepresentations and calumnies in Mr Marsh's Review of Sir George Barlow*]. SB, v (52/3), 197-200.
K. Curry.

SOUTHOUSE, Thomas
The Southouse text of *Arden of Feversham*. LIB, v (50/1), 113-29.
J. M. Nosworthy.

SOUTHWELL, Lady Anne
The library of Lady Southwell and Captain Sibthorpe. SB, xx (67), 243-54.
J. C. Cavanaugh.

SOWERBY, Emily Millicent
Beaumont, Francis (1584-1616) and Fletcher, John (1579-1625). *A King and no King*, London, for Thomas Walkley, 1619. PBSA, xxxiv (40), 270.

C.I.. *A Pleasant Comedie, Called the Two Merry Milke-Maids.* London, Bernard Alsop, 1620. PBSA, xxxiv (40), 270.

Hieron, Samuel (?1576-1617). *A Helpe vnto Deuotion . . . the fifth edition.* London, H. L[ownes], 1613. PBSA, xxxiv (40), 271.

—. *A Verry merry wherry-ferry-voyage.* PBSA, xxxiv (40), 271.

—. PBSA, xxxiv (40), 358.

Walbancke, Matthew (?1596-?1667). *Editor. Annalia Dvbrensia. Vpon the yeerely celebration of Mr. Robert Dovers Olimpick Games vpon Cotswold-Hills . . .* London, Robert Raworth, 1636. PBSA, xxxiv (40), 271.

Blanchard, Jean Pierre (1753-1809). *Journal de ma Quarante-cinquième Ascension, . . .* Philadelphie, Charles Cist, 1793. PBSA, xxxiv (40), 358.

Heywood, John (c1497-c1580). *A dialogue conteining the nomber in effect of all the prouerbes in the Englishe tongue.* PBSA, xxxiv (40), 358.

Raleigh, Sir Walter (1552-1618). *A Declaration of the demeanor and cariage of Sir W. Raleigh, 1618.* PBSA, xxxiv (40), 358.

Taylor, John, the water poet (1580-1653). *A Shilling, or, The Trauailes of Twelue-pence.* [E. Allde, 1621]. PBSA, xxxiv (40), 358.

Hymns and sequences of the Use of Salisbury. *Hymnorum cum notis opusculum.* [1530]. PBSA, xxxv (41), 157.

Mervin. *The most famous and renowned Historie, of that woorthie and Illustrious Knight Meruine . . .* By I. M. Gent. London, R. Blower and Val. Sims, 1612. PBSA, xxxv (41), 157.

Tuvill, Daniel (d. 1660). *The Dove and the Serpent*, London, 1614. PBSA, xxxv (41), 158.

Davies, John (1565?-1618). *Wittes Pilgrimage.* London [1605?] PBSA, xxxvi (42), 63.

Thomas Jefferson and his library. PBSA, l (56), 213-28.

SPAIN
The earliest books printed in Spain. PBSA, liii (59), 91-113.
L. Witten.

SPANISH BOOKS
The printing of Spanish books in Elizabethan England. LIB, xx (65), 177-229.
G. Ungerer.

Spanish books in England: 1800-1850. TCBS, iii (59/63), 70-92.
N. Glendinning.

SPARGO, John Webster
Some reference books of the sixteenth and seventeenth centuries: a finding-list. PBSA, xxxi (37), 133-75.

SPARROW, John Hanbury A.
Samuel Parr, 1747-1825. (Some uncollected authors, 9). BC, v (56), 63-72.

Robert Bloomfield. Addenda. (Note, 116). BC, viii (59), 299.

Some later editions of Sir John Davies's *Nosce Teipsum*. LIB, i (46/7), 136-42.

A manuscript from Queen Christina's Library: the *Amores* of Sigismondo Boldini. Illus. LIB, xvii (62), 281-315.

—. *and* CARTER, John Waynflete
A. E. Housman, an annotated check-list. LIB, xxi (40/1), 160-91.

—. Additions and corrections. LIB, xxiii (42/3), 42-3.

SPAULDING, Thomas Marshall
A manuscript of Sir John Smythe's *Certain Discourses*. PBSA, xxxi (37), 180-4.

Cockle, Maurice J. D. *A Bibliography of English Military Books up to 1642 and Contemporary Foreign Works*. London, 1900. Additions and corrections. PBSA, xxxiv (40), 186.

The first printing in Hawaii. PBSA, l (56), 313-27.

SPAWN, Carol *and* SPAWN, Willman
The Aitken shop. Identification of an eighteenth-century bindery and its tools. Illus. PBSA, lvii (63), 422-37.

SPECHTSHART, Hugo
The *Forma Scribendi* of Hugo Spechtshart. LIB, xxi (40/1), 264-78.
S. H. Steinberg.

SPECTATOR
A coloured frontispiece to the *Spectator*. (Query, 195). BC, xiv (65), 546.
H. A. Hammelmann.

The text of the *Spectator*. SB, v (52/3), 109-28.
D. F. Bond.

SPECULUM CHRISTIANI
The Morgan copy of Machlinia's *Speculum Christiani*. SB, v (52/3), 159-60.
C. F. Bühler.

SPECULUM IUDICIALE
The Strasbourg *Speculum iudiciale*, 1473: with a note on the career of Johann Bekenhub. LIB, xi (56), 273-7.
J. V. Scholderer.

SPEED, John
A long use of a setting of type [i.e. of John Speed's *The Genealogies Recorded in the Holy Scriptures*]. SB, ii (49/50), 173-5.
E. E. Willoughby.

SPEGHT, Thomas
Speght's Chaucer and MS. GG. 4.27 [a *Canterbury Tales* MS. in Cambridge University Library]. SB, xxi (68), 225-35.
G. B. Pace.

SPELLING
Principles governing the use of variant spellings as evidence of alternate setting by two compositors. LIB, xxi (40/1), 78-94.
C. Hinman.

Spelling and the bibliographer. LIB, xviii (63), 1-28.
T. H. Hill.

Spelling tests and the first quarto of *King Lear*. LIB, xx (65), 310-15.
E. A. J. Honigmann.

Author, compositor, and metre: copy-spelling in *Titus Andronicus* and other Elizabethan printings. PBSA, liii (59), 160-87.
H. T. Price.

These careless Elizabethans: names bewitched. PBSA, liv (60), 115-19.
F. B. Williams.

The rationale of old-spelling editions of the plays of Shakespeare and his contemporaries. SB, xiii (60), 49-67.
J. R. Brown.

The rationale of old-spelling editions of the plays Shakespeare and his contemporaries: a rejoinder [to J. R. Brown's article]. SB, xiii (60), 69-76.
A. Brown.

The influence of justification on spelling in Jaggard's compositor B. SB, xx (67), 235-9.
W. S. Kable.

Compositor B, the Pavier quartos, and copy spellings. SB, xxi (68), 131-61.
W. S. Kable.

The Oxford old-spelling Shakespeare concordances. SB, xxii (69), 143-64.
T. H. Howard-Hill.

SPENCER, Charles *3rd earl of Sunderland*
The Sunderland copy of Jacques Auguste de Thou's *History of his time*. BC, xv (66), 446-53.
S. Kinser.

SPENCER, Hazelton
The undated quarto of *I Honest Whore*. [A letter]. LIB, xvi (35/6), 241-2.

SPENCER, Lois
The professional and literary connexions of George Thomason. LIB, xiii (58), 102-18.

The politics of George Thomason. LIB, xiv (59), 11-27.

The printing of Sir George Croke's *Reports*. SB, xi (58), 231-46.

SPENDER, Stephen Harold
The printing of Auden's *Poems*, 1928, and Spender's *Nine experiments*. LIB, xxii (67), 149-50.
A. T. Tolley.

SPENSER, Edmund
Edmund Spenser's first printer, Hugh Singleton. LIB, xiv (33/4), 121-56.
H. J. Byrom.

Spenser's *Colin Clout;* the poem and the book. PBSA, lvi (62), 397-413.
S. Meyer.

Prior's copy of Spenser's *Works*, 1679. PBSA, xli (67), 52-5.
W. L. Godshalk.

A note on the printing of E. K's glosses [to *The Shepheardes Calender*]. SB, xiv (61), 203-5.
J. Stillinger.

The printing of Spenser's *Faerie Queene* in 1596. SB, xviii (65), 49-67.
F. B. Evans.

SPIELMANN, Percy Edwin
A travelling library. (Query, 91). BC, vii (58), 77.

Collections of miniature books. (Query, 114). BC, viii (59), 74.

Napoleon's travelling library. (Query, 113). BC, viii (59), 74.

SPINNEY, G. H.
Cheap repository tracts: Hazard and Marshall edition. LIB, xx (39/40), 295-340.

SPIRIT OF THE FARMERS' MUSEUM
Attribution of authorship in *The spirit of the Farmers' museum*, 1801. PBSA, lix (65), 170-6.
G. T. Tanselle.

SPIRIT OF THE TIMES
Sue, Eugene. *The King of the Winds* [*The Godolphin Arabian*]. translated for the *Spirit of the Times*. PBSA, xl (40), 162-4.
C. Collins *and* R. W. Henderson.

Spirit of the Times. PBSA, xl (46), 164-8.
C. Collins.

The passing of a noble *Spirit*. PBSA, xliv (50), 372-3.
L. Eberstadt.

An Extra issue of the *Spirit of the Times*. PBSA, xlviii (54), 198.
C. Collins.

The *Spirit of the Times*. [A letter]. Illus. PBSA, xlviii (54), 300-1.
C. S. Brigham.

The *Spirit of the Times*; its early history and some of its contributors. PBSA, xlviii (54), 117-48.
N. Yates.

SPIVEY, Herman E.
Manuscript resources for the study of William Cullen Bryant. PBSA, xliv (50), 254-68.

SPOELBERCH DE LOVENJOUL, Charles de
See SPOELBERCH DE LOVENJOUL, Alfred Charles-Joseph *viscomte de.*

SPOELBERCH DE LOVENJOUL, Alfred Charles-Joseph *vicomte de*
Charles de Spoelberch de Lovenjoul, 1836-1907. (Portrait of a bibliophile, 6). BC, x (61), 18-27.
H. Crampton.

SPOERRI, James Fuller
The Odyssey Press edition of James Joyce's *Ulysses*. PBSA, l (56), 195-8.

SPOONER, Mr.
Was Mr. Spooner advertising? (Note, 195). BC, xii (63), 204.
D. Parikian.

SPORER, Hans
Concerning the dating of Rüst's and Sporer's world maps. PBSA, xlviii (53), 156-8.
E. Rosenthal.

SPROTT, Samuel Ernest
The Osler manuscript of Herbert's *Religio Laici*. LIB, xi (56), 120-2.

SPYRI, Johanna
Spyri, Johanna (1827-1901). *Heidi, her years of wandering and learning*. Boston, 1884. PBSA, xxxv (41), 75.
G. C. Weaver.

SQUIER, Ephraim George
The Ephraim George Squier manuscripts in the Library of Congress: a checklist. PBSA, liii (59), 309-26.
J. E. Patterson *and* W. R. Stanton.

SQUIRE, William Barclay
William Barclay Squire, 1855-1927, music librarian. LIB, xii (57), 1-10.
A. H. King.

STAFFORD, Henry *1st baron*
The books and interests of Henry, lord Stafford. LIB, xxi (66), 87-114.
A. H. Anderson.

STALLMAN, Robert Wooster
The Red Badge of Courage: a collation of two pages of manuscript expunged from chapter xii. PBSA, xlix (55), 273-7.

STAM, J. F.
J. F. Stam, Amsterdam, and English Bibles. Illus. LIB, ix (54), 185-93.
A. F. Johnson.

STAMP ACT 1764
David Hall and the Stamp Act. PBSA, lxi (67), 13-37.
R. D. Harlan.

STANDING TYPE
See TYPE

STANFORD, Leland
Leland Stanford and H. H. Bancroft's *History*: a bibliographical curiosity. PBSA, xxvii (33), 12-23.
G. T. Clark.

STANFORD UNIVERSITY *Hoover inst. and libr.*
The Hoover Library on War, Revolution, and Peace. PBSA, xxxiii (39), 107-15.
H. H. Fisher.

STANHOPE, Philip Dormer *4th earl of Chesterfield*
Lord Chesterfield, 1694-1773. (English literary autographs, 28). BC, vii (58), 397.
T. J. Brown.

The Edinburgh edition of Chesterfield's *Letters to his son*. LIB, v (50/1), 271-2.
C. Price.

A Chesterfield bibliography to 1800. Illus. PBSA, xxix (35), 3-114.
S. L. Gulick, *jr*.

The number, order, and authorship of the Hanover pamphlets attributed to Chesterfield. PBSA, xliv (56), 224-38.
W. B. Todd.

Issued in parts: the seventh edition of Chesterfield's *Letters to his son*. PBSA, lx (66), 159-65.
S. L. Gulick, *jr*.

STANLEY, Thomas
Thomas Stanley, 1625-1678: a bibliography of his writings in prose and verse, 1647-1743. TCBS, i (49/53), 139-72.
M. Flower.

Thomas Stanley's manuscript of his poems and translations. TCBS, ii (54/8), 359-65.
G. M. Crump.

STANSBY, William
George Sandys *v.* William Stansby: the 1632 edition of Ovid's *Metamorphosis*. LIB, iii (48/9), 193-212.
R. B. Davis.

STANTON, Ralph G. *and* DUST, Alvin I.
A defense of Innocencio [Francisco de Silva]. PBSA, lxi (67), 241-3.

STANTON, William R. *and* PATTERSON, Jerry E.
The Ephraim George Squier manuscripts in the Library of Congress: a checklist. PBSA, liii (59), 309-26.

STANZ, Bernard Perger von
Bernard Perger von Stanz. PBSA, xxxvii (43), 69-74.
P. G. W. Skarshaug.

STAPYLTON, Sir Robert
The first editions of Sir Robert Stapylton's *The Slighted Maid*, 1663, and *The Step-Mother*, 1664. PBSA, xlv (51), 143-8.
F. T. Bowers.

THE STAR ROVER
The Star Rover and Daniel Foss's Oar. PBSA, xliv (50), 182-5.
C. R. Toothaker.

STAR SPANGLED BANNER
The star spangled banner. [A bibliography]. PBSA, lx (66), 176-84.
J. Blanck.

STARK, Lewis Morgrage
Fisher, Jonathan (1768-1847). *Two elegies, on the Deaths of Mrs. Marianne Burr . . . and of Mrs. Rebekah Walker*. Hanover, Dunham and True, 1796. PBSA, xxxiv (40), 86.

Mexico [Legal form]. *(S)Epan quantos esta carta vieren como yo . . .* [Mexico, Pedro Ocharte, 156-?]. PBSA, xxxiv (40), 87.

—. *Sepan quantos esta carta vieren como yo . . .* [Mexico, Pedro Ocharte, before Oct. 25, 1565]. PBSA, xxxiv (40), 87.

—. *(E)Nla ciudad de Mexico a [diezeocho] dias del mes de [Abrill] de Mil y quinientos y ochenta y [seys] años . . .* [Mexico 158-?]. PBSA, xxxiv (40), 87.

To all brave, healthy, able bodied, and well disposed young men, in this neighbourhood, who have any inclination to join the troops, now raising under General Washington . . . take notice [n.p., 1799]. PBSA, xxxvi (42), 67.

United Christian Friends. *Hymns for the use of the Society of United Christian Friends*. New-York, J. Tiebout, 1797. PBSA, xxxvii (43), 77.

Authorship of *A Poem, Addressed to a Young Lady*, Antigua, 1757 and Boston, 1773. PBSA, lii (58), 55-6.

STARKEY, Lawrence Granville
The printing by the Cambridge [Mass.] press of *A Platform of Church Discipline*, 1649. SB, ii (49/50), 79-93.

Benefactors of the Cambridge [Mass.] press: a reconsideration. SB, iii (50/1), 267-70.

—. *and* ROPP, Philip
The printing of *A Declaration of the Demeanor and Cariage of Sir Walter Raleigh*, 1618. LIB, iii (48/9), 124-34.

STATES
Criteria for classifying hand-printed books as issues and variant states. PBSA, xli (47), 271-92.
F. T. Bowers.

The state of the issue. PBSA, xlii (48), 239-55.
P. S. Dunkin.

—. [A letter] in reply to P. S. Dunkin's article. PBSA, xlii (48), 341-3.
F. T. Bowers.

—. [A letter] in reply to F. T. Bowers. PBSA, xliii (49), 83.
P. S. Dunkin.

The issues and states of the second folio and Milton's *Epitaph on Shakespeare*. Illus. SB, v (52/3) 81-108.
W. B. Todd.

STATIONERS' COMPANY
Charter trouble. Written on the occasion of the quater-centenary of the grant of a charter to the Stationers' Company. BC, vi (57), 369-77.
C. C. Blagden.

William A. Jackson and the Stationers' Company. (Note, 281). BC, xv (66), 485.
S. Hodgson.

Parliament and the press, 1643-7. LIB, xiii (32/3), 399-424; xiv (33/4) 39-58.
W. M. Clyde.

Alice [Norton] and the Stationers. LIB, xv (34/5), 499-500.
Sir W. W. Greg.

The Company of Stationers before 1557. LIB, xviii (37/8), 1-38.
H. G. Pollard.

The early constitution of the Stationers' Company. LIB, xviii (37/8), 235-60.
H. G. Pollard.

Entrance, licence, and publication. LIB, xxv (44/5), 1-22.
Sir W. W. Greg.

—. [A letter]. LIB, xxvi (45/6), 195.
L. Kirschbaum.

—. [A letter]. LIB, xxvi (45/6), 308-10.
Sir W. W. Greg.

Papers and documents recently found at Stationers' Hall. LIB, xxv (44/5), 23-6.
S. Hodgson.

Richard Smith: 'foreign to the Company'. LIB, iii (48/9), 186-92.
S. Thomas.

The English stock of the Stationers' Company. LIB, x (55), 163-85.
C. C. Blagden.

—. [A letter]. LIB, xi (56), 53.
Sir W. W. Greg.

The English stock of the Stationers' Company in the time of the Stuarts. LIB, xii (57), 167-86.
C. C. Blagden.

The Stationers' Company in the Civil War period. LIB, xiii (58), 1-17.
C. C. Blagden.

Apprenticeship in the Stationers' Company, 1555-1640. LIB, xiii (58), 292-9.
D. F. McKenzie.

The laws of Elizabethan copyright: the Stationers' view. LIB, xv (60), 8-20.
C. J. Sisson.

Variant entry fees of the Stationers' Company. PBSA, li (57), 103-10.
W. A. Jackson.

Henry Walley of the Stationers' Company and John Marston. PBSA, lvi (62), 366-8.
P. J. Finkelpearl.

The accounts of the Wardens of the Stationers' Company. SB, ix (57), 69-93.
C. C. Blagden.

The distribution of almanacks in the second half of the seventeenth century. SB, xi (58), 107-16.
C. C. Blagden.

The 'Company' of printers. SB, xiii (60), 3-17.
C. C. Blagden.

Thomas Carnan and the almanack monopoly. SB, xiv (61), 23-43.
C. C. Blagden.

George Wither's quarrel with the stationers: an anonymous reply to *The Schollers Purgatory*. SB, xvi (63), 27-42.
A. Pritchard.

John Partridge and the Company of Stationers. SB, xvi (63), 61-80.
R. P. Bond.

Privilege to print. SB, xvi (63), 201-3.
J. G. McManaway.

Wither and the stationers. SB, xix (66), 210-15.
N. E. Carlson.

Stationers made free of the City in 1551/2 and 1552. TCBS, i (49/53), 194-5.
B. Dickins.

Early Cambridge printers and the Stationers' Company. TCBS, ii (54/8), 275-89.
C. C. Blagden.

Restrictive practices in the Elizabethan book trade: the Stationers' Company *v.* Thomas Thomas 1583-8. TCBS, iv (64/8), 276-90.
J. Morris.

STATIUS, Publius Papinius
Statius, Publius Papinius (*c.* 45-96 A.D.) *Opera*. PBSA, xxxiv (40), 85.
F. R. Goff.

STECK, James S.
Center rules in folio printing: a new kind of bibliographical evidence. SB, i (48/9), 188-91.

Dryden's *Indian Emperour*: the early editions and their relation to the text. SB, ii (49/50), 139-52.

STEDMAN, John
A rare copy of John Stedman's *Laelius and Hortensia*. PBSA, li (57), 241-4.
P. A. Doyle.

STEEDMAN, J. W.
R. S. Surtees: *The horseman's manual* 1831. Which issue was the earlier? (Query, 231). BC, xvii (68), 492.

STEELE, Geoffrey
A rare color-plate book. PBSA, lviii (64), 293-5.

STEELE, Oliver Lee
Early impressions of Ellen Glasgow's *The Miller of Old Church*, 1911. LIB, xvi (61), 50-2.

On the imposition of the first edition of Hawthorne's *The Scarlet Letter*. Illus. LIB, xvii (62), 250-5.

A note on early impressions of Ellen Glasgow's *They Stooped to Folly*. PBSA, lii (58), 310-12.

The Case of the Planters of Tobacco in Virginia, 1733: an extraordinary use of standing type. SB, v (52/3), 184-6.

Half-sheet imposition of eight-leaf quires in formes of thirty-two and sixty-four pages. SB, xv (62), 274-8.

Evidence of plate damage as applied to the first impression of Ellen Glasgow's *The Wheel of Fire*. Illus. SB, xvi (63), 223-31.

STEELE, Sir Richard
See also SPECTATOR

Richard Steele, 1672-1729; Joseph Addison, 1672-1719. (English literary autographs, 25). Illus. BC, vii (58), 63.
T. J. Brown.

Gibbon's copy of Steele's *Dramatick Works*. (Note, 217). BC, xiii (64), 207.
C. C. Nickerson.

The piracy of Steele's *The Lying Lover*. LIB, x (55), 127-9.
D. F. Foxon.

The publication of Steele's *Conscious Lovers*. SB, ii (48/50), 169-73.
R. M. Baine.

Two scenes by Addison in Steele's *Tender husband*. SB, xix (66), 217-26.
S. S. Kenny.

Eighteenth-century editions of Steele's *Conscious Lovers*. SB, xxi (68), 253-61.
S. S. Kenny.

STEERE, Elizabeth B.
Observations sur le Mémoire de la France, envoyées dans les cours de l'Europe, par le ministère Britannique, pour justifier la réponse faite à la réquisition de S.M.T.C. du 21 décembre 1755. [Paris, 1756?]. PBSA, xxxiv (40), 361.

Who shall be governor, Strong or Sullivan? . . . . N.P., 1806. PBSA, xxxv (41), 74.

A Sketch of the life of General Lafayette. Translated from the French by James P. Cobbett. London, 1830. PBSA, xxxv (41), 207.

STEFFAN, Truman Guy
Byron's dramas: three untraced MSS. (Query, 191). BC, xiv (65), 367.

STEIN, Harold
Six tracts about women: a volume in the British Museum. [*The Deceyte of women*. A. Vele, n.d.; *The scole house of women*, J. King, 1560; Edward More, *The defence of women*. J. King, 1560; *The proude wyues pater noster*. J. King, 1560; Robert Copland, *The Seuen sorowes*, W. Copland, n.d.,; and *Frederyke of Iennen*. A. Vele n.d.]. LIB, xv (34/5), 38-48.

STEINBERG, Sigfrid Heinrich
The *Forma Scribendi* of Hugo Spechtshart. LIB, xxi (40/1), 264-78.

Medieval writing-masters. Illus. LIB, xxii (41/2), 1-24.

A French version of Duranti's prescriptions on the presentation of papal bulls. LIB, xxiii (42/3), 84-9.

A hand-list of specimens of medieval writing-masters. LIB, xxiii (42/3), 191-4.

—. [A letter]. LIB, ii (47/8), 203.

STEPHANUS
See ESTIENNE

STEPHENS, James
James Stephens' contributions to *The Irish Review*. PBSA, xlvi (52), 398-9.
G. B. Saul.

A holograph notebook and the publication of its contents: a bibliographical note on James Stephens. PBSA, lvii (63), 226.
P. McFate.

STEPHENS, Robert
Robert Stephens, Messenger of the Press: an episode in 17th-century censorship. PBSA, xlix (55), 131-52.
L. Rostenberg.

'Robin Hog' Stephens: Messenger of the Press. Press. PBSA, l (56), 381-7.
J. R. Moore.

STEREOTYPE
William Ged and the invention of stereotype. (Query, 102). BC, vii (58), 296-7.
J. W. Carter.

—. [A letter]. LIB, xiii (58), 141.

William Ged and the invention of stereotype. Illus. LIB, xv (60), 161-92.
J. W. Carter.

—. A postscript. Illus. LIB, xvi (61), 143-5.
R. Donaldson.

A plate from Ged's *Sallust*, Edinburgh, 1739, 1744. BTHK, iv (64/6), 76.
J. P. W. Gaskell.

A note on the first stereotyping in England. JPHS, i (65), 97-8.
J. Morris.

William Ged and the invention of stereotype, a second postscript. Illus. LIB, xxii (67), 352-4.
R. Donaldson.

A mirror for bibliographers: duplicate plates in modern printing. PBSA, liv (60), 83-8.
M. J. Bruccoli.

Imposition figures and plategangs in *The Rescue*. Illus. SB, xiv (61), 258-62.
M. J. Bruccoli *and* C. A. Rheault.

Evidence of plate damage as applied to the first impressions of Ellen Glasgow's *The Wheel of Fire*. Illus. SB, xvi (63), 223-31.
O. L. Steele.

STERN, Madeleine Bettina
Sherlock Holmes: rare-book collector: a study in book detection. PBSA, xlvii (53), 135-55.

STERNE, Laurence
Sterne: *Sentimental Journey*. First edition. (Query, 9). BC, i (52), 57.
A., R. F.

On collecting Sterne. Illus. BC, i (52), 246-58.
J. C. T. Oates.

The advertisement in the *Sentimental Journey*. (Query, 9). BC, ii (53), 157.
C. Benson.

Lawrence Sterne, 1713-1768. (English literary autographs, 27). Illus. BC, vii (58), 285.
T. J. Brown.

Early editions of *Tristram Shandy*. (Query, 217). BC, xvi (67), 377.
K. Monkman.

Notes on the bibliography of Sterne. TCBS, ii (54/8), 155-69.
J. C. T. Oates.

STEVENS, Arretta J.
The edition of Montaigne read by Melville. PBSA, lxii (68), 130-4.

STEVENS, Henry
Proposal of Henry Stevens for a *Bibliographia Americana* to the year 1700, to be published by the Smithsonian Institution. Illus. PBSA, xxxvi (42), 245-66.
V.H. Paltsits.

Henry Stevens: the making of a bookseller. PBSA, xlviii (54), 149-69.
W. W. Parker.

Henry Stevens sweeps the States. PBSA, lii (58), 249-61.
W. W. Parker.

STEVENS, Joan
'Woodcuts dropped into the text': the illustrations in *The Old Curiosity Shop* and *Barnaby Rudge*. Illus. SB, xx (67), 113-34.

STEVENSON, Allan Henry
Shirley's publishers: the partnership of Crooke and Cooke. LIB, xxv (44/5), 140-61.

Thomas Thomas makes a dictionary. [i.e. his *Dictionarium linguae Latinae et Anglicanae*, 1587]. Illus. LIB, xiii (58), 234-46.

Paper as bibliographical evidence. Illus. LIB, xvii (62), 197-212.

A critical study of Heawood's *Watermarks mainly of the 17th and 18th centuries*. PBSA, xlv (51), 23-36.

New uses of watermarks as bibliographical evidence. SB, i (48/9), 149-82.

Watermarks are twins. Illus. SB, iv (51/2), 57-91.

Shakespearian dated watermarks. Illus. SB, iv (51/2), 159-64.

Chain-indentations in paper as evidence. SB. vi (54), 181-95.

Tudor roses from John Tate. Illus. SB, xx (67), 15-34.

STEVENSON, George
Bulwer Lytton and George Stevenson. (Query, 84). BC, vi (57), 291-2.
K. T. Barrow.

STEWART, Powell
See STEWART, Walter Powell

STEWART, Thomas
Thomas Stewart, Robert Burns, and the law. PBSA, lvi (62), 46-55.
J. Egerer.

STEWART, Walter Powell
A bibliographical contribution to biography: James Miller's *Seasonable Reproof*. LIB, iii (48/9), 295-8.

STICKLAND, Irina
Bibliography of G. W. M. Reynolds. (Query, 170). BC, xii (63), 357.

STILLINGER, Jack Clifford
A note on the printing of E. K.'s glosses [to *The Shepheardes Calender*]. SB, xiv (61), 203-5.

Dwight's *Triumph of Infidelity*: text and interpretation. SB, xv (62), 259-66.

The text of *The Eve of St. Agnes*. SB, xvi (63), 207-12.

The text of Keats's *Ode on indolence*. SB, xxii (69), 255-8.

STILLWELL, Margaret Bingham
Incunabula and fine printing in Argentina. PBSA, xxxvi (42), 315-18.

A Book of Hours for the use of Autun printed for Simon Vostre, *ca.* 1507. A correction to the Stillwell census. PBSA, xli (47), 341-2.
H. Bober.

STIRLING-MAXWELL COLLECTION
See GLASGOW *univ., libr.*

STOCK, Elliot
Elliot Stock's devices. (Query, 76). BC, v (56), 384.
H. R. Page.

STOCKER, Arthur Frederick
A possible new source for Servius Danielis on *Aeneid* III-V. SB, iv (51/2), 129-41.

The Servius of Cassel for *Aeneid* III-V. SB, vi (54), 93-100.

STODDARD, Elizabeth
An unpublished review by Henry James [of E. Stoddard's *Two Men*]. SB, xx (67), 267-73.
J. Kraft.

STODDARD, Roger E.
Dashiell Hammett, 1894-1961. (Some uncollected authors, 31). BC, xi (62), 71-8.

Oscar Wegelin, pioneer bibliographer of American literature. PBSA, lvi (62), 237-47.

C. Fiske Harris, collector of American poetry and plays. PBSA, lvii (63), 14-32.

STONE, Alan Reynolds
The Albion press. Illus. JPHS, ii (66), 58-73.

The Albion press, addenda and corrigenda. JPHS, iii (67), 97-100.

STONE, Frank
Boyd, James (1888-   ). *Drums.* Charles Scribner's Sons', New York, 1925. PBSA, xxxv (41), 207-8.

STONE AND KIMBALL
See KRAMER, Sidney

STONLEY, Richard
The library of Elizabeth's embezzling teller [Richard Stonley]. SB, ii (49/50), 49-61.
L. Hotson.

STONYHURST COLLEGE
Stonyhurst College. (Unfamiliar libraries, 2). BC, vi (57), 343-9.
H. Chadwick.

STORER, Anthony Morris
The Storer collection in Eton College library. Illus. BC, v (56), 115-26.
Sir R. Birley.

STORM, Colton
Congress of the United States. *Acts passed at a Congress of the United States of America, Begun and held at the city of New-York on Wednesday the fourth of March, in the year M,DCC, LXXXIX* . . . New York, Francis Childs and John Swaine. PBSA, xxxv (41), 70-1.

A further note on *Novello Cattanio.* PBSA, xlvi (52), 274-5.

STORY, Patrick L.
William Hazlitt's *The spirit of the age*, third edition, 1858. (Query, 206). BC, xv (66), 356.

STOTHARD, Thomas
Samuel Rogers, his illustrators, J. M. W. Turner and Thomas Stothard, and other friends. (Among my books, 3). Illus. BH, i (47/51), 198-218.
H. Rycroft.

STOTT, Raymond Toole
Boz's *Memoirs of Joseph Grimaldi* 1838. (Note, 277). BC, xv (66), 354-6.

[Reply to Laurence's 'In Search of Henry James'. A letter].PBSA, lii (59), 329-30.

STOW, John
John Stow's editions of Skelton's *Workes* and of *Certaine Worthye Manuscript Poems.* SB, viii (56), 215-17.
W. Ringler.

Lydgate's *Serpent of Division*, 1559, edited by John Stow. SB, xiv (61), 201-3.
W. Ringler.

STOWE, Harriet Elizabeth Beecher
Cruickshank's *Uncle Tom's Cabin,* 1852. (Note, 183). BC, xi (62), 345-7.
W. B. Todd.

Mrs. Stowe first writes of Kentuckians for Kentuckians. PBSA, li (57), 340-1.
J. J. Weisert.

STRABOLGI, David *baron*
Paul Verlaine's *Les Amies.* (Note, 114). BC, viii (59), 296-7.

STRAHAN, William
Some additional figures of distribution of eighteenth-century English books. [Based on W. Strahan's papers in the Bodleian]. PBSA, lix (65), 160-70.
R. D. Harlan.

William Strahan's ledgers: standard charges for printing, 1733-1785. SB, xx (67), 89-111.
P. Hernlund.

—. II: charges for papers, 1738-1785. SB, xxii (69), 179-95.
P. Hernlund.

STRAMBOTTI D'OGNI SORTE E SONETTI ALLA BERGAMASCA
Two undescribed incunabula. [Justiniano, Leonardo: *Sonetti d'amore. El desperato.* (Rome: Johann Besicken, c. 1500). *Strambotti D'Ogni Sorte e Sonetti alla Bergamasca.* (Rome: Eucharius Silber, c. 1500)]. PBSA, xxxix (45), 162-3.
C. F. Bühler.

STRASSBURG
A Strassburg incunable in the Euing collection in Glasgow University Library. BTHK, iii (60/2), 165-73.
F. W. Ratcliffe.

Two Strassburg reprints [by W. and J. Rihel] of Aldine classics. LIB, viii (53), 274-5.
J. V. Scholderer.

The Strasbourg *Speculum Iudiciale* 1473: with a note on the career of Johann Bekenhub. LIB, xi (56), 273-7.
J. V. Scholderer.

The printers of Strassburg and humanism, from 1501 until the advent of the Reformation. PBSA, xxxiv (40), 68-77.
L. Rostenberg.

A West Baden incunbulum [*Sermones Thesauri novi de tempore*, Strassburg, 1486]. PBSA, xli (47), 147-8.
E. R. Smothers.

The printer of Jordanus de Quedlinburg, Strassburg, 1481-1502. PBSA, xlvi (52), 179-85.
J. V. Scholderer.

STRATMAN, Carl Joseph
Tancred and Sigismunda. (Note, 109). BC, ix (60), 188.

Problems in *The Prompter,* a guide to plays. PBSA, lv (61), 36-40.

Cotes's Weekly Journal; or, The English Stage-Player. PBSA, lvi (62), 104-6.

John Dryden's *All for Love*: unrecorded edition. PBSA, lvii (63), 77-9.

STRATTON, Royal B.
Bound for Bashan [Rev. R. B. Stratton's *Captivity of the Oatman Girls, being an interesting narrative of Life Among the Apache and Mohave Indians*.] PBSA, lvii (63), 449-53.
R. H. Dillon.

STRAUS, Ralph
John Baskerville. Proposals for a revised edition of Straus and Dent's bibliography and memoir. TCBS, i (49/53), 191-2.
J. Dreyfus *and* R. J. L. Kingsford.

—. *and* DENT, Robert K. Prolegomena to the revised edition of Straus and Dent's *John Baskerville.* TCBS, i (49/53), 288-95.
J. P. W. Gaskell.

STRAWBERRY HILL
The booksellers' 'Ring' at Strawberry Hill in 1842. SB, vii (55), 194-8.
A. T. Hazen.

STREETER, Thomas Winthrop
[Vandeleur]. *Travels to the Westward . . . or the Unknown Parts of America in the years 1786 and 1787.* Windsor (Vt.), Alden Spooner, 1794. PBSA, xxxiv (40), 190.

Notes on North American regional bibliographies. PBSA, xxxvi (42), 171-86.

STRONKS, James B.
Stephen Crane's English years: the legend corrected. PBSA, lvii (63), 340-9.

STROUP, Thomas Bradley
The Christmas Ordinary: manuscript and authorship. PBSA, l (56), 184-90.

STROUT, Alan Lang
Writers on German literature in *Blackwood's Magazine,* with a footnote on Thomas Carlyle. LIB, ix (54), 35-44.

The anonymous works of Mrs. A. Gillespie Smyth. LIB, x (55), 208-9.

The authorship of articles in *Blackwood's Magazine,* numbers xvii-xxiv, August 1818-March 1819. LIB, xi (56), 187-201.

The first twenty-three numbers of the *Noctes Ambrosianae.* LIB, xii (57), 108-18.

STRUNK, Oliver
Early music publishing in the United States. PBSA, xxxi (37), 176-9.

STUART, Daniel
Wordsworth's poetry and Stuart's newspapers: 1797-1803. SB, xv (62), 149-89.
R. S. Woof.

STUART, G. William
Concerning two anonymous printings by John Dawson. PBSA, lvii (63), 218-19.

Two more anonymous printings by John Dawson. PBSA, lvii (63), 445-6.

STUART, Henry Benedict M.C. *cardinal*
Books and Henry Stuart, Cardinal Duke of York. Illus. BH, ii (51/2), 191-205.
I. S. Munro.

STUART, James
A binding designed by James Stuart, 1762. (English bookbindings, 55). Illus. BC, xiv (65), 538.
H. M. Nixon.

STUBBE, Henry
Stubbe and Wotton. (Note, 63). BC, v (56), 78.
H. W. Jones.

—. (Note, 63). BC, v (56), 276.
C. S. Bliss.

An unexplained 17th-century cancel; [in Stubbe's *Legends, no histories*]. (Query, 129). BC, xi (62), 351-2.
R. J. F. Carnon.

STULL, Joseph S.
An early annotated edition of *The Eve of St. Agnes.* PBSA, xlvi (52), 269-73.

STURGIS, Howard Overing
A binding variant. [H.O. Sturgis: *Belchamber.* Constable, 1904]. (Query, 13). BC, i (52), 130.
J. W. Carter.

STURMAN, Berta
The second quarto of *A King and No King,* 1625. SB, iv (51/2), 166-70.

A date and a printer for *A looking glasse for London and England,* Q4. SB, xxi (68), 248-53.

STURT, J.
J. Sturt, facsimilist. LIB, xxv (44/5), 72-9.
A. T. Hazen.

—. LIB, xxvi (45/6), 307-8.
H. Macdonald.

STUTLER, Boyd B.
Early West Virginia imprints. Illus. PBSA, xlv (50), 237-45.

STUTTGART
Notes on bindings from English collections at Stuttgart. BC, v (56), 158-61.
E. Kyriss.

SUBERS, Helen D.
Jacobus de Voragine (*c.* 1230-*c.* 1298). *Legenda aurea* [German:] *Passional oder Leben der Heiligen, Sommerteil.* Augsburg: Johann Schönsperger, 23 Aug. 1487. PBSA, xxxiv (40), 268-9.

SUBSCRIPTION PUBLISHING
A subscription list to Mozart's *Così fan tutte*. LIB, vii (52), 132-3.
A. H. King.

Dryden, Tonson, and subscriptions for the 1697 *Virgil*. PBSA, lvii (63), 129-51.
J. Barnard.

SUCKLING, Sir John
The printer of a 1641 Suckling pamphlet. PBSA, xlvii (53), 70.
J. C. Wyllie.

An editorial experiment: Suckling's *A Session of the Poets*. SB, xvi (63), 43-60.
L. A. Beaurline.

Identification of New York Public Library manuscript 'Suckling Collection' and of Huntington Manuscript 198. SB, xix (66), 215-16.
C. M. Armitage.

SUDBURY *Ontario*
The War Memorial at Sudbury, Ontario. PBSA, liv (60), 186-8.
T. B. Haber.

SUE, Marie Joseph Eugène
Eugene's Sue's *The King of the Winds* [*The Godolphin Arabian*] translated for the *Spirit of the Times*. PBSA, xl (46), 162-4.
C. Collins *and* R. W. Henderson.

SUIDAS
Press-figures: a case-history of 1701-1703. [*Suidae Lexicon*, 1705]. TCBS, iii (59/63), 32-46.
D. F. McKenzie.

SULLIVAN, Sir Arthur Seymour
The Gondoliers. PBSA, lix (65), 193-8.
D. A. Randall.

Gilbert and Sullivan's *Princess Ida*. PBSA, lix (65), 322-6.
D. A. Randall.

SULLIVAN, Frank
Breton, Nicholas (?1545-?1626). *A Poste with a Packet of Madde Letters*. PBSA, xxxvii (43), 233.

SULPITIUS, Joannes *Verulanus*
Two rare books in the University Library, Glasgow. [Michael Scott's *Mensa Philosophica* and the *Grammar of Sulpitius*]. BTHK, i/1 (56), 22-3.
P. Forman.

Sulpitius Verulanus, Johannes (15th-cent.) *De versuum scansione*. [Milan, Johannes Angelus Scinzenzeler, about 1500]. PBSA, xxxv (41), 156-7.
H. R. Mead.

SUNDERLAND, *3rd earl of*
See SPENCER, Charles *3rd earl of Sunderland*

SUNDERLAND LIBRARY
Jacob Bryant and the Sunderland Library, Illus. LIB, ii (47/8), 192-9.
A. N. L. Munby.

SUPER, Robert Henry
The authorship of *Guy's Porridge Pot* and *The Dun Cow*. LIB, v (50/1), 55-8.

Notes on some obscure Landor editions. PBSA, xlvi (52), 58-62.

None was worth my strife: Landor and the Italian police. PBSA, xlvii (53), 113-32.

SUPPLICATIONS
Registers of supplications: Registra supplicationum. EBST, ii (38/45), 383-4.
A. I. Dunlop.

SURREY *Earl of*
See HOWARD, Henry *earl of Surrey*

SURTEES, Robert Smith
R. S. Surtees: *The horseman's manual* 1831. Which issue was the earlier? BC, xvii (68), 492.
J. W. Steedman.

SURVIVAL OF BOOKS
The survival of English books printed before 1640: a theory and some illustrations. LIB, xxiii (42/3), 171-90.
O. M. Willard.

SUSENBROTUS, Joannes
The *Grammaticae Artis Institutio* of Joannes Susenbrotus: a bibliographical note. SB, xiv (61), 197-200.
J. X. Brennan.

SUTHERLAND, James Rancieman
The circulation of newspapers and literary periodicals, 1700-30. LIB, xv (34/5), 110-24.

SUTHERLAND, Raymond Carter
A critical view of the recent literature of British heraldry. PBSA, lvi (62), 445-53.

SWAINE, Charles
See also: An Account of a voyage . . .

The Great Probability of a North-West Passage. London, Thomas Jeffreys, 1768. [Attributed to C. Swaine]. PBSA, xxxix (45), 319-20.
B. Solis-Cohen.

SWAN, Bradford Fuller
The Ruysch map of the world, 1507-1508. PBSA, xlv (51), 219-36.

A checklist of early printing on the island of Antigua, 1748-1800. PBSA, l (56), 285-92.

SWAN, Marshall W. S.
Shakespeare's *Poems*: the first three Boston editions. PBSA, xxxvi (42), 27-36.

—. *and* CARSON, Marian S.
John Bioren: printer to Philadelphia publishers. PBSA, xliii (49), 321-34.

SWAYZE, Walter E.
Sir William Watson: additions and corrections. (Some uncollected authors, 12). BC, vi (57), 285-6.

—. [Addenda]. BC, vi (57), 402.

SWEDISH IMPRINTS
The earliest Swedish imprints in the United States. Illus. PBSA, xxxix (45), 181-91.
A. G. Renstrom.

SWEEP-EMBARGO'S NEW YEAR'S MESSAGE
Sweep-embargo's New Year's message. [Albany, 1809]. PBSA, xxxiv (40), 189.
O. Wegelin.

SWEET, Forest H.
Prices, collectors, and librarians. PBSA, xxxvi (42), 46-55.

SWEET SINGER OF MICHIGAN
See MOORE, Julia A.

SWIFT, Jonathan
Jonathan Swift, 1667-1745. (English literary autographs, 5). Illus. BC, ii (53), 68-9.
T. J. Brown.

Swift's April Fool for a bibliophile. BC, ii (53), 205-8.
I. Ehrenpreis.

Jonathan Swift and the Four Last Years of the Queen. Illus. LIB, xvi (35/6), 61-90.
H. Williams.

—. [A letter]. LIB, xvi (35/6), 343-4.
H. Williams.

—. [A letter]. LIB, xvi (35/6), 344-6.
H. Davis.

The publication of the first Drapier Letter. LIB, xix (38/9), 107-15.
N. M. Rothschild.

On Swift's marginalia in copies of Macky's Memoirs. LIB, xix (38/9), 354-62.
W. F. Trench and K. B. Garrett.

The first printing of the letters of Pope and Swift. LIB, xix (38/9), 465-85.
M. Mack.

New light on the first printing of the letters of Pope and Swift. LIB, xxiv (43/4), 74-80.
V. E. Dearing.

Swift's Discourse . . . Contests . . . Athens and Rome, 1701. LIB, iv (49/50), 201-5.
H. Teerink.

An uncancelled copy of the first collected edition of Swift's poems. [Swift's Works, 1735, Dublin edition]. LIB, xxii (67), 44-56.
M. J. P. Weedon.

An unpublished letter from Swift. LIB, xxii (67), 57-66.
P. V. Thompson.

Another attribution to Swift. PBSA, xlv (51), 82-3.
W. B. Todd.

The 1735 Dublin edition of Swift's Poems. PBSA, liv (60), 57-60.
J. E. Dustin.

When Swift first employed George Faulkner. PBSA, lvi (62), 354-6.
B. Slepian.

The publication history of Faulkner's edition of Gulliver's Travels. PBSA, lvii (63), 219-21.
B. Slepian.

The Ford changes and the text of Gulliver's Travels. PBSA, lxii (68), 1-23.
C. Jenkins.

Swift, Pope, and 'the sin of wit'. PBSA, lxii (68), 80-5.
J. M. Aden.

A checklist of illustrated editions of Gulliver's Travels, 1727-1914. PBSA, lxii (68), 85-123.
D. S. Lenfest.

Swift's Verses on the death of doctor Swift. [and Addendum]. SB, iv (51/52), 183-8; vii (55) 238-9.
H. Teerink.

The earliest London printings of Verses on the death of doctor Swift. SB, xv (62), 243-7.
A. H. Scouten.

The text of Scott's edition of Swift [The works of Jonathan Swift, D.D., Dublin, 1814]. SB, xxii (69), 240-55.
L. H. Potter.

SWINBURNE, Algernon Charles
Swinburne problems. (Query, 51). BC, iii (54), 227-8.
E. E. Bissell.

Swinburne's Atalanta in Calydon. (Note, 39). BC, iii (54), 307.
J. S. Mayfield.

A Swinburne puzzle. (Note, 42). Illus. BC, iv (55), 74-8.
J. S. Mayfield.

The first edition of Atalanta in Calydon. (Query, 71). BC, v (56), 281.
A. Rogers.

Gosse, Wise and Swinburne. (Note, 115). BC, viii (59), 297-9.
E. E. Bissell.

Algernon Charles Swinburne, 1837-1909. (English literary autographs, 37). Illus. BC, x (61), 57.
T. J. Brown.

Swinburne's The Queen-Mother [and] Rosamond, 1860. (Query, 184). BC, xiii (64), 357-9.
S. H. Nowell-Smith.

An unrecorded Wiseian issue [of the Dead love entry in The Bibliography of Swinburne]. (Note, 318). BC, xviii (69), 385-6.
W. B. Todd.

Swinburne's letter concerning Poe. PBSA, xliv (50), 185-90.
I. B. Cauthen, jr.

Two presentation copies of Swinburne's Atalanta in Calydon. PBSA, xlix (55), 360-5.
J. S. Mayfield.

Swinburne's Heptalogia improved. SB, xxii (69), 258-66.
R. A. Greenberg.

SWITZER, Stephen
The first edition of Switzer's *Brocoli*. LIB, vii (52), 58.
R. Hagedorn.

—. [A letter]. LIB, vii (52), 211-12.
C. C. Blagden.

SYLVESTER, Richard Standish
Cavendish's *Life of Wolsey*. (Query, 54). BC, iii (54), 310.

SYMONDS, John Addington
John Addington Symonds: the 'peccant' pamphlets. (Note, 215). BC, xiii (64), 68-70.
T. d'A. Smith.

J. A. Symonds and the 'peccant' pamphlets. (Note, 215). BC, xiii (64), 206-7.
Elkin Mathews *ltd*.

SYMSON, Patrick
A Gorbals imprint of 1701, with notes on Patrick Simpson's *Spiritual Songs*. Illus. GBSR, vi (20), 1-13.
W. J. Couper.

SZLADITS, Lola L.
Addenda to Sidnell: Yeats's *The shadowy waters*. PBSA, lxii (68), 614-17.

T

TAHITI
Tahitian imprints, 1817-1833. PBSA, xxxv (41), 48-57.
G. L. Harding.

TALAEUS, Audomarus
Hobbes and Talon's Ramist rhetoric in English. TCBS, i (49/53), 260-9.
W. J. Ong.

TALES FROM BLACKWOOD
Tales from Blackwood. EBST, ii (38/45), 443-5.
M. Sadleir.

TALES OF THE WILD AND THE WONDER-FUL
Tales of the Wild and the Wonderful, 1925. (Query, 104), BC, vii (58), 417.
J. Park.

T. J. Wise and *Tales of the Wise and the Wonderful*. (Query, 104). BC, viii (59), 300-3.
J. E. Alden.

—. BC, viii (59), 303-6.
J. Rubinstein.

TALFOURD, Sir Thomas Noon
Magazine and other contributions by Mary Russell Mitford and Thomas Noon Talfourd. SB, xii (59), 218-26.
W. A. Coles.

TALON, Omer
See TALAEUS, Audomarus

TANNER, Lawrence Edward
William Caxton's houses at Westminster. Illus. LIB, xii (57), 153-66.

TANSELLE, George Thomas
The Mitchell Kennerley imprint. BC, xiii (64), 185-93.

The case of the missing apostrophes. (Note, 219). BC, xiii (64), 210-11.

Royall Tyler, 1757-1826. (Some uncollected authors, 42). BC, xv (66), 303-20.

Samuel Roth's *Love secrets*, 1927. (Note, 282). BC, xv (66), 486-7.

Signatures on versos: Luce's *The woodman* 1887. (Note, 316). BC, xviii (69), 384.

The specification of binding cloth. LIB, xxi (66), 246-7.

The recording of press figures. Illus. LIB, xxi (66), 318-25.

Tolerances in bibliographical description. LIB, xxiii (68), 1-12.

Three unrecorded issues of Masefield's *Tragedy of Nan*. LIB, xxiii (68), 145-7.

Lindsay's *General William Booth*: a bibliographical and textual note. PBSA, lv (61), 371-80.

Whitman's short stories: another reprint. PBSA, lvi (62), 115.

Unrecorded early reprintings of two Poe tales. PBSA, lvi (62), 252.

Additional reviews of Sherwood Anderson's work. PBSA, lvi (62), 358-65.

The Lyric Year: a bibliographical study. PBSA, lvi (62), 454-71.

Floyd Dell in the *Friday Literary Review.* PBSA, lvii (63), 371-6.

Additions to the bibliography of Maxwell Anderson. PBSA, lvii (63), 90-1.

Charles A. Beard in the *Freeman.* PBSA, lvii (63), 226-9.

Two more appearances of *The Raven.* PBSA, lvii (63), 229-30.

A further note on Hart Crane's critics. PBSA, lviii (64), 180-1.

The Thomas Seltzer imprints. Illus. PBSA, lviii (64), 380-448.

Attribution of authorship in *The spirit of the Farmers' Museum*, 1801. PBSA, lix (65), 170-6.

Early American fiction in England: the case of *The Algerine captive* [by R. Tyler]. PBSA, lix (65), 367-84.

The identification of type faces in bibliographical description. PBSA, lx (66), 185-202.

The ABA issue of Meredith Nicholson's *A Hoosier Chronicle*, 1912. PBSA, lx (66), 223-4.

Some Stone & Kimball addenda. [S. Kramer's *A history of Stone & Kimball and Herbert S. Stone & company*]. PBSA, lx (66), 476-8.

An unrecorded Chicago ante-fire imprint: Whipple's *Ethzelda*. PBSA, lxi (67), 123-4.

The Laurence Gomme imprint. PBSA, lxi (67), 225-40.

A proposal for recording additions to bibliographies. PBSA, lxii (68), 227-36.

BAL addendum: Ambrose Bierce — entry No. 1112.* PBSA, lxii (68), 451.

Stone & Kimball addendum: Blossom's *Checkers.* PBSA, lxii (68), 451-2.

Addenda to Irish [W. R. Irish's *The modern American muse*]: Brown, North, and Wild. PBSA, lxii (68), 452.

Typee and De Voto once more. PBSA, lxii (68), 601-4.

The Little Leather Library Corporation's *Fifty best poems of America.* PBSA, lxii (68), 604-7.

An unknown early appearance of *The Raven.* SB, xvi (63), 220-3.

Unsigned and initialed contributions to *The Freeman.* SB, xvii (64), 153-75.

The historiography of American literary publishing. SB, xviii (65), 3-39.

Press figures in America: some preliminary observations. SB, xix (66), 123-60.

A system of color identification for bibliographical description. SB, xx (67), 203-34.

The descriptive bibliography of American authors. SB, xxi (68), 1-24.

Copyright records and the bibliographer. SB, xxii (69), 77-124.

TAPLIN, Gardner B.
Mrs. Browning's contributions to periodicals: addenda. PBSA, xliv (50), 275-6.

TARDIVUS, Guilelmus
Tardivus, Guilelmus, *Grammatica, elegantia et rhetorica*. [Poitiers, Jean Bouyer, about 1488]. PBSA, xxxvi (42), 229-30.
H. R. Mead.

Tardivus, Guilelmus. *In invidiosam falsamque detractionem ubicunque gentium responsio ac defensio*. [Paris, Atelier du Soufflet Vert (Louis Simonel and associates), about 1480]. PBSA, xxxvi (42), 230.
H. R. Mead.

TARKINGTON, Newton Booth
The pre-publication printings of Tarkington's *Penrod*. SB, v (52), 153-7.
C. R. Coxe.

TARR, John Charles
Measurement of type. [A letter]. LIB, i (46/7), 248-9.

TATE, John
Tudor roses from John Tate. Illus. SB, xx (67), 15-34.
A. Stevenson.

TATE, Nahum
The laureate as huckster: Nahum Tate and an early eighteenth century example of publisher's advertising. SB, xxi (68), 261-6.
S. L. Astor.

TATLER
Early editions of *The Tatler*. SB, xv (62), 121-33.
W. B. Todd.

TAUCHNITZ, Bernhard, Verlag
The Tauchnitz *David Copperfield*, 1849. (Note, 53). BC, iv (55), 253-4.
P. H. Muir.

Dickens and Tauchnitz. (Note, 55). BC, iv (55), 329.
P. H. Muir.

Firma Tauchnitz 1837-1900. Illus. BC, xv (66), 423-6.
S. Nowell-Smith.

TAXES
Printers' lobby: model 1802. SB, iii (50), 207-28.
R. G. Silver.

TAYLOR, Anne
For works by J. and A. Taylor *see* TAYLOR, Jane

TAYLOR, Donald Stewart
The authenticity of Chatterton's *Miscellanies in Prose and Verse*. PBSA, lv (61), 289-96.

TAYLOR, Eva G. R.
Margarita philosophica. (Among my books, 2). Illus. BH, i (47/51), 65-71.

TAYLOR, Henry C.
The Henry C. Taylor collection. (Contemporary collectors, 40). Illus. BC, xiv (65), 34-48.
J. S. Kebabian.

TAYLOR, Isaac
Eighteenth-century English illustrators: Isaac Taylor the elder. [Together with a list of] Books with illustrations designed and engraved by Isaac Taylor the elder. Illus. BC, i (52), 14-27.
H. A. Hammelmann.

Engravings by Isaac Taylor. (Note, 2). BC, i (52), 126.
W. B. Todd.

Engravings by Isaac Taylor. (Note, 3). BC, i (52), 126-7.
F. Algar.

TAYLOR, Jane
Blake's *Holy Thursday* in Anne and Jane Taylor's *City Scenes*. (Note, 128). BC, ix (60), 75-6.
Sir G. L. Keynes.

TAYLOR, Jeremy *bp. of Down and Connor*
Some notes on the bibliography of Jeremy Taylor. Illus. LIB, ii (47/8), 233-49.
R. Gathorne-Hardy.

—. [A letter]. LIB, iii (48/9), 66.

Jeremy Taylor and Elizabeth Grymeston. [A letter]. LIB, xv (34/5), 247-8.
G. Bone.

TAYLOR, John
John Taylor's *Booke of Martyrs*, 1633. (Note, 49). BC, iv (55), 171-2.
J. Hayward.

—. (Note, 49). BC, iv (55), 327.
W. A. Jackson.

—. (Note, 49). BC, iv (55), 327.
B. Juel-Jensen.

Two unrecorded editions of John Taylor's *Verbum Sempiternum*. LIB, xii (57), 46-8.
L. H. Kendall, *jr.*

Octavo nonce collections of John Taylor. LIB, xviii (63), 51-7.
A. Freeman.

Taylor, John, *the water poet*. (1580-1653). *A shilling, or, The Trauailes of twelve-pence*. [E. Allde, 1621]. PBSA, xxxiv (40), 358.
E. M. Sowerby.

A verry merry wherry-ferry-voyage. London, PBSA, xxxiv (40), 271.
E. M. Sowerby.

—. PBSA, xxxiv (40), 358.
E. M. Sowerby.

John Taylor's piracy of *The Packmans Paternoster*. PBSA, lvii (63), 201-10.
L. H. Kendall, *jr.*

TAYLOR, John Russell
The Hotten piracy of Tennyson's *Poems MDCCCXXX-MDCCCXXXIII*. (Note, 208). BC, xii (63), 492-3.

TAYLOR, Richard
Richard Taylor, a preliminary note. Illus. JPHS, ii (66), 45-8.
N. Barker.

TAYLOR, Robert H.
The Robert Taylor library. (Contemporary collectors, 3). BC, iii (54), 272-8.

Henry Bradley Martin. (Contemporary collectors, 35). Illus. BC, xii (63), 184-93.

The manuscript of Trollope's *The American Senator*, collated with the first edition. PBSA, xli (47), 123-39.

Bibliothecohimatiourgomachia. PBSA, xlviii (54), 230-8.

TAYLOR, Theodora
Addenda to Irish [W. R. Irish's *The modern American Muse*]: Theodora Taylor, Rixford J. Lincoln, David Bailey, Lester S. Parker. PBSA, lxiii (69), 198-200.
R. C. Johnson.

TAYLOR, Thomas
Thomas Taylor's biography. SB, xiv (61), 234-6.
G. E. Bentley.

TEERINK, Herman
Swift's *Discourse . . . contests . . . Athens and Rome*, 1701. LIB, iv (49/50), 201-5.

Swift's *Verses on the death of doctor Swift*. [*And* Addendum]. SB, iv (51/2), 183-8; vii (55), 238-9.

TEMPLE, Sir William *bart.*
Sir William Temple on Orinda: neglected publication. Illus. PBSA, lvii (63), 328-36.
W. Roberts.

TEMPLEMAN, William Darby
Additions to the check-list of Young's *Night-Thoughts* in America. PBSA, xliii (49), 348-9.

TENNYSON *family*
[Tennyson, A., C., & F.]. *Poems by Two Brothers,* 1827. (Note, 172). BC, xi (62), 80.
S. Nowell-Smith.

The Tennysons' *Poems by Two Brothers,* 1827. (Note, 172). BC, xii (63), 68.
S. Nowell-Smith.

TENNYSON, Alfred *1st baron*
Some uncatalogued manuscripts of Tennyson. Illus. BC, iv (55), 158-62.
K. W. Grandsen.

Extant copies of Tennyson's *Timbuctoo*, 1829. (Query, 101). BC, vii (58), 296.
B., A.C.

Tennyson's *In Memoriam*, 1850. (Note, 129). BC, ix (60), 76-7.
S. Nowell-Smith.

Lord Tennyson, 1809-1892. (English literary autographs, 45). Illus. BC, xii (63), 61.
T. J. Brown.

How rare are Montagu Butler's translations of Tennyson? (Query, 162). BC, xii (63), 72-3.
R. L. Collins.

Montagu Butler's translation of Tennyson. (Query, 162). BC, xii (63), 356.
C. S. Bliss.

A Latin translation of Tennyson's *In Memoriam*. (Note, 207). BC, xii (63), 490-2.
P. E. Hall.

The Hotten piracy of Tennyson's *Poems MDCCCXXX-MDCCCXXXIII*. (Note, 208). BC, xii (63), 492-3.
J. R. Taylor.

Wise, Wrenn and Tennyson's *Enoch Arden*, 1864. (Note, 214). BC, xiii (64), 67-8.
W. B. Todd.

A nonexistent variant in Tennyson's *Poems, Chiefly Lyrical*, 1830. (Note, 245). BC, xiv (65), 214-15.
C. de L. Ryals.

The 'green' Tennysons. (Note, 246). BC, xiv (65), 215.
P. F. Hinton.

A copy of Tennyson's *The princess*, 1848. (Query, 207). BC, xv (66), 356-7.
P. Bartlett.

A Latin translation of *In Memoriam*. (Note, 207). BC, xvii (68), 78.
P. E. Hall.

Tennyson's *Idylls of the king* and *The Holy grail*. (Query, 222). BC, xvii (68), 218.
P. E. Hall.

Tennyson's *In memoriam* 1850. (Note, 129). BC, xvii (68), 350-1.
S. H. Nowell-Smith.

Tennyson's *Idylls* and *The holy grail*. (Query, 222). BC, xvii (68), 490.
M. Trevanion.

Tennyson's *Carmen Saeculare*, 1887. LIB, ii (47/8), 200-2.
J. Carter.

A note on the variants of *In Memoriam* and *Lucretius*. LIB, viii (53), 259-73.
W. D. Paden.

The variants of *In Memoriam*. [A letter]. LIB, xviii (63), 64.
C. Ricks.

Tennyson's *Lucretius*. LIB, xx (65), 63-4.
C. Ricks.

Tennyson's *Tiresias*, 1885. LIB, xxiv (69), 55-6.
S. H. Nowell-Smith.

The proofs of *Gareth and Lynette* in the Widener collection. PBSA, xli (47), 321-40.
E. F. Shannon.

The Hallam-Tennyson *Poems,* 1830. SB, i (48), 193-9.
M. V. Bowman.

The history of a poem: Tennyson's *Ode on the death of the duke of Wellington*. SB, xiii (60), 149-77.
E. F. Shannon.

Tennyson's *The Lover's Tale*, R. H. Shepherd, and T. J. Wise. SB, xviii (65), 111-45.
W. D. Paden.

A note on Tennyson's *Ode on the Death of the Duke of Wellington*. SB, xviii (65), 282.
C. Ricks.

TERENTIUS, Publius *Afer*
Terentius, Publius, *Afer* (c. 190 - c. 159 B.C.) *Flowers for latine speakinge*. Selected out of Terence, and . . . translated into Englishe, 1572. London, Robert Marshe. PBSA, xxxv (41), 294.
F. R. Goff.

The *Terence* of Turin, 1483. Illus. SB, xvii (64), 195-6.
C. F. Bühler.

TERESA, St.
The first publication of Abraham Woodhead's translation of St. Teresa. LIB, xxi (66), 234-40.
J. Buchanan-Brown.

TERM CATALOGUES
The genesis of the *Term Catalogues*. LIB, viii (53), 30-5.
C. C. Blagden.

The missing *Term Catalogue*. [Michaelmas 1695]. SB, vii (55), 185-90.
C. C. Blagden.

TESTAMENT, New
A brief history of the English version of the *New Testament* first published at Rheims in 1582, continued down to the present day. LIB, xx (39/40), 351-76; xxi, 44-77.
H. Pope.

The New Testament 1611. (Dublin: George Grierson 1799). (Query, 242). BC, xviii (69), 520-1.
D. W. Adams.

The Rheims version of the New Testament. [A letter]. LIB, xxi (40/1), 216.
F. B. Williams, *jr*.

The first testaments printed in New Jersey. PBSA, xlv (51), 148-51.
G. C. Rockefeller.

The first edition of the New Testament in French. PBSA, li (57), 61-7.
H. Lehmann-Haupt.

TEXTILE INDUSTRIES
The Scottish textile industries. GBSR, xi (33), 96-107.
I. F. M. Dean.

TEXTUAL CRITICISM
See EDITORIAL PROBLEMS

TEXTUAL PROBLEMS
See EDITORIAL PROBLEMS

THACKERAY, George
The library of George Thackeray, Provost of King's College, Cambridge. Illus. BC, vi (57), 143-9.
A. N. L. Munby.

THACKERAY, William Makepeace
Thackeray: *Pendennis*, (Query, 3). BC, i (52), 54.
G. Waynflete.

Thackeray: *The Rose and the Ring*, 1855. (Query, 10). BC, i (52), 57-8.
W., C.

The Rose and the Ring, 1855. (Query, 10). BC, ii (53), 77.
J. D. Gordan.

Thackeray, W. M. (1811-1863). *Vanity Fair*. 20 parts in 19. London, 1847-1848. PBSA, xxxiv (40), 191-2.
D. A. Randall.

—. PBSA, xxxiv (40), 276-8.

Notes towards a correct collation of the first edition of *Vanity Fair*. Illus. PBSA, xlii (48), 95-109.
D. A. Randall.

Thackeray's contributions to *Fraser's Magazine*. SB, xix (66), 67-84.
E. M. White.

William Makepeace Thackeray, 1811-63. (English literary autographs, 2). Illus. BC, i (52), 96-7.
T. J. Brown.

THAT LASS O'LOWRIES
A further printing of *That Lass O'Lowries*. PBSA, lvii (63), 222.
N. Kane.

THEATRE
Theatrical collecting. Illus. BC, i (52), 41-51.
I. K. Fletcher.

An unrecognized document in the history of French Renaissance staging. Illus. LIB, xvi (35/6), 232-5.
S. L. England.

The theatrical collectanea of Daniel Lysons. PBSA, li (57), 333-4.
J. G. McManaway.

THEOPHILUS
De Thou and Theophilus's *Institutes*, [in Trinity College, Cambridge]. TCBS, iii (59/63), 160-3.
G. G. Barber.

THEOPHRASTUS
A newly-discovered Oxford Book [Theophrastus's *Characters*, 1628]. PBSA, xxxii (38), 98-101.
M. Harman.

THERE WAS A LITTLE GIRL
There was a little girl: its first printings, its authorship, its variants. PBSA, xl (46), 287-310.
S. Kramer.

THESES
Two unrecorded Edinburgh theses of 1676 and 1680. BTHK, ii (59/60), 63-6.
R. J. Durling.

THIBAULT, Jacques Anatole
First edition of *L'Ile des Pingouins*. (Note, 144). BC, ix (60), 332-3.
P. H. Muir.

THOMAS *à Kempis*
For *De imitatione Christi* [sometimes ascr. to Thomas à Kempis] *See* IMITATIO CHRISTI

THOMAS, Alan Gradon
Ralph Willett of Merly, 1719-1795. (Portrait of a bibliophile, 10). Illus. BC, xii (63), 439-48.

G. M. Hopkins and the Silver Jubilee album. Illus. LIB, xx (65), 148-52.

—. *and* POWELL, Lawrence Clark
Recollections of a Durrell collector. (Some uncollected authors, 23). BC, ix (60), 56-63.

THOMAS, David
Catalogue of Specimens of Printing Types by English and Scottish Printers and Founders, 1665-1830. [A letter]. LIB, xvii (36/7), 232-4.

THOMAS, Donald Serrell
Prosecutions of *Sodom: or, The quintessence of debauchery*, and *Poems on several occasions by the E of R,* 1689-1690 and 1693. LIB, xxiv (69). 51-5.

Ulysses and the Attorney-General 1936. LIB, xxiv (69), 343-5.

THOMAS, Dylan Marlais
The bibliography of Dylan Thomas. (Note, 81). BC, vi (57), 71-3.
W. B. Todd.

Issues of Dylan Thomas's *The Map of Love*. (Note, 82). BC, vi (57), 73-4.
J. Campbell.

The second edition of Dylan Thomas's *18 poems*. (Note, 227). BC, xiii (64), 351-2.
T. d'A. Smith.

Dylan Thomas and A.E.H. PBSA, lii (58), 309-10.
W. White.

Dylan Thomas, Mr. Rolph, and *John O'London's Weekly*. PBSA, lx (66), 370-2.
W. White.

THOMAS, Sir Henry
Watermarks. EBST, ii (38/45), 449-50.

Juan de Vingles (Jean de Vingle), a sixteenth-century book illustrator. Illus. LIB, xviii (37/8), 121-76.

Copperplate engravings in early Spanish books. Illus. LIB, xxi (40/1), 109-42.

An unknown impression by the printer of the first edition of the *Lusiadas*. Illus. LIB, xxi (40/1), 309-19.

Copperplate engravings in Portuguese books of the late sixteenth century. Illus. LIB, xxii (41/2), 145-62.

Antonio [Martínez] de Salamanca, printer of *La Celestina*, Rome, *c.* 1525. LIB, viii (53), 45-50.

THOMAS, Isaiah
British authorship of ballads in the Isaiah Thomas collection. SB, ix (57), 255-8.
T. L. Philbrick.

THOMAS, Milton Halsey
The Reverend Samuel Johnson's *Collection of Prayers*, 1759. PBSA, xlviii (54), 416-21.

THOMAS, P. Jones
The birds at Osterley Park. Illus. BH, i (47/52), 193-7.

THOMAS, Sidney
A note on the reporting of Elizabethan sermons. LIB, iii (48/9), 120-1.

Richard Smith: 'foreign to the Company'. LIB, iii (48/9), 186-92.

The printing of *Greenes Groatsworth of witte* and *Kind-harts dreame* [by H. Chettle]. SB, xix (66), 196-7.

THOMAS, Thomas
Thomas Thomas makes a dictionary. Illus. LIB, xii (58), 234-46.
A. H. Stevenson.

Restrictive practices in the Elizabethan book trade: the Stationers' Company *v.* Thomas Thomas 1583-8. TCBS, iv (64/8), 276-90.
J. Morris.

The hand of Thomas Thomas. Illus. TCBS, iv (64/8), 291-2.
Sir G. L. Keynes.

Thomas Thomas, printer to the university of Cambridge 1583-8. Part II: Some account of his materials and bookbindings with a short-title list of his printing. Illus. TCBS, iv (64/8), 339-62.
J. Morris.

THOMASON, George
The professional and literary connexions of George Thomason. LIB, xiii (58), 102-18.
L. Spencer.

The politics of George Thomason. LIB, xiv (59), 11-27.
L. Spencer.

THOMPSON, Daniel Varney
Medieval parchment-making. LIB, xvi (35/6), 113-7.

THOMPSON, Henry Yates
Portman Square to New Bond Street, or, How to make money though rich. [The dispersal of the Yates Thompson collection]. BC, xvi (67), 323-39.
J. Q. Bennett.

THOMPSON, Lawrence Sidney
The printing and publishing activities of the American Tract Society from 1825 to 1850. Illus. PBSA, xxxv (41), 81-114.

The first non-serial Puerto Rican imprint. PBSA, xliv (50), 181-2.

Notes on Turkish bibliography. PBSA, xlvi (52), 159-63.

Sällskapet Bokvännerna and its publications. PBSA, xlvi (52), 263-9.

Wagner-camp. PBSA, lv (61), 45-6.

THOMPSON, Nathaniel
Nathaniel Thompson, Catholic printer and publisher of the Restoration. LIB, x (55), 186-202.
L. Rostenberg.

THOMPSON, Paul V.
An unpublished letter from Swift. LIB, xxii (67), 57-66.

THOMPSON, W. D. J. Cargill
Notes on King's College Library, 1500-1570, in particular for the period of the Reformation. [With] Appendix. The inventory of 1556/7. TCBS, ii (54/8), 38-54.

The two editions of Thomas Bilson's *True difference between Christian subjection and unchristian rebellion*. TCBS, ii (54/8), 199-203.

The sixteenth-century editions of *A supplication unto King Henry the Eighth* by Robert Barnes, D. D.,: a footnote to the history of the royal supremacy. TCBS, iii (59/63), 133-42.

THOMSON, Mrs.
Mrs Thomson and Miss Pigott. (Note, 86). BC, vi (57), 293-6.
D. E. Rhodes.

—. (Note, 86). BC, vi (57), 405.
H. W. Edwards.

—. (Note, 86). BC, vii (58), 77-8.
D. E. Rhodes.

THOMSON, Frances Mary
A Newcastle collection of wood blocks [in the University library, Newcastle upon Tyne]. Illus. BC, xvii (68), 443-57.

A Newcastle collection of wood blocks [by F. M. Thomson]. BC, xviii (69), 384-5.
S. Roscoe.

John Wilson, an Ayrshire printer, publisher and bookseller. BTHK, v (67/70), 41-61.

THOMSON, George
Thomson's collections of national song with special reference to the contributions of Haydn and Beethoven. Illus. EBST, ii (38/45), 1-64.
C. Hopkinson *and* C. B. Oldman.

—. Addenda and Corrigenda. EBST, iii (48/55), 121-4.
C. Hopkinson *and* C. B. Oldman.

THOMSON, J. C.
T. J. Wise and J. C. Thomson. (Query, 164). BC, xii (63), 74.
M. Trevanion.

THOMSON, James
A variant issue of Thomson's *Summer*, 1727. (Note, 77). BC, v (56), 383.
T. R. Francis.

Some Dublin editions of James Thomson's *Tancred and Sigismunda*. (Note, 96). BC, vii (58), 190.
T. R. Francis.

James Thomson's *Tancred and Sigismunda*. (Note, 109). BC, viii (59), 181-2.
T. R. Francis.

—. (Note, 109). BC, ix (60), 188.
C. J. Stratman.

Variants in the 1746 edition of Thomson's *Seasons*. LIB, xvii (36/7), 214-20.
J. E. Wells.

Thomson's *Spring*: early editions true and false. LIB, xxii (41/2), 223-43.
J. E. Wells.

Unauthorised readings in the first edition of Thomson's *Coriolanus*. PBSA, xlvi (52), 62-6.
W. B. Todd.

Oh! *Sophonisba! Sophonisba!* Oh! SB, xii (59), 204-13.
D. F. Foxon.

THOMSON, William
William Thomson's *Orpheus Caledonius*. BTHK, i/2 (57), 26-7.
L. Jolley.

THORDARSON, Chester H.
Bibliotheca Thordarsoniana: the sequel. PBSA, xliv (50), 29-54.
R. Hagedon.

THOREAU, Henry David
The bibliographical history of Thoreau's *A week on the Concord and Merrimack Rivers*. PBSA, xliii (49), 39-47.
R. Adams.

THORKELIN COLLECTION
See NATIONAL LIBRARY OF SCOTLAND

THORNDIKE, Lynn
A problem as to incunabula of the *Phisionomia* of Michael Scot. PBSA, xlviii (54), 411-13.

THORNTON, John Leonard
Andrew Boorde's *Dyetary of Health* and its attribution to Thomas Linacre. LIB, ii (47/8), 172-3.

THORNTON, Weldon
Joyce's *Ulysses*, 1922. (Note, 175). BC, xi (62), 85-6.

THORPE, James
Issues of the first edition of *The Vicar of Wakefield*. PBSA, xlii (48), 312-15.

THORPE, Thomas
Thomas Thorpe, publisher of *Shake-Speares Sonnets*. PBSA, liv (60), 16-37.
L. Rostenberg.

THORSON, James L.
The publication of *Hudibras*. Illus. PBSA, lx (66), 418-38.

THOU, Jacques Auguste de
Press-marks of the de Thou library. (Note, 69). BC, v (56), 173-4.
R. Birley.

The Sunderland copy of Jacques Auguste de Thou's *History of his time*. BC, xv (66), 446-53.
S. Kinser.

An unknown manuscript catalogue of the library of J. A. de Thou. Illus. BC, xvii (68), 168-76.
S. Kinser.

Books from the library of Jacques Auguste de Thou. Illus. BH, i (47/51), 1-17.
L. J. Lloyd.

De Thou and Theophilus's *Institutes*, [in Trinity College, Cambridge]. TCBS, iii (59/63), 160-3.
G. G. Barber.

THREE-DECKERS
The nineteenth century three-volume novel. PBSA, li (57), 263-302.
C. E. *and* E. S. Lauterbach.

THUCYDIDES
Henry Stephanus and Thucydides. [A letter]. LIB, xvii (36/7), 361-2.
J. E. Powell.

THUMB-INDEXES
Early thumb-indexes. (Query, 131). BC, ix (60), 456.
A. Ehrman.

TICKNOR AND FIELDS
Book distribution in mid-nineteenth century America, illustrated by the publishing records of Ticknor and Fields, Boston. PBSA, xli (47), 210-30.
W. S. Tryon.

TIGHE, Mary
A ghost of [Mary Tighe's] *Psyche*? (Query, 193). BC, xiv (65), 545.
S. Nowell-Smith.

TILLET, Titus
A Cambridge binding by Titus Tillet, 1677. (English bookbindings, 27). Illus. BC, vii (58), 396.
H. M. Nixon.

TILLOTSON, Arthur *and* SHEARER, Thomas
Percy's relations with Cadell and Davies. LIB, xv (34/5), 224-36.

—. *and* TILLOTSON, Geoffrey
Pen-and-ink corrections in mid-seventeenth-century books. LIB, xiv (33/4), 59-72.

TILLOTSON, Geoffrey
Eighteenth-century capitalization. LIB, ix (54), 268-70.

—. *and* TILLOTSON, Arthur
Pen-and-ink corrections in mid-seventeenth-century books. LIB, xiv (33/4), 59-72.

TILLOTSON, John *abp. of Canterbury*
The text of John Tillotson's sermons. LIB, xiii (58), 18-36.
D. D. Brown.

The Dean's dilemma: a further note on a Tillotson passage. Illus. LIB, xiv (59), 282-7.
D. D. Brown.

TILLOTSON, Kathleen Mary
Oliver Twist in three volumes. LIB, xviii (63), 113-32.

TILNEY, Edmund
Edmund Tilney's *The Flower of Friendshippe*. LIB, xxvi (45/6), 175-81.
J. G. Tilney Bassett.

TILNEY-BASSETT, J. G.
See BASSETT, J. G. Tilney-

TILTON, Eleanor Marguerite
Literary Bantlings: addenda to the Holmes bibliography. PBSA, li (57), 1-18.

TIMES, The
Henry Hallam, *The Times* newspaper, and the Halliwell case. LIB, xviii (63), 133-40.
W. H. Bond.

TIMKO, Michael
H. G. Wells's dramatic criticism for the *Pall Mall Gazette*. LIB, xvii (62), 138-45.

TIMMER, B. J.
The history of a manuscript. [Bodleian MS. Junius 11]. Illus. BC, i (52), 6-13.

TINKER, Edward Larocque
Charles Gayarré, 1805-95. PBSA, xxvii (33), 24-64.

TIPTOFT, John *earl of Worcester*
A Renaissance library: the collection of John Tiptoft, Earl of Worcester. LIB, xviii (37/8), 67-83.
R. J. Mitchell.

TISSOT, Samuel Auguste
A note on Tissot's *Advice to the People*, London, 1767. PBSA, xxxiv (40), 262-6.
J. E. Alden.

TITLE-PAGES
Architectural design on English title-pages. LIB, xiv (33/4), 289-98.
W. H. Smith.

Additions to *Title-page borders*. 1485-1640. Illus. LIB, xvii (36/7), 264-311.
F. S. Ferguson.

English pictorial music title-pages, 1820-1885. Illus. LIB, iv (50), 262-72.
A. H. King.

Penny-pinching printers and tampered titles. SB, xix (61), 209-11.
F. B. Williams.

TITLING-SLIPS
Titling-slips in 17th century books. (Query, 128). BC, ix (60), 203.
A. W. G. Lowther.

—. BC, ix (60), 333.
H. G. Pollard.

TIXALL MANUSCRIPT
The Tixall manuscript of Sir Philip Sidney's and the Countess of Pembroke's paraphrase of the Psalms. (Note, 314). BC, xviii (69), 222-3.
B. Juel-Jensen.

TO ALL BRAVE, HEALTHY, ABLE BODIED . . . YOUNG MEN
To all brave, healthy, able bodied and well disposed young men. [*n.p.,* 1799]. PBSA, xxxvi (42), 67.
L. M. Stark.

TOBACCO
Where there's smoke there's — literature. PBSA, xxxv (41), 145-50.
G. Arents.

A warning for tabacconists. PBSA, xlii (48), 148-50.
P. S. Dunkin.

TOD, James
Tod's *Annals of Rajast'han.* Illus. BH, i (47/51), 293-303.
F. Noyce.

TODD, William Burton
Engravings by Isaac Taylor. (Note, 2). BC, i (52), 126.

Pope: *One thousand seven hundred and eight, Dialogue II.* (Note, 5). BC, i (52), 127.

The 1748 editions of the *Castle of Indolence.* (Note, 9). BC, i (52), 192-3.

William Collins's *Odes,* 1747. (Query, 17). BC, i (52), 195.

Goldsmith, *The Traveller,* 1770. (Note, 13). BC, i (52), 264-5.

Concealed editions of Samuel Johnson. BC, ii (53), 59-65.

Goldsmith's *Millenium Hall,* 1762. (Note, 15). BC, ii (53), 72.

Johnson's *Marmor Norfolciense.* (Note, 18). BC, ii (53), 73.

The Duke of Norfolk's press. (Query, 40). BC, ii (53), 283.

The '1651' editions of *Leviathan.* (Note, 29). BC, iii (54), 68-9.

Early children's books. (Query, 46). BC, iii (54), 150-1.

Burke's *Reflections on the Revolution in France.* (Query, 58). BC, iv (55), 81.

Concealed Pope editions. BC, v (56), 48-52.

Sheridan's *The Critic.* (Note, 68). BC, v (56), 172-3.

Fielding's *The Modern Husband,* 1732. (Note, 61). BC, v (56), 276.

The bibliography of Dylan Thomas. (Note, 81). BC, vi (57), 71-3.

Copleston, *Advice to a Young Reviewer.* (Note, 85). BC, vi (57), 293.

Ritson, *Observations on . . . the history of English Poetry,* 1782. (Note, 90). BC, vi (57), 408.

Dickens, *A Tale of Two Cities,* 1859. (Note, 94). BC, vii (58), 80.

First edition of *The Gentleman's Magazine.* (Query, 96). BC, vii (58), 188-9.

Hume, *Exposé succinct.* (Note, 97). BC, vii (58), 191.

Hannah Cowley: re-impressions, not reissues. (Note, 102). BC, vii (58), 301.

Reynolds's *Discourses.* 1769-1791. (Note, 103). BC, vii (58), 417-18.

Macpherson's *Fingal* and *Temora.* (Note, 122). BC, viii (59), 429-30.

Variant issues of *On the Origin of Species,* 1859. (Note, 131). BC, ix (60), 78.

Whitehead's *State Dunces,* 1733. (Note, 135). BC, ix (60), 195.

D. G. Rossetti's *Early Italian Poets,* 1861. (Note, 142). BC, ix (60), 329-31.

—. BC, x (61), 447.

Philips's *Cyder,* 1708. (Note, 150). BC, x (61), 68.

Borrow's *Lavengro and Faustus.* (Note, 153). BC, x (61), 70.

Mary Astell's *Serious proposal to the ladies,* 1694. (Note, 164). BC, x (61), 334-5.

A curious form of cancellation. (Query, 140). BC, x (61), 454-5.

Dickens's *Christmas Carol.* (Note, 170). BC, x (61), 449-54.

Cruikshank's *Uncle Tom's Cabin,* 1852. (Note, 183). BC, xi (62), 345-7.

An early state of Charlotte Brontë's *Shirley,* 1849. (Note, 204). BC, xii (63), 355-6.

Wise, Wrenn, and Tennyson's *Enoch Arden,* 1864. (Note, 214). BC, xiii (64), 67-8.

The first power-printed sheet. (Query, 176). BC, xiii (64), 71-2.

Liber Chronicarum, 1493. (Note, 231). BC, xiii (64), 497-8.

Variants in Johnson's *Dictionary,* 1755. (Note, 242). BC, xiv (65), 212-13.

A bibliographical misprint. (Note, 243). BC, xiv (65), 214.

A binder's misprint. (Note, 244). BC, xiv (65), 214.

Holcroft's *Follies of a day*, 1785. (Note, 260). BC, xiv (65), 544.

Scott's *Vision of Don Roderick*, 1811. (Note, 261). BC, xiv (65), 544.

Dickens's *Battle of Life*: round six. Illus. BC, xv (66), 48-54.

Le compost et calendrier des bergiers. 1529. (Query, 64). BC, xviii (69), 93.

Horne, *Orion: an epic poem* 1843. (Note, 309). BC, xviii (69), 219.

Some Wiseian advertisements. (Note, 310). BC, xviii (69), 219-20.

Blackmore, *Fringilla* 1895. (Query, 239). BC, xviii (69), 226.

An unrecorded Wiseian issue [of the *Dead Love* entry in the *Bibliography of Swinburne*]. (Note, 318). BC, xviii (69), 385-6.

The bibliographical history of Burke's *Reflections on the Revolution in France.* LIB, vi (51), 100-8.

The first printing of Hume's *Life*, 1777. LIB, vi (51), 123-5.

On the use of advertisements in bibliographical studies. LIB, viii (53), 174-87.

The printing of eighteenth-century periodicals: with notes on the *Examiner* and the *World.* LIB, x (55), 49-54.

The first edition of *The World.* LIB, xi (56), 283-4.

The Ferrara Bible. LIB, xii (57), 44-53.

A bibliographical account of *The Annual Register*, 1758-1825. LIB, xvi (61), 104-20.

London printers' imprints, 1800-1848. LIB, xxi (66), 46-62.

Some Wiseian ascriptions in the Wrenn catalogue. LIB, xxiii (68), 95-107.

The number, order, and authorship of the Hanover pamphlets attributed to Chesterfield. PBSA, xliv (50), 224-38.

Variant editions of Lyttelton's *To the Memory of a Lady lately deceased.* PBSA, xliv (50), 274-5.

A previously undescribed *Horace.* Illus. PBSA, xlv (51), 70-6.

Press figures and book reviews as determinants of priority: A study of Hume's *Douglas*, 1751, and Cumberland's *The Brothers*, 1770. PBSA, xlv (51), 72-6.

Another attribution to Swift. PBSA, xlv (51), 82-3.

Two issues of Crabbe's *Works*, 1823. PBSA, xlv (51), 250-1.

Twin titles in Scott's *Woodstock*, 1826. PBSA, xlv (51), 256.

A hidden edition of Whitehead's *Variety*, 1776. PBSA, xlv (51), 357-8.

Concurrent printing: an analysis of Dodsley's *Collection of Poems by Several Hands.* PBSA, xlvi (52), 45-57.

Unauthorised readings in the first edition of Thomson's *Coriolanus.* PBSA, xlvi (52), 62-6.

Texts and pretexts. PBSA, xlvi (52), 164.

Duplicate editions of Mason's *Musaeus*, 1747. PBSA, xlvi (52), 397-8.

The 1680 editions of Rochester's *Poems* with notes on earlier texts. PBSA, xlvii (53), 43-58.

Three notes on Fielding. PBSA, xlvii (53), 70-5.

Three notes on Charles Hanbury Williams. PBSA, xlvii (53), 159-60.

Multiple editions of Lyttelton's *The Court-Secret*, 1741. PBSA, xlvii (53), 380-1.

Aldine anchors, initials, and the 'counterfeit' Cicero [*Le Pistole ad Attico*]. Illus. PBSA, lx (66). 413-17.

The early editions and issues of *The Monk*, with a bibliography. SB, ii (49/50), 3-24.

Observations on the incidence and interpretation of press figures. SB, iii (50/1), 171-205.

Bibliography and the editorial problem in the eighteenth century. SB, iv (51/2), 41-55.

The issues and states of the second folio and Milton's *Epitaph on Shakespeare.* Illus. SB, v (52/3), 81-108.

The 'private issues' of *The Deserted Village.* [*and* Addendum]. SB, vi (54), 25-44; vii (55), 239.

The printing of Johnson's *Journey*, 1775. SB, vi (54), 247-54.

Patterns in press figures: a study of Lyttelton's *Dialogues of the Dead.* SB, viii (56), 230-5.

The early editions and issues of Scott's *Border Antiquities.* SB, ix (57), 244-51.

The first editions of *The good natur'd man* and *She stoops to conquer.* SB, xi (58), 133-42.

Recurrent printing. SB, xii (59), 189-98.

Early editions of *The Tatler.* SB, xv (62), 121-33.

A bibliographical account of *The Gentleman's Magazine*, 1731-1754. SB, xviii (65), 81-109. 81-109.

Arithmetic colophons in nineteenth-century books. SB, xix (66), 244-5.

—. *and* FOXON, David Fairweather
Thomas J. Wise and the pre-Restoration drama: a supplement. LIB, xvi (61), 287-93.

TOKEN
Hawthorne's income from *The Token.* SB, viii (56), 236-8.
S. L. Gross.

TOLLEMACHE *family*
The book-stamps of the Tollemache family of Helmingham and Ham. Illus. BC, xvi (67), 178-85.

TOLLEY, A. T.
The printing of Auden's *Poems*, 1928, and Spender's *Nine experiments*. LIB, xxii (67), 149-50.

TOMKIS, Thomas
Standing type in Tomkis's *Albumazar*. LIB, xiii (58), 175-85.
R. K. Turner.

TOMLINSON, Henry Major
H. M. Tomlinson's *A Bluebell at Thiepval*. (Query, 149). BC, xi (62), 219.
P. R. Haack.

TONGUE COMBATANTS
The Tongue combatants . . . 1684. (Note, 299). BC, xvii (68), 217.
R. J. Roberts.

TONSON, Jacob
Dryden, Tonson, and subscriptions for the 1697 *Virgil*. PBSA, lvii (63), 129-51.
J. Barnard.

TOON, Mabel Mary A. Chan-
See CHAN-TOON, Mabel Mary A.

TOOTHAKER, Charles R.
The Star Rover and Daniel Foss's *Oar*. PBSA, xliv (50), 182-5.

TOPOGRAPHY
Travel and topography in seventeenth-century England, a bibliography of sources for social and economic history. LIB, xiii (32/3), 292-311.
G. E. Fussell *and* V. G. B. Atwater.

TORRESANO DI ASOLA *family*
Some documents concerning the Torresani and the Aldine press. LIB, xxv (44/5), 111-21.
C. F. Bühler.

TORSVAN, Berick Traven
A checklist of the works of B. Traven and the critical estimates and biographical essays on him; together with a brief biography. PBSA, liii (59), 37-67.
E. R. Hagemann.

TOUCH-STONE
The Touch-stone, London, 1728. (Query, 145). BC, x (61), 337.
J. B. Shipley.

The authorship of *The Touch-stone*, 1728 [attributed to J. Ralph]. PBSA, lxii (68), 189-98.
J. B. Shipley.

TOURGÉE, Albion Winegar
A checklist of the writings of Albion W. Tourgée, 1838-1905. SB, xviii (65), 269-79.
D. H. Keller.

TOURNEISEN, J. J.
J. J. Tourneisen of Basle and the publication of English books on the Continent *c.* 1800. LIB, xv (60), 193-200.
G. G. Barber.

TOURNEUR, Cyril
The authorship and the bibliography of *The Revenger's Tragedy*. LIB, xv (60), 262-77.
G. R. Price.

The authorship of *The Revenger's Tragedy*. PBSA, lvi (62), 195-218.
P. B. Murray.

TOUSSAINT, Auguste
An American printing equipment in Mauritius in the eighteenth century. Illus. PBSA, xliv (50), 175-81.

TRACY, Clarence
Richard Savage d. 1743. (Some uncollected authors, 36). Illus. BC, xii (63), 340-9.

TRACY, Walter
A note on Eric Gill's Pilgrim type. BC, ii (53), 50-3.

TRADE BINDINGS
See BOOKBINDINGS

TRADE CARDS
Trade card as frontispiece. (Query, 49). BC, iii (54), 227.
N. Latimer.

TRADE SALES
Booksellers' trade sales 1718-1786. LIB, v (50/1), 243-57.
C. C. Blagden.

TRAHERNE, Thomas
Whereabouts of books owned by Traherne, Hopton, Bridgemon. (Query, 236). BC, xviii (69), 225-6.
L. Sauls.

Traherne's hand in the Credenhill records. LIB, xxiv (69), 50.
L. Sauls.

Thomas Traherne's commonplace book. PBSA, lviii (64), 458-65.
C. L. Marks.

Traherne's *Church's year-book*. [MS. Bodl. Eng. th. e. 51]. PBSA, lx (66), 31-72.
C. L. Marks.

Thomas Traherne's early studies. PBSA, lxii (68), 511-36.
C. L. Marks.

Traherne's Ficino notebook [MS. Burney 126]. PBSA, lxiii (69), 73-81.
C. M. Sicherman.

The careless compositor for *Christian ethicks*. PBSA, lxiii (69), 123-6.
L. Sauls.

TRANQUEBAR
Printing at Tranquebar, 1712-1845. Illus. LIB, iv (49/50), 179-95.
V. Rosenkilde.

TRANS-MISSISSIPPI PRINTING
The first trans-Mississippi imprint. PBSA, lii (58), 306-9.
D. Kaser.

TRANSCRIPTION
Photographic reproduction versus quasi-facsimile transcription. [A letter]. LIB, vii (52), 135-7.
J. P. W. Gaskell.

TRANSLATIONS
Translations for the Elizabethan middle class. LIB, xii (31/2), 312-31.
L. B. Wright.

Editions of the classics and English translations. [A letter]. LIB, viii (53), 204.
C. C. Blagden.

A numerical survey of Elizabethan translations. Illus. LIB, xxii (67), 104-27.
J. G. Ebel.

TRAUBE, Ludwig
Latin palaeography since Traube. TCBS, iii (59/63), 361-81.
T. J. Brown.

TRAVEL
Travel and topography in seventeenth-century England, a bibliography of sources for social and economic history. LIB, xiii (32/3), 292-311.
G. E. Fussell *and* V. G. B. Atwater.

TRAVELLING LIBRARIES
A travelling library. (Query, 91). BC, vii (58), 77.
P. E. Spielmann.

—. BC, vii (58), 188.
J. E. Norton.

Napoleon's travelling library. (Query, 113). BC, viii (59), 74.
P. E. Spielmann.

—. BC, viii (59), 308-9.
E. R. Gill.

TRAVEN, B. *pseud.*
See TORSVAN, Berick Traven

TREATISE OF LOVE
Seven variants in *The Treatise of Love*. PBSA, xlvi (52), 393-6.
J. H. Fisher.

TREATISE OF THE THREE EVILS
A note on *God's Judgement upon the Gentile Apostatized Church* & *A Treatise of the Three Evils of the Last Times* with special reference to a volume in the library of St. Paul's Cathedral, Dundee, which contains both title-pages. BTHK, iii (60/2), 31-4.
R. C. Rider.

TREES
America — a hunting ground for eighteenth-century naturalists with special reference to their publications about trees. PBSA, xxxii (38), 1-16.
J. R. Butler.

TRENCH, W. F. *and* GARRATT, K. B.
On Swift's marginalia in copies of Macky's *Memoirs*. LIB, xix (38/9), 354-62).

TREUTTEL AND WÜRTZ
Treuttel and Würtz: some aspects of the importation of books from France, c. 1825. Illus. LIB, xxiii (68), 118-44.
G. G. Barber.

TREVANION, Michael
Pompeii the Fourth. (Query, 145). BC, xi (62), 86.

T. J. Wise and J. C. Thomson. (Query, 164). BC, xii (63), 74.

Thomas J. Wise's descriptive formula. (Query, 181). BC, xiii (64), 355-6.

'A contract of eternall bond of love, confirmed by . . .'? [The leaflet printed at the Chiswick Press announcing the marriage of M. Lee and R. Le Gallienne]. BC, xv (66), 215.

Tennyson's *Idylls* and *The holy grail*. (Query, 222). BC, xvii (68), 490.

TREWE ENCOUNTRE
The trewe encountre: a pamphlet on Flodden Field [and one of the earliest English news-pamphlets, c. 1513]. Illus. TCBS, i (49/53), 126-9.
J. C. T. Oates.

TRIBUNE
Walt Whitman's correspondence with Whitelaw Reid, editor of the New York *Tribune*. SB, viii (56), 242-9.
E. H. Miller.

TRILLING, Lionel
The anthologist: editor *vs.* compiler. [L. Trilling's *The experience of literature*]. PBSA, lxiii (69), 321-3.
R. M. Davis.

TRINIDAD WEEKLY COURANT
Trinidad Weekly Courant. PBSA, xxxvii (43), 235.
D. C. McMurtrie.

TRIUMPH OF PEACE
The Triumph of Peace, a bibliographer's nightmare. Illus. LIB, i (46/7), 113-26.
Sir W. W. Greg.

TROLLOPE, Anthony
Orley Farm: an underline variant. (Query, 16). BC, i (52), 195.
M. Sadleir.

Orley Farm. (Query, 16). BC, i (52), 267.
F. R. Powell.

—. BC, ii (53), 157.
G. Green.

Can you forgive her? (Query, 35). BC, ii (53), 158.
G. Green.

Trollope's *La Vendée*, London, 1850. (Note, 152). BC, x (61), 69-70.
J. Carter.

The manuscript of Trollope's *The American Senator* collated with the first edition. PBSA, xli (47), 123-39.
R. H. Taylor.

TROTTUS, Albertus
Albertus Trottus and Albertus de Ferrariis. LIB, ii (47/8), 158-9.
L. A. Sheppard.

TROXELL, Gilbert McCoy
The Elizabethan Club of Yale University. PBSA, xxvii (33), 83-8.

TRUMBULL, Benjamin
Trumbull, Benjamin, 1735-1820. PBSA, xl (46), 160-1.
J. E. Alden.

TRUMBULL, James Hammond
James Hammond Trumbull, bibliographer of Connecticut. PBSA, xlviii (54), 239-47.
D. B. Engley.

TRUMP, James D. Van
See VAN TRUMP, James D.

TRUXTON, Thomas
Truxton, Thomas (1755-1822). *Remarks, instructions, and examples relating to latitude and longitude.* Philadelphia, 1794. PBSA, xxxiv (40), 362.
A. W. Paine.

TRYON, Warren Stenson
Book distribution in mid-nineteenth century America, illustrated by the publishing records of Ticknor and Fields, Boston. PBSA, xli (47), 210-30.

TUCKER, Joseph Eagon
John Davies of Kidwelly, 1627?-1693, translator from the French. With an annotated bibliography of his translations. PBSA, xliv (50), 119-52.

Castillo Solórzano's *Garduña de Sevilla* in English translation. PBSA, xlvi (52), 154-8.

Wing's *Short-title Catalogue* and translations from the French, 1641-1700. PBSA, xlix (55), 37-67.

On the authorship of the *Turkish Spy*: an *état présent*. PBSA, lii (58), 34-47.

TULK, Charles Augustus
Blake, Tulk and Garth Wilkinson. LIB, xxvi (45/6), 190-2.
Sir G. L. Keynes.

TURBERVILLE, George
Richard Hakluyt and Turberville's poems on Russia. PBSA, lxi (67), 350-1.
L. E. Berry.

TURKISH BIBLIOGRAPHY
Notes on Turkish bibliography. PBSA, xlvi (52), 159-63.
L. S. Thompson.

TURKISH SPY
On the authorship of the *Turkish Spy*: an *état* PBSA, lii (58), 34-47.
J. E. Tucker.

TURNBULL, G. H.
Notes on John Durie's *Reformed Librarie-Keeper*. LIB, i (46/7), 64-7.

TURNED SHEETS
The ghost of the turned sheet. PBSA, xlv (51), 246-50.
P. S. Dunkin.

TURNER, Dawson William
A bibliography of the printed works of Dawson Turner. TCBS, iii (59/63), 232-56.
W. R. Dawson.

TURNER, Daymond
Biblioteca Ovetense: a speculative reconstruction of the library of the first chronicler of the Indies. PBSA, lvii (63), 157-83.

TURNER, J. W.
Boswell's crest. (Query, 23). BC, i (52), 268.

TURNER, Joseph Mallord W.
Samuel Rogers, his illustrators, J. M. W. Turner and Thomas Stothard, and other friends. (Among my books, 3). Illus. BH, i (47/51), 197-218.
H. Rycroft.

TURNER, Michael Laurence
Conrad and T. J. Wise. (Note, 272). BC, xv (66), 350-1.

TURNER, Robert K.
Standing type in Tomkis's *Albumazar*. LIB, xiii (58), 175-85.

The printing of *Philaster* Q1 and Q2. LIB, xv (60), 21-32.

Notes on the text of *Thierry and Theodoret* Q1. SB, xiv (61), 218-31.

The relationship of *The Maid's Tragedy* Q1 and Q2. PBSA, li (57), 322-7.

Coxe's *A description of Carolina*, 1722-1741. SB, ix (57), 252-5.

The composition of *The Insatiate Countess*, Q2. SB, xii (59), 198-203.

The printing of Beaumont and Fletcher's *The Maid's Tragedy*, Q1, 1619. SB, xiii (60), 199-220.

The text of Heywood's *The fair maid of the West*. Illus. LIB, xxii (67), 299-325.

Printing methods and textual problems in *A Midsummer Night's Dream* Q1. SB, xv (62), 33-55.

The printing of *A King and No King* Q1. SB, xviii (65), 255-61.

Reappearing types as bibliographical evidence. Illus. SB, xix (66), 198-209.

The printers and the Beaumont and Fletcher folio of 1647, section 2. SB, xx (67), 35-59.

TURNER, Tom
The Tom Turner library. Illus. BC, ii (53), 258-63.
G. N. Ray.

TUTHILL, Louisa Caroline
Addenda to Wright [*American fiction 1774-1850*]: Mancur, Pise, Tuthill, Weld. PBSA, lxiii (69), 294.
W. S. Kable.

TUVILL, Daniel
Tuvill, Daniel (d. 1660). *The Dove and the Serpent*, London, 1614. PBSA, xxxv (41), 158.
E. M. Sowerby.

TWAIN, Mark *pseud.*
See CLEMENS, Samuel Langhorne

TWYMAN, Michael
The tinted lithograph. Illus. JPHS, i (65), 39-56.

The lithographic hand press 1796-1850. Illus. JPHS, iii (67), 3-50.

TWYNE, Brian
Brian Twyne's library [with a catalogue]. OBSP, iv (52), 1-42.
R. F. Ovenell.

TYLER, Annette E.
The chronology of the Estienne editions, Paris, 1526-50; Old Style or New? LIB, iv (49/50), 64-8.

Robert Estienne and his privileges, 1526-1550. LIB, iv (49/50), 225-37.

TYLER, Royall
Royall Tyler, 1757-1826. (Some uncollected authors, 42). BC, xv (66), 303-20.
G. T. Tanselle.

Some additional facts about Royall Tyler. (Note, 292). BC, xvi (67), 511.
M. B. Péledeau.

Early American fiction in England: the case of *The Algerine captive* [by R. Tyler]. PBSA, lix (65), 367-84.
G. T. Tanselle.

TYPE
A note on Eric Gill's Pilgrim type. BC, ii (53), 50-3.
W. Tracy.

In search of an archetype. (Query, 125). BC, ix (60), 80.
G. G. Barber.

Type-designs and type-founding in Scotland. EBST, ii (38/45), 253-61.
A. F. Johnson.

Caslon punches: an interim note. JPHS, i (65), 68-70.
H. Carter.

Académisme et typographie. The making of the Romain du roi. JPHS, i (65), 71-95.
A. Jammes.

New music types. Invention in the eighteenth century. Illus. 2 pts. JPHS, i (65), 21-38, ii (66), 23-44.
H. E. Poole.

Nineteenth-century decorated types at Oxford. Illus. JPHS, ii (66), inset.
J. Mosley.

Elizabethan roman and italic types. Illus. LIB, xiv (33/4), 85-100, 212-28.
F. Isaac.

Type faces, old and new. Illus. LIB, xiv (33/4), 121-43.
B. Warde.

Sources of roman and italic types used by English printers in the sixteenth century. Illus. LIB, xvii (36/7), 70-82.
A. F. Johnson.

Some types used by Paolo Manuzio. Illus. LIB, xix (38/9), 167-75.
A. F. Johnson.

Adolf Rusch and the earliest roman types. Illus. LIB, xx (39/40), 43-50.
J. V. Scholderer.

The 'goût hollandois'. Illus. LIB, xx (39/40), 180-96.
A. F. Johnson.

The italic types of Robert Granjon. Illus. LIB, xxi (40/1), 291-308.
A. F. Johnson.

Early humanistic script and the first roman type. LIB, xxiv (43/4), 1-29.
S. Morison.

The supply of types in the sixteenth century. LIB, xxiv (43/4), 47-65.
A. F. Johnson.

Measurement of type. [A letter]. LIB, i (46/7), 248-9.
J. C. Tarr.

Typographical studies [A letter]. LIB, i (46/7), 250-3.
E. Howe.

Stephen Parker's fount of Irish type. LIB, x (55), 278-80.
J. W. Phillips.

The types of Christopher Plantin. Illus. LIB, xi (56), 170-9.
H. Carter.

Standing type in Tomkis's *Albumazar*. LIB, xiii (58), 175-85.
R. K. Turner.

Cardinal Cervini and the printing of Greek. [A letter]. LIB, xiii (58), 299.
A. F. Johnson.

The longevity of a type-face. Illus. LIB, xvii (62), 242-6.
H. Carter.

The design of Day's Saxon. Illus. LIB, xxii (67), 283-98.
G. Wakeman.

Notes on standing type in Elizabethan printing. PBSA, xl (46), 205-21.
F. T. Bowers.

The identification of type faces in bibliographical description. PBSA, lxi (66), 185-202.
G. T. Tanselle.

A long use of a setting of type. [John Speed's *The Genealogies recorded in the Holy Scriptures.*]. SB, ii (49/50), 173-5.
E. E. Willoughby.

Scotch type in eighteenth-century America. SB, iii (50), 270-4.
J. E. Alden.

Type sizes in the eighteenth century. [*And*] Addendum. SB, v (52/54), 147-51, vi (54), 286.
J. P. W. Gaskell.

The Case of the Planters of Tobacco in Virginia, 1733: an extraordinary use of standing type. SB, v (52), 184-6.
O. L. Steele.

Benjamin Franklin's Philadelphia type. SB, xi (58), 179-206.
C. W. Miller.

Reappearing types as bibliographical evidence. Illus. SB, xix (66), 198-209.
R. K. Turner, *jr*.

The Irish broadside of 1571 and Queen Elizabeth's types. Illus. TCBS, i (49/53), 48-60.
B. Dickins.

The first book printed in Anglo-Saxon types. [Aelfric: *A testimonie of antiquitie*]. Illus. TCBS, iii (59/63), 265-9.
J. Bromwich.

TYPE-COMPOSING MACHINE
An assessment of Mackie's steam type-composing machine. JPHS, i (65), 57-67.
J. Moran.

TYPE FOUNDERS AND FOUNDRIES
See also LONDON SOCIETY OF MASTER LETTER-FOUNDERS

Type-designs and type-founding in Scotland. EBST, ii (38/45), 253-61.
A. F. Johnson.

Aperçu sur la fonderie typographique parisienne au xviiie siècle. LIB, xxiv (69), 200-18.
J. Veyrin-Forrer.

John Heaz, Elizabethan letter-founder to the printers. TCBS, i (49/53), 287.
B. Dickins.

TYPE SIZES
Type sizes in the eighteenth century. [*And*] Addendum. SB, v (52/3), 147-51; vi (54), 286.
J. P. W. Gaskell.

TYPE SPECIMENS
Typographical specimen books, a check-list of the Broxbourne collection with an introduction. Illus. BC, v (56), 256-72.
W. T. Berry *and* A. M. Fern.

Specimens of printing types before 1850 in the typographical library at the University Press, Oxford. BC, viii (59), 397-410.
J. S. G. Simmons.

Two states of a Bodoni type specimen. (Note, 218). BC, xiii (64), 207-10.
M. J. Faigel.

Anthony Bessemer, London, 1830. (19th century type-specimen books, 1). JPHS, v (69), 99.
A. Bessemer.

Catalogue of Specimens of Printing Types by English and Scottish Printers and Founders, 1665-1830. [A letter]. LIB, xvii (36/7), 230-1.
A. F. Johnson.

—. LIB, xvii (36/7), 232-4.
D. Thomas.

The type-specimen books of Claude Lamesle and Nicolas Gando. Illus. LIB, xviii (37/8), 201-12.
A. F. Johnson.

A list of type specimens. LIB, xxii (41/2), 185-204.
H. Carter *and others*.

Two Caslon specimens. LIB, ii (47/8), 199-200.
L. W. Hanson.

French type specimen books. LIB, vi (51), 28-41.
E. Howe.

The undated Oxford broadsheet *Specimen*. Illus. LIB, xi (56), 11-17.
J. S. G. Simmons.

Unrecorded type specimens at the University of Vermont. PBSA, li (57), 162-3.
H. McArthur.

TYRELL, James
Concerning James Tyrell, 1642-1718. (Query, 159). BC, xii (63), 72.
J. L. Axtell.

TYRRELL, E. P. *and* SIMMONS, John Simon G.
Slavonic books before 1700 in Cambridge libraries. Illus. TCBS, iii (59/62), 382-400.

Slavonic books of the eighteenth century in Cambridge libraries. TCBS, iv (64/8), 225-45.

TYRWHITT, Thomas
Printer's copy for Tyrwhitt's *Chaucer*. SB, iii (50), 265-6.
A. L. Hench.

U

UDALL, Nicholas
The Vesalian compendium [*De Humani Corporis Fabrica*] of Geminus and Nicholas Udall's translation; their relation to Vesalius, Caius, Vicary and De Mondeville. Illus. LIB, xiii (32/3), 367-94.
S. V. Larkey.

ULLMAN, Berthold Louis
Abecedaria and their purpose. Illus. TCBS, iii (59/62), 181-6.

ULRIC IN PERSONAS
Ulric in personas. EBST, iii (48/55), 82-3.
W. Beattie.

UNGERER, Gustav
The printing of Spanish books in Elizabethan England. LIB, xx (65), 177-229.

UNICORN BINDER
Notes on some new tools used by the 'Unicorn binder'. Illus. LIB, ii (47/8), 283-4.
J. B. Oldham.

UNITED CHRISTIAN FRIENDS
United Christian Friends. *Hymns for the use of the Society of* . . . . New York, 1797. PBSA, xxxvii (43), 77.
L. M. Stark.

UNITED STATES
Special collections for the study of history and literature in the South east. PBSA, xxviii (34), 97-131.
R. B. Downs *and* L. R. Wilson.

UNITED STATES *Congress*
Congress of the United States. *Acts passed at a Congress of the United States of America, begun and held at the city of New York.* PBSA, xxxv (41), 70-1.
C. Storm.

Congress of the United States. *Acts of the First Congress.* New-York. [*And*] *Acts passed at a Congress . . . begun . . . On Wednesday the fourth of March, In the year MDCCLXXXIX* Philadelphia. PBSA, xxxv (41), 158.
L. E. Osborne.

The story of the United States Senate documents, 1st Congress, 1st session, New York, 1789. PBSA, lvi (62), 175-94.
J. B. Childs.

'Disappeared in the Wings of Oblivion'. The story of the United States House of Representatives printed documents at the first session of the First Congress, New York, 1789. Illus. PBSA, lviii (64), 91-132.
J. B. Childs.

UNITED STATES *constitutions*
The first printing of the Constitution in a book. PBSA, xlii (48), 256-8.
S. Jackson.

French publications of the Declaration of Independence and the American Constitutions, 1776-1783. PBSA, xlvii (53), 313-38.
D. Echeverria.

The authentic archetype of the United States Constitution. PBSA, lvi (62), 372-4.
J. B. Childs.

UNITED STATES *Inspector's Office.*
United States. Inspector's Office, Washington, Feb. 19, 1812. *At a General Court-Martial, . . . Brigadier General James Wilkinson was tried.* PBSA, xxxiv (40), 189-90.
L. W. Dunlap.

UNITED STATES *nat. libr. of med.*
An Ulm unicum of 1501 [M. Puff von Schrick's *Ain guts nutzlichs büchlin von den auss geprenten wassern*], in the National library of medicine, Bethesda, Maryland. Illus. LIB, xx (65), 55-7.
R. J. *and* S. M. Durling.

UNIVERSAL CHRONICLE
John Newbery, projector of the *Universal Chronicle*: a study of the advertisements. SB, xi (58), 249-51.
G. J. Kolb.

UNIVERSAL PENMAN
See BICKHAM, George

THE UNIVERSAL VISITER
Christopher Smart, Richard Rolt, and *The Universal Visiter*. LIB, xvii (36/7), 212-14.
C. Jones.

Christopher Smart and the *Universal Visiter*. LIB, x (55), 203-5.
A. Sherbo.

UPCOTT, William
William Upcott and John Evelyn's papers. LIB, xx (65), 320-5.
W. G. Hiscock.

URIE, Robert
The parentage of Robert Urie, printer in Glasgow. BTHK, v (67/70), 38-40.
R. A. Gillespie.

URQUHART, Sir Thomas
Milton, N.LL, and Sir Tho. Urquhart. Illus. LIB, xiv (33/4), 470-6.
H. C. H. Candy.

—. [A letter]. LIB, xv (34/5), 249-50.
J. W. Pendleton.

URSPRUNG VND ORDNUNGEN DER BERG-WERGE
Ursprung vnd Ordnungen der Bergwerge . . . (Leipzig 1616): location of copies. (Query, 223). BC, xvii (68), 219.
R. L. King.

USHAW *St. Cuthbert's coll.*
Note on the binding of Ushaw College XVIII *c.* 9b. TCBS, i (49/53), 46-7.
J. B. Oldham.

USTICK, W. Lee
   'Parchment' and 'vellum'. LIB, xvi (35/6),
   439-43.

UTRECHT, Treaty of
   The provisions made by the Treaties of Utrecht,
   etc. Lond., 1762. PBSA, xxxv (41), 73.
   A. B. Forbes.

V

VAIL, Joseph
An address to a Deist, a poem. PBSA, xxxvi (42), 64.
C. S. Brigham.

VAIL, Robert William G.
James Johns, Vermont pen printer. Illus. PBSA, xxvii (33), 89-132.

Sabin's *Dictionary.* PBSA, xxxi (37), 1-9.

Sketch of an Indian irruption into the town of Shawangunk, in the year 1780. PBSA, xxxvii (43), 77-8.

Bibliographical notes on certain Eastern mining companies of the California Gold Rush, 1849-1850. Illus. PBSA, xliii (49), 247-78.

Adventures of Jonathan Corncob, Loyal American Refugee, 1787, a commentary. PBSA, l (56), 101-14.

In memoriam: Robert William Glenroie Vail 1890-1966. PBSA, lxii (68), 579-80.
J. J. Heslin.

VALERIUS MAXIMUS
The printing of a Valerius Maximus dated 1671. SB, vii (55), 177-81.
C. F. Bühler.

VALLETTA
Some notes on the public library, Valletta. EBST, ii (38/45), 437-40.
J. Purves.

VAN ARDSEL, Rosemary
John Chapman and *The Westminster Review.* (Note, 66). BC, v (56), 171-2.

VANBURGH, Sir John
William Wycherley, 1640?-1716. Sir John Vanburgh, 1664-1726. (English literary autographs, 41). Illus. BC, xi (62), 63.
T. J. Brown.

VANDELEUR
Travels to the Westward . . . Windsor, (Ut.) Alden Spooner, 1794. PBSA, xxxiv (40), 190.
T. W. Streeter.

VAN DEN KEERE, Pieter
Pieter van den Keere. LIB, v (50/1), 130-2.
R. A. Skelton.

VANDERBANK, John
Eighteenth-century English illustrators, John Vanderbank, 1694-1739. Illus. BC, xvii (68), 285-99.
H. A. Hammelmann.

VANDERSEE, Charles
James's *Pandora*: the mixed consequences of revision. SB, xxi (68), 93-108.

VAN DIEST, Gillis *the elder*
The birth-year of Gillis van Diest I, Antwerp printer of English books. LIB, iii (48/9), 213.
H. R. Hoppe.

VAN HOESEN, Henry B.
The Bibliographical Society of America — its leaders and activities, 1904-1939. PBSA, xxxv (41), 177-202.

VAN PATTEN, Nathan
A presentation copy of Coleridge's *Sibylline Leaves*, with manuscript notes, altered readings, and deletions by the author. LIB, xvii (36/7), 221-4.

A newly discovered issue of Scott's *The Vision of Don Roderick.* LIB, xviii (37/8), 109-13.

An Eskimo translation of Defoe's *Robinson Crusoe.* Godthaab, Greenland, 1862-1865. Illus. PBSA, xxxvi (42), 56-8.

The Yerba Buena Press and some related privately printed books. Illus. PBSA, xliii (49), 202-9.

Icelandic translations of Maugham. PBSA, xlv (51), 158-9.

VAN REGEMORTER, Berthe
The binding of the Archangel Gospels. Illus. BC, xiii (64), 481-5.

Ethiopian bookbindings. LIB, xvii (62), 85-8.

VAN SCHREEVEN, William
The Journal of the Convention of the State of Georgia, on the Federal Constitution. Augusta: Printed by John E. Smith, Printer to the State. MDCCLXXXVIII. PBSA, xl (46), 161.

VAN TRUMP, James D. *and* ZIEGLER, Arthur P. *jr.*
Thomas Bird Mosher, publisher and pirate. Illus. BC, xi (62), 295-312.

VAN VECHTEN, Carl
Additions to the bibliography of Carl Van Vechten. PBSA, lv (61), 42-5.
K. W. Jonas.

VARADI, A.
A Landor rarity. (Note, 32). BC, iii (54), 71-3.

Early Czech books (Note, 41). BC, iv (55), 73-4.

VARBANETS, N. V.
Incunabula in the Saltykov-Shchedrin Library, Leningrad. Illus. BC, iv (55), 273-8.

VARGA, Nicholas
Damon and Alexis: Nuptial satire or political squib? PBSA, xlix (55), 354-8.

VATICAN *archivio*
Registers of supplications: Registra supplicationum [in the Vatican archives]. EBST, ii (38/45), 383-4.
A. I. Dunlop.

VAUGHAN, Henry
Henry Vaughan and his publishers. LIB, xx (40), 401-11.
W. R. Parker.

VAUGHAN, Richard
The handwriting of Matthew Paris. [*With*] List of MSS. containing the handwriting of Matthew Paris. Illus. TCBS, i (49/53), 376-94.

—. *and* FINES, John
A handlist of manuscripts in the Library of Corpus Christi College, Cambridge, not described by M. R. James. TCBS, iii (59/63), 113-23.

VAUGHAN, Robert
Two ghosts: Herbert's *Baripenthes* and the Vaughan-Holland portrait of Sidney. LIB, xxiv (43/4), 175-81.
W. H. Bond.

VAUTROLLIER, Thomas
Francis Clement's *Petie schole* at the Vautrollier press, 1587. LIB, xxii (67), 1-12.
R. D. Pepper.

VEEVERS, Erica
Albions Triumph: a further corrected state of the text. LIB, xvi (61), 294-9.

VEGETIUS RENATUS, Flavius
The device on plate E5v of Vegetius's *De re militari*. (Query, 240). BC, xviii (69), 226-7.
H. Bohem.

A note on some fragments of Vegetius from Augsburg. LIB, viii (53), 36-7.
D. E. Rhodes.

VELLEKOOP, Jacques
Ernst Philip Goldschmidt 1887-1954. The evolution of a great bookseller. Illus. BC, iii (54), 118-24.

VELLUM
'Parchment' and 'vellum'. LIB, xvi (35/6), 439-43.
W. L. Ustick.

VELZ, John William
'Pirate Hills' and the quartos of *Julius Caesar*. PBSA, lxiii (69), 177-93.

VENICE
Venice revisited. BC, xvii (68), 37-41.
A. Rau.

VENNAR, Richard
Richard Vennar and *The Double PP*. PBSA, xliii (49), 199-202.
P. Shaw.

VENUS IN THE CLOISTER
The reappearance of two lost black sheep. [*Venus in the Cloister*, 1725; and Cleland's own abridgement of the *Memoirs of a Woman of Pleasure*, entitled *Memoirs of Fanny Hill*]. (Note, 239). BC, xiv (65), 75-6.
D. F. Foxon.

VERGILIUS MARO, Publius
An unpublished commentary by George Buchanan on Virgil. EBST, iii (48/55), 269-88.
C. P. Finlayson.

Further notes on a Milanese edition of Virgil [published by N. de Gorgonzola]. LIB, xxiv (69), 142.
D. E. Rhodes.

Dryden, Tonson, and subscriptions for the 1697 *Virgil*. PBSA, lvii (63), 129-51.
J. Barnard.

A possible new source for Servius Danielis on *Aeneid* III-V. SB, iv (51), 129-41.
A. F. Stocker.

The Servius of Cassel for *Aeneid* III-V. SB, vi (54), 93-100.
A. F. Stocker.

VERLAINE, Paul Marie
Paul Verlaine's *Les Amies*. (Note, 114). BC, viii (59), 296-7.
D. Strabolgi.

VERMONT
A bibliography of Vermont bibliography and printing. PBSA, lv (61), 17-33.
M. A. McCorison.

VERMONT *univ.*
Unrecorded type specimens at the University of Vermont. PBSA, li (57), 162-3.
H. McArthur.

VERNE, Jules
Julies Verne. (Note, 54). BC, iv (55), 327-9.
P. H. Muir.

VERNER, Coolie
Some observations on the Philadelphia 1794 editions of Jefferson's *Notes*. SB, ii (49/50), 201-4.

The several states of the Farrer map of Virginia. SB, iii (50/1), 281-4.

—. *and* CONKWRIGHT, P. J.
The printing of Jefferson's *Notes*, 1793-94. SB, v (52/3), 201-3.

VERNER, Mathilde
Johann Albert Fabricius, eighteenth-century scholar and bibliographer. PBSA, lx (66), 281-326.

VERSTEGHEN, Richard *pseud.*
See ROWLANDS, Richard

VERVLIET, Hendrik Désiré L.
The Garamond types of Christopher Plantin. Illus. JPHS, i (65), 14-20.

VESALIUS, Andreas
The engraved title-page of the *Fabrica* of Vesalius (1543 & 1555) and a drawing in the Hunterian Library, Glasgow University. Illus. BTHK, iii (60/2), 96-7.
R. Donaldson.

The Vesalian compendium [*De Humani Corporis Fabrica*] of Geminus and Nicholas Udall's translation: their relation to Vesalius, Caius, Vicary and De Mondeville. Illus. LIB, xiii (33), 367-94.
S. V. Larkey.

VETUS REPERTORIUM
'Vetus repertorium', an early memorandum book of the diocese of Lincoln. TCBS, iv (64/8), 100-6.
D. M. Owen.

VEYRIN-FORRER, Jeanne
Aperçu sur la fonderie typographique parisienne au xviiie siècle. LIB, xxiv (69), 200-18.

VICARY, Thomas
The Vesalian compendium [*De Humani Corporis Fabrica*] of Geminus and Nicholas Udall's translation; their relation to Vesalius, Caius, Vicary, and De Mondeville. Illus. LIB, xiii (33), 367-94.
S. V. Larkey.

VICENTE, Gil
Gil Vicente and Shakespeare. Illus. BH, ii (51/2), 1-12.
A. Livermore.

VICENTINO, Arrighi
A royal manuscript by Arrighi Vicentino in the B. M. (Note, 91). Illus. BC, vii (58), 78-9.
B. Wolpe.

VIDA DE CRISTO
Corrected misprinting in the *Vida de Cristo*, Lisbon, 1495. PBSA, liv (60), 290-1.
C. F. Bühler.

VIETH, David M.
The text of Rochester and the editions of 1680. Illus. PBSA, l (56), 243-63.

Order of contents as evidence of authorship: Rochester's *Poems* of 1680. PBSA, liii (59), 293-308.

A textual paradox: Rochester's *To a Lady in a Letter*. PBSA, liv (60), 147-62.

An unsuspected cancel in Tonson's 1691 *Rochester*. PBSA, lv (61), 130-3.

VIETS, Henry R.
The printings in America of Polidori's *The Vampyre* in 1819. PBSA, lxii (68), 434-5.

The London editions of Polidori's *The Vampyre*. PBSA, lxiii (69), 83-103.

VILJOEN, Helen Gill
Ruskin, Millais and Effie Gray. (Query, 22). BC, i (52), 268.

VILLANI, Francesco
Francesco Villani, a forgotten poet of the Lunigiana. (Some uncollected authors, 2). BC, iii (54), 45-9.
D. E. Rhodes.

VILLETTE, Charlotte de
Marie Antoinette and Charlotte de Villette. (Note, 89). BC, vi (57), 408.
C. Hesketh.

VINCENT, Augustine
Cancels and corrections in *A Discovery of Errors*, 1622. LIB, xiii (58), 124-7.
E. R. Wood.

VINER, Charles
Charles Viner's *General abridgment of law and equity*. OBSP, ii (27/30), 227-325.
S. Gibson *and* sir W. Holdsworth.

VINER, G. H.
The origin and evolution of the book-plate. Illus. LIB, i (46/7), 39-44.

VINGLES, Juan de
Juan de Vingles (Jean de Vingle), a sixteenth-century book illustrator. Illus. LIB, xviii (37), 121-76.
H. Thomas.

VINIARD OF DEVOTION
Three little Tudor books [Xenophon's *Treatise of Household*, tr. G. Hervet, T. Berthelet, 1532; Philip Moore's *The Hope of Health*, J. Kingston 1564; *The Viniard of Devotion*. Newly corrected for Edw. White, 1599]. Illus. LIB, xiv (33/4), 178-206.
E. F. Bosanquet.

VIRGILIUS MARO, Publius
See VERGILIUS MARO, Publius

VIRGIN AND CHILD BINDER
The Virgin and Child binder, LVL, and William Horman. Illus. LIB, xvii (62), 77-85.
N. R. Ker.

VIRGINIA
The classical tradition in colonial Virginia. PBSA, xxxiii (39), 85-97.
L. B. Wright.

A short account of the first settlement of the Provinces of Virginia, Maryland, New-York, New-Jersey and Pennsylvania by the English. London, 1735. PBSA, xxxvi (42), 231.
N. B. Wainwright.

A West Virginia broadside. Illus. PBSA, xliii (48), 322-3.
J. C. Wyllie.

Early West Virginia imprints. Illus. PBSA, xlv (51), 237-45.
B. B. Stutler.

The several states of the Farrer map of Virginia. SB, iii (50), 281-4.
C. Verner.

Jefferson as collector of Virginiana. SB, xiv (61), 117-44.
R. B. Davis.

VIRTUE
The fragments *Virtue* and *The Assemble of Goddes*. STC 24844a and 17005-17007a. PBSA, xlvii (53), 378-80.
W. Ringler.

VLIMMERIUS, Johannes
English manuscripts owned by Johannes Vlimmerius and Cornelius Duyn. LIB, xxii (41/2), 205-7.
N. R. Ker.

VOET, Leon B.
The printers' chapel in the Plantinian House. LIB, xvi (61), 1-14.

VOLTAIRE, François Marie Arouet de
Voltaire's *La Henriade*. (Query, 47). BC, iii (54), 151.
H. Williams.

Voltaire's *La Henriade*. (Query, 47). BC, iii (54), 307-8.
D. Flower.

Voltaire and his library. Illus. BC, vii (58), 139-51.
V. Lublinsky.

Candide: a perennial problem. BC, viii (59), 284-8.
D. Flower.

Montesquieu, Voltaire and Rousseau in eighteenth-century Scotland: a checklist of editions and translations of their works published in Scotland before 1801. BTHK, ii (59/60), 40-63.
A. K. Howard.

Some aspects of the bibliography of Voltaire. LIB, i (46/7), 223-36.
D. Flower.

—. [A letter]. LIB, iv (49/50), 74.
P. H. Muir.

Voltaire at Stationers' Hall. LIB, x (55), 126-7.
F. J. Crowley.

Some early editions of Voltaire printed in London. LIB, xiv (59), 287-93.
K. I. Maslen.

VON RICHENTHAL, Ulrich
See RICHENTHAL, Ulrich von

VORAGINE, Jacobus de
Legenda aurea [German]: *Passional oder Leben der Heiligen, Sommerteil*. Augsburg: Johann Schönsperger, 1487. PBSA, xxxiv (40), 268-9.
H. D. Subers.

VORONOVA, T. P.
Western MSS in the Saltykov-Shchedrin library, Leningrad. Illus. BC, v (56), 12-18.

VOSPER, Robert
A pair of bibliomanes for Kansas: Ralph Ellis and Thomas Jefferson Fitzpatrick. PBSA, lv (61), 207-25.

Rare books in redbrick cases. BC, xi (62), 21-34.

VOSTRE, Simon
A Book of Hours for the use of Autun printed for Simon Vostre (*c.* 1507). A correction to the Stillwell census. PBSA, xli (47), 341-2.
H. Bober.

W., C.
Thackeray: *The Rose and the Ring*, 1855. (Query, 10). BC, i (52), 57-8.

WADDESDON MANOR
Waddesdon Manor. (Unfamiliar libraries, 5). Illus. BC, viii (59), 131-9.
A. R. A. Hobson.

WADDELL, David
The writings of Charles Davenant, 1656-1714. LIB, xi (56), 206-12.

WAGNER, H. R.
Wagner-Camp. [Notes on H. R. Wagner's *The plains and the rockies*. 3rd ed., revised by C. L. Camp]. PBSA, lv (61), 45-6.
L. S. Thompson.

WAGNER G.
James Leslie Mitchell/Lewis Grassic Gibbon: a chronological checklist. BTHK, i (56/8), 3-21.

WAGNER, Henry Raup
Commercial printers of San Francisco from 1851 to 1880. PBSA, xxxiii (39), 69-84.

Two unknown American incunabula. PBSA, xxxix (45), 318-19.

WAINWRIGHT, Nicholas B.
A short account of the first settlement of the Provinces of Virginia, Maryland, New-York, New-Jersey and Pennsylvania, by the English. London, 1735. PBSA, xxxvi (42), 231.

WAKEMAN, Geoffrey
Gems from The Poets, 1859. (Note, 199). BC, xii (63), 207-8.

Two editions of 'Cruikshank's Grimm'. (Note, 286). BC, xvi (67), 82-3.

Anastatic printing for Sir Thomas Phillipps. Illus. JPHS, v (69), 24-40.

Henry Bradbury's nature-printed books. Illus. LIB, xxi (66), 63-7.

The design of Day's Saxon. Illus. LIB, xxii (67), 283-98.

WALBANCKE, Matthew
Walbancke, Matthew (?1596-?1667). *Annalia Dubrensia. Vpon the yeerely celebration of Mr. Robert Dovers Olimpick Games vpon Cotswold-Hills*. London, Robert Raworth, 1636. PBSA, xxxiv (40), 271.
E. M. Sowerby.

WALBANK, Alan
Country collecting. BC, vi (57), 54-9.

Railway reading. BC, ix (60), 285-91.

Gothic romances and yellowbacks. (Contemporary collectors, 32). Illus. BC, xi (62), 313-22.

WALBRIDGE, Earle F.
An additional note on *The Cardboard Box*. PBSA, xlvii (53), 75-6.

Key novels, American and European: a supplement to *Literary Characters Drawn From Life*. PBSA, xlvii (53), 161-91.

A Critical History of Children's Literature [by C. Meigs and others]: a second list of errata. PBSA, xlviii (54), 263-7.

The Whole Family and Henry James. PBSA, lii (58), 144-5.

WALCOTE, William de
Two medieval book lists [the libraries of Simon Burley and William de Walcote]. LIB, xxiii (68), 236-9.
V. J. Scattergood.

WALDEGRAVE, Robert
Robert Waldegrave and the books he printed or published in 1603. Illus. LIB, xiii (58), 225-33.
W. A. Jackson.

WALE, Samuel
Samuel Wale. (Eighteenth-century English illustrators). Illus. BC, i (52), 150-65.
H. A. Hammelmann.

WALES
Developments in the book trade in eighteenth-century Wales. LIB, xxiv (69), 33-43.
E. Rees.

WALEY, Arthur
The privately printed *Chinese Poems*, 1916. (Query, 136). BC, ix (60), 458.
F. A. Johns.

—. BC, x (61), 72.
G. F. Sims.

Arthur Waley's *Chinese Poems*, 1916. (Note, 210). BC, xii (63), 494.
F. A. Johns.

WALKER, Alice
The cancelled lines in *2 Henry IV*, IV,i.93, 95. LIB, vi (51/2), 115-16.

The folio text of *1 Henry IV*. SB, vi (54), 45-59.

Compositor determination and other problems in Shakespearian texts. SB, vii (55), 3-15.

Collateral substantive texts, with special reference to *Hamlet*. SB, vii (5), 51-67.

Some editorial principles, with special reference to *Henry V*. SB, viii (56), 95-111.

Principles of annotation: some suggestions for editors of Shakespeare. SB, ix (57), 95-105.

WALKER, Anthony
Anthony Walker. (Eighteenth-century English illustrators). BC, iii (54), 87-102.
H. A. Hammelmann.

WALKER, Ralph Spence
Charles Burney's theft of books at Cambridge. Illus. TCBS, iii (59/63), 313-26.

WALKER, Robert
Robert Walker, printer, c. 1755. [A letter]. LIB, xi (56), 286.
J. R. Hetherington.

—. [A letter]. LIB, xii (57), 125.
C. C. Blagden

WALKLEY, Thomas
Walkley's supposed piracy of Wither's *Workes* in 1620. LIB, xix (38), 339-46.
L. Kirschbaum.

WALL, Alexander J.
American genealogical research, its beginning and growth. PBSA, xxxvi (42), 305-14.

WALLACE, James
James Wallace's *An account of the Islands of Orkney*, London, 1700. BTHK, iv (63/6), 36-8.
I. R. Grant.

WALLER, Frederick O.
Three 1695 editions of Jevon's *Devil of a Wife*. SB, iii (50/1), 255.

Printer's copy for *The Two Noble Kinsmen*. SB, xi (58), 61-84.

WALLEY, Henry
Henry Walley of the Stationers' Company and John Marston. PBSA, lvi (62), 366-8.
P. J. Finkelpearl.

WALLING, Henry Francis
Nineteenth-century cadastral maps in Ohio. [Based on a paper by H. F. Walling]. PBSA, lix (65), 306-15.
W. W. Ristow.

WALLIS, Peter John
Doctoring the date; two Glasgow examples. BTHK, v (67/70), 144-6.

William Oughtred's *Arithmeticae in numeris* or *Clavis mathematicae*, 1647; an unrecorded (unique?) edition in Aberdeen university library. BTHK, v (67/70), 147-50.

The library of William Crashawe. Illus. TCBS, (54/8), 213-28.

William Oughtred's *Circles of proportion* and *Trigonometries*. TCBS, iv (64/8), 372-82.

WALMSLEY, D. M.
Unrecorded article by T. S. Eliot. (Note, 139). BC, ix (60), 198-9.

WALPOLE, Horace
Horace Walpole, 1717-1797. (English literary autographs, 8). Illus. BC, ii (53), 273-5.
T. J. Brown.

The 1796 edition of Walpole's *Anecdotes*, a fifth volume (Note, 279). BC, xv (66), 484.
J. H. C. Gerson.

Horace Walpole's library. LIB, ii (47), 45-52.
W. S. Lewis.

The booksellers' 'Ring' at Strawberry Hill in 1842. SB, vii (55), 194-8.
A. T. Hazen.

WALPOLE, Sir Hugh
Sir Hugh Walpole. (Bibliomanes, 2). Illus. 3 pts. BC, iv (55), 217-28, 299-307; v (56), 38-47.
P. H. Muir.

WALSH, James E.
'The librarian's library': the William A. Jackson bibliographical collection. Illus. 2 pts. BC, xiv (65), 499-510; xv (66), 34-45.

Notes on the Philip Hofer reference collection. (Contemporary collectors, 45). Illus. BC, xviii (69), 159-69.

American printings of Longfellow's *The Golden Legend*, 1851-1855. PBSA, lvii (63), 81-8.

WALSH, John
John Walsh, music publisher: the first twenty-five years. LIB, i (46/7), 1-5.
W. C. Smith.

John Walsh and his successors. LIB, iii (48/9), 291-5.
W. C. Smith.

WÄLSUNGENBLUT
Concerning the affair *Wälsungenblut*. BC, xiii (64), 463-72.
M. Walter.

WALT WHITMAN FELLOWSHIP
The Walt Whitman fellowship: an account of its organization and a check-list of its papers. PBSA, li (57), 67-84.
W. White.

—. Additions and corrections. PBSA, li (57), 167-9.

WALTER, Marie
Concerning the affair *Wälsungenblut*. BC, xiii (64), 463-72.

WALTERS, William T.
See also WALTERS ART GALLERY

The publishing ventures of a Victorian connoisseur. A sidelight on William T. Walters. Illus. PBSA, lvii (63), 271-311.
D, Miner.

WALTERS ART GALLERY
The collection of manuscripts and rare books in the Walters Art Gallery. PBSA, xxx (30), 104-9.
D. Miner.

WALTON, Francis R.
Joannes Gennadius, 1844-1932. (Portrait of a bibliophile, 12). Illus. BC, xiii (64), 305-26.

A faked Henri II — Diane de Poitiers binding. (Note, 236). BC, xiv (65), 72.

Two anonymous translations of Pseudo-Xenophon [in the Gennadius library]. BC, xvi (67), 218.

WALTON, Isaak
A bibliography of Isaak Walton's *Lives*. [Limited to the 17th-century editions]. OBSP, ii (27/30), 327-40.
J. E. Butt.

WALTS, Robert W.
William Dean Howells and his *Library Edition*. PBSA, lii (58), 283-94.

Howells's plans for two travel books. PBSA, lvii (63), 453-9.

WARBURTON, William
Warburton, Hanmer and the 1745 edition of Shakespeare. SB, ii (49), 35-48.
G. E. Dawson.

WARD, Artemus *pseud*.
See BROWNE, C. F.

WARD, Roger
Roger Ward's Shrewsbury stock: an inventory of 1585. LIB, xiii (58), 247-268.
A. Rodger.

WARDE, Beatrice Lamberton
Type faces, old and new. Illus. LIB, xvi (35/6), 121-43.

WARNER, Charles Dudley
That *Gilded Age* again: an attempt to unmuddle the mystery of the fifty-seven variants. PBSA, xxvii (43), 141-56.
F. C. Willson.

The fake title-page of the *Gilded Age*: a solution. PBSA, l (56), 292-6.
D. Woodfield.

Toward a critical text of *The gilded age* [by Mark Twain and C. D. Warner]. PBSA, lix (65), 142-9.
H. Hill.

WARNING FOR TOBACCONISTS
A warning for Tobacconists. PBSA, xlii (48), 148-50.
P. S. Dunkin.

WARRANTIES
Booksellers' warranties. LIB, i (46/7), 244-5.
Sir F. C. Francis.

WARRILOW, Alice Georgina, GASKELL, John Philip W. *and* BARBER, Giles Gaudard
An annotated list of printers' manuals to 1850. Illus. JPHS, iv (68), 11-32.

WARTON, Thomas
A Dublin reprint of Thomas Warton's *History of English Poetry*. LIB, i (46), 69-70.
J. M. G. Blakiston.

WARWICK, *St. Mary's church*
The Caxton Legenda at St. Mary's, Warwick. Illus. LIB, xii (57), 225-39.
P. Morgan *and* G. D. Painter.

WARWICK, Arthur
Arthur Warwick, 1603/4-1633: the author of *Spare minutes*. Illus. LIB, xxi (66), 223-30.
K. J. Höltgen *and* J. Horden.

WARWICKSHIRE TALENTS
The Warwickshire Talents, 1809. (Query, 156).
BC, xi (62), 486.
S. Nowell-Smith.

WASHINGTON D. C., *Folger Shakespeare libr.*
The Harmsworth collection and the Folger Library. BC, vi (57), 123-8.
L. B. Wright.

Some Folger academic drama manuscripts. SB, xii (59), 117-30.
R. H. Bowers.

WASHINGTON D.C., *libr. of Congress.*
The A. E. Housman manuscripts in the Library of Congress. BC, iv (55), 110-14.
J. Carter.

The Ephraim George Squier manuscripts in the Library of Congress: a checklist. PBSA, liii (59), 309-26.
J. E. Patterson *and* W. R. Stanton.

Two autographs of a 'Sienese Gentleman' in the Library of Congress. PBSA, liv (60), 291-3.
J. M. Edelstein.

WASHINGTON, George
To all brave, healthy, able-bodied, and well disposed young men, in this neighbourhood, who have any inclination to join the troops, now raising under General Washington. [n.p., 1799]. PBSA, xxxvi (42), 67.
L. M. Stark.

Washington's manuscript diaries of 1795 and 1798. PBSA, xlv (51), 117-24.
R. Baughman.

WATER LANE PRESS
The first two years of the Water Lane press. [*With*] A check-list. TCBS, ii (54/8), 170-84.
J. P. W. Gaskell.

WATERMARKS
See also CHAIN LINES

The Leningrad method of watermark reproduction. (Note, 160). Illus. BC, x (61), 329-30.
J. S. G. Simmons.

Watermark copying by an X-ray method. Illus. (Note, 248). BC, xiv (65), 217-18.
H. D. Jamieson.

The Delft method of watermark reproduction. (Note, 320). BC, xviii (69), 514-15.
J. S. G. Simmons.

Watermarks. EBST, ii (38/45), 449-50.
Sir H. Thomas.

Eighteenth-century quartos with vertical chain lines. LIB, xvi (35/6), 337-42.
A. T. Hazen.

Watermark dates in English paper. LIB, xxv (44), 70-1.
C. B. Oldman.

Turned chain-lines. Illus. LIB, v (50/1), 184-200.
K. Povey *and* I. J. C. Foster.

A critical study of Heawood's *Watermarks mainly of the 17th and 18th centuries*. PBSA, xlv (51), 23-36.
A. H. Stevenson.

Russian watermarks and embossed paper stamps of the eighteenth and nineteenth centuries. PBSA, lvii (63), 121-8.
S. A. Klepikov.

New uses of watermarks as bibliographical evidence. SB, i (48/9), 149-82.
A. H. Stevenson.

Watermarks are twins. Illus. SB, iv (51/2), 57-91.
A. H. Stevenson.

Shakespearian dated watermarks. Illus. SB, iv (51/2), 150-64.
A. H. Stevenson.

Watermarks and the dates of fifteenth-century books. SB, ix (57), 217-24.
C. F. Bühler.

Tudor roses from John Tate. Illus. SB, xx (67), 15-34.
A. H. Stevenson.

WATSON, Andrew George
An identification of some manuscripts owned by Dr. John Dee and Sir Simonds D'Ewes. LIB, xiii (58), 194-8.

Two unrecorded items of 1603. Illus. LIB, xvi (61), 299-302.

Christopher and William Carye, collectors of monastic manuscripts, and 'John Carye'. LIB, xx (65), 135-42.

Prices of some second-hand law books in 1620. PBSA, lvii (63), 212-17.

WATSON, George
A manuscript of Hector Boece. EBST, ii (38/45), 392-3.

WATSON, Sir William
Sir William Watson. (Some uncollected authors, 12). BC, v (56), 375-80.
C. Woolf.

—. Additions and corrections. BC, vi (57), 66-7.
N. Colbeck.

—. BC, vi (57), 285-6.
W. E. Swayze.

—. [Addenda]. BC, vi (57), 402.

WATSON, W. M. *and* ISAAC, Peter Charles G.
The history of the book trade in the north, a review of a research project. Illus. JPHS, iv (68), 87-98.

WATSON, William Davy
William Davy Watson, author of *Trevor: or the New St. Francis*. PBSA, lix (65), 55-7.
D. B. Green.

WATT, Frank William
Early Canadiana. BC, x (61), 28-39.

WATT, Ian
Publishers and sinners: the Augustan view. SB, xii (59), 3-20.

WATT, James
James Watt, 1736-1819. (English scientific autographs, 7). Illus. BC, xv (66), 47.
T. J. Brown.

WATT, Robert
Do you know your Lowndes? A bibliographical essay on William Thomas Lowndes and incidentally on Robert Watt and Henry G. Bohn. PBSA, xxxiii (39), 1-22.
G. W. Cole.

WAUGH, Evelyn
Textual problems in the novels of Evelyn Waugh. PBSA, lxii (68), 259-63.
R. M. Davis.

—. PBSA, lxiii (69), 41-6.
R. M. Davis.

WAYLAND, John
Wayland's edition of *The Mirror for Magistrates*. Illus. LIB, xiii (32/3), 155-7.
W. A. Jackson.

WAYNFLETE, George *pseud*.
Thackeray: *Pendennis*. (Query, 3). BC, i (52), 54.

WEAD, Eunice
Early binding stamps of religious significance in certain American libraries. A supplementary report. Illus. Addendum [by E. Kyriss]. SB, ii (49/50), 63-77; v (52/3), 210.

WEALE, W. H. James
W. H. James Weale, the pioneer. LIB, vi (51), 200-11.
M. W. Brockwell.

WEAVER, Gustine Courson
Spyri, Johanna (1827-1901). *Heidi, her years of wandering and learning*. Boston, 1884. PBSA, xxxv (41), 75.

WEAVER, Harriet Shaw
Harriet Weaver and James Joyce. (Query, 212). BC, xv (66), 488-9.
J. H. Lidderdale.

Harriet Weaver's letters to James Joyce, 1915-1920. SB, xx (67), 151-88.
J. Firth.

WEBB, C. A. *and* SCHOLDERER, Julius Victor
Berthold Ruppel, printer of the *Sermones Meffreth*. Illus. LIB, xv (60), 1-7.

WEBBE, Joseph
An ambitious printing project of the early seventeenth century. [Joseph Webbe's works]. LIB, xvi (61), 190-6.
V. Salmon.

WEBER, Carl Jefferson
Hardy's grim note in *The Return of the Native*. PBSA, xxxvi (42), 37-45.

The manuscript of Hardy's *Two on a Tower*. Illus. PBSA, xl (46), 1-21.

Hardy's debut — how a literary 'career was determined' one hundred years ago. PBSA, lix (65), 319-22.

WEBER, David C.
Bibliographical blessings. PBSA, lxi (67), 307-14.

WEBSTER, John
The collaboration of Dekker and Webster in *Northward Ho* and *Westward Ho*. PBSA, lvi (62), 482-6.
P. B. Murray.

The printing of John Webster's plays. 3 pts. SB, vi (54), 117-40; viii (54), 113-22; xv (54), 57-69.
J. R. Brown.

WEBSTER, Noah
Salesmanship of an early American best seller. [Noah Webster's *Grammatical Institute*]. PBSA, xxxi (38), 38-46.
Mrs. R. Skeel, *jr*.

WECHEL, Christian
A letter written by Andrea Alciato to Christian Wechel. LIB, xvi (61), 201-5.
C. F. Bühler.

WEDDERBURN, Alexander
Some errors in the bibliography of the library edition of John Ruskin's works [by E. Cook and A. Wedderburn]. PBSA, lxii (68), 127-9.
J. Halladay.

WEEDON, Margaret J. P.
Richard Johnson and the successors to John Newbery. LIB, iv (49/50), 25-63.

Mother Goose's Melody. LIB, vi (51-2), 216-18.

An uncancelled copy of the first collected edition of Swift's poems. [Swift's *Works*, 1735, Dublin edition]. LIB, xxii (67), 44-56.

WEEKLEY, A. S.
A concealed edition? (Query, 33). BC, ii (53) 158.

WEEKS, William Raymond
Addenda to Wright [*American fiction 1774-1850*]: Burdett, Curtis, Ludson, Weeks. PBSA, lxii (68),452-3.
W. S. Kable.

WEGELIN, Oscar
Cree, Joseph. *Verses Addressed by Joseph Cree, To the Gentlemen and Ladies, To whom he carries the New-York Gazetteer. January 1, 1775*. PBSA, xxxiv (40), 187.

Sweep-Embargo's New Year's Message. [Albany, 1809]. PBSA, xxxiv (40), 189.

Oscar Wegelin, pioneer bibliographer of American literature. PBSA, lvi (62), 237-47.
R. E. Stoddard.

WEIL, Ernst
William Fitzer, the publisher of Harvey's *De Motu Cordis*, 1628. LIB, xxiv (43/4), 132-64.

Samuel Browne, printer to the University of Heidelberg, 1655-1662. LIB, v (50/1), 14-25.

WEINREB, Ben
A 17th-century bookseller's circular. (Query, 153). BC, xi (62), 484-5.

WEISERT, John J.
Mrs. Stowe first writes of Kentuckians for Kentuckians. PBSA, li (57), 340-1.

WEISS, Roberto
Humfrey, Duke of Gloucester *d*. 1447. (Portrait of a bibliophile, 11). Illus. BC, xiii (64), 161-70.

WEITENKAMPF, Frank
What is a facsimile? PBSA, xxxvii (43), 114-30.

WELCH, C. E.
Julian Notary and Andrew Rowe: two contemporary records. LIB, xi (56), 277-8.

WELD, J. H.
Addenda to Wright [*American fiction 1774-1850*]: Mancur, Pise, Tuthill, Weld. PBSA, lxiii (69), 294.
W. S. Kable.

WELLCOME HISTORICAL MEDICAL LIBRARY
See LONDON *Wellcome historical medical libr*.

WELLESLEY, John
The Penguin collector. (Penguin books; three short essays, 3). BC, i (52), 213-14.

A sixteenth-century fragment. (Query, 26). Illus. BC, i (52), 269.

Microbibliography. (Note, 24). BC, ii (53), 219.

Author's certificate to printer. (Note, 37). BC, iii (54), 226.

WELLESLEY COLLEGE *libr*.
A slashed copy [in Wellesley College library] of *Reliques of Robert Burns* [collected and published by R. H. Cromek], 1808. (Note, 265). H. D. French.

WELLS, Gabriel
Mr Muir and Gabriel Wells: a rejoinder. BC, x (61), 53-5.
D. A. Randall.

WELLS, Herbert George
H. G. Wells's contributions to the *Saturday Review*. LIB, xvi (61), 29-36.
G. N. Ray.

H. G. Wells's dramatic criticism for the *Pall Mall Gazette*. LIB, xvii (62), 138-45.
M. Timko.

WELLS, James M.
The John M. Wing Foundation of the Newberry Library. Illus. BC, viii (59), 157-62.

The Bureau Académique d'Écriture: a footnote to the history of French calligraphy. Illus. PBSA, li (57), 203-13.

WELLS, John Edwin
Variants in the 1746 edition of Thomson's *Seasons*. LIB, xvii (36/7), 214-20.

Lyrical Ballads, 1800: a paste-in. LIB, xix (38/9), 486-91.

Thompson's *Spring*: early editions true and false. LIB, xxii (41/2), 223-43.

WELSH, Robert Ford
The printer of the 1594 octavo of Marlowe's *Edward II*. SB, xvii (64), 197-8.

WERKEN, T.
A fifteenth century scribe: T. Werken. [*With*] a List of manuscripts written by T. Werken. TCBS, i (49/53), 97-104.
Sir R. A. B. Mynors.

WERKMEISTER, Lucyle Thomas, WOOF, Robert Samuel *and* ERDMAN, David Vorse
Unrecorded Coleridge variants: additions and corrections. SB, xiv (61), 236-45.

WESSEN, Ernest J.
Lincoln bibliography — its present status and needs. PBSA, xxxiv (40), 327-48.

Debates of Lincoln and Douglas. A bibliographical discussion. PBSA, xl (46), 91-106.

Jones' *Nests and Eggs of the Birds of Ohio*. PBSA, xlvii (53), 218-30.

WESSON, A.
'Drawback' in the book trade. (Query, 168). BC, xii (63), 356.

WEST, Elsie L.
Another reprint of Irving's *Biography of James Lawrence*. PBSA, lvii (63), 448-9.

WEST, Herbert Faulkner
The Dartmouth college library. (Unfamiliar libraries, 10). Illus. BC, xv (66), 175-82.

WEST, James
A London panel-stamped binding, *c.* 1530, rebacked for James West, *c.* 1755. (English bookbindings, 59). Illus. BC, xv (66), 460.
H. M. Nixon.

Book-collecting in the eighteenth century: the library of James West. LIB, iii (48/9), 265-78.
R. C. Lucas.

WEST, Nathanael
Nathanael West, 1903?-1940. (Some uncollected authors, 32). BC, xi (62), 206-10.
W. White.

Bibliography of Nathanael West. (Note, 187). BC, xi (62), 351.
W. White.

Nathanael West's *Balso Snell* in cloth. PBSA, lx (66), 474-6.
W. White.

Nathanael West: a bibliography. SB, xi (58), 207-24.
W. White.

West's revisions of *Miss Lonelyhearts*. SB, xvi (63), 232-43.
C. A. Daniel.

WEST, Paul
The Dome. An aesthetic periodical of the 1890's. BC, vi (57), 160-9.

WESTERN AMERICAN
The *Western American* — an early California newspaper. PBSA, xxxiv (40), 349-55.
L. C. Powell.

WESTMINSTER LIBRARY
The Westminster Library: history and mystery. LIB, xxi (66), 240-5.
P. Kaufman.

WESTMINSTER REVIEW
John Chapman and *The Westminster Review*. (Note, 66). BC, v (56), 171-2.
R. Van Arsdel.

WESTON, John Charles
Burke's authorship of the historical articles in Dodsley's *Annual Register*. PBSA, li (57), 244-9.

The text of Burns' *The Jolly Beggars*. SB, xiii (60), 239-47.

Predecessors to Burke's and Dodsley's *Annual Register*. SB, xvii (64), 215-20.

WHALLEY, Arthur George C.
Samuel Taylor Coleridge, 1772-1834. (Portrait of a bibliophile, 7). BC, x (61), 275-90.

Coleridge marginalia lost. Illus. BC, xvii (68), 428-42.

Coleridge marginalia lost. (Note, 315). BC, xviii (69), 223.

The Bristol Library borrowings of Southey and Coleridge, 1793-8. LIB, iv (49/50), 114-32.

WHALLEY, George
See WHALLEY, Arthur George C.

WHARTON, Edith
Hidden printings in Edith Wharton's *The Children*. SB, xv (62), 269-73.
M. J. Bruccoli.

WHATMAN, James
Whatman paper in a book dated 1757. (Query, 108). BC, viii (59), 72.
E. Wolf.

—. BC, viii (59), 306-8.
T. Balston.

Baskerville and James Whatman. SB, v (52), 187-9.
A. T. Hazen.

WHEAT, Carl Irving
Mapping the American West. PBSA, l (56), 1-16.

WHEBLE, John
The missing third edition of Wheble's *Junius*, 1771. SB, xiii (60), 235-8.
B. G. Evans.

WHIPPLE, T. H.
An unrecorded Chicago ante-fire imprint: Whipple's *Ethzelda*. PBSA, lxi (67), 123-4.
G. T. Tanselle.

WHISTON
Parnell on Whiston. PBSA, lvii (63), 91-2.
C. J. Rawson.

WHITAKER, J. *and sons, ltd.*
An ancient Whitaker. [E. Chamberlayne's *The present state of England compleat*, 1687]. BH, i (47/51), 417-21.
A. C. Prance.

WHITAKER, S. F.
The first edition of Shaftesbury's *Moralists*. LIB, vii (52), 235-41.

WHITE, Cathcart
See EDINBURGH *univ., libr.*

WHITE, Edward M.
Thackeray's contributions to *Fraser's magazine*. SB, xix (66), 67-84.

WHITE, Gilbert
Gilbert White, 1720-1793. (English literary autographs, 29). Illus. BC, viii (59), 51.
T. J. Brown.

—. (Some uncollected authors, 43). BC, xvii (68), 300-21.
C. A. Prance.

Gilbert White's *The natural history of Selborne*. (Note, 304). BC, xviii (69), 89-90.
W. S. Scott.

WHITE, James
A manuscript of James White's translation of *The Clouds*. LIB, xxvi (46), 304-7.
N. S. Angus.

WHITE, Norman *and* DUNNE, Tom
A Hopkins discovery [in L. Magnus and C. Headlam, *Prayers from the poets: a calendar of devotion*]. LIB, xxiv (69), 56-8.

WHITE, Richard
La Cava; or Recollections of the Neapolitans. (Query, 19). BC, i (52), 197.

WHITE, Robert
See NEWCASTLE-UPON-TYNE *univ., libr.*

WHITE, William
Variant readings in Housman's *More Poems*. (Note, 20). BC, ii (53), 73-7.

Variant readings in Housman's *Collected Poems*. (Note, 34). BC, iii (54), 145-8.

Housman's *Epitaph on an army of mercenaries*. (Query, 63). BC, iv (55), 173.

A variant reading in Housman's *Collected Poems*. (Note, 80). BC, vi (57), 71.

Press copies of Joyce's *Ulysses*. (Note, 156). BC, x (61), 72.

Nathanael West, 1903?-1940. (Some uncollected authors, 32). BC, xi (62), 206-10.

Bibliography of Nathanael West. (Note, 187). BC, xi (62), 351.

A. E. Housman's *Collected Poems*. (Note, 192). BC, xii (63), 71.

Ernest Bramah, 1869?-1942. (Some uncollected authors, 37). BC, xiii (64), 54-63.

Emendations in Housman. (Note, 234). BC, xiii (64), 500-1.

Ernest Bramah's dates (Note, 228). BC, xiv (65), 72.

Misprints in Housman's *Last poems*. (Note, 255). BC, xiv (65), 540-1.

A. E. Housman — an annotated check-list. Additions and corrections. LIB, xxiii (42/3), 31-42.

—. LIB, vii (52), 201-10.

A Shropshire Lad in process: the textual evolution of some A. E. Housman poems. LIB, ix (54), 255-64.

[Housman, A. E. (1859-1936).] *Odes from the Greek Dramatists*. London, 1890. PBSA, xxxiv (40), 274.

—. PBSA, xxxv (41), 297-8.

Jeffers, Robinson (1887-). *The Cardinal*. November '05. University California. PBSA, xxxiv (40), 362-3.

Osler, Sir William (1849-1919). *The principles and practice of medicine*. New York, 1892. [&c.]. PBSA, xxxv (41), 162.

—. PBSA, xxxvi (42), 233.

Housman, A. E. (1859-1936). *The Oracles*. PBSA, xxxvii (43), 78.

James Joyce: addenda to Alan Parker's bibliography. PBSA, xliii (49), 401-11.

Titles from Housman: IV. PBSA, xliv (50), 190-2.

More Dos Passos: bibliographical addenda. PBSA, xlv (51), 156-8.

Two problems in A. E. Housman bibliography. PBSA, xlv (51), 358-9.

Abercrombie and Housman: a coincidence in parodies. PBSA, xlviii (54), 98-99.

An unrecorded Housman MS item. PBSA, xlix (55), 78-9.

The Walt Whitman Fellowship: an account of its organization and a checklist of its papers. PBSA, li (57), 67-84.

—. Additions and corrections. PBSA, li (57), 167-9.

Housman's Sydney address. PBSA, lii (58), 138-9.

Walt Whitman's short stories: some comments and a bibliography. PBSA, lii (58), 300-6.

—. Two addenda. PBSA, liv (60), 126.

—. Addenda. PBSA, lvii (63), 221-2.

Dylan Thomas and A. E. Housman. PBSA, lii (58), 309-10.

A checklist of A. E. Housman's writings in Latin. PBSA, liv (60), 188-90.

Housman in Sudbury, Ontario. PBSA, liv (60), 295.

Mr. Ciardi, Mr. Adams, and Mr. White. [C. M. Adams' review of *John Ciardi, a bibliography* by W. White]. PBSA, lv (61), 393.
C. E. Feinberg.

Housman in French and music. PBSA, lvi (62), 257-9.

Snodgrass peoples his universe: II. PBSA, lvii (63), 94.

Haiku: an addendum. PBSA, lvii (63), 233.

The first, 1855, *Leaves of Grass*: how many copies? PBSA, lvii (63), 352-4.

Hemingway in Korea. PBSA, lix (65), 190-2.

The old man and the sea as a German textbook. PBSA, lx (66), 89-90.

The text of A. E. Housman's *Collected poems*. PBSA, lx (66), 221-3.

Dylan Thomas, Mr. Rolph, and *John O'London's weekly*. PBSA, lx (66), 370-2.

Two versions of F. Scott Fitzgerald's *Babylon revisited*: a textual and bibliographical study. PBSA, lx (66), 439-52.

Nathanael West's *Balso Snell* in cloth. PBSA, lx (66), 474-6.

Robinson Jeffers' *The beginning and the end*: another error. PBSA, lxi (67), 126.

Two Bramah variants [of *A little flutter* and *The moon of much gladness*]. PBSA, lxii (68), 254-6.

Addendum to Hanneman: Hemingway's *The old man and the sea*. [Audre Hanneman's *Ernest Hemingway*: a comprehensive bibliography]. PBSA, lxii (68), 613-4.

Nathanael West: a bibliography. SB, xi (58), 207-24.

Whitman's *Leaves of Grass*: notes on the pocket book, 1889, edition. SB, xviii (65), 280-1.

WHITECHAPEL *School Press*
The School Press. (Query, 44). BC, iii (54), 149-50.
A. Muirhead.

—. BC, iii (54), 73.
A. Ehrman.

WHITEHEAD, Paul
Whitehead's *State Dunces*, 1733. (Note, 135). BC, ix (60), 195.
W. B. Todd.

WHITEHEAD, William
A hidden edition of Whitehead's *Variety*, 1776. PBSA, xlv (51), 357-8.
W. B. Todd.

WHITING, F. Brooke
The authorship of *A proposition for the safety and happiness of the King*. 1667. PBSA, l (56), 182-3.

WHITMAN, Marcus
Authentic account of the murder of Dr. Whitman: the history of a pamphlet. PBSA, lv (61), 319-46.
G. N. Belknap.

WHITMAN, Sarah Helen
Poe and Sarah Helen Whitman. BC, xii (63), 490.
C. S. Bliss.

WHITMAN, Walt
See also WALT WHITMAN FELLOWSHIP

The centenary, of *Leaves of Grass*. Two Whitman catalogues. BC, iv (55), 324-6.
D. Daiches.

Walt Whitman's reception in Scandinavia. PBSA, xl (46), 259-75.
G. W. Allen.

The manuscripts of Whitman's *Song of the Redwood-Tree*. PBSA, l (56), 53-85.
F. T. Bowers.

A Whitman collector destroys a Whitman myth. Illus. PBSA, lii (58), 73-92.
C. E. Feinberg.

W. Whitman's short stories: some comments and bibliography. PBSA, lii (58), 300-6.
W. White.

—. Two addenda. PBSA, liv (60), 126.

—. Addenda. PBSA, lvii (63), 221-2.

A note on a Whitman holograph poem. PBSA, lv (61), 233-6.
A. Golden.

Whitman's short stories: another reprint. PBSA, lvi (62), 115.
G. T. Tanselle.

The first, 1855, *Leaves of Grass*: how many copies? PBSA, lvii (63), 352-4.
W. White.

A recovered Whitman fair copy of a *Drum-taps* poem, and a *Sequel to drum-taps* fragment. PBSA, lix (65), 439-41.
A. Golden.

A sheaf of Whitman letters. SB, v (52), 203-10.
W. Harding.

Whitman's manuscripts for the original *Calamus* poems. SB, vi (54), 257-65.
F. T. Bowers.

Walt Whitman's correspondence with Whitelaw Reid, editor of the New York *Tribune*. SB, viii (56), 242-9.
E. H. Miller.

Whitman's *Leaves of Grass*: notes on the pocket book, 1889, edition. SB, viii (65), 280-1.
W. White.

WHITTIER, John Greenleaf
The first separate printing of *Maud Miller*. PBSA, li (47), 148-51.
C. A. Wilson.

John Greenleaf Whittier in *The Independent*. PBSA, lx (66), 91.
G. Monteiro.

WHITTINTON, Robert
A checklist of Robert Whittinton's grammars. LIB, vii (52), 1-14.
H. S. Bennett.

The gilt binding of the Whttinton *Epigrams*, MS. Bodley 523. LIB, vii (52), 120-1.
H. M. Nixon.

WHYTE, William
Haydn's settings of Scottish songs in the collections of Napier and Whyte. Illus. EBST, iii (48/55), 85-120.
C. Hopkinson *and* C. B. Oldman.

WIDNALL, Samuel Page
Samuel Page Widnall and his press at Granchester, 1871-1892. Illus. TCBS, ii (54/8), 366-72.
B. Dickins.

—. Addenda. TCBS, iii (59/63), 95.
B. Dickins.

—. Further addenda. TCBS, iii (59/63), 176-8.
B. Dickins.

WIER, Richard
Richard Wier and Count MacCarthy-Reagh. Illus. BC, ii (53), 247-57.
C. Ramsden.

WILD, Payson Sibley
Addenda to Irish [W. R. Irish's *The modern American muse*]: Brown, North, and Wild. PBSA, lxii (68), 452.
G. T. Tanselle.

WILD, Robert
Two editions of *Iter Boreale*, 1668. (Note, 196). BC, xii (63), 204-5.
R. S. Pirie.

WILDE, Oscar
Who wrote *For Love of the King*? Oscar Wilde or Mrs. Chan Toon? BC, vii (58), 269-72.
G. Sims.

WILDER, Thornton
Thornton Wilder and the reviewers. PBSA, lviii (64), 35-49.
J. R. Bryer.

WILES, A. G. D.
The date of publication and composition of Sir William Alexander's supplement to Sidney's *Arcadia*. PBSA, l (56), 387-92.

WILES, Roy McKeen
Dates in English imprints, 1700-52. LIB, xii (57), 190-3.

Further additions and corrections to G. A. Cranfield's *Handlist of English Provincial Newspapers and Periodicals 1700-1760*. TCBS, ii (54/8), 385-9.

WILEY, Margaret Lee
A supplement to the bibliography of *Shakespeare Idolatry* [by R. W. Babcock]. SB, iv (51/2), 164-6.

WILKINS, George
Manuscript evidence for dates of two *Short-title Catalogue* books: George Wilkins's *Three Miseries of Barbary* and the third edition of Elizabeth Grymeston's *Miscelanea*. LIB, xvi (61), 141-2.
R. Krueger.

WILKINS, John
Two editions of John Wilkins's *Mathematicall Magick*, London, 1648. PBSA, xliii (49), 195.
A. E. Lownes.

WILKINS-FREEMAN, Mary E.
See FREEMAN, Mary E. Wilkins-

WILKINSON, Cyril Hackett
A small collection at Oxford. (Contemporary collectors, 9). BC, v (56), 127-36.

WILKINSON, J. J. Garth
Blake, Tulk and Garth Wilkinson. LIB, xxvi (45), 190-2.
Sir G. L. Keynes.

WILKINSON, brig. gen. James.
United States Inspector's Office, Washington, Feb. 18, 1812. *At A General Court-Martial, . . . Brigadier General James Wilkinson was tried . . .* PBSA, xxxiv (40), 189-90.
L. W. Dunlap.

WILKINSON, Kenneth Douglas
Withering on The Foxglove. [Dr. W. Withering's *An account of the foxglove*]. Illus. BH, i (47/51), 184-92.

WILKINSON, Robert
An eighteenth-century forgery of Robert Wilkinson's *Merchant Royall*, 1607. LIB, v (50/1), 274.
F. Cordasco.

WILKS, John
Presentation-copies of Everard Digby's *Theoria Analytica*. LIB, xii (57), 121-2.

WILLARD, Oliver M.
The survival of English books printed before 1640: a theory and some illustrations. LIB, xxiii (42/3), 171-90.

WILLET, Ralph
Ralph Willet of Merly, 1719-1795. (Portraits of bibliophiles, 10). Illus. BC, xii (63), 439-48.
A. G. Thomas.

An admonition to borrowers [in a sale catalogue of 1813 of the library of Ralph Willet]. (Note, 210). BC, xiii (64), 211.
A. Ehrman.

WILLIAM *de Machlinia*
See WILLIAM *of Mechlin*

WILLIAM *of Mechlin*
The headlines of William de Machlinia's *Year-Book, 37 Henry VI*. SB, i (48/9), 123-32.
C. F. Bühler.

The Morgan copy of Machlinia's *Speculum Christiani*. SB, v (52/3), 159-60.
C. F. Bühler.

WILLIAM *of Ockham*
A variant edition of Ockham's *Summa Logicae*. PBSA, liv (60), 176.
L. W. Riley.

WILLIAM AND MARGARET
See MALLOCH, David

WILLIAM AND MARY COLLEGE *libr.*
Notes on the original library of the College of William and Mary in Virginia, 1693-1705. PBSA, xli (47), 239-67.
J. M. Jennings.

WILLIAMS, Charles
A checklist of reviews by Charles Williams. PBSA, lv (61), 100-17.
L. R. Dawson, *jr.*

WILLIAMS, Sir Charles Hanbury
Three notes on C. H. Williams. PBSA, xlvii (53), 159-60.
W. B. Todd.

WILLIAMS, Franklin Burleigh
Fragosa, King of Aragon, ?1618. (Query, 105). BC, viii (59), 70-1.

Wormholes in stored sheets. [A letter]. LIB, xviii (37/8), 463-4.

The Rheims version of the New Testament. [A letter]. LIB, xxi (40/1), 216.

Special presentation epistles before 1641: a preliminary checklist. Illus. LIB, vii (52), 15-20.

An index of dedications and commendatory verse. Illus. LIB, xii (57), 11-22.

The Laudian imprimatur. Illus. LIB, xv (60), 96-104.

These careless Elizabethans: names bewitched. PBSA, liv (60), 115-19.

Josse Glover breaks into print. PBSA, lv (61), 383-5.

An initiation into initials. SB, ix (57), 163-78.

Penny-pinching printers and tempered titles. SB, xix (61), 209-11.

Commendatory verses: the rise of the art of puffing. SB, xix (66), 1-14.

Photo-facsimiles of *STC* books: a cautionary check list. SB, xxi (68), 109-30.

WILLIAMS, George Walton
The printer of the first folio of Sidney's *Arcadia*. LIB, xii (57), 274-5.

Textual revision in Crashaw's *Upon the bleeding crucifix*. SB, i (48/9), 191-3.

A note on *King Lear*, III, ii, 1-3. SB, ii (49/50), 175-82.

Setting by formes in quarto printing. SB, xi (58), 39-53.

The printer and the date of *Romeo and Juliet* Q4. SB, xviii (65), 253-4.

Roberts' compositors in *Titus Andronicus* Q2. SB, viii (56), 27-38.

The order of stanzas in Cowley and Crashaw's 'On hope' [by C. H. Miller, SP, lxi 1964]. SB, xxii (69), 207-10.

—. *and* CANTRELL, Paul L.
The printing of the second quarto of *Romeo and Juliet*, 1599. SB, ix (57), 107-28.

WILLIAMS, Sir Harold Herbert
La Henriade, (Query, 47). BC, iii (54), 151.

Jonathan Swift and the *Four Last Years of the Queen*. Illus. LIB, xvi (35/6), 61-90.

—. [A letter]. LIB, xvi (35/6), 343-4.

Robert Brunlees McKerrow, 12 Dec., 1872 - 20 Jan. 1940. Illus. LIB, xx (39/40), 345-9.

WILLIAMS, Inez
A 'table' in Heylyn's *Observations*. (Query, 171). BC, xiii (64), 354.

WILLIAMS, Iolo Aneurin
English book-illustration, 1700-1775. Illus. LIB, xvii (36/7), 1-21.

WILLIAMS, Philip
The compositor of the 'Pied Bull' *Lear*. SB, i (48/9), 59-68.

The 'second issue' of Shakespeare's *Troilus and Cressida*, 1609. SB, ii (49/50), 25-33.

Shakespeare's *Troilus and Cressida*: the relationship of quarto and folio. SB, iii (50/1), 131-43.

New approaches to textual problems in Shakespeare. SB, viii (56), 3-14.

WILLIAMS, T. E.
The private press of T. E. Williams. (Query, 160). BC, xii (63), 72.
A. Ehrman.

WILLIAMS, Tennessee
Tennesee Williams by another name. PBSA, lvii (63), 377-8.
A. Brown.

WILLIAMS, William P.
The F1 *Othello* copy-text. PBSA, lxiii (69), 23-5.

WILLIAMSBURG
The Williamsburg paper mill of William Parks the printer. Illus. PBSA, xxxi (37), 21-44.
R. Goodwin.

WILLIAMSON, Karina
Another edition of Smart's *Hymns for the amusement of children.* LIB, x (55), 280-2.

WILLIAMSTOWN *Mass., Williams coll., Chapin libr.*
Notes on errata from books in the Chapin library. LIB, xiii (32), 259-71.
L. E. Osborne.

WILLOUGHBY, Edwin Eliott
Bacon's copy of a Douai-Rheims bible. LIB, iii (48/9), 54-6.

The reading of Shakespeare in colonial America. PBSA, xxxi (37), 45-56.

Forbes, John (1568?-1634). *Four sermons.* [probably printed by Giles Thorp, Amsterdam] 1635. PBSA, xxxiv (40), 85.

Bible. English. *The Holy Bible.* London, R. Barker, 1618. PBSA, xxxiv (40), 185.

A 1642 American item. PBSA, xlii (48), 321.

A long use of a setting of type. [John Speed's *The Genealogies Recorded in the Holy Scriptures*]. SB, ii (49/50), 173-5.

WILLSON, Frank C.
That *Gilded Age* again: an attempt to unmuddle the mystery of the fifty-seven variants. PBSA, xxvii (43), 141-56.

WILMOT, John *earl of Rochester*
Rochester rarities. (Query, 41). BC, ii (53), 224.
J. D. Hayward.

Rochester's *Poems on several occasions,* new light on the dated and undated editions, 1680. Illus. LIB, xix (38/9), 185-97.
P. Gray.

The 1680 'Antwerp' edition of Rochester's *Poems.* LIB, xx (39/40), 105.
D. Dale.

Prosecutions of *Sodom: or, The quintessence of debauchery,* and *Poems on several occasions by the E. of R.,* 1689-1690 and 1693. LIB, xxiv (69), 51-5.
D. S. Thomas.

The 1680 editions of Rochester's *Poems* with notes on earlier texts. PBSA, xlvii (53), 43-58.
W. B. Todd.

Order of contents as evidence of authorship: Wilmot's *Poems* of 1680. PBSA, xlvii (53), 43-58.
D. M. Vieth.

The text of Wilmot and the editions of 1680. PBSA, l (56), 243-63.
D. M. Vieth.

A textual paradox: Rochester's *To a Lady in a Letter.* PBSA, liv (60), 147-62.
D. M. Vieth.

An unsuspected cancel in Tonson's 1691 *Rochester.* PBSA, lv (61), 130-3.
D. M. Vieth.

WILSON, Alexander
The early work of the Foulis Press and the Wilson Foundry. Illus. LIB, vii (52), 77-110, 149-77.
J. P. W. Gaskell.

WILSON, Arthur
Arthur Wilson's *The Inconstant Lady.* Illus. LIB, xviii (37/8), 287-313.
R. C. Bald.

WILSON, Carroll Atwood
The first separate printing of *Maud Muller.* PBSA, li (47), 148-51.

A bibliographical footnote: 'Long' and 'Lo' [in a line of Longfellow's *Evangeline*]. PBSA, xli (47), 204-9.

WILSON, Edward
The book-stamps of the Tollemache family of Helmingham and Ham. Illus. BC, xvi (67), 178-85.

WILSON, Edward Meryon
The two editions of Calderón's *Primera Parte* of 1640. Illus. LIB, xiv (59), 175-91.

On the *Tercera Parte* of Calderón — 1664. Illus. SB, xv (62), 223-30.

Samuel Pepys's Spanish chap-books. 3 pts. TCBS, ii (54/8), 127-54, 229-68, 305-22.

Some Spanish verse chap-books of the seventeenth century. Illus. TCBS, iii (59/63), 327-34.

A Cervantes item from Emmanuel college library: Barros's *Filosofía cortesana,* 1587. Illus. TCBS, iv (64/8), 363-71.

WILSON, Frank Percy
Some English mock-prognostications. LIB, xix (38/9), 6-43.

English proverbs and dictionaries of proverbs. LIB, xxvi (45/6), 51-71.

A Merie and Pleasant Prognostication, 1577. LIB, iv (49/50), 135-6.

Nicholas Breton's *I would and would not,* 1619. LIB, xii (57), 273-4.

WILSON, John
John Wilson, an Ayrshire printer, publisher and bookseller. BTHK, v (67), 41-61.
F. M. Thomson.

A manuscript of John Wilson's songs. LIB, x (55), 55-7.
M. C. Crum.

WILSON, John Dover
A note on the porter in *Macbeth*. EBST, ii (38/45), 413-16.

The origins and development of Shakespeare's *Henry IV*. LIB, xxvi (45/6), 2-16.

WILSON, Louis Round *and* DOWNS, Robert Bingham
Special collections for the study of history and literature in the South-east. PBSA, xxviii (34), 97-131.

WILSON, Robert
A political cancel in *The Coblers Prophesie*. LIB, xxiii (42/3), 94-100.
I. Mann.

Notes on the Malone Society reprint of *The Cobler's Prophecy*. LIB, xxvi (45/6), 181-9.
I. Mann.

The variants in Robert Wilson's *The Three Lords of London*. LIB, xviii (63), 142-4.
H. S. D. Mithal.

—. LIB, xiii (58), 57-9.
L. Nathanson.

WILSON, Samuel Mackay
The *Kentucky Gazette* and John Bradford its founder. PBSA, xxi (37), 102-32.

WILSON, William
'Future' and 'Fortune' in *A Night at an Inn*. PBSA, lviii (64), 477-8.

WILSON, William Jerome
The textual relations of the Thacker manuscript on Columbus and early Portuguese navigations. PBSA, xxxiv (40), 199-220.

WILSON FOUNDRY
See WILSON, Alexander

WINANS, Robert B.
Works by and about Samuel Johnson in eighteenth-century America. PBSA, lxii (68), 537-46.

WINCHESTER *coll., libr.*
Winchester college. (Unfamiliar libraries, 11). Illus. BC, xvi (67), 297-304.
J. M. G. Blakiston.

Winchester College library before 1750. Illus. LIB, ix (54), 1-16.
W. Oakeshott.

Winchester College library in the eighteenth and early nineteenth centuries. Illus. LIB, xvii (62), 23-45.
J. M. G. Blakiston.

WINDHAM, William
Johnson's last gifts to Windham. BC, v (56), 354-6.
R. W. Ketton-Cremer.

Windham and Gauffecourt. TCBS, i (49/53), 186-90.
A. N. L. Munby.

WINDSOR *St. George's chapel, libr.*
The manuscripts of St. George's chapel, Windsor. LIB, xiii (32/3), 55-76.
M. R. James.

WINE AND FOOD
See FOOD AND WINE

WING, Donald Godard
The making of the *Short-title catalogue, 1641-1700*. PBSA, xlv (51), 59-69.

Wing's *Short-title catalogue* and translations from the French, 1641-1700. PBSA, xlix (55), 37-67.
J. E. Tucker.

WING, John M.
For J. M. Wing Foundation
See NEWBERRY LIBRARY *John M. Wing foundation.*

WINSHIP, George Parker
A document concerning the first Anglo-American press. Illus. LIB, xx (39/40), 51-70.

Prince, Thomas (1687-1758). *The case of Heman considered*. Boston, 1756. PBSA, xxxvi (41), 73.

WINSTANLEY, Denys Arthur
Halliwell Phillipps and Trinity College library. LIB, ii (47/8), 250-77.

WISE, John S.
Wise words from Virginia: the published writings of John S. Wise, of the Eastern Slope and New York City. PBSA, liv (60), 273-85.
C. C. Davis.

WISE, Thomas James
Thomas J. Wise's *Verses*, 1882 & 1883. (Query, 36). BC, ii (53), 158-9.
J. Carter.

—. (Query, 36). BC, ii (53), 283.
M. P. Pariser.

Tales of the Wild and the Wonderful. 1825. (Query, 104). BC, vii (58), 417.
J. Park.

T. J. Wise and *Tales of the Wild and the Wonderful*. (Query, 104). BC, viii (59), 300-3.
J. E. Alden.

—. (Query, 104). BC, viii (59), 300-6.
J. Rubinstein.

Gosse, Wise and Swinburne. (Note, 115). BC, viii (59), 297-9.
E. E. Blissell.

Thomas J. Wise and 'Richard Gullible'. (Note, 110). BC, viii (59), 182-3.
J. Carter.

—. (Query, 152). BC, xi (62), 353.
G. C. Singer.

Who was Mr. Y.Z.? (Query, 152). BC, xi (62), 484.
J. Carter.

T. J. Wise and the technique of promotion. (Note, 184). BC, xi (62), 347-8.
G. C. Singer.

—. (Note, 184). BC, xi (62), 480-2; xii (63), 202.
J. Carter.

T. J. Wise and J. C. Thomson. (Query, 164). BC, xii (63), 74.
M. Trevanion.

—. BC. xii (63), 68-71.
G. C. Singer.

A unique copy of *The Runaway Slave*, 1849. (Note, 191). BC, xii (63), 202-3.
J. Carter.

Wise, Wrenn, and Tennyson's *Enoch Arden*, 1864. (Note, 214). BC, xiii (64), 67-8.
W. B. Todd.

Thomas J. Wise's descriptive formula. (Query, 181). BC, xiii (64), 214-15.
J. Carter.

—. (Query, 181). BC, xiii (64), 355-6.
M. Trevanion.

So Gosse was in it after all? (Note, 235). BC, xiii (64), 501-3.
N. J. Barker.

Conrad and T. J. Wise. (Note, 272). BC, xv (66), 350-1.
M. L. Turner.

Wise forgeries in Doves bindings. (Query, 226). BC, xvii (68), 352-3.
J. Carter.

Wise and Ruskin. I. BC, xviii (69), 45-56.
J. S. Dearden.

—. II. (II and III). Illus. BC, xviii (69), 170-88.
J. S. Dearden.

—. III (IV and V). BC, xviii (69), 318-39.
J. S. Dearden.

Some Wiseian advertisements. (Note, 310). BC, xviii (69), 219-20.
W. B. Todd.

Wise, Smart & Moody. (Note, 319). BC, xviii (69), 386-7.
S. Nowell-Smith.

An unrecorded Wiseian issue [of the *Dead Love* entry in the *Bibliography of Swinburne*]. (Note, 318). BC, xviii (69), 385-6.
W. B. Todd.

The Wise Shelley letter. [A letter]. LIB, v (50/1), 63-4.
T. G. Ehrsam.

Thomas J. Wise and the Pre-Restoration drama: a supplement. LIB, xvi (61), 287-93.
D. F. Foxon *and* W. B. Todd.

Some Wiseian ascriptions in the Wrenn catalogue. LIB, xxiii (68), 95-107.
W. B. Todd.

T. J. Wise as bibliographer. LIB, xxiv (69), 129-41.
S. Nowell-Smith.

Thomas J. Wise's *Verses*, 1882/1883. LIB, xxiv (69), 246-9.
J. Carter.

Thomas J. Wise to John Henry Wrenn on nineteenth-century bibliography. PBSA, xxxvi (42), 215-28.
F. E. Ratchford.

'A certain 4° *Elegy*'. Re — T. J. Wise and Sir Edmund Gosse). PBSA, lv (61), 229-31.
D. K. Adams.

The not-so-gentle art of puffing: William G. Kingsland and Thomas J. Wise. PBSA, lxii (68), 25-37.
L. H. Kendall, *jr*.

Tennyson's *The Lover's Tale,* R. H. Shepherd, and T. J. Wise. SB, xviii (65), 111-45.
W. D. Paden.

WISTER, Owen
Fifty years of *The Virginian*. Illus. PBSA, xlvi (52), 99-120.
N. O. Rush.

WITCH
Some notes on Crane's manuscript of *The Witch*. LIB, xxii (41/2), 208-22.
Sir W. W. Greg.

WITCH HUNTING
Recent witch hunting research, or where do we go from here? [With a bibliography]. PBSA, lxii (68), 373-420.
H. C. E. Midelfort.

WITHER, George
George Wither's *Three Private Meditations*. (Note, 87). BC, vi (57), 405-6.
L. H. Kendall, *jr*.

Walkley's supposed piracy of Wither's *Workes* in 1620. LIB, xix (38/9), 339-46.
L. Kirschbaum.

George Wither's quarrel with the stationers: an anonymous reply to *The Schollers Purgatory*. SB, xvi (63), 27-42.
A. Pritchard.

Wither and the stationers. SB, xix (66), 210-15.
N. E. Carlson.

WITHERBEE, Sidney A.
Towards a descriptive bibliography of Stephen Crane: *Spanish-American war songs* [by S. A. Witherbee]. PBSA, lxi (67), 267-9.
J. Katz *and* M. J. Bruccoli.

WITHERING, William
Withering on the foxglove. [Dr. W. Withering's *An account of the foxglove*]. Illus. BH, i (47/51), 184-92.
K. D. Wilkinson.

WITT, Mario M.
The flood of 4 November 1966 [in Florence]. BC, xvi (67), 13-25.

WITTEN, Laurence
James Marshall Osborn. (Contemporary collectors, 23). Illus. BC, viii (59). 383-96.

The earliest books printed in Spain. PBSA, liii (59), 91-113.

WODHULL, Michael
Michael Wodhull. (Note, 65). BC, v (56), 76.
C. Severne.

Bindings in the M. Wodhull library. [A letter]. LIB, viii (53), 279.
C. Ramsden.

WOLF, Edwin
Blake exhibitions in America on the occasion of the bicentenary of the birth of William Blake. BC, vi (57), 378-85.

Whatman paper in a book dated 1757. (Query, 108). BC, viii (59), 72.

Some books of early English provenance in the Library Company of Philadelphia. Illus. BC, ix (60), 275-84.

An untraced 18th-century catalogue. (Query, 142). BC, x (61), 201-2.

Edward Halle's *The Union of the Two Noble and Illustre Famelies of Lancastre and Yorke,* and its place among English Americana. PBSA, xxxiii (39), 40-54.

Press corrections in sixteenth and seventeenth-century quartos. PBSA, xxxvi (42), 187-98.

The Blake-Linnell accounts in the library of Yale University. PBSA, xxxvii (43), 1-22.

The year after Franklin's year. PBSA, li (57), 227-35.

The reconstruction of Benjamin Franklin's library: an unorthodox jigsaw puzzle. Illus. PBSA, lvi (62), 1-16.

Thoughts on books and libraries. PBSA, lvii (63), 438-44.

The library of Ralph Assheton: the book background of a colonial Philadelphia lawyer. PBSA, lviii (64), 345-79.

A 235-year-old library moves 235,000 books. [The Library Company of Philadelphia]. Illus. PBSA, lx (66), 166-75.

Evidence indicating the need for some bibliographical analysis of American-printed historical works. PBSA, lxiii (69), 261-77.

WOLF, Georg
The devices of J. Phillippe and G. Wolf. (Note, 193). BC, xii (63), 203.
O. L. Shaw.

WOLFE, John
John Wolfe, printer and publisher, 1579-1601. Illus. LIB, xiv (33/4), 241-88.
H. R. Hoppe.

John Wolfe and a Spanish book. LIB, iii (48/9), 214-16.

WOLFE, Richard J.
Caleb Bingham's *American preceptor*, Lexington, 1805. PBSA, lix (65), 177-82.

WOLFE, Thomas
The editing of *Look Homeward, Angel.* PBSA, lvii (63), 1-13.
F. E. Skipp.

WOLFF, Jakob *de Pforzheim*
The undated *Aesop* attributed to Jakob Wolff de Pforzheim (Hain-Copinger, 327). LIB, xii (57), 119-21.
C. C. Rattey.

WOLFF, Robert Lee
Nineteenth-century fiction. (Contemporary collectors, 42). Illus. 2 pts. BC, xiv (65), 355-47, 511-22.

WOLPE, Berthold Ludwig
A royal manuscript by Arrighi Vicentino in the British Museum. (Note, 91). Illus. BC, vii (58), 78-9.

—. and CARTER, Harry
Pepys's copy of Moxon's *Mechanick Exercises.* LIB, xiv (59), 124-6.

WOMEN
Some unconventional women before 1800: printers, booksellers, and collectors. PBSA, xlix (55), 300-14.
F. Hamill.

WOOD, Anthony
Wood's life of Milton: its sources and significance. PBSA, lii (58), 1-22.
W. Parker.

WOOD, Edward Rudolf
Cancels and corrections in *A Discovery of Errors*, 1622. LIB, xiii (58), 124-7.

WOODBERRY, George Edward
A finding list of manuscript materials relating to George Edward Woodberry. PBSA, xlvi (52), 165-8.
J. Doyle.

WOOD BLOCKS
A Newcastle collection of wood blocks [in the University library, Newcastle-upon-Tyne]. Illus. BC, xvii (68), 443-57.
F. M. Thomson.

'A Newcastle collection of wood blocks' [by F. M. Thomson]. BC, xviii (69), 384-5.
S. Roscoe.

Phototransfer of drawings in wood-block engravings. Illus. JPHS, v (69), 87-97.
Sir P. Fildes.

WOODCUTS
Woodcuts for an almanac. (Query, 64). Illus. BC, iv (55), 254-5.
M. Frost.

Woodcuts for an almanac. (Query, 64). BC, v (56), 174.
B. A. Gross.

The earliest dated woodcut book-plate. (Note, 119). Illus. BC, viii (59), 426-7.
A. Ehrman.

—. BC, ix (60), 325.

The source of the woodcuts in Wynkyn de Worde's edition of Mandeville's *Travels*, 1499. LIB, vi (51), 154-61.
M. Letts.

The woodcut illustrations in the English editions of *Mandeville's Travels*. PBSA, xlvii (53), 59-69.
J. W. Bennett.

'Woodcuts dropped into the text'; the illustrations in *The Old Curiosity Shop* and *Barnaby Rudge*. Illus. SB, xx (67), 113-34.
J. Stevens.

WOOD-ENGRAVING
The progress of wood-engraving in current book-illustration. Illus. BH, i (47/51), 254-62.
C. Sandford.

WOODFIELD, Denis Buchanan
The fake title-page of the *Gilded Age*: a solution. PBSA, l (56), 292-6.

WOODHEAD, Abraham
The first publication of Abraham Woodhead's translation of St. Teresa [of Avila, *Works*]. LIB, xxi (66), 234-40.
J. Buchanan-Brown.

WOODRESS, James Leslie
A note on Lowell bibliography: the review [in the *North American Review*] of Howells' *Venetian Life*. SB, iv (51/2), 210-11.

WOODS, Frederick Basil
Churchilliana. (Note, 230). BC, xiii (64), 497.

WOODWARD, Arthur Maurice
A grammarian's fraud. (Note, 132). BC, ix (60), 188-92.

A manuscript of the Latin version of Appian's *Civil Wars*. Illus. LIB, xxvi (45/6), 149-57.

WOODWARD, Daniel Holt
A Baconian and Cervantes. (Note, 146). BC, ix (60), 454.

Not in Madan. (Note, 168). BC, x (61), 448.

An 18th-century list of books with prices. (Note, 212). BC, xiii (64), 65-6.

An unrecorded Oxford *Quæstiones*, 1617. (Note, 284). BC, xvi (67), 81-2.

The manuscript corrections and printed variants in the quarto edition of *Gondibert*, 1615. LIB, xx (65), 298-309.

Sir Philip Sidney's *Arcadia*, 1638: an unrecorded issue. LIB, xxii (67), 67-70.

John Quinn and T. S. Eliot's first book of criticism. PBSA, lvi (62), 259-65.

Notes on the publishing history and text of *The Waste Land*. PBSA, lviii (64), 252-69.

Thomas Fuller, William Dugard, and the pseudonymous *Life of Sidney*, 1655 [prefixed to Sidney's *Arcadia*]. PBSA, lxii (68), 501-10.

Thomas Fuller, the Protestant divines, and plagiary yet speaking. [*Abel redivivus*]. TCBS, iv (64/8), 201-24.

WOODWARD, Philip
Philip Woodward: Elizabethan pamphleteer and translator. LIB, iv (49/50), 14-24.
G. H. Russell.

WOODWARD, Robert H.
Harold Frederic: a bibliography. SB, xvii (60), 247-57.

WOOF, Robert Samuel
A Coleridge-Wordsworth manuscript and 'Sarah Hutchinson's poets'. SB, xix (66), 226-31.

WOOF, Robert Samuel, ERDMAN, David Vorse *and* WERKMEISTER, Lucyle Thomas
Unrecorded Coleridge variants: additions and corrections. SB, xiv (61), 236-45.

Wordsworth's poetry and Stuart's newspapers: 1797-1803. SB, xv (62), 149-89.

WOOLF, Cecil
Norman Douglas. (Query, 34). BC, ii (53), 158.

Sir William Watson. (Some uncollected authors, 12). BC, v (56), 375-80.

William Lisle Bowles, 1762-1850. (Some uncollected authors, 18). 2 pts. BC, vii (58), 286-94, 407-16.

George Darley, 1795-1846. (Some uncollected authors, 28). BC, x (61), 186-92.

Hawker of Morwenstow, 1803-1875. (Some uncollected authors, 39). 2 pts. BC, xiv (65), ʊ2-71, 202-11.

Frederick Rolfe. (Some uncollected authors, 5). BC, iv (55), 63-8.

Peter Cheyney's *Poems of Love and War* and *To Corona and Other Poems*. (Query, 192). BC, xiv (65), 367.

WOOLF, Virginia
Additions to the bibliography of Virginia Woolf. (Note, 216). BC, xiii (64), 70.
B. J. Kirkpatrick.

WORDE, Wynkyn de
Wynkyn de Worde's use of the Plimpton manuscript of *De Proprietatibus Rerum*. Illus. LIB, vi (51), 7-18.
R. W. Mitchner.

The source of the woodcuts in Wynkyn de Worde's edition of Mandeville's *Travels*, 1499. LIB, vi (51), 154-61.
M. Letts.

A new title from De Worde's press. [*Here begynneth Octauyan, the emperoure of Rome*, in the Huntington library]. Illus. LIB, ix (54), 45-9.
H. R. Mead.

Printing evidence in Wynkyn de Worde's edition of *The Life of Johan Picus*, by St. Thomas More. PBSA, xliii (49). 398-9.
F. T. Bowers.

Wynkyn de Worde's printing of Lydgate's *Horse, Sheep and Goose*. PBSA, xlvi (52), 392-3.
C. F. Bühler.

Notes on the Wynkyn de Worde editions of the *Boke of St. Albans*, and its separates. SB, v (52), 43-52.
E. Pafort.

The date of *Cocke Lorelles bote* [printed by Wynkyn de Worde]. SB, xix (66), 175-81.
P. R. Baumgartner.

WORDSWORTH, William
Wordsworth and his amanuenses. (English literary autographs, 13). Illus. BC, iv (55), 48-9.
T. J. Brown.

Lyrical Ballads, 1800: a paste-in. LIB, xix (38/9), 489-91.
J. E. Wells.

Letters of Longman & Co. to Wordsworth, 1814-36. LIB, ix (54), 25-34.
W. J. B. Owen.

The printing of *Lyrical Ballads*, 1798. Illus. LIB, ix (54), 221-41.
D. F. Foxon.

Costs, sales, and profits of Longman's editions of Wordsworth. LIB, xii (57), 93-107.
W. J. B. Owen.

A bibliography of Wordsworth in American periodicals through 1825. PBSA, lii (58), 205-19.
J. C. Barnes.

Wordsworth's poetry and Stuart's Newspapers: 1797-1803. SB, xv (62), 149-89.
R. S. Woof.

A Coleridge-Wordsworth manuscript and 'Sarah Hutchinson's poets'. SB, xix (66), 226-31.
R. S. Woof.

WORKING TO RULE
Working to rule, 1600-1800; a study of pressmen's practice. LIB, xx (65), 13-54.
K. Povey.

WORLD
The printing of eighteenth-century periodicals: with notes on the *Examiner* and the *World*. LIB, x (55), 49-54.
W. B. Todd.

The first edition of *The World*. LIB, xi (56), 283-4.
W. B. Todd.

WORLD WAR, 1914-1918.
American poetry of the first World War and the book trade. PBSA, lxi (67), 109-24.
J. A. Hart.

WORMALD, Francis *and* GILES, Phyllis Margaret
A handlist of the additional manuscripts in the Fitzwilliam Museum, received since the publication of the catalogue by Dr M. R. James in 1895 (excluding the McClean bequest). Pt. I. TCBS, i (49/53), 197-207.

—. Pt. II. TCBS, i (49/53), 297-309.

—. Pt. III. TCBS, i (49/53), 365-75.

—. Pt. IV. Index. TCBS, ii (54/8), 1-13.

Description of Fitzwilliam Museum MS.3-1954. Illus. TCBS, iv (64/8), 1-28.

WORMHOLES
Wormholes in stored sheets. [A letter]. LIB, xviii (37/8), 463-4.
F. B. Williams, *jr*.

WORMSER, Richard S.
Lincoln, Waldo. *Bibliography of American Cookery Books, 1742-1860*. Worcester, Mass., 1929. Additions. PBSA, xxxiv (40), 360.

Bosworth, Newton (d. 1848). *The Accidents of Human Life*. New York, 1814. PBSA, xxxv (41), 207.

Fabulous fiction. PBSA, xlvii (53), 231-47.

WOTTON, Sir Henry
Stubbe and Wotton. (Note, 63). BC, v (56), 78.
H. W. Jones.

—. (Note, 63). BC, v (56), 276.
C. S. Bliss.

You meaner beauties of the night, a study in transmission and trans-mogrification. LIB, xxvi (45/6), 99-121.
J. B. Leishman.

Wotton's *The Character of a Happy Life*. LIB, x (55), 270-4.
C. F. Main.

WRANGHAM, Francis
An unrecorded pamphlet by Archdeacon Wrangham. (Note, 203). BC, xii (63), 355.
B. C. Bloomfield.

—. BC, xiii (64), 64-5, 206.
C. B. L. Barr.

Archdeacon Francis Wrangham, 1769-1842, and his books. LIB, xvii (36/7), 129-30.
M. Sadleir.

Archdeacon Francis Wrangham, a supplement. LIB, xix (38/9), 422-61.
M. Sadleir.

Archdeacon Wrangham's *Poems*. LIB, iv (49/50), 205-11.
P. A. Shelley.

WRATISLAW, Theodore William
Theodore Wratislaw's *Caprices* 1893. (Note, 306). BC, xviii (69), 90-2.
T.d'A. Smith.

WREITTOUN, John
A hitherto unrecorded Wreittoun pamphlet. BTHK, i/3 (58), 42-4.
D. M. Lloyd.

A handlist of works from the press of John Wreittoun at Edinburgh, 1627-*c.* 1639. EBST, ii (38/45), 89-104.
W. Beattie.

WRENN, John Henry
Wise, Wrenn, and Tennyson's *Enoch Arden*, 1864. (Note, 214). BC, xiii (64), 67-8.
W. B. Todd.

Some Wiseian ascriptions in the Wrenn catalogue. LIB, xxiii (68), 95-107.
W. B. Todd.

Thomas J. Wise to John Henry Wrenn on nineteenth-century bibliography. PBSA, xxxvi (42), 215-28..
F. E. Ratchford.

WRIGHT, Andrew Howell
An authoritative text of *The horse's mouth.* PBSA, lxi (67), 100-9.

WRIGHT, Cyril Ernest
Edward Harley, 2nd Earl of Oxford, 1689-1741. (Portrait of a bibliophile, 8). Illus. BC, xi (62), 158-74.

The dispersal of the monastic libraries and the beginnings of Anglo-Saxon studies. Matthew Parker and his circle: a preliminary study. Illus. TCBS, i (49/53), 208-37.

WRIGHT, Louis Booker
The Harmsworth collection and the Folger Library. BC, vi (57), 123-8.

Translations for the Elizabethan middle class. LIB, xiii (32/3), 312-31.

The classical tradition in colonial Virginia. PBSA, xxxiii (39), 85-97.

WRIGHT, Lyle Henry
Propaganda in early American fiction. PBSA, xxxiii (39), 98-106.

Addenda to Wright [*American fiction 1774-1850*]: Burdett, Curtis, Judson, Weeks. PBSA, lxii (68), 452-3.
W. S. Kable.

—. Mancur, Pise, Tuthill, Weld. PBSA, lxiii (69), 294.
W. S. Kable.

WROTH, Lawrence Counselman
The Jesuit relations from New France. PBSA, xxx (36), 110-49.

The early cartography of the Pacific. Illus. PBSA, xxxviii (44), 87-268.

The frontier presidios of New Spain: books, maps, and a selection of manuscripts relating to the Rivera expedition of 1724-1728. PBSA, xlv (51), 191-218.

Lathrop Colgate Harper: a happy memory. PBSA, lii (58), 161-72.

WYATT, Sir Thomas
Wyatt and the several editions of *The court of Venus.* SB, xix (66), 181-95.
C. A. Huttar.

WYCHERLEY, William
William Wycherley, 1640?-1716; Sir John Vanbrugh, 1664-1726. (English literary autographs, 41). Illus. BC, xi (62), 63.
T. J. Brown.

A letter with a character of Mr. Wycherly. BH, i (47/51), 177-83.
Lord Lansdowne.

The two 1695 editions of Wycherley's *Country Wife.* SB, iii (50/1), 252-3.
R. N. E. Megaw.

WYLLIE, John Cook
Gilmer, Francis Walker (1790-1826). *A Vindication of the laws, limiting the rate of interest on loans.* Richmond, 1820. PBSA, xxxiv (40), 86.

Smith, John (1580-1631). *The true travels.* Richmond, 1819. PBSA, xxxiv (40), 88.

Clives [pseud.] *The following publication . . . to William Smith.* [New York, 1783]. PBSA, xxxiv (40), 359.

[Collier, Robert Ruffin] 1805-1870. *Original and miscellaneous essays. By a Virginian.* Richmond, 1829. PBSA, xxxiv (40), 359.

Jefferson, Thomas (1743-1826). *Observations sur la Virginie.* Paris, 1786. PBSA, xxxv (41), 71.

[Jodrell, Richard Paul] (1745-1831). *The Knight and Friars: an historical tale.* New York, 1786. PBSA, xxxv (41), 72.

Quesnay de Beaurepaire, Alexandre Marie, (fl. 1780). *Mémoire et Prospectus, concernant L'Académie des Sciences et Beaux Arts des Étas-Unis de l'Amérique.* Paris, 1788. PBSA, xxxv (41), 73-4.

Dow, Lorenzo (1777-1834). *The opinion of Dow;* on Lorenzo's thoughts, on different religious subjects. Windham, 1804. PBSA, xxxv (41), 205.

A West Virginian broadside. Illus. PBSA, xlii (48), 322-3.

William Parks' errata. PBSA, xlvi (52), 275.

The printer of a 1641 Suckling pamphlet. PBSA, xlvii (53), 70.

The forms of twentieth-century cancels. PBSA, xlvii (53), 95-112.

A 19th century American two-city cancel. PBSA, lii (58), 140.

Bledsoe's *Is Davis a Traitor?* A note on an imprint changed without cancellation. PBSA, lii (58), 220.

The bibliographer and the collecting of historical materials. PBSA, lviii (64), 148-53.

Footnote for Andrew Jackson bibliography. PBSA, lix (65), 437.

WYNNE, Marjorie Gray
Bibliographical files for research in the Yale University libraries. PBSA, xlix (55), 199-211.

In memoriam: James Tinkham Babb, 1899-1968. PBSA, lxiii (69), 1-3.

X

XENOPHON
Three little Tudor books [i.e. Xenophon's *Treatise of Household*, tr. G. Hervet, T. Berthelet, 1532; Philip Moore's *The Hope of Health*, J. Kingston, 1564; *The Viniard of Devotion*. Newly corrected for Edw. White, 1599]. Illus. LIB, xiv (33), 178-256.
E. F. Bosanquet.

XEREZ, Francisco de
Early editions of Xerez: *Verdadera Relacion de la Conquista del Peru*. Illus. PBSA, xxx (36), 57-84.
A. Pogo.

X-RAY METHOD
Watermark copying by an x-ray method. (Note, 24). Illus. BC, xiv (65), 217-18.
H. D. Jamieson.

Y

YALE UNIVERSITY *Elizabethan club*
The Elizabethan Club of Yale University.
PBSA, xxvii (33), 83-8.
McCoy Troxell.

YALE UNIVERSITY *libr.*
The Blake-Linnell accounts in the library of
Yale University. PBSA, xxxvii (43), 1-22.
E. Wolf.

Aldis, Foley and the collection of American
literature at Yale. PBSA, xlii (48), 41-9.
D. C. Gallup.

Bibliographical files for research in the Yale
University libraries. PBSA, xlix (55), 199-211.
M. G. Wynne.

YAMADA, Akihiro
A proof-sheet in *An humorous day's mirth*
(1599) printed by Valentine Simmes. Illus. LIB,
xxi (66), 155-7.

YATES, Norris
The *Spirit of the Times*: its early history and
some of its contributors. PBSA, xlviii (54),
117-48.

YEAR BOOK, 37 Henry VI
The headlines of William de Machlinia's *Year
Book, 37 Henry VI.* SB, i (48), 123-32.
C. F. Bühler.

YEATS, William Butler
William Butler Yeats, 1865-1939. (English
literary autographs, 49). Illus. BC, xiii (64),
53.
T. J. Brown.

Manuscript versions of Yeats' *The Countess
Cathleen*. PBSA, lvi (62), 79-103.
M. J. Sidnell.

Unrecorded variants in two Yeats poems.
PBSA, lx (66), 367-8.
G. Monteiro.

Manuscript version of Yeats's *The Shadowy
Waters*, an abbreviated description and chron-
ology of the papers relating to the play in the
National Library of Ireland. PBSA, lxii (68),
39-57.
M. J. Sidnell.

Addenda to Sidnell [in PBSA, lxii (68)]: Yeats'
The shadowy waters. PBSA, lxii (68), 614-17.
L. L. Szladits.

Some textual problems in Yeats. SB, ix (57),
51-67.
R. K. Alspach.

Yeat's *Vision* and *The Two Trees*. SB, xvii
(64), 220-2.
R. Mortenson.

YELLOWBACKS
Gothic romances and yellowbacks. (Contem-
porary collectors, 32). Illus. BC, xi (62), 313-22.
A. Walbank.

YERBA BUENA PRESS
The Yerba Buena Press and some related
privately printed books. Illus. PBSA, xliii (49),
202-9.
N. Van Patten.

YONGE, Theodore
Samuel Rogers's *Poems*, 1812. (Query, 169).
BC, xii (63), 356-7.

YORK
The King's printer at York and Shrewsbury,
1642-3. LIB, xxiii (42/3), 129-31.
L. W. Hanson.

YORK, *dean and chapter libr.*
The Library of the dean and chapter of York.
EBST, ii (39/45), 390-1.
F. Harrison.

YORKSHIRE TRAGEDY
Variants in Q1 of *A Yorkshire Tragedy*. LIB,
xi (56), 262-7.
G. H. Blayney.

YOST, Genevieve
The reconstruction of the library of Norborne
Berkeley, Baron de Botetourt, governor of
Virginia, 1768-1770. PBSA, xxxvi (42), 97-123.

YOUNG, Douglas F.
James Leslie Mitchell/Lewis Grassic Gibbon:
a chronological checklist. Additions I. BTHK,
v (67/70), 169-73.

YOUNG, Edward, *1683-1765*
Young's *Night-Thoughts* re-examined. LIB, iii
(49), 299-301.
H. Pettit.

A check-list of Young's *Night-Thoughts in
America*. PBSA, xlii (48), 150-6.
H. Pettit.

Additions to the check-list of Young's *Night-
Thoughts in America*. PBSA, xliii (49), 348-9.
W. D. Templeman.

—. Further additions. PBSA, xliv (50), 192-5.
H. Pettit.

The Edward Young-Edmund Curll quarrel: a
review. Illus. PBSA, lxii (68), 321-35.
H. Leek.

YOUNG, Edward
The early days of Penguins. (Penguin books:
three short essays, 1). BC, i (52), 210-11.

YOUNG AMERICA
Poe and 'Young America'. SB, xxi (68),
25-58.
C. Richard.

Z

Z, mr. Y.
Who was Mr. Y.Z? (Query, 152). BC, xi (62), 484.
J. Carter.

—. BC, xi (62), 353.
G. C. Singer.

ZAGORIN, Perez
The authorship of *Mans Mortallitie*. LIB, v (50/1), 179-83.

ZÁRATE, Agustin de
Some observations on the Spanish and foreign editions of Zárate's *Historia del descubrimiento y conquista del Perú*. PBSA, xlix (55), 95-111.
D. McMahon.

ZATHEY, Jerzy
The Jagellonian Library, Cracow. (Unfamiliar libraries, 8). Illus. BC, xiii (64), 24-32.

ZEDLER, Gottfried
A note on Zedler's Coster theory. PBSA, xxxvii (43), 61-8.
C. F. Bühler.

ZEITLIN, Jacob
Small renaissance: Southern California style. PBSA, l (56), 17-27.

ZEL, Ulrich
Two benefactions of Ulrich Zel. LIB, xii (57), 271-3.
L. A. Sheppard.

ZIEGLER, Arthur P. *and* VAN TRUMP James D.
Thomas Bird Mosher, publisher and pirate. Illus. BC, xi (62), 295-312.

ZION'S TEMPLE
See MANCHESTER *Zion's temple, libr.*

ZUCCARO, Taddeo
A lost drawing by Taddeo Zuccaro. (Query, 166). BC, xii (63), 208.
J. A. Gere.